Business Essentials

Supporting HNC/HND and Foundation degrees

Finance: Management Accounting and Financial Reporting

Course Book

In this July 2010 edition:

- Full and comprehensive coverage of the key topics within the subject
- Activities, examples and quizzes
- Practical illustrations and case studies
- Index
- Fully up to date as at July 2010
- Coverage mapped to the Edexcel Guidelines for the HNC/HND in Business

BPP LEARNING MEDIA

First edition July 2010

Published ISBN 9780 7517 9039 9
e-ISBN 9780 7517 9155 6

British Library Cataloguing-in-Publication Data
A catalogue record for this book is available from the British Library

Published by
BPP Learning Media Ltd
BPP House, Aldine Place
London W12 8AA

www.bpp.com/learningmedia

Printed in the United Kingdom

Your learning materials, published by BPP Learning Media Ltd, are printed on paper sourced from sustainable, managed forests.

We are grateful to Edexcel for permission to reproduce the Guidelines for the BTEC Higher Nationals in Business.

A note about copyright

Dear Customer

What does the little © mean and why does it matter?

Your market-leading BPP books, course materials and e-learning materials do not write and update themselves. People write them: on their own behalf or as employees of an organisation that invests in this activity. Copyright law protects their livelihoods. It does so by creating rights over the use of the content.

Breach of copyright is a form of theft – as well as being a criminal offence in some jurisdictions, it is potentially a serious breach of professional ethics.

With current technology, things might seem a bit hazy but, basically, without the express permission of BPP Learning Media:

- Photocopying our materials is a breach of copyright
- Scanning, ripcasting or conversion of our digital materials into different file formats, uploading them to facebook or e-mailing them to your friends is a breach of copyright

You can, of course, sell your books, in the form in which you have bought them – once you have finished with them. (Is this fair to your fellow students? We update for a reason.) But the e-products are sold on a single user licence basis: we do not supply 'unlock' codes to people who have bought them second-hand.

And what about outside the UK? BPP Learning Media strives to make our materials available at prices students can afford by local printing arrangements, pricing policies and partnerships which are clearly listed on our website. A tiny minority ignore this and indulge in criminal activity by illegally photocopying our material or supporting organisations that do. If they act illegally and unethically in one area, can you really trust them?

BPP LEARNING MEDIA

Contents

Introduction

BPP Learning Media's **Business Essentials** range is the ideal learning solution for all students studying for business-related qualifications and degrees. The range provides concise and comprehensive coverage of the key areas that are essential to the business student.

Qualifications in business are traditionally very demanding. Students therefore need learning resources which go straight to the core of the topics involved, and which build upon students' pre-existing knowledge and experience. The BPP Learning Media Business Essentials range has been designed to meet exactly that need.

Features include:

- In-depth coverage of essential topics within business-related subjects
- Plenty of activities, quizzes and topics for discussion to help retain the interest of students and ensure progress
- Up-to-date practical illustrations and case studies that really bring the material to life
- A full index, with key terms highlighted in bold

In addition, the contents of the chapters are comprehensively mapped to the **Edexcel Guidelines**, providing full coverage of all topics specified in the HND/HNC qualifications in Business.

Each chapter contains:

- An introduction and a list of specific study objectives
- Summary diagrams and signposts to guide you through the chapter
- A chapter roundup, quick quiz with answers and answers to activities

Other titles in this series:

Generic titles

Economics

Accounts

Business Maths

Mandatory units for the Edexcel HND/HNC in Business qualification

Unit 1	Business Environment
Unit 2	Managing Finance
Unit 3	Organisations and Behaviour
Unit 4	Marketing Principles
Unit 5	Business Law
Unit 6	Business Decision Making
Unit 7	Business Strategy
Unit 8	Research Project

Pathways for the Edexcel HND/HNC in Business qualification

Units 9 and 10	Finance: Management Accounting and Financial Reporting
Units 11 and 12	Finance: Auditing and Financial Systems and Taxation
Units 13 and 14	Management: Leading People and Professional Development
Units 15 and 16	Management: Communications and Achieving Results
Units 17 and 19	Marketing and Promotion
Units 18 and 20	Marketing and Sales Strategy
Units 21 and 22	Human Resource Management
Units 23 and 24	Human Resource Development and Employee Relations
Units 25-28	Company and Commercial Law

For more information, or to place an order, please call 0845 0751 100 (for orders within the UK) or +44(0)20 8740 2211 (from overseas), e-mail learningmedia@bpp.com, or visit our website at www.bpp.com/learningmedia.

If you would like to send in your comments on this Course Book, please turn to the review form at the back of this book.

Study Guide

This Course Book includes features designed specifically to make learning effective and efficient.

- Each chapter begins with a summary diagram which maps out the areas covered by the chapter. There are detailed summary diagrams at the start of each main section of the chapter. You can use the diagrams during revision as a basis for your notes.

- After the main summary diagram there is an introduction, which sets the chapter in context. This is followed by learning objectives, which show you what you will learn as you work through the chapter.

- Throughout the Course Book, there are special aids to learning. These are indicated by symbols in the margin:

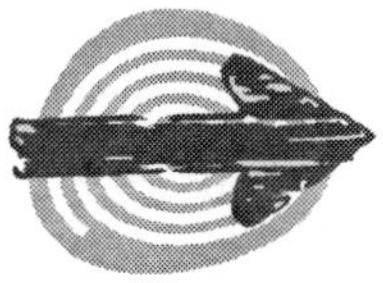

Signposts guide you through the book, showing how each section connects with the next.

Definitions give the meanings of key terms. The *glossary* at the end of the book summarises these.

Activities help you to test how much you have learned. An indication of the time you should take on each is given. Answers are given at the end of each chapter.

Topics for discussion are for use in seminars. They give you a chance to share your views with your fellow students. They allow you to highlight holes in your knowledge and to see how others understand concepts. If you have time, try 'teaching' someone the concepts you have learned in a session. This helps you to remember key points and answering their questions will consolidate your knowledge.

Examples relate what you have learned to the outside world. Try to think up your own examples as you work through the Course Book.

Chapter roundups present the key information from the chapter in a concise format. Useful for revision.

- The wide **margin** on each page is for your notes. You will get the best out of this book if you interact with it. Write down your thoughts and ideas. Record examples, question theories, add references to other pages in the Course Book and rephrase key points in your own words.

- At the end of each chapter, there is a **chapter roundup** and a **quick quiz** with answers. Use these to revise and consolidate your knowledge. The chapter roundup summarises the chapter. The quick quiz tests what you have learned (the answers often refer you back to the chapter so you can look over subjects again).

- At the end of the book, there is an index.

Part A

Management Accounting

Chapter : 1

COST ACCOUNTING, COST CLASSIFICATION AND COST BEHAVIOUR

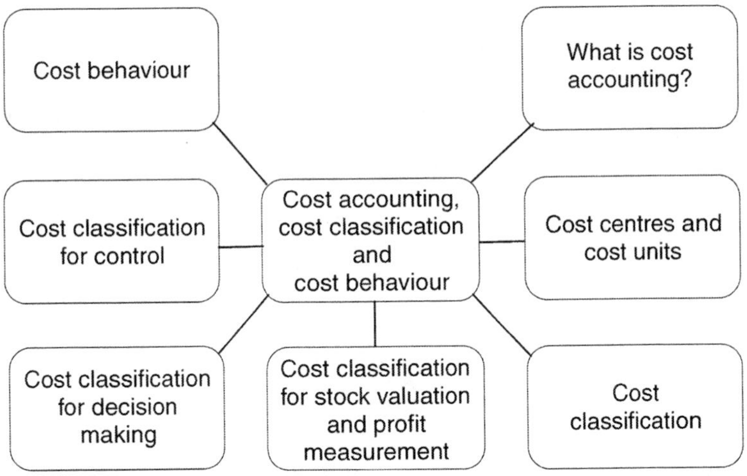

Introduction

Involvement with costs is fundamental to the role of management accountants. Any business, whether it manufactures goods or provides a service, needs to know how much its products or services cost and how these costs might change in response to decisions made. They will use this information to manage the business effectively, for example, in setting prices and determining which products are most profitable, in planning and budgeting for future periods and for monitoring and controlling costs.

Your objectives

In this chapter you will learn about the following.

(a) Cost centres and cost units

(b) Cost classification

(c) Cost behaviour

1 WHAT IS COST ACCOUNTING?

Who can provide the answers to the following questions?

- What was the cost of goods produced or services provided last period?
- What was the cost of operating a department last month?
- What revenues were earned last week?

Yes, you've guessed it, the cost accountant.

Knowing about costs incurred or revenues earned enables management to do the following.

(a) Assess the profitability of a product, a service, a department, or the whole organisation.

(b) Set selling prices with some regard for the costs of sale.

(c) Put a value to stocks of goods (raw materials, work in progress, finished goods) that are still held in store at the end of a period, for preparing a balance sheet of the company's assets and liabilities.

The managers of a business have the responsibility of planning and controlling the resources used. To carry out this task effectively they must be provided with sufficiently accurate and detailed information, and the cost accounting system should provide this. Cost accounting is a management information system which analyses past, present and future data to provide the basis for managerial action.

It would be wrong to suppose that cost accounting systems are restricted to manufacturing operations. Cost accounting information is also used in service industries, government departments and welfare organisations. Within a manufacturing organisation, the cost accounting system should be applied not only to manufacturing operations but also to administration, selling and distribution, research and development and so on.

So, cost accounting is concerned with providing information to assist the following.

- Establishing stock valuations, profits and balance sheet items
- Planning
- Control
- Decision making

2 THE ORGANISATION, COST CENTRES AND COST UNITS

An organisation, whether it is a manufacturing company, a provider of services (such as a bank or a hotel) or a public sector organisation (such as a hospital), may be divided into a number of different **functions** within which there are a number of **departments**. A manufacturing organisation might be structured as follows.

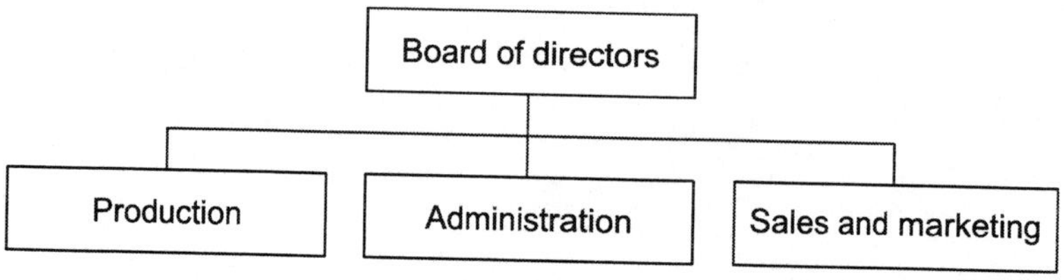

Figure 1.1 Structure of manufacturing organisation

Suppose an organisation produces chocolate cakes for a number of supermarket chains. The production function is involved with the making of the cakes, the administration department with the preparation of accounts and the employment of staff and the marketing department with the selling and distribution of the cakes.

Within the production function there are three departments, two of which are production departments (the mixing department and the baking department) which are actively involved in the production of the cakes and one of which is a service department (stores department) which provides a service or back-up to the production departments.

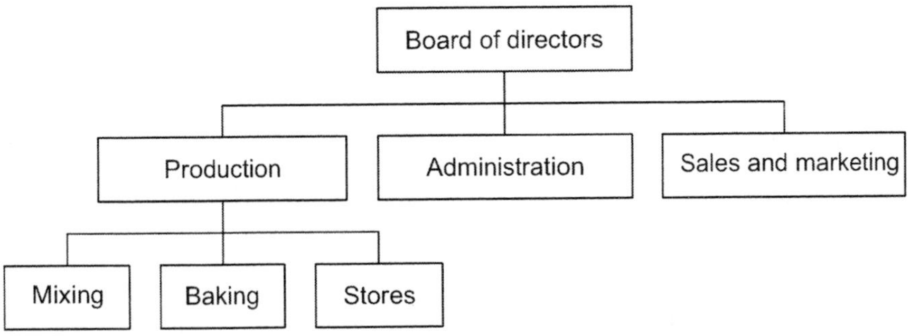

Figure 1.2 Detailed structure of manufacturing organisation

2.1 Cost centres

In general, for cost accounting purposes, departments are termed **cost centres** and the product produced by an organisation is termed the **cost unit**. In our example, the cost centres of the production function could be the mixing department, the baking department and the stores department and the organisation's cost unit could be one chocolate cake.

When costs are incurred, they are generally allocated to a **cost centre**. A cost centre acts as a **collecting place** for certain costs before they are analysed further. Cost centres may include the following.

- A department (as in our example above);
- A machine, or group of machines;
- A project (eg the installation of a new computer system);
- A new product (to enable the costs of development and production to be identified).

2.2 Cost units

Once costs have been traced to cost centres, they can be further analysed in order to establish a cost per cost unit. Alternatively, some items of costs may be charged directly to a cost unit, for example direct materials and direct labour costs, which you will meet later in this text.

Definition

> A **cost unit** is a unit of product or service to which costs can be related. The cost unit is the basic control unit for costing purposes.

Different organisations use different cost units. Here are some suggestions.

Organisation	Possible cost unit
Steelworks	Tonne of steel produced Tonne of coke used
Hospital	Patient/day Operation Out-patient visit
Freight organisation	Tonne/kilometre
Passenger transport organisation	Passenger/kilometre
Accounting firm	Audit performed Chargeable hour
Restaurant	Meal served

One of the principal purposes of cost accounting is therefore to determine the cost of a single cost unit (for stock valuation, cost planning and control and profit reporting purposes).

3 COST CLASSIFICATION

Before any attempt is made to establish stock valuations and measure profits, to plan, make decisions or exercise control (in other words, do any cost accounting), costs must be classified. Classification involves arranging costs into groupings of similar items in order to make stock valuation, profit measurement, planning, decision making and control easier.

4 COST CLASSIFICATION FOR STOCK VALUATION AND PROFIT MEASUREMENT

For the purposes of stock valuation and profit measurement, the cost accountant must calculate the cost of one unit. The total cost of a cost unit is made up of the following three elements of cost.

- Materials
- Labour
- Other expenses (such as rent and rates, interest charges and so on)

Cost elements can be classified as direct costs or indirect costs.

4.1 Direct cost

Definition

A **direct cost** is a cost that can be traced in full to the product, service, or department that is being costed.

(a) **Direct materials costs** are the costs of materials that are known to have been used in making and selling a product (or providing a service).

(b) **Direct labour costs** are the specific costs of the workforce used to make a product or provide a service. Direct labour costs are established by measuring the time taken for a job, or the time taken in 'direct production work'.

(c) **Other direct expenses** are those expenses that have been incurred in full as a direct consequence of making a product, or providing a service, or running a department.

Each of these will be reviewed in more detail later.

4.2 Indirect cost/overhead

Definition

> An **indirect cost** or overhead is a cost that is incurred in the course of making a product, providing a service or running a department, but which cannot be traced directly and in full to the product, service or department. Examples might be the cost of supervisors' wages, cleaning materials and buildings insurance.

Total expenditure may therefore be analysed as follows.

Materials cost	=	Direct materials cost	+	Indirect materials cost
+		+		+
Labour cost	=	Direct labour cost	+	Indirect labour cost
+		+		+
Expenses	=	Direct expenses		Indirect expenses
Total cost	=	Direct cost	+	Overhead cost

Total direct cost is often referred to as **prime cost**. Some authorities restrict the term **prime cost** to direct materials and direct labour, but you will often find that examination questions and assessments also include direct expenses in prime cost.

You should be able to specify whether an item of expenditure is classed as a direct materials cost, a direct labour cost, a production overhead and so on. Further information on such cost items is given below.

4.3 Direct material

Definition

> **Direct material** is all material becoming part of the product (unless used in negligible amounts and/or having negligible cost).

Direct material costs are charged to the product as part of the prime cost. Examples of direct material are as follows.

- **Component parts** or other materials specially purchased for a particular job, order or process.
- **Part-finished work** which is transferred from department 1 to department 2 becomes finished work of department 1 and a direct material cost in department 2.
- **Primary packing materials** like cartons and boxes.

Materials used in negligible amounts and/or having negligible cost can be grouped under indirect materials as part of overhead.

4.4 Direct wages

Definition

> **Direct wages** are all wages paid for labour (either as basic hours or as overtime) expended on work on the product itself.

Direct wages costs are charged to the product as part of the **prime cost**.

Examples of groups of labour receiving payment as direct wages are as follows.

(a) Workers engaged in **altering** the condition, conformation or composition of the product.

(b) Inspectors, analysts and testers **specifically required** for such production.

> **Activity 1** **(15 minutes)**
>
> Classify the following labour costs as either direct or indirect.
>
> (a) The basic pay of direct workers (cash paid, tax and other deductions)
> (b) The basic pay of indirect workers
> (c) Overtime premium, ie the premium above basic pay, for working overtime
> (d) Bonus payments under a group bonus scheme
> (e) Employer's National Insurance contributions
> (f) Idle time of direct workers, paid while waiting for work
> (g) Work on installation of equipment

4.5 Direct expenses

Definition

> **Direct expenses** are any expenses which are incurred on a specific product other than direct material cost and direct wages.

Direct expenses are charged to the product as part of the **prime** cost. Examples of direct expenses are as follows.

- The cost of **special** designs, drawings or layouts
- The **hire of tools** or equipment for a particular job
- **Maintenance costs** of tools, jigs, fixtures and so on

Direct expenses are also referred to as **chargeable expenses.**

4.6 Overheads

Definition

> **Overheads** include all indirect material cost, indirect wages and indirect expenses incurred by a business.

Overheads associated with the **production** process itself include the following.

(a) **Indirect materials** which cannot be traced in the finished product.

- Consumable stores, eg material used in negligible amounts

(b) **Indirect wages**, meaning all wages not charged directly to a product.

- Salaries and wages of non-productive personnel in the production department, eg production supervisors

(c) **Indirect expenses** (other than material and labour) not charged directly to production.

- Rent, rates and insurance of a factory
- Depreciation, fuel, power, repairs and maintenance of plant, machinery and factory buildings

Overheads associated with the **administration** of the business include the following examples.

- **Depreciation** of office equipment.
- **Office salaries**, including salaries of secretaries and accountants.
- Rent, rates, insurance, lighting, cleaning and heating of general offices, telephone and postal charges, bank charges, legal charges, audit fees.

Overheads may also be incurred in the **selling and distribution** of the goods produced. Some examples are as follows.

- **Printing** and **stationery**, such as catalogues and price lists.
- Cost of packing cases.
- **Salaries** and **commission** of sales representatives and sales department staff and wages of packers, drivers and despatch clerks.
- **Advertising** and **sales promotion**, market research.

- **Rent, rates** and **insurance** of sales offices and showrooms, bad debts and collection charges, cash discounts allowed, after sales service.
- **Freight and insurance charges**, rent, rates, insurance and depreciation of warehouses, depreciation and running expenses of delivery vehicles.

Activity 2 **(10 minutes)**

A direct labour employee's wage in week 5 consists of the following.

		£
(a)	Basic pay for normal hours worked, 36 hours at £4 per hour =	144
(b)	Pay at the basic rate for overtime, 6 hours at £4 per hour =	24
(c)	Overtime shift premium, with overtime paid at time-and-a-quarter ¼ × 6 hours × £4 per hour =	6
(d)	A bonus payment under a group bonus (or 'incentive') scheme - bonus for the month =	30
Total gross wages in week 5 for 42 hours of work		204

What is the direct labour cost for this employee in week 5?

4.7 Product costs and period costs

Definitions

- **Product costs** are costs identified with a finished product. Such costs are initially identified as part of the value of stock. They become expenses (in the form of cost of goods sold) only when the stock is sold.
- **Period costs** are costs that are deducted as expenses during the current period without ever being included in the value of stock held.

Consider a retailer who acquires goods for resale without changing their basic form. The only product cost is therefore the purchase cost of the goods. Any unsold goods are held as stock, valued at the lower of purchase cost and net realisable value, and included as an asset in the balance sheet. As the goods are sold, their cost becomes an expense in the form of 'cost of goods sold'. A retailer will also incur a variety of selling and administration expenses. Such costs are period costs because they are deducted from revenue without ever being regarded as part of the value of stock.

Now consider a manufacturing firm in which direct materials are transformed into saleable goods with the help of direct labour and factory overheads. All these costs are product costs because they are allocated to the value of stock until the goods are sold. As with the retailer, selling and administration expenses are regarded as period costs.

5 COST CLASSIFICATION FOR DECISION MAKING

Decision making is concerned with future events and hence management require information on expected future costs and revenues. Although cost accounting systems are designed to accumulate **past** costs and revenues this historical information may provide a starting point for forecasting future events.

5.1 Fixed costs and variable costs

A knowledge of how costs will vary at different levels of activity (or volume) is essential for decision making.

Definitions

- A **fixed cost** is a cost which is incurred for a particular period of time and which, within certain activity levels, is unaffected by changes in the level of activity.
- A **variable cost** is a cost which varies with the level of activity.

EXAMPLES

Some examples are as follows.

(a) Direct material costs are **variable costs** because they rise as more units of a product are manufactured.

(b) Sales commission is often a fixed percentage of sales turnover, and so is a **variable cost** that varies with the level of sales.

(c) Telephone call charges are likely to increase if the volume of business expands, and so they are a **variable overhead cost.**

(d) The rental cost of business premises is a constant amount, at least within a stated time period, and so it is a **fixed cost.**

Note that costs can be classified as direct costs or indirect costs/overheads, or as fixed costs or variable costs. These alternative classifications are not, however, mutually exclusive, but are complementary to each other, so that we can find some direct costs that are fixed costs (although they are commonly variable costs) and some overhead costs that are fixed and some overhead costs that are variable.

6 COST CLASSIFICATION FOR CONTROL

6.1 Controllable and uncontrollable costs

One of the purposes of cost accounting is to provide control information to management who wish to know whether or not a particular cost item can be controlled by management action.

Definitions

- A **controllable cost** is a cost which can be influenced by management decisions and actions.
- An **uncontrollable cost** is any cost that cannot be affected by management within a given time span.

7 COST BEHAVIOUR AND LEVELS OF ACTIVITY

Definition

Cost behaviour is 'The variability of input costs with activity undertaken'.

The level of activity refers to the amount of work done, or the number of events that have occurred. Depending on circumstances, the level of activity may refer to measures such as the following.

- The volume of production in a period.
- The number of items sold.
- The value of items sold.
- The number of invoices issued
- The number of units of electricity consumed.

7.1 Basic principles of cost behaviour

The basic principle of cost behaviour is that as the level of activity rises, costs will usually rise. It will probably cost more to produce 2,000 units of output than it will cost to produce 1,000 units; it will usually cost more to make five telephone calls than to make one call and so on. The problem for the accountant is to determine, for each item of cost, the way in which costs rise and by how much as the level of activity increases.

For our purposes in this chapter, the level of activity will generally be taken to be the volume of production/output.

8 COST BEHAVIOUR PATTERNS

8.1 Fixed costs

We discussed fixed costs briefly in Section 5. A **fixed cost** is a cost which tends to be unaffected by increases or decreases in the volume of output. Fixed costs are a **period charge**, in that they relate to a span of time; as the time span increases, so too will the fixed costs. A sketch graph of a fixed cost would look like this.

NOTES

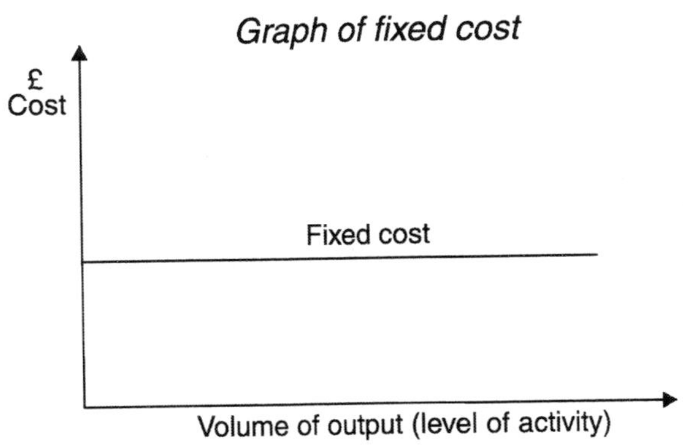

Figure 1.3 Graph of fixed cost

Examples of a fixed cost would be as follows.

- The salary of the managing director (per month or per annum)
- The rent of a single factory building (per month or per annum)
- Straight line depreciation of a single machine (per month or per annum)

8.2 Step costs

Definition

> A **step cost** is a cost which is fixed in nature but only within certain levels of activity.

Consider the depreciation of a machine which may be fixed if production remains below 1,000 units per month. If production exceeds 1,000 units, a second machine may be required, and the cost of depreciation (on two machines) would go up a step. A sketch graph of a step cost could look like this.

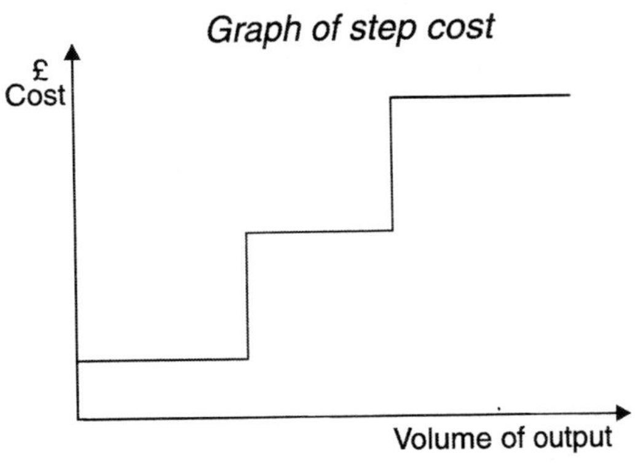

Figure 1.4 Graph of step cost

Other examples of step costs are as follows.

- Rent is a step cost in situations where accommodation requirements increase as output levels get higher.
- Basic pay of employees is nowadays usually fixed, but as output rises, more employees (direct workers, supervisors, managers and so on) are required.

8.3 Variable costs

We discussed variable costs briefly earlier in this chapter. A **variable cost** is a cost which tends to vary directly with the volume of output. The variable cost **per unit** is the same amount for each unit produced whereas **total** variable cost increases as volume of output increases. A sketch graph of a variable cost would look like this.

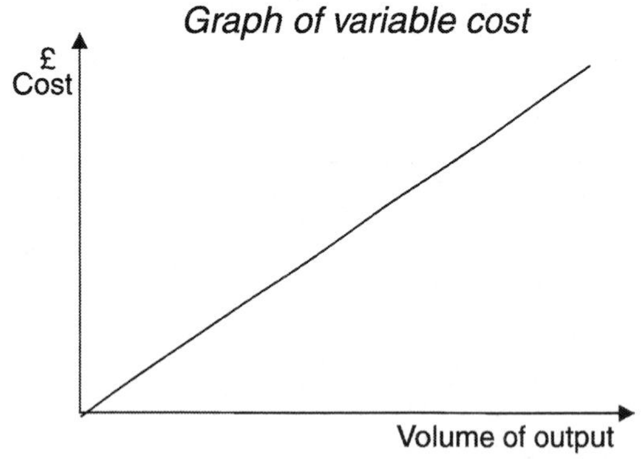

Figure 1.5 Graph of variable cost

Examples of variable costs are as follows.

- The cost of raw materials (where there is no discount for bulk purchasing since bulk purchase discounts reduce the unit cost of purchases).
- Direct labour costs are, for very important reasons which you will study later, usually classed as a variable cost even though basic wages are often fixed.
- Sales commission is variable in relation to the volume or value of sales.

8.4 Semi-variable costs (or semi-fixed costs or mixed costs)

Definition

> A **semi-variable/semi-fixed/mixed cost** is a cost which contains both fixed and variable components and so is partly affected by changes in the level of activity.

Examples of semi-variable costs include the following.

- **Electricity and gas bills**. There is a basic charge plus a charge per unit of consumption.
- **Sales representative's salary**. The sales representative may earn a basic monthly amount of, say, £1,000 and then commission of 10% of the value of sales made.

The behaviour of a semi-variable cost can be presented graphically as follows.

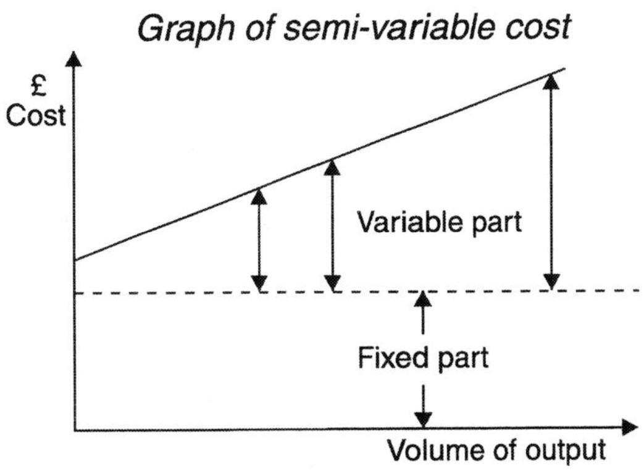

Figure 1.6 Graph of semi-variable cost

8.5 Cost behaviour and total and unit costs

If the variable cost of producing a unit is £5 per unit then it will remain at that cost per unit no matter how many units are produced. However if the business's fixed costs are £5,000 then the fixed cost *per unit* will decrease the more units are produced: one unit will have fixed costs of £5,000 per unit; if 2,500 are produced the fixed cost per unit will be £2; if 5,000 are produced the fixed cost per unit will be only £1. Thus as the level of activity increases the total costs *per unit* (fixed cost plus variable cost) will decrease.

In sketch graph form this may be illustrated as follows.

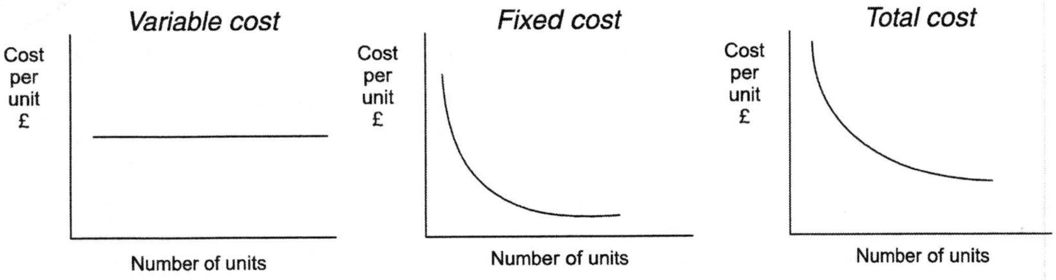

Figure 1.7 Cost behaviour

Activity 3 **(5 minutes)**

Are the following likely to be fixed, variable or mixed costs?

(a) Telephone bill

(b) Annual salary of the chief accountant

(c) The management accountant's annual membership fee to his professional body (paid by the company)

(d) Cost of materials used to pack 20 units of product X into a box

8.6 Assumptions about cost behaviour

It is often possible to assume that, within the normal or relevant range of output, costs are either fixed, variable or semi-variable.

9 DETERMINING THE FIXED AND VARIABLE ELEMENTS OF SEMI-VARIABLE COSTS

There are several ways in which fixed cost elements and variable cost elements within semi-variable costs may be ascertained. Each method only gives an estimate, and can therefore give differing results from the other methods. The principal methods are the high-low method and the scattergraph method.

9.1 High-low method

(a) Records of costs in previous periods are reviewed and the costs of the following two periods are selected.

- The period with the highest volume of activity
- The period with the lowest volume of activity

(b) The difference between the total cost of these two periods will be the variable cost of the difference in activity levels (since the same fixed cost is included in each total cost).

(c) The variable cost per unit may be calculated from this (difference in total costs ÷ difference in activity levels), and the fixed cost may then be determined by substitution.

EXAMPLE: THE HIGH-LOW METHOD

The costs of operating the maintenance department of a computer manufacturer, Sillick and Chips Ltd, for the last four months have been as follows.

Month	*Cost*	*Production volume*
	£	Units
1	110,000	7,000
2	115,000	8,000
3	111,000	7,700
4	97,000	6,000

Calculate the costs that should be expected in month five when output is expected to be 7,500 units. Ignore inflation.

ANSWER

(a)

	Units		£
High output or volume	8,000	Total cost	115,000
Low output or volume	6,000	Total cost	97,000
	2,000	Variable cost of	18,000
Variable cost per unit	£18,000/2,000 =		£9

(b) Substituting in either the high or low volume cost:

		High		*Low*
		£		£
Total cost		115,000		97,000
Variable costs	(8,000 × £9)	72,000	(6,000 × £9)	54,000
Fixed costs		43,000		43,000

(c) Estimated maintenance costs when output is 7,500 units:

	£
Fixed costs	43,000
Variable costs (7,500 × £9)	67,500
Total costs	110,500

Activity 4 **(15 minutes)**

The Valuation Department of a large firm of surveyors wishes to develop a method of predicting its total costs in a period. The following past costs have been recorded at two activity levels.

	Number of valuations (V)	*Total cost (£) (TC)*
Period 1	420	82,200
Period 2	515	90,275

The total cost model for a period could be represented as follows.

A TC = £46,500 + 85V
B TC = £42,000 + 95V
C TC = £46,500 – 85V
D TC = £51,500 – 95V

Which option is correct?

9.2 Scattergraph method

A scattergraph of costs in previous periods can be prepared (with cost on the vertical axis and volume of output on the horizontal axis). A **line of best fit**, which is a line drawn **by judgement** to pass through the middle of the points, thereby having as many points above the line as below it, can then be drawn and the fixed and variable costs determined.

A scattergraph of the cost and volume data in the high-low method example on the previous page is shown below.

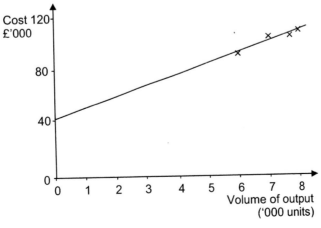

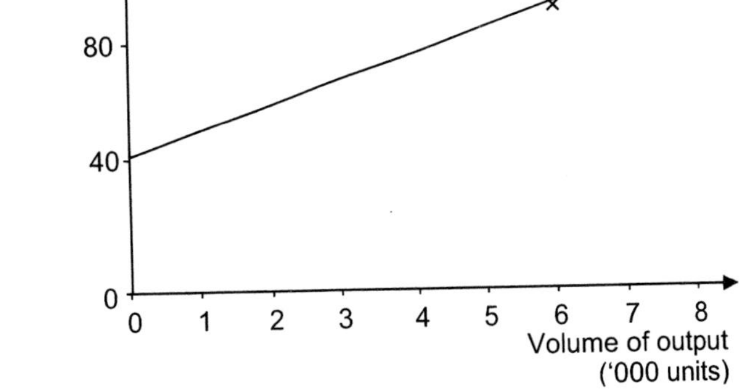

Figure 1.8 Scattergraph

The point where the line cuts the vertical axis (approximately £40,000) is the fixed cost (the cost if there is no output). If we take the value of one of the plotted points which lies close to the line and deduct the fixed cost from the total cost, we can calculate the variable cost per unit.

Total cost for 8,000 units	= £115,000
Variable cost for 8,000 units	= £(115,000 – 40,000) = £75,000
Variable cost per unit	= £75,000/8,000 = £9.375

Chapter roundup

- Cost accounting is a method of establishing stock valuations, profits and balance sheet items as well as a system for planning, control and decision making.
- Cost centres are collecting places for costs before they are further analysed. Cost units are the basic control units for costing purposes.
- A direct cost is a cost that can be traced in full to the product, service or department being costed. An indirect cost (or overhead) is a cost that is incurred in the course of making a product, providing a service or running a department, but which cannot be traced directly and in full to the product, service or department.
- For the preparation of financial statements, costs are often classified as either product costs or period costs. Product costs are costs identified with goods produced or purchased for resale. Period costs are costs deducted as expenses during the current period.
- Costs which are not affected by the level of activity are fixed costs or period costs.
- Step costs are fixed within a certain range of activity.
- Variable costs increase or decrease with the level of activity.
- Semi-fixed, semi-variable or mixed costs are costs which are part fixed and part variable.
- The fixed and variable elements of semi-variable costs can be determined by the high-low method or the scattergraph method.
- For control purposes, costs can be analysed as controllable or uncontrollable.

Quick quiz

1 What are cost centres and cost units?

2 Suggest a suitable cost unit for an accounting firm.

3 What is a direct cost?

4 Give three examples of a direct expense.

5 Give three examples of overheads.

6 What are product costs and period costs?

7 Give an example of a fixed cost and a step cost.

8 Describe the high-low method.

Answers to Quick quiz

1 Cost centres are collecting places for costs before they are further analysed (see Section 2.1). Cost units are units of product or service to which costs can be related.

2 Audit performed or chargeable hour.

3 A direct cost is a cost that can be traced in full to the product, service, or department that is being costed.

4 The cost of special designs, the hire of equipment, or the maintenance of tools, all incurred for a specific job.

5 Any three of the following:

Production overheads: consumable stores, foreman's salary, factory rent, rates and insurance, depreciation and maintenance of plant, fuel and power.

Administration overheads: depreciation of office equipment, office salaries, and other office expenses such as rent, electricity and postage.

Selling overheads: printing of catalogues, sales department salaries, advertising, and other sales department expenses such as bad debts, rent and settlement discounts allowed.

Distribution overheads: packing cases, wages of packers, clerks and van drivers, and other distribution expenses such as depreciation of vans and warehouses, and freight charges.

6 Product costs are costs identified with a finished product, and are included in the value of stock. Period costs are deducted as expenses in the current period and are not included in the value of stock.

7 Fixed costs: rent, managing director's salary, straight line depreciation of a single fixed asset.

Step cost: rent and supervisor's salary, when output increases such that additional resources are acquired (another factory or supervisor).

8 The high-low method of finding the fixed and variable components of a semi-variable cost involves three steps.

(i) Find the variable cost per unit using the data for the highest and lowest **output** levels.

Variable cost per unit =

$$\frac{\text{(Total cost at highest output level – total cost at lowest output level)}}{\text{(Highest output in units – lowest output in units)}}$$

(ii) Calculate the variable cost at the highest or lowest output (either will do).

Variable cost at highest output = Variable cost per unit x highest output (units)

(iii) Find the fixed costs using the total costs and variable costs at the output level used in (ii).

	£
Total costs at highest output level	x
Less: variable costs at highest output level	(x)
Fixed costs	x

The variable cost per unit and the total fixed costs can now be used to estimate the total costs at any output levels within the range covered by the original observed data (ie between the highest and lowest output levels referred to).

Answers to Activities

1 (a) Direct

(b) Indirect, however, if a customer asks for an order to be carried out which involves the dedicated use of indirect workers' time, the cost of this time would be a direct labour cost of the order as it is a cost which is traceable to a specific order.

(c) Overtime **premium** paid to both direct and indirect workers is usually an indirect cost because it is 'unfair' that an item made in overtime should be more costly just because, by chance, it was made after the employee normally clocks off for the day.

There are two particular circumstances in which the overtime premium might be a direct cost.

(i) Overtime worked at the specific request of a customer to get his order completed.

(ii) Overtime worked regularly by a production department in the normal course of operations.

(d) Generally indirect

(e) Employer's national insurance contributions (which are added to employees' total pay as a wages cost) are normally treated as an indirect labour cost.

(f) Indirect

(g) The cost of work on capital equipment is incorporated into the capital cost of the equipment and is therefore neither a direct nor an indirect production cost

2

		Direct cost	*Indirect cost*
		£	£
(a)	Basic pay	144	
(b)	Basic rate on overtime	24	
(c)	Overtime shift premium		6
(d)	Bonus payment		30
		168	36

Note the basic rate for overtime is a part of direct wages cost. It is only the overtime **premium** that is usually regarded as an overhead or indirect cost.

3 (a) Mixed
(b) Fixed
(c) Fixed
(d) Variable

4 Apply the high-low method.

	Valuations	*Total cost*
	V	£
Period 2 – high	515	90,275
Period 1 – low	420	82,200
Change due to variable cost	95	8,075

∴ Variable cost valuation = £8,075/95 = £85.

Period 2: fixed cost = £90,275 – (515 × £85)
= £46,500

Therefore TC = 46,500 + 85V, option A.

Chapter : 2

MATERIALS AND LABOUR COSTS

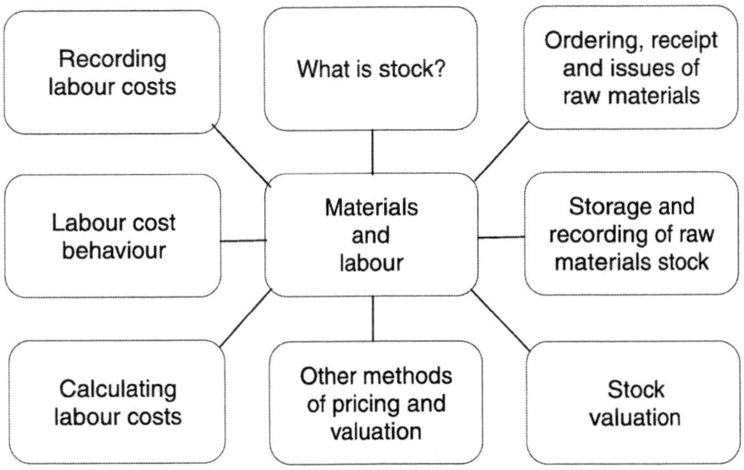

Introduction

The investment in stock is a very important one for most businesses, both in terms of monetary value and relationships with customers (no stock, no sale, loss of customer goodwill). It is therefore vital that management establish and maintain an **effective stock control system** and that they are aware of the major costing problem relating to materials, that of pricing materials issues and valuing stock at the end of each period.

You should note that this chapter does not include detailed material on stock control levels and re-ordering. This topic is covered in Unit 6 (and previously in Unit 5) of the HNC/HND Business qualification, and you should refer back to the work you did for those units.

Your objectives

In this chapter you will learn about the following.

(a) The nature of stock
(b) The ordering, receipt and issue of raw materials
(c) The storage and recording of raw materials
(d) Stock valuation
(e) FIFO (first in, first out)
(f) LIFO (last in, first out)
(g) Cumulative weighted average pricing
(h) Other methods of pricing and valuation
(i) Stock valuation and profitability
(j) Calculating labour costs
(k) Labour cost behaviour
(l) Recording labour costs

1 WHAT IS STOCK?

The stocks held in any organisation can generally be classified under four main headings.

- Raw materials
- Work in progress
- Finished goods
- Spare parts/consumables

Not all organisations will have stock of all four general categories. It is worth noting that the terms 'stock' and 'inventory' are often used interchangeably in many organisations.

This chapter will concentrate on raw materials, but similar problems and considerations apply to all forms of stock.

2 THE ORDERING, RECEIPT AND ISSUE OF RAW MATERIALS

2.1 Ordering and receiving materials

Proper records must be kept of the physical procedures for ordering and receiving a consignment of materials to ensure the following.

- That enough stock is held
- That there is no duplication of ordering
- That quality is maintained
- That there is adequate record keeping for accounts purposes

---

EXAMPLE

A typical series of procedures might be as follows.

(a) Current stocks run down to the level where a reorder is required. The stores department issues a **purchase requisition** which is sent to the purchasing department, authorising the department to order further stock. An example of a purchase requisition is shown below.

PURCHASE REQUISITION Req. No.

Department/job number:
Suggested Supplier:

Date

Requested by:
Latest date required:

Quantity	Code number	Description	Estimated Cost	
			Unit	£

Authorised signature:

(b) The purchase department draws a **purchase order** which is sent to the supplier. (The supplier may be asked to return an acknowledgement copy as confirmation of his acceptance of the order.) Copies of the purchase order must be sent to the accounts department and the storekeeper (or receiving department).

Purchase Order/Confirmation

Our Order Ref: Date

To

(Address)

Please deliver to the above address

Ordered by:

Passed and checked by:

Total Order Value £

		Subtotal		
		VAT (@ 17.5%)		
		Total		

(c) The purchasing department may have to obtain a number of quotations if either a new stock line is required, the existing supplier's costs are too high or the existing supplier no longer stocks the goods needed. Trade discounts (reduction in the price per unit given to some customers) should be negotiated where possible.

(d) The supplier delivers the consignment of materials, and the storekeeper signs a **delivery note** for the carrier. The packages must then be checked against the copy of the purchase order, to ensure that the supplier has delivered the types and quantities of materials which were ordered. (Discrepancies would be referred to the purchasing department.)

(e) If the delivery is acceptable, the storekeeper prepares a **goods received note (GRN)**, an example of which is shown below.

GOODS RECEIVED NOTE		WAREHOUSE COPY NO 5565
DATE:	TIME:	
OUR ORDER NO:		WAREHOUSE A
SUPPLIER AND SUPPLIER'S ADVICE NOTE NO:		
QUANTITY	CAT NO	DESCRIPTION
RECEIVED IN GOOD CONDITION:		(INITIALS)

(f) A copy of the **GRN** is sent to the accounts department, where it is matched with the copy of the purchase order. The supplier's invoice is checked against the purchase order and GRN, and the necessary steps are taken to pay the supplier. The invoice may contain details relating to discounts such as trade discounts, quantity discounts (order in excess of a specified amount) and settlement discounts (payment received within a specified number of days).

Activity 1 **(10 minutes)**

What are the possible consequences of a failure of control over ordering and receipt of materials?

2.2 Issue of materials

Materials can only be issued to production against a **materials/stores requisition**. This document must record not only the quantity of goods issued, but also the cost centre or the job number for which the requisition is being made. The materials requisition note may also have a column, to be filled in by the cost department, for recording the cost or value of the materials issued to the cost centre or job.

Materials requisition note			
Date required		Cost centre No/ Job No	
Quantity	*Item code*	*Description*	£
Signature of requisitioning Manager/ Foreman			Date ......

2.3 Materials transfers and returns

Where materials, having been issued to one job or cost centre, are later transferred to a different job or cost centre, without first being returned to stores, a **materials transfer note** should be raised. Such a note must show not only the job receiving the transfer, but also the job from which it is transferred. This enables the appropriate charges to be made to jobs or cost centres.

Material returns must also be documented on a **materials returned note**. This document is the 'reverse' of a requisition note, and must contain similar information. In fact it will often be almost identical to a requisition note. It will simply have a different title and perhaps be a distinctive colour, such as red, to highlight the fact that materials are being returned.

2.4 Impact of computerisation

Many stock control systems these days are computerised. Computerised stock control systems vary greatly, but most will have the features outlined below.

(a) **Data must be input into the system**. For example, details of goods received may simply be written on to a GRN for later entry into the computer system. Alternatively, this information may be keyed in directly to the computer: a GRN will be printed and then signed as evidence of the transaction, so that both the warehouse and the supplier can have a hard copy record in case of dispute. Some systems may incorporate the use of devices such as bar code readers.

Other types of transaction which will need to be recorded include the following.

- **Transfers** between different categories of stock (for example from work in progress to finished goods)
- **Despatch**, resulting from a sale of items of finished goods to customers
- **Adjustments** to stock records if the amount of stock revealed in a physical stock count differs from the amount appearing on the stock records

(b) **A stock master file is maintained**. This file will contain details for every category of stock and will be updated for new stock lines. A database file may be maintained.

Activity 2 **(5 minutes)**

What type of information do you think should be held on a stock master file?

The file may also hold details of stock movements over a period, but this will depend on the type of system in operation. In a **batch system**, transactions will be grouped and input in one operation and details of the movements may be held in a separate transactions file, the master file updated in total only. In an **on-line system**, transactions may be input directly to the master file, where the record of movements is thus likely to be found. Such a system will mean that the stock records are constantly up to date, which will help in monitoring and controlling stock.

The system may generate orders automatically once the amount in stock has fallen to the reorder level.

(c) **The system will generate outputs**. These may include, depending on the type of system, any of the following.

- **Hard copy** records, for example a printed GRN, of transactions entered into the system.
- Output on a **VDU** screen in response to an enquiry (for example the current level of a particular line of stock, or details of a particular transaction).
- Various **printed reports**, devised to fit in with the needs of the organisation. These may include stock movement reports, detailing over a period the movements on all stock lines, listings of GRNs, despatch notes and so forth.

A computerised stock control system is usually able to give more up to date information and more flexible reporting than a manual system but remember that both manual and computer based stock control systems need the same types of data to function properly.

3 THE STORAGE AND RECORDING OF RAW MATERIALS STOCK

Storekeeping involves storing materials to achieve the following objectives.

- Speedy **issue** and **receipt** of materials
- Full **identification** of all materials at all times
- Correct **location** of all materials at all times
- **Protection** of materials from damage and deterioration
- Provision of **secure stores** to avoid pilferage, theft and fire
- **Efficient** use of storage space
- **Maintenance** of correct stock levels
- Keeping correct and up-to-date **records** of receipts, issues and stock levels

3.1 Recording stock levels

One of the objectives of storekeeping is to maintain accurate records of current stock levels. This involves the accurate recording of stock movements (issues from and receipts into stores). The most frequently encountered system for recording stock movements is the use of bin cards and stores ledger accounts.

3.2 Bin cards

A **bin card** shows the level of stock of an item at a particular stores location. It is kept with the actual stock and is updated by the storekeeper as stocks are received and issued. A typical bin card is shown below.

NOTES

Bin card

Part code no................ Location ....

Bin number .... Stores ledger no ....

Receipts			*Issues*			Stock balance
Date	Quantity	G.R.N. No.	Date	Quantity	Req. No.	

The use of bin cards is decreasing, partly due to the difficulty in keeping them updated and partly due to the merging of stock recording and control procedures, frequently using computers.

3.3 Stores ledger accounts

A typical stores ledger account is shown below. Note that it shows the value of stock.

Stores ledger account

Material .... Maximum Quantity ....

Code .... Minimum Quantity ....

Date	Receipts				Issues				Stock		
	G.R.N. No.	Quantity	Unit Price £	Amount £	Stores Req. No.	Quantity	Unit Price £	Amount £	Quantity	Unit Price £	Amount £

The above illustration shows a card for a manual system, but even when the stock records are computerised, the same type of information is normally included in the computer file. The running balance on the stores ledger account allows stock levels and valuation to be monitored.

3.4 Free stock

Managers need to know the **free stock balance** in order to obtain a full picture of the current stock position of an item. Free stock represents what is really **available for future use** and is calculated as follows.

	Materials in stock	X
+	Materials on order from suppliers	X
–	Materials requisitioned, not yet issued	(X)
	Free stock balance	X

Knowledge of the level of physical stock assists stock issuing, stocktaking and controlling maximum and minimum stock levels: knowledge of the level of free stock assists ordering.

Activity 3 **(10 minutes)**

A wholesaler has 8,450 units outstanding for Part X100 on existing customers' orders; there are 3,925 units in stock and the calculated free stock is 5,525 units.

How many units does the wholesaler have on order with his supplier?

3.5 Identification of materials: stock codes (materials codes)

Materials held in stores are **coded** and **classified**. Advantages of using code numbers to identify materials are as follows.

- Ambiguity is avoided.
- Time is saved. Descriptions can be lengthy and time-consuming.
- Production efficiency is improved. The correct material can be accurately identified from a code number.
- Computerised processing is made easier.
- Numbered code systems can be designed to be flexible, and can be expanded to include more stock items as necessary.

The digits in a code can stand for the type of stock, supplier, department and so forth.

3.6 Stocktaking

Stocktaking involves counting the physical stock on hand at a certain date, and then checking this against the balance shown in the stock records. There are two methods of carrying out this process, **periodic stocktaking** and **continuous stocktaking**.

Periodic stocktaking is a process whereby all stock items are physically counted and then valued. This is usually carried out **annually** and the objective is to count all items of stock on a specific date.

Continuous stocktaking is the process of counting and valuing selected items at different times on a rotating basis. This involves a specialist team counting and checking a number of stock items each day, so that each item is checked at least once a year. Valuable items or items with a high turnover could be checked more frequently. The advantages of this system compared to periodic stocktaking are as follows.

(a) The annual stocktaking is unnecessary and the disruption it causes is avoided.

(b) Regular skilled stocktakers can be employed, reducing likely errors.

(c) More time is available, reducing errors and allowing investigation.

(d) Deficiencies and losses are revealed sooner than they would be if stocktaking were limited to an annual check.

(e) Production hold-ups are eliminated because the stores staff are at no time so busy as to be unable to deal with material issues to production departments.

(f) Staff morale is improved and standards raised.

(g) Control over stock levels is improved, and there is less likelihood of overstocking or running out of stock.

3.7 Stock discrepancies

There will be occasions when stock checks disclose discrepancies between the physical amount of an item in stock and the amount shown in the stock records. When this occurs, the cause of the discrepancy should be investigated, and appropriate action taken to ensure that it does not happen again.

3.8 Perpetual inventory

A perpetual inventory system involves recording every receipt and issue of stock as it occurs on bin cards and stores ledger accounts. This means that there is a continuous record of the balance of each item of stock. The balance on the stores ledger account therefore represents the stock on hand and this balance is used in the calculation of closing stock in monthly and annual accounts. In practice, physical stocks may not agree with recorded stocks and therefore continuous stocktaking is necessary to ensure that the perpetual inventory system is functioning correctly and that minor stock discrepancies are corrected.

3.9 Obsolete, deteriorating and slow-moving stocks and wastage

Obsolete stocks are those items which have become out-of-date and are no longer required. Obsolete items are written off to the profit and loss account and disposed of.

Stock items may be wasted because, for example, they get broken. All **wastage** should be noted on the stock records immediately so that physical stock equals the stock balance on records and the cost of the wastage written off to the profit and loss account.

Slow-moving stocks are stock items which are likely to take a long time to be used up. For example, 5,000 units are in stock, and only 20 are being used each year. This is often caused by overstocking. Managers should investigate such stock items and, if it is felt that the usage rate is unlikely to increase, excess stock should be written off as for obsolete stock, leaving perhaps four or five years' supply in stock.

4 STOCK VALUATION

For financial accounting purposes, stocks are valued at the **lower of cost and net realisable value** (ie the lower of what they cost the business and what the business is likely to receive selling them). In practice, stocks will usually be valued at cost in the stores records throughout the course of an accounting period. Only when the period ends will the value of the stock in hand be reconsidered so that items with a net realisable value below their original cost will be revalued downwards, and the stock records altered accordingly.

4.1 Charging units of stock to cost of production or cost of sales

It is important to be able to distinguish between the way in which the physical items in stock are actually issued. In practice a storekeeper may issue goods in the following way.

- The oldest goods first
- The latest goods received first

- Randomly
- Those which are easiest to reach

By comparison the cost of the goods issued must be determined on a **consistently applied basis**, and must ignore the likelihood that the materials issued will be costed at a price different to the amount paid for them.

This may seem a little confusing at first, and it may be helpful to explain the point further. Suppose that there are three units of a particular material in stock.

Units	*Date received*	*Purchase cost*
A	June 20X1	£100
B	July 20X1	£106
C	August 20X1	£109

In September, one unit is issued to production. As it happened, the physical unit actually issued was B. The accounting department must put a value or cost on the material issued, but the value would not necessarily be the cost of B, £106. The principles used to value the materials issued are not concerned with the actual unit issued, A, B, or C. Nevertheless, the accountant may choose to make one of the following assumptions.

(a) The unit issued is valued as though it were the earliest unit in stock, ie at the purchase cost of A, £100. This valuation principle is called FIFO, or first in, first out.

(b) The unit issued is valued as though it were the most recent unit received into stock, ie at the purchase cost of C, £109. This method of valuation is LIFO, or last in, first out.

(c) The unit issued is valued at an average price of A, B and C, ie £105.

In the following sections we will consider each of the pricing methods detailed above (and a few more), using the following transactions to illustrate the principles in each case.

EXAMPLE

TRANSACTIONS DURING MAY 20X3

	Quantity Units	*Unit cost* £	*Total cost* £	*Market value per unit on date of transaction* £
Opening balance, 1 May				
(the opening stock, or o/s)	100	2.00	200	
Receipts, 3 May	400	2.10	840	2.11
Issues, 4 May	200			2.11
Receipts, 9 May	300	2.12	636	2.15
Issues, 11 May	400			2.20
Receipts, 18 May	100	2.40	240	2.35
Issues, 20 May	100			2.35
Closing balance, 31 May	200			2.38
			1,916	

---

5 FIFO (FIRST IN, FIRST OUT)

FIFO assumes that materials are issued out of stock in the order in which they were delivered into stock: issues are priced at the cost of the earliest delivery remaining in stock. (Remember this has nothing to do with how the physical stock is issued – we are dealing with stock valuation.)

Using **FIFO**, the cost of issues and the closing stock value in the example would be as follows.

Date of issue	*Quantity issued*	*Value*		
	Units		£	£
4 May	200	100 o/s at £2	200	
		100 at £2.10	210	
				410
11 May	400	300 at £2.10	630	
		100 at £2.12	212	
				842
20 May	100	100 at £2.12		212
Cost of issues				1,464
Closing stock value	200	100 at £2.12	212	
		100 at £2.40	240	
				452
				1,916

Notes

(a) The cost of materials issued plus the value of closing stock equals the cost of purchases plus the value of opening stock (£1,916).

(b) The market price of purchased materials is rising dramatically. In a period of inflation, there is a tendency with FIFO for materials to be issued at a cost lower than the current market value, although closing stocks tend to be valued at a cost approximating to current market value.

5.1 The advantages and disadvantages of the FIFO method

(a) **Advantages**

(i) It is a logical pricing method which probably represents what is physically happening: in practice the oldest stock is likely to be used first.

(ii) It is easy to understand and explain to managers.

(iii) The stock valuation can be near to a valuation based on replacement cost.

(b) **Disadvantages**

(i) FIFO can be cumbersome to operate because of the need to identify each batch of material separately.

(ii) Managers may find it difficult to compare costs and make decisions when they are charged with varying prices for the same materials.

(iii) In a period of high inflation, stock issue prices will lag behind current market value.

Activity 4 **(30 minutes)**

Draw up an extract from a stores ledger account using the columns shown below. Complete the columns in as much details as possible using the information in the example on the previous page.

STORES LEDGER ACCOUNT

	Receipts				Issues				Stock		
Date	GRN No.	Quantity	Unit price £	Amount £	Stores Req. No.	Quantity	Unit price £	Amount £	Quantity	Unit price £	Amount £

6 LIFO (LAST IN, FIRST OUT)

LIFO assumes that materials are issued out of stock in the reverse order to which they were delivered: the most recent deliveries are issued before earlier ones, and are priced accordingly.

Using **LIFO**, the cost of issues and the closing stock value in the example above would be as follows.

Date of issue	*Quantity issued* Units	*Valuation*	£	£
4 May	200	200 at £2.10		420
11 May	400	300 at £2.12	636	
		100 at £2.10	210	
				846
20 May	100	100 at £2.40		240
Cost of issues				1,506
Closing stock value	200	100 at £2.10	210	
		100 at £2.00	200	
				410
				1,916

Notes

(a) The cost of materials issued plus the value of closing stock equals the cost of purchases plus the value of opening stock (£1,916).

(b) In a period of inflation there is a tendency with **LIFO** for the following to occur.

(i) Materials are issued at a price which approximates to current market value.

(ii) Closing stocks become undervalued when compared to market value.

NOTES

6.1 The advantages and disadvantages of the LIFO method

(a) **Advantages**

(i) Stocks are issued at a price which is close to current market value.

(ii) Managers are continually aware of recent costs when making decisions, because the costs being charged to their department or products will be current costs.

(b) **Disadvantages**

(i) The method can be cumbersome to operate because it sometimes results in several batches being only part-used in the stock records before another batch is received.

(ii) LIFO is often the opposite to what is physically happening and can therefore be difficult to explain to managers.

(iii) As with FIFO, decision making can be difficult because of the variations in prices.

7 CUMULATIVE WEIGHTED AVERAGE PRICING

The **cumulative weighted average pricing method, AVCO,** calculates a weighted average price for all units in stock. Issues are priced at this average cost, and the balance of stock remaining would have the same unit valuation. The average price is determined by dividing the total cost by the total number of units.

A new weighted average price is calculated whenever a new delivery of materials into store is received. This is the key feature of cumulative weighted average pricing.

EXAMPLE

In our example, issue costs and closing stock values would be as follows.

Date	*Received* Units	*Issued* Units	*Balance* Units	*Total stock value* £	*Unit cost* £	£
Opening stock			100	200	2.00	
3 May	400			840	2.10	
			* 500	1,040	2.08	
4 May		200		(416)	2.08	416
			300	624	2.08	
9 May	300			636	2.12	
			* 600	1,260	2.10	
11 May		400		(840)	2.10	840
			200	420	2.10	
18 May	100			240	2.40	
			* 300	660	2.20	
20 May		100		(220)	2.20	220
						1,476
Closing stock value			200	440	2.20	440
						1,916

* A new stock value per unit is calculated whenever a new receipt of materials occurs.

Notes

(a) The cost of materials issued plus the value of closing stock equals the cost of purchases plus the value of opening stock (£1,916).

(b) In a period of inflation, using the cumulative weighted average pricing system, the value of material issues will rise gradually, but will tend to lag a little behind the current market value at the date of issue. Closing stock values will also be a little below current market value.

7.1 The advantages and disadvantages of cumulative weighted average pricing

(a) **Advantages**

- (i) Fluctuations in prices are smoothed out, making it easier to use the data for decision making.
- (ii) It is easier to administer than FIFO and LIFO, because there is no need to identify each batch separately.

(b) **Disadvantages**

- (i) The resulting issue price is rarely an actual price that has been paid, and can run to several decimal places.
- (ii) Prices tend to lag a little behind current market values when there is gradual inflation.

Activity 5 **(30 minutes)**

An organisation has recorded the following details on an item of stock for the month of June.

	Units	*Cost per unit*
Opening stock	300	£5
4 June – issue	50	
7 June – receipt	100	£5.56
10 June – issue	75	
11 June – issue	100	
15 June – receipt	100	£5.27
20 June – issue	200	

What would be the cost of issues and valuation of the closing stock if:

(a) LIFO is used to value stocks
(b) AVCO is used to value stocks

8 OTHER METHODS OF PRICING AND VALUATION

8.1 Standard cost pricing

Under the standard cost pricing method, all issues are at predetermined standard price. Such a method is used with a system of standard costing, which will be covered later in this text.

8.2 Replacement cost pricing

Arguments for **replacement cost pricing** include the following.

- When materials are issued out of stores, they will be replaced with a new delivery; issues should therefore be priced at the current cost to the business of replacing them in stores.
- Closing stocks should be valued at current replacement cost in the balance sheet to show the true value of the assets of the business.

The advantages and disadvantages of **replacement costing** are as follows.

(a) **Advantages**

(i) Issues are at up-to-date costs so that managers can take recent trends into account when making decisions based on their knowledge of the costs being incurred.

(ii) It is recommended as a method of accounting for inflation.

(iii) It is easy to operate once the replacement cost has been determined.

(b) **Disadvantages**

(i) The price may not be an actual price paid, and a difference will then arise on issues.

(ii) It can be difficult to determine the replacement cost.

(iii) The method is not acceptable to the HM Revenue and Customs or for SSAP 9, although this should not be a major consideration in internal cost accounts.

Activity 6 **(5 minutes)**

Which pricing method can be used as a practical alternative to replacement cost pricing?

8.3 Specific price

This method values issues at their individual price and the stock balance is made up of individual items valued at individual prices. It is only really suitable for expensive stock lines where stock holdings and usage rates are low.

9 STOCK VALUATION AND PROFITABILITY

In the previous descriptions of FIFO, LIFO, average costing and so on, the example used raw materials as an illustration. Each method produced different figures for both the value of closing stocks and also the cost of material issues. Since raw materials costs affect the cost of production, and the cost of production works through eventually into the cost of sales, it follows that different methods of stock valuation will provide different profit figures.

10 CALCULATING LABOUR COSTS

Labour remuneration methods need to be considered very carefully as they will affect the following.

- The cost of finished products or services.
- The morale and efficiency of employees

There are three basic groups of remuneration method.

- Time work
- Piecework schemes
- Bonus/incentive schemes

We will discuss each of these in the next few paragraphs.

10.1 Time work

Formula to learn

> The most common form of **time work** is a **day-rate system** in which wages are calculated by the following formula.
>
> Wages = Hours worked × Rate of pay per hour

If an employee works for more hours than the basic daily requirement he may be entitled to an **overtime payment**. Hours of overtime are usually paid at a premium rate. For instance, if the basic day-rate is £8 per hour and overtime is paid at time-and-a-quarter, eight hours of overtime would be paid the following amount.

	£
Basic pay (8 × £4)	64
Overtime premium (8 × £1)	15
Total (8 × £5)	80

The **overtime premium** is the extra rate per hour which is paid, not the whole of the payment for the overtime hours. Overtime can be at any agreed rate; common examples are time-and-a-half or double time.

If employees work unsocial hours, for instance overnight, they may be entitled to a **shift premium**. This is similar to an overtime premium and means that the employee is paid an increased hourly rate. The extra amount paid per hour, above the basic hourly rate, is the shift premium.

Day-rate systems are most appropriate when the quality of output is more important than the quantity, or where there is no basis for payment by performance because there is no incentive for employees who are paid on this basis to improve their performance.

10.2 Piecework schemes

Formula to learn

> In a **piecework scheme**, wages are calculated by the following formula.
>
> Wages = Units produced × Rate of pay per unit

Suppose for example, an employee is paid £5 for each unit produced and works a 40 hour week. Production overhead is added at the rate of £2 per direct labour hour.

Weekly production	*Pay (40 hours)*	*Overhead*	*Conversion cost*	*Conversion cost per unit*
Units	£	£	£	£
40	200	80	280	7.00
50	250	80	330	6.60
60	300	80	380	6.33
70	380	80	430	6.15

As his output increases, his wage increases and at the same time unit costs of output are reduced.

It is normal for pieceworkers to be offered a **guaranteed minimum wage,** so that they do not suffer loss of earnings when production is low through no fault of their own.

If an employee makes several different types of product, it may not be possible to add up the units for payment purposes. Instead, a **standard time allowance** is given for each unit to arrive at a total of piecework hours for payment.

WORKED EXAMPLE: PIECEWORK

An employee is paid £6 per piecework hour produced. In a 40 hour week he produces the following output.

	Piecework time allowed per unit
15 units of product X	0.5 hours
20 units of product Y	2.0 hours

Calculate the employee's pay for the week.

ANSWER

Piecework hours produced are as follows.

Product X	15 × 0.5 hours	7.5 hours
Product Y	20 × 2.0 hours	40.0 hours
Total piecework hours		47.5 hours

Therefore employee's pay = 47.5 × £6 = £285.00 for the week.

10.3 Differential piecework schemes

These offer an incentive to employees to increase their output by paying higher rates for increased levels of production. For example:

up to and including 80 units, rate of pay per unit in this band	=	£1.00
81 to 90 units, rate of pay per unit in this band	=	£1.20
above 90 units, rate of pay per unit in this band	=	£1.30

An employee producing 97 units would therefore receive (80 × £1.00) + (10 × £1.20) + (7 × £1.30) = £101.10.

Employers should obviously be careful to make it clear whether they intend to pay the increased rate on all units produced, or on the extra output only.

10.4 Summary

Piecework schemes may be summarised as follows.

- They enjoy fluctuating popularity.
- They are occasionally used by employers as a means of increasing pay levels.
- They are frequently condemned as a means of driving employees to work too hard to earn a satisfactory wage.
- Careful inspection of output is necessary to ensure that quality is maintained as production increases.

10.5 Bonus/incentive schemes

In general, bonus schemes were introduced to compensate workers paid under a time-based system for their inability to increase earnings by working more efficiently. Various types of incentive and bonus schemes have been devised which encourage greater productivity. The characteristics of such schemes are as follows.

(a) A target is set and actual performance is compared with target.

(b) Employees are paid more for their efficiency.

(c) In spite of the extra labour cost, the unit cost of output is reduced and the profit earned per unit of sale is increased; in other words the profits arising from productivity improvements are shared between employer and employee.

(d) Morale of employees should be expected to improve since they are seen to receive extra reward for extra effort.

There are many possible types of incentive schemes.

(a) A **high day-rate system** is an incentive scheme where employees are paid a high hourly wage rate in the expectation that they will work more efficiently than similar employees on a lower hourly rate in a different company.

(b) Under an **individual bonus scheme**, individual employees qualify for a bonus on top of their basic wage, with each person's bonus being calculated separately.

(c) Where individual effort cannot be measured, and employees work as a team, an individual incentive scheme is impractical but a **group bonus scheme** is feasible.

(d) In a **profit sharing scheme**, employees receive a certain proportion of their company's year-end profits (the size of their bonus being related to their position in the company and the length of their employment to date).

(e) Companies operating **incentive schemes involving shares** use their shares, or the right to acquire them, as a form of incentive.

Note that an employer may provide other bonuses and benefits (company cars, non-contributory pension schemes, subsidised canteen). Such benefits do not always improve production so much as reduce labour turnover.

10.6 Labour turnover

Labour turnover is a measure of the rate at which employees are leaving an organisation. It is usually calculated as follows.

$$\text{Labour turnover for the period} = \frac{\text{number of employees leaving and replaced}}{\text{average workforce}} \times 100$$

A high turnover can be costly for an organisation. For example new employees must be recruited and trained, they may work at a slower rate and there may be a loss of output due to a delay in the new labour becoming available.

The level of labour turnover should obviously be minimised and well-designed remuneration and incentive schemes can contribute towards this.

WORKED EXAMPLE: INCENTIVE SCHEMES

Swetton Tyres Ltd manufactures a single product. Its work force consists of 10 employees, who work a 36-hour week exclusive of lunch and tea breaks. The standard time required to make one unit of the product is two hours, but the current efficiency (or productivity) ratio being achieved is 80%. No overtime is worked, and the work force is paid £8 per attendance hour.

Because of agreements with the work force about work procedures, there is some unavoidable idle time due to bottlenecks in production, and about four hours per week per person are lost in this way.

The company can sell all the output it manufactures, and makes a 'cash profit' of £40 per unit sold, deducting currently achievable costs of production but *before* deducting labour costs.

An incentive scheme is proposed whereby the work force would be paid £10 per hour in exchange for agreeing to new work procedures that would reduce idle time per employee per week to two hours and also raise the efficiency ratio to 90%. Evaluate the incentive scheme from the point of view of profitability.

SOLUTION

The current situation

Hours paid for: 10 employees × 36 hours per week = 360 hours

Hours working 10 employees × 32 hours working = 320 hours

Note: there are 4 hours per week of idle time per employee hence 36 – 4 = 32 hours working.

At 80% efficiency:

Expected units produced = 320 hours worked ÷ 2 hours per unit
= 160 expected units

Note: each unit takes 2 hours to produce

At 80% efficiency: $160 \times \frac{80}{100}$ = 128 units actually produced

	£
Cash profits before deducting labour costs (128 × £40)	5,120
Less labour costs (£8 × 360 hours paid for)	2,880
Net profit	2,240

The incentive scheme

Hours working: 10 employees × 34 hours = 340 hours

Note: idle time has now been reduced to 2 hours per week per employee so 36 – 2 = 34 hours.

Units produced, at 90% efficiency $\frac{340}{2} \times \frac{90}{100}$ = 153 units

	£
Cash profits before deducting labour costs (153 × £40)	6,120
Less labour costs (£10 × 360)	3,600
Net profit	2,520

In spite of a 25% increase in labour costs, profits would rise by £280 per week. The company and the workforce would both benefit provided, of course, that management can hold the work force to their promise of work reorganisation and improved productivity.

Activity 7 **(10 minutes)**

The following data relate to work at a certain factory.

Normal working day 8 hours

Basic rate of pay per hour £12

Standard time allowed to produce 1 unit 2 minutes

Premium bonus 75% of time saved at basic rate

What will be the labour cost in a day when 340 units are made?

11 LABOUR COST BEHAVIOUR

(a) When employees are paid on a piecework basis their pay is a variable cost.

(b) When employees are paid a basic day-rate wage, their pay per week is fixed, regardless of the volume of output. The high cost of redundancy payments and the scarcity of skilled labour will usually persuade a company to retain its employees at a basic wage even when output is low.

(c) Because of productivity bonuses, overtime premium, commission and so on, labour costs are often mixed semi-variable costs.

Labour costs tend to behave in a step cost fashion.

(a) Where the steps are short (that is where extra labour is needed for small increases in output volumes), the labour costs tend to approximate a variable cost.

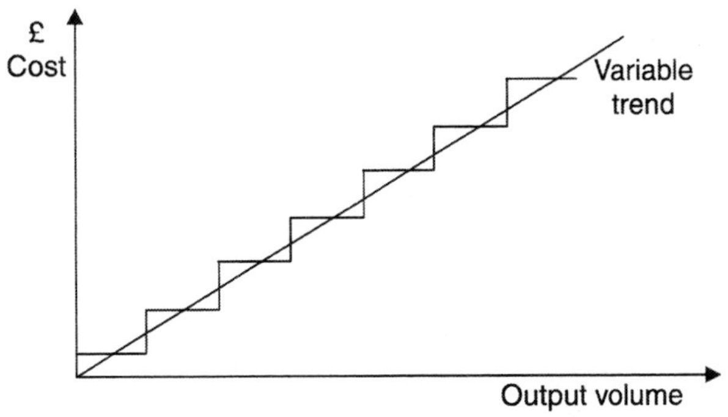

In this graph, the short steps approximate closely to a variable cost line, and for most purposes, it will be sufficiently accurate to treat labour as a purely variable cost.

(b) If, on the other hand, the labour force is static for wide ranges of output, the cost tends to be fixed in nature.

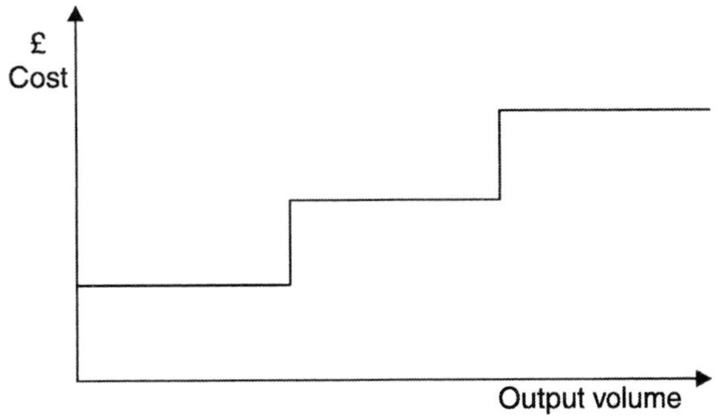

Figure 2.1 Volume cost graphs

The cost accountant has to treat labour costs as fixed or variable.

(a) Direct labour is usually regarded as being a variable cost in labour-intensive work. In highly automated industries it may be regarded as a fixed cost.

(b) For control purposes, direct labour is regarded as a variable cost so that measures of efficiency or productivity can be obtained.

NOTES

12 RECORDING LABOUR COSTS

12.1 Organisation for controlling and measuring labour costs

Several departments and management groups are involved in the collection, recording and costing of labour. These include the following.

- Personnel
- Production planning
- Timekeeping
- Wages
- Cost accounting

From a cost accounting point of view, the **timekeeping department** provides the most important information to facilitate the recording of labour cost. The timekeeping department is responsible for accurately recording the time spent in the factory by each worker and time spent by each worker on each job or operation: attendance time and job time respectively. Such timekeeping provides basic data for statutory records, payroll preparation, labour costs of an operation or overhead absorption (where based on wages or labour hours) and statistical analysis of labour records for determining productivity and control of labour costs.

12.2 Attendance time

The bare minimum record of employees' time is a simple **attendance record** showing days absent because of holiday, sickness or other reason.

It is also necessary to have a record of the following.

- Time of arrival
- Time of breaks
- Time of departure

These may be recorded as follows.

- In a signing-in book
- By using a time recording clock which stamps the time on a clock card
- By using swipe cards (which make a computer record)

An example of a clock card is shown on the next page.

NOTES

No Name			Ending	
HOURS	RATE	AMOUNT	DEDUCTIONS	
Basic O/T Others			Income Tax NI Other	
			Total deduction	
Total Less deductions Net due				
Time	Day		Basic time	Overtime
1230	T			
0803	T			
1700	M			
1305	M			
1234	M			
0750	M			

Signature _ _ _ _ _ _ _ _ _ _ _

12.3 Job time

The next step is to analyse the hours spent at work according to what was done during those hours. The method adopted depends upon the size of the organisation, the nature of the work and the type of incentive scheme in operation.

Continuous production. Where **routine, repetitive** work is carried out it might not be practical to record the precise details. For example if a worker stands at a conveyor belt for seven hours his work can be measured by keeping a note of the number of units that pass through his part of the process during that time.

Job costing. When the work is not of a repetitive nature the records required might be one or several of the following.

(a) **Daily or weekly time sheets**. A time sheet is filled in by the employee as a record of how their time has been spent. The total time on the time sheet should correspond with time shown on the attendance record.

Time Sheet No. _ _ _ _ _ _ _ _ _ _ _ _ _ _ _

Employee Name _ _ _ _ _ _ _ _ _ Clock Code _ _ _ _ _ _ _ _ _ Dept _ _ _ _ _ _ _

Date _ _ _ _ _ _ _ _ _ _ _ _ _ _ _ _ _ Week No. _ _ _ _ _ _ _ _ _ _ _ _ _ _

Job No.	Start Time	Finish Time	Qty	Checker	Hrs	Rate	Extension

The time sheet will be filled in by the employee, for hours worked on each job (job code) or area of work (cost code). The cost of the hours worked will be entered at a later stage in the accounting department.

(b) **Job cards**. Cards are prepared for each job or batch, unlike time sheets which are made out for each employee and which may contain bookings relating to numerous jobs. When employees work on a job they record on the job card the time spent on that job and so job cards are likely to contain entries relating to numerous employees. On completion of the job it will contain a full record of the times involved in the job or batch. The problem of job cards, however, is that the reconciliation of job time and attendance time can be a difficult task, especially for jobs which stretch over several weeks. It is therefore difficult to incorporate them directly into wage calculation procedures. They do, however, reduce the amount of writing to be done by the employee and therefore the possibility of error. A typical job card is shown below.

JOB CARD			
Department ________	Job no ________		
Date ________	Operation no ________		
Time allowance ________	Time started ________		
	Time finished ________		
	Hours on the job ________		
Description of job	Hours	Rate	Cost
Employee no ________	Certified by ________		
Signature ________			

12.4 Piecework

The wages of pieceworkers and the labour cost of work done by them is determined from what is known as a **piecework ticket** or an **operation card**. The card records the total number of items (or 'pieces') produced and the number of rejects. Payment is only made for 'good' production. A typical operation card is shown below.

OPERATION CARD				
Operator's Name ________			Total Batch Quantity ________	
Clock No ________			Start Time ________	
Pay week No ________	Date ________		Stop Time ________	
Part No ________			Works Order No ________	
Operation ________			Special Instructions ________	
Quantity Produced	No Rejected	Good Production	Rate	£
Inspector ________			Operative ________	
Foreman ________			Date ________	
PRODUCTION CANNOT BE CLAIMED WITHOUT A PROPERLY SIGNED CARD				

Note that the attendance record of a pieceworker is still required for calculations of holidays, sick pay and so on.

12.5 Salaried labour

Even though salaried staff are paid a flat rate monthly, they may be required to complete timesheets. The reasons are as follows.

(a) Timesheets provide management with information (eg product costs).

(b) Timesheet information may provide a basis for billing for services provided, for example, a firm of solicitors or accountants may bill clients based on the number of hours work done.

(c) Timesheets are used to record hours spent and so support claims for overtime payments by salaried staff.

12.6 Idle time

In many jobs there are times when, through no fault of their own, employees cannot get on with their work. They may be waiting for another department to finish its contribution to a job, or a machine may break down or there may simply be a temporary shortage of work.

Idle time has a cost because employees will still be paid their basic wage or salary for these unproductive hours and so there should be a record of idle time. This may simply comprise an entry on time sheets coded to 'idle time' generally, or separate idle time cards may be prepared. A supervisor might enter the time of a stoppage, its cause, its duration and the employees made idle on an idle time record card. Each stoppage should have a separate reference number which can be entered on time sheets or job cards as appropriate.

12.7 Cost accounting department

The cost accounting department has the following responsibilities.

- The accumulation and classification of all cost data (which includes labour costs).
- Preparation of cost data reports for management.
- Analysing information on time cards and payroll to obtain details of direct and indirect labour, overtime and so on.

In order to establish the labour cost involved in products, operations, jobs and cost centres, the following documents are used.

- Clock cards
- Job cards
- Idle time cards
- Payroll

Analyses of labour costs are used for the following.

(a) Charging wages directly attributable to production to the appropriate job or operation.

(b) Charging wages which are not directly attributable to production as follows.

   (i) Idle time of production workers is charged to indirect costs as part of the overheads.

   (ii) Wages costs of supervisors, or store assistants are charged to the overhead costs of the relevant department.

(c) Producing idle time reports which show a summary of the hours lost through idle time, and the cause of the idle time. Idle time may be analysed as follows.

   (i) Controllable eg lack of materials.
   (ii) Uncontrollable eg power failure.

Formula to learn

$$\textbf{Idle time ratio} = \frac{\text{Idle hours}}{\text{Total hours}} \times 100\%$$

The idle time ratio is useful because it shows the proportion of available hours which were lost as a result of idle time.

NOTES

Chapter roundup

- Every movement of material in a business should be documented using the following as appropriate: purchase requisition, purchase order, GRN, materials requisition note, materials transfer note and materials returned note.
- Perpetual inventory refers to a stock recording system whereby the records (bin cards and stores ledger accounts) are updated for each receipt and issue of stock as it occurs.
- Stocktaking can be carried out on a continuous or periodic basis.
- Free stock balance calculations take account of stock on order from suppliers, and of stock which has been requisitioned but not yet delivered.
- The valuation of stock is of the utmost importance because it has a direct effect on the calculation of profit.
- FIFO assumes that materials are issued out of stock in the order in which they were delivered into stock: issues are priced at the cost of the earliest delivery remaining in stock.
- LIFO assumes that materials are issued out of stock in the reverse order to which they were delivered: the most recent deliveries are issued before earlier ones and issues are priced accordingly.
- Cumulative weighted average, AVCO, requires a calculation of the average cost of all units of stock after each new receipt.
- There are three basic groups of remuneration method for labour - time work, piecework schemes and bonus/incentive schemes.
- Although labour costs tend to behave in a step cost fashion, cost accountants usually treat labour costs as fixed or variable.
- Labour turnover is the rate at which employees leave a company and this rate should be kept as low as possible.
- Labour attendance time is recorded on, for example, an attendance record or clock card. Job time may be recorded on daily time sheets, weekly time sheets or job cards.
- The labour cost of pieceworkers is recorded on a piecework ticket/operation card.
- Idle time has a cost and must therefore be recorded.

Quick quiz

1 List five steps in the ordering and receipt of raw materials.

2 Name two key items of information that must be shown on a Materials Requisition.

3 What is the purpose of a Materials Transfer Note?

4 What is free stock?

5 What are the advantages and disadvantages of using LIFO in materials issues pricing?

6 How would you calculate a cumulative weighted average price?

7 What is a differential piecework scheme?

8 What types of document are used in recording job time.

9 What is idle time?

10 What is the idle time ratio?

Answers to Quick quiz

1
   1 Purchase requisition sent from stores to purchasing.
   2 Purchase order sent from purchasing to supplier.
   3 Goods received and checked against supplier's delivery note.
   4 Goods received note (GRN) sent by storekeeper to accounts department.
   5 Supplier's invoice matched with purchase order and GRN in accounts department.

2 Any two of the following.

Description of goods required
Quantity of goods required
Date goods required by
Department or job requiring the goods
Signature and date of authorisation

3 A materials transfer note provides details of goods transferred from one job or cost centre to another so that the costs incurred can be correctly allocated to those jobs or cost centres.

4 Free stock is the stock available for future use and is calculated as follows.

Materials in stock	X
Add: materials on order from suppliers	X
Less: materials requisitioned, not yet issued	(X)
Free stock balance	X

5 Advantages of LIFO: Stocks are issued at a price which is close to current market value and managers are made aware of recent costs when making decisions because their department will be charged with these 'current' costs.

Disadvantages of LIFO: stock records will be 'untidy' as they may include part-used batches; it rarely reflects the actual usage of stock; and decision-making can be difficult because of fluctuating prices.

6 After each receipt calculate: $\frac{\text{Total cost of units in stock}}{\text{Total number of units in stock}}$

7 A differential piecework scheme offers incentives to employees by paying higher rates for increased levels of production. For example, the rate of pay could increase as follows.

Up to 2000 units	50p per unit in this band
2000 to 2200 units	54p per unit in this band
2200 to 2400 units	56p per unit in this band

8 Daily time sheets
Weekly time sheets
Job cards

9 Idle time is time when employees are not able to get on with their work through no fault of their own.

10 Idle time ratio $= \frac{\text{Idle hours}}{\text{Total hours}} \times 100\%$

Answers to Activities

1 (a) Incorrect materials being delivered, disrupting operations

(b) Incorrect prices being paid

(c) Deliveries other than at the specified time (causing disruption)

(d) Insufficient control over quality

(e) Invoiced amounts differing from quantities of goods actually received or prices agreed

You may, of course, have thought of equally valid consequences.

2 Here are some examples.

(a) Stock code number, for reference
(b) Brief description of stock item
(c) Reorder level
(d) Reorder quantity
(e) Cost per unit
(f) Selling price per unit (if finished goods)
(g) Amount in stock
(h) Frequency of usage

3 Since this is a wholesaler, materials requisitioned are the same as customer orders – they are movements of stock out of stores, so:

Free stock balance = units in stock + units on order – units requisitioned, but not yet issued or in this case customer orders.

5,525 = 3,925 + units on order – 8,450

5,525 – 3,925 + 8,450 = units on order, therefore:

Units on order = 10,050

4

STORES LEDGER ACCOUNT (extract)

Date	GRN No.	Receipts Quantity	Receipts Unit price £	Receipts Amount £	Stores Req. No.	Issues Quantity	Issues Unit price £	Issues Amount £	Stock Quantity	Stock Unit price £	Stock Amount £
1.5.X3									100	2.00	200.00
3.5.X3		400	2.10	840.00					100	2.00	200.00
									400	2.10	840.00
									500		1,040.00
4.5.X3						100	2.00	200.00			
						100	2.10	210.00	300	2.10	630.00
9.5.X3		300	2.12	636.00					300	2.10	630.00
									300	2.12	636.00
									600		1,266.00
11.5.X3						300	2.10	630.00			
						100	2.12	212.00	200	2.12	424.00
18.5.X3		100	2.40	240.00					200	2.12	424.00
									100	2.40	240.00
									300		664.00
20.5.X3						100	2.12	212.00	100	2.12	212.00
									100	2.40	240.00
31.5.X3									200		452.00

Note: The opening balance on 1 May of 100 units is not a receipt for the period as it would have been received in a previous period. It is just brought forward in the stock column.

5 (a)

Date	Receipts Quantity	Receipts Unit price £	Receipts Amount £	Issues Quantity	Issues Unit price £	Issues Amount £	Stock Quantity	Stock Unit price £	Stock Amount £
Opening stock							300	5.00	1,500
4 June				50	5.00	250	250	5.00	1,250
7 June	100	5.56	556				250	5.00	1,250
							100	5.56	566
							350		1,806
10 June				75	5.56	417	250	5.00	1,250
							25	5.56	139
							275		1,389
11 June				25	5.56	139			
				75	5.00	375	175	5.00	875
				100		514			
15 June	100	5.27	527				175	5.00	875
							100	5.27	527
							275		1,402
20 June				100	5.27	527			
				100	5.00	500	75	5.00	375
				200		1,027			

Value of issues under LIFO: 250 + 417 + 514 + 1,027 = £2,208.

Value of closing stock: £375

(b)

Date	*Received units*	*Issued units*	*Balance units*	*Total stock value*	*Unit cost*
				£	£
Opening stock			300	1,500	5.00
4 June		(50)		(250)	5.00
			250	1,250	5.00
7 June	100			556	5.56
			350	1,806	5.16
10 June		(75)		(387)	5.16
			275	1,419	5.16
11 June		(100)		(516)	5.16
			175	903	5.16
15 June	100			527	5.27
			275	1,430	5.20
20 June		(200)		(1,040)	5.20
			75	390	5.20

Value of issues under AVCO = 250 + 387 + 516 + 1,040
= £2,193

Value of closing stock = £390

6 LIFO is a reasonably accurate method of accounting for inflation provided that closing stock values are periodically reviewed and revalued.

7

Standard time for 340 units (× 2 minutes)	680 minutes
Actual time (8 hours per day) (8 × 60 minutes)	480 minutes
Time saved	200 minutes

	£
Bonus = 75% × 200 minutes × £12 per hour (see note)	30
Basic pay = 8 hours × £12	96
Total labour cost	126

Note: £12 per hour is £0.10 per minute (£12 ÷ 60 = 0.2).

Chapter : 3

OVERHEAD APPORTIONMENT AND ABSORPTION

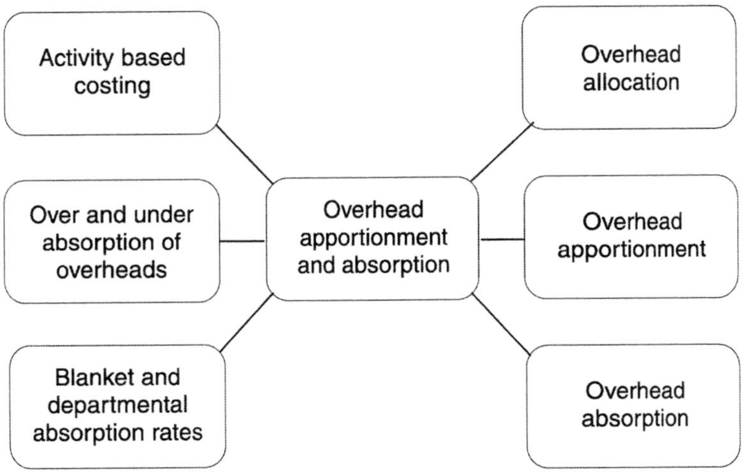

Introduction

There are basically two schools of thought as to the correct method of dealing with overheads: **marginal costing** (which we will be looking at in the next chapter) and **absorption costing**, the topic of this chapter.

Absorption costing is a method for sharing overheads between a number of different products on a fair basis. The chapter begins by looking at the three stages of absorption costing: **allocation, apportionment and absorption.** We then move on to the important issue of **over/under absorption**, a frequently examined topic. The chapter concludes with a brief look at a relatively recent development in the treatment of overheads, **activity based costing.**

Your objectives

In this chapter you will learn about the following.

(a) Overhead allocation

(b) Overhead apportionment

(c) Overhead absorption

(d) Blanket absorption rates and departmental absorption rates

(e) Over and under absorption of overheads

(f) Activity based costing

NOTES

1 OVERHEAD ALLOCATION

Definition

> **Allocation** is the process by which whole cost items are charged direct to a cost unit or cost centre.

1.1 Cost centres

Cost centres may be one of the following types.

(a) A **production department**, to which production overheads are charged

(b) A **production area service department**, to which production overheads are charged

(c) An **administrative department**, to which administration overheads are charged

(d) A **selling** or a **distribution department**, to which sales and distribution overheads are charged

(e) An **overhead cost centre**, to which items of expense which are shared by a number of departments, such as rent and rates, heat and light and the canteen, are charged

1.2 Allocation

The following are examples of costs which would be charged directly to cost centres via the process of allocation.

(a) The cost of a warehouse security guard will be charged to the warehouse cost centre.

(b) Paper on which computer output is recorded will be charged to the computer department.

EXAMPLE

As an example of overhead allocation, consider the following costs of a company.

Wages of the supervisor of department A	£200
Wages of the supervisor of department B	£150
Indirect materials consumed in department A	£50
Rent of the premises shared by departments A and B	£300

The cost accounting system might include three cost centres.

Cost centre:	101	Department A
	102	Department B
	201	Rent

Overhead costs would be allocated directly to each cost centre, ie £200 + £50 to cost centre 101, £150 to cost centre 102 and £300 to cost centre 201. The rent of the factory will be subsequently shared between the two production departments, but for the purpose of day to day cost recording in this particular system, the rent will first of all be charged in full to a separate cost centre.

---

2 OVERHEAD APPORTIONMENT

2.1 First stage: apportioning general overheads

Overhead apportionment follows on from overhead allocation. The first stage of overhead apportionment is to identify all overhead costs as production department, production area service department, administration or selling and distribution overhead. This means that the costs for heat and light, rent and rates, the canteen and so on (that is, costs which have been allocated to general overhead cost centres) must be shared out between the other cost centres.

2.2 Bases of apportionment

Overhead costs should be shared out on a fair basis. You will appreciate that because of the complexity of items of cost it is rarely possible to use only one method of apportioning costs to the various departments of an organisation. The bases of apportionment for the most usual cases are given below.

Overhead to which the basis applies	**Basis**
Rent, rates, heating and light, repairs and depreciation of buildings	Floor area occupied by each cost centre
Depreciation, insurance of equipment	Cost or book value of equipment
Personnel office, canteen, welfare, wages and cost offices, first aid	Number of employees, or labour hours worked in each cost centre
Heating, lighting (possible alternative)	Volume of space occupied by each cost centre

WORKED EXAMPLE: OVERHEAD APPORTIONMENT

Millie Ltd has incurred the following overhead costs.

	£'000
Depreciation of factory	100
Factory repairs and maintenance	60
Factory office costs (treat as production overhead)	150
Depreciation of equipment	80
Insurance of equipment	20
Heating	39
Lighting	10
Canteen	90
	549

Information relating to the production and service departments in the factory is as follows.

	Department			
	Production 1	*Production 2*	*Service 100*	*Service 101*
Floor space (square metres)	1,200	1,600	800	400
Volume (cubic metres)	3,000	6,000	2,400	1,600
Number of employees	30	30	15	15
Book value of equipment	£30,000	£20,000	£10,000	£20,000

Determine how the overhead costs should be apportioned between the four departments.

ANSWER

Costs are apportioned using the following general formula.

$$\frac{\text{Total overhead cost}}{\text{Total value of apportionent basis}} \times \text{value of apportionment basis of cost centre}$$

So for the factory depreciation, the most reasonable way of sharing the costs would be based on floor area.

	Production 1	*Production 2*	*Service 100*	*Service 101*
Floor space	1,200	1,600	800	400

The total floor area is: 1,200 + 1,600 + 800 + 400 = 4,000 sq metres.

So using the general formula given above the overhead of factory depreciation of £100,000 would be apportioned to the departments as follows.

	Total cost	*Departments* 1	2	*100*	*101*
	£'000	£'000	£'000	£'000	£'000
Factory depreciation	100	30	40	20	10

Department 1: $\frac{100{,}000}{4{,}000} \times 1{,}200 = 30{,}000$

Department 2: $\frac{100{,}000}{4{,}000} \times 1{,}600 = 40{,}000$

Department 100: $\frac{100{,}000}{4{,}000} \times 800 = 20{,}000$

Department 101: $\frac{100{,}000}{4{,}000} \times 400 = 10{,}000$

Always check to ensure the total of the costs you have apportioned is the same as the total cost. In this example: 30,000 + 40,000 + 20,000 + 10,000 = 100,000 which is the total cost of the factory depreciation. The rest of the table can be completed.

Item of cost	*Basis of apportionment*	*Total cost*	*To Department* 1	2	100	101
		£'000	£'000	£'000	£'000	£'000
Factory depreciation	(floor area)	100	30.0	40	20.0	10.0
Factory repairs	(floor area)	60	18.0	24	12.0	6.0
Factory office costs	(number of employees)	150	50.0	50	25.0	25.0
Equipment depreciation	(book value)	80	30.0	20	10.0	20.0
Equipment insurance	(book value)	20	7.5	5	2.5	5.0
Heating	(volume)	39	9.0	18	7.2	4.8
Lighting	(floor area)	10	3.0	4	2.0	1.0
Canteen	(number of employees)	90	30.0	30	15.0	15.0
Total		549	177.5	191	93.7	86.8

2.3 Second stage: service cost centre cost apportionment

The second stage of overhead apportionment concerns the treatment of **service cost centres**. A factory is divided into several production departments and also a number of service departments, but only the production departments are directly involved in the manufacture of the units. In order to be able to add production overheads to unit costs, it is necessary to have all the overheads charged to (or located in) the production departments. The next stage in absorption costing is, therefore, to apportion the costs of service cost centres to the production cost centres. Examples of possible apportionment bases are as follows.

Service cost centre	Possible basis of apportionment
Stores	Number of materials requisitions
Maintenance	Hours of maintenance work done for each cost centre
Production planning	Direct labour hours worked in each production cost centre

WORKED EXAMPLE: APPORTIONING SERVICE COST CENTRE COSTS TO PRODUCTION COST CENTRES

Mac Ltd incurred the following overhead costs.

	Production departments		*Stores*	*Maintenance*
	X	*Y*	*department*	*department*
	£	£	£	£
Allocated costs	6,000	4,000	1,000	2,000
Apportioned costs	2,000	1,000	1,000	500
	8,000	5,000	2,000	2,500

The maintenance department worked 500 hours for department X and 750 hours for department Y. Production department X raised 12,000 material requisitions. Department Y raised 8,000 material requisitions.

Calculate the total production overhead costs of departments X and Y.

SOLUTION

The stores cost can be allocated to the production centres using the number of requisitions and the maintenance departments cost can be allocated using maintenance hours.

The formula used in the previous worked example can be used here too.

Stores cost to department X:

$$\frac{\text{Total cost in stores}}{\text{Total number of material requisitions}} \times \text{requisitions by department X}$$

$$\frac{2{,}000}{(12{,}000 + 8{,}000)} \times 12{,}000 = 1{,}200$$

Stores cost to department Y

$$\frac{\text{Total cost in stores}}{\text{Total number of material requisitions}} \times \text{requisitions by department Y}$$

$$\frac{2{,}000}{(12{,}000 + 8{,}000)} \times 8{,}000 = 800$$

Similar calculations would be made to reapportion the maintenance department costs to X and Y:

Maintenance to X: $\frac{2,500}{(500+750)} \times 500 = 1,000$

Maintenance to Y: $\frac{2,500}{(500+750)} \times 750 = 1,500$

In summary then:

Service department	*Basis of apportionment*	*Total cost*	*Dept X*	*Dept Y*
		£	£	£
Stores	Number of requisitions	2,000	1,200	800
Maintenance	Hours	2,500	1,000	1,500
		4,500	2,200	2,300
Previously allocated and apportioned costs		13,000	8,000	5,000
Total overhead		17,500	10,200	7,300

Never forget to include the directly allocated costs when determining overheads to be apportioned.

NOTES

Activity 1 **(30 minutes)**

Pippin Ltd has three production departments (forming, machines and assembly) and two service departments (maintenance and general).

The following is an analysis of budgeted overhead costs for a twelve-month period.

	£	£
Rent and rates		8,000
Power		750
Light, heat		5,000
Repairs, maintenance:		
Forming	800	
Machines	1,800	
Assembly	300	
Maintenance	200	
General	100	
		3,200
Departmental expenses:		
Forming	1,500	
Machines	2,300	
Assembly	1,100	
Maintenance	900	
General	1,500	
		7,300
Depreciation:		
Plant		10,000
Fixtures and fittings		250
Insurance:		
Plant		2,000
Buildings		500
Indirect labour:		
Forming	3,000	
Machines	5,000	
Assembly	1,500	
Maintenance	4,000	
General	2,000	
		15,500
		52,500

Other available data are as follows.

	Floor area sq.ft	*Plant value* £	*Fixtures & fittings* £	*Effective horse-power*	*Direct cost for year* £	*Labour hours worked*	*Machine hours worked*
Forming	2,000	25,000	1,000	40	20,500	14,400	12,000
Machines	4,000	60,000	500	90	30,300	20,500	21,600
Assembly	3,000	7,500	2,000	15	24,200	20,200	2,000
Maintenance	500	7,500	1,000	5	-	-	-
General	500	-	500	-	-	-	-
	10,000	100,000	5,000	150	75,000	55,100	35,600

Using the data provided, apportion overheads to the five departments.

Activity 2 **(20 minutes)**

Using your solution to Activity 1 and the following information about the apportionment of service department costs, apportion the costs of the two service departments of Pippin Ltd to the three production departments and hence determine the total overhead for those departments.

	Maintenance	*General*
	%	%
Forming	20	30
Machines	50	60
Assembly	30	10
	100	100

3 OVERHEAD ABSORPTION

Having allocated and/or apportioned all overheads, the next stage in absorption costing is to add them to, or **absorb them into**, the cost of production or sales.

(a) **Production overheads** are added to the prime cost (direct materials, labour and expenses: see Chapter 1, para 4.2), the total of the two being the factory cost, or full cost of production. Production overheads are therefore included in the value of stocks of finished goods.

(b) **Administration and selling and distribution overheads** are then added, the sum of the factory cost and these overheads being the total cost of sales. These overheads are not however included in the value of closing stock.

3.1 Use of a predetermined absorption rate

Overheads are not absorbed on the basis of the actual overheads incurred but on the basis of estimated or budgeted figures (calculated prior to the beginning of the period). The rate at which overheads are included in cost of sales (**absorption rate**) is predetermined before the accounting period actually begins for a number of reasons.

(a) Goods are produced and sold throughout the year, but many actual overheads are not known until the end of the year. It would be inconvenient to wait until the year end in order to decide what overhead costs should be.

(b) An attempt to calculate overhead costs more regularly (such as each month) is possible, although estimated costs must be added for occasional expenditures such as rent and rates (incurred once or twice a year). The difficulty with this approach would be that actual overheads from month to month would fluctuate randomly; therefore, overhead costs charged to production would depend to a certain extent on random events and changes. A unit made in one month might be charged with £4 of overhead, in a subsequent month with £5, and in a third month with £4.50. Only units made in winter would be charged with the heating overhead. Such changes are considered misleading for costing purposes and administratively and clerically inconvenient to deal with.

(c) Similarly, production output might vary each month. For example actual overhead costs might be £20,000 per month and output might vary from, say, 1,000 units to 20,000 units per month. The unit rate for overhead would be £20 and £1 per unit respectively, which would again lead to administration and control problems.

3.2 Predetermination

Overhead absorption rates are therefore predetermined as follows.

(a) The overhead **likely to be incurred** during the coming year is estimated.

(b) The total hours, units, or direct costs on which the overhead absorption rates are to be based (activity level) are estimated.

(c) The estimated overhead is divided by the budgeted activity level to arrive at an absorption rate.

3.3 Selecting the appropriate absorption base

There are a number of different **bases of absorption** (or 'overhead recovery rates') which can be used. Examples are as follows.

- A percentage of direct materials cost
- A percentage of direct labour cost
- A percentage of prime cost
- A rate per machine hour
- A rate per direct labour hour
- A rate per unit

The choice of an absorption basis is a matter of judgement and common sense. There are no strict rules or formulae involved, although factors which should be taken into account are set out below. What is required is an absorption basis which realistically reflects the characteristics of a given cost centre and which avoids undue anomalies.

It is safe to assume, for example, that the overhead costs for producing brass screws are similar to those for producing steel screws. The cost of brass is, however, very much greater than that of steel. Consequently, the overhead charge for brass screws would be too high and that for steel screws too low, if a percentage of cost of materials rate were to be used.

Using prime cost as the absorption base would lead to anomalies because of the inclusion of the cost of material, as outlined above.

If the overhead actually attributable to units was incurred on, say a time basis, but one highly-paid employee was engaged on producing one item, while a lower-paid employee was producing another item, the overhead charged to the first item using a percentage of wages rate might be too high while the amount absorbed by the second item might be too low. This method should therefore only be used if similar wage rates are paid to all direct employees in a production department. A direct labour hour rate might be considered 'fairer'.

It is for this reason that many factories use a **direct labour hour rate** or **machine hour rate** in preference to a rate based on a percentage of direct materials cost, wages or prime cost.

(a) A **direct labour** hour basis is most appropriate in a **labour intensive** environment.

(b) A **machine hour** rate would be used in departments where production is controlled or dictated by **machines**. This basis is becoming more appropriate as factories become more heavily automated.

A **rate per unit** would be effective only if all units were identical.

WORKED EXAMPLE: OVERHEAD ABSORPTION

The budgeted production overheads and other budget data of Calculator Ltd are as follows.

Budget	*Production dept 1*	*Production dept 2*
Overhead cost	£36,000	£5,000
Direct materials cost	£32,000	
Direct labour cost	£40,000	
Machine hours	10,000	
Direct labour hours	18,000	
Units of production		1,000

Calculate the absorption rate using the various bases of apportionment.

ANSWER

(a) Department 1

(i) Percentage of direct materials cost $\frac{£36{,}000}{£32{,}000} \times 100\% = 112.5\%$

(ii) Percentage of direct labour cost $\frac{£36{,}000}{£40{,}000} \times 100\% = 90\%$

(iii) Percentage of prime cost $\frac{£36{,}000}{£72{,}000} \times 100\% = 50\%$

Prime cost = direct materials + direct labour = 32,000 + 40,000 = £72,000

(iv) Rate per machine hour $\frac{£36{,}000}{10{,}000 \text{ hrs}} = £3.60$ per machine hour

(v) Rate per direct labour hour $\frac{£36{,}000}{18{,}000 \text{ hrs}} = £2$ per direct labour hour

(b) The department 2 absorption rate will be based on units of output.

$\frac{£5{,}000}{1{,}000 \text{ units}} = £5$ per unit produced

---

3.4 Importance of the basis of absorption

The choice of the basis of absorption is significant in determining the cost of individual units, or jobs, produced. Using the previous example, suppose that an individual product has a material cost of £80, a labour cost of £85, and requires 36 labour hours and 23 machine hours to complete. The overhead cost of the product would vary, depending on the basis of absorption used by the company for overhead recovery.

(a) As a percentage of direct materials cost, the overhead cost would be
112.5% × £80 = £90.00

(b) As a percentage of direct labour cost, the overhead cost would be
$90\% \times £85 =$ £76.50

(c) As a percentage of prime cost, the overhead cost would be
$50\% \times £165 =$ £82.50

(d) Using a machine hour basis of absorption, the overhead cost would be
23 hrs × £3.60 = £82.80

(e) Using a labour hour basis, the overhead cost would be 36 hrs × £2 = £72.00

In theory, each basis of absorption would be possible, but the company should choose a basis for its own costs which seems to be 'fairest'. In our example, this choice will be significant in determining the cost of individual products, as the following summary shows, but the **total cost** of production overheads is the budgeted overhead expenditure, no matter what basis of absorption is selected. It is the relative share of overhead costs borne by individual products and jobs which is affected by the choice of overhead absorption basis.

3.5 Summary

A summary of the product costs in the previous example is shown below.

	Basis of overhead recovery				
	Percentage of materials cost	*Percentage of labour cost*	*Percentage of prime cost*	*Machine hours*	*Direct labour hours*
	£	£	£	£	£
Direct material	80	80.00	80.00	80.00	80
Direct labour	85	85.00	85.00	85.00	85
Production overhead	90	76.50	82.50	82.80	72
Total production cost	255	241.50	247.50	247.80	237

Activity 3 **(15 minutes)**

Using your solution to Activity 2 and the following information, determine suitable overhead absorption rates for Pippin Ltd's three production departments.

	Forming	*Machines*	*Assembly*
Budgeted direct labour hours per annum	5,556	790	5,240
Budgeted machine hours per annum	1,350	5,626	147

4 BLANKET ABSORPTION RATES AND DEPARTMENTAL ABSORPTION RATES

Definition

A **blanket overhead absorption rate** is an absorption rate used throughout a factory and for all jobs and units of output irrespective of the department in which they were produced.

For example, if total overheads were £500,000 and there were 250,000 direct machine hours during the period, the **blanket overhead rate** would be £2 per direct machine hour and all jobs passing through the factory would be charged at that rate.

Such a rate is not appropriate, however, if there are a number of departments and jobs do not spend an equal amount of time in each department.

It is argued that if a single factory overhead absorption rate is used, some products will receive a higher overhead charge than they ought 'fairly' to bear, whereas other products will be under-charged. By using a separate absorption rate for each department, charging of overheads will be equitable and the full cost of production of items will be more representative of the cost of the efforts and resources put into making them.

Activity 4 **(5 minutes)**

The following data relate to one year in department A.

Budgeted machine hours	25,000
Actual machine hours	21,875
Budgeted overheads	£350,000
Actual overheads	£320,000

Based on the data above, what is the machine hour absorption rate as conventionally calculated?

5 OVER AND UNDER ABSORPTION OF OVERHEADS

5.1 Estimates

The rate of overhead absorption is based on **estimates** (of both numerator and denominator) and it is quite likely that either one or both of the estimates will not agree with what *actually* occurs. Actual overheads incurred will probably be either greater than or less than overheads absorbed into the cost of production.

(a) **Over absorption** means that the overheads charged to the cost of production are greater than the overheads actually incurred.

(b) **Under absorption** means that insufficient overheads have been included in the cost of production.

EXAMPLE

Suppose that the budgeted overhead in a production department is £80,000 and the budgeted activity is 40,000 direct labour hours. The overhead recovery rate (using a direct labour hour basis) would be £2 per direct labour hour.

Actual overheads in the period are, say £84,000 and 45,000 direct labour hours are worked.

	£
Overhead incurred (actual)	84,000
Overhead absorbed (45,000 × £2)	90,000
Over-absorption of overhead	6,000

In this example, the cost of produced units or jobs has been charged with £6,000 more than was actually spent. An adjustment to reconcile the overheads charged to the actual overhead is necessary and the over-absorbed overhead will be written as a credit to the **profit and loss account** at the end of the accounting period.

Activity 5 **(10 minutes)**

A company has recorded the following information on overheads for a period.

Budgeted information

	Production departments	
	X	*Y*
Allocated overheads	£4,000	£3,000
Apportioned overheads	£2,500	£2,750
	£6,500	£5,750
Direct labour hours	2,500 hrs	1,000 hrs
Machine hours	300 hrs	5,000 hrs
Actual information		
Actual overheads incurred	£7,300	£4,500
Direct labour hours	2,600 hrs	1,300 hrs
Machine hours	400 hrs	4,800 hrs

Calculate the under- or over-absorption of overheads for each of the production departments.

5.2 The reasons for under-/over-absorbed overhead

The overhead absorption rate is **predetermined from budget estimates** of overhead cost and the expected volume of activity. Under or over recovery or absorption of overhead will occur in the following circumstances.

- Actual overhead costs are different from budgeted overheads.
- The actual activity level is different from the budgeted activity level.
- Both actual overhead costs and actual activity level are different from budget.

WORKED EXAMPLE: UNDER AND OVER ABSORPTION OF OVERHEADS

Rioch Havery Ltd is a small company which manufactures two products, A and B, in two production departments, machining and assembly. A canteen is operated as a separate production service department.

The budgeted production and sales in the year to 31 March 20X3 are as follows.

	Product A	*Product B*
Sales price per unit	£100	£140
Sales (units)	2,200	1,400
Production (units)	2,000	1,500
Material cost per unit	£28	£24

	Product A Hours per unit	*Product B* Hours per unit
Direct labour:		
Machining department (£8 per hour)	2	3
Assembly department (£6 per hour)	1	2
Machine hours per unit:		
Machining department	3	4
Assembly department	1/2	

Budgeted production overheads are as follows.

	Machining department	*Assembly department*	*Canteen*	*Total*
	£	£	£	£
Allocated costs	20,000	50,000	24,000	94,000
Apportionment of other general production overheads	52,000	24,000	16,000	92,000
	72,000	74,000	40,000	106,000
Number of employees	30	20	1	51
Floor area (square metres)	5,000	2,000	500	7,500

Required

(a) Calculate an absorption rate for overheads in each production department for the year to 31 March 20X3 and the budgeted cost per unit of products A and B.

(b) Suppose that in the year to 31 March 20X3, 2,200 units of Product A are produced and 1,500 units of Product B. Direct labour hours per unit and machine hours per unit in both departments were as budgeted.

Actual production overheads are as follows.

	Machining department	*Assembly department*	*Canteen*	*Total*
	£	£	£	£
Allocated costs	61,400	55,000	20,000	136,600
Apportioned share of general production overheads	34,000	16,000	10,000	60,000
	95,400	71,200	30,000	196,600

Calculate the under- or over-absorbed overhead in each production department and in total.

ANSWER

(a) **Apportion budgeted overheads**

First we need to apportion budgeted overheads to the two production departments. Canteen costs will be apportioned on the basis of the number of employees in each department. (Direct labour hours in each department are an alternative basis of apportionment, but the number of employees seems to be more directly relevant to canteen costs.)

	Machining department	*Assembly department*	*Total*
	£	£	£
Budgeted allocated costs	20,000	50,000	70,000
Share of general overheads	52,000	24,000	76,000
Apportioned canteen costs (30:20)	24,000	16,000	40,000
	96,000	90,000	186,000

Notice when reapportioning the canteen cost we have ignored the number of employees in the canteen. The idea of reapportionment is to remove **all** service centre overheads and share them amongst the production departments on a fair basis. It therefore makes sense to ignore the employee working for the canteen, otherwise costs would remain in the canteen service centre. So costs are shared on the ratio of 30:20.

Choose absorption rates

Since machine time appears to be more significant than labour time in the machining department, a machine hour rate of absorption will be used for overhead recovery in this department. On the other hand, machining is insignificant in the assembly department, and a direct labour hour rate of absorption would seem to be the basis which will give the fairest method of overhead recovery.

	Product A		*Product B*		*Total*
Total direct labour hours					
Machining department	2 × 2,000	+	3 × 1,500	=	8,500 hours
Assembly department	1 × 2,000	+	2 × 1,500	=	5,000 hours
Total machine hours					
Machining department	3 × 2,000	+	4 × 1,500	=	12,000 hours
Assembly department	½ × 2,000			=	1,000 hours

	Direct labour hours	*Machine hours*	
Machining	8,500	12,000	Machine intensive
Assembly	5,000	1,000	Labour intensive

Calculate overhead absorption rates

The overhead absorption rates are predetermined, using budgeted estimates. Since the overheads are production overheads, the budgeted activity relates to the volume of production, in units (the production hours required for volume of sales being irrelevant).

	Product A	*Product B*	*Total*
Budgeted production (units)	2,000	1,500	
Machining department:			
machine hours	6,000 hrs	6,000 hrs	12,000 hrs
Assembly department:			
direct labour hours	2,000 hrs	3,000 hrs	5,000 hrs

The overhead absorption rates will be as follows.

	Machining department	*Assembly department*
Budgeted overheads	£96,000	£90,000
Budgeted activity	12,000 hrs	5,000 hrs
Absorption rate	£8 per machine hour	£18 per direct labour hour

Determine a budgeted cost per unit

The budgeted cost per unit would be as follows.

	Product A		Product B	
	£	£	£	£
Direct materials		28		24
Direct labour:				
Machining department (@ £8/hr)	16		24	
Assembly department (@ £6/hr)	6		12	
		22		36
Prime cost		50		60
Production overhead:				
Machining department (@£8/machine hr)	24		32	
Assembly department (@ £18/direct labour hr)	18		36	
		41		68
Full production cost		92		128

(b) **Apportion actual service department overhead to production departments**

When the actual costs are analysed, the 'actual' overhead of the canteen department (£30,000) would be split between the machining and assembly departments.

	Machining department	*Assembly department*	*Total*
	£	£	£
Allocated cost	61,400	55,200	116,600
Apportioned general overhead	34,000	16,000	50,000
Canteen (30:20) (as before)	13,000	12,000	30,000
	113,400	83,200	196,600

Establish the over- or under-absorption of overheads

There would be an over- or under-absorption of overheads as follows.

		Machining department		*Assembly department*	*Total*
		£		£	£
Overheads absorbed					
Product A (2,200 units)	(× £8 × 3hrs)	52,800	(× £18 × 1hr)	39,600	92,400
Product B (1,500 units)	(× £8× 4hrs)	48,000	(× £18 × 2hrs)	54,000	102,000
		100,800		93,600	194,400
Overheads incurred		113,400		83,300	196,600
Over-/(under)-absorbed overhead		(12,600)		10,400	(2,200)

The total under-absorbed overhead of £1,100 will be written off to the profit and loss account at the end of the year, to compensate for the fact that overheads charged to production (£97,200) were less than the overheads actually incurred (£98,300).

5.3 Recording the under-/over-absorbed overheads in the profit and loss account

Once the under-/over-absorbed overheads have been calculated the amount is recorded in the profit and loss account under cost of sales.

6 ACTIVITY BASED COSTING

Absorption costing appears to be a relatively straightforward way of adding overhead costs to units of production using, more often than not, a volume-related absorption basis (such as direct labour hours or direct machine hours). The assumption that all overheads are related primarily to production volume is implied in this system. Absorption costing was developed at a time when most organisations produced only a narrow range of products and when overhead costs were only a very small fraction of total costs, direct labour and direct material costs accounting for the largest proportion of the costs. Errors made in adding overheads to products were therefore not too significant.

6.1 Development

Nowadays, however, with the advent of **advanced manufacturing technology**, overheads are likely to be far more important and, in fact, direct labour may account for as little as 5% of a product's cost. Moreover, there has been an increase in the costs of **non-volume related support activities**, such as setting-up, production scheduling, inspection and data processing, which assist the efficient manufacture of a wide range of products. These overheads are not, in general, affected by changes in production volume. They tend to vary in the long term according to the **range and complexity** of the products manufactured rather than the volume of output.

Because traditional absorption costing methods tend to allocate too great a proportion of overheads to high volume products (which cause relatively little diversity), and too small a proportion of overheads to low volume products (which cause greater diversity and therefore use more support services), alternative methods of costing have been developed. **Activity based costing (ABC)** is one such development.

6.2 The major ideas behind activity based costing

These are:

(a) **Activities cause costs**. Activities include ordering, materials handling, machining, assembly, production scheduling and despatching.

(b) **Products create demand for the activities.**

(c) Costs are assigned to products **on the basis of a product's consumption of the activities.**

6.3 Outline of an ABC system

An ABC costing system operates as follows.

Step 1. Identify an organisation's major activities.

Step 2. Identify the factors which determine the size of the costs of an activity/cause the costs of an activity. These are known as **cost drivers**. Look at the following examples.

Activity	*Possible cost driver*
Ordering	Number of orders
Materials handling	Number of production runs
Production scheduling	Number of production runs
Despatching	Number of despatches

For those costs that vary with production levels in the short term, ABC uses **volume-related cost drivers** such as labour or machine hours. The cost of oil used as a lubricant on the machines would therefore be added to products on the basis of the number of machine hours since oil would have to be used for each hour the machine ran.

Step 3. Collect the costs of each activity into what are known as **cost pools** (equivalent to cost centres under more traditional costing methods).

Step 4. Charge support overheads to products on the basis of their usage of the activity. A product's usage of an activity is measured by the number of the activity's cost driver it generates.

Suppose, for example, that the cost pool for the ordering activity totalled £100,000 and that there were 10,000 orders (the cost driver). Each product would therefore be charged with £10 for each order it required. A batch requiring five orders would therefore be charged with £50 as its share of the ordering costs for the period.

6.4 Comparison with absorption costing

Absorption costing and **ABC** are similar in many respects. In both systems, direct costs go straight to the product and overheads are allocated to production cost centres/cost pools. The difference lies in the manner in which overheads are absorbed into products.

- **Absorption costing** most commonly uses two **absorption bases** (labour hours and/or machine hours) to charge overheads to products.
- **ABC** uses many **cost drivers** as absorption bases (number of orders, number of despatches and so on).

Absorption rates under ABC should therefore be more closely linked to the causes of overhead costs and hence product costs should be more realistic, especially where support overheads are high.

WORKED EXAMPLE: ABSORPTION COSTING VERSUS ABC

The following example illustrates the point that traditional cost accounting techniques result in a misleading and inequitable division of costs between low-volume and high-volume products, and that ABC can provide a more meaningful allocation of cots.

Suppose that Cooplan Ltd manufactures four products, W, X, Y and Z. Output and cost data for the period just ended are as follows.

	Output units	*Number of production runs in the period*	*Material cost per unit*	*Direct labour hours per unit*	*Machine hours per unit*
			£		
W	10	2	20	1	1
X	10	2	80	3	3
Y	100	5	20	1	1
Z	100	5	80	3	3
		14			

Direct labour cost per hour £5

Overhead costs	£
Short run variable costs	3,080
Set-up costs	10,920
Expediting and scheduling costs	9,100
Materials handling costs	7,700
	30,800

Required

Prepare unit costs for each product using conventional costing and ABC.

ANSWER

Using a **conventional absorption costing approach** and an absorption rate for overheads based on either direct labour hours or machine hours, the product costs would be as follows.

	W	*X*	*Y*	*Z*	*Total*
	£	£	£	£	£
Direct material	200	800	2,000	8,000	
Direct labour	50	150	500	1,500	
Overheads *	700	2,100	7,000	21,000	
	950	3,050	9,500	30,500	44,000
Units produced	10	10	100	100	
Cost per unit	£95	£305	£95	£305	

* £30,800 ÷ 440 hours = £70 per direct labour or machine hour.

Using **activity based costing** and assuming that the number of production runs is the cost driver for set-up costs, expediting and scheduling costs and materials handling costs and that machine hours are the cost driver for short-run variable costs, unit costs would be as follows.

	W	*X*	*Y*	*Z*	*Total*
	£	£	£	£	£
Direct material	200	800	2,000	8,000	
Direct labour	50	150	500	1,500	
Short-run variable overheads (W1)	70	210	700	2,100	
Set-up costs (W2)	1,560	1,560	3,900	3,900	
Expediting, scheduling costs (W3)	1,300	1,300	3,250	3,250	
Materials handling costs (W4)	1,100	1,100	2,750	2,750	
	4,280	5,120	13,100	21,500	44,000
Units produced	10	10	100	100	
Cost per unit	£428	£512	£131	£215	

Workings

1	£3,080 ÷ 440 machine hours =	£7 per machine hour
2	£10,920 ÷ 14 production runs =	£780 per run
3	£9,100 ÷ 14 production runs =	£650 per run
4	£7,700 ÷ 14 production runs =	£550 per run

Summary

Product	*Conventional costing unit cost*	*ABC unit cost*	*Difference per unit*	*Difference in total*
	£	£	£	£
W	95	428	+ 333	+3,330
X	305	512	+ 207	+2,070
Y	95	131	+ 36	+3,600
Z	305	215	– 90	–9,000

The figures suggest that the traditional volume-based absorption costing system is flawed.

(a) It **underallocates overhead costs to low-volume products** (here, W and X) and **over-allocates overheads to higher-volume products** (here Z in particular).

(b) It underallocates overhead costs to smaller-sized products (here W and Y with just one hour of work needed per unit) and over allocates overheads to larger products (here X and particularly Z).

Chapter roundup

- Product costs are built up using absorption costing by a process of allocation, apportionment and absorption.
- The absorption rate is calculated by dividing the budgeted overhead by the budgeted level of activity. For production overheads, the level of activity is often budgeted direct labour hours or budgeted machine hours.
- Management should try to establish an absorption rate that provides a reasonably 'accurate' estimate of overhead costs for jobs, products or services.
- Under- or over-absorbed overhead is inevitable in estimates of absorption costing because the predetermined overhead absorption rates are based on estimates of overhead expenditure and the level, or volume, of activity.
- If overheads absorbed exceed overheads incurred, the cost of production (or sales) will have been too high. The amount of over absorption will be written as a 'favourable' adjustment to the profit and loss account. Similarly, if overheads absorbed are lower than the amount of overheads incurred, the cost of production (or sales) will have been too low. The amount of under absorption will be written as an 'adverse' adjustment to the profit and loss account.
- Activity based costing (ABC) is an alternative to the more traditional absorption costing. ABC involves the identification of the factors (cost drivers) which cause the costs of an organisation's major activities. Support overheads are charged to products on the basis of their usage of an activity.

Quick quiz

1 What is overhead allocation?

2 What basis might be applied to apportion heat and light?

3 What is service cost centre cost apportionment?

4 Why is it common to use **predetermined** overhead absorption rates?

5 What is the problem with using a single factory overhead absorption rate?

6 Why does under- or over-absorbed overhead occur?

7 What is a cost driver?

8 What is a cost pool?

Answers to Quick quiz

1 Overhead allocation is the process of charging a cost, in full, directly to a cost centre.

2 Volume of space occupied is an appropriate basis for the apportionment of heat and light.

3 Service cost centre cost apportionment is the apportionment of costs allocated or apportioned to a service cost centre to production cost centres directly involved in the production of cost units.

4 Overhead absorption rates are often predetermined as this avoids two problems.

The value of overheads to be apportioned may not be known until the end of the year, but the cost of the cost unit needs to be ascertained as they are being produced and sold.

Costs and output vary, with a resulting variability in unit cost. This is unhelpful for costing, administration and control purposes.

5 A single overhead absorption rate will charge unfair amounts of overheads to products unless the product range is homogeneous. A misleading cost will then result.

6 Under- and over-absorption of overheads occur because estimates are used of costs and output in the calculation of an overhead absorption rate. The actual overhead costs and activity levels are unlikely to be the same as the estimates. (5.1-5.2)

7 A cost driver is a factor that causes a cost and determines the size of the cost of a major activity in a business.

8 A cost pool is a collection of all the costs of an activity.

Answers to Activities

1

	Basis	Forming £	Machines £	Assembly £	Maint'nce £	General £	Total £
Directly allocated overheads:							
Repairs, maintenance	Note 1	800	1,800	300	200	100	3,200
Departmental expenses	Note 1	1,500	2,300	1,100	900	1,500	7,300
Indirect labour Note 1		3,000	5,000	1,500	4,000	2,000	15,500
Apportionment of other overheads:							
Rent, rates	1	1,600	3,200	2,400	400	400	8,000
Power	2	200	450	75	25	0	750
Light, heat	1	1,000	2,000	1,500	250	250	5,000
Dep'n of plant	3	2,500	6,000	750	750	0	10,000
Dep'n of F & F	4	50	25	100	50	25	250
Insurance of plant	3	500	1,200	150	150	0	2,000
Insurance of buildings	1	100	200	150	25	25	500
Note 2		11,250	22,175	8,025	6,750	4,300	52,500

Basis of apportionment:

1 floor area
2 effective horsepower
3 plant value
4 fixtures and fittings value

Notes:

1 Some of the overheads have already been attributed or allocated to a specific department. These costs should just be recorded in that department.

2 Do not forget to include the allocated costs in this total.

2 Maintenance costs are reapportioned using the percentages given so 20% goes to forming, 50% to machines and 30% to assembly.

Forming 6,750 × 20% = 1,350
Machines 6,750 × 50% = 3,375
Assembly 6,750 × 30% = 2,025

Similarly for general.

Service department	*Basis of apportionment*	*Total cost* £	*Forming* £	*Machines* £	*Assembly* £
Maintenance	2:5:3	6,750	1,350	3,375	2,025
General	3:6:1	4,300	1,290	2,580	430
		11,050	2,640	5,955	2,455
Previously allocated and apportioned costs		41,450	11,250	22,175	8,025
Total overhead		52,500	13,890	28,130	10,480

3

Forming (labour intensive) $\frac{£13,890}{5,556}$ = £2.50 per direct labour hour

Machines (machine intensive) $\frac{£28,130}{5,626}$ = £5 per machine hour

Assembly (labour intensive) $\frac{£10,480}{5,240}$ = £2 per direct labour hour

Note. Since there are more labour hours than machine hours in the forming department this would be considered a labour intensive department thus an overhead absorption rate per direct labour hour is used.

In the machines department there are considerably more machine hours than labour hours. So, being a machine intensive department, a machine hour overhead absorption rate is used.

Assembly is clearly labour intensive as the direct labour hours are far more than the machine hours and so a direct labour hour rate is used to absorb overheads.

4 Overhead absorption rate $= \frac{\text{Budgeted overheads}}{\text{Budgeted machine hours}} = \frac{£350,000}{25,000}$

= £14 per machine hour

5 **Production Department X**

Overhead absorption rate will be based on direct labour hours

OAR = $\frac{£6,500}{2,500 \text{ hours}}$ = £2.60/labour hour

	£
Actual overheads	7,300
Absorbed overheads 2,600 × £2.60	6,760
Under absorbed	540

Production Department Y

Overhead absorption rate will be based on machine hours

OAR = $\frac{£5,750}{5,000 \text{ hours}}$ = £1.15/machine hour

	£
Actual overheads	4,500
Absorbed overheads 4,800 × £1.15	5,520
Over absorbed	1,020

Chapter : 4

MARGINAL AND ABSORPTION COSTING

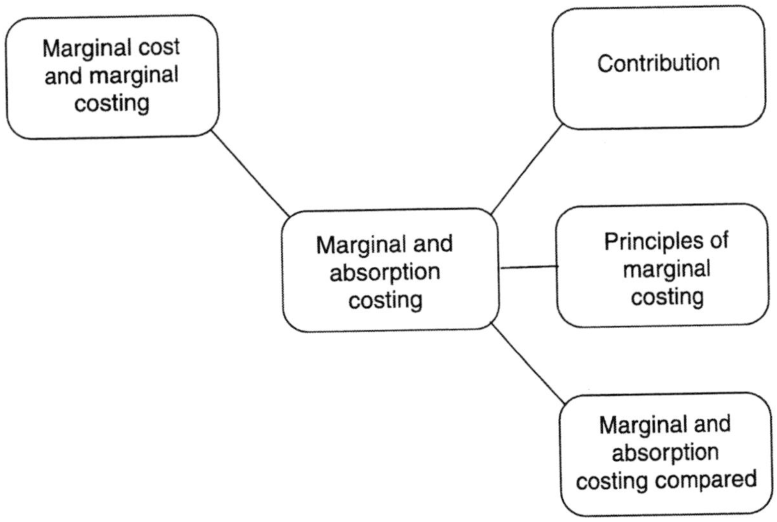

Introduction

In an earlier chapter we introduced the idea of **product costs** and **period costs**. **Product costs** are costs identified with goods produced or purchased for resale. Such costs are initially identified as part of the value of stock and only become expenses when the stock is sold. In contrast, **period costs** are costs that are deducted as expenses during the current period without ever being included in the value of stock held. In the previous chapter we saw how product costs are absorbed into the cost of units of output.

This chapter describes **marginal costing** and compares it with **absorption costing**. Whereas absorption costing recognises fixed costs (usually fixed production costs) as part of the cost of a unit of output and hence as product costs, marginal costing treats all fixed costs as period costs. Two such different costing methods obviously each have their supporters and we will be looking at the arguments both in favour of and against each method. Each costing method, because of the different stock valuation used, produces a different profit figure and we will be looking at this particular point in detail.

Your objectives

In this chapter you will learn about the following.

- Marginal cost and marginal costing
- Contribution
- The principles of marginal costing
- The differences between marginal costing and absorption costing

1 MARGINAL COSTING AND MARGINAL COST

Definitions

> **Marginal costing** is an alternative method of costing to absorption costing. In marginal costing, only variable costs are charged as a cost of sales and a contribution is calculated which is sales revenue minus the variable cost of sales. Closing stocks of work in progress or finished goods are valued at marginal (variable) production cost. Fixed costs are treated as a period cost, and are charged in full to the profit and loss account of the accounting period in which they are incurred.
>
> **Marginal cost** is the cost of a unit of a product or service which would be avoided if that unit were not produced or provided.

The marginal production cost per unit of an item usually consists of the following.

- Direct materials
- Direct labour
- Variable production overheads

2 CONTRIBUTION

Definition

> **Contribution** is the difference between sales value and the marginal cost of sales.

Contribution is of fundamental importance in marginal costing, and the term 'contribution' is really short for 'contribution towards covering fixed overheads and making a profit'.

3 THE PRINCIPLES OF MARGINAL COSTING

The principles of marginal costing are as follows.

(a) Period fixed costs are the same for any volume of sales and production (provided that the level of activity is within the 'relevant range'). Therefore, by selling an extra item of product or service the following will happen.

- Revenue will increase by the sales value of the item sold.
- Costs will increase by the variable cost per unit.
- Profit will increase by the amount of contribution earned from the extra item.

(b) Similarly, if the volume of sales falls by one item, the profit will fall by the amount of contribution earned from the item.

(c) Profit measurement should therefore be based on an analysis of total contribution. Since fixed costs relate to a period of time, and do not change with increases or decreases in sales volume, it is misleading to charge units of sale with a share of fixed costs. Absorption costing is therefore misleading, and it is more appropriate to deduct fixed costs from total contribution for the period to derive a profit figure.

(d) When a unit of product is made, the extra costs incurred in its manufacture are the **variable production costs**. Fixed costs are unaffected, and no extra fixed costs are incurred when output is increased. It is therefore argued that the valuation of closing stocks should be at variable production cost (direct materials, direct labour, direct expenses (if any) and variable production overhead) because these are the only costs properly attributable to the product.

Before explaining marginal costing principles any further, it will be helpful to look at a numerical example.

WORKED EXAMPLE: MARGINAL COSTING

Water Ltd makes a product, the Splash, which has a variable production cost of £6 per unit and a sales price of £10 per unit. At the beginning of September 20X4, there were no opening stocks and production during the month was 20,000 units. Fixed costs for the month were £45,000 (production, administration, sales and distribution). There were no variable marketing costs.

Required

Calculate the contribution and profit for September 20X4, using marginal costing principles, if sales were as follows.

(a) 10,000 Splashes
(b) 15,000 Splashes
(c) 20,000 Splashes

ANSWER

The first stage in the profit calculation must be to identify the variable costs, and then the contribution. Fixed costs are deducted from the total contribution to derive the profit. All closing stocks are valued at marginal production cost (£6 per unit).

	10,000 Splashes		*15,000 Splashes*		*20,000 Splashes*	
	£	£	£	£	£	£
Sales (at £10)		100,000		150,000		200,000
Opening stock	0		0		0	
Variable production cost	120,000		120,000		120,000	
	120,000		120,000		120,000	
Less value of closing stock (at marginal cost)	60,000		30,000		-	
Variable cost of sales		60,000		90,000		120,000
Contribution		40,000		60,000		80,000
Less fixed costs		45,000		45,000		45,000
Profit/(loss)		(5,000)		15,000		35,000
Profit/(loss) per unit		£(0.50)		£1		£1.75
Contribution per unit		£4		£4		£4

Conclusions

Note. Closing stock figures are calculated as production minus sales units, so at sales of 10,000 Splashes closing stock would be 10,000 units as 20,000 units were produced. At sales of 15,000 units, 5,000 units will be left in stock at the end of the month. If sales are for 20,000 units then all units produced are sold and no stocks remain.

The conclusions which may be drawn from this example are as follows.

(a) The **profit per unit varies** at differing levels of sales, because the average fixed overhead cost per unit changes with the volume of output and sales.

(b) The **contribution per unit is constant** at all levels of output and sales. Total contribution, which is the contribution per unit multiplied by the number of units sold, increases in direct proportion to the volume of sales.

(c) Since the **contribution per unit does not change**, the most effective way of calculating the expected profit at any level of output and sales would be as follows.

   (i) First calculate the total contribution.
   (ii) Then deduct fixed costs as a period charge in order to find the profit.

(d) In our example the expected profit from the sale of 17,000 Splashes would be as follows.

	£
Total contribution (17,000 × £4)	68,000
Less fixed costs	45,000
Profit	23,000

3.1 Summary

(a) If total contribution exceeds fixed costs, a profit is made.

(b) If total contribution exactly equals fixed costs, no profit and no loss is made and breakeven point is reached.

(c) If total contribution is less than fixed costs, there will be a loss.

Activity 1 **(10 minutes)**

Plumber Ltd makes two products, the Loo and the Wash. Information relating to each of these products for April 20X4 is as follows.

	Loo		*Wash*
Opening stock	nil		nil
Production (units)	15,000		6,000
Sales (units)	10,000		5,000
	£		£
Sales price per unit	20		30
Unit costs			
Direct materials	8		14
Direct labour	4		2
Variable production overhead	2		1
Variable sales overhead	2		3
Total variable costs per unit	16		20
Fixed costs for the month		£	
Production costs		40,000	
Administration costs		15,000	
Sales and distribution costs		25,000	

Using marginal costing principles, calculate the profit in April 20X4. Use the approach set out in the conclusions above.

4 MARGINAL COSTING AND ABSORPTION COSTING COMPARED

Marginal costing as a cost accounting system is significantly different from absorption costing. It is an **alternative method** of accounting for costs and profit, which rejects the principles of absorbing fixed overheads into unit costs.

4.1 Marginal costing

In marginal costing

(i) Closing stocks are valued at **marginal production cost.**

(ii) Fixed costs are charged in full against the profit of the period in which they are incurred.

4.2 Absorption costing

In absorption costing (sometimes referred to as **full costing**)

(i) Closing stocks are valued at full production cost, and include a share of fixed production costs.

(ii) This means that the cost of sales in a period will include some fixed overhead incurred in a previous period (in opening stock values) and will exclude some fixed overhead incurred in the current period but carried forward in closing stock values as a charge to a subsequent accounting period.

This distinction between marginal costing and absorption costing is very important and the contrast between the systems must be clearly understood. Work carefully through the following example to ensure that you are familiar with both methods.

WORKED EXAMPLE: MARGINAL AND ABSORPTION COSTING COMPARED

Two Left Feet Ltd manufactures a single product, the Claud. The following figures relate to the Claud for a one-year period.

Activity level		50%	100%
Sales and production (units)		400	800
		£	£
Sales		8,000	16,000
Production costs:	variable	3,200	6,400
	fixed	1,600	1,600
Sales and distribution costs:			
	variable	1,600	3,200
	fixed	2,400	2,400

The normal level of activity for the year is 800 units. Fixed costs are incurred evenly throughout the year, and actual fixed costs are the same as budgeted.

There were no stocks of Claud at the beginning of the year.

In the first quarter, 220 units were produced and 160 units sold.

(a) Calculate the fixed production costs absorbed by Clauds in the first quarter if absorption costing is used.

(b) Calculate the under/over recovery of overheads during the quarter.

(c) Calculate the profit using absorption costing.

(d) Calculate the profit using marginal costing.

(e) Explain why there is a difference between the answers to (c) and (d).

ANSWER

(a) $\dfrac{\text{Budgeted fixed production costs}}{\text{Budgeted output (normal level of activity)}} = \dfrac{£1{,}600}{800 \text{ units}}$

Absorption rate = £2 per unit produced.

During the quarter, the fixed production overhead absorbed was 220 units × £2 = £440.

(b)

	£
Actual fixed production overhead	400 (¼ of £1,600)
Absorbed fixed production overhead	440
Over absorption of overhead	40

(c) Profit for the quarter, absorption costing

	£	£
Sales (160 × £20)		3,200
Production costs		
Variable (220 × £8)	1,760	
Fixed (absorbed overhead (220 × £2))	440	
Total (220 × £10)	2,200	
Less closing stocks (60 × £10)	600	
Production cost of sales	1,600	
Adjustment for over-absorbed overhead	40	
Total production costs		1,560
Gross profit		1,640
Less: sales and distribution costs		
variable (160 × £4)	640	
fixed (1/4 of £2,400)	600	
		1,240
Net profit		400

(d) Profit for the quarter, marginal costing

	£	£
Sales		3,200
Variable production costs	1,760	
Less closing stocks (60 × £8)	480	
Variable production cost of sales	1,280	
Variable sales and distribution costs (Note)	640	
Total variable costs of sales		1,920
Total contribution		1,280
Less:		
Fixed production costs incurred	400	
Fixed sales and distribution costs	600	
		1,000
Net profit		280

Note. Variable sales and distribution costs will be based on units **sold** not produced.

(e) The difference in profit is due to the different valuations of closing stock. In absorption costing, the 60 units of closing stock include absorbed fixed overheads of £120 (60 × £2), which are therefore costs carried over to the next quarter and not charged against the profit of the current quarter. In marginal costing, all fixed costs incurred in the period are charged against profit.

	£
Absorption costing profit	400
Fixed production costs carried forward in stock values (60 × £2)	120
Marginal costing profit	280

4.3 Conclusions

We can draw a number of conclusions from this example.

(a) **Marginal costing** and **absorption costing** are different techniques for assessing profit in a period.

(b) If there are **changes in stocks during a period, marginal costing and absorption costing give different results for profit obtained.**

(i) **If stock levels increase, absorption costing will report the higher profit** because some of the fixed production overhead incurred during the period will be carried forward in closing stock (which reduces cost of sales) to be set against sales revenue in the following period instead of being written off in full against profit in the period concerned (as in the example).

(ii) **If stock levels decrease, absorption costing will report the lower profit** because as well as the fixed overhead incurred, fixed production overhead which had been brought forward in opening stock is released and is included in cost of sales.

(c) If the opening and closing stock volumes and values are the same, marginal costing and absorption costing will give the same profit figure.

(d) In the long run, total profit for a company will be the same whether marginal costing or absorption costing is used because in the long run, total costs will be the same by either method of accounting. Different accounting conventions merely affect the profit of individual accounting periods.

Activity 2 **(10 minutes)**

The overhead absorption rate for product X is £10 per machine hour. Each unit of product X requires five machine hours. Stock of product X on 1.1.X1 was 150 units and on 31.12.X1 it was 100 units. What is the difference in profit between results reported using absorption costing and results reported using marginal costing?

EXAMPLE: COMPARISON OF TOTAL PROFITS

Let us suppose that a company makes and sells a single product. At the beginning of period 1, there are no opening stocks of the product, for which the variable production cost is £4 and the sales price £6 per unit. Fixed costs are £2,000 per period, of which £1,500 are fixed production costs.

	Period 1	*Period 2*
Sales	1,200 units	1,800 units
Production	1,500 units	1,500 units

What would the profit be in each period using the following methods of costing?

(a) Absorption costing. Assume normal output is 1,500 units per period.
(b) Marginal costing.

ANSWER

It is important to notice that although production and sales volumes in each period are different (and therefore the profit for each period by absorption costing will be different from the profit by marginal costing), over the full period, total production equals sales volume, the total cost of sales is the same, and therefore the total profit is the same by either method of accounting.

NOTES

(a) **Absorption costing**: the absorption rate for fixed production overhead is

$$\frac{£1{,}500}{1{,}500 \text{ units}} = £1 \text{ per unit}$$

	Period 1		*Period 2*		*Total*	
	£	£	£	£	£	£
Sales (× £6)		7,200		10,800		18,000
Opening stock	-		1,500		-	
Production costs						
Variable (× £4)	6,000		6,000		12,000	
Fixed	1,500		1,500		3,000	
	7,500		9,000		15,000	
Less closing stock c/f	1,500		-		-	
Production cost of sales	6,000		9,000		15,000	
(Under-)/over-absorbed overhead (*Note*)	-		-		-	
Total production costs		6,000		9,000		15,000
Gross profit		1,200		1,800		3,000
Other costs		500		500		1,000
Net profit		700		1,300		2,000

Note. As actual production is the same as the normal output there will not be any under or over absorption of overheads.

(b) **Marginal costing**

	Period 1		*Period 2*		*Total*	
	£	£	£	£	£	£
Sales		7,200		10,800		18,000
Opening stock	-		1,200		-	
Variable production cost	6,000		6,000		12,000	
	6,000		7,200		12,000	
Less closing stock c/f	1,200		-		-	
Variable production cost of sales		4,800		7,200		12,000
Contribution		2,400		3,600		6,000
Fixed costs		2,000		2,000		4,000
Profit		400		1,600		2,000

Note that the total profit over the two periods is the same for each method of costing, but the profit in each period is different.

Activity 3 **(10 minutes)**

When opening stocks were 8,500 litres and closing stocks 6,750 litres, a firm had a profit of £62,100 using marginal costing.

Assuming that the fixed overhead absorption rate was £3 per litre, what would be the profit using absorption costing?

4.4 Marginal costing and absorption costing compared: which is better?

There are accountants who favour each costing method.

(a) Arguments in favour of absorption costing are as follows.

   (i) Fixed production costs are incurred in order to make output; it is therefore 'fair' to charge all output with a share of these costs.

   (ii) Closing stock values, by including a share of fixed production overhead, will be valued on the principle required for the financial accounting valuation of stocks by SSAP 9.

   (iii) A problem with calculating the contribution of various products made by a company is that it may not be clear whether the contribution earned by each product is enough to cover fixed costs, whereas by charging fixed overhead to a product it is possible to ascertain whether it is profitable or not.

(b) Arguments in favour of marginal costing are as follows.

   (i) It is simple to operate.

   (ii) There are no apportionments, which are frequently done on an arbitrary basis, of fixed costs. Many costs, such as the managing director's salary, are indivisible by nature.

   (iii) Fixed costs will be the same regardless of the volume of output, because they are period costs. It makes sense, therefore, to charge them in full as a cost to the period.

   (iv) The cost to produce an extra unit is the variable production cost. It is realistic to value closing stock items at this directly attributable cost.

   (v) Under or over absorption of overheads is avoided.

   (vi) Marginal costing information can be used for decision making but absorption costing information is not suitable for decision making.

   (vii) Fixed costs (such as depreciation, rent and salaries) relate to a period of time and should be charged against the revenues of the period in which they are incurred.

Activity 4 **(20 minutes)**

Kanga Ltd manufactures a single product, the Roo. Details on the product are given below.

	Roo
	£
Selling price	25
Unit costs	
Direct materials	5
Direct labour	6
Variable production overhead	2
Variable sales overhead	1
Budgeted production for period	500 units

Fixed costs for the month are given below.

	Budgeted costs	*Actual costs*
	£	£
Production overhead	1,500	1,700
Administration costs	900	800
Selling costs	500	625

Budgeted sales for the period were 400 units although actual sales were 500 units. There was no opening stock and actual production for the month was 600 units.

(a) Calculate the net profit using absorption costing
(b) Calculate the net profit using marginal costing
(c) Explain the difference between (a) and (b)

Chapter roundup

- Absorption costing is most often used for routine profit reporting and must be used for financial accounting purposes. Marginal costing provides better management information for planning and decision making.
- Marginal cost is the variable cost of one unit of product or service (the cost which would be avoided if that unit were not produced).
- Contribution is an important measure in marginal costing, and it is calculated as the difference between sales value and marginal or variable cost.
- In marginal costing, fixed production costs are treated as period costs and are written off as they are incurred. In absorption costing, fixed production costs are absorbed into the cost of units and are carried forward in stock to be charged against sales for the next period. Stock values using absorption costing are therefore greater than those calculated using marginal costing.
- Reported profit figures using marginal costing or absorption costing will differ if there is any change in the level of stocks in the period. If production is equal to sales, there will be no difference in calculated profits using these costing methods.

Quick quiz

1 Define contribution.

2 How are stocks valued in marginal costing?

3 If opening and closing stock volumes and values are the same, does absorption costing or marginal costing give the higher profit?

4 Describe three arguments in favour of absorption costing.

5 What are the arguments in favour of the use of marginal costing?

Answers to Quick quiz

1 Contribution is the difference between sales value and the marginal cost of sales.

2 In marginal costing stocks are valued at variable production cost.

3 If there is no change in stocks during a period, both methods will give the same profit.

4 Arguments for absorption costing.

(i) Fixed costs are incurred in order to make output, therefore it is fair to charge output with a share of these costs.

(ii) Stock valuation which includes a share of fixed production cost complies with SSAP 9.

(iii) The calculation of a profit figure for each product shows which products are profitable.

5 Arguments for marginal costing.

(i) Simple to operate.

(ii) Avoids the arbitrary apportionment of fixed costs.

(iii) Avoids under- and over-absorption of overheads.

(iv) Information produced can be used for decision-making.

(v) It makes sense to charge fixed costs to the period as they do not change with volume of production.

(vi) Closing stock is valued at its directly attributable cost.

Answers to Activities

1

	£
Contribution from Loos	
(unit contribution = £20 – £16 = £4 × 10,000)	40,000
Contribution from Washes	
(unit contribution = £30 – £20 = £10 × 5,000)	50,000
Total contribution	90,000
Fixed costs for the period (40,000 + 15,000 + 25,000)	80,000
Profit	10,000

2 The key is the change in the volume of stock. Stock levels have decreased therefore absorption costing will report a lower profit.

The correct answer based on the **change** in stock levels × fixed overhead absorption per unit = (150 – 100) × £10 × 5 = £2,500 lower profit, because stock levels decreased.

3 Stock levels reduced, therefore the absorption costing profit would be lower.

Difference in profit = (8,500 – 6,750) × £3 = £5,250
Absorption costing profit = £62,100 – £5,250 = £56,850

NOTES

4 (a) Profit for the period using absorption costing.

	£	£
Sales (500 × 25)		12,500
Opening stock	-	
Production costs		
Variable production costs		
(600 × (5 + 6 + 2))	7,800	
Fixed production costs		
$(600 \times \left(\frac{1,500}{500}\right)$ Note	1,800	
	9,600	
Closing stock (100 × 16)	(1,600)	
Production cost of sales	8,000	
Adjustment for over absorption (see below)	(100)	
Total production costs		(7,900)
Gross profit		4,600
Administration costs (actual)		(800)
Selling costs:		
Variable (500 × 1)		(500)
Fixed		(625)
Net profit under absorption costing		2,675

Note. Full cost per unit:

	£
Direct materials	5
Direct labour	6
Variable production overhead	2
Fixed production overhead $\left(\frac{1,500}{500}\right) =$	3
	16

	£
Actual production overheads	1,700
Absorbed production overheads (600 × 3)	1,800
Over absorbed	100

(b) Profit for the period using marginal costing.

	£	£
Sales (500 × 25)		12,500
Opening stock	-	
Production costs		
Variable (600 × (5 + 6 + 2))	7,800	
	7,800	
Closing stock (100 × 13)	(1,300)	
Variable production cost of sales	6,500	
Variable sales and distribution costs (500 × 1)	500	
		(7,000)
Total contribution		5,500
Less: Fixed production overheads	1,700	
Fixed administration costs	800	
Fixed selling costs	625	
		(3,125)
Net profit under marginal costing		2,375

(c) The difference in profit is caused by the valuation of stock. Under absorption costing fixed production costs are carried forward in closing stock to the next period whereas under marginal costing these fixed production costs are charged in full to the period.

	£
Absorption costing profit	2,675
Fixed production costs carried forward in stock values (100 × 3)	(300)
Marginal costing profit	2,375

Chapter : 5
PRICE, VALUE AND QUALITY

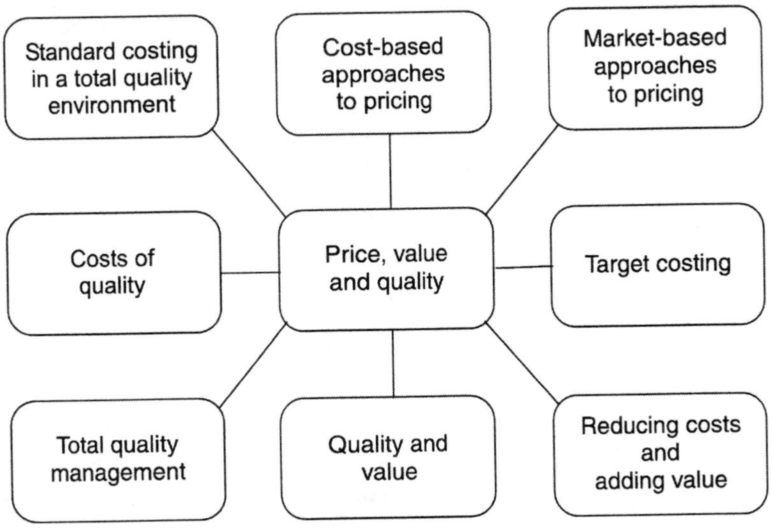

Introduction

Finding the cost of a product or service means, amongst other things, that you have a basis for setting a **selling price** that will earn the business the profit it wants. Recently, however, some businesses have approached the problem from the opposite side: they have decided what the selling price should be in order for the product to sell, and then they deduct the profit they want, which leaves the **target cost**. In this chapter we look at methods of pricing that are based on cost, as well as target costing.

The need to cut costs is something which affects most businesses these days if they want to price their products competitively and remain in business. In this chapter we look at ways in which costs can be reduced and managed. Central to these techniques is the need to maintain and improve **quality** and add **value**.

Your objectives

In this chapter you will learn about the following.

(a) Pricing based on cost

(b) Market-based pricing

(c) Target costing

(d) Cost reduction and value analysis

(e) Total Quality Management

1 COST-BASED APPROACHES TO PRICING

1.1 Full cost-plus pricing

Definition

> **Full cost-plus pricing** is a method of determining the sales price by calculating the full cost of the product and adding a percentage mark-up for profit.

In practice cost is one of the most important influences on price. Many firms base price on simple cost-plus rules (costs are estimated and then a mark-up is added in order to set the price). A traditional approach to pricing is full cost-plus pricing.

The 'full cost' may be a fully absorbed production cost only, or it may include some absorbed administration, selling and distribution overhead.

A business might have an idea of the percentage profit margin it would like to earn, and so might **decide on an average profit mark-up** as a general guideline for pricing decisions. This would be particularly **useful for** businesses that carry out a large amount of **contract work or jobbing work**, for which individual job or contract prices must be quoted regularly to prospective customers. However, the percentage profit **mark-up does not have to be rigid and fixed**, but can be varied to suit the circumstances. In particular, the percentage mark-up can be varied to suit demand conditions in the market.

> **Activity 1** **(5 minutes)**
>
> A product's full cost is £4.70 and is sold at full cost plus 70%.
>
> What is the selling price?

WORKED EXAMPLE: FULL COST-PLUS PRICING

Markup Ltd has begun to produce a new product, Product X, for which the following cost estimates have been made.

	£
Direct materials	54
Direct labour: 4 hrs at £10 per hour	40
Variable production overheads: machining, ½ hr at £12 per hour	6
	100

Fixed production overheads are budgeted at £600,000 per month and, because of the shortage of available machining capacity, the company will be restricted to 10,000 hours of machine time per month. The absorption rate will be a direct labour rate, however, and budgeted direct labour hours are 25,000 per month.

The company wishes to make a profit of 20% on full production cost from product X.

Required

What is the full cost-plus based price?

ANSWER

	£
Direct materials	54.00
Direct labour (4 hours)	40.00
Variable production overheads	6.00
Fixed production overheads	
(at $\frac{£600,000}{25,000}$ = £24 per direct labour hour)	96.00
Full production cost	196.00
Profit mark-up (20%)	39.20
Selling price per unit of product X	235.20

Problems with and advantages of full cost-plus pricing

There are several serious **problems** with relying on a full cost approach to pricing.

(a) It **fails to recognise** that demand may be determining price. For many products, the price set will determine the quantity sold. The price we set using this method may not lead to selling the quantity that gives us the biggest profit. In other words, the price we set might not be competitive.

(b) There may be a need to **adjust prices to market and demand conditions.**

(c) **Budgeted output volume** needs to be established. Output volume is a key factor in the overhead absorption rate.

(d) A **suitable basis for overhead absorption** must be selected, especially where a business produces more than one product.

However, it is a **quick, simple and cheap** method of pricing which can be delegated to junior managers (which is particularly important with jobbing work where many prices must be decided and quoted each day) and, since the size of the profit margin can be varied, a decision based on a price in excess of full cost should ensure that a company working at normal capacity will **cover all of its fixed costs and make a profit.**

1.2 Marginal cost-plus pricing

Definition

> **Marginal cost-plus pricing/mark-up pricing** is a method of determining the sales price by adding a profit margin on to either marginal cost of production or marginal cost of sales.

Whereas a full cost-plus approach to pricing draws attention to net profit and the net profit margin, a variable cost-plus approach to pricing **draws attention to gross profit** and the **gross profit margin**, or **contribution**.

Activity 2 **(20 minutes)**

A product has the following costs.

	£
Direct materials	5
Direct labour	3
Variable overheads	7

Fixed overheads are £10,000 per month. Budgeted sales per month are 400 units.

What is the mark up on marginal cost if the selling price is £20?

There are several **advantages** of a marginal cost-plus approach to pricing

(a) It is a **simple and easy** method to use.

(b) The **mark-up percentage can be varied**, and so mark-up pricing can be adjusted to reflect demand conditions.

(c) It **draws management attention to contribution**, and the effects of higher or lower sales volumes on profit. In this way, it helps to create a better awareness of the concepts and implications of marginal costing and cost-volume-profit analysis. For example, if a product costs £10 per unit and a mark-up of 150% is added to reach a price of £25 per unit, management should be clearly aware that every additional £1 of sales revenue would add 60 pence to contribution and profit.

(d) In practice, mark-up pricing is used in businesses where there is a readily-identifiable basic variable cost. Retail industries are the most obvious example, and it is quite common for the prices of goods in shops to be fixed by adding a mark-up (20% or 33.3%, say) to the purchase cost.

There are, of course, **drawbacks** to marginal cost-plus pricing.

(a) Although the size of the mark-up can be varied in accordance with demand conditions, it **does not ensure that sufficient attention is paid to demand** conditions, competitors' prices and profit maximisation.

(b) It **ignores fixed overheads** in the pricing decision, but the sales price must be sufficiently high to ensure that a profit is made after covering fixed costs.

1.3 Cost-plus pricing and stock valuation

Many retail businesses price their goods by applying a fixed mark up to their cost. When it comes to stocktaking, it is therefore very convenient to take the selling price of the goods as shown on the price ticket or the price list, and deduct the profit element to arrive at the cost of the goods for stock valuation purposes.

Activity 3 **(5 minutes)**

The price tags on six boxes of cutlery show that the selling price of each is £187.50. The retailer has a uniform mark up on cost of 25%.

What is the cost of the cutlery stock?

2 MARKET-BASED APPROACHES TO PRICING

2.1 Product life cycle

The product life concept is relevant to pricing policy. The concept states that a typical product moves through four stages.

(a) **Introduction**

The product is introduced to the market. Heavy **capital expenditure** will be incurred on product development and perhaps also on the purchase of new fixed assets and building up stocks for sale.

On its introduction to the market, the product will begin to earn some revenue, but initially demand is likely to be small. Potential customers will be unaware of the product or service, and the organisation may have to spend further on **advertising** to bring the product or service to the attention of the market.

(b) **Growth**

The product gains a bigger market as demand builds up. Sales revenues increase and the product begins to make a profit. The initial costs of the **investment** in the new product are gradually **recovered**.

(c) **Maturity**

Eventually, the growth in demand for the product will slow down and it will enter a period of relative maturity. It will continue to be profitable. The product may be **modified or improved, as a means of sustaining its demand**.

(d) **Saturation and decline**

At some stage, the market may reach 'saturation point'. Demand will start to fall. For a while, the product will still be profitable in spite of declining sales, but eventually it will become a **loss-maker** and this is the time when the organisation should decide to stop selling the product or service, and so the product's life cycle should reach its end.

Remember, however, that some mature products will **never decline**: staple food products such as milk or bread are the best example.

Not all products follow this cycle, but it remains a useful tool when considering decisions such as pricing. **The life cycle concept is relevant when considering what pricing policy will be adopted.**

2.2 Markets

The price that an organisation can charge for its products will also be influenced by the market in which it operates.

Definition

- **Perfect competition**: many buyers and many sellers all dealing in an identical product. Neither producer nor user has any market power and both must accept the prevailing market price.
- **Monopoly**: one seller who dominates many buyers. The monopolist can use his market power to set a profit-maximising price.
- **Oligopoly**: relatively few competitive companies dominate the market. Whilst each large firm has the ability to influence market prices, the unpredictable reaction from the other giants makes the final industry price indeterminate.

2.3 Competition

In **established industries** dominated by a few major firms, a price initiative by one firm will usually be countered by a price reaction by competitors. In these circumstances, **prices tend to be stable**.

If a **rival cuts its prices** in the expectation of increasing its market share, a **firm has several options**.

(a) It will **maintain its existing prices** if the expectation is that only a small market share would be lost, so that it is more profitable to keep prices at their existing level. Eventually, the rival firm may drop out of the market or be forced to raise its prices.

(b) It may maintain its prices but respond with a **non-price counter-attack**. This is a more positive response, because the firm will be securing or justifying its current prices with a product change, advertising, or better back-up services.

(c) It may **reduce its prices**. This should protect the firm's market share so that the main beneficiary from the price reduction will be the consumer.

(d) It may **raise its prices** *and respond with a* **non-price counter-attack**. The extra revenue from the higher prices might be used to finance an advertising campaign or product design changes. A price increase would be based on a campaign to emphasise the quality difference between the firm's own product and the rival's product.

2.4 Price leadership

Given that price competition can have disastrous consequences in conditions of oligopoly, it is not unusual to find that large corporations emerge as price leaders. The price leader **indicates to the other firms in the market what the price will be**, and **competitors then set their prices with reference to the leader's price**.

2.5 Market penetration pricing

This is a policy of **low prices** when the product is **first launched** in order to obtain sufficient penetration into the market. A penetration policy may be appropriate:

- If the firm wishes to **discourage new entrants** into the market.
- If the firm wishes to **shorten the initial period of the product's life cycle** in order to enter the growth and maturity stages as quickly as possible.
- If there are significant **economies of scale** to be achieved from a high volume of output, so that quick penetration into the market is desirable in order to gain unit cost reductions.
- If **demand is likely to increase as prices fall.**

2.6 Market skimming pricing

In contrast, market skimming involves charging **high prices** when a product is **first launched** and **spending heavily on advertising** and sales promotion to obtain sales. As the product moves into the **later stages** of its life cycle (growth, maturity and decline) **progressively lower prices** will be charged. The profitable 'cream' is thus skimmed off in stages until sales can only be sustained at lower prices.

The aim of market skimming is to gain **high unit profits early** in the product's life. High unit prices make it more likely that **competitors** will enter the market than if lower prices were to be charged.

Such a policy is appropriate:

- Where the **product is new and different**, so that customers are prepared to pay high prices so as to be one up on other people who do not own it. For example games systems.
- Where the strength of **demand** and the sensitivity of demand to price are **unknown**. It is better from the point of view of marketing to start by charging high prices and then reduce them if the demand is insufficient.
- Where products may have a **short life cycle**, and so need to recover their development costs and make a profit quickly.

2.7 Differential pricing

In certain circumstances the **same product** can be sold at **different prices** to **different customers**. There are a number of bases on which such prices can be set.

Basis	Example
By **market segment**	A cross-channel ferry company would market its services at different prices in England, Belgium and France, for example. Services such as cinemas and hairdressers are often available at lower prices to old age pensioners and/or juveniles.
By **product version**	Many car models have 'add on' extras which enable one brand to appeal to a wider cross-section of customers. The final price need not reflect the cost price of the add on extras directly: usually the top of the range model would carry a price much in excess of the cost of provision of the extras, as a prestige appeal.

Basis	Example
By **place**	Theatre seats are usually sold according to their location so that patrons pay different prices for the same performance according to the seat type they occupy.
By **time**	This is perhaps the most popular type of price discrimination. Railway companies, for example, are successful price discriminators, charging more to rush hour rail commuters whose demand remains the same whatever the price charged at certain times of the day.

2.8 Price and the price elasticity of demand

Economists argue that the higher the price of a good, the lower will be the quantity demanded. We have already seen that in practice it is by no means as straightforward as this (some goods are bought *because* they are expensive, for example), but you know from your personal experience as a consumer that the theory is essentially true.

An important concept in this context is **price elasticity of demand (PED).**

Definition

> The **price elasticity of demand** measures the extent of change in demand for a good following a change to its price.

Price elasticity (η)is measured as:

$$\frac{\text{\% change in sales demand}}{\text{\% change in sales price}}$$

Demand is said to be **elastic** when a **small change in the price** produces a **large change in the quantity demanded**. The PED is then greater than 1. Demand is said to be **inelastic** when a **small change in the price** produces only a **small change in the quantity demanded**. The PED is then less than 1.

There are two special values of price elasticity of demand.

- Demand is **perfectly inelastic (η = 0)**. There is **no change in quantity** demanded, **regardless of the change in price.**
- Demand is **perfectly elastic ($\eta = \infty$)**. Consumers will want to **buy an infinite amount**, but only **up to a particular price level**. Any price increase above this level will reduce demand to zero.

An awareness of the concept of elasticity can assist management with pricing decisions.

- In circumstances of **inelastic demand, prices should be increased** because revenues will increase and total costs will reduce (because quantities sold will reduce).
- In circumstances of **elastic demand,** increases in prices will bring decreases in revenue and decreases in price will bring increases in revenue.

Management therefore have to **decide whether the increase/decrease in costs will be less than/greater than the increases/decreases in revenue.**

- In situations of **very elastic demand**, overpricing can lead to a massive drop in quantity sold and hence a massive drop in profits, whereas underpricing can lead to costly stock outs and, again, a significant drop in profits. **Elasticity must therefore be reduced by creating a customer preference which is unrelated to price** (through advertising and promotional activities).
- In situations of **very inelastic demand**, customers are not sensitive to price. **Quality, service, product mix and location are therefore more important** to a firm's pricing strategy.

2.9 The demand-based approach to pricing

Price theory or **demand** theory is based on the idea that a connection can be made between price, quantity demanded and sold, and total revenue. Demand varies with price, and so if an estimate can be made of demand at different price levels, it should be **possible to derive either a profit-maximising price** or a revenue-maximising price.

The theory is dependent on realistic estimates of demand being made at different price levels. Making accurate estimates of demand is often difficult as price is only one of many variables that influence demand. Some larger organisations go to considerable effort to estimate the demand for their products or services at differing price levels by producing estimated demand curves.

For example a large transport authority might be considering an increase in bus fares or underground fares. The effect on total revenues and profit of the increase in fares could be estimated from a knowledge of the demand for transport services at different price levels. If an increase in the price per ticket caused a **large** fall in demand, because demand was price elastic, total revenues and profits would fall whereas a fares increase when demand is price inelastic would boost total revenue, and since a transport authority's costs are largely fixed, this would probably boost total profits too.

Many businesses enjoy something akin to a monopoly position, even in a competitive market. This is because they develop a unique marketing mix, for example a unique combination of price and quality. The significance of a monopoly situation is:

(a) The business does not have to 'follow the market' on price, in other words it is not a 'price-taker', but has more choice and flexibility in the prices it sets.

   (i) At higher prices, demand for its products or services will be less.

   (ii) At lower prices, demand for its products or services will be higher.

(b) There will be a selling price at which the business can maximise its profits.

WORKED EXAMPLE: DEMAND-BASED APPROACH

Moose Ltd sells a product which has a variable cost of £8 per unit. The sales demand at the current sales price of £14 is 3,000 units. It has been estimated by the marketing department that the sales volume would fall by 100 units for each addition of 25 pence to the sales price.

We want to establish whether the current price of £14 is the optimal price which maximises contribution. In order to do this we can look at unit contribution, sales volume and total contribution at different sales prices.

ANSWER

Sales price	*Unit contribution*	*Sales volume*	*Total contribution*
£	£	Units	£
13.00	5.00	3,400	17,000
13.25	5.25	3,300	17,325
13.50	5.50	3,200	17,600
13.75	5.75	3,100	17,825
14.00	*6.00 (14 – 8)*	*3,000*	*18,000*
14.25	6.25	2,900	18,125
14.50	6.50	2,800	18,200
14.75	6.75	2,700	18,225*
15.00	7.00	2,600	18,200

* Contribution would be maximised at a price of £14.75, and sales of 2,700 units.

The current price is not optimal.

3 TARGET COSTING

3.1 The target costing approach

Japanese companies developed target costing as a **response to the problem of controlling and reducing costs over the entire product life cycle**, but **especially** during the **design and development stages**. It has been used successfully **by car manufacturers** in particular, including Toyota and Mercedes Benz.

Target costing requires managers to change the way they think about the relationship between cost, price and profit. The traditional approach is to **develop a product, determine the expected standard production cost** of that product and then **set a selling price** (probably **based on cost**), with a **resulting profit or loss**. Costs are **controlled** through **variance analysis** at monthly intervals.

The target costing approach is to **develop a product concept** and the primary specifications for performance and design and then to **determine the price customers would be willing to pay** for that concept. The **desired profit margin** is **deducted from the price, leaving** a figure that represents **total cost**. This is the **target cost**. The product must be capable of being produced for this amount otherwise it will not be manufactured.

During the product's life the **target cost** will be **continuously reviewed and reduced** so that the **price can fall**. Continuous **cost reduction techniques** must therefore be used.

3.2 Achieving the target cost

If the **anticipated product cost** (based on the design specifications) is **above the target cost**, the product must be **modified** so that it is cheaper to produce.

The total target cost can be split into broad cost categories such as development, marketing, manufacturing and so on. A team of designers, engineers, marketing and production staff, as well as the management accountant, should then endeavour to produce a product with planned development, marketing, manufacturing (and so on) costs below the target costs. The cost reduction techniques explored in the next section will need to be used to achieve this.

If any of the target costs cannot be achieved given the product design, other individual targets must be reduced, the product redesigned yet again or scrapped.

Activity 4 **(10 minutes)**

Seven League Boots Ltd wishes to sell 14,000 units of its product, which has a variable cost of £15 to make and sell. Fixed costs are £47,000 and the required profit is £23,000.

Calculate the sales price per unit.

4 REDUCING COSTS AND ADDING VALUE

4.1 Cost reduction

Budgetary control and **standard costing** are examples of **cost control techniques**. Cost control is all about **keeping costs within predetermined limits** (usually standard cost). If actual costs differ from planned costs by an excessive amount, cost control action is necessary.

Cost reduction is different. It aims to **reduce costs below a previously accepted level, without adversely affecting the quality of the product** or service being provided.

Significant **cost reduction** can be **achieved** simply by using a **little common sense**. Here are some examples.

- **Improve the efficiency of materials usage** by reducing levels of wastage.
- **Improve labour productivity** by giving pay incentives or changing work methods to eliminate unnecessary procedures.
- **Improve the efficiency of equipment usage** by achieving a better balance between preventive maintenance and machine 'down time' for repairs.
- **Reduce material costs** by taking advantage of bulk purchase discounts or by improving stores control.
- **Reduce labour costs** by replacing people with machinery or by improving work methods following a work study (see below).
- **Save on finance costs** by taking advantage of early payment discounts or reassessing sources of finance.

- **Improve control over spending decisions** so that junior managers are not able to commit an organisation without consideration of long-term cost. For example, the hire of two office assistants at wages of £200 per week each would cost £200,000 over a ten-year period. Such a decision might be taken by an office manager whereas the purchase of a piece of machinery for the same cost would probably need board authorisation.

Activity 5 **(10 minutes)**

How can wastage be reduced?

A successful **cost reduction programme** will **cover all aspects** of an organisation's activities, systems and products and will be **supported by senior management**.

As well as the common sense ways of reducing costs, there are a number of formal techniques that can improve products or services, reduce waste, simplify systems and hence reduce costs.

4.2 Value analysis

Value analysis involves **assessing the value of every aspect of a product** (or service) in order to **devise ways** of **achieving** the product's (or service's) **purpose** as **economically** as possible while **maintaining** the required standard of **quality** and **reliability**.

Conventional cost reduction techniques aim to **produce a particular design of a product as cheaply as possible. Value analysis,** on the other hand, tries to **find the least-cost method of making a product that achieves its intended purpose.**

A value analysis assessment is likely to be carried out by a **team of experts** from the engineering, technical production and finance departments. It will involve the systematic investigation of every source of cost and every technique of production with the aim of getting rid of all unnecessary costs. An **unnecessary cost** is a cost that **does not add value**.

Value is **only added** to a product **while it is actually being processed**. Whilst it is being inspected for quality, moving from one part of the factory to another, waiting for further processing and held in store, value is not being added. Non value-adding activities should therefore be eliminated.

A **value-adding activity cannot be eliminated without the customer perceiving a deterioration in the performance, function or other quality of a product**.

Activity 6 **(5 minutes)**

Which of the following are value-adding activities?

(a) Setting up a machine so that it drills holes of a certain size
(b) Repairing faulty production work
(c) Painting a car, if the organisation manufactures cars
(d) Storing materials

There are some areas of that are of special importance.

- *Product design*

  At the design stage value analysis is called **value engineering.** The designer should be cost conscious and avoid unnecessary complications. Simple product design can avoid production and quality control problems, thereby resulting in lower costs.

- *Components and material costs*

  The purchasing department should beware of lapsing into habit with routine buying decisions. It has a crucial role to play in reducing costs and improving value by procuring the desired quality materials at the lowest possible price.

- *Production methods*

  These ought to be reviewed continually, on a product-by-product basis, especially with changing technology.

Value analysis typically involves consideration of the following.

- **Can the function of the product be achieved in another way**, using less expensive methods?
- **Are all the functions of the product essential**, or can some be removed without affecting quality?
- **Can a cheaper substitute material be found** which is as good, if not better, than the material currently used?
- **Can unnecessary weight or embellishments be removed** without reducing the product's attractions or desirability?
- **Can a new product/service be standardised** so it can be produced in conjunction with existing products/services?
- **Is it possible to use standardised components** (or to make components to a particular standard) thereby reducing the variety of units used and produced? **Variety reduction (standardisation)** is cost effective because it allows a range of finished products to be produced from a common, relatively small pool of components. In general, if there are fewer product varieties, production is more straight-forward, which makes it easier to automate and so costs are likely to reduce. Fitted kitchens, for example, come in a wide variety of colours and finishes but it is only the cupboard doors that differ; the bodies of the cupboards are standardised.
- **Is it possible to reduce the number of components,** for example could a product be assembled safely with a smaller number of screws?

Activity 7 **(15 minutes)**

Standardisation of parts and components might offer enormous cost reduction potential for some manufacturing industries. Can you think why this might be the case? What are the disadvantages of standardisation?

The origins of value analysis were in the engineering industry, but it **can be applied to services or to aspects of office work.**

If applied thoroughly and on a **continuous** basis, value analysis should result in a planned, ongoing search for cost reductions.

4.3 Work study

Work study is used to **determine the most efficient methods of using labour, materials and machinery**. There are two main parts to work study.

- **Method study** involves **systematically recording** and **critically examining** existing and proposed **ways** of **doing work**. The aim of this is to **develop** and **apply easier** and **more effective methods**, and so **reduce costs.**
- **Work measurement** involves **establishing the time for a qualified worker** to carry out a **specified job** at a **specified level of performance.**

Areas where work study can be applied

- Plant facilities, layout and space utilisation
- Analysis, design and improvement of work systems (say forms used or the telephone system), work places and work methods
- Setting standards
- Determining the most profitable, alternative combinations of personnel, materials and equipment

4.4 Organisation and methods (O&M)

Organisation and methods (O&M) is a term for **techniques**, including method study and work measurement, that are used to **examine clerical, administrative and management procedures in order to make improvements.**

O&M is **primarily concerned with office work** and looks in particular at areas such as the following.

- Organisation
- Office layout
- Office mechanisation
- Documentation and the design of forms
- Duties
- Staffing
- Methods of procedure

Work study and O&M are perhaps associated in your mind with establishing standard times for work, but the real aim is to decide the most efficient methods of getting work done. More efficient methods and tighter standards will improve efficiency and productivity, and so reduce costs.

4.5 Difficulties with introducing cost reduction programmes

- There may be **resistance from employees** to the pressure to reduce costs, usually because the nature and purpose of the campaign has not been properly explained to them, and because they feel threatened by the change.

- The programme may be limited to a small area of the business with the result that **costs are reduced in one cost centre, only to reappear as an extra cost in another**.
- Cost reduction campaigns are **often introduced as a rushed, desperate measure** instead of a carefully organised, well thought-out exercise.
- **Long-term factors** must be considered. Reduction in expenditure on maintenance, advertising or research and development in the short term could have serious long-term consequences.
- It is becoming increasingly apparent that the **key area** for cost reduction is **product design**. Once manufacturing begins there is less scope for reducing costs, especially if production is heavily automated.

5 QUALITY AND VALUE

In the past, many organisations focused on **quantity** – producing as many 'units' as possible as cheaply as possible. **Customers** used to accept late delivery of the same old unreliable products from organisations which appeared to care little for their customers. But **now** they **want more.**

- New products
- High levels of quality
- On-time delivery
- Immediate response to their requests

Businesses **today** are therefore **concentrating** on **quality** in the hope of becoming the success stories of the 21st century.

5.1 Quality

Definition

> **Quality** means 'the **degree of excellence of a thing**' – how well made it is, or how well it is performed if it is a service, how well it serves its purpose, and how it measures up against its rivals.
>
> The quality of a product or service has also been defined as 'its **fitness for the customer's purpose**'.

So if we are looking for an '**excellent**' **product** or service, we expect it to be **completely satisfactory for its purpose** from the **point of view of the customer.**

The **degree** to which a product or service is **fit for its purpose** will depend on the product or service in question.

- **Cost**. Customers expect some products to be cheap because of their short life. Pencils and daily newspapers are examples.
- **Life**. Other products are expected to last for longer and to be reliable and hence are more expensive. Televisions are an example.

- **Manner of production**. With some products, customers expect the use of highly skilled labour and/or expensive raw materials. A meal in a highly-commended restaurant is an example.
- **Esteem**. If a customer is looking for esteem or status from a product, the product is likely to have a high price, a designer label and/or expensive package. An example is designer-label clothing.

A **quality service** is likely to be **efficient**, be provided by **courteous staff** who have **knowledge of the service** and take place within a **pleasant environment**. For example, if a train arrives on time, is clean and comfortable and the guard gives out accurate announcements over the tannoy, many customers would feel they had enjoyed a quality service.

5.2 Value

The **value** of a product or service **to a customer** can therefore be considered in terms of its **fitness for purpose** and the **prestige or esteem attached**. From the **point of view of the producer of the product or the provider of the service,** however, other aspects are important.

- All organisations need to control costs and so the **cost of making the product or providing the service** is one aspect.
- The other aspect, the product's or service's **selling price** (its **market value),** is of importance to profit-making organisations.

The value of a product therefore has four distinct aspects.

- **Cost value** is the cost of producing and selling an item/providing a service.
- **Exchange value** is the market value of the product or service.
- **Use value** is what the product or service does, the purpose it fulfils.
- **Esteem value** is the prestige the customer attaches to a product.

Activity 8 **(5 minutes)**

Classify the following features of a product, using the types of value set out above.

(a) The product can be sold for £27.50.
(b) The product is available in six colours to suit customers' tastes.
(c) The product will last for ten years.

5.3 Enhancing value

The **producer** of a product or **provider** of a service will want to **increase exchange value** (the selling price) **without increasing cost value. To do this, the value the customer attaches** to the product or service **must be enhanced** (its **use value** or its **esteem value**) so that they will pay the higher price.

- Extended opening hours may add to the use value of a local shop.
- The esteem value of certain products such as expensive jewellery can be increased by increasing the price!

6 TOTAL QUALITY MANAGEMENT (TQM))

If the level of quality is to be controlled, a **control system** is needed.

Step 1.

Establish **standards of quality** for a product or service.

↓

Step 2.

Establish **procedures or production methods** which ought to ensure that these required standards of quality are met in a suitably high proportion of cases.

↓

Step 3.

Monitor actual quality.

↓

Step 4.

Take **control action** when actual quality falls below standard.

Activity 9 **(5 minutes)**

How is this system of control similar to budgetary control and standard costing control systems?

EXAMPLE

How might the postal service control quality? It might establish a standard that 90% of first class letters will be delivered on the day after they are posted, and 99% will be delivered within two days of posting.

- Procedures would have to be established for ensuring that these standards could be met (attending to such matters as frequency of collections, automated letter sorting, frequency of deliveries and number of staff employed).
- Actual performance could be monitored, perhaps by taking samples from time to time of letters that are posted and delivered.
- If the quality standard is not being achieved, management should take control action (employ more postmen or advertise the use of postcodes again).

Quality management becomes **total *(Total Quality Management (TQM))* when it is applied to everything a business does.**

6.1 Get it right, first time

One of the basic principles of TQM is that the **cost of preventing mistakes is less than the cost of correcting them** once they occur. The aim should therefore be **to get things right first time**. Every mistake, delay and misunderstanding, directly costs an organisation money through **wasted time and effort**, including time taken in pacifying customers. The **lost potential for future sales because of poor customer service must also be taken into account.**

6.2 Continuous improvement

A second basic principle of TQM is dissatisfaction with the *status quo*: the belief that it is **always possible to improve** and so the aim should be to '**get it more right next time**'.

6.3 Quality assurance procedures

Because TQM embraces every activity of a business, quality assurance procedures **cannot be confined to the production process** but must also cover the work of sales, distribution and administration departments, the efforts of external suppliers, and the reaction of external customers.

(a) *Quality assurance of goods inwards*

The quality of output depends on the quality of input materials. Quality control should therefore include **procedures over acceptance and inspection of goods inwards** and **measurement of rejects.** Each supplier can be given a 'rating' for the quality of the goods they tend to supply, and preference with purchase orders can be given to well-rated suppliers. This method is referred to as 'vendor rating'.

Where a **quality assurance scheme** is in place the supplier guarantees the quality of goods supplied and allows the customers' inspectors access while the items are being manufactured. The **onus is on the supplier to carry out the necessary quality checks**, or face cancellation of the contract.

Suppliers' quality assurance schemes are being used increasingly, particularly where extensive sub-contracting work is carried out, for example in the motor industries. One such scheme is **BS EN ISO 9000** certification. A company that gains registration has a certificate testifying that it is operating to a structure of written policies and procedures which are designed to ensure that it can consistently deliver a product or service to meet customer requirements.

(b) *Inspection of output*

This will take place at various key stages in the production process and will provide a continual check that the production process is under control. The aim of inspection is *not* really to sort out the bad products from the good ones after the work has been done. The **aim is to satisfy management that quality control in production is being maintained.**

The **inspection of samples** rather than 100% testing of all items will keep inspection costs down, and smaller samples will be less costly to inspect than larger samples. The greater the confidence in the reliability of production methods and process control, the smaller the samples will be.

(c) *Monitoring customer reaction*

Some sub-standard items will inevitably be produced. Checks during production will identify some bad output, but other items will reach the customer who is the ultimate judge of quality. **Complaints ought to be monitored** in the form of letters of complaint, returned goods, penalty discounts, claims under guarantee, or requests for visits by service engineers. Some companies actually survey customers on a regular basis.

6.4 Employees and quality

Workers themselves are frequently the best source of information about how (or how not) to improve quality. **Empowerment** makes use of this. It has two key aspects.

- Allowing workers to have the **freedom to decide how to do** the necessary work, using the skills they possess and acquiring new skills as necessary to be an effective team member.
- Making workers **responsible** for achieving production targets and for quality control.

Quality circles can also be used to draw upon the knowledge and experience of the workforce.

A quality circle is a group of employees who meet regularly to discuss **problems of quality** and **quality control** in their area of work, and perhaps to suggest ways of improving quality.

6.5 Quality control and inspection

A distinction should be made between **quality control** and **inspection.**

Quality control involves setting controls for the process of manufacture or service delivery. It is aimed at **preventing the manufacture of defective items** or the provision of defective services.

Inspection is a technique of **identifying when defective items are being produced at an unacceptable level.** Inspection is usually carried out at three main points.

- Receiving inspection – for raw materials and purchased components
- Floor or process inspection for WIP
- Final inspection or testing for finished goods

7 COSTS OF QUALITY

When we talk about quality-related costs you should remember that a concern for **good quality saves money**; it is **poor quality that costs money.** There are four main quality-related costs.

(a) **Prevention costs** are the costs of any action taken to investigate, prevent or reduce defects and failures.

(b) **Appraisal costs** are the costs of assessing the quality achieved.

(c) **Internal failure costs** are the costs arising within the organisation of failing to achieve the required level of quality.

NOTES

(d) **External failure costs** are the costs arising outside the organisation of failing to achieve the required level of quality (after transfer of ownership to the customer).

Quality-related cost	Example
Prevention costs	Quality engineering
	Design/development of quality control/inspection equipment
	Maintenance of quality control/inspection equipment
	Administration of quality control
	Training in quality control
Appraisal costs	Acceptance testing
	Inspection of goods inwards
	Inspection costs of in-house processing
	Performance testing
Internal failure costs	Failure analysis
	Re-inspection costs
	Losses from failure of purchased items
	Losses due to lower selling prices for sub-quality goods
	Costs of reviewing product specifications after failures
External failure costs	Administration of customer complaints section
	Costs of customer service section
	Product liability costs
	Cost of repairing products returned from customers
	Cost of replacing items due to sub-standard products/marketing errors

The introduction of TQM will cause a drop in internal and external failure costs but prevention and appraisal costs will increase. Management need to ensure that the cost savings are never outweighed by the additional costs.

WORKED EXAMPLE: COST OF POOR QUALITY

A manufacturer's inspection procedures indicate that one faulty item out of every 1,000 good items produced is sent to a customer. The management regards this as acceptable, as a replacement will be supplied free of charge. Unit sales are 10,000,000 per year, and each unit costs £20 to manufacture and makes a profit of £5. It is probable that every customer who buys a faulty product will return it, and will thenceforth buy a similar product from another company. The average customer buys two units a year. Marketing costs per new customer are £10 per year.

(a) What is your best estimate of the net cost of this policy for a year?

(b) What name(s) would you give to quality-related costs of this type?

(c) Could the situation be improved by incurring other types of quality-related cost?

ANSWER

(a) Presumed number of bad units delivered a year = 10,000,000/1,000= 10,000

	£
Cost of defects 10,000 × £20	200,000
Cost of free replacement 10,000 × £20	200,000
Manufacturing cost	400,000
Marketing costs for replacement customers £10 × 10,000	100,000
Gross cost of poor quality	500,000
Less income from original sale	250,000
Net cost of poor quality	250,000

Although the cost of the original defective item is recovered, the company **does not get it right first time**. The company has still suffered the cost of the replacement and the cost of replacing the customer by marketing to new customers.

(b) The cost of replacements is an external failure cost; the cost of defects and the new marketing costs are internal failure costs.

(c) It appears that the manufacturer already incurs *appraisal* costs, since there are inspection procedures for goods about to be despatched. The reason(s) for the fault should be established (a further *internal failure* cost) and the extent of the problem should be more precisely ascertained (further *appraisal* costs), since it is not certain that all dissatisfied customers return their goods, though it is highly likely that their business is lost. Once this has been done it will be possible to decide whether, by spending more on *prevention*, the overall cost of poor quality can be reduced.

7.1 Traditional accounting systems and the cost of quality

Traditionally, the **costs** of **scrapped units, wasted materials and reworking** have been **lost within the costs of production** by incorporating the costs of an expected level of loss (a normal loss) to the costs of good production. **Other costs of poor quality have been included within production or marketing overheads.** So such costs are not only **considered as inevitable** but are not highlighted for management attention.

Traditional accounting reports **tend also to ignore the hidden but real costs of excessive stock levels** (held to enable faulty material to be replaced without hindering production) **and the facilities necessary for storing that stock.**

The introduction of a system of **just-in-time (JIT)** purchasing and manufacturing should eradicate such costs. A just-in-time production system is driven by demand from customers for finished products. Components on a production line are only produced when needed for the next stage of production. Stocks of work in progress and finished goods are therefore not needed. In a just-in-time purchasing system, materials are not delivered until they are needed in production, thereby eradicating stock of raw materials.

To **implement a TQM programme, costs of quality** must be **highlighted separately** within accounting reports so that *all* employees are aware of the cost of poor quality.

7.2 Explicit and implicit costs of quality

Explicit costs of quality are those that are recorded in accounting records, to be separately highlighted with the implementation of a TQM programme.

Implicit costs of quality are not recorded in accounting records. They tend to be of two forms.

- **Opportunity costs** such as the loss of future sales to a customer dissatisfied with faulty goods
- **Costs which tend to be subsumed** within other account headings such as costs which result from the disruptions caused by stockouts due to faulty purchases

Activity 10 **(5 minutes)**

Elyard Ltd defines the cost of quality as the total of all costs incurred in preventing faults in production of its single product, plus the costs involved in correcting faults once they have occurred. It only includes explicit costs of quality.

Task

Determine which of the following costs Elyard Ltd would include in the cost of quality.

(a) Remedial work required as a result of faulty raw material
(b) Cost of customer support department which deals with faulty products
(c) Loss of customer goodwill following delivery of faulty products
(d) Cost of detailed inspection of raw materials due to poor quality of supplies
(e) Cost of products returned by customers due to faults
(f) Sales revenue lost as a result of returns in (e)

8 STANDARD COSTING IN A TOTAL QUALITY ENVIRONMENT

It has been argued that traditional variance analysis is unhelpful and potentially misleading in the modern organisation, and causes managers to focus their attention on the wrong issues.

Standard costing concentrates on **quantity** and ignores other factors contributing to an organisation's effectiveness. In a **total quality** environment, however, quantity is not an issue, **quality** is. Effectiveness in such an environment therefore centres on high quality output (produced as a result of high quality input); the cost of failing to achieve the required level of effectiveness is not measured in variances, but in terms of the **internal and external failure costs** which would not be identified by traditional standard costing analysis.

Standard costing might measure, say, **labour efficiency** in terms of individual tasks and the level of **output**. In a **total quality environment**, the effectiveness of labour is more appropriately measured in terms of **re-working** required, **returns** from customers, **defects** identified in subsequent stages of production and so on.

In a **TQM** environment there are likely to be **minimal rate variances** if the workforce are paid a guaranteed weekly wage. Fixed price contracts, with suppliers guaranteeing levels of quality, are often a feature, and so there are likely to be **few, if any, material price and usage variances.**

So **can standard costing and TQM exist together?**

- Predetermined standards conflict with the TQM philosophy of continual improvement.
- Continual improvements should alter quantities of inputs, prices and so on, whereas standard costing is best used in a stable, standardised, repetitive environment.
- Standard costs often incorporate a planned level of scrap in material standards. This is at odds with the TQM aim of 'zero defects'.

On the other hand, variance analysis can contribute towards the aim of improved product quality by keeping track of quality control information. This is because variance analysis measures both the planned use of resources and actual use of resources in order to compare the two.

As variance analysis is generally expressed in terms of purely quantitative measures, such as quantity of raw materials used and price per unit of quantity, issues of quality would appear to be excluded from the reporting process. Quality would appear to be an excuse for spending more time, say, or buying more expensive raw materials.

Variance analysis, as it currently stands, therefore needs to be adapted to take account of quality issues.

(a) Variance analysis reports should routinely include measures such as defect rates. Although zero defects will be most desirable, such a standard of performance may not be reached at first. However there should be an expected rate of defects: if this is exceeded then management attention is directed to the excess.

(b) The absolute number of defects should be measured *and* their type. If caused by certain materials and components this can shed light on, say, a favourable materials price variance which might have been caused by substandard materials being purchased more cheaply. Alternatively, if the defects are caused by shoddy assembly work this can shed light on a favourable labour efficiency variance if quality is being sacrificed for speed.

(c) It should also be possible to provide financial measures for the cost of poor quality. These can include direct costs such as the wages of inspection and quality control staff, the cost of time in rectifying the defects, and the cost of the materials used in rectification.

(d) Measures could be built into materials price and variance analysis, so that the materials price variance as currently reported includes a factor reflecting the quality of materials purchased.

Activity 11 **(10 minutes)**

Read the following extract from an article in the *Financial Times* and then explain how the bank could monitor the impact of the initiative.

'If you telephone a branch of Lloyds Bank and it rings five times before there is a reply; if the person who answers does not introduce him or herself by name during the conversation; if you are standing in a queue with more people in it than the number of tills, then something is wrong.'

'If any of these things happen then the branch is breaching standards of customer service set by the bank since last July ... the "service challenge" was launched in the bank's 1,888 branches last summer after being tested in 55 branches ...'

'Lloyds already has evidence of the impact. Customers were more satisfied with pilot branches ... than with others.'

Chapter roundup

- In full-cost pricing the sales price is determined by calculating the full cost of the product and then adding a percentage mark-up for profit.
- Marginal cost-plus pricing involves adding a profit margin to the marginal cost of production/sales.
- Cost-plus pricing makes it easy to find the cost for stock valuation purposes of retail goods for which the selling price is available.
- Three alternative pricing strategies for new products are market penetration pricing, market skimming pricing and premium pricing.
- A typical product has a life cycle of four stages.
- The price that an organisation can charge for its products will be determined to a certain extent by the market (perfect competition, monopoly, oligopoly) in which it operates.
- Competition can affect pricing policy.
- A price leader indicates to the other firms in the market what the price will be.
- Differential pricing involves selling the same product at different prices to different customers.
- The price elasticity of demand measure the extent of change in demand for a good following a change in price. Demand can be elastic or inelastic.
- The demand-based approach to pricing involves determining a profit-maximising price.
- The target costing approach is to develop a product concept and the primary specifications for performance and design and then to determine the price customers would be willing to pay for that concept. The desired profit margin is deducted from the price leaving a figure that represents the total cost. This is the target cost. The product must be capable of being produced for this amount otherwise it will not be manufactured.
- Value engineering is cost reduction before production.
- Cost reduction aims to reduce costs below a previously acceptable level, without adversely affecting the quality of the product or service being provided.
- Value analysis involves assessing the value of every aspect of a product (or service) in order to devise ways of achieving the product's (or service's) purpose as economically as possible whilst maintaining the required standard of quality and reliability.
- Other techniques of cost reduction include variety reduction (standardisation), work study and O&M.

Quick quiz

1 Fill in the blanks.

Full cost pricing is a method of determining the .... by calculating the .... of the product and adding a .... for profit.

2 Market penetration pricing is appropriate if market research reveals that a small cut in the selling price of the product will lead to a large increase in the quantity demanded. True or False?

3 What are the four stages of the product life cycle?

4 What is an oligopoly?

5 What price is first charged for a product under a policy of market penetration pricing?

6 When target costing is in use, a product concept is developed. What is determined next?

A Profit margin
B Price
C Full cost
D Production cost

7 Choose the correct words from those highlighted.

Cost reduction/control is about regulating the costs of operating a business and keeping costs within acceptable limits whereas **cost reduction/control** is a planned and positive approach to reducing expenditure.

8 The cost of inspecting a product for quality is a value-added cost. True or False?

9 Match the cost to the correct cost category.

Costs

(a) Administration of quality control
(b) Product liability costs
(c) Acceptance testing
(d) Losses due to lower selling prices for sub-quality goods

Cost categories

- Prevention costs
- Appraisal costs
- Internal failure costs
- External failure costs

10 Match the terms to the correct definitions.

Terms

Cost value
Exchange value
Use value
Esteem value

Definitions

(a) The prestige the customer attaches to the product
(b) The market value of the product
(c) What the product does
(d) The cost of producing and selling the product

11 Choose the correct word from those highlighted.

Explicit/implicit costs of quality are not recorded in accounting records.

12 Fill in the blanks.

There are two basic principles of TQM.

……………………………………………

……………………………………………

Answers to Quick quiz

1 Selling price
Full cost
Markup

2 True

3 Introduction, growth, maturity, decline

4 A market dominated by relatively few competitive companies.

5 Low prices

6 B

7 The first term should be cost control, the second term cost reduction.

8 False

9 (a) Prevention costs
(b) External failure costs
(c) Appraisal costs
(d) Internal failure costs

10 (a) Esteem value
(b) Exchange value
(c) Use value
(d) Cost value

11 Implicit

12 Get it right, first time

Continuous improvement

NOTES

Answers to Activities

1 £7.99 (£4.70 × 170%)

2

	£
Selling price	20
Marginal (variable) cost (5 + 3 + 7)	15
	5

$$\text{Mark up} = \frac{\text{Profit}}{\text{Marginal cost}} \times 100\%$$

$$= \frac{5}{15} \times 100\%$$

$$= 33^1/_3\%$$

Note that the fixed overheads are not included in the marginal cost.

3 The selling price is obtained as shown below, firstly in general (%) terms, and than using the actual values.

	%	£	
Cost	100	150.00	(187.5 × 100/125)
Profit	25	37.50	(187.5 × 25/125)
Selling price	125	187.50	

The cost of the stock is £900 (6 × £150) in total.

4 Required contribution = fixed costs plus profit
= £47,000 + £23,000
= £70,000
14,000 units

	£
Required contribution per unit sold	5
Variable cost per unit	15
Required sales price per unit	20

5 Here are some suggestions

- Changing the specifications for cutting solid materials
- Introducing new equipment that reduces wastage in processing or handling materials
- Identifying poor quality output at an earlier stage in the operational processes
- Using better quality materials

6 All but (c) are **non** value-adding activities.

7 If a manufacturer has fewer types of components to manufacture, he will be able to increase the length of production runs, and so reduce production costs. Non-standard parts tend to be produced in small runs, and unit costs will be higher as a consequence.

Standardisation also helps to cut purchasing cost because there are fewer items to buy and stock. The company can purchase in bulk, and so perhaps obtain bulk purchase discounts. It may also be possible to buy standard parts from more than one supplier, and so purchasing will be more competitive.

The disadvantage of standardisation is that it may result in a loss of sales revenue or customer loyalty.

8 (a) Exchange value
(b) Esteem value
(c) Use value

9 Standard costing and budgetary control systems also require standards to be set, actual results to be monitored and control action to be taken if actual results differ from those expected.

10 (c) and (f) would not be included because they would not be recorded within the accounting records and hence are implicit costs.

11 A wide variety of answers is possible. The article goes on to explain how the bank has monitored the initiative.

(a) It has devised a 100 point scale showing average satisfaction with branch service.

(b) It conducts a 'first impressions' survey of all new customers.

(c) There is also a general survey carried out every six months which seeks the views of a weighted sample of 350 customers per branch.

(d) A survey company telephones each branch anonymously twice a month to test how staff respond to enquiries about products.

(e) A quarter of each branch's staff answer a monthly questionnaire about the bank's products to test their knowledge.

(f) Groups of employees working in teams in branches are allowed to set their own additional standards. This is to encourage participation.

(g) Branches that underperform are more closely watched by 24 managers who monitor the initiative.

NOTES

Chapter : 6

COSTING SYSTEMS

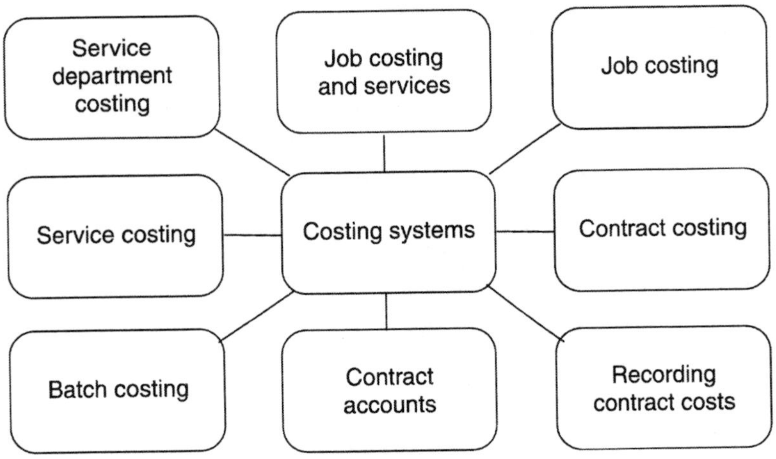

Introduction

A cost accounting method is designed to suit the way goods are processed or manufactured or the way services are provided. Each organisation's cost accounting method will therefore have unique features but costing methods of firms in the same line of business will usually have common aspects. On the other hand, organisations involved in completely different activities, such as hospitals and car part manufacturers, will use very different methods.

This chapter looks at four types of costing system. We will see the circumstances in which each system should be used and how the costs are calculated. A fifth costing system, **process costing**, is dealt with in the next chapter.

Your objectives

In this chapter you will learn about the following.

(a) Job costing

(b) Contract costing

(c) Batch costing

(d) Service costing

1 JOB COSTING

Definitions

A **job** is a cost unit which consists of a single order or contract.

Job costing is a costing method applied where work is undertaken to customers' special requirements and each order is of comparatively short duration.

The work relating to a job is usually carried out within a factory or workshop and moves through processes and operations as a **continuously identifiable unit**. The term job may also be applied to work such as property repairs, and the job costing method may be used in the costing of internal capital expenditure jobs.

Note that job costing is one type of **specific order costing** (another type is **contract costing**, which you will meet shortly).

1.1 Procedure

In job costing, production is usually carried out in accordance with the special requirements of each customer. It is therefore usual for each job to differ in one or more respects from every other job, which means that a separate record must be maintained to show the details of a particular job.

When an **order** is received from a customer, the estimating department will prepare an **estimate** for the job. If the customer accepts the estimate, the job will be given a separate job number, to identify it from all other jobs.

1.2 Collection of job costs

Once work has begun on the job, careful record keeping is necessary to accurately collect the job costs.

(a) **Materials requisitions are sent to stores**. The material requisition note will be used to cost the materials issued to the job concerned, and this cost may then be recorded on a **job cost sheet**, which records all costs relating to a particular job. The cost may include items already in stock, at an appropriate valuation, and/or items specially purchased.

(b) **A job ticket is given to the worker who is to perform the first operation of the job**. The times of his starting and finishing the operation are recorded on the ticket, which is then passed to the person who is to carry out the second operation, where a similar record of the times of starting and finishing is made. When the job is completed, the job ticket is sent to the cost office, where the time spent will be costed and recorded on the job cost sheet.

(c) The job's share of the **factory overhead**, based on the absorption rate(s) in operation, is recorded on the job cost sheet.

(d) The **relevant costs** of materials issued, direct labour performed and direct expenses incurred as recorded on the job cost sheet are charged to the job account in the work in progress ledger. The total value of the jobs in progress will represent the balance on the work in progress control account since each job is represented by an account in the WIP ledger.

(e) **On completion of the job,** the job account is charged with the appropriate administration, selling and distribution overhead, after which the total cost of the job can be ascertained.

(f) The difference between the agreed selling price and the total actual cost will be the supplier's profit (or loss).

1.3 Job cost sheet (or card)

An example of a job cost sheet (or job card) is as follows. It may show the detail of relatively small jobs or may be used to summarise the cost elements for larger jobs.

JOB COST SHEET

Customer Mr J White	Customer's Order No.	Job No. B641
Job Description Repair damage to offside front door		Vehicle make Peugot 205 GTE
Estimate Ref. 2599	Invoice No.	Vehicle reg. no. G 614 SOX
Quoted price £338.68	Invoice price £355.05	Date to collect 14.6.X3

Material						Labour								Overheads			
Date	Req. No.	Qty.	Price	Cost £	Cost p	Date	Employee	Cost Ctre	Hrs.	Rate	Bonus	Cost £	Cost p	Hrs	OAR	Cost £	Cost p
12.6	36815	1	75.49	75	49	12.6	018	B	1.98	6.50	-	12	87	7.9	2.50	19	75
12.6	36816	1	33.19	33	19	13.6	018	B	5.92	6.50	-	38	48				
12.6	36842	5	6.01	30	05						13.65	13	65				
13.6	36881	5	3.99	19	95												
Total C/F				158	68	Total C/F						65	00	Total C/F		19	75

Expenses				
Date	Ref.	Description	Cost £	Cost p
12.6	-	N. Jolley Panel-beating	50	-
Total C/F			50	-

Job Cost Summary	Actual £	Actual p	Estimate £	Estimate p
Direct Materials B/F	158	68	158	68
Direct Expenses B/F	50	00		
Direct Labour B/F	65	00	180	00
Direct Cost	273	68		
Overheads B/F	19	75		
	293	43		
Admin overhead (add 10%)	29	34		
= Total Cost	322	77	338	68
Invoice Price	355	05		
Job Profit/Loss	32	28		

Comments

Job Cost Card Completed by ____________________

NOTES

Activity 1 **(20 minutes)**

Frisbee Ltd is a company that carries out jobbing work. One of the jobs carried out in February was job 1357, to which the following information relates.

Direct material Y: 400 kilos were issued from stores at a cost of £10 per kilo.

Direct material Z: 800 kilos were issued from stores at a cost of £12 per kilo. 60 kilos were returned.

Department P: 320 labour hours were worked, of which 100 hours were done in overtime.

Department Q: 200 labour hours were worked, of which 100 hours were done in overtime.

Overtime work is not normal in Department P, where basic pay is £8 per hour plus an overtime premium of £2 per hour. Overtime work was done in Department Q in February because of a request by the customer of another job to complete his job quickly. Basic pay in Department Q is £10 per hour and overtime premium is £3 per hour.

Overhead is absorbed at the rate of £6 per direct labour hour in both departments.

The organisation adds 30% to full production cost to arrive at a price for a job.

Calculate the following.

(a) The direct materials cost of job 1357
(b) The direct labour cost of job 1357
(c) The full production cost of job 1357
(d) The price of job 1357

1.4 Work in progress at the end of an accounting period

At the end of an accounting period any jobs which are still in progress are regarded as work in progress, which is a form of stock. Stock and work in progress need to be valued at the lower of cost and net realisable value for financial accounting purposes. Job cost sheets will provide details of the costs incurred in bringing a job to its present condition. Net realisable value will be the price agreed with the customer, less any further costs to complete the job as per any budgets or estimates made at the time of tendering for the job. Generally, if the job is expected to make a profit the cost per the job sheet will be the value of the incomplete job at the period end.

1.5 Completed jobs

When jobs are completed, job cost sheets are transferred from the work in progress category to finished goods. When delivery is made to the customer, the costs become a cost of sale.

1.6 Job costing and computerisation

Job cost sheets exist in **manual systems**, but it is increasingly likely that in large organisations the job costing system will be **computerised**, using accounting software specifically designed to deal with job costing requirements. A computerised job accounting system is likely to contain the following features.

(a) Every job will be given a job code number, which will determine how the data relating to the job is stored.

(b) A separate set of codes will be given for the type of costs that any job is likely to incur. Thus, 'direct wages', say, will have the same code whichever job they are allocated to.

(c) In a sophisticated system, costs can be analysed both by job (for example all costs related to Job 456), but also by type (for example direct wages incurred on all jobs). It is thus easy to perform control analysis and to make comparisons between jobs.

An example may help to illustrate the way in which the costing of individual jobs fits in with the recording of total costs in control accounts. Study the following example very carefully and make sure that you understand the solution.

WORKED EXAMPLE: JOB COSTING

Pistachio Ltd is a jobbing company. On 1 June 20X2, there was one uncompleted job in the factory. The job cost sheet for this work is summarised as follows.

Job Cost Sheet, Job No 6832

Costs to date	£
Direct materials	1,890
Direct labour (120 hours)	1,050
Factory overhead (£6 per direct labour hour)	720
Factory cost to date	3,660

During June, three new jobs were started in the factory, and costs of production were as follows.

Direct materials		£
Issued to:	Job 6832	7,170
	Job 6833	5,040
	Job 6834	11,800
	Job 6835	13,260

Material transfers	£
Job 6834 to job 6833	1,000
Job 6832 to 6834	1,860

Materials returned to store	£
From job 6832	1,110
From job 6835	510

Labour hours recorded	
Job 6832	430 hrs
Job 6833	650 hrs
Job 6834	280 hrs
Job 6835	410 hrs

The cost of labour hours during June 20X2 was £9 per hour, and production overhead is absorbed at the rate of £6 per direct labour hour. Production overheads incurred during the month amounted to £11,400. Completed jobs were delivered to customers as soon as they were completed, and the invoiced amounts were as follows.

Job 6832	£16,500
Job 6834	£24,000
Job 6835	£22,500

Administration and marketing overheads are added to the cost of sales at the rate of 20% of factory cost on completion of jobs. Actual costs incurred during June 20X2 amounted to £9,600.

(a) Prepare T-accounts accumulating the production costs for each individual job during June 20X2.

(b) Prepare summaries of the costs of each job, and calculate the profit on each completed job.

ANSWER

(a) **Job accounts**

JOB 6832

	£		£
Balance b/f	3,660	Job 6834 a/c (materials transfer)	1,860
Materials (stores a/c)	7,170	Stores a/c (materials returned)	2,610
Labour (wages a/c)	3,870	Cost of sales a/c (balance)	12,810
Production overhead (o'hd a/c)	2,580		
	17,280		17,280

JOB 6833

	£		£
Materials (stores a/c)	5,040	Balance c/f	15,540
Labour (wages a/c)	5,850		
Production overhead (o'hd a/c)	3,900		
Job 6834 a/c (materials transfer)	750		
	15,540		15,540

JOB 6834

	£		£
Materials (stores a/c)	11,850	Job 6833 a/c (materials transfer)	750
Labour (wages a/c)	2,520	Cost of sales a/c (balance)	17,160
Production overhead (o'hd a/c)	1,680		
Job 6832 a/c (materials transfer)	1,860		
	17,910		17,910

JOB 6835

	£		£
Materials (stores a/c)	13,260	Stores a/c (materials returned)	510
Labour (wages a/c)	3,690	Cost of sales a/c (balance)	18,900
Production overhead (o'hd a/c)	2,460		
	19,410		19,410

(b) **Job costs, summarised**

	Job 6832	*Job 6833*	*Job 6834*	*Job 6835*
	£	£	£	
Materials	*4,590	5,790	**12,960	12,750
Labour	4,920	5,850	2,520	3,690
Production overhead	3,300	3,900	1,680	2,460
Factory cost	12,810	15,540(c/f)	17,160	18,900
Admin & marketing o'hd (20%)	2,562		3,432	3,780
Cost of sale	15,372		20,592	22,680
Invoice value	16,500		2,400	2,250
Profit/(loss) on job	1,128		3,408	(180)

* £(1,890 + 7,170 – 1,860 – 2,610) ** £(11,850 + 1,860 – 750)

Activity 2 **(10 minutes)**

A firm uses job costing and recovers overheads on direct labour.

Three jobs were worked on during a period, the details of which are as follows.

	Job 1	*Job 2*	*Job 3*
	£	£	£
Opening work in progress	8,500	0	46,000
Material in period	17,150	29,025	0
Labour for period	12,500	23,000	4,500

The overheads for the period were exactly as budgeted, £140,000.

Jobs 1 and 2 were the only incomplete jobs.

What was the value of closing work in progress?

2 CONTRACT COSTING

Imagine trying to build up job costs on a job ticket in the way described in the previous section during the excavation of the tunnel under the English Channel or the construction of a skyscraper. It would be impossible. In industries such as building and construction work, civil engineering and shipbuilding, job costing is not usually appropriate. Contract costing is.

Definitions

> A **contract** is a cost unit or cost centre which is charged with the direct costs of production and an apportionment of head office overheads.
>
> **Contract costing** is the name given to a method of job costing where the job to be carried out is of such magnitude that a formal contract is made between the customer and supplier. It applies where work is undertaken to customers' special requirements and each order is of long duration (compared with the time to which job costing applies). The work is usually constructional and *in general* the method is similar to job costing, although there are, of course, a few differences.

2.1 Features of contract costing

- A **formal contract** is made between customer and supplier.
- Work is undertaken to **customers' special requirements.**
- The work is for a **relatively long duration**. Large jobs may take a long time to complete, perhaps two or three years. Even when a contract is completed within less than twelve months, it is quite possible that the work may have begun during one financial year and ended during the supplier's next financial year; therefore the profit on the contract will relate to more than one accounting period.
- The work is frequently **constructional** in nature.
- The method of costing is **similar to job costing**.
- The work is frequently **based on site**.
- It is not unusual for a site to have its **own cashier and time-keeper**.

2.2 Problems

The problems which may arise in contract costing are as follows.

Problem	Comment
Identifying direct costs	Because of the large size of the job, many cost items which are usually thought of as production overhead are charged as direct costs of the contract (for example supervision, hire of plant, depreciation or loss in value of plant which is owned, sub-contractors' fees or charges and so on).
Low indirect costs	Because many costs normally classed as overheads are charged as direct costs of a contract, the absorption rate for overheads should only apply a share of the cost of those cost items which are not already direct costs. For most contracts the only item of indirect cost would be a charge for head office expenses.
Difficulties of cost control	Because of the size of some contracts and some sites, there are often cost control problems (material usage and losses, pilferage, labour supervision and utilisation, damage to and loss of plant and tools, vandalism and so on).

Problem	Comment
Dividing the profit between different accounting periods	When a contract covers two or more accounting periods, how should the profit (or loss) on the contract be divided between the periods? This problem is, fortunately, outside the scope of your syllabus.

3 RECORDING CONTRACT COSTS

3.1 Direct materials

The direct materials used on a contract may be obtained from the company's central stores or they may be delivered direct to the site by the company's suppliers. In both cases carefully prepared documentation must ensure that the **correct contract is charged with the correct materials**. A materials requisition note would record the movement of materials from stores; the supplier's invoice supported by a goods received note would document the cost of materials delivered direct to site.

Materials issued from a central store or delivered by a supplier are often in excess of the quantities actually required. The surplus quantities are eventually returned to store, a material returns note prepared and the cost of the materials credited to the contract account.

At the end of an accounting period, a contract may be incomplete and if this is the case, there will probably be materials on site which have not yet been used. (Indeed some of them may never be used, but eventually returned to store.) Materials on site at the end of an accounting period should be carried forward as 'closing stock of materials on site' and brought forward as opening stock at the beginning of the next accounting period.

3.2 Direct labour

Since all the work done by direct labour on a contract site is spent exclusively on a single contract, the direct labour cost of the contract should be easily identified from the wages sheets. If some employees work on several contracts at the same time, perhaps travelling from one site to another, their time spent on each contract will have to be recorded on time sheets, and each contract charged with the cost of these recorded hours. The cost of supervision, which is usually a production overhead in job costing, will be a direct cost of a contract.

3.3 Subcontractors

On large contracts, **much work may be done by subcontractors**. The invoices of subcontractors will be **treated as a direct expense of the contract**, although if the invoiced amounts are small, it may be more convenient to account for them as 'direct materials' rather than as direct expenses.

3.4 The cost of plant

A feature of most contract work is the amount of plant used. Plant used on a contract may be owned by the company, or hired from a plant hire firm.

Activity 3 **(5 minutes)**

If plant is hired from a plant hire firm, how should the cost be treated?

If the **plant is owned by the company**, a variety of accounting methods may be employed.

(a) **Method one: charging depreciation**. The contract may be charged depreciation on the plant, on a straight line or reducing balance basis. For example if a company has some plant which cost £10,000 and which is depreciated at 10% per annum straight line (to a residual value of nil) and a contract makes use of the plant for six months, a depreciation charge of £500 would be made against the contract. The disadvantage of this simple method of costing for plant is that the contract site foreman is not made directly responsible and accountable for the value of the actual plant in his charge. The foreman must be responsible for receipt of the plant, returning the plant after it has been used and proper care of the plant whilst it is being used.

(b) **Method two: charging the contract with current book value**. A more common method of costing for plant is to charge the contract with the current book value of the plant. A numerical example will help to illustrate this method.

Contract number X795 obtained some plant and loose tools from central store on 1 January 20X2. The book value of the plant was £100,000 and the book value of the loose tools was £8,000. On 1 October 20X2, some plant was removed from the site: this plant had a book value on 1 October of £20,000. At 31 December 20X2, the plant remaining on site had a book value of £60,000 and the loose tools had a book value of £5,000.

CONTRACT X795 ACCOUNT

	£		£
1 January 20X2		*1 October 20X2*	
Plant issued to site	100,000	Plant transferred	20,000
Loose tools issued to site	8,000	*31 December 20X2*	
		Plant value c/f	60,000
		Loose tools value c/f	5,000
		Depreciation (bal fig)	23,000
	108,000		108,000

The difference between the values on the debit and the credit sides of the account (£20,000 for plant and £3,000 for loose tools) is the depreciation cost of the equipment for the year.

(c) **Method three: using a plant account**. A third method of accounting for plant costs is to open a *plant account*, which is debited with the depreciation costs and the running costs (repairs, fuel and so on) of the equipment. A notional hire charge is then made to contracts using the plant, at a rate of £x per day. For example suppose that a company owns some equipment which is depreciated at the rate of £100 per month. Running costs in May 20X3 are £300. The plant is used on 20 days in the month, 12 days on Contract X and 8 days on Contract Y. The accounting entries would be as follows.

PLANT ACCOUNT

	£		£
Depreciation	100	Contract X (hire for 12 days)	240
Running costs	300	Contract Y (hire for 8 days)	160
	400		400

CONTRACT X

	£		£
Plant account (notional hire)	240		

CONTRACT Y

	£		£
Plant account (notional hire)	160		

3.5 Overhead costs

Overhead costs are added periodically (for example at the end of an accounting period) and are based on predetermined overhead absorption rates for the period. You may come across examples where a share of head office general costs is absorbed as an overhead cost to the contract, but this should not happen if the contract is unfinished at the end of the period, because only *production* overheads should be included in the value of any closing work in progress.

4 CONTRACT ACCOUNTS

The **account for a contract is a job account, or work in progress account**, and is a record of the direct materials, direct labour, direct expenses and overhead charges on the contract. A typical contract account might appear as shown below. Check the items in the account carefully, and notice how the cost (or value) of the work done emerges as work in progress.

NOTES

EXAMPLE: A CONTRACT ACCOUNT

CONTRACT 794 - TEN-LANE MOTORWAY

	£'000		£'000
Book value of plant on site b/d	14,300	Materials returned to stores or transferred to other sites	2,100
Materials requisition from stores	15,247	Proceeds from sale of materials on site and jobbing work for other customers	600
Materials and equipment purchased	36,300	Book value of plant transferred	4,800
Maintenance and operating costs of plant and vehicles	14,444	Materials on site c/d	7,194
Hire charges for plant and vehicles not owned	6,500	Book value of plant on site c/d	6,640
Tools and consumables	8,570		21,334
Direct wages	23,890	Cost of work done c/d (balancing item)	139,917
Supervisors' and engineers' salaries (proportion relating to time spent on the contract)	13,000		
Other site expenses	12,000		
Overheads (apportioned perhaps on the basis of direct labour hours)	17,000		
	161,251		161,251
Materials on site b/d	7,194		
Book value of plant on site b/d	6,640		
Cost of work done b/d	139,917		

On an unfinished contract, where no profits are taken mid-way through the contract, this cost of work in progress is carried forward as a closing stock balance.

4.1 Progress payments

Because a contract price may run into millions of pounds, a customer is likely to be required under the terms of the contract to make progress payments to the contractor throughout the course of the work so that the contractor does not suffer from significant cash flow problems.

The amount of the payments will be based on the value of work done (as a proportion of the contract price). This value is known as the **value certified** and will be **assessed by an architect or surveyor** (for a building contract) or qualified engineer in his certificate. A certificate provides confirmation that work to a certain value has been completed, and that some payment to the contractor is now due. The **amount of the payment** will be calculated as follows.

	The value of work done and certified by the architect or engineer
minus	**a retention (see below)**
minus	**the payments made to date**
equals	**payment due.**

Thus, if an architect's certificate assesses the value of work done on a contract to be £125,000 and if the retention is 10%, and if £92,000 has already been paid in progress payments the current payment will be:

£125,000 – £12,500 – £92,000 = £20,500

4.2 Retention monies

A customer is unlikely to want to pay the full amount of the value certified in case the contractor fails to complete the work or it later turns out that some of the work is of an unacceptable standard. There is therefore often a retention (usually between 2% and 10% of the certified value). **Retention monies are released when the contract is fully completed and accepted by the customer.** Until then the retention is regarded by the contractor as a debtor.

4.3 Profits on contracts

You may have noticed that the progress payments do not necessarily give rise to profit immediately because of retentions. Let us now turn our attention to how profits are calculated on contracts completed in one accounting period.

If a contract is started and completed in the same accounting period, the calculation of the profit is straightforward, sales minus the cost of the contract. Suppose that contract FM102 has the following costs.

	£'000
Direct materials (less returns)	80
Direct labour	70
Direct expenses	16
Plant costs	12
Overhead	22
	200

The work began on 1 April 20X5 and was completed on 15 October 20X5 in the contractor's same accounting year.

The contract price was £240,000 and on 20 October the inspecting engineer issued the final certificate of work done. At that date the customer had already paid £180,000 and the remaining £60,000 was still outstanding at the end of the contractor's accounting period. The contract accounts would appear as follows.

CONTRACT FM102 ACCOUNT

	£'000		£'000
Materials less returns	80	Cost of sales (P&L)	200
Labour	70		
Expenses	16		
Plant cost	12		
Overhead	22		
	200		200

We need to determine the **turnover figure** to be matched against the cost of sales figure of £200,000. For the purposes of profit reporting, we **take the contract price** of £240,000 (and not the amount already paid).

The profit on the contract will therefore be treated in the profit and loss account as follows.

	£'000
Turnover	240
Cost of sales	200
	40

5 BATCH COSTING

Definition

A **batch** is a cost unit which consists of a separate, readily identifiable group of product units which maintain their separate identity throughout the production process.

The procedures for **costing batches** are very similar to those for costing jobs.

(a) The batch is treated as a **job** during production and the costs are collected in the manner already described in this chapter.

(b) Once the batch has been completed, the **cost per unit** can be calculated as the total batch cost divided by the number of units in the batch.

EXAMPLE: BATCH COSTING

A company manufactures model cars to order and has the following budgeted overheads for the year, based on normal activity levels.

Department	*Budgeted overheads* £	*Budgeted activity*
Welding	60,000	1,500 labour hours
Assembly	100,000	1,000 labour hours

Selling and administrative overheads are 20% of factory cost. An order for 250 model cars type XJS1, made as Batch 8638, incurred the following costs.

Materials	£120,000
Labour	100 hours welding shop at £25/hour
	200 hours assembly shop at £10/hour

£5,000 was paid for the hire of special X-ray equipment for testing the welds.

Task

Calculate the cost per unit for Batch 8638.

ANSWER

The first step is to calculate the overhead absorption rate for the production departments.

Welding $= \frac{£60,000}{1,500} =$ £40 per labour hour

Assembly $= \dfrac{£100{,}000}{1{,}000} =$ £100 per labour hour

Total cost - Batch no 8638

	£	£
Direct material		120,000
Direct expense		5,000
Direct labour 100 × 25 =	2,500	
200 × 10 =	2,000	
		4,500
Prime cost		129,500
Overheads 100 × 40=	4,000	
200 × 100 =	20,000	
		24,000
Factory cost		153,500
Selling and administrative cost (20% of factory cost)		3,070
Total cost		184,200

Cost per unit $= \dfrac{£184{,}200}{250} = £736.80$

Activity 4 **(30 minutes)**

Lyfsa Kitchen Units Ltd crafts two different sizes of standard unit and a DIY all-purpose unit for filling up awkward spaces. The units are built to order in batches of around 250 (although the number varies according to the quality of wood purchased), and each batch is sold to NGJ Furniture Warehouses Ltd.

The costs incurred in May 20X4 were as follows.

	Big unit	*Little unit*	*All-purpose*
Direct materials purchased	£10,480	£13,420	£7,640
Direct labour			
Skilled (hours)	1,580	1,700	160
Semi-skilled (hours)	3,160	1,900	300
Direct expenses	£2,360	£3,400	£500
Selling price of batch	£66,360	£55,000	£39,000
Completed at 31 May 20X4	100%	80%	25%

The following information is available.

All direct materials for the completion of the batches have been recorded. Skilled labour is paid £10 per hour, semi-skilled £8 per hour. Administration expenses total £4,400 per month and are to be allocated to the batches on the basis of direct labour hours. Direct labour costs, direct expenses and administration expenses will increase in proportion to the total labour hours required to complete the little units and the all-purpose units. On completion of the work the practice of the manufacturer is to divide the calculated profit on each batch 20% to staff as a bonus, 80% to the company. Losses are absorbed 100% by the company.

Tasks

(a) Calculate the profit or loss made by the company on big units.

(b) Project the profit or loss likely to be made by the company on little units and all-purpose units.

(c) Comment on any matters you think relevant to management as a result of your calculations.

6 SERVICE COSTING

Definition

Service costing is 'Cost accounting for services or functions, eg canteens, maintenance, personnel. These may be referred to as service centres, departments or functions'. CIMA *Official Terminology*

What are service organisations?

Service organisations do not make or sell tangible goods. Profit-seeking service organisations include accountancy firms, law firms, management consultants, transport companies, banks, insurance companies and hotels. Almost all not-for-profit organisations - hospitals, schools, libraries and so on - are also service organisations.

Service costing differs from the other costing methods (product costing methods) for a number of reasons.

(a) With many services, the cost of direct materials consumed will be relatively small compared to the labour, direct expenses and overheads cost. In product costing the direct materials are often a greater proportion of the total cost.

(b) Because of the difficulty of identifying costs with specific cost units in service costing, the indirect costs tend to represent a higher proportion of total cost compared with product costing.

(c) The output of most service organisations is often intangible and hence difficult to define. It is therefore difficult to establish a measurable cost unit.

(d) The service industry includes such a wide range of organisations which provide such different services and have such different cost structures that costing will vary considerably from one service to another.

Specific characteristics of services are **intangibility, simultaneity, perishability** and **heterogeneity.** Consider the service of providing a haircut.

(a) A haircut is **intangible** in itself, and the performance of the service comprises many other intangible factors, like the music in the salon, the personality of the hairdresser, the quality of the coffee.

(b) The production and consumption of a haircut are **simultaneous,** and therefore it cannot be inspected for quality in advance, nor can it be returned if it is not what was required.

(c) Haircuts are **perishable,** that is, they cannot be stored. You cannot buy them in bulk, and the hairdresser cannot do them in advance and keep them stocked away in case of heavy demand. The incidence of work in progress in service organisations is less frequent than in other types of organisation.

(d) A haircut is **heterogeneous** and so the exact service received will vary each time: not only will two hairdressers cut hair differently, but a hairdresser will not consistently deliver the same standard of haircut.

6.1 Unit cost measures

A particular problem with service costing is the difficulty in defining a realistic cost unit that represents a suitable measure of the service provided. Frequently, a **composite cost unit** may be deemed more appropriate if the service is a function of two activity variables. Hotels, for example, may use the '**occupied bed-night**' as an appropriate unit for cost ascertainment and control.

Typical cost units used by companies operating in a service industry are shown below.

Service	Cost unit
Road, rail and air transport services	Passenger-kilometre, tonne-kilometre
Hotels	Occupied bed-night
Education	Full-time student
Hospitals	Patient-day
Catering establishments	Meal served

Each organisation will need to ascertain the cost unit most appropriate to its activities. If a number of organisations within an industry use a common cost unit, valuable **comparisons** can be made between similar establishments. This is particularly applicable to hospitals, educational establishments and local authorities. Unit costs are also useful control measures as we shall see in the examples that follow.

Activity 5 **(10 minutes)**

Suggest cost units that are appropriate to a transport business.

6.2 Cost per service unit

Whatever cost unit is decided upon, the calculation of a cost per unit is as follows.

Formula to learn

$$\text{Cost per service unit} = \frac{\text{Total costs for period}}{\text{Number of service units in the period}}$$

The following examples will illustrate the principles involved in service industry costing and the further considerations to bear in mind when costing services.

WORKED EXAMPLE: COSTING AN EDUCATIONAL ESTABLISHMENT

A university offers a range of degree courses. The university organisation structure consists of three faculties each with a number of teaching departments. In addition, there is a university administrative/management function and a central services function.

(a) The following cost information is available for the year ended 30 June 20X3.

(i) **Occupancy costs**

Total £1,500,000

Such costs are apportioned on the basis of area used which is as follows.

	Square metres
Faculties	7,500
Teaching departments	20,000
Administration/management	7,000
Central services	3,000

(ii) **Administrative/management costs**

Direct costs: £1,775,000
Indirect costs: an apportionment of occupancy costs

Direct and indirect costs are charged to degree courses on a percentage basis.

(iii) **Faculty costs**

Direct costs: £700,000
Indirect costs: an apportionment of occupancy costs and central service costs

Direct and indirect costs are charged to teaching departments.

(iv) **Teaching departments**

Direct costs: £5,525,000
Indirect costs: an apportionment of occupancy costs and central service costs plus all faculty costs

Direct and indirect costs are charged to degree courses on a percentage basis.

NOTES

(v) **Central services**

Direct costs: £1,000,000
Indirect costs: an apportionment of occupancy costs

(b) Direct and indirect costs are charged to users in proportion to the estimated external costs of service provision, as follows.

	£'000
Faculties	240
Teaching departments	800
Degree courses:	
Business studies	32
Mechanical engineering	48
Catering studies	32
All other degrees	448
	1,600

(c) Additional data relating to the degree courses is as follows.

	Business studies	*Degree course Mechanical engineering*	*Catering studies*
Number of undergraduates	80	50	120
Apportioned costs (as % of totals)			
Teaching departments	3.0%	2.5%	7%
Administration/management	2.5%	5.0%	4%

Central services are to be apportioned as detailed in (b) above.

The total number of undergraduates from the university in the year to 30 June 20X3 was 2,500.

Tasks

(a) Calculate the average cost per undergraduate for the year ended 30 June 20X3.

(b) Calculate the average cost per undergraduate for each of the degrees in business studies, mechanical engineering and catering studies, showing all relevant cost analysis.

ANSWER

(a) The average cost per undergraduate is as follows.

	Total costs for university £'000
Occupancy	1,500
Admin/management	1,775
Faculty	700
Teaching departments	5,525
Central services	1,000
	10,500
Number of undergraduates	2,500
Average cost per undergraduate for year ended 30 June 20X3	£4,200

(b) Average cost per undergraduate for each course is as follows.

	Business studies	*Mechanical engineering*	*Catering studies*
	£	£	£
Teaching department costs (W1 and using % in question)	241,590	201,325	563,710
Admin/management costs (W1 and using % in question)	51,375	102,750	82,200
Central services (W2)	22,400	33,600	22,400
	315,365	337,675	668,310
Number of undergraduates	80	50	120
Average cost per undergraduate for year ended 30 June 20X3	£3,942	£6,754	£5,569

Workings

1 Cost allocation and apportionment

Cost item	*Basis of apportionment*	*Teaching departments*	*Admin/ management*	*Central services*	*Faculties*
		£'000	£'000	£'000	£'000
Direct costs	allocation	5,525	1,775	1,000	700
Occupancy costs	area used	800	280	120	300
Central services reapportioned	(W2)	560	-	(1,120)	168
Faculty costs reallocated	allocation	1,168	-	-	(1,168)
		8,053	2,055		

2 Central services apportionment of internal costs in proportion to the external costs.

	External costs	*Apportionment of internal central service costs*
	£'000	£'000
Faculties	240	168.0 $(\frac{240}{1,600} \times 1,120)$
Teaching	800	560.0
Degree courses:		
Business studies	32	22.4
Mechanical engineering	48	33.6
Catering studies	32	22.4
All other degrees	448	313.6
	1,600	1,120.0

Note. Some costs will be charged to the degree courses but this has not been considered in this example.

Activity 6 **(20 minutes)**

Carry Ltd operates a small fleet of delivery vehicles. Expected costs are as follows.

Loading	1 hour per tonne loaded
Loading costs:	
Labour (casual)	£6 per hour
Equipment depreciation	£80 per week
Supervision	£300 per week
Drivers' wages (fixed)	£350 per man per week
Petrol	20p per kilometre
Repairs	10p per kilometre
Depreciation	£80 per week per vehicle
Supervision	£400 per week
Other general expenses (fixed)	£200 per week

There are two drivers and two vehicles in the fleet.

During a slack week, only six journeys were made.

Journey	*Tonnes carried (one way)*	*One-way distance of journey* Kilometres
1	5	100
2	8	20
3	2	60
4	4	50
5	6	200
6	5	300

What is the expected average full cost per tonne-kilometre for the week?

Activity 7 **(20 minutes)**

Mary Manor Hotel has 80 rooms and these are all either double or twin-bedded rooms offered for either holiday accommodation or for private hire for conferences and company gatherings.

In addition the hotel has a recreation area offering swimming pool, sauna and so on. This area is for the use of all residents with some days being available for paying outside customers.

The restaurant is highly regarded and widely recommended. This is used by the guests and is also open to the general public.

Discuss the possible features of an accounting information system that might be used in this organisation.

7 SERVICE DEPARTMENT COSTING

Service department costing is used to establish a specific cost for an '**internal service**' which is a service provided by one department for another, rather than sold externally to customers. Examples of some internal service departments include the following.

- Canteen
- Data processing
- Maintenance

7.1 The purposes of service department costing

The costing of internal services has two basic purposes.

(a) **To control the costs and efficiency in the service department.** If we establish a distribution cost per tonne-km, a canteen cost per employee, a maintenance cost per machine hour, job cost per repair, or a mainframe computer operating cost per hour, we can do the following in order to establish control measures.

(i) Compare actual costs against a target or standard

(ii) Compare actual costs in the current period against actual costs in previous periods

(b) **To control the costs of the user departments, and prevent the unnecessary use of services.** If the costs of services are charged to the user departments in such a way that the charges reflect the use actually made by each user department of the service department's services then the following will occur.

(i) The overhead costs of user departments will be established more accurately. Some service department variable costs might be identified as costs which are directly attributable to the user department.

(ii) If the service department's charges for a user department are high, the user department might be encouraged to consider whether it is making an excessively costly and wasteful use of the service department's service.

(iii) The user department might decide that it can obtain a similar service at a lower cost from an external service company and so the service department will have priced itself out of the market. This is clearly not satisfactory from the point of view of the organisation as a whole.

Service costing also provides a **fairer basis** for charging service costs to user departments, instead of charging service costs as overheads on a broad direct labour hour basis, or similar arbitrary apportionment basis. This is because service costs are related more directly to **use**.

Some examples of situations where the costing of internal services would be useful are as follows.

(a) If repair costs in a factory are costed as jobs with each bit of repair work being given a job number and costed accordingly, repair costs can be charged to the departments on the basis of repair jobs actually undertaken, instead of on a more generalised basis, such as apportionment according to machine hour capacity in each department. Departments with high repair costs could then consider their high incidence of repairs, the age and reliability of their machines, or the skills of the machine operators.

(b) If mainframe computer costs are charged to a user department on the basis of a cost per hour, the user department would make the following assessment.

(i) Whether it was getting good value from its use of the mainframe computer.

(ii) Whether it might be better to hire the service of a computer bureau, or perhaps install a stand-alone microcomputer system in the department.

Activity 8 **(5 minutes)**

The maintenance department of FA Ltd charges user departments for its services as follows.

- A predetermined hourly rate for labour hours worked on maintenance jobs
- Specifically identifiable materials are charged at actual cost

The budgeted maintenance labour hours for the latest period were 800 hours, during which maintenance costs of £8,400 were budgeted to be incurred.

During the period, 22 maintenance hours were worked in production department 1, and materials costing £18 were used on these maintenance jobs.

What is the charge to production department 1 for its use of the maintenance service department during the period?

8 JOB COSTING AND SERVICES

Service costing is one of the subdivisions of **continuous operation costing** and as such should theoretically be applied when the services result from a sequence of continuous or repetitive operations or processes. Service costing is therefore ideal for catering establishments, road, rail and air transport services and hotels. However, just because an organisation provides a service, it does not mean that service costing should automatically be applied.

Remember that job costing applies where work is undertaken to customers' special requirements. An organisation may therefore be working in the service sector but may supply one-off services which meet particular customers' special requirements; in such a situation job costing may be more appropriate than service costing. For example, a consultancy business, although part of the service sector, could use job costing.

(a) Each job could be given a separate number.

(b) Time sheets could be used to record and analyse consultants' time.

(c) The time spent against each job number would be shown as well as, for example, travelling time and mileage.

(d) Other costs such as stationery could be charged direct to each job as necessary.

Chapter roundup

- Job costing is the costing method used where each cost unit is separately identifiable.
- Each job is given a number to distinguish it from other jobs.
- Costs for each job are collected on a job cost sheet or job card.
- Material costs for each job are determined from material requisition notes.
- Labour times on each job are recorded on a job ticket, which is then costed and recorded on the job cost sheet.
- Overhead is absorbed into the cost of jobs using the predetermined overhead absorption rates.
- Contract costing is a form of job costing which applies where the job is on a large scale and for a long duration. The majority of costs relating to a contract are direct costs.
- Contract costs are collected in a contract account.
- A customer is likely to be required to make progress payments which are calculated as the value of work done and certified by the architect or engineer minus a retention minus the payments made to date.
- Batch costing is similar to job costing in that each batch of similar articles is separately identifiable. The cost per unit manufactured in a batch is the total batch cost divided by the number of units in the batch.
- Service costing can be used by companies operating in a service industry or by companies wishing to establish the cost of services carried out by some of their departments.
- Specific characteristics of services
  - Intangibility
  - Simultaneity
  - Perishability
  - Heterogeneity
- One main problem with service costing is being able to define a realistic cost unit that represents a suitable measure of the service provided. If the service is a function of two activity variables, a composite cost unit may be more appropriate.
- Cost per service unit = $\dfrac{\text{Total costs for period}}{\text{Number of service units in the period}}$
- Service department costing is also used to establish a specific cost for an internal service which is a service provided by one department for another, rather than sold externally to customers eg canteen, maintenance.

Quick quiz

1 Describe the procedures by which job costs are collected.

2 How is a job valued at the end of an accounting period if it is incomplete?

3 List the features of contract costing.

4 How is the amount of a progress payment calculated?

5 What are retention monies?

6 How would you calculate the cost per unit of a completed batch?

7 Define service costing.

8 Match up the following services with their typical cost units.

Service	**Cost unit**
Hotels	Patient-day
Education	Meal served
Hospitals	Full-time student
Catering organisations	Occupied bed-night

9 What is the advantage of organisations within an industry using a common cost unit?

10 Cost per service unit = ____________________

11 Service department costing is used to establish a specific cost for an 'internal service' which is a service provided by one department for another.

True ☐

False ☐

Answers to Quick quiz

1 Job costs are collected on a job cost sheet from materials requisitions, which details the materials issued to the job, and job tickets, on which the time spent by each person on the particular job are recorded. The job's share of factory overheads, based on the appropriate absorption rate is also noted on the job sheet.

2 Incomplete work at the end of the period is known as Work In Progress, and forms part of stock. It is therefore valued at the lower of cost and net realisable value. The job sheet will detail the cost of bringing the stock to its present location and condition. The net realisable value will be the selling price agreed with the customer, less any further costs to be incurred to complete the job. These details should be obtainable from the estimated costings of the job.

3 A formal contract is made between customer and supplier
Work is undertaken to the customer's special requirements
The work is for a relatively long duration
It is often construction work
The costing method is similar to job costing
The work is often based on-site
The site may have its own cashier and time-keeper

4 The value of work done and certified by the architect or engineer

minus	a retention
minus	the payments made to date
equals	payment due.

5 Retention monies are withheld by a customer until the contract is fully completed and accepted by the customer.

6 $\dfrac{\text{Total batch cost}}{\text{Number of units in the batch}}$

7 Cost accounting for services or functions eg canteens, maintenance, personnel (service centres/functions).

8

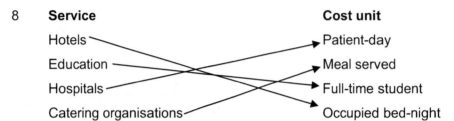

Service	**Cost unit**
Hotels	Patient-day
Education	Meal served
Hospitals	Full-time student
Catering organisations	Occupied bed-night

9 It is easier to make comparisons.

10 Cost per service unit = $\dfrac{\text{Total costs for period}}{\text{Number of service units in the period}}$

11 True

Answers to Activities

1 (a)

	£
Direct material Y (400 kilos × £10)	4,000
Direct material Z (800 – 60 kilos × £12)	8,880
Total direct material cost	12,880

(b)

	£
Department P (320 hours × £8)	2,560
Department Q (200 hours × £10)	2,000
Total direct labour cost	4,560

Overtime premium will be charged to overhead in the case of Department P, and to the job of the customer who asked for overtime to be worked in the case of Department Q.

(c)

	£
Direct material cost	12,880
Direct labour cost	4,560
Production overhead (520 hours × £6)	3,120
	20,560

(d) Price = £20,560 × 130% = £26,728

2 Total labour cost = £12,500 + £23,000 + £4,500 = £40,000

Overhead absorption rate = $\dfrac{£140{,}000}{£40{,}000} \times 100\% = 350\%$ of direct labour cost

Closing work in progress valuation

		Job 1		*Job 2*	*Total*
		£		£	£
Costs given in question		38,150		52,025	90,175
Overhead absorbed	(12,500 × 350%)	43,750	(23,000 × 350%)	80,500	124,250
					214,425

3 If the plant is hired, the cost will be a direct expense of the contract.

4 (a) Big units

	£	£
Direct materials		10,480
Direct labour		
Skilled 1,580 hours at £10	15,800	
Semi-skilled 3,160 hours at £8	25,280	
		41,080
Direct expenses		2,360
Administrative expenses 4,740 hours at £1.00 (see below)		4,740
		58,660
Selling price		66,360
Calculated profit		7,700
Divided: staff bonus 20%		£1,540
profit for company 80%		£6,160

Administration expenses absorption rate $= \frac{£8,800}{8,800}$ per labour hour

= £1.00 per labour hour

(b)

		Little units			*All-purpose*	
		£	£		£	£
Direct materials			13,420			7,640
Direct labour						
Skilled	1,700 hrs at £10	17,000		160 hrs at £10	1,600	
Semi-skilled	1,900 hrs at £8	15,200		300 hrs at £8	2,400	
Direct expenses		3,400			500	
Administration expenses:	3,600 hrs at £1.00	3,600		460 hrs at £1.00	460	
		39,200			4,960	
Costs to completion	20/80 × 39,200	9,800		75/25 × 5,680	14,880	
			49,000			19,840
Total costs			62,420			27,480
Selling price			55,000			39,000
Calculated profit/(loss)			(7,420)			11,520
Divided:	Staff bonus 20%		–			2,304
	(Loss)/profit for company		(7,420)			9,218

Note that whilst direct labour costs, direct expenses and administration expenses increase in proportion to the total labour hours required to complete the little units and the all-purpose units, there will be no further material costs to complete the batches.

(c) Little units are projected to incur a loss. There are two possible reasons for the loss.

   (i) The estimation process may be inadequate. For example, it may have been incorrect to assume that the make-up of the costs to completion is the same as the make-up of the costs already incurred. It is possible that all of the skilled work has already been carried out and only unskilled labour is required to complete the batch. If the loss is the result of inadequate estimating, the estimation procedure should be reviewed to prevent recurrence.

   (ii) It is the result of a lack of cost control. If this is the case, appropriate action should be taken to exercise control in future.

5 The cost unit is the basic measure of control in an organisation, used to monitor cost and activity levels. The cost unit selected must be measurable and appropriate for the type of cost and activity. Possible cost units which could be suggested are as follows.

Cost per kilometre

- Variable cost per kilometre
- Fixed cost per kilometre – however this is not particularly useful for control purposes because it will tend to vary with the kilometres run
- Total cost of each vehicle per kilometre – this suffers from the same problem as above
- Maintenance cost of each vehicle per kilometre

Cost per tonne-kilometre

This can be more useful than a cost per kilometre for control purposes, because it combines the distance travelled and the load carried, both of which affect cost.

Cost per operating hour

Once again, many costs can be related to this cost unit, including the following.

- Total cost of each vehicle per operating hour
- Variable costs per operating hour
- Fixed costs per operating hour – this suffers from the same problems as the fixed cost per kilometre in terms of its usefulness for control purposes.

6 Variable costs

Journey	*1*	*2*	*3*	*4*	*5*	*6*
	£	£	£	£	£	£
Loading labour	30	48	12	24	36	30
(£6 per hour, 1 hour per tonne)						
Petrol (both ways)	40	8	24	20	80	120
Repairs (both ways)	20	4	12	10	40	60
	90	60	48	54	156	210

Total costs

	£
Variable costs (total for journeys 1 to 6 from above)	618
Loading equipment depreciation	80
Loading supervision	300
Drivers' wages (2 drivers)	700
Vehicles depreciation (2 vehicles)	160
Drivers' supervision	400
Other costs	200
	2,458

Journey	*Tonnes*	*One-way distance Kilometres*	*Tonne-kilometres*
1	5	100	500
2	8	20	160
3	2	60	120
4	4	50	200
5	6	200	1,200
6	5	300	1,500
			3,680

Cost per tonne-kilometre $\frac{£2,458}{3,680} = £0.668$

Note that the large element of fixed costs may distort this measure but that a variable cost per tonne-kilometre of £618/3,680 = £0.168 may be useful for budgetary control.

7 The accounting information system that might be used in this organisation would require the following features.

(a) The hotel should be divided into a number of responsibility centres, with one manager responsible for the performance of each centre. Examples of such centres could be rooms, recreation area and restaurant.

(b) The costing system must be capable of identifying the costs and revenues to be allocated to each responsibility centre.

(c) The system must also include a fair method of apportioning those costs and revenues which cannot be directly allocated to a specific centre.

(d) Each responsibility centre would have a detailed budget against which the actual results would be compared for management control purposes.

(e) The information system must be capable of providing rapid feedback of information to managers so that prompt control action can be taken where appropriate.

(f) Key control measures should also be used, perhaps with standard targets set in advance. Examples include the following.

- Cost per bed per night
- Cost per sauna hour
- Cost per meal in the restaurant

These control measures would also provide the basic information from which a pricing decision can be made.

8 Predetermined labour hour rate for maintenance = £8,400/800
= £10.50 per hour

∴ Charge to production department 1:

	£
Maintenance labour (22 hours × £10.50)	231
Materials	18
	249

Chapter : 7
PROCESS COSTING

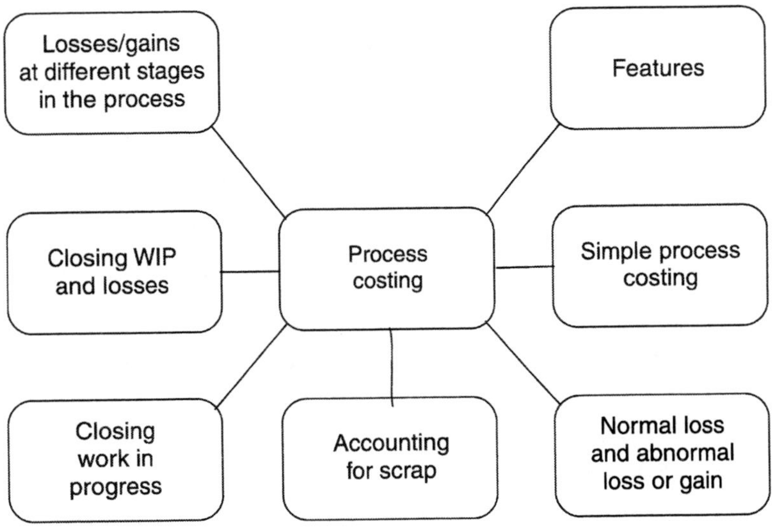

Introduction

We looked at four cost accounting methods, **job costing, contract costing, batch costing** and **service costing** in the previous chapter. In this chapter we will consider another, **process costing**. We will begin from basics and look at how to account for the most simple of processes. We will then move on to how to account for any **losses** which might occur, as well as what to do with any **scrapped units** which are sold. Next we will consider how to deal with **closing work in progress** before examining situations involving closing work in progress and losses. Throughout the chapter we will be looking at how to record process costs in **process accounts** which are simply WIP ledger accounts.

Your objectives

In this chapter you will learn about the following.

(a) The distinguishing features of process costing

(b) Simple process costing

(c) Normal loss and abnormal loss or gain

(d) Accounting for scrap

(e) Closing work in progress

(f) Closing work in progress and losses

(g) Identification of losses/gains at different stages in the process

1 THE DISTINGUISHING FEATURES OF PROCESS COSTING

Definition

> **Process costing** is a costing method used where it is not possible to identify separate units of production, or jobs, usually because of the continuous nature of the production processes involved.

It is common to identify process costing with **continuous production** such as the following.

- Oil refining
- The manufacture of soap
- Paint
- Food and drink

The features of process costing which make it different from job or batch costing are as follows.

(a) The continuous nature of production in many processes means that there will usually be **closing work in progress which must be valued**. In process costing it is not possible to build up cost records of the cost of each individual unit of output because production in progress is an indistinguishable homogeneous mass.

(b) There is often a **loss in process** due to spoilage, wastage, evaporation and so on.

(c) The **output** of one process becomes the **input** to the next until the finished product is made in the final process.

(d) Output from production may be a single product, but there may also be a **by-product** (or by-products) and/or **joint products**.

2 SIMPLE PROCESS COSTING

Before tackling the more complex areas of process costing, we will begin by looking at a very simple process costing example which will illustrate the basic techniques which we will build upon in the remainder of this chapter.

WORKED EXAMPLE

Suppose that Purr and Miaow Ltd make squeaky toys for cats. Production of the toys involves two processes, shaping and colouring. During the year to 31 March 20X3, 1,000,000 units of material worth £500,000 were input to the first process, shaping. Direct labour costs of £200,000 and production overhead costs of £200,000 were also incurred in connection with the shaping process. There were no opening or closing stocks in the shaping department. The process account for shaping for the year ended 31 March 20X3 is as follows.

PROCESS 1 (SHAPING) ACCOUNT

	Units	£		Units	£
Direct materials	1,000,000	500,000	Output to Process 2	1,000,000	900,000
Direct labour		200,000			
Production overheads		200,000			
	1,000,000	900,000		1,000,000	900,000

2.1 Double entry

You will see that a **process account** is nothing more than a **ledger account with debit and credit entries** although it does have an additional column on both the debit and credit sides showing **quantity**. When preparing process accounts you are advised to include these memorandum quantity columns and to balance them off (ie ensure they total to the same amount on both sides) **before** attempting to complete the monetary value columns since they will help you to check that you have missed nothing out. This becomes increasingly important as more complications are introduced into questions.

Because process accounts are simply ledger accounts, the double entry works as it does for any other ledger account. For example, the corresponding credit entry of £200,000 for labour in the process 1 account above will be in the **wages and salaries control account**. Students often think process costing is difficult but if you bear in mind that you are simply completing a normal ledger account which is part of a system of double entry cost bookkeeping you will find this topic much more straightforward.

WORKED EXAMPLE

After that slight digression let us go back to Purr and Miaow Ltd. When using process costing, if a series of separate processes is needed to manufacture the finished product, the output of one process becomes the input to the next until the final output is made in the final process. In our example, all output from shaping was transferred to the second process, colouring, during the year to 31 March 20X3. An additional 500,000 units of material, costing £300,000, were input to the colouring process. Direct labour costs of £150,000 and production overhead costs of £150,000 were also incurred. There were no opening or closing stocks in the colouring department. The process account for colouring for the year ended 31 March 20X3 is as follows.

PROCESS 2 (COLOURING) ACCOUNT

	Units	£		Units	£
Materials from process 1	1,000,000	900,000	Output to finished		
Added materials		300,000	goods	1,000,000	1,500,000
Direct labour		150,000			
Production overhead		150,000			
	1,000,000	1,500,000		1,000,000	1,500,000

Direct labour and production overhead may be treated together in some contexts as **conversion cost.**

Notice that although figures are given for the number of units of additional material these are not recorded in the process account. This is because added materials are usually materials which enhance the existing production units – in this example, we would be colouring the squeaky toys from process 1, we are not making any new toys but improving old ones we already have. So we do not need to add any extra units for added material and the number of units of material added are **never** recorded in the process account.

Added materials, labour and overhead in process 2 are usually **added gradually** throughout the process. Materials from process 1, in contrast, will often be **introduced in full at the start of the second process**.

2.2 Framework for dealing with process costing

Process costing is centred around **four key steps**. The exact work done at each step will depend on the circumstances of the question, but the approach can always be used. Don't worry about the terms used. We will be looking at their meaning as we work through the chapter.

Step 1. **Determine output and losses**

- Determine expected output.
- Calculate normal loss and abnormal loss and gain.
- Calculate equivalent units if there is closing work in progress.

Step 2. **Calculate cost per unit of output, losses and WIP**

Calculate cost per unit or cost per equivalent unit.

Step 3. **Calculate total cost of output, losses and WIP**

In some examples this will be straightforward. In cases where there is closing work in progress, a statement of evaluation will have to be prepared.

Step 4. **Complete accounts**

- Complete the process account.
- Write up the other accounts required by the question such as abnormal loss/gain accounts, scrap accounts and so on.

Activity 1 **(15 minutes)**

Palm Ltd manufactures a product, the Wombat, which goes through two separate processes, mixing and shaping.

10,000 units of material costing £30,000 were input into the mixing process along with direct labour costs of £45,000 and production overheads of £22,500.

The output from mixing was transferred to the shaping process where materials were added costing £5,000 for 5,000 units and further direct labour and production overheads were £10,000 and £4,500 respectively.

What was the total value of the output from the shaping process? From this, calculate the full cost per unit.

3 NORMAL LOSS AND ABNORMAL LOSS OR GAIN

During a production process, a loss may occur due to wastage, spoilage, evaporation, and so on.

Definitions

Normal loss is the loss expected during a process. It is not given a share of the input costs.

Abnormal loss is the extra loss resulting when actual loss is greater than normal or expected loss, and it is given a share of the input costs.

Abnormal gain is the gain resulting when actual loss is less than the normal or expected loss, and it is given a 'negative cost'.

Since normal loss is not given a cost, the cost of producing these units is borne by the 'good' units of output.

Abnormal loss and gain units are valued at the same unit rate as 'good' units. Abnormal events do not therefore affect the cost of good production. Their costs are **analysed separately** in an **abnormal loss or abnormal gain account**.

WORKED EXAMPLE: ABNORMAL LOSSES AND GAINS

Suppose that input to a process is 1,000 units at a cost of £4,500. Normal loss is 10% and there are no opening or closing stocks. Determine the accounting entries for the cost of output and the cost of the loss if actual output is 860 units.

Before we demonstrate the use of the 'four step framework' we will summarise the way that the losses are dealt with.

(a) Normal loss is given no share of the input cost.

(b) The cost of output is therefore based on the **expected** units of output, which in our example amount to 90% of 1,000 = 900 units.

(c) Abnormal loss is given a cost, which is written off to the profit and loss account via an abnormal loss/gain account.

(d) Abnormal gain is treated in the same way, except that being a gain rather than a loss, it appears as a **debit** entry in the process account (whereas a loss appears as a **credit** entry in this account).

ANSWER

Step 1. **Determine output and losses**

If actual output is 860 units and the actual loss is 140 units:

	Units
Actual loss	140
Normal loss (10% of 1,000)	100
Abnormal loss (balancing figure)	40

Step 2. **Calculate cost per unit of output and losses**

The cost per unit of output and the cost per unit of abnormal loss are based on expected output.

$$\frac{\text{Costs incurred}}{\text{Expected output}} = \frac{£4{,}500}{900 \text{ units}} = £5 \text{ per unit}$$

Step 3. **Calculate total cost of output and losses**

Normal loss is not assigned any cost.

	£
Cost of output (860 × £5)	4,300
Normal loss	0
Abnormal loss (40 × £5)	200
	4,500

Step 4. **Complete accounts**

PROCESS ACCOUNT

	Units	£		Units		£
Cost incurred	1,000	4,500	Normal loss	100		0
			Output (finished goods a/c)	860	(× £5)	4,300
			Abnormal loss	40	(× £5)	200
	1,000	4,500		1,000		4,500

ABNORMAL LOSS ACCOUNT

	Units	£		Units	£
Process a/c	40	200	Profit and loss a/c	40	200

If there is a closing balance in the abnormal loss or gain account when the profit for the period is calculated, this balance is taken to the profit and loss account: an abnormal gain will be a credit to profit and loss and an abnormal loss will be a debit to profit and loss.

Activity 2 **(20 minutes)**

Charlton Ltd manufactures a product in a single process operation. Normal loss is 10% of input. Loss occurs at the end of the process. Data for June are as follows.

Opening and closing stocks of work in progress	Nil
Cost of input materials (3,300 units)	£59,100
Direct labour and production overhead	£30,000
Output to finished goods	2,750 units

What was the full cost of finished output in June?

4 ACCOUNTING FOR SCRAP

4.1 Loss may have a scrap value

The following basic rules are applied in accounting for this value in the process accounts.

(a) **Revenue from scrap** is treated, not as an addition to sales revenue, but as a **reduction in costs.**

(b) The scrap value of **normal loss** is therefore used to reduce the material costs of the process.

DEBIT Scrap account
CREDIT Process account

with the scrap value of the normal loss.

(c) The scrap value of **abnormal loss** is used to reduce the cost of abnormal loss.

DEBIT Scrap account
CREDIT Abnormal loss account

with the scrap value of abnormal loss, which therefore reduces the write-off of cost to the profit and loss account.

(d) The scrap value of **abnormal gain** arises because the actual units sold as scrap will be less than the scrap value of normal loss. Because there are fewer units of scrap than expected, there will be less revenue from scrap as a direct consequence of the abnormal gain. The abnormal gain account should therefore be debited with the scrap value.

DEBIT Abnormal gain account
CREDIT Scrap account

with the scrap value of abnormal gain.

(e) The **scrap account** is completed by recording the **actual cash received** from the sale of scrap.

DEBIT Cash account
CREDIT Scrap account

with the cash received from the sale of the actual scrap.

The same basic principle therefore applies that only **normal losses** should affect the cost of the good output. The scrap value of **normal loss only** is credited to the process account. The scrap values of abnormal losses and gains are analysed separately in the abnormal loss or gain account.

WORKED EXAMPLE: SCRAP AND ABNORMAL LOSS OR GAIN

A factory has two production processes. Normal loss in each process is 10% and scrapped units sell for £0.50 each from process 1 and £3 each from process 2. Relevant information for costing purposes relating to period 5 is as follows.

	Process 1	*Process 2*
Direct materials added:		
units	2,000	1,250
cost	£8,100	£1,900
Direct labour	£4,000	£10,000
Production overhead	150% of direct labour cost	120% of direct labour cost
Output to process 2/finished goods	1,750 units	2,800 units
Actual production overhead	£17,800	

Required

Prepare the accounts for process 1, process 2, scrap, abnormal loss or gain and production overhead.

ANSWER

Step 1. Determine output and losses

	Process 1	*Process 2*
	Units	Units
Output	1,750	2,800
Normal loss (10% of input)	200	300
Abnormal loss (balancing figure)	50	-
Abnormal gain (balancing figure)	-	(100)
	2,000	3,000*

* 1,750 units from process 1 + 1,250 units input to process.

Notice in this example further direct materials have been added in process 2. This will then increase the number of production units. This is very different to the situation where materials are added, remember this type of material enhances the production units and does not increase the number of units.

Step 2. Calculate cost per unit of output and losses

		Process 1		*Process 2*
		£		£
Cost of input				
- material		8,100		1,900
- from Process 1		-	(1,750 × £10)	17,500
- labour		4,000		10,000
- overhead	(150% × £4,000)	6,000	(120% × £10,000)	12,000
		18,100		41,400
less: scrap value of **normal loss**	(200 × £0.50)	(100)	(300 × £3)	(900)
		18,000		40,500
Expected output				
90% of 2,000		1,800		
90% of 3,000				2,700
Cost per unit				
£18,000 ÷ 1,800		£10		
£40,500 ÷ 2,700				£15

Step 3. Calculate total cost of output and losses

	Process 1		*Process 2*
	£		£
Output (1,750 × £10)	17,500	(2,800 × £15)	42,000
Normal loss (200 × £0.50)*	100	(300 × £3)*	900
Abnormal loss (50 × £10)	500		-
	18,100		42,900
Abnormal gain	-	(100 × £15)	(1,500)
	18,100		41,400

* Remember that normal loss is valued at scrap value only.

Step 4. **Complete accounts**

PROCESS 1 ACCOUNT

	Units	£		Units	£
Direct material	2,000	8,100	Scrap a/c (normal loss)	200	100
Direct labour		4,000	Process 2 a/c	1,750	17,500
Production overhead a/c		6,000	Abnormal loss a/c	50	500
	2,000	18,100		2,000	18,100

PROCESS 2 ACCOUNT

	Units	£		Units	£
Direct material			Scrap a/c (normal loss)	300	900
From process 1	1,750	17,500	Output	2,800	42,000
Further direct material added	1,250	1,900			
Direct labour		10,000			
Production overhead		12,000			
	3,000	41,400			
Abnormal gain	100	1,500			
	3,100	42,900		3,100	42,900

ABNORMAL LOSS ACCOUNT

	£		£
Process 1 (50 units)	500	Scrap a/c: sale of scrap of extra loss (50 units)	25
		Profit and loss a/c	475
	500		500

ABNORMAL GAIN ACCOUNT

	£		£
Scrap a/c (loss of scrap revenue due to abnormal gain, 100 units × £3)	300	Process 2 abnormal gain (100 units)	1,500
Profit and loss a/c	1,200		
	1,500		1,500

SCRAP ACCOUNT

	£		£
Scrap value of normal loss		Cash a/c - cash received	
Process 1 (200 units)	100	Loss in process 1 (250 units)	125
Process 2 (300 units)	900	Loss in process 2 (200 units)	600
Abnormal loss a/c (process 1)	25	Abnormal gain a/c (process 2)	300
	1,025		1,025

PRODUCTION OVERHEAD ACCOUNT

	£		£
Overhead incurred	17,800	Process 1 a/c	6,000
Over-absorbed overhead a/c (or P & L a/c)	200	Process 2 a/c	12,000
	18,000		18,000

Activity 3 **(20 minutes)**

JPC Ltd uses a process to manufacture its single product. Details for the latest period were as follows.

	Quantity	£
Direct material input	750	5,175
Direct labour		33,750
Production overheads		2,235

Normal losses are expected to be at 10% of input and JPC Ltd can usually sell any losses for £1.60 per unit. Actual losses for the period were 70 units.

Prepare the ledger account for the process for the period.

5 CLOSING WORK IN PROGRESS

In the examples we have looked at so far we have assumed that opening and closing stocks of work in process have been nil. We must now look at more realistic examples and consider how to allocate the costs incurred in a period between completed output (ie finished units) and partly completed closing stock.

Some examples will help to illustrate the problem, and the techniques used to share out (apportion) costs between finished output and closing work in progress.

WORKED EXAMPLE: VALUATION OF CLOSING STOCK

Trotter Ltd is a manufacturer of processed goods. In March 20X3, in one process, there was no opening stock, but 5,000 units of input were introduced to the process during the month, at the following cost.

	£
Direct materials	16,560
Direct labour	7,360
Production overhead	5,520
	29,440

Of the 5,000 units introduced, 4,000 were completely finished during the month and transferred to the next process. Closing stock of 1,000 units was only 60% complete with respect to materials and conversion costs.

ANSWER

(a) The problem in this example is to divide the costs of production (£29,440) between the finished output of 4,000 units and the closing stock of 1,000 units. It is argued, with good reason, that a division of costs in proportion to the number of units of each (4,000:1,000) would not be 'fair' because closing stock has not been completed, and has not yet 'received' its full amount of materials and conversion costs, but only 60% of the full amount. The 1,000 units of closing stock, being only 60% complete, are the equivalent of 600 fully worked units.

(b) To apportion costs fairly and proportionately, units of production must be converted into the equivalent of completed units, ie into **equivalent units of production**.

Definition

> **Equivalent units** are notional whole units which represent incomplete work, and which are used to apportion costs between work in process and completed output.

Step 1. **Determine output**

For this step in our framework we need to prepare a statement of equivalent units.

STATEMENT OF EQUIVALENT UNITS

	Total units	*Completion*	*Equivalent units*
Fully worked units	4,000	100%	4,000
Closing stock	1,000	60%	600
	5,000		4,600

Step 2. **Calculate cost per unit of output, and WIP**

For this step in our framework we need to prepare a statement of costs per equivalent unit because equivalent units are the basis for apportioning costs.

STATEMENT OF COSTS PER EQUIVALENT UNIT

$$\frac{\text{Total cost}}{\text{Equivalent units}} = \frac{£29{,}440}{4{,}600}$$

Cost per equivalent unit £6.40

Step 3. **Calculate total cost of output and WIP**

For this stage in our framework a statement of evaluation may now be prepared, to show how the costs should be apportioned between finished output and closing stock.

STATEMENT OF EVALUATION

Item	*Equivalent units*	*Cost of equivalent unit*	*Valuation* £
Fully worked units	4,000	£6.40	25,600
Closing stock	600	£6.40	3,840
	4,600		29,440

Step 4. **Complete accounts**

The process account would be shown as follows.

PROCESS ACCOUNT

	Units	£		Units	£
(Stores a/c) Direct materials	5,000	16,560	Output to next process	4,000	25,600
(Wages a/c) Direct labour		7,360	Closing stock c/f	1,000	3,840
(O'hd a/c) Production o'hd		5,520			
	5,000	29,440		5,000	29,440

When preparing a process 'T' account, it might help to make the entries as follows.

(a) **Enter the units first**. The units columns are simply memorandum columns, but they help you to make sure that there are no units unaccounted for (for example as loss).

(b) **Enter the costs of materials, labour and overheads next**. These should be given to you.

(c) **Enter your valuation of finished output and closing stock next**. The value of the credit entries should, of course, equal the value of the debit entries.

5.1 Different rates of input

In many industries, materials, labour and overhead may be added at **different rates** during the course of production.

(a) Output from a previous process (for example, the output from process 1 to process 2) may be introduced into the subsequent process all at once, so that closing stock is 100% complete in respect of these materials.

(b) Further materials may be **added gradually** during the process, so that closing stock is only **partially complete** in respect of these added materials.

(c) Labour and overhead may be 'added' at yet another different rate. When production overhead is absorbed on a labour hour basis, however, we should expect the degree of completion on overhead to be the same as the degree of completion on labour.

When this situation occurs, equivalent units, and a cost per equivalent unit, should be **calculated separately for each type of material, and also for conversion costs.**

WORKED EXAMPLE: EQUIVALENT UNITS AND DIFFERENT DEGREES OF COMPLETION

Suppose that Shaker Ltd is a manufacturer of processed goods, and that results in process 2 for April 20X3 were as follows.

Opening stock	nil
Material input from process 1	4,000 units
Costs of input:	£
material from process 1	6,000
added materials in process 2	1,080
conversion costs	1,720

Output is transferred into the next process, process 3.

Closing work in process amounted to 800 units, complete as to:

process 1 material	100%
added materials	50%
conversion costs	30%

Prepare the account for process 2 for April 20X3.

ANSWER

Step 1. **Determine output and losses**

STATEMENT OF EQUIVALENT UNITS (OF PRODUCTION IN THE PERIOD)

			Equivalent units of production					
			Process 1		*Added*		*Labour and*	
Input	*Output*	*Total*	*material*		*materials*		*overhead*	
Units		Units	Units	%	Units	%	Units	%
4,000	Completed production	3,200	3,200	100	3,200	100	3,200	100
	Closing stock	800	800	100	400	50	240	30
4,000		4,000	4,000		3,600		3,440	

Note. Since 3,200 units were completed these units must be 100% complete for all costs. It is only the closing stock which is partially complete.

Step 2. **Calculate cost per unit of output, losses and WIP**

STATEMENT OF COST (PER EQUIVALENT UNIT)

Input	*Cost*	*Equivalent production in units*	*Cost per unit*
	£		£
Process 1 material	6,000	4,000	1.50
Added materials	1,080	3,600	0.30
Labour and overhead	1,720	3,440	0.50
	8,800		2.30

Step 3. **Calculate total cost of output, losses and WIP**

STATEMENT OF EVALUATION (OF FINISHED WORK AND CLOSING STOCKS)

Production	*Cost element*	*Number of equivalent units*	*Cost per equivalent unit*	*Total*	*Cost*
			£	£	£
Completed production		3,200	2.30		7,360
Closing stock:	process 1 material	800	1.50	1,200	
	added material	400	0.30	120	
	labour and overhead	240	0.50	120	
					1,440
					8,800

Step 4. **Complete accounts**

PROCESS ACCOUNT

	Units	£		Units	£
Process 1 material	4,000	6,000	Process 3 a/c	3,200	7,360
Added material		1,080	(finished output)		
Conversion costs		1,720	Closing stock c/f	800	1,440
	4,000	8,800		4,000	8,800

6 CLOSING WORK IN PROGRESS AND LOSSES

The previous paragraphs have dealt separately with the following.

(a) The treatment of **loss** and **scrap**

(b) The use of **equivalent units** as a basis for apportioning costs between units of output and units of **closing stock**

We must now look at a situation where both problems occur together, that is there is closing work in progress, and also losses occurring during the process. We shall begin with an example where loss has no scrap value.

The rules are as follows.

(a) Costs should be **divided** between **finished output, closing stock** and **abnormal loss/gain** using equivalent units as a basis of apportionment.

(b) Units of **abnormal loss/gain** are often taken to be **one full equivalent unit** each, and are valued on this basis.

(c) **Abnormal loss units** are an **addition** to the total equivalent units produced but **abnormal gain units** are **subtracted** in arriving at the total number of equivalent units produced.

(d) Units of normal loss are 'equivalent to' zero equivalent units.

WORKED EXAMPLE: CHANGES IN STOCK LEVEL AND LOSSES

The following data has been collected.

Opening stock	none	Output to finished goods	2,000 units
Input units	2,800 units	Closing stock	450 units, 70% complete
Cost of input	£16,695	Total loss	350 units
Normal loss	10%; nil scrap value		

Required

Prepare the process account for the period.

ANSWER

Step 1. **Determine output and losses**

STATEMENT OF EQUIVALENT UNITS

	Total units		*Equivalent units of work done this period*
Completely worked units	2,000	(× 100%)	2,000
Closing stock	450	(× 70%)	315
Normal loss	280		0
Abnormal loss	70	(× 100%)	70
	2,800		2,385

Step 2. **Calculate cost per unit of output, losses and WIP**

STATEMENT OF COST PER EQUIVALENT UNIT

$$\frac{\text{Costs incurred}}{\text{Equivalent units of work done}} = \frac{£16{,}695}{2{,}385}$$

Cost per equivalent unit = £7

Step 3. **Calculate total cost of output, losses and WIP**

STATEMENT OF EVALUATION

	Equivalent units	£
Completely worked units	2,000	14,000
Closing stock	315	2,205
Abnormal loss	70	490
	2,385	16,695

Step 4. **Complete accounts**

PROCESS ACCOUNT

	Units	£		Units	£
Input costs	2,800	16,695	Normal loss	280	0
			Finished goods a/c	2,000	14,000
			Abnormal loss a/c	70	490
			Closing stock c/d	450	2,205
	2,800	16,695		2,800	16,695

6.1 Closing work in progress, loss and scrap

When loss has a **scrap value**, the accounting procedures are the same as those previously described. However, if the equivalent units are a different percentage (of the total units) for materials, labour and overhead, it is a convention that the **scrap value of normal loss** is **deducted from the cost of materials** before a cost per equivalent unit is calculated.

Activity 4 **(30 minutes)**

Prepare a process account from the following information.

Opening stock	Nil
Input units	10,000
Input costs	
Material	£5,150
Labour	£2,700
Normal loss	5% of input
Scrap value of units of loss	£1 per unit
Output to finished goods	8,000 units
Closing stock	1,000 units
Completion of closing stock	80% for material
	50% for labour

7 IDENTIFICATION OF LOSSES/GAINS AT DIFFERENT STAGES IN THE PROCESS

In our previous examples, we have assumed that loss occurs at the completion of processing, so that units of abnormal loss or abnormal gain count as a full equivalent unit of production. It may be, however, that units are rejected as scrap or 'loss' at an inspection stage **before the completion of processing**. When this occurs, units of abnormal loss should count as a proportion of an equivalent unit, according to the volume of work done and materials added **up to the point of inspection**. An example may help as an illustration.

WORKED EXAMPLE: INCOMPLETE REJECTED ITEMS

Coffee Ltd manufactures product X, and the following information relates to process 3 during September 20X2.

During the month 1,600 units of product X were transferred from process 2, at a valuation of £10,000. Other costs in process 3 were as follows.

Added materials	£4,650
Labour and overhead	£2,920

Units of product X are inspected in process 3 when added materials are 50% complete and conversion cost 30% complete. No losses are normally expected, but during September 20X2, actual loss at the inspection stage was 200 units of product X, which were sold as scrap for £2 each.

Required

Prepare the process 3 account and abnormal loss account for September 20X2.

ANSWER

Step 1. **Determine output and losses**

The equivalent units of work done this period are as follows.

STATEMENT OF EQUIVALENT UNITS

			Equivalent units			
Item	*Total units*	*Process 2 material*		*Added material*		*Conversion costs*
Units from process 2	1,600					
Abnormal loss	(200)	200	(50%)	100	(30%)	60
Fully worked units, Sept 20X2	1,400	1,400	(100%)	1,400	(100%)	1,400
		1,600		1,500		1,460

Step 2. **Calculate cost per unit of output, losses and WIP**

STATEMENT OF COST PER EQUIVALENT UNIT

	Process 2 material	*Added material*	*Conversion costs*
Costs incurred, Sept 20X2	£10,000	£4,650	£2,920
Equivalent units	1,600	1,500	1,460
Cost per equivalent unit	£6.25	£3.10	£2

Step 3. **Calculate total cost of output, losses and WIP**

STATEMENT OF EVALUATION

	Process 2 material	*Added material*	*Conversion costs*	*Total*
	£	£	£	£
Fully worked units	8,750	4,340	2,800	15,890
Abnormal loss	1,250	310	120	1,680
	10,000	4,650	2,920	17,570

The only difference between this example and earlier examples is that abnormal loss has been valued at less than one equivalent unit, for added materials and conversion costs.

Step 4. **Complete accounts**

PROCESS 3 ACCOUNT

	Units	£		Units	£
Process 2 output	1,600	10,000	*Output*		
Added materials	-	4,650	Good units	1,400	15,890
Labour and overhead	-	2,920	Abnormal loss	200	1,680
	1,600	17,570		1,600	17,570

ABNORMAL LOSS ACCOUNT

	Units	£		Units	£
Process 3 account	200	1,680	Cash (sale of scrap)	200	400
			Profit and loss a/c		1,280
	200	1,680	Cash (sale of scrap)	200	1,680

NOTES

Activity 5 **(30 minutes)**

JM Ltd manufactures a single product, AS, through two continual processes.

Information regarding these processes is given below.

		Process 1	*Process 2*
Direct materials:	units	10,000 units	
	cost	£24,500	
Material added:	units		5,000 units
	cost		£7,460
Direct labour		£15,500	£18,580
Production overheads		£8,260	£6,900
Normal losses:	Expected	10%	5%
	Scrap value	£2 per unit	£5.50 per unit
Output		8,000 units	7,000 units
Closing stock		1,800 units	500 units

Losses in process 1 are noted at the end of the process whereas in process 2 this occurs when 60% of the material is added and it is 30% complete with regard to conversion costs.

Closing stocks are completed as follows.

	Process 1	*Process 2*
Direct material	100%	
Material added		80%
Conversion costs	40%	50%

Prepare the process accounts for the period.

Chapter roundup

- Use our suggested four-step approach when dealing with process costing questions.

  Step 1. Determine output and losses
  Step 2. Calculate cost per unit of output, losses and WIP
  Step 3. Calculate total cost of output, losses and WIP
  Step 4. Complete accounts

- Process costing is used where there is a continuous flow of identical units.
- When units are partly complete at the end of a period, it is necessary to calculate the equivalent units of production in order to determine the cost of a complete unit.
- Losses may occur in process. If a certain level of loss is expected, this is known as normal loss. If losses are greater than expected, the extra loss is abnormal loss. If losses are less than expected, the difference is known as abnormal gain.
- The valuation of normal loss is either at scrap value or nil.
- It is conventional for the scrap value of normal loss to be deducted from the cost of materials before a cost per equivalent unit is calculated.
- Abnormal loss and gain units are valued at the same full cost as a good unit of production.
- If units are rejected as scrap or loss before the completion of processing, units of loss should count as a proportion of an equivalent unit, according to the volume of work done and materials added up to the point of inspection.

Quick quiz

1 What are the distinguishing features of process costing?

2 Distinguish between normal loss and abnormal loss.

3 How are normal losses and abnormal losses valued?

4 Is an abnormal gain a debit or credit entry in the process account?

5 What are the different accounting treatments for the scrap value of normal loss and the scrap value of abnormal loss?

6 What is an equivalent unit?

Answers to Quick quiz

1 Production is continuous

Individual units of output cannot be distinguished

There is often loss in process due to spoilage/wastage/evaporation etc

The output of one process may be the input for another process

Output may be a single product, by products and/or joint products

2 Normal loss is expected during a process, whereas abnormal loss is the unexpected loss over and above the normal loss.

3 Normal losses are valued at their scrap value or nil. Abnormal losses are valued at the cost of good production.

4 Debit.

5 The scrap value of a normal loss is used to reduce the material costs of the process by debiting the process account. The scrap value of an abnormal loss is used to reduce the value of the abnormal loss by crediting the abnormal loss account.

6 An equivalent unit is a notional whole unit which represents incomplete work. It is used to apportion costs between work in process and completed output.

Answers to Activities

1 PROCESS 1: MIXING

	Units	£		Units	£
Direct materials	10,000	30,000	Output to		
Direct labour		45,000	process 2	10,000	97,500
Production overhead		22,500			
	10,000	97,500		10,000	97,500

PROCESS 2: SHAPING

	Units	£		Units	£
Input from process 1	10,000	97,500	Output to		
Added material		5,000	finished goods	10,000	117,000
Direct labour		10,000			
Production overhead		4,500			
	10,000	117,000		10,000	117,000

Total value of output = £117,000

Full cost/unit= $\frac{£117{,}000}{10{,}000}$ = £11.70

2 ***Step 1.*** **Determine output and losses**

	Units
Actual output	2,750
Normal loss (10% × 3,300)	330
Abnormal loss (balancing figure)	220
	3,300

Step 2. **Calculate cost per unit of output and losses**

$$\frac{\text{Cost of input}}{\text{Expected units of output}} = \frac{£89,100}{3,300 - 330} = £30 \text{ per unit}$$

Step 3. **Calculate total cost of output and losses**

	£
Cost of output (2,750 × £30)	82,500
Normal loss	0
Abnormal loss (220 × £30)	6,600
	89,100

3 ***Step 1*** ***Determine output and losses***

	Units
Actual loss	70
Normal loss (750 × 10%)	75
Abnormal gain	5

Step 2 **Calculate cost per unit of output and losses**

	£
Cost of input	
Direct materials	5,175
Direct labour	33,750
Production overheads	2,235
	41,160
Less: Normal loss scrap proceeds 75 × 1.60	(120)
	41,040
Expected output 90% × 750	675
Cost per unit £41,040 ÷ 675	£60.80

Step 3 **Calculate total cost of output and losses**

	£
Cost of output (750 – 70) × £60.80	41,344
Normal loss (75 × £1.60)	120
Abnormal gain (5 × £60.80)	(304)
	41,160

Step 4 **Complete account**

PROCESS

	Units	£		Units	£
Direct material	750	5,175	Scrap – normal loss	75	120
Direct labour		33,750	Output	680	41,344
Production overheads		2,235			
Abnormal gain	5	304			
	755	41,464		755	41,464

4 ***Step 1.*** **Determine output and losses**

STATEMENT OF EQUIVALENT UNITS

	Total	*Equivalent units*			
		Material		*Labour*	
	Units	%	Units	%	Units
Completed production	8,000	100	8,000	100	8,000
Closing stock	1,000	80	800	50	500
Normal loss	500				
Abnormal loss (balancing figure)	500	100	500	100	500
	10,000		9,300		9,000

Step 2. **Calculate cost per unit of output, losses and WIP**

STATEMENT OF COST PER EQUIVALENT UNIT

	Cost	*Equivalent units*	*Cost per equivalent unit*
	£		£
Material (£(5,150 – 500))	4,650	9,300	0.50
Labour	2,700	9,000	0.30
	7,350		0.80

Normal loss scrap proceeds = 500 units × £1 per unit
= £500

Step 3. **Calculate total cost of output, losses and WIP**

STATEMENT OF EVALUATION

	Equivalent units	*Cost per equivalent unit*	*Total*	
		£	£	£
Completed production	8,000	0.80		6,400
Closing stock: material	800	0.50	400	
labour	500	0.30	150	
				550
Abnormal loss	500	0.80		400
				7,350

Step 4. **Complete accounts**

PROCESS ACCOUNT

	Units	£		Units	£
Material	10,000	5,150	Completed production	8,000	6,400
Labour		2,700	Closing stock	1,000	550
			Normal loss	500	500
			Abnormal loss	500	400
	10,000	7,850		10,000	7,850

5 It is easier in this example to deal with each process separately.

Process 1

Step 1. **Determine output and losses**

The equivalent units of work done for process 1 this period are as follows.

STATEMENT OF EQUIVALENT UNITS

	Total	*Direct material*		*Conversion costs*	
Output	8,000	8,000	100%	8,000	100%
Normal loss	1,000	-		-	
Abnormal gain	(800)	(800)	100%	(800)	100%
Closing stock	1,800	1,800	100%	720	40%
	10,000	9,000		7,920	

Step 2. **Calculate cost per unit of output, losses and WIP**

	Direct material	*Conversion costs*
	£	£
Costs incurred	24,500	15,500 + 8,260
Less scrap proceeds	(2,000)	= £23,760
	£22,500	
Equivalent units	9,000 units	7,920 units
Cost per equivalent unit	£2.50	£3

Step 3. **Calculate total cost of output, losses and WIP**

	Direct material	*Conversion costs*	*Total*
	£	£	£
Output	20,000	24,000	44,000
Abnormal gain	(2,000)	(2,400)	(4,400)
Closing stock	4,500	2,160	6,660

Process 2

Step 1. **Determine output and losses**

	Total	*Process 1 material*	%	*Material added*	%	*Conversion costs*	%
Output	7,000	7,000	100	7,000	100	7,000	100
Normal loss	400	-		-		-	
Abnormal loss	100	100	100	60	60	30	30
Closing stock	500	500	100	400	80	250	50
	8,000	7,600		7,460		7,280	

Although the question did not say, closing stock must be 100% for process 1 otherwise it would still be in process 1.

Step 2. **Calculate cost per unit of output losses and WIP**

	Process 1	*Material added*	*Conversion costs*
	£	£	£
Costs incurred	44,000	7,460	25,480
Less: Scrap proceeds	(2,200)		
	41,800		
Equivalent units	7,600	7,460	7,280
Cost per equivalent unit	£5.50	£1.00	£3.50

Step 3. **Calculate total cost of output, losses and WIP**

	Process 1	*Material added*	*Conversion costs*	*Total*
	£	£	£	£
Output	38,500	7,000	24,500	70,000
Abnormal loss	550	60	105	715
Closing stock	2,750	400	875	4,025

Step 4. **Complete accounts**

PROCESS 1

	Units	£		Units	£
Direct materials	10,000	24,500	Scrap: normal loss	1,000	2,000
Direct labour		15,500	Output to process 2	8,000	44,000
Production overheads		8,260	Closing stock	1,800	6,660
Abnormal gain	800	4,400			
	10,800	52,660		10,800	52,660

PROCESS 2

	Units	£		Units	£
From process 1	8,000	44,000	Scrap: normal loss	400	2,200
Materials added		7,460	Output to finished goods	7,000	70,000
Direct labour		18,580	Abnormal loss	100	715
Production overheads		6,900	Closing stock	500	4,025
	8,000	76,940		8,000	76,940

Chapter : 8
BUDGETING

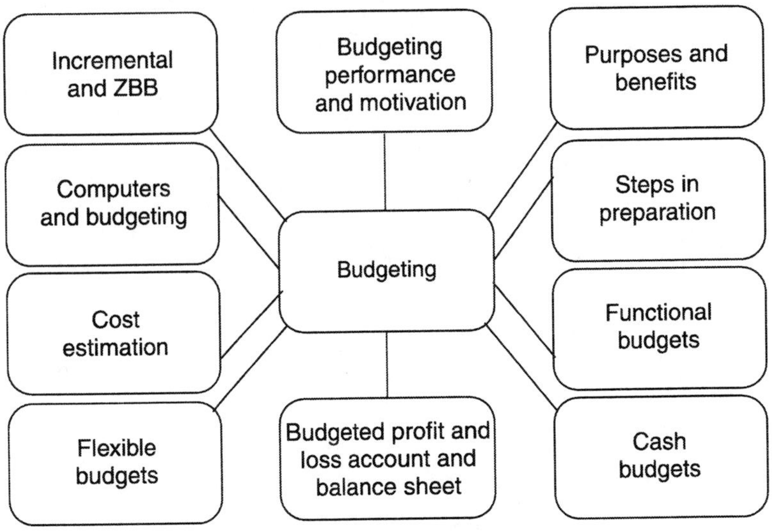

Introduction

The chapter begins by explaining the **reasons** why an organisation might prepare a budget and goes on to detail the **steps in the preparation of a budget**. The method of preparing, and the relationship between the various **functional budgets** is then set out.

The chapter also considers the construction of **cash budgets** and **budgeted profit and loss accounts and balance sheets**, the budgeted profit and loss account and balance sheet making up what is known as a **master budget**. Two different budgeting systems are described: the more traditional **incremental** approach, and a more recent development – **zero-based budgeting (ZBB).** The difference between these two approaches is that the first builds on the previous year's budgets, whereas ZBB begins from scratch each time the budget is prepared.

Finally, we will look at the way in which budgets can affect the **behaviour** and performance of employees, for better and for worse.

Your objectives

In this chapter you will learn about the following.

(a) The purposes and benefits of a budget

(b) Steps in the preparation of a budget

(c) Preparing functional budgets

(d) Cash budgets

(e) Budgeted profit and loss account and balance sheet

(f) Flexible budgets

(g) Cost estimation

(h) Computers and budgeting

(i) Incremental and zero-based budgeting systems

(j) Budgeting, performance and motivation

1 THE PURPOSES AND BENEFITS OF A BUDGET

Definition

A **budget** is 'A quantitative statement, for a defined period of time, which may include planned revenues, expenses, assets, liabilities and cash flows'.

1.1 Purposes and benefits

The main purpose and benefit of using a budget is:

(a) **To ensure the achievement of the organisation's objectives**

The organisation's objectives are quantified and drawn up as targets to be achieved within the timescale of the budget plan.

Using a budget has six further purposes/benefits, all of which contribute to the main purpose, as listed here.

(b) **To compel planning**

Planning **forces management to look ahead**, to set out detailed plans for achieving the targets for each department, operation and (ideally) each manager and to anticipate problems.

(c) **To communicate ideas and plans**

A **formal system** is necessary to ensure that each person affected by the plans is aware of what he or she is supposed to be doing. Communication might be one-way, with managers giving orders to subordinates, or there might be a two-way dialogue.

(d) **Co-ordinate activities**

The activities of different departments need to be **co-ordinated** to ensure maximum integration of effort towards **common goals**. This implies, for example, that the purchasing department should base its budget on production requirements and that the production budget should in turn be based on sales expectations.

(e) **To provide a framework for responsibility accounting**

Budgets require that managers of budget centres are made **responsible** for the achievement of budget targets for the operations under their personal control.

(f) **To establish a system of control**

Control over actual performance is provided by the comparisons of **actual results against the budget** plan. Departures from budget can then be **investigated** and the reasons for the departures can be found and acted upon

(g) **Motivate employees to improve their performance**

The interest and commitment of employees can be retained if there is a system which lets them know how well or badly they are performing. The identification of controllable reasons for departures from budget with managers responsible provides an **incentive for improving future performance**.

The remainder of the chapter explain further how budgets are used to achieve these benefits. We will being by looking at the planning and control aspects of budgeting.

1.2 Budgets in the context of planning and control

The diagram below represents the planning and control cycle. **Planning** involves making choices between alternatives and is primarily a decision-making activity. The **control** process involves measuring and correcting actual performance to ensure that the strategies that are chosen and the plans for implementing them are carried out. The link between these two is the budget.

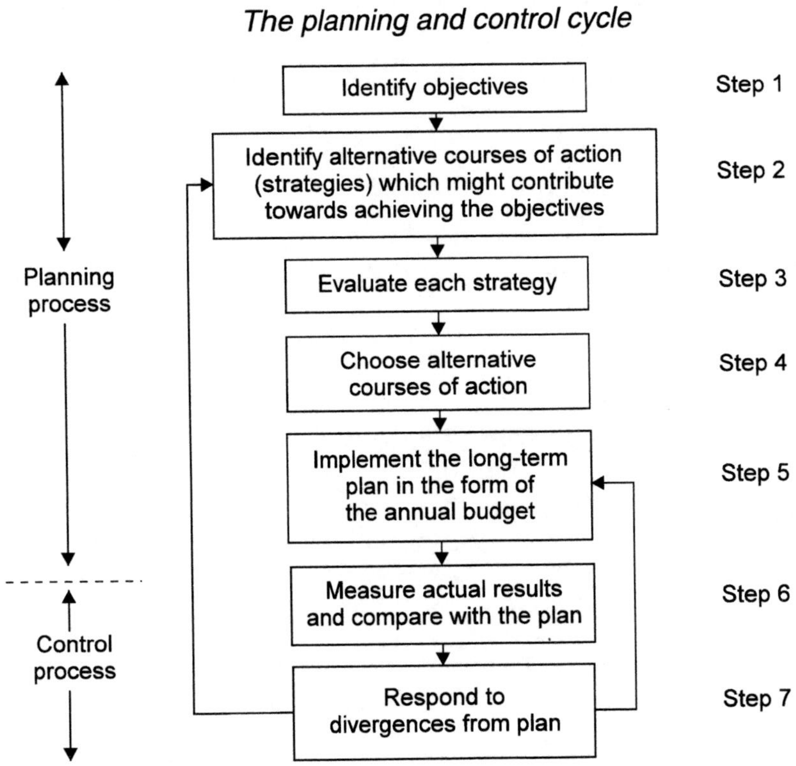
The planning and control cycle
Identify objectives
Step 1
Identify alternative courses of action (strategies) which might contribute towards achieving the objectives
Step 2
Evaluate each strategy
Step 3
Choose alternative courses of action
Step 4
Implement the long-term plan in the form of the annual budget
Step 5
Measure actual results and compare with the plan
Step 6
Respond to divergences from plan
Step 7
Planning process
Control process

Figure 8.1 Planning and control cycle

Step 1. **Identify objectives**

Objectives establish the direction in which the management of the organisation wish it to be heading. Typical objectives include the following.

- To maximise profits
- To increase market share
- To produce a better quality product than anyone else

Objectives answer the question: '**where do we want to be**?'.

Step 2. **Identify potential strategies**

Once an organisation has decided 'where it wants to be', the next step is to identify a range of possible courses of action or **strategies that might enable the organisation to get there.**

The organisation must therefore carry out an **information-gathering exercise** to ensure that it has a full **understanding of where it is now.** This is known as a '**position audit**' or '**strategic analysis**' and involves **looking** both **inwards** and **outwards**.

- The organisation must **gather information from all of its internal parts** to find out what resources it possesses: what its manufacturing capacity and capability is, what is the state of its technical know-how, how well it is able to market itself, how much cash it has in the bank, how much it could borrow and so on.
- It must also **gather information externally** so that it can assess its position in the environment. Just as it has assessed its **own strengths and weaknesses**, it must do likewise for its competitors (**threats**). Its market must be analysed (and any other markets that it is intending to enter) to identify possible new **opportunities**. The 'state of the world' must be considered. Is it in recession or is it booming? What is likely to happen in the future? This process is known as SWOT analysis.

Having carried out a strategic analysis, alternative strategies can be identified.

Step 3. **Evaluate strategies**

The strategies must then be evaluated **in terms of suitability, feasibility and acceptability in the context of the strategic analysis**. Management should select those strategies that have the greatest potential for achieving the organisation's objectives. One strategy may be chosen or several.

Step 4. **Choose alternative courses of action**

The next step in the process is to collect the **chosen strategies** together and **co-ordinate them into a long-term plan**, commonly expressed in financial terms.

Typically a long-term financial plan would show the following.

- Projected cash flows
- Projected long-term profits
- Capital expenditure plans
- Balance sheet forecasts
- A description of the long-term objectives and strategies in words

Step 5. **Implement the long-term plan**

The **long-term plan** should then be **broken down into smaller parts**. It is unlikely that the different parts will fall conveniently into successive time periods. Strategy A may take two and a half years, while Strategy B may take five months, but not start until year three of the plan. It is usual, however, to break down the plan as a whole into equal time periods (usually one year). The resulting **short-term plan** is the **budget**.

Steps 6 and 7. **Measure actual results and compare with plan. Respond to divergences from plan**

At the end of the year actual results should be compared with those expected under the long-term plan. The **long-term plan should be reviewed** in the light of this comparison and the progress that has been made towards achieving the organisation's objectives should be assessed. Management can also **consider the feasibility of achieving the objectives** in the light of unforeseen circumstances which have arisen during the year. If the plans are now **no longer attainable then alternative strategies must be considered** for achieving the organisation's objectives, as indicated by the feedback loop (the arrowed line) linking step 7 to step 2. This aspect of control is carried out by senior management, normally on an annual basis.

The control of **day-to-day operations** is exercised by lower-level managers. At frequent intervals they must be provided with **performance reports** which consist of **detailed comparisons of actual results and budgeted results**. Performance reports provide **feedback information** by comparing planned and actual outcomes. Such reports should highlight those activities that do not conform to plan, so that managers can devote their scarce time to focusing on these items. Effective control requires that **corrective action** is taken so that **actual outcomes conform to planned outcomes**, as indicated by the feedback loop linking steps 5 and 7. Isolating past inefficiencies and the reasons for them will enable managers to take action that will avoid the same inefficiencies being repeated in the future. The system that provides reports that compare actual performance with budget figures is known as **responsibility accounting.** We will return to this topic later in the Unit.

2 STEPS IN THE PREPARATION OF A BUDGET

Towards the end of the planning stage, the budget will be prepared. Whilst we need to concentrate here on the mechanics of budget preparation, it is important to appreciate the co-ordinating role of budgets. You will see how the activities of all aspects of the business are brought together in the budget.

2.1 Budget committee

The **co-ordination** and **administration** of budgets is usually the responsibility of a **budget committee** (with the managing director as chairman). The budget committee is assisted by a **budget officer** who is usually an accountant. Every part of the organisation should be represented on the committee, so there should be a representative from sales, production, marketing and so on. Functions of the budget committee include the following.

- **Co-ordination and allocation of responsibility** for the preparation of budgets
- Issuing of the **budget manual**
- **Timetabling**
- **Provision of information** to assist in the preparation of budgets
- **Communication** of final budgets to the appropriate managers
- **Monitoring** the budgeting and planning process by **comparing actual and budgeted results**

2.2 Responsibility for budgets

The responsibility for preparing the budgets should, ideally, lie with the managers who are responsible for implementing them. For example, the preparation of particular budgets might be allocated as follows.

- The sales manager should draft the sales budget and the selling overhead cost centre budgets.
- The purchasing manager should draft the material purchases budget.
- The production manager should draft the direct production cost budgets.

Activity 1 **(5 minutes)**

Which one of the following is the budget committee *not* responsible for?

A Preparing functional budgets
B Timetabling the budgeting operation
C Allocating responsibility for the budget preparation
D Monitoring the budgeting process

2.3 The budget manual

Definition

The **budget manual** is a collection of instructions governing the responsibilities of persons and the procedures, forms and records relating to the preparation and use of budgetary data.

A budget manual may contain the following.

(a) An explanation of the **objectives** of the budgetary process including the following.

- The purpose of budgetary planning and control
- The objectives of the various stages of the budgetary process

- The importance of budgets in the long-term planning and administration of the enterprise

(b) **Organisational structures**, including the following

- An organisation chart
- A list of individuals holding budget responsibilities

(c) An outline of the **principal budgets** and the **relationship between them**

(d) **Administrative details of budget preparation** such as the following

- Membership, and terms of reference of the budget committee
- The sequence in which budgets are to be prepared
- A timetable

(e) **Procedural matters** such as the following

- Specimen forms and instructions for their completion
- Specimen reports
- Account codes (or a chart of accounts)
- The name of the budget officer to whom enquiries must be sent

2.4 Steps in budget preparation

The procedures for preparing a budget will differ from organisation to organisation but the steps described below will be indicative of the steps followed by many organisations. The preparation of a budget may take weeks or months and the **budget committee** may meet several times before the **master budget** (budgeted profit and loss account and budgeted balance sheet) is finally agreed. **Functional budgets** (sales budgets, production budgets, direct labour budgets and so on), which are amalgamated into the master budget, may need to be amended many times over as a consequence of discussions between departments, changes in market conditions and so on during the course of budget preparation.

2.5 Identifying the principal budget factor

Definition

> The **principal budget factor** is the factor which limits the activities of an organisation.

The first task in the budgetary process is to identify the principal budget factor. This is also known as the key budget factor or limiting budget factor.

The **principal budget factor** is usually **sales demand**: a company is usually restricted from making and selling more of its products because there would be no sales demand for the increased output at a price which would be acceptable/profitable to the company. The principal budget factor may also be machine capacity, distribution and selling resources, the availability of key raw materials or the availability of cash. Once this factor is defined then the remainder of the budgets can be prepared. For example, if sales are the principal budget factor then the production manager can only prepare his budget after the sales budget is complete.

NOTES

Once the principal budget factor has been identified, the stages involved in the preparation of a budget can be summarised as follows (assuming that sales are the principal budget factor).

(a) The **sales budget** is prepared in units of product and sales value. The **finished goods stock budget** can be prepared at the same time. This budget decides the planned increase or decrease in finished goods stock levels.

(b) With the information from the sales and stock budgets, the **production budget** can be prepared. This is, in effect, the sales budget in units plus (or minus) the increase (or decrease) in finished goods stock. The production budget will be stated in terms of units.

(c) This leads on logically to budgeting the **resources for production**. This involves preparing a **materials usage budget, machine usage budget and a labour budget**.

(d) In addition to the materials usage budget, a **materials stock budget** will be prepared, to decide the planned increase or decrease in the level of stocks held. Once the raw materials usage requirements and the raw materials stock budget are known, the purchasing department can prepare a **raw materials purchases budget** in quantities and value for each type of material purchased.

(e) During the preparation of the sales and production budgets, the managers of the cost centres of the organisation will prepare their draft budgets for the department **overhead costs**. Such overheads will include maintenance, stores, administration, selling and research and development.

(f) From the above information a **budgeted profit and loss account** can be produced.

(g) In addition several other budgets must be prepared in order to arrive at the **budgeted balance sheet**. These are the **capital expenditure budget** (for fixed assets), the **working capital budget** (for budgeted increases or decreases in the level of debtors and creditors as well as stocks), and a **cash budget**.

Activity 2 **(20 mins)**

The data for the output of Tango is as follows:

Material per unit	6 kg
Labour per unit	1 hr
Maximum demand	2,150 units
Stock of finished goods:	
Opening	200
Closing	50

Maximum availability of materials is 14,000 kg and of labour is 1500 hours.

Required

Prepare sales, production, materials usage and labour budgets

3 PREPARING FUNCTIONAL BUDGETS

Having seen the theory of budget preparation, let us look at **functional** (or **departmental**) budget preparation.

WORKED EXAMPLE: PREPARING A MATERIALS PURCHASES BUDGET

ECO Ltd manufactures two products, S and T, which use the same raw materials, D and E. One unit of S uses 3 litres of D and 4 kilograms of E. One unit of T uses 5 litres of D and 2 kilograms of E. A litre of D is expected to cost £3 and a kilogram of E £7.

The sales budget for 20X2 comprises 8,000 units of S and 6,000 units of T; finished goods in stock at 1 January 20X2 are 1,500 units of S and 300 units of T, and the company plans to hold stocks of 600 units of each product at 31 December 20X2.

Stocks of raw material are 6,000 litres of D and 2,800 kilograms of E at 1 January and the company plans to hold 5,000 litres and 3,500 kilograms respectively at 31 December 20X2.

The warehouse and stores managers have suggested that a provision should be made for damages and deterioration of items held in store, as follows.

Product S :	loss of 50 units
Product T :	loss of 100 units
Material D :	loss of 500 litres
Material E :	loss of 200 kilograms

Task

Prepare a material purchases budget for the year 20X2.

ANSWER

To calculate material purchases requirements it is first necessary to calculate the material usage requirements. That in turn depends on calculating the budgeted production volumes.

	Product S	*Product T*
	Units	Units
Production required		
To meet sales demand	8,000	6,000
To provide for stock loss	50	100
For closing stock	600	600
	8,650	6,700
Less stock already in hand	1,500	300
Budgeted production volume	7,150	6,400

	Material D	*Material E*
	Litres	Kgs
Usage requirements		
To produce 7,150 units of S	21,450	28,600
To produce 6,400 units of T	32,000	12,800
To provide for stock loss	500	200
For closing stock	5,000	3,500
	58,950	45,100
Less stock already in hand	6,000	2,800

NOTES

Budgeted material purchases	52,950	42,300
Unit cost	£3	£7
Cost of material purchases	£158,850	£296,100
Total cost of material purchases	£454,950	

The basics of the preparation of each functional budget are similar to those above.

4 CASH BUDGETS

Definition

A **cash budget** is a statement in which estimated **future cash receipts and payments** are tabulated in such a way as to show the forecast cash balance of a business at defined intervals.

EXAMPLE

For example, in December 20X2 an accounts department might wish to estimate the cash position of the business during the three following months, January to March 20X3. A cash budget might be drawn up in the following format.

	Jan	*Feb*	*Mar*
	£	£	£
Estimated cash receipts			
From credit customers	14,000	16,500	17,000
From cash sales	3,000	4,000	4,500
Proceeds on disposal of fixed assets		2,200	
Total cash receipts	17,000	22,700	21,500
Estimated cash payments			
To suppliers of goods	8,000	7,800	10,500
To employees (wages)	3,000	3,500	3,500
Purchase of fixed assets		16,000	
Rent and rates			1,000
Other overheads	1,200	1,200	1,200
Repayment of loan	2,500		
	14,700	28,500	16,200
Net surplus/(deficit) for month	2,300	(5,800)	5,300
Opening cash balance	1,200	3,500	(2,300)
Closing cash balance	3,500	(2,300)	3,000

In the example above (where the figures are purely for illustration) the accounts department has calculated that the cash balance at the beginning of the budget period, 1 January, will be £1,200. Estimates have been made of the cash which is likely to be received by the business (from cash and credit sales, and from a planned disposal of fixed assets in February). Similar estimates have been made of cash due to be paid out by the business (payments to suppliers and employees, payments for rent, rates and other overheads, payment for a planned purchase of fixed assets in February and a loan repayment due in January).

From these estimates it is a simple step to calculate the excess of cash receipts over cash payments in each month. In some months cash payments may exceed cash receipts and there will be a **deficit** for the month; this occurs during February in the above example because of the large investment in fixed assets in that month.

The last part of the cash budget above shows how the business's estimated cash balance can then be rolled along from month to month. Starting with the opening balance of £1,200 at 1 January a cash surplus of £2,300 is generated in January. This leads to a closing January balance of £3,500 which becomes the opening balance for February. The deficit of £5,800 in February throws the business's cash position into **overdraft** and the overdrawn balance of £2,300 becomes the opening balance for March. Finally, the healthy cash surplus of £5,300 in March leaves the business with a favourable cash position of £3,000 at the end of the budget period.

4.1 The usefulness of cash budgets

The cash budget is one of the most important planning tools that an organisation can use. It shows the **cash effect of all plans made within the budgetary process** and hence its preparation can lead to a **modification of budgets** if it shows that there are insufficient cash resources to finance the planned operations.

It can also give management an indication of **potential problems** that could arise and allows them the opportunity to take action to avoid such problems. A cash budget can show **four positions**. Management will need to take appropriate action depending on the potential position. This is part of the process of the management of working capital.

Cash position	Appropriate management action
Short-term surplus	• Pay creditors early to obtain discount • Attempt to increase sales by increasing debtors and stocks • Make short-term investments
Short-term deficit	• Increase creditors • Reduce debtors • Arrange an overdraft
Long-term surplus	• Make long-term investments • Expand • Diversify • Replace/update fixed assets
Long-term deficit	• Raise long-term finance (such as via issue of share capital) • Consider shutdown/disinvestments opportunities

WORKED EXAMPLE: CASH BUDGET

Peter Blair has worked for some years as a sales representative, but has recently been made redundant. He intends to start up in business on his own account, using £15,000 which he currently has invested with a building society. Peter maintains a bank account showing a small credit balance, and he plans to approach his bank for the necessary additional finance. Peter asks you for advice and provides the following additional information.

(a) Arrangements have been made to purchase fixed assets costing £8,000. These will be paid for at the end of September 20X3 and are expected to have a five-year life, at the end of which they will possess a nil residual value.

(b) Stocks costing £5,000 will be acquired on 28 September and subsequent monthly purchases will be at a level sufficient to replace forecast sales for the month.

(c) Forecast monthly sales are £3,000 for October, £6,000 for November and December, and £10,500 from January 20X4 onwards.

(d) Selling price is fixed at the cost of stock plus 50%.

(e) Two months' credit will be allowed to customers but only one month's credit will be received from suppliers of stock.

(f) Running expenses, including rent but excluding depreciation of fixed assets, are estimated at £1,600 per month.

(g) Peter intends to make monthly cash drawings of £1,000.

Required

Prepare a cash budget for the six months to 31 March 20X4.

ANSWER

The opening cash balance at 1 October will consist of Peter's initial £15,000 less the £8,000 expended on fixed assets purchased in September. In other words, the opening balance is £7,000. Cash receipts from credit customers arise two months after the relevant sales.

Payments to suppliers are a little more tricky. We are told that cost of sales is 100/150 × sales. Thus for October cost of sales is 100/150 × £3,000 = £2,000. These goods will be purchased in October but not paid for until November. Similar calculations can be made for later months. The initial stock of £5,000 is purchased in September and consequently paid for in October.

Depreciation is not a cash flow and so is *not* included in a cash budget.

The cash budget can now be constructed.

CASH BUDGET FOR THE SIX MONTHS ENDING 31 MARCH 20X4

	Oct	*Nov*	*Dec*	*Jan*	*Feb*	*Mar*
	£	£	£	£	£	£
Payments						
Suppliers	5,000	2,000	4,000	4,000	7,000	7,000
Running expenses	1,600	1,600	1,600	1,600	1,600	1,600

NOTES

Drawings	1,000	1,000	1,000	1,000	1,000	1,000
	7,600	4,600	6,600	6,600	9,600	9,600
Receipts						
Debtors	-	-	3,000	6,000	6,000	10,500
Surplus/(shortfall)	(7,600)	(4,600)	(3,600)	(600)	(3,600)	900
Opening balance	7,000	(600)	(5,200)	(8,800)	(9,400)	(13,000)
Closing balance	(600)	(5,200)	(8,800)	(9,400)	(13,000)	(12,100)

Activity 3 **(30 minutes)**

You are presented with the budgeted data shown in Annex A for the period November 20X4 to June 20X5 for your firm. It has been extracted from the other functional budgets that have been prepared.

You are also told the following.

(a) Sales are 40% cash, 60% credit. Credit sales are paid two months after the month of sale.

(b) Purchases are paid the month following purchase.

(c) 75% of wages are paid in the current month and 25% the following month.

(d) Overheads are paid the month after they are incurred.

(e) Dividends are paid three months after they are declared.

(f) Capital expenditure is paid two months after it is incurred.

(g) The opening cash balance is £15,000.

The managing director is pleased with these figures as they show sales will have increased by more than 100% in the period under review. In order to achieve this he has arranged a bank overdraft with a ceiling of £50,000 to accommodate the increased stock levels and wage bill for overtime worked.

Annex A

	Nov X4	*Dec X4*	*Jan X5*	*Feb X5*	*Mar X5*	*Apr X5*	*May X5*	*June X5*
	£	£	£	£	£	£	£	£
Sales	80,000	100,000	110,000	130,000	140,000	150,000	160,000	180,000
Purchases	40,000	60,000	80,000	90,000	110,000	130,000	140,000	150,000
Wages	10,000	12,000	16,000	20,000	24,000	28,000	32,000	36,000
Overheads	10,000	10,000	15,000	15,000	15,000	20,000	20,000	20,000
Dividends		20,000						
Capital expenditure			30,000			40,000		

Required

(a) Prepare a cash budget for the 6 month period January to June 20X5.

(b) Comment upon your results in the light of your managing director's comments and offer advice.

4.2 Other working capital budgets

It may also be useful for a business monitoring its cash situation to look at other components of working capital: stock, debtors and creditors. Stock usually gets detailed consideration when the functional budgets are prepared. Debtors budgets and creditors budgets are very straightforward when patterns of payment to creditors and from debtors are considered for the purpose of preparing the cash budget.

Activity 4 **(15 minutes)**

Using the information in Activity 2 above, calculate the debtors and creditors budgets for January to June 20X5.

5 BUDGETED PROFIT AND LOSS ACCOUNT AND BALANCE SHEET

As well as wishing to forecast its cash position, a business might want to estimate its profitability and its financial position for a coming period. This would involve the preparation of a budgeted profit and loss account and balance sheet, both of which form the **master budget**.

WORKED EXAMPLE: PREPARING A BUDGETED PROFIT AND LOSS ACCOUNT AND BALANCE SHEET

Using the information in the example above involving Peter you are required to prepare Peter Blair's budgeted profit and loss account for the six months ending on 31 March 20X4 and a budgeted balance sheet as at that date.

ANSWER

The profit and loss account is straightforward. The first figure is sales, which can be computed very easily from the information in Paragraph 4.1(c). It is sufficient to add up the monthly sales figures given there; for the profit and loss account there is no need to worry about any closing debtor. Similarly, cost of sales is calculated directly from the information on gross margin contained in the previous example.

FORECAST TRADING AND PROFIT AND LOSS ACCOUNT
FOR THE SIX MONTHS ENDING 31 MARCH 20X4

	£	£
Sales (3,000 + (2 × 6,000) + (3 × 10,500))		46,500
Cost of sales ($^2/_3$ × £46,500)		31,000
Gross profit		15,500
Expenses		
Running expenses (6 × £1,600)	9,600	
Depreciation (£8,000 × 20% × 6/12)	800	
		10,400
Net profit		5,100

Stock, debtors and creditors' budgets for each period are not needed; we can find the figures for the balance sheet as follows.

(a) Stock will comprise the initial purchases of £5,000.

(b) Debtors will comprise sales made in February and March (not paid until April and May respectively).

(c) Creditors will comprise purchases made in March (not paid for until April).

(d) The bank overdraft is the closing cash figure computed in the cash budget.

FORECAST BALANCE SHEET AT 31 MARCH 20X4

	£	£
Fixed assets £(8,000 – 800)		7,200
Current assets		
Stocks	5,000	
Debtors (2 × £10,500)	21,000	
	26,000	
Current liabilities		
Bank overdraft	12,100	
Trade creditors (March purchases)	7,000	
	19,100	
Net current assets		6,900
		14,100
Proprietor's interest		
Capital introduced		15,000
Profit for the period	5,100	
Less drawings	6,000	
Deficit retained		(900)
		14,100

Budget questions are often accompanied by a large amount of sometimes confusing detail. This should not blind you to the fact that many figures can be entered very simply from the logic of the trading situation described. For example in the case of Peter Blair you might feel tempted to begin a T-account to compute the closing debtors figure. This kind of working is rarely necessary, since you are told that debtors take two months to pay. Closing debtors will equal total credit sales in the last two months of the period.

Similarly, you may be given a simple statement that a business pays rates at £1,500 a year, followed by a lot of detail to enable you to calculate a prepayment at the beginning and end of the year. If you are preparing a budgeted profit and loss account for the year do not lose sight of the fact that the rates expense can be entered as £1,500 without any calculation at all.

6 FLEXIBLE BUDGETS

Definitions

- A **fixed budget** is a budget which is set for a single activity level.
- A **flexible budget** is 'A budget which, by recognising different cost behaviour patterns, is designed to change as volume of activity changes'.

Master budgets are based on planned volumes of production and sales but do not include any provision for the event that actual volumes may differ from the budget. In this sense they may be described as **fixed budgets**.

A **flexible budget** has two advantages.

(a) At the **planning** stage, it may be helpful to know what the effects would be if the actual outcome differs from the prediction. For example, a company may budget to sell 10,000 units of its product, but may prepare flexible budgets based on sales of, say, 8,000 and 12,000 units. This would enable **contingency plans** to be drawn up if necessary.

(b) At the end of each month or year, actual results may be compared with the relevant activity level in the flexible budget as a **control** procedure.

Flexible budgeting uses the principles of marginal costing. In estimating future costs it is often necessary to begin by looking at cost behaviour in the past. For costs which are wholly fixed or wholly variable no problem arises. But you may be presented with a cost which appears to have behaved in the past as a semi-variable cost (partly fixed and partly variable). A technique for estimating the level of the cost for the future is called the high/low method. We looked at this technique in Chapter 1: attempt the following question to ensure that you can remember what to do.

Activity 5 **(15 minutes)**

The cost of factory power has behaved as follows in past years.

	Units of output produced	*Cost of factory power* £
20X1	7,900	38,700
20X2	7,700	38,100
20X3	9,800	44,400
20X4	9,100	42,300

Budgeted production for 20X5 is 10,200 units. Estimate the cost of factory power which will be incurred. Ignore inflation.

We can now look at a full example of preparing a flexible budget.

WORKED EXAMPLE: PREPARING A FLEXIBLE BUDGET

(a) Prepare a budget for 20X6 for the direct labour costs and overhead expenses of a production department at the activity levels of 80%, 90% and 100%, using the information listed below.

(i) The direct labour hourly rate is expected to be £7.50.

(ii) 100% activity represents 60,000 direct labour hours.

(iii) Variable costs

Indirect labour	£1.50 per direct labour hour
Consumable supplies	£0.75 per direct labour hour
Canteen and other welfare services	6% of direct and indirect labour costs

(iv) Semi-variable costs are expected to relate to the direct labour hours in the same manner as for the last five years.

Year	Direct labour hours	Semi-variable costs £
20X1	64,000	41,600
20X2	59,000	39,600
20X3	53,000	37,200
20X4	49,000	35,600
20X5	40,000 (estimate)	32,000 (estimate)

(v) Fixed costs

	£
Depreciation	36,000
Maintenance	20,000
Insurance	3,000
Rates	30000
Management salaries	50,000

(vi) Inflation is to be ignored.

(b) Calculate the budget cost allowance (ie expected expenditure) for 20X6 assuming that 57,000 direct labour hours are worked.

ANSWER

(a)

	80% level 48,000 hrs £'000	*90% level 54,000 hrs* £'000	*100% level 60,000 hrs* £'000
Direct labour	360.00	405.00	450.00
Other variable costs			
Indirect labour	72.00	81.00	90.00
Consumable supplies	36.00	40.50	45.00
Canteen etc	25.92	29.16	32.40
Total variable costs (£10.29 per hour)	493.92	555.66	617.40
Semi-variable costs (W)	35.20	37.60	40.00
Fixed costs			
Depreciation	36.00	36.00	36.00
Maintenance	20.00	20.00	20.00
Insurance	8.00	8.00	3.00
Rates	30.00	30.00	30.00
Management salaries	50.00	50.00	50.00
Budgeted costs	673.12	737.26	801.40

Working

Using the high/low method:

	£
Total cost of 64,000 hours	41,600
Total cost of 40,000 hours	32,000
Variable cost of 24,000 hours	9,600
Variable cost per hour (£9,600/24,000)	£0.40

	£
Total cost of 64,000 hours	41,600
Variable cost of 64,000 hours (× £0.40)	25,600
Fixed costs	16,000

Semi-variable costs are calculated as follows.

			£
60,000 hours	(60,000 × £0.40) + £16,000	=	40,000
54,000 hours	(54,000 × £0.40) + £16,000	=	37,600
48,000 hours	(48,000 × £0.40) + £16,000	=	35,200

(b) The budget cost allowance for 57,000 direct labour hours of work would be as follows.

		£
Variable costs	(57,000 × £10.29)	586,530
Semi-variable costs	(£16,000 + (57,000 × £0.40))	38,800
Fixed costs		144,000
		769,330

6.1 Budgetary control

This is the practice of establishing budgets which identify areas of responsibility for individual managers (for example production managers, purchasing managers and so on) and of regularly comparing actual results against expected results. The most important method of budgetary control, for the purpose of your examination, is **variance analysis**, which involves the comparison of actual results achieved during a control period (usually a month, or four weeks) with a flexible budget. The differences between actual results and expected results are called **variances** and these are used to provide a guideline for **control action** by individual managers. We will be looking at variances in some detail later in the following chapter.

The wrong approach to budgetary control is to compare actual results against a fixed budget. Consider the following example.

EXAMPLE

Windy Ltd manufactures a single product, the cloud. Budgeted results and actual results for June 20X2 are shown below.

	Budget	*Actual results*	*Variance*
Production and sales of the cloud (units)	2,000	3,000	
	£	£	£
Sales revenue (a)	20,000	30,000	10,000 (F)
Direct materials	6,000	8,500	2,500 (A)
Direct labour	4,000	4,500	500 (A)
Maintenance	1,000	1,400	400 (A)
Depreciation	2,000	2,200	200 (A)
Rent and rates	1,500	1,600	100 (A)
Other costs	3,600	5,000	1,400 (A)
Total costs (b)	18,100	23,200	5,100
Profit (a) – (b)	1,900	6,800	4,900 (F)

(a) In this example, the variances are meaningless for purposes of control. Costs were higher than budget because the volume of output was also higher; variable costs would be expected to increase above the budgeted costs in the fixed budget. There is no information to show whether control action is needed for any aspect of costs or revenue.

(b) For control purposes, it is necessary to know the answers to questions such as the following.

- Were actual costs higher than they should have been to produce and sell 3,000 clouds?
- Was actual revenue satisfactory from the sale of 3,000 clouds?

The correct approach to budgetary control is as follows.

(a) Identify fixed and variable costs.
(b) Produce a flexible budget using marginal costing techniques.

WORKED EXAMPLE

In the previous example of Windy Ltd, let us suppose that we have the following estimates of cost behaviour.

(a) Direct materials, direct labour and maintenance costs are variable.

(b) Rent and rates and depreciation are fixed costs.

(c) Other costs consist of fixed costs of £1,600 plus a variable cost of £1 per unit made and sold.

ANSWER

The budgetary control analysis should be as follows.

	Fixed budget (a)	*Flexible budget (b)*	*Actual results (c)*	*Budget variance (b) - (c)*
Production & sales (units)	2,000	3,000	3,000	
	£	£	£	£
Sales revenue	20,000	30,000	30,000	0
Variable costs				
Direct materials	6,000	9,000	8,500	500 (F)
Direct labour	4,000	6,000	4,500	1,500 (F)
Maintenance	1,000	1,500	1,400	100 (F)
Semi-variable costs				
Other costs	3,600	4,600	5,000	400 (A)
Fixed costs				
Depreciation	2,000	2,000	2,200	200 (A)
Rent and rates	1,500	1,500	1,600	100 (A)
Total costs	18,100	24,600	23,200	1,400 (F)
Profit	1,900	5,400	6,800	1,400 (F)

Note. (F) denotes a **favourable** variance and (A) an **adverse** or unfavourable variance. Adverse variances are sometimes denoted as (U) for 'unfavourable'.

We can analyse the above as follows.

(a) In selling 3,000 units the expected profit should have been, not the fixed budget profit of £1,900, but the flexible budget profit of £5,400. Instead, actual profit was £6,800 ie £1,400 more than we should have expected. The reason for this £1,400 improvement is that, given output and sales of 3,000 units, overall costs were lower than expected (and sales revenue was exactly as expected). For example the direct material cost was £500 lower than expected.

(b) Another reason for the improvement in profit above the fixed budget profit is the sales volume. Windy Ltd sold 3,000 clouds instead of 2,000 clouds, with the following result.

	£	£
Budgeted sales revenue increased by		10,000
Budgeted variable costs increased by:		
direct materials	3,000	
direct labour	2,000	
maintenance	500	
variable element of other costs	1,000	
Budgeted fixed costs are unchanged		6,500
Budgeted profit increased by		3,500

Budgeted profit was therefore increased by £3,500 because sales volumes increased. This is the difference in profit between the fixed budget and the flexible budget (5,400 – 1,900 = 3,500).

(c) A full variance analysis statement would be as follows.

	£	£
Fixed budget profit		1,900
Variances		
Sales volume	3,500 (F)	
Direct materials cost	500 (F)	
Direct labour cost	1,500 (F)	
Maintenance cost	100 (F)	
Other costs	400 (A)	
Depreciation	200 (A)	
Rent and rates	100 (A)	
		4,900 (F)
Actual profit		6,800

If management believes that any of these variances are large enough to justify it, they will investigate the reasons for them to see whether any corrective action is necessary.

Activity 6 **(5 minutes)**

The budgeted variable cost per unit was £2.75. When output was 18,000 units, total expenditure was £98,000 and it was found that fixed overheads were £11,000 over budget whilst variable costs were in line with budget.

What was the amount budgeted for fixed costs?

7 COST ESTIMATION

It should be obvious that the production of a budget calls for the preparation of **cost estimates** and **sales forecasts**. In fact, budgeting could be said to be as much a test of estimating and forecasting skills than anything else. In this section we will consider various cost estimation techniques.

7.1 Cost estimation methods

Cost estimation involves the measurement of **historical costs** to predict **future costs**. Some estimation techniques are more sophisticated than others and are therefore likely to be more reliable but, in practice, the simple techniques are more commonly found and should give estimates that are sufficiently accurate for their purpose. It is these simple techniques which we will be examining here.

7.2 Account-classification method or engineering method

By this method, the manager responsible for estimating costs will go through a list of the individual expenditure items which make up the total costs. Each item will be **classified** as fixed, variable or semi-variable, and values will be assigned to these, probably by reference to the historical cost accounts with an adjustment for estimated cost inflation.

This, in rough terms, is how the direct cost items (materials and labour costs) might be built-up when a budgeted direct cost per unit of output is estimated. It is also commonly used by cost centre managers in budgeting overhead costs and is quick and inexpensive. The technique does, however, depend on the **subjective judgement** of each manager and his skill and realism in estimating costs, and so only an approximate accuracy can be expected from its use.

7.3 High/low method

We met the **high/low method** in Chapter 1 (refer back to this chapter to refresh your memory of how it works). The major drawback to the high/low method is that **only two historical cost records from previous periods are used** in the cost estimation. Unless these two records are a reliable indicator of costs throughout the relevant range of output, which is unlikely, only a 'loose approximation' of fixed and variable costs will be obtained. The advantage of the method is its relative **simplicity**.

7.4 The scattergraph method

You should recall from Chapter 1 that a **graph** can be plotted of the historical costs from previous periods, and from the resulting scatter diagram, a '**line-of-best-fit**' can be drawn by visual estimation.

The advantage of the scattergraph over the high/low method is that a **greater quantity of historical data is used** in the estimation, but its disadvantage is that the cost line is drawn by visual judgement and so is a **subjective approximation**.

8 COMPUTERS AND BUDGETING

The examples we have looked at so far have demonstrated the need for a great number of **numerical manipulations** to produce a budget, be it a cash budget or a master budget. It is highly unlikely that the execution of the steps in the process will be problem free. Functional budgets will be out of balance with each other and will require modification so that they are **compatible**. The revision of one budget may well lead to the revision of all of the budgets. The manual preparation of a master budget and a cash budget in the real world would therefore be daunting to say the very least.

8.1 Advantages of computers

Computers, however, can take the hard work out of budgeting: a computerised system will have four basic advantages over a manual system.

- A computer has the ability to process a **larger volume of data**.
- A computerised system can **process data more rapidly** than a manual system.
- Computerised systems tend to be **more accurate** than manual systems.
- Computers have the ability to **store large volumes of data** in a readily accessible form.

Such advantages make computers ideal for taking over the manipulation of numbers, leaving staff to get involved in the real planning process.

8.2 Methods

Budgeting is usually computerised using either a computer program written specifically for the organisation or by a commercial spreadsheet package.

Both methods of computerisation of the budgeting process will involve a **mathematical model** which represents the real world in terms of financial values. The model will consist of several, or many, **interrelated variables**, a variable being an item in the model which has a value. For example a cash budgeting model would include variables for sales, credit periods, purchases, wages and salaries and so on.

Once the planning model has been constructed, the same model can be used again and again, simply by changing the values of the variables to produce new results for cash inflows, cash outflows, net cash flows and cash/bank balance.

A major advantage of **budget models** is the ability to evaluate different options and carry out '**what if' analysis**. By changing the value of certain variables (for example altering the ratio of cash sales to credit sales, increasing the amount of bad debts or capital expenditure, increasing the annual pay award to the workforce and so on) management are able to assess the effect of potential changes in their environment.

Computerised models can also incorporate **actual results**, period by period, and carry out the necessary calculations to produce **budgetary control reports**.

The use of a model also allows the **budget for the remainder of the year to be adjusted** once it is clear that the circumstances on which the budget was originally based have changed.

8.3 Spreadsheets

Most organisations do not have budgeting programs written for them but use standard spreadsheet packages.

Definition

'Spreadsheet' has been defined as 'the term commonly used to describe many of the modelling packages available for microcomputers, being loosely derived from the likeness to a "spreadsheet of paper" divided into rows and columns'.

The idea behind a spreadsheet is that the model builder should construct a model in rows and columns format.

(a) Variables are represented by a row or column of items, or even by just one 'cell' in the spreadsheet.

(b) Numerical values for the **variables** are derived as follows.

(i) They can be inserted into the model via **keyboard input**.

(ii) They can be calculated from other data in the model using **formulae** specified within the construction of the model itself. In other words formulae can be included in the cells of the spreadsheet and referenced to other cells containing numerical information.

(iii) They can be obtained from data held on **disk file** - in another spreadsheet, for example.

(c) **Text** can also be entered and manipulated to some extent.

The more sophisticated modern packages can handle information in **'3D' format** (a 'pad' of paper, as it were, rather than a single sheet) and can present results as charts or graphs.

To assess the **use of spreadsheets in budgeting** let us consider a cash budget. A cash budget needs frequent updating to reflect current and forecast conditions, changes in credit behaviour and so on. Each period (week, month or whatever) up-to-date information is input and in combination with brought forward file data, the cash budget will be automatically projected forward by the spreadsheet program. Surpluses and deficiencies may well be highlighted.

Both abbreviated and detailed versions of the cash budget may be produced along with graphical representations of the same information.

	A	B	C	D	E	F	G	H
2			Summary Cash Budget (Ref. Details Budgets A-L)					
3								
4			*Jan*	*Feb*	*Mar*	*Apr*	*May*	*June*
5			£'000	£'000	£'000	£'000	£'000	£'000
6	Opening balance		15	22	20	-36	-50	-83
7	add							
8	Total receipts		92	112	122	138	148	162
9	less							
10	Total payments		-85	-114	-178	-152	-181	-235
11	equals							
12	Closing balance		22	20	-36	-50	-83	-156
13								
14	Current overdraft limit		40	40	40	40	60	120
15								
16	Warning indicator					*	*	*
17						*	*	*
18							*	*
19								*

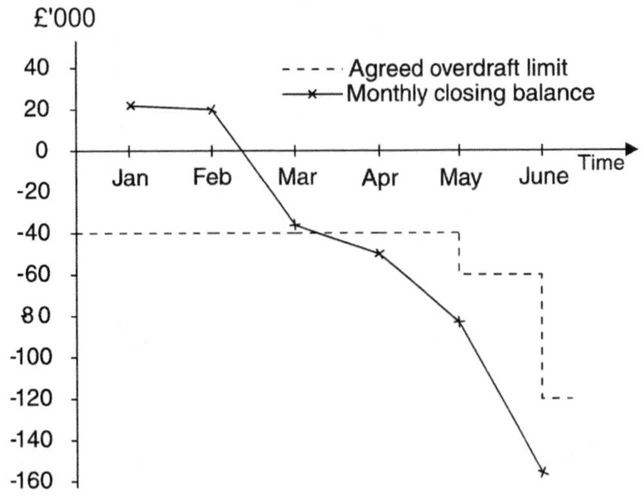

Figure 8.2 Examples of spreadsheets

Perhaps the greatest benefit that can be obtained from a spreadsheet package is its facility to perform '**what if' calculations** at great speed. For example, the consequences throughout the organisation of sales growth per month of nil, $^1/_2$%, 1%, $1^1/_2$% and so on can be calculated at the touch of a button.

9 INCREMENTAL AND ZERO BASED BUDGETING SYSTEMS

9.1 Incremental budgeting

The traditional approach to budgeting is to base next year's budget on the current year's results plus an extra amount for estimated growth or inflation next year. This approach is known as incremental budgeting since it is concerned mainly with the increments in costs and revenues which will occur in the coming period.

Incremental budgeting is a reasonable procedure if current operations are as effective, efficient and economical as they can be, and the organisation and the environment are largely unchanged.

In general, however, it is an **inefficient form of budgeting** as it **encourages slack** and **wasteful spending** to creep into budgets: managers will spend to budget, even if the amount added for inflation proved not to be necessary, so that the level of next year's budget is maintained. The result is that past inefficiencies are perpetuated because cost levels are rarely subjected to close scrutiny.

To ensure that inefficiencies are not concealed, alternative approaches to budgeting have been developed. One such approach is **zero based budgeting (ZBB)**, the use of which was pioneered by P Pyhrr in the United States in the early 1970s.

9.2 The principles of zero based budgeting

ZBB rejects the assumption inherent in incremental budgeting that next year's budget can be based on this year's costs. Every aspect of the budget is examined in terms of its cost and the benefits it provides and the selection of better alternatives is encouraged.

Definition

Zero based budgeting involves preparing a budget for each cost centre from a zero base. Every item of expenditure has then to be justified in its entirety in order to be included in the next year's budget.

9.3 Implementing zero based budgeting

The implementation of ZBB involves a number of steps but of greater importance is the **development of a questioning attitude** by all those involved in the budgetary process. Existing practices and expenditures must be challenged and searching questions, such as the following must be asked.

- Does the activity need to be carried out?
- What would be the consequences if the activity was not carried out?
- Does the activity benefit the organisation?
- Is the current level of provision current?
- Are there alternative ways of providing the function?
- How much should the activity cost?
- Is the expenditure worth the benefits achieved?

The basic approach of ZBB has three steps.

Step 1. **Define decision packages**

A **decision package** is a comprehensive **description of a specific organisational activity which management can use to evaluate the activity and rank it in order of priority against other activities.** Managers prepare decision packages for the activities within the budget centre for which they have responsibility.

There are two types of decision package.

- **Mutually exclusive packages** contain **alternative methods of getting the same job done**. The best option among the packages must be selected by comparing costs and benefits and the other packages are then discarded. For example, an organisation might consider two alternative decision packages for the preparation of the payroll: Package 1 might be in-house preparation of the payroll whereas Package 2 could involve the use of an outside agency.
- **Incremental packages divide one aspect of an activity into different levels of effort**. The 'base' package will describe the minimum amount of work that must be done to carry out the activity and the other packages describe what additional work could be done, at what cost and for what benefits.

NOTES

EXAMPLE

Suppose that a cost centre manager is preparing a budget for maintenance costs. He might first consider two mutually exclusive packages. Package A might be to keep a maintenance team of two men per shift for two shifts each day at a cost of £60,000 per annum, whereas package B might be to obtain a maintenance service from an outside contractor at a cost of £50,000. A cost-benefit analysis will be conducted because the quicker repairs obtainable from an in-house maintenance service might justify its extra cost.

If we now suppose that package A is preferred, the budget analysis must be completed by describing the incremental variations in this chosen alternative.

(a) The 'base' package would describe the minimum requirement for the maintenance work. This might be to pay for one man per shift for two shifts each day at a cost of £30,000.

(b) Incremental package 1 might be to pay for two men on the early shift and one man on the late shift, at a cost of £45,000. The extra cost of £15,000 would need to be justified, for example by savings in lost production time, or by more efficient machinery.

(c) Incremental package 2 might be the original preference, for two men on each shift at a cost of £60,000. The cost-benefit analysis would compare its advantages, if any, over incremental package 1.

(d) Incremental package 3 might be for three men on the early shift and two on the late shift, at a cost of £75,000; and so on.

Step 2. **Evaluate and rank packages**

Each activity (decision package) is evaluated and ranked on the basis of its benefit to the organisation.

The ranking process provides managers with a technique to **allocate scarce resources** between different activities. Minimum work requirements (those that are essential to get a job done) will be given high priority and so too will work which meets legal obligations. In the accounting department these would be minimum requirements to operate the payroll, purchase ledger and sales ledger systems, and to maintain and publish a set of accounts which satisfies the external auditors.

The **ranking process can be lengthy** because large numbers of different packages will have been prepared by managers throughout the organisation. In large organisations the number of packages might be so huge that senior management cannot do the ranking unaided. In such circumstances, the following occurs.

(a) Cost centre managers will be asked to rank the packages for their own cost centre.

(b) The manager at the next level up the hierarchy of seniority will consolidate the rankings of his or her subordinates into a single ranking list for the group of cost centres, using the rankings of each cost centre as a guide.

(c) These consolidated rankings will be passed in turn one stage further up the management hierarchy for further consolidation. At higher levels of consolidation, the ranking process might be done by a committee of managers rather than by an individual.

Once a consolidated ranking of packages has been prepared, it should be reviewed to make sure that there is a general agreement that the rankings are reasonable and there are no anomalies in them.

Step 3. **Allocate resources**

Resources in the budget are then **allocated** according to the funds available and the evaluation and ranking of the competing packages. Packages involving small expenditures can be dealt with by junior managers but senior managers must make decisions involving larger amounts of expenditure. The ZBB process must, however, run through the entire management structure.

9.4 The advantages of implementing ZBB

- It is possible to identify and **remove inefficient or obsolete operations.**
- Cost reductions are possible.
- It forces employees to **avoid wasteful expenditure**.
- It can **increase motivation**.
- It provides a **budgeting and planning tool** for management which responds to changes in the business environment; 'obsolescent' items of expenditure are identified and dropped.
- The **documentation** required **provides** all management with a coordinated, in-depth **appraisal of an organisation's operations.**
- It **challenges the status quo** and forces an organisation to examine alternative activities and existing expenditure levels.
- In summary, ZBB should result in a **more efficient allocation and utilisation of resources** to an organisation's activities and departments.

9.5 The disadvantages of ZBB

The major disadvantage of zero based budgeting is the **time and energy required**. The assumptions about costs and benefits in each package must be continually updated and new packages developed as soon as new activities emerge. The following problems might also occur.

- **Short-term benefits** might be **emphasised** to the detriment of long-term benefits.
- The **false idea that all decisions have to be made in the budget might be encouraged**. Management must be able to meet unforeseen opportunities and threats at all times, and must not feel restricted from carrying out new ideas simply because they were not approved by a decision package, cost benefit analysis and the ranking process.

- It may be a **call for management skills** both in constructing decision packages and in the ranking process **which the organisation does not possess**. Managers may therefore have to be trained in ZBB techniques so that they can apply them sensibly and properly.
- It may be **difficult to 'sell' ZBB to managers as a useful technique** for the following reasons.
  - Incremental costs and benefits of alternative courses of action are hard to quantify accurately.
  - Employees or trade union representatives may resist management ideas for changing the ways in which work is done.
- The organisation's **information systems may not be capable of providing suitable** incremental cost and incremental benefit **analysis**.
- **The ranking process can be difficult**. Managers face three common problems.
  - A large number of packages may have to be ranked.
  - There is often a conceptual difficulty in having to rank packages which managers regard as being equally vital, for legal or operational reasons.
  - It is difficult to rank completely different types of activity, especially where activities have qualitative rather than quantitative benefits - such as spending on staff welfare and working conditions - where ranking must usually be entirely subjective.

In summary, perhaps the **most serious drawback to ZBB is that it requires a lot of management time and paperwork**. One way of obtaining the benefits of ZBB but of overcoming the drawbacks is to apply it selectively on a rolling basis throughout the organisation. This year finance, next year marketing, the year after personnel and so on. In this way all activities will be thoroughly scrutinised over a period of time.

9.6 Using zero based budgeting

ZBB can be used by both **profit-making** and **non-profit-making** organisations. It is popular in the US and Canada but its adoption has been slow in the UK.

The procedures of zero base budgeting do not lend themselves easily to direct manufacturing costs where standard costing, work study and the techniques of management planning and control have long been established as a means of budgeting expenditure.

ZBB is best applied to expenditure incurred in **departments that support** the essential production function. These include marketing, finance, quality control, repairs and maintenance, production planning, research and development, engineering design, personnel, data processing, sales and distribution. In many organisations, these expenses make up a large proportion of the total expenditure. These activities are less easily quantifiable by conventional methods and are **more discretionary** in nature.

ZBB can also be successfully applied to **service industries** and **non-profit-making organisations** such as local and central government departments, educational establishments, hospitals and so on.

ZBB can be applied in any organisation where alternative levels of provision for each activity are possible and where the costs and benefits are separately identifiable.

Some particular uses of ZBB are:

(a) **Budgeting for discretionary cost items**, such as advertising, R & D and training costs. The priorities for spending money could be established by ranking activities and alternative levels of spending or service can be evaluated on an incremental basis. For example, is it worth spending £2,000 more to increase the numbers trained on one type of training course by 10%? If so, what priority should this incremental spending on training be given, when compared with other potential training activities?

(b) **Rationalisation measures.** 'Rationalisation' means cutting back on production and activity levels, and cutting costs. ZBB can be used to make rationalisation decisions when an organisation is forced to make spending cuts. (This use of ZBB might explain any unpopularity it might have among managers.)

10 BUDGETING, PERFORMANCE AND MOTIVATION

In this chapter we have concentrated on the importance of the budgeting process for planning and control by management. A further aspect of the budgeting process is the human behavioural aspect, the effect that the budgeting process and resulting budgets has on the performance of managers and employees alike.

10.1 Budgets and motivation

Much has been written about the motivational effect of the budgeting process on managers in a business and there are many conflicting views. However it is well recognised that the budgetary process has the potential to be a powerful motivating tool, but conversely can also quite easily have a de-motivating effect on managers.

The effect of the eventual budgets on the motivation of managers will largely be due to the level of difficulty of the targets set by the budget, and the manner in which the budgets are set – are these imposed budgets or have the managers taken part in the budgeting process?

10.2 Budgets and standards as targets

Once decided, budgets become targets. But **how difficult** should the targets be? And how might people react to targets which are easy to achieve, or difficult to achieve?

The **quantity of material and labour time included in the budget** will **depend on the level of performance** required by management. Four types of performance standard might be set.

Ideal standards are based on **perfect operating conditions**: no wastage, no spoilage, no inefficiencies, no idle time, no breakdowns. Employees will often feel that the goals are unattainable, become demotivated and not work so hard.

Attainable standards are based on the hope that a standard amount of work will be carried out efficiently, machines properly operated or materials properly used. **Some**

allowance is made for wastage and inefficiencies. If well-set they provide a useful psychological incentive by giving employees a realistic, but challenging target of efficiency.

Current standards are based on **current working conditions** (current wastage, current inefficiencies). They do not attempt to improve on current levels of efficiency.

Basic standards are kept unaltered over a long period of time, and may be out of date. They are used to show change in efficiency or performance over a long period of time. They are perhaps the least useful and least common type of standard in use.

The impact on employee behaviour of budgets based on these different standards is summarised in the table below.

Type of standard	Impact
Ideal standards:	Some say that they provide employees with an incentive to be more efficient even though it is highly unlikely that the standard will be achieved. Others argue that they are likely to have an unfavourable effect on employee motivation because the differences between standards and actual results will always be adverse. The employees may feel that the goals are unattainable and so they will not work so hard.
Attainable standards:	Might be an incentive to work harder as they provide a realistic but challenging target of efficiency.
Current standards:	Will not motivate employees to do anything more than they are currently doing.
Basic standards:	May have an unfavourable impact on the motivation of employees. Over time they will discover that they are easily able to achieve the standards. They may become bored and lose interest in what they are doing if they have nothing to aim for.

Similar comments apply to budgets.

Budgets and standards are **more likely to motivate** employees if employees accept that the budget or standard is **achievable.** If it can be achieved too easily, it will not provide sufficient motivation. If it is too difficult, employees will not accept it because they will believe it to be unachievable. In extreme circumstances, if employees believe a budget is impossible to achieve, they might be so demotivated that they attempt to prove that the budget is wrong. This is obviously the completely opposite effect to that intended.

The various **research** projects into the behavioural effects of budgeting have given **conflicting views** on certain points. However, there appears to be **general agreement** that a **target must fulfil certain conditions** if it is to motivate employees to work towards it.

- It must be **sufficiently difficult** to be a **challenging** target.
- It must **not be so difficult** that it is not achievable.
- It must be **accepted** by the employees as their personal goal.

10.3 Participation

There are basically two ways in which a budget can be set: from the **top down** (**imposed** budget) or from the **bottom up** (**participatory** budget).

10.4 Imposed style of budgeting

In this approach to budgeting, **top management prepare a budget with little or no input from operating personnel.** This budget is then **imposed** upon the employees who have to work to the budgeted figures.

The times when imposed budgets are **effective** are as follows.

- In newly-formed organisations, because of employees' lack of knowledge
- In very small businesses, because the owner/manager has a complete overview of the business
- When operational managers lack budgeting skills
- When the organisation's different units require precise co-ordination
- When budgets need to be set quickly

They are, of course, advantages and disadvantages to this style of setting budgets.

Advantages

- The aims of long-term plans are more likely to be incorporated into short-term plans.
- They improve the co-ordination between the plans and objectives of divisions.
- They use senior management's overall awareness of the organisation.
- There is less likelihood of input from inexperienced or uninformed lower-level employees.
- Budgets can be drawn up in a shorter period of time because a consultation process is not required.

Disadvantages

- Dissatisfaction, defensiveness and low morale amongst employees who have to work to meet the targets. It is hard for people to be motivated to achieve targets set by somebody else. Employees might put in only just enough effort to achieve targets, without trying to beat them.
- The feeling of team spirit may disappear.
- Organisational goals and objectives might not be accepted so readily and/or employees will not be aware of them.
- Employees might see the budget as part of a system of trying to find fault with their work: if they cannot achieve a target that has been imposed on them they will be punished.
- If consideration is not given to local operating and political environments, unachievable budgets for overseas divisions could be produced.

- Lower-level management initiative may be stifled if they are not invited to participate.

10.5 Participative style of budgeting

In this approach to budgeting, **budgets are developed by lower-level managers who then submit the budgets to their superiors**. The budgets are based on the lower-level managers' perceptions of what is achievable and the associated necessary resources.

> **Activity 7** **(10 minutes)**
>
> In what circumstances might participative budgets be effective?

The **advantages** of participative budgets are as follows.

- They are based on information from employees most familiar with the department. Budgets should therefore be more realistic.
- Knowledge spread among several levels of management is pulled together, again producing more realistic budgets.
- Because employees are more aware of organisational goals, they should be more committed to achieving them.
- Co-ordination and cooperation between those involved in budget preparation should improve.
- Senior managers' overview of the business can be combined with operational-level details to produce better budgets.
- Managers should feel that they 'own' the budget and will therefore be more committed to the targets and more motivated to achieve them.
- Participation will broaden the experience of those involved and enable them to develop new skills.

Overall, participation in budget setting should give those involved a more positive attitude towards the organisation, which should lead to better performance.

There are, on the other hand, a number of **disadvantages** of participative budgets.

- They consume more time.
- Any changes made by senior management to the budgets submitted by lower-level management may cause dissatisfaction.
- Budgets may be unachievable if managers are not qualified to participate.
- Managers may not co-ordinate their own plans with those of other departments.
- Managers may include budgetary slack (padding the budget) in their budgets. This means they have over-estimated costs or under-estimated income. Actual results are then more likely to be better than the budgeted target results.
- An earlier start to the budgeting process could be required.

The research projects do not appear to provide definite conclusions about the motivational effects of budgeting. The **attitudes of the individuals** involved have an impact.

- Some managers may complain that they are too busy to spend time on setting standards and budgeting.
- Others may feel that they do not have the necessary skills.
- Some may think that any budget they set will be used against them.

In such circumstances participation could be seen as an **added pressure rather than as an opportunity**. For such employees an imposed approach might be better.

10.6 Negotiated style of budgeting

At the two extremes, budgets can be dictated from above or simply emerge from below but, in practice, different levels of management often agree budgets by a process of negotiation.

- In the imposed budget approach, operational managers will try to negotiate with senior managers the budget targets which they consider to be unreasonable or unrealistic.
- Likewise senior management usually review and revise budgets presented to them under a participative approach through a process of negotiation with lower level managers.
- **Final budgets are therefore most likely to lie between what top management would really like and what junior managers believe is feasible.**

10.7 Creative budgets

In the process of preparing budgets, managers might **deliberately overestimate costs and underestimate sales**, so that they will not be blamed in the future for overspending and poor results.

In controlling actual operations, managers must then **ensure that their spending rises to meet their budget**, otherwise they will be 'blamed' for careless budgeting.

A typical situation is for a manager to **pad the budget** and waste money on non-essential expenses so that he uses all his budget allowances. The reason behind his action is the fear that unless the allowance is fully spent it will be reduced in future periods thus making his job more difficult as the future reduced budgets will not be so easy to attain. Because inefficiency and slack are allowed for in budgets, achieving a budget target means only that costs have remained within the accepted levels of inefficient spending.

Budget bias can **work in the other direction** too. It has been noted that, after a run of mediocre results, some managers **deliberately overstate revenues and understate cost estimates**, no doubt feeling the need to make an immediate favourable impact by promising better performance in the future. They may merely delay problems, however, as the managers may well be censured when they fail to hit these optimistic targets.

10.8 Goal congruence and dysfunctional decision making

Individuals are motivated by personal desires and interests. These desires and interests may tie in with the objectives of the organisation – after all, some people 'live for their jobs'. Other individuals see their job as a chore, and their motivations will have nothing to do with achieving the objectives of the organisation for which they work.

It is therefore important that **some of the desires, interests and goals motivating employees correspond with the goals of the organisation as a whole.** This is known as **goal congruence**. Such a state would exist, for example, if the manager of department A worked to achieve a 10% increase in sales for the department, this 10% increase being part of the organisation's overall plan to increase organisational sales by 20% over the next three years.

On the other hand, **dysfunctional behaviour** can occur if a **manager's goals are not in line with those of the organisation as a whole**. Attempts to enhance his or her own situation or performance (typically '**empire building**' – employing more staff, cutting costs to achieve favourable variances but causing quality problems in other departments) will be at the expense of the best interests of the organisation as a whole. **Participation is not necessarily the answer**. Goal congruence does not necessarily result from allowing managers to develop their own budgets.

A well designed standard costing and budgetary control system can help to ensure goal congruence: continuous feedback prompting appropriate control action should steer the organisation in the right direction. The next chapter goes on to explore how such systems operate.

Activity 8 **(30 minutes)**

Eskafield Industrial Museum opened ten years ago and soon became a market leader with many working exhibits. In the early years there was a rapid growth in the number of visitors but with no further investment in new exhibits, this growth has not been maintained in recent years.

Two years ago, John Derbyshire was appointed as the museum's chief executive. His initial task was to increase the number of visitors to the museum and, following his appointment, he had made several improvements to make the museum more successful.

Another of John's tasks is to provide effective financial management. This year the museum's Board of Management has asked him to take full responsibility for producing the 20X9 budget. He has asked you to prepare estimates of the number of visitors next year.

Shortly after receiving your notes, John Derbyshire contacts you. He explains that he had prepared a draft budget for the Board of Management based on the estimated numbers for 20X9. This had been prepared on the basis that:

- most of the museum's expenses such as salaries and rates are fixed costs;
- the museum has always budgeted for a deficit;
- the 20X9 deficit will be £35,000.

At the meeting with the Board of Management, John was congratulated on bringing the deficit down from £41,000 in 20X7 to £37,000 (latest estimate) in 20X8. However, the Board of Management raised two issues.

They felt that the planned deficit of £35,000 should be reduced to £29,000 as this would represent a greater commitment.

They also queried why the budget had been prepared without any consultation with the museum staff, ie a top down approach.

Task

Draft a memo to John Derbyshire. Your memo should:

(a) discuss the motivational implications of imposing the budget reduction from £35,000 to £29,000;

(b) consider the arguments for and against using a top-down budgeting approach for the museum.

11 BUDGETING AND QUALITY

Many businesses, both manufacturing and service businesses, are wholly concerned with quality. The concept behind quality control is the principle of 'get it right first time'.

11.1 Total Quality Management (TQM)

Total Quality Management (TQM) is a philosophy that means that quality management is the aim of every part of the organisation. The aim is to 'get it right first time' which means that there is a striving for continuous improvement in order to eliminate faulty work and prevent mistakes. It must apply to every part of the business and every activity that the business undertakes, whether it is in making the product, providing the service, selling the product or general administration. Under TQM each person within the business, in every function of the business, has to recognise that he/she has customers. In some cases these are external customers but in many cases these are internal customers, the employees' colleagues and managers.

11.2 Budgeting and TQM

The budgeting process is about setting standards or targets for all aspects and functions of the business to meet. If the budgeting process is successful it can help in this continuous process of improvement by setting targets that eventually eliminate all unnecessary waste and mistakes.

We looked at TQM in more detail earlier in the text.

Chapter roundup

- The purposes of a budget are as follows.

  1 To ensure the achievement of the organisation's objective.
  2 To compel planning
  3 To communicate ideas and plans
  4 To co-ordinate activities
  5 To provide a framework for responsibility accounting
  6 To motivate employees and improve their performance
  7 To establish a system of control

- A budget is a financial or quantitative plan of operations for a forthcoming accounting period.
- The sales budget is usually the first functional budget prepared because sales is usually the principal budget factor. The order of preparation of the remaining budgets could be finished goods stock budget, production budget, budgets for resources of production, materials stock budget, raw materials purchases budget and overhead cost budgets.
- Cash budgets show the expected receipts and payments during a budget period. The usefulness of cash budgets is that they enable management to make any forward planning decisions that may be needed, such as advising their bank of estimated overdraft requirements or strengthening their credit control procedures to ensure that debtors pay more quickly.
- The master budget consists of a budgeted profit and loss account and a budgeted balance sheet.
- Budgeted profit and cash flow for a period are unlikely to be the same.
- Fixed budgets remain unchanged regardless of the level of activity; flexible budgets are designed to flex or change with the level of activity.
- For control purposes, the actual results should be compared with the flexed budget. The differences between the components of the flexed budget and the actual results are budget variances.
- Simple cost estimation techniques include the account classification/ engineering method, the high/low method and the scattergraph method.
- Computers can provide substantial assistance to the budgeting process. 'What if' analysis, budget versus actual comparisons and adjustments to the budget following pertinent changes to the circumstances on which the budget was based are all facilitated.
- Incremental budgeting bases next year's budget on the current year's. Zero-based budgeting prepares each year's budget from a zero base; every item of expenditure has to be justified in its entirety.
- Budgets and standards are most likely to motivate employees if employees accept that the budget/standard is achievable.
- Budgets can be set from the top down (imposed budget) or from the bottom up (participatory budget). You need to be aware of the conditions needed for either one to be the preferred approach.

- Goal congruence occurs when the goals of an individual tie in with the goals of the organisation as a whole. If this is not the case dysfunctional behaviour can occur.

Quick quiz

1 Who, ideally, should prepare budgets?

2 What is the master budget?

3 What is the principal budget factor and why is it important in the budgetary planning process?

4 Why are cash budgets useful?

5 What are the advantages of a flexible budget over a fixed budget?

6 Flexible budgets are normally prepared on a marginal costing basis. True or false?

7 What is the wrong approach to budgetary control?

8 What is the correct approach to budgetary control?

9 Match the descriptions to the budgeting style.

Description

(a) Budget allowances are set without the involvement of the budget holder.

(b) All budget holders are involved in setting their own budgets.

(c) Budget allowances are set on the basis of discussions between budget holders and those to whom they report.

Budgeting style

Negotiated budgeting
Participative budgeting
Imposed budgeting

10 Budgetary slack is necessary to ensure that managers are able to meet their targets. True or false?

NOTES

Answers to Quick quiz

1 The managers responsible for the implementation of the budgets should prepare those budgets.

2 The master budget comprises a budgeted balance sheet and a budgeted profit and loss account.

3 The principal budget factor is the factor which limits the activities of an organisation. It is important as it must be identified and a budget for this factor produced first, as all the other budgets will depend on it.

4 Cash budgets show the cash effects of all the plans, and indicate where potential problems can arise. The organisation can then amend its plans, if necessary, to take advantage of forecast cash surpluses and avoid deficits.

5 It helps at the planning stage to look at the effects of different activity levels and draw up contingency plans, if necessary

At the year end, actual results will be compared with the flexed budget as a control measure

6 True.

7 The wrong approach to budgetary control is to compare actual results to the fixed budget.

8 The correct approach to budgetary control is to compare actual results to the budget flexed to the actual level of activity.

9 (a) Imposed budgeting
(b) Participative budgeting
(c) Negotiated budgeting

10 False. Budgets should be reviewed to ensure that operational managers have not included slack.

Answers to Activities

1 A is correct because it is the manager responsible for implementing the budget that must prepare it, not the budget committee.

2 Identify the principle budget factor.

Maximum demand	2,150
To meet demand	
Opening stock	(200)
Closing stock	50
Demand	2,150
Required production to meet demand	2,000

Materials required = 6 kg × 2,000 = 120,000 kg. As 14,000 kg are available materials are not limiting factor.

Labour required = 1 hr × 2,000 = 2,000 hrs. As only 1,500 hours are available. Labour is the limiting factor.

With only 1,500 hours of labour maximum production = 1,500 units.

Sales can therefore be 1,500 + 200 – 50 = 1,650 units.

Materials usage = production of 1,500 units × 6 kg = 9,000 kg.

Summary:

Sales	= 1,650 units.
Production	= 1,500 units
Materials usage	= 9,000 kg
Labour	= 1,500 hours

3 Cash budget for January to June 20X5

(a)

	January £'000	February £'000	March £'000	April £'000	May £'000	June £'000
Receipts						
Sales revenue						
Cash	44	52	56	60	64	72
Credit	48	60	66	78	84	90
	92	112	122	138	148	162
Payments						
Purchases	60	80	90	110	130	140
Wages						
75%	12	15	18	21	24	27
25%	3	4	5	6	7	8
Overheads	10	15	15	15	20	20
Dividends			20			
Capital expenditure			30			40
	85	114	178	152	181	235
b/f	15	22	20	(36)	(50)	(83)
Net cash flow	7	(2)	(56)	(14)	(33)	(73)
c/f	22	20	(36)	(50)	(83)	(156)

(b) The overdraft arrangements are quite inadequate to service the cash needs of the business over the six month period. If the figures are realistic then action should be taken now to avoid difficulties in the near future. The following are possible courses of action.

- Activities could be curtailed.
- Other sources of cash could be explored, for example a long-term loan to finance the capital expenditure and a factoring arrangement to provide cash due from debtors more quickly.
- Efforts to increase the speed of debt collection could be made.
- Payments to creditors could be delayed.
- The dividend payments could be postponed (the figures indicate that this is a small company, possibly owner-managed).
- Staff might be persuaded to work at a lower rate in return for, say, an annual bonus or a profit-sharing agreement.
- Extra staff might be taken on to reduce the amount of overtime paid.
- The stockholding policy should be reviewed: it may be possible to meet demand from current production and minimise cash tied up in stocks.

NOTES

4

Month-end	*Jan X5*	*Feb X5*	*Mar X5*	*Apr X5*	*May X5*	*Jun X5*
	£'000	£'000	£'000	£'000	£'000	£'000
Debtors	126	144	162	174	186	204
Creditors	80	90	110	130	140	150

Example of the calculation of debtors budget:

Debtors at the end of March = 60% × (February sales + March sales)
= 60% × (£130,000 + £140,000)
= £162,000

5

	Units	£
20X3 (highest output)	9,800	44,400
20X2 (lowest output)	7,700	38,100
	2,100	6,300

The variable cost per unit is therefore £6,300/2,100 = £3.
The level of fixed cost can be calculated by looking at any output level.

	£
Total cost of factory power in 20X3	44,400
Less variable cost of factory power (9,800 × £3)	29,400
Fixed cost of factory power	15,000

An estimate of costs is 20X5 is as follows.

	£
Fixed cost	15,000
Variable cost of budgeted production (10,200 × £3)	30,600
Total budgeted cost of factory power	45,600

6

	£
Total expenditure	98,000
Budgeted variable cost (18,000 × £2.75)	49,500
Actual fixed costs incurred	48,500
Fixed overhead expenditure variance	11,000
Budgeted fixed costs	37,500

7 Participative budgets might be effective:

- In well-established organisations, because systems are in place and past experience can be used as a basis for forward planning
- In very large businesses, where senior management do not have enough knowledge of all of the organisation's activities to enable them to draw up budgets
- When operational managers have strong budgeting skills
- When the organisation's different units act autonomously

8 **Tutorial note**. In task (b) you may have felt that the top-down approach to budgeting was more appropriate at the museum. Justify your answer and you will receive marks.

MEMORANDUM

To: John Derbyshire
From: Consultant
Date: 5 October 20X8
Subject: **Behavioural aspects of budgeting**

(a) Motivational implications of imposing the budget reduction

When setting budgets, certain managers establish a budgeted figure and then add on a bit extra (when budgeting costs) or take off a bit (when estimating revenue) 'just in case'. This extra, which is known as **budgetary slack**, is included or deducted 'just in case' they haven't estimated accurately, costs turn out to be higher than expected or revenue lower than expected or there is some other unforeseeable event which stops them meeting their budget target.

This slack **needs to be removed** from the budget. Senior management therefore have to make an estimate of the slack and ask for the budget submitted by the lower-level manager to be adjusted accordingly. If the manager has not incorporated slack, this can be very demotivating; the entire budgeting process has to begin again and costs reduced/revenues increased to the level required. Moreover, the manager is likely to feel no sense of ownership of the budget, it having been imposed on him/her, and hence he or she will be less inclined to make efforts to meet the targets.

The size of the reduction/increase will determine the effect on morale; a small change is likely to have less effect than a large change.

Given that the Board of Management appear to have requested the reduction from £35,000 to £29,000 with no reason to believe that you have incorporated budgetary slack (£35,000 being £2,000 less than the estimated deficit for 20X8), it is likely have a negative impact on both your motivation and that of other museum staff.

(b) Top-down budgeting

In the top-down or **imposed** approach to budgeting, **top management prepare a budget with little or no input from operating personnel** and it is then imposed upon the employees who have to work to the budgeted figures.

In the **bottom-up** or **participatory** approach to budgeting, **budgets are developed by lower-level managers** who then submit the budgets to their superiors. The budgets are based on lower-level managers' perceptions of what is achievable and the associated necessary resources.

Imposed budgets tend to be effective in newly-formed organisations and/or in very small businesses whereas participatory budgets are most often seen in more mature organisations, of medium to large size.

The imposed style of budgeting uses senior management's awareness of total resource availability, decreases the possibility of input from inexperienced or uninformed lower-level employees and ensures that an organisation's strategic plans are incorporated into planned activities.

On the other hand, the bottom-up approach ensures that information from employees most familiar with each department's needs and constraints is included, knowledge spread among several levels of management is pulled together, morale and motivation is improved and acceptance of and commitment to organisational goals and objectives by operational managers is increased. What's more, they tend to be more realistic.

Given that the museum is well established and in view of the advantages set out above, the **bottom-up approach** would seem to be the **more suitable** of the two approaches for the museum.

Chapter : 9

STANDARD COSTING AND VARIANCE ANALYSIS

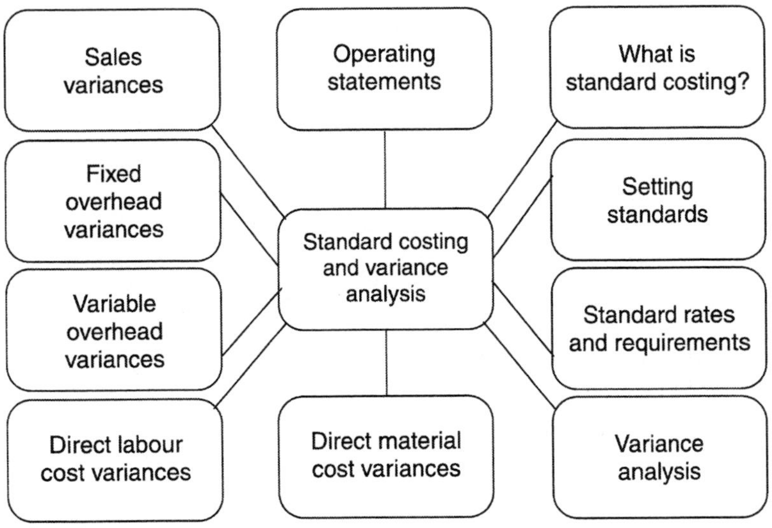

Introduction

Just as there are **standards** for most things in our daily lives (cleanliness in hamburger restaurants, educational achievement of eleven year olds, number of trains running on time), there are standards for the costs of products and services. Moreover, just as the standards in our daily lives are not always met, the standards for the costs of products and services are not always met. We will not, however, be considering the standards of cleanliness of hamburger restaurants in this chapter but we will be looking at standards for **costs**, what they are used for and how they are set.

We will then see how **standard costing** forms the basis of a process called **variance analysis**, which was introduced in the last chapter. Variance analysis is a vital management control tool, and we will spend a large part of this chapter explaining the calculations, and part of the next chapter looking at how the control is actually exercised.

Your objectives

In this chapter you will learn about the following.

(a) Standard costing

(b) Variance analysis

(c) Operating statements

1 WHAT IS STANDARD COSTING?

The building blocks of standard costing are standard costs and so before we look at standard costing in any detail you really need to know what a standard cost is.

1.1 Standard cost

The standard cost of product 1234 is set out below.

STANDARD COST CARD - PRODUCT 1234

	£	£
Direct materials		
Material X – 3 kg at £40 per kg	120	
Material Y – 9 litres at £20 per litre	180	
		300
Direct labour		
Grade A – 6 hours at £15 per hour	90	
Grade B – 8 hours at £20 per hour	160	
		250
Standard direct cost		550
Variable production overhead – 14 hours at £5 per hour		70
Standard variable cost of production		620
Fixed production overhead – 14 hours at £15 per hour		630
Standard full production cost		1,250
Administration and marketing overhead		150
Standard cost of sale		1,400
Standard profit		200
Standard sales price		1,600

Definition

A **standard cost** is a planned unit cost.

Notice how the total standard cost is built up from standards for each cost element: standard quantities of materials at standard prices, standard quantities of labour time at standard rates and so on. It is therefore determined by management's estimates of the following.

- The expected prices of materials, labour and expenses
- Efficiency levels in the use of materials and labour
- Budgeted overhead costs and budgeted volumes of activity

We will see how management arrives at these estimates in Section 2.

But why should management want to prepare standard costs? Obviously to assist with standard costing, but what is the point of standard costing?

1.2 The uses of standard costing

Standard costing has a variety of uses but its two principal ones are as follows.

(a) To **value stocks** and **cost production** for cost accounting purposes. It is an alternative method of valuation to methods like FIFO and LIFO which we saw earlier in this text.

(b) To act as a **control device** by establishing standards (planned costs), highlighting (via **variance analysis** which we will cover shortly) activities that are not conforming to plan and thus **alerting management** to areas which may be out of control and in need of corrective action.

Activity 1 **(20 minutes)**

Bloggs Ltd makes one product, the Joe. Two types of labour are involved in the preparation of a Joe, skilled and semi-skilled. Skilled labour is paid £20 per hour and semi-skilled £10 per hour. Twice as many skilled labour hours as semi-skilled labour hours are needed to produce a Joe, four semi-skilled labour hours being needed.

A Joe is made up of three different direct materials. Seven kilograms of direct material A, four litres of direct material B and three metres of direct material C are needed. Direct material A costs £1 per kilogram, direct material B £2 per litre and direct material C £3 per metre.

Variable production overheads are incurred at Bloggs Ltd at the rate of £2.50 per direct labour (skilled) hour.

A system of absorption costing is in operation at Bloggs Ltd. The basis of absorption is direct labour (skilled) hours. For the forthcoming accounting period, budgeted fixed production overheads are £250,000 and budgeted production of the Joe is 5,000 units.

Administration, selling and distribution overheads are added to products at the rate of £10 per unit.

A mark-up of 25% is made on the Joe.

Required

Using the above information draw up a standard cost card for the Joe.

Although the use of standard costs to simplify the keeping of cost accounting records should not be overlooked, we will be concentrating on the **control** and **variance analysis** aspect of standard costing.

Definition

Standard costing is 'A control technique which compares standard costs and revenues with actual results to obtain variances which are used to stimulate improved performance'.

Notice that the above definition highlights the control aspects of standard costing.

1.3 Standard costing as a control technique

Standard costing therefore involves the following.

- The establishment of predetermined estimates of the costs of products or services
- The collection of actual costs
- The comparison of the actual costs with the predetermined estimates.

The predetermined costs are known as **standard costs** and the difference between standard and actual cost is known as a **variance**. The process by which the total difference between standard and actual results is analysed in known as **variance analysis**.

Although standard costing can be used in a variety of costing situations (batch and mass production, process manufacture, jobbing manufacture (where there is standardisation of parts) and service industries (if a realistic cost unit can be established)), the greatest benefit from its use can be gained if there is a **degree of repetition** in the production process. It is therefore most suited to **mass production** and **repetitive assembly work**.

2 SETTING STANDARDS

Standard costs may be used in both absorption costing and in marginal costing systems. We shall, however, confine our description to standard costs in absorption costing systems.

As we noted earlier, the standard cost of a product (or service) is made up of a number of different standards, one for each cost element, each of which has to be set by management. We have divided the next section into two: the first part looks at setting the monetary part of each standard, whereas the second part looks at setting the resources requirement part of each standard.

3 STANDARD RATES AND REQUIREMENTS

3.1 Direct material prices

Direct material prices will be estimated by the purchasing department from their knowledge of the following.

- Purchase contracts already agreed
- Pricing discussions with regular suppliers
- The forecast movement of prices in the market
- The availability of bulk purchase discounts

Price inflation can cause difficulties in setting realistic standard prices. Suppose that a material costs £10 per kilogram at the moment and during the course of the next twelve months it is expected to go up in price by 20% to £12 per kilogram. What standard price should be selected?

- The current price of £10 per kilogram
- The average expected price for the year, say £11 per kilogram

Either would be possible, but neither would be entirely satisfactory.

(a) If the **current price** were used in the standard, the reported price variance will become adverse as soon as prices go up, which might be very early in the year. If prices go up gradually rather than in one big jump, it would be difficult to select an appropriate time for revising the standard.

(b) If an **estimated mid-year price** were used, price variances should be favourable in the first half of the year and adverse in the second half of the year, again assuming that prices go up gradually throughout the year. Management could only really check that in any month, the price variance did not become excessively adverse (or favourable) and that the price variance switched from being favourable to adverse around month six or seven and not sooner.

3.2 Direct labour rates

Direct labour rates per hour will be set by discussion with the personnel department and by reference to the payroll and to any agreements on pay rises with trade union representatives of the employees.

(a) A separate hourly rate or weekly wage will be set for each different labour grade/type of employee.

(b) An average hourly rate will be applied for each grade (even though individual rates of pay may vary according to age and experience).

Similar problems when dealing with inflation to those described for material prices can be met when setting labour standards.

3.3 Overhead absorption rates

When standard costs are fully absorbed costs, the **absorption rate** of fixed production overheads will be **predetermined,** usually each year when the budget is prepared, and based in the usual manner on budgeted fixed production overhead expenditure and budgeted production.

For selling and distribution costs, standard costs might be absorbed as a percentage of the standard selling price.

3.4 Standard resource requirements

To estimate the materials required to make each product (**material usage**) and also the labour hours required (**labour efficiency**), **technical specifications** must be prepared for each product by production experts (either in the production department or the work study department).

(a) The '**standard product specification**' for materials must list the quantities required per unit of each material in the product. These standard input quantities must be made known to the operators in the production department so that control action by management to deal with **excess material wastage** will be understood by them.

(b) The '**standard operation sheet**' for labour will specify the expected hours required by each grade of labour in each department to make one unit of product. These standard times must be carefully set (for example by work study) and must be understood by the labour force. Where necessary, **standard procedures** or **operating methods** should be stated.

3.5 Performance standards

The quantity of material and labour time required will depend on the level of performance required by management. Standards may be set at '**attainable levels** which assume efficient levels of operation, but which include **allowances** for normal loss, waste and machine downtime, or at **ideal levels**, which make **no allowance** for the above losses, and are only attainable under the most favourable conditions' (CIMA *Official Terminology*).

When setting standards, managers must be aware of two requirements.

- The need to establish a useful control measure
- The need to set a standard which will have the desired motivational effect.

These two requirements are often conflicting, so that the final standard cost might be a compromise between the two.

3.6 Taking account of wastage, losses etc

If, during processing, the quantity of material input to the process is likely to reduce (due to wastage, evaporation and so on), the quantity input must be greater than the quantity in the finished product and a material standard must take account of this.

Suppose that the fresh raspberry juice content of a litre of Purple Pop is 100ml and that there is a 10% loss of raspberry juice during process due to evaporation. The standard material usage of raspberry juice per litre of Purple Pop will be:

$$100\text{ml} \times \frac{100\%}{(100-10)\%} = 100\text{ml} \times \frac{100\%}{90\%} = 111.11\text{ml}$$

Activity 2 **(10 minutes)**

A unit of product X requires 24 active labour hours for completion. It is anticipated that there will be 20% idle time which is to be incorporated into the standard times for all products. If the wage rate is £10 per hour, what is the standard labour cost of one unit of product X?

3.7 Problems in setting standards

Setting standards is not as straightforward as the above examples might imply. A number of problems can arise.

(a) Deciding how to incorporate **inflation** into planned unit costs

(b) Agreeing on a **performance standard** (attainable or ideal)

(c) Deciding on the **quality** of materials to be used (a better quality of material will cost more, but perhaps reduce material wastage)

(d) Estimating materials **prices** where seasonal price variations or bulk purchase discounts may be significant

(e) Finding sufficient **time** to construct accurate standards as standard setting can be a **time-consuming process**

(f) Incurring the **cost of setting up and maintaining a system** for establishing standards

(g) Dealing with possible **behavioural problems**, managers responsible for the achievement of standards possibly resisting the use of a standard costing control system for fear of being blamed for any adverse variances

Note that standard costing is most difficult in times of inflation but it is still worthwhile.

(a) **Usage** and **efficiency** variances will still be meaningful

(b) **Inflation is measurable**: there is no reason why its effects cannot be removed from the variances reported.

(c) Standard costs can be **revised** so long as this is **not done too frequently**.

3.8 The advantages of standard costing

The advantages for **control** in having a standard costing system in operation can be summarised as follows.

(a) Carefully planned standards are an **aid to more accurate budgeting**.

(b) Standard costs provide a **yardstick** against which actual costs can be measured.

(c) The **setting of standards** involves determining the best materials and methods which may lead to **economies**.

(d) A **target of efficiency** is set for employees to reach and **cost consciousness** is stimulated.

(e) Variances can be calculated which enable the principle of '**management by exception**' to be operated. Only the variances which exceed acceptable tolerance limits need to be investigated by management with a view to control action.

(f) Standard costs **simplify the process of bookkeeping** in cost accounting, because they are easier to use than LIFO, FIFO and weighted average costs.

(g) Standard times **simplify the process of production scheduling**.

(h) Standard performance levels might provide an **incentive for individuals** to achieve targets for themselves at work.

4 INTRODUCTION TO VARIANCE ANALYSIS

The actual results achieved by an organisation during a reporting period (week, month, quarter, year) will, more than likely, be **different** from the expected results (the expected results being the **standard costs**). Such differences may occur between individual items, such as the cost of labour, and between the total expected profit and the total actual profit.

Management will have spent considerable time and trouble setting **standards** as we have seen. Actual results have differed from the standards. Have costs been controlled? What do wise managers do? Ignore the difference and continue trying to attain the standards? Hopefully not. Wise managers will consider the differences that have occurred and use the results of their considerations in their attempts to attain the standards. The wise manager will use **variance analysis** as a **control** method.

NOTES

The following sections examine variance analysis and set out the method of calculating material cost variances, labour cost variances, variable and fixed overhead variances and sales variances.

5 VARIANCE ANALYSIS

Definition

A **variance** is the 'Difference between a planned, budgeted, or standard cost and the actual cost incurred. The same comparisons may be made for revenues.'

The process by which the **total** difference between standard and actual results is analysed is known as **variance analysis**. When actual results are better than expected results, we have a **favourable** variance (F). If, on the other hand, actual results are worse than expected results, we have an **adverse** variance (A).

The **total profit variance** (the difference between budgeted profit and actual profit) can be split into three: **sales variances**, **production cost variances** and **non-production cost variances**. In the remainder of this chapter we will consider production cost variances, both fixed and variable, and sales variances.

6 DIRECT MATERIAL COST VARIANCES

The **total direct material cost variance** (the difference between what the output actually cost and what it should have cost, in terms of material) can be divided into two sub-variances.

(a) **The direct material price variance**

This is the difference between the standard cost and the actual cost for the actual quantity of material used or purchased. In other words, it is the difference between what the material did cost and what it should have cost.

(b) **The direct material usage variance**

This is the difference between the standard quantity of materials that should have been used for the number of units actually produced, and the actual quantity of materials used, valued at the standard cost per unit of material. In other words, it is the difference between how much material should have been used and how much material was used, valued at standard cost.

WORKED EXAMPLE: DIRECT MATERIAL COST VARIANCES

Product A has a standard direct material cost as follows.

5 kilograms of material M at £2 per kilogram = £10 per unit of A.

During April 20X3, 100 units of A were manufactured, using 520 kilograms of material M which cost £1,025.

Calculate the following variances.

(a) The total direct material cost variance
(b) The direct material price variance
(c) The direct material usage variance

ANSWER

(a) **The total direct material cost variance**

This is the difference between what 100 units should have cost and what they did cost.

	£
100 units should have cost (× £10)	1,000
but did cost	1,025
Total direct material cost variance	25 (A)

The variance is adverse because the units cost more than they should have cost.

(b) **The direct material price variance**

This is the difference between what 520 kgs should have cost and what 520 kgs did cost.

	£
520 kgs of M should have cost (× £2)	1,040
but did cost	1,025
Material M price variance	15 (F)

The variance is favourable because the material cost less than it should have.

(c) **The direct material usage variance**

This is the difference between how many kilograms of M should have been used to produce 100 units of A and how many kilograms were used, valued at the standard cost per kilogram.

100 units should have used (× 5 kgs)	500 kgs
but did use	520 kgs
Usage variance in kgs	20 kgs (A)
× standard cost per kilogram	× £2
Usage variance in £	£40 (A)

The variance is adverse because more material than should have been used was used.

(d) **Summary**

	£
Material price variance	15 (F)
Material usage variance	40 (A)
Total direct material cost variance	25 (A)

6.1 Material variances and opening and closing stock

Suppose that a company uses raw material P in production, and that this raw material has a standard price of £3 per metre. During one month 6,000 metres are bought for £18,600, and 5,000 metres are used in production. At the end of the month, stock will have been increased by 1,000 metres. In variance analysis, the problem is to decide whether the **material price variance** should be calculated on the basis of **materials purchased** (6,000 metres) or on the basis of **materials used** (5,000 metres).

The answer to this problem depends on how **closing stocks** of the raw materials will be valued.

(a) If they are valued at **standard cost** (1,000 units at £3 per unit) the price variance is calculated on material **purchases** in the period.

(b) If they are valued at **actual cost** *(FIFO)* (1,000 units at £3.10 per unit) the price variance is calculated on materials **used in production** in the period.

A **full standard costing system** is usually in operation and therefore the price variance is calculated on **purchases** in the period. The variance on the full 6,000 metres will be written off to the costing profit and loss account, even though only 5,000 metres are included in the cost of production.

There are two main advantages in extracting the material price variance **at the time of receipt**.

(a) If variances are extracted at the time of receipt they will be **brought to the attention of managers earlier** than if they are extracted as the material is used. If it is necessary to correct any variances then management action can be more timely.

(b) Since variances are extracted at the time of receipt, **all stocks will be valued at standard price**. This is administratively easier and it means that all issues from stocks can be made at standard price. If stocks are held at actual cost it is necessary to calculate a separate price variance on each batch as it is issued. Since issues are usually made in a number of small batches this can be a time consuming task, especially with a manual system.

The price variance would be calculated as follows.

	£
6,000 metres of material P purchased should cost (× £3)	18,000
but did cost	18,600
Price variance	600 (A)

7 DIRECT LABOUR COST VARIANCES

The calculation of **direct labour variances** is very similar to the calculation of direct material variances.

The **total direct labour cost variance** (the difference between what the output should have cost and what it did cost, in terms of labour) can be divided into two sub-variances.

(a) The **direct labour rate variance**

This is similar to the direct material price variance. It is the difference between the standard cost and the actual cost for the actual number of hours paid for.

In other words, it is the difference between what the labour did cost and what it should have cost.

(b) The **direct labour efficiency variance**

This is similar to the direct material usage variance. It is the difference between the hours that should have been worked for the number of units actually produced, and the actual number of hours worked, valued at the standard rate per hour.

In other words, it is the difference between how many hours should have been worked and how many hours were worked, valued at the standard rate per hour.

7.1 Idle time variance

A company may operate a costing system in which any **idle time** is recorded. Idle time may be caused by machine breakdowns or not having work to give to employees, perhaps because of bottlenecks in production or a shortage of orders from customers. When idle time occurs, the labour force is still paid wages for time at work, but no actual work is done. Time paid for without any work being done is unproductive and therefore inefficient. In variance analysis, **idle time is an adverse efficiency variance.**

When idle time is recorded separately, it is helpful to provide control information which identifies the cost of idle time separately and in variance analysis there will be an idle time variance **as a separate part of the labour efficiency variance**. The remaining efficiency variance will then relate only to the productivity of the labour force during the hours spent **actively working.**

WORKED EXAMPLE: LABOUR VARIANCES WITH IDLE TIME

The direct labour cost of product C is as follows.

3 hours of grade T labour at £10.00 per hour = £30.00 per unit of product C.

During June 20X3, 300 units of product C were made, and the cost of grade T labour was £6,600 for 910 hours. During the month, there was a machine breakdown, and 40 hours were recorded as idle time.

Calculate the following variances.

(a) The total direct labour cost variance
(b) The direct labour rate variance
(c) The idle time variance
(d) The direct labour efficiency variance

ANSWER

(a) **The total direct labour cost variance**

	£	
300 units of product C should cost (× £30.00)	9,000	
but did cost	8,800	
Total direct labour cost variance	200	(F)

Actual cost is less than standard cost. The variance is therefore favourable.

(b) **The direct labour rate variance**

The rate variance is a comparison of what the hours paid should have cost and what they did cost.

	£	
910 hours of grade T labour should cost (× £10.00)	9,100	
but did cost	8,800	
Direct labour rate variance	300	(F)

Actual cost is less than standard cost. The variance is therefore favourable.

(c) **The idle time variance**

The idle time variance is the hours of idle time, valued at the standard rate per hour.

Idle time variance = 40 hours (A) × £10.00 = £400 (A)

Idle time is always an adverse variance.

(d) **The direct labour efficiency variance**

The efficiency variance considers the hours actively worked (the difference between hours paid for and idle time hours). In our example, there were (910 – 40) = 870 hours when the labour force was not idle. The variance is calculated by taking the amount of output produced (300 units of product C) and comparing the time it should have taken to make them, with the actual time spent *actively* making them (870 hours). Once again, the variance in hours is valued at the standard rate per labour hour.

300 units of product C should take (× 3 hrs)	900 hrs	
but did take (910 – 40)	870 hrs	
Direct labour efficiency variance in hours	30 hrs	(F)
× standard rate per hour	× £10.00	
Direct labour efficiency variance in £	£300	(F)

(e) **Summary**

	£
Direct labour rate variance	300 (F)
Idle time variance	400 (A)
Direct labour efficiency variance	300 (F)
Total direct labour cost variance	200 (F)

Remember that, if idle time is recorded, the actual hours used in the efficiency variance calculation are the **hours worked and not the hours paid for.**

8 VARIABLE OVERHEAD VARIANCES

The total variable overhead variance is the difference between what the output actually cost and what it should have cost, in terms of variable overhead.

Like the materials and labour variances already discussed, the total variable overhead variance can be split into the part relating to a difference in the price of the overheads absorbed (the expenditure variance) and another relating to the quantity of overheads used (the efficiency variance). If overheads are absorbed on the basis of direct labour hours worked, the calculations will be very similar to those used for direct labour variances.

(a) **The variable overhead expenditure variance**

This is the difference between the standard overheads that would have been absorbed over the actual labour hours worked and the actual variable overheads. If there is any idle time then the hours paid will be ignored as variable overheads are only incurred when labour is working.

(b) **The variable overhead efficiency variance**

This is the difference between the actual hours worked and the number of hours that should have been worked for the quantity of output produced, valued at the standard absorption rate.

WORKED EXAMPLE: VARIABLE OVERHEAD VARIANCES

The variable overhead cost of product D is £10 per direct labour hour. Two labour hours are required to make one unit of product D. In July 20X3 225 labour hours were worked to produce 120 units of product D. The total cost for variable overhead was £2,350.

Calculate the following variances.

(a) The total variable overhead variance
(b) The variable overhead expenditure variances
(c) The variable overhead efficiency variance

ANSWER

(a) **The total variable overhead variance**

	£
120 units of product D should have cost (× £10 × 2 hrs)	2,400
but did cost	2,350
Total variable overhead variance	50 (F)

The variance is favourable because the actual cost was less than the standard cost.

Note that variable overheads are assumed to be incurred during active working hours only (and not during hours of idle time).

NOTES

(b) **The variable overhead expenditure variance**

	£
Overheads should have been incurred at £10 per hr over 225 hrs	2,250
but the actual amount incurred was	2,350
Variable overhead expenditure variance	100 (A)

The variance is adverse because the actual cost of variable overheads was more than would have been expected.

(c) **The variable overhead efficiency variance**

120 units of D should take (× 2 hrs)	240 hrs
but did take	225 hrs
Variable overhead efficiency variance in hours	15 hrs (F)
× standard rate per hour	× £10
Variable overhead efficiency variance	£150 (F)

In many organisations, as in this example, the absorption rate is based on direct labour hours worked. This means that the labour and overheads efficiency variances will always be in the same 'direction' as each other; the efficiency of the workforce is reflected in the efficient use of overheads. This is because the amount of labour hours worked on a product bears a relation to the amount of overhead incurred. So, the longer the workforce works, the more overheads are incurred. A favourable variance therefore means that the workforce has worked fewer hours than expected to produce the goods, and fewer overheads will have been incurred in making those goods.

9 FIXED OVERHEAD VARIANCES

The **total fixed overhead variance** is the difference between the overhead absorbed and the actual cost incurred (where the overhead absorbed is based on the standard number of hours for the units actually produced).

Fixed overheads do not follow the same pattern as the other costs so far considered because of their fixed nature. The total variance can be split into the expenditure and volume variances.

(a) **The fixed overhead expenditure variance**

This is simply the difference between the actual fixed overheads and budgeted fixed overheads that were originally planned (ie not the flexed budget).

(b) **The fixed overhead volume variance**

This looks at the change in the volume of production from the original budgeted level to the actual level. Again, assuming that overheads are absorbed using a labour hours rate, the volume variance is the difference between the budgeted level of production and the actual level of production, valued at the standard overhead absorption rate × standard hours per unit.

If further information is required, the volume variance can be further analysed into capacity and efficiency variances.

(c) **The fixed overhead capacity variance**

This calculates the amount by which the capacity of the workforce has exceeded or fallen short of the budgeted level. It is the difference between the planned hours to be worked and the actual hours worked, valued at the standard fixed overhead absorption rate.

(d) **The fixed overhead efficiency variance**

The efficiency variance is calculated along the same lines as before, to see if more or less hours were used to make the actual level of production, as compared with the standard. It is the difference between the hours that should have been worked for the number of units produced and the actual hours that were worked, valued at the standard fixed overhead absorption rate.

WORKED EXAMPLE: OVERHEAD VARIANCES

A company budgets to produce 1,000 units of product E during August 20X3. The expected time to produce a unit of E is five hours. The budgeted fixed overhead is £20,000 and fixed overheads are absorbed on a labour hours basis. Actual fixed overhead turns out to be £20,450. Actual productive hours during the period were 5,150 and 1,010 units were produced.

Required

Calculate the following variances.

(a) The total fixed overhead variance
(b) The fixed overhead expenditure variance
(c) The fixed overhead volume variance
(d) The fixed overhead capacity variance
(e) The fixed overhead efficiency variance

ANSWER

(a) **The total fixed overhead variance**

We begin by calculating a predetermined overhead absorption rate.

$$\text{Fixed overhead absorption rate} = \frac{\text{Budgeted fixed overheads}}{\text{Budgeted activity level}}$$

$$= \frac{\pounds 20{,}000}{1{,}000 \text{ units} \times 5\text{hrs}}$$

$$= \pounds 4 \text{ per hour}$$

We can now turn our attention to calculating the total fixed overhead variance.

	£
Actual overhead cost incurred	20,450
Standard overhead absorbed (1,010 × 5 × £4)	20,200
	250 (A)

The variance is adverse since actual overheads were greater than overheads absorbed.

Note how the overhead absorbed is based on the **standard number of hours for actual production**.

(b) **The fixed overhead expenditure variance**

	£	
Actual cost	20,450	
Budgeted cost	20,000	
Fixed overhead expenditure variance	450	(A)

The variance is adverse as the actual cost is greater than that planned in the original budget.

(c) **The fixed overhead volume variance**

Budgeted volume of production	1,000	units
Actual volume	1,010	units
Fixed overhead volume variance in units	10	(F)
× standard hours	× 5	hrs
× standard fixed overhead absorption rate	× £4	
Fixed overhead volume variance	£200	(F)

The volume variance is favourable as the volume of production achieved was greater than the budget.

(d) **The fixed overhead capacity variance**

Budgeted capacity	5,000	hrs
Actual hours worked	5,150	hrs
Fixed overhead capacity variance in hours	150	hrs (F)
× standard rate per hour	× £4	
Fixed overhead capacity variance	£600	(F)

The capacity variance is favourable because the actual capacity achieved is greater than the budgeted capacity of 5,000 hours.

(e) **The fixed overhead efficiency variance**

1,010 units of E should take (× 5 hrs)	5,050	hrs
but did take	5,150	hrs
Variable overhead efficiency variance in hours	100	hrs (A)
× standard rate per hour	× £4	
Fixed overhead efficiency variance	£400	(A)

The efficiency variance is adverse as it has taken longer to produce 1,010 units than was expected.

Activity 3 **(10 minutes)**

Using the information in the example above, calculate the under/over absorption of fixed overheads relating to product E for August 20X3. Be careful to absorb overheads into units of production based on the standard hours per unit and the standard rate per hour.

What do you notice about this figure and the variances above?

Activity 4 **(30 minutes)**

Brain Ltd produces and sells one product only, the Blob, the standard cost for one unit being as follows.

	£
Direct material - 10 kilograms at £20 per kg	200
Direct wages - 5 hours at £6 per hour	30
Variable production overhead - 5 hours at £1 per hour	5
Fixed production overhead – 5 hours at £10 per hour	50
Total standard cost	285

The fixed production overhead included in the standard cost is based on an expected monthly output of 900 units.

During April 20X3 the actual results were as follows.

Production	800 units
Direct material	7,800 kg used, costing £159,900
Direct wages	4,200 hours worked for £24,150
Variable production overhead	£4,900
Fixed production overhead	£47,000

Required

(a) Calculate direct material price and usage variances.
(b) Calculate direct labour rate and efficiency variances.
(c) Calculate the variable overhead expenditure and efficiency variances.
(d) Calculate the fixed overhead expenditure and volume variances
(e) Calculate the fixed overhead capacity and efficiency variances

10 SALES VARIANCES

Referring back to our definition of standard costing earlier in this chapter, you will see that revenues are an important part of this control technique. As well as exercising some control over costs, we need to keep an eye on sales and whether they are in line with expectation.

The cost variances we have calculated have all had a direct effect on profit. In other words, any change in the quantity or cost will increase or decrease profit to this extent also. Sales are a little different, however, as an increase in the quantity sold not only increases the sales revenue, but it also means that we bring in all the costs of those extra units sold. We have to take account of this in the calculations, and generally look at the effect on profit of any sales variances.

The total sales variance is the difference between actual sales and budgeted sales, less standard cost in each case. The total variance can be split into two further variances.

(a) *The sales price variance*

This is the difference between the actual selling price and the standard selling price for the actual sales volume in units. The price variance can be calculated in terms of revenue as this will have a direct effect on profit.

(b) *The sales volume variance*

This variance looks at the effect on budgeted profit of selling more or less units than were budgeted-for. It is the difference between the budgeted sales volume and the actual sales volume, valued at the standard profit per unit.

EXAMPLE: SALES VARIANCES

The sales budget for product F for March 20X4 is 500 units at a price of £25 per unit. Each unit of F has a standard cost of £17.

The actual sales revenue for March 20X4 is £13,260, with 520 units of product F sold.

Calculate the following variances.

(a) The sales price variance
(b) The sales volume variance
(c) The total sales variance

ANSWER

(a) **The sales price variance**

	£	
520 units of F should have sold for (× £25)	13,000	
But did sell for	13,260	
	260	(F)

The variance is favourable as the selling price was higher than expected, at £25.50 (£13,260/520).

Note that this variance can also be calculated in terms of profit; it is not quite such an easy method to remember, but it does tie-in with the total sales variance below.

	£	
Standard selling price – standard cost (£25 – £17)	8.00	
Actual selling price – standard cost (£25.50 – £17)	8.50	
Sales price variance per unit	0.50	
× units sold	× 520	
sales price variance	260	(F)

(b) **The sales volume variance**

Budgeted sales volume	500	units
Actual sales volume	520	units
Sales volume variance in units	20	units
× standard profit per unit (£25 – £17)	× £8	
	160	(F)

The variance is favourable as the sales volume was larger than expected.

(c) **The total sales variance**

	£	
Sales evaluated at the standard profit should be (500 × £8)	4,000	
But actual sales less standard costs were (520 × £8.50)	4,420	
	420	(F)

---

11 OPERATING STATEMENTS

So far, we have considered how variances are calculated without considering how they combine to **reconcile the difference between budgeted profit and actual profit** during a period. This reconciliation is usually presented as a report to senior management at the end of each control period. The report is called an operating statement or statement of variances.

Definition

The CIMA *Official Terminology* definition of an **operating statement** is 'A regular report for management of actual costs and revenues, as appropriate. Usually compares actual with budget and shows variances'.

WORKED EXAMPLE: VARIANCES AND OPERATING STATEMENTS

Sydney Ltd manufactures one product, and the entire product is sold as soon as it is produced. There are no opening or closing stocks and work in progress is negligible. The company operates a standard costing system and analysis of variances is made every month. The standard cost card for the product, a boomerang, is as follows.

STANDARD COST CARD - BOOMERANG		£
Direct materials	0.5 kilos at £4 per kilo	2.00
Direct wages	2 hours at £10.00 per hour	20.00
Variable overheads	2 hours at £0.30 per hour	0.60
Fixed overhead	2 hours at £3.70 per hour	7.40
Standard cost		30.00
Standard profit		6.00
Standing selling price		36.00

Selling and administration expenses are not included in the standard cost, and are deducted from profit as a period charge.

Budgeted output for the month of June 20X5 was 5,100 units. Actual results for June 20X5 were as follows.

Production of 4,850 units was sold for £169,750.
Materials consumed in production amounted to 2,300 kgs at a total cost of £9,800.
Labour hours paid for amounted to 8,500 hours at a cost of £84,000.
Actual operating hours amounted to 8,000 hours.
Variable overheads amounted to £2,600.
Fixed overheads amounted to £42,300.
Selling and administration expenses amounted to £18,000.

Task

Calculate all variances and prepare an operating statement for the month ended 30 June 20X5.

ANSWER

		£
(a)	2,300 kg of material should cost (× £4)	9,200
	but did cost	9,800
	Material price variance	600 (A)
(b)	4,850 boomerangs should use (× 0.5 kgs)	2,425 kg
	but did use	2,300 kg
	Material usage variance in kgs	125 kg (F)
	× standard cost per kg	× £4
	Material usage variance in £	£ 500 (F)
		£
(c)	8,500 hours of labour should cost (× £10)	85,000
	but did cost	84,000
	Labour rate variance	1,000 (F)
(d)	4,850 boomerangs should take (× 2 hrs)	9,700 hrs
	but did take (active hours)	8,000 hrs
	Labour efficiency variance in hours	1,700 hrs (F)
	× standard cost per hour	× £10
	Labour efficiency variance in £	£17,000 (F)
(e)	Idle time variance 500 hours (A) × £10	£5,000 (A)
	Hours paid – operating hours	
		£
(f)	8,000 hours incurring variable o/hd expenditure should cost (× £0.30)	2,400
	but did cost	2,600
	Variable overhead expenditure variance	200 (A)
(g)	Variable overhead efficiency variance in hours is the same as the labour efficiency variance:	
	1,700 hours (F) × £0.30 per hour	£ 510 (F)
		£
(h)	Budgeted fixed overhead (5,100 units × 2 hrs × £3.70)	37,740
	Actual fixed overhead	42,300
	Fixed overhead expenditure variance	4,560 (A)
(i)	Actual production volume	4,850 units
	Budgeted production volume	5,100 units
	Fixed overhead volume variance in units	250 units (A)
	× Standard hours × standard fixed overhead absorption rate	× 2 hours
	Fixed overhead volume variance	× £3.70
		1,850 (A)
(j)	Fixed overhead efficiency variance in hours is the same as the labour efficiency variance:	
	1,700 hrs (F) × £3.70 per hour	£6,290 (F)
(k)	Budgeted capacity (5,100 units × 2 hours)	10,200 hrs
	Actual hours of work	8,000 hrs
	Capacity variance in hours	2,200 hrs (A)
	× standard fixed overhead absorption rate per hour	× £3.70
	Fixed overhead capacity variance	£8,140 (A)
(l)	Revenue from 4,850 boomerangs should be (× £36)	174,600
	but was	169,750
	Selling price variance	4,850 (A)

NOTES

(m)	Budgeted sales volume	5,100 units
	Actual sales volume	4,850 units
	Sales volume profit variance in units	250 units
	× standard profit per unit	× £6 (A)
	Sales volume profit variance in £	£1,500 (A)

There are several ways in which an operating statement may be presented. Perhaps the most common format is one which reconciles budgeted profit to actual profit. In this example, sales and administration costs will be introduced at the end of the statement, so that we shall begin with 'budgeted profit before sales and administration costs'.

Sales variances are reported first, and the total of the budgeted profit and the two sales variances results in a figure for 'actual sales minus the standard cost of sales'. The cost variances are then reported, and an actual profit (before sales and administration costs) calculated. Sales and administration costs are then deducted to reach the actual profit.

EXAMPLE

SYDNEY LTD - OPERATING STATEMENT JUNE 20X5

		£	£
Budgeted profit before sales and administration costs (£6 × 5,100)			30,600
Sales volume variance			1,500 (A)
Budgeted profit from actual sales (flexed budget profit)			29,100
Selling price variance			4,850 (A)
Actual sales minus the standard cost of sales			24,250
Cost variances	(F)	(A)	
	£	£	
Material price		600	
Material usage	500		
Labour rate	1,000		
Labour efficiency	17,000		
Labour idle time		5,000	
Variable overhead expenditure		200	
Variable overhead efficiency	510		
Fixed overhead expenditure		4,560	
Fixed overhead efficiency	6,290		
Fixed overhead capacity		8,140	
	25,300	18,500	6,800 (F)
Actual profit before sales and admin costs			31,050
Sales and administration costs			18,000
Actual profit, June 20X5			13,050

Check	£	£
Sales		169,750
Materials	9,800	
Labour	84,000	
Variable overhead	2,600	
Fixed overhead	42,300	
Sales and administration	18,000	
		156,700
Actual profit		13,050

Activity 5 **(45 minutes)**

Bromill Limited makes a single product, LI, using a single raw material AN.

Standard costs relating to LI have been calculated as follows.

Standard cost schedule - LI	*Per unit*
	£
Direct material, AN, 100 kg at £5 per kg	500
Direct labour, 10 hours at £8 per hour	80
Variable production overhead, 10 hours at £2 per hour	20
Fixed production overhead 10 hours at £1 per hour	10
	610

The standard selling price of a LI is £900 and Bromill aim to produce 1,020 units a month.

During December, 1,000 units of LI were produced and sold. Relevant details of this production are as follows.

Direct material AN

90,000 kgs costing £720,000 were bought and used.

Direct labour

8,200 hours were worked during the month and total wages were £63,000.

Variable production overhead

The actual cost for the month was £25,000.

Fixed production overhead

The actual cost for the month was £9,800

Each LI was sold for £975.

Tasks

Calculate the following for the month of December, and use them to prepare an operating statement.

(a) Direct labour cost variance, analysed into rate and efficiency variances

(b) Direct material cost variance, analysed into price and usage variances

(c) Variable production overhead variance, analysed into expenditure and efficiency variances

(d) Fixed production overhead variance analysed into expenditure, capacity and efficiency

(e) Selling price variance

(f) Sales volume variance

NOTES

Chapter roundup

- A standard cost is a predetermined estimated unit cost, used for stock valuation and control.
- There are a number of advantages and disadvantages associated with standard costing.
- Variances explain the difference between actual results using actual costs and expected results, at standard cost.
- Management should only receive information of significant variances. This is known as 'management by exception'.
- The total direct material cost variance can be subdivided into the direct material price variance and the direct material usage variance.
- Direct material price variances are extracted at the time of receipt of the materials, not at the time of usage, assuming that stock is valued at standard cost.
- The total direct labour cost variance can be subdivided into the direct labour rate variance and the direct labour efficiency variance.
- If idle time arises, it is usual to calculate a separate idle time variance, and to base the calculation of the efficiency variance on active hours (when labour actually worked) only.
- The total variable overhead variance is the difference between what the total variable overhead cost should have been and what the overhead cost was.
- The total variable overhead variance can be subdivided into the variable overhead expenditure variance and the variable overhead efficiency variance
- The total fixed overhead variance is the difference between the actual fixed overhead incurred and the overhead absorbed (based on standard hours for actual production).
- The total fixed overhead variance can be subdivided into the fixed overhead expenditure variance and the fixed overhead volume variance; the fixed overhead volume variance can be further subdivided into the fixed overhead capacity variance and the fixed overhead efficiency variance.
- The total sales variance can be subdivided into the sales price variance and the sales volume variance.
- An operating statement can be used to reconcile the difference between budgeted profit and actual profit for a period, with variances being the reconciling items.

Quick quiz

1 What is a standard cost?

2 What are the two principal uses of standard costing?

3 What is a standard product specification?

4 Name two types of performance standard.

5 Which two variances subdivide the total direct material cost variance?

6 What are the two main advantages in calculating the material price variance at the time of receipt?

7 Why might idle time occur?

8 What does the total fixed overhead variance measure?

9 Which variance compares budgeted labour hours and actual labour hours and values the difference at the fixed overhead adsorption rate?

10 Which two figures are reconciled in an operating statement?

Answers to Quick quiz

1 A standard cost is a planned unit cost.

2 To value stocks and cost production

To act as a control device by analysing the variances between actual and expected results

3 A standard product specification lists the different materials and the quantities of each type of material used in the product.

4 Attainable and ideal standards.

5 Materials price and materials usage.

6 Variances are brought to the attention of managers, and potential problems resolved, earlier

As the price variance is calculated immediately, all further stock movements will be recorded at standard price which is easier for administrative purposes

7 Idle time might occur due to machine breakdown, lack of customer orders or bottlenecks in production.

8 The total fixed overhead variance measures the difference between overheads actually incurred and overheads absorbed, based on the standard number of hours for the units actually produced.

9 The fixed overhead capacity variance (where fixed overheads are recovered using a labour hour rate).

10 Budgeted profit and actual profit.

Answers to Activities

1 STANDARD COST CARD - PRODUCT JOE

	£	£
Direct materials		
A - 7 kgs × £1	7	
B - 4 litres × £2	8	
C - 3 m × £3	9	
		24
Direct labour		
Skilled - 8 × £20	160	
Semi-skilled - 4 × £10	40	
		200
Standard direct cost		224
Variable production overhead - 8 × £2.50		20
Standard variable cost of production		244
Fixed production overhead - 8 × £6.25 (W)		50
Standard full production cost		294
Administration, selling and distribution overhead		10
Standard cost of sale		304
Standard profit (25% × 304)		76
Standard sales price		380

Working

$$\text{Overhead absorption rate} = \frac{£250{,}000}{5{,}000 \times 8} = £6.25 \text{ per skilled labour hour}$$

2 The basic labour cost for 24 hours is £240. However with idle time it will be necessary to pay for more than 24 hours in order to achieve 24 hours of actual work, in fact 30 hours will need to be paid for.

$$\text{Standard labour cost} = \text{active hours for completion} \times \frac{125}{100} \times £10$$

$$= 24 \times 1.25 \times £10 = £300$$

3

		£
Fixed overheads for the period		20,450
Fixed overheads absorbed	(1,010 units × 5 hrs per unit × £4 per hr)	20,200
Underabsorption		250

The amount by which the fixed overheads are underabsorbed is the total fixed overhead variance. In dealing with overheads, estimates are made in advance so that an overhead absorption rate can be found and overheads can be recovered as the production process progresses. This is the same process of costing in advance that is used for standard costing. So when we calculate an under or over absorption of overheads, we are basically calculating a variance on fixed overheads.

4 (a) Price variance

	£
7,800 kgs should have cost (× £20)	156,000
but did cost	159,900
Price variance	3,900 (A)

Usage variance

800 units should have used (× 10 kgs)	8,000 kgs
but did use	7,800 kgs
Usage variance in kgs	200 kgs (F)
× standard cost per kilogram	× £20
Usage variance in £	£4,000 (F)

(b) Labour rate

	£
4,200 hours should have cost (× £6)	25,200
but did cost	24,150
Rate variance	1,050 (F)

Labour efficiency

800 units should have taken (× 5 hrs)	4,000 hrs
but did take	4,200 hrs
Efficiency variance in hours	200 hrs (A)
× standard rate per hour	× £6
Efficiency variance in £	£1,200 (A)

(c) Variable overhead expenditure

	£
Overheads should have been incurred at £1 per hr over 4,200 hrs	4,200
but the actual cost was	4,900
Variable overhead expenditure variance	700 (A)

Variable overhead efficiency

800 Blobs should take (× 5 hrs)	4,000 hrs
but did take	4,200 hrs
Variable overhead efficiency variance in hours	200 hrs (A)
× standard rate per hour	× £1
Variable overhead efficiency variance	£200 (A)

(d) Fixed overhead expenditure

	£
Actual cost	47,000
Budgeted cost (900 units × £50 per unit)	45,000
Fixed overhead expenditure variance	2,000 (A)

Fixed overhead volume

Budgeted volume of production	900 units
Actual volume	800 units
Fixed overhead volume variance in units	100 (A)
× standard hours	× 5 hrs
× standard fixed overhead absorption rate	× £10
Fixed overhead volume variance	£5,000 (A)

(e) Fixed overhead capacity

Budgeted capacity (900 Blobs × 5 hrs per Blob)	4,500 hrs
Actual hours worked	4,200 hrs
Fixed overhead capacity variance in hours	300 hrs (A)
× standard rate per hour	× £10
Fixed overhead capacity variance	£3,000 (A)

Fixed overhead efficiency

800 Blobs should take (× 5 hrs)	4,000 hrs
but did take	4,200 hrs
Variable overhead efficiency variance in hours	200 hrs (A)
× standard rate per hour	× £10
Fixed overhead efficiency variance	£2,000 (A)

5 (a) Direct labour cost variances

	£
8,200 hours should cost (× £8)	65,600
but did cost	63,000
Direct labour rate variance	2,600 (F)

1,000 units should take (× 10 hours)	10,000 hrs
but did take	8,200 hrs
Direct labour efficiency variance in hrs	1,800 hrs (F)
× standard rate per hour	× £8
Direct labour efficiency variance in £	£14,400 (F)

Summary	£
Rate	2,600 (F)
Efficiency	14,400 (F)
Total	17,000 (F)

(b) Direct material cost variances

	£
90,000 kg should cost (× £5)	450,000
but did cost	720,000
Direct material price variance	270,000 (A)

1,000 units should use (× 100 kg)	100,000 kg
but did use	90,000 kg
Direct material usage variance in kgs	10,000 kg (F)
× standard cost per kg	× £5
Direct material usage variance in £	£50,000 (F)

Summary	£
Price	270,000 (A)
Usage	50,000 (F)
Total	220,000 (A)

(c) Variable production overhead variances

	£
8,200 hours incurring o/hd should cost (× £2)	16,400
but did cost	25,000
Variable production overhead expenditure variance	8,600 (A)

Efficiency variance in hrs (from (b))	1,800 hrs (F)
× standard rate per hour	× £2
Variable production overhead efficiency variance	£3,600 (F)

Summary

	£
Expenditure	8,600 (A)
Efficiency	3,600 (F)
Total	5,000 (A)

(d) Fixed overhead variances

	£
Actual cost	9,800
Budgeted cost (1,020 units × £10 per unit)	10,200
Fixed overhead expenditure variance	400 (F)
Budgeted capacity (1,020 units of LI × 10 hrs per LI)	10,200 hrs
Actual hours worked	8,200 hrs
Fixed overhead capacity variance in hours	2,000 hrs (A)
× standard rate per hour	× £1
Fixed overhead capacity variance	£2,000 (A)
1,000 LI should take (× 10 hrs)	10,000 hrs
but did take	8,200 hrs
Fixed overhead efficiency variance in hours	1,800 hrs (F)
× standard rate per hour	× £1
Fixed overhead efficiency variance	£1,800 (F)

Summary

	£
Expenditure	400 (F)
Capacity	2,000 (A)
Efficiency	1,800 (F)
Total	200 (F)

(e) Selling price variance

	£
Revenue from 1,000 units should have been (× £900)	900,000
but was (× £975)	975,000
Selling price variance	75,000 (F)

(f) Sales volume variance

Budgeted sales	1,020 units
Actual sales	1,000 units
Sales volume variance in units	20 units (A)
× standard contribution margin (£(900 – 610))	× £290
Sales volume contribution variance in £	£5,800 (A)

BROMILL LIMITED – OPERATING STATEMENT FOR DECEMBER

			£	
Budgeted profit (£290 × 1,020)			295,800	
Sales volume variance			5,800	(A)
Budgeted profit from actual sales			290,000	
Selling price variance			75,000	(F)
Actual sales minus standard cost of sales			365,000	
Cost variances	*(F)*	*(A)*		
	£	£		
Labour rate	2,600			
Labour efficiency	14,400			
Materials price		270,000		
Materials usage	50,000			
Variable production overhead expenditure		8,600		
Variable production overhead efficiency	3,600			
Fixed production overhead expenditure	400			
Fixed production overhead capacity		2,000		
Fixed production overhead efficiency	1,800			
	72,800	280,600	207,800	(A)
Actual profit (£975,000 - £817,800 (Working))			157,200	

Working

	£
Direct material	720,000
Total wages	63,000
Variable production overhead	25,000
Fixed production overhead	9,800
	817,800

Chapter : 10
RESPONSIBILITY ACCOUNTING

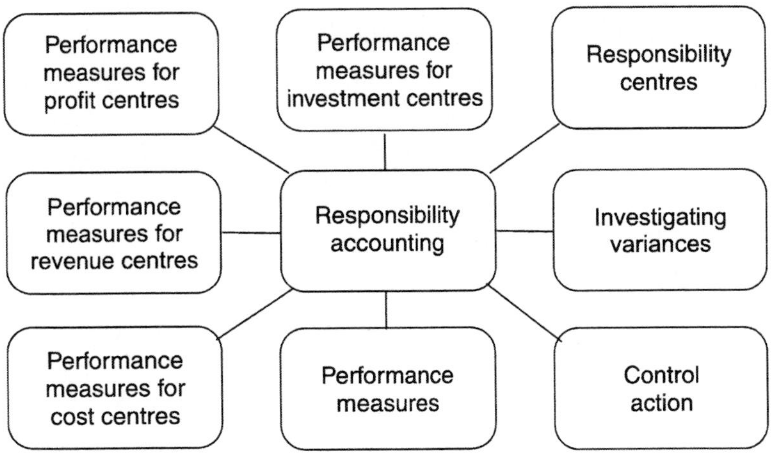

Introduction

In the last chapter we learnt the mechanics of calculating variances and preparing operating statements. But, for the purposes of operating a budgetary control system, this is not the end of the matter. The information must be given to the people responsible for the parts of the organisation that are experiencing variances, so that they can take action to bring the situation under control. Having a set-up which gives this responsibility to managers is known as **responsibility accounting**.

Variances provide one way of highlighting a possible problem area to managers, and is therefore a type of **performance indicator**. We will have a look at other performance indicators, which can be used to monitor the performance of individual departments in the organisation and the organisation as a whole.

Your objectives

In this chapter you will learn about the following.

(a) Responsibility centres

(b) Investigating variances

(c) Control action

(d) Performance indicators

1 RESPONSIBILITY CENTRES

Definitions

- **Responsibility accounting** is a system of accounting that **makes revenues and costs the responsibility of particular managers** so that the performance of each part of the organisation can be **monitored** and **assessed**.
- A **responsibility centre** is a **section** of an organisation that is headed by a manager who has **direct responsibility** for its performance.

A budget will be prepared for each responsibility centre, and its manager will be responsible for achieving the budget targets of that centre. The performance of the centre will be monitored, and the manger will be expected to take appropriate action if there are significant variances or other targets are not met.

Responsibility centres are usually divided into different categories. Here we shall describe cost (expense), revenue, profit and investment centres.

1.1 Cost centres

Definition

A **cost** (or **expense**) **centre** is any part of an organisation which incurs costs.

Cost centres can be quite small, sometimes one person or one machine or one expenditure item. They can also be quite big, for example an entire department. An organisation might establish a hierarchy of cost centres. For example, within a transport department, individual vehicles might each be made a cost centre, the repairs and maintenance section might be a cost centre, there might be cost centres for expenditure items such as rent or building depreciation on the vehicle depots, vehicle insurance and road tax. The transport department as a whole might be a cost centre at the top of this hierarchy of sub-cost centres.

To charge actual costs to a cost centre, each cost centre will have a cost code, and items of expenditure will be recorded with the appropriate **cost code**. When costs are eventually analysed, there may well be some apportionment of the costs of one cost centre to other cost centres.

Information about cost centres might be collected in terms of **total actual costs, total budgeted costs** and **total cost variances**. In addition, the information might be analysed in terms of **ratios**, such as cost per unit produced (budget and actual), hours per unit produced (budget and actual) and transport costs per tonne/ kilometre (budget and actual).

NOTES

1.2 Revenue centres

Definition

> A **revenue centre** is a **section** of an organisation which **raises revenue** but has **no responsibility for production**. A sales department is an example.

The term 'revenue centre' is often used in non-profit-making organisations. Revenue centres are similar to cost centres, except that whereas cost centres are for costs only, revenue centres are for recording revenues only. Information collection and reporting could be based on a comparison of budgeted and actual revenues earned by that centre.

1.3 Profit centres

Definition

> A **profit centre** is any section of an organisation (for example, division of a company) which **earns revenue** and **incurs costs**. The profitability of the section can therefore be measured.

Profit centres differ from cost centres in that they **account for both costs and revenues.** The **key performance measure** of a profit centre is therefore **profit. The manager of the profit centre must be able to influence both revenues and costs** (in other words, have a say in both sales and production policies).

A profit centre manager is likely to be a fairly senior person within an organisation, and a profit centre is likely to cover quite a large area of operations. A profit centre might be an entire division within the organisation, or there might be a separate profit centre for each product, brand or service or each geographical selling area. Information requirements need to be similarly focused.

In the hierarchy of responsibility centres within an organisation, there are likely to be several cost centres within a profit centre.

1.4 Investment centres

Definition

> An **investment centre manager** has some say **in investment policy** in his area of operations as well as **being responsible for costs and revenues**.

Several profit centres might share the same capital items, for example the same buildings, stores or transport fleet, and so investment centres are likely to include several profit centres, and provide a basis for control at a very senior management level, like that of a subsidiary company within a group.

The performance of an investment centre is measured by the **return on capital employed.** It shows how well the investment centre manager has used the resources under his control to generate profit.

NOTES

Activity 1 **(10 minutes)**

Motorway Minibreaks Limited owns a chain of motels situated at strategic points alongside the major motorways in the UK. It is a high-volume, low-margin business which operates a strict system of budgetary control, central to which is a hierarchy of responsibility centres. Bookings can be made directly with the hotels, or via a central call centre. Each hotel has a restaurant which is open to the public as well as guests. The hotel manager has a capital expenditure budget, although the Head Office makes all decisions regarding the purchase of new hotels.

Suggest which of the following responsibility centres would be categorised as a cost centre, a revenue centre, a profit centre, and an investment centre.

(a) The central bookings call centre.

(b) The Shap Fell Minibreak Hotel

(c) The Bridgeview Restaurant at the Avonmouth Minibreak Hotel

(d) The domestic services (cleaning and maintenance) function in the Tamworth Minibreak Hotel

2 INVESTIGATING VARIANCES

Having identified the areas over which managers have responsibility, each manager will have to decide whether or not to investigate the reasons for the occurrence of a particular variance. There are a number of factors which should be considered.

2.1 Materiality

Small variations in a single period between actual and standard are bound to occur and are unlikely to be significant. Obtaining an 'explanation' of the reasons why they occurred is likely to be time-consuming and irritating for the manager concerned. For such variations further investigation is not worthwhile.

2.2 Controllability

Managers of responsibility centres should only be held responsible for costs over which they have some control. These are known as controllable costs, which are items of expenditure which can be directly influenced by a given manager within a given time span.

If there is a general worldwide price increase in the price of an important raw material there is nothing that can be done internally to control the effect of this. If a central decision is made to award all employees a 10% increase in salary, staff costs in division A will increase by this amount and the variance is not controllable by division A's manager. Uncontrollable variances call for a change in the standard, not an investigation into the past.

2.3 Variance trend

Although small variations in a single period are unlikely to be significant, small variations that occur consistently may need more attention. Variance trend is more important than a single set of variances for one accounting period. The trend provides an indication of whether the variance is fluctuating within acceptable control limits or becoming out of control.

(a) If, say, an efficiency variance is £1,000 adverse in month 1, the obvious conclusion is that the process is out of control and that corrective action must be taken. This may be correct, but what if the same variance is £1,000 adverse every month? The **trend** indicates that the process is in control and the standard has been wrongly set.

(b) Suppose, though, that the same variance is consistently £1,000 adverse for each of the first six months of the year but that production has steadily fallen from 100 units in month 1 to 65 units by month 6. The variance trend in absolute terms is constant, but relative to the number of units produced, efficiency has got steadily worse.

Individual variances should therefore not be looked at in isolation; **variances should be scrutinised for a number of successive periods** if their full significance is to be appreciated.

Activity 2 **(10 minutes)**

What might the following variance trend information indicate?

(a) Regular, perhaps fairly slight, increases in adverse price variances
(b) A rapid, large increase in adverse price variances
(c) Gradually improving labour efficiency variances
(d) Worsening trends in machine running expense variances

2.4 The significance of variances

A variance can be considered significant if it will influence management's actions and decisions. Significant variances usually need investigating.

Variances which are simply random deviations, in other words fluctuations which have arisen by chance, are uncontrollable. This is because a standard cost is really only an *average* expected cost and is not a rigid specification. Some variances either side of this average must be expected to occur and are hence outside management's control.

The problem for both management and the accountant is therefore to decide whether a variation from standard is attributable to chance and hence *not* significant or whether it is due to a controllable cause and therefore significant.

2.5 Control limits and control charts

Because standard costs are only estimates of average costs, it would be incorrect to treat them as being rigid. **Tolerance limits** should be set, and only variances which exceed these limits should be reported as being significant and investigated. The following variances would lie within the tolerance limits.

- **Normal variations around average performance**, with variations above and below the average (adverse and favourable variances) cancelling each other out in the course of time.

- **Minor operational variances** which are too small to justify the cost of investigation and control action by management. Small variances might 'sort themselves out' in time, and only if they persist and grow larger should investigative action be worthwhile.
- A **minor planning error** in the standard cost for the year.

The control limits may be illustrated on a **variance control chart** as follows.

Variance control chart

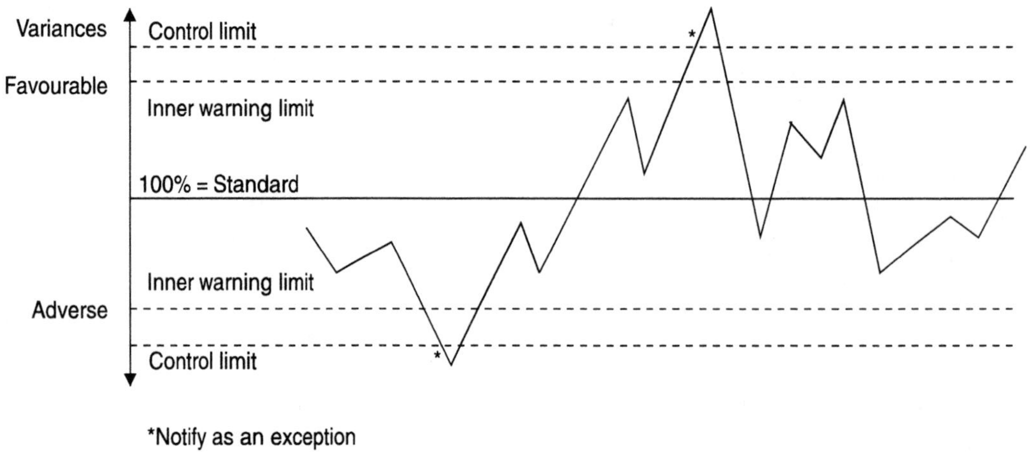

Figure 10.1 Variance control chart

There are several ways of establishing control limits.

- Management might establish a rule that any variance should be deemed significant if it exceeds a certain percentage of standard, for example if it exceeds 10% of standard in any one period based on judgement or experience.
- Management can use statistics, and estimate not only the standard cost, but the expected standard deviation (a measure of the spread or dispersion) of actual costs around the standard. Variances would then be deemed significant if actual costs were significantly different from standard.

Not all variances which are outside the control limits require detailed investigation. Often the cause is already known. A variance will only be investigated if the expected value of benefits from investigation and any control action exceed the costs of investigation.

For example it may be known from past experience that the cost of investigating a particular variance is £150 and that cost savings amounting to £1,200 can be made if the variance is corrected successfully. However it is also known that there is only a 30% possibility of the variance being corrected once the cause is found.

Expected value of an investigation = (£1,200 × 0.3) – £150 = £210

In this particular case it is worth investigating the variance.

NOTES

> **Activity 3** **(10 minutes)**
>
> Every month the operating statement of Jefferson Ltd shows a direct material efficiency variance of between £1,500 and £2,500 relating to a product that is only to be produced for a further six months. The company management accountant believes that if the variance is investigated, there is a 70% chance that its cause can eliminated. The cost of the investigation, however, is £5,000.
>
> Should the investigation take place?

Another approach is to **look at the variances over a number of accounting periods**, instead of just looking at variances in a single period.

The variance in each period is added to the total of the variances that have occurred over a longer period of time. If the variances are not significant, the total will simply fluctuate in a random way above and below the average (favourable and unfavourable variances), to give an insignificant total or cumulative sum. If the cumulative sum develops a positive or negative drift, it may exceed a set tolerance limit. Then the situation must be investigated, and control action will probably be required. The cumulative sum of variances over a period of time can be shown on a **cusum chart**.

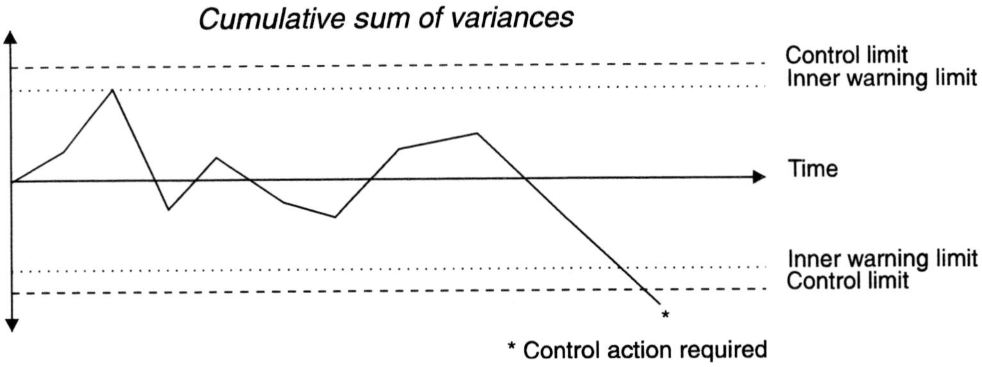

Figure 10.2 Cumulative sum of variances

The advantage of the multiple period approach is that trends are detectable earlier, and control action can be introduced sooner than might have been the case if only current-period variances were investigated.

3 CONTROL ACTION

If a variance is assessed as significant then the responsible manager may need to take control action.

Since a variance compares historical actual costs with standard costs, it is a statement of what has gone wrong (or right) in the past. By taking control action, managers can do nothing about the past, but they can use their analysis of past results to identify where the 'system' is out of control. If the cause of the variance is controllable, action can be taken to bring the system back under control in future. If the variance is uncontrollable, on the other hand, but *not* simply due to chance, it will be necessary to revise forecasts of expected results, and perhaps to revise the budget.

It may be possible for control action to restore actual results back on course to achieve the original budget. For example, if there is an adverse labour efficiency variance in month 1 of 1,100 hours, control action by the production department might succeed in increasing efficiency above standard by 100 hours per month for the next 11 months.

It is also possible that control action might succeed in restoring better order to a situation, but the improvements might not be sufficient to enable the company to achieve its original budget. For example if for three months there has been an adverse labour efficiency in a production department, so that the cost per unit of output was £8 instead of a standard cost of £5. Control action might succeed in improving efficiency, so that unit costs are reduced to £7, £6 or even £5, but the earlier excess spending means that the profit in the master budget will not be achieved.

Depending on the situation and the control action taken, the action may take immediate effect, or it may take several weeks or months to implement. The effect of control action might be short-lived, lasting for only one control period; but it is more likely to be implemented with the aim of long-term improvement.

3.1 Possible control action

The control action which may be taken will depend on the reason why the variance occurred. Some reasons for variances are outlined in the paragraphs below.

(a) **Measurement errors**

In practice it may be extremely difficult to establish that 1,000 units of product A used 32,000 kg of raw material X. Scales may be misread, the pilfering or wastage of materials may go unrecorded, items may be wrongly classified (as material X3, say, when material X8 was used in reality), or employees may make adjustments to records to make their own performance look better.

An investigation may show that control action is required to improve the accuracy of the recording system so that measurement errors do not occur.

(b) **Out of date standards**

Price standards are likely to become out of date when changes to the costs of material, power, labour and so on occur, or in periods of high inflation. In such circumstances an investigation of variances is likely to highlight a general change in market prices rather than efficiencies or inefficiencies in acquiring resources.

Standards may also be out of date where operations are subject to technological development or if learning curve effects have not been taken into account. Investigation of this type of variance will provide information about the inaccuracy of the standard and highlight the need to frequently review and update standards.

(c) **Random or chance fluctuations**

A standard is an average figure. It represents the midpoint of a range of possible values and therefore actual results are likely to deviate unpredictably within the predictable range.

As long as the variance falls within this range, it will be classified as a random or chance fluctuation and control action will not be necessary.

(d) **Efficient or inefficient operations**

Spoilage and better quality material/more highly skilled labour than standard are all likely to affect the efficiency of operations and hence cause variances. Investigation of variances in this category should highlight the cause of the inefficiency or efficiency and will lead to control action to eliminate the inefficiency being repeated or action to compound the benefits of the efficiency. For example, stricter supervision may be required to reduce wastage levels. The table below looks at possible reasons for the occurrence of the variances we calculated in the previous chapter.

Variance	Favourable	Adverse
Material price	Unforeseen discounts received More care taken in purchasing Change in material standard	Price increase Careless purchasing Change in material standard
Material usage	Material used of higher quality than standard More effective use made of material Errors in allocating material to jobs	Defective material Excessive waste Theft Stricter quality control Errors in allocating material to jobs
Labour rate of pay	Use of apprentices or other workers at a rate of pay lower than standard	Wage rate increase
Idle time	The idle time variance is always adverse	Machine breakdown Non-availability of material Illness or injury to worker
Labour efficiency (also fixed and variable overhead efficiency where overheads are recovered based on direct labour hours)	Output produced more quickly than expected because of work motivation, training, better quality of equipment or materials Errors in allocating time to jobs	Lost time in excess of standard allowed Output lower than standard set because of deliberate restriction, lack of training, or sub-standard material used Errors in allocating time to jobs
Variable overhead expenditure	Savings in costs incurred More economical use of services	Increase in cost of services used Excessive use of services Change in type of services used
Fixed overhead expenditure	Savings in costs incurred More economical use of services	Increase in cost of services used Excessive use of services Change in type of services used
Sales price	Price increase to cover unforeseen costs Price increase following increased demand	Price cut to stimulate demand due to increase in competition
Sales volume	Increased sales resulting from a new advertising campaign or a change in perception of the product by the public	Unexpected slump in the economy/demand for the product

3.2 Interdependence between variances

The cause of one variance may be wholly or partly explained by the cause of another variance. Examples could be as follows.

(a) If the purchasing department buys a cheaper material which is poorer in quality than the expected standard, the material price variance will be favourable, but this may cause material wastage and an adverse usage variance.

(b) Similarly, if employees used to do some work are highly experienced, they may be paid a higher rate than the standard wage per hour, but they should do the work more efficiently than employees of 'average' skill. In other words, an adverse rate variance may be compensated by a favourable efficiency variance.

(c) An adverse efficiency variance may be reported following the purchase of cheaper material (favourable material price variance) because operatives find difficulty in processing the cheaper material.

(d) A rise in selling price very often leads to a fall in the volume of goods sold, so sales price and volume variances can be interdependent.

Activity 4 **(25 minutes)**

VARIANCE REPORT: SEPTEMBER 20X5

	Variance (Adverse)	*Variance (Favourable)*	*Total variance*
	£	£	£
Material			–2,000
Usage	5,500		
Price		3,500	
Labour			–1,500
Efficiency	3,000		
Rate		1,500	
Overhead			–500
Expenditure		4,500	
Efficiency	2,000		
Capacity	3,000		

Actual costs for September 20X5 were as follows.

	£
Materials	100,000
Labour	80,000
Overheads	75,000
Total	255,000

The total adverse variance of £4,000 is 1.57% of total costs.

Comment on the possible causes of these variances and whether they warrant investigation.

4 PERFORMANCE MEASURES

Management **measure** the **performance** of an organisation in a number of areas to **see** whether **objectives or targets are being met**.

- In the organisation as a whole
- In each of the main sub-divisions of the organisation
- In individual activities
- In relationships with customers, the market, suppliers and competitors

The process of performance measurement is carried out using a variety of **performance indicators**, which are individual measurements. We look at performance indicators **in general** below before moving on to look at performance indicators **derived from the profit and loss account and balance sheet.** As well as being of use to management, **parties external** to the organisation can use these as a guide to how well the organisation is performing.

4.1 Performance indicators

In the previous section we looked at the analysis of **variances**. Cost variances are examples of performance indicators and can provide assistance to management in a number of ways.

- Monitoring the use of resources
- Controlling the organisation
- Planning for the future

In this section we will look at a wide variety of performance indicators. Let's have a look at some examples and the possible uses they could have.

- The direct labour efficiency variance, which could **identify problems** with labour productivity
- Distribution costs as a percentage of turnover, which could help with the **control of costs**
- Number of hours during which labour are idle, which could indicate **how well resources are being used**
- Profit as a percentage of turnover, which could highlight **how well the organisation is being managed**
- Number of units returned by customers, which could help with **planning** production and finished stock levels

Given this **wide range of uses**, you should be able to appreciate the importance of performance indictors and their value to managers in allowing them to see where improvements in organisational performance can be made.

A performance indicator is only useful if it is given meaning in relation to something else. Here is a list of **yardsticks** against which indicators can be compared so as to become useful.

- **Standards, budgets or targets**
- **Trends over time** (comparing last year with this year, say). An upward trend in the number of rejects from a production process, say, would indicate a

problem that needed investigating. The effects of inflation would perhaps need to be recognised if financial indicators were being compared over time.

- **The results of other parts of the organisation**. Large manufacturing companies may compare the results of their various production departments, supermarket chains will compare the results of their individual stores, while a college may compare pass rates in different departments.
- **The results of other organisations.** For example, trade associations or the government may provide details of key indicators based on averages for the industry.

As with all comparisons, it is vital that the performance measurement process compares '**like with like**'. There is little to be gained in comparing the results of a small supermarket in a high street with a huge one in an out-of-town shopping complex. We return to the importance of consistency in comparisons later in this chapter.

4.2 Qualitative and quantitative measures

It is possible to distinguish between quantitative data, which is capable of being expressed in numbers, and qualitative data, which can only be expressed in numerical terms with difficulty.

- An example of a **quantitative** performance measure is 'You have been late for work **twice** this week and it's only Tuesday!'.
- An example of a **qualitative** performance measure is 'My bed is **very** comfortable'.

The first measure is likely to find its way into a staff appraisal report. The second would feature in a bed manufacturer's customer satisfaction survey. Both are indicators of whether their subjects are doing as good a job as they are required to do.

Qualitative measures are by nature **subjective** and **judgmental** but this does not mean that they are not valuable. They are especially valuable when they are derived from several different sources because then they can be expressed in a mixture of quantitative and qualitative terms which is more meaningful overall.

Consider the statement 'Seven out of ten customers think our beds are very comfortable'. This is a quantitative measure of customer satisfaction as well as a qualitative measure of the perceived performance of the beds. (But it does not mean that only 70% of the total beds produced are comfortable, nor that each bed is 70% comfortable and 30% uncomfortable: 'very' is the measure of comfort.)

4.3 Productivity, efficiency and effectiveness

In general, performance indicators are established to measure productivity, efficiency and effectiveness.

- Effectiveness is about meeting targets and objectives.
- Productivity is a measure of output relative to some form of input.

5 PERFORMANCE MEASURES FOR COST CENTRES

5.1 Productivity

This is the quantity of the product or service produced **(output) in relation to** the resources put in (**input**). For example so many units produced per hour, or per employee, or per tonne of material. It measures **how efficiently resources are being used.**

5.2 Cost per unit

For the manager of a cost centre which is also a production centre one of the most important performance measures will be cost per unit. This is simply the total costs of production divided by the number of units produced in the period.

EXAMPLE: COST PER UNIT

The total costs and number of units produced for a production cost centre for the last two months are as follows:

	May	*June*
Production costs	£128,600	£143,200
Units produced	12,000	13,500
Cost per unit	$\frac{£128,600}{12,000}$	$\frac{£143,200}{13,500}$
	= £10.72	£10.61

5.3 Indices

Indices can be used in order to measure activity.

Indices show **how a particular variable has changed relative to a base value**. The base value is usually the level of the variable at an earlier date. The 'variable' may be just one particular item, such as material X, or several items may be incorporated, such as 'raw materials' generally.

In its simplest form an index is calculated as **(current value ÷ base value) × 100%.**

Thus if materials cost £15 per kg in 20X0 and now (20X3) cost £27 per kg the 20X0 value would be expressed in index form as 100 (15/15 × 100) and the 20X3 value as 180 (27/15 × 100). If you find it easier to think of this as a percentage, then do so.

EXAMPLE: WORK STANDARDS AND INDICES

Standards for work done in a service department could be expressed as an index. For example, suppose that in a sales department, there is a standard target for sales representatives to make 25 customer visits per month each. The budget for May might be for ten sales representatives to make 250 customer visits in total. Actual results in May might be that nine sales representatives made 234 visits in total. Performance could then be measured as:

Budget	100	(Standard = index 100)
Actual	104	$(234 \div (9 \times 25)) \times 100)$

This shows that 'productivity' per sales representative was actually 4% over budget.

6 PERFORMANCE MEASURES FOR REVENUE CENTRES

Traditionally sales performance is measured against price and volume targets. Other possible measures include revenue targets and target market share. They may be analysed in detail: by country, by region, by individual products, by salesperson and so on.

In a customer-focused organisation the basic information 'Turnover is up by 14%' can be supplemented by a host of other indicators.

(a) **Customer rejects/returns: total sales**. This ratio helps to monitor customer satisfaction, providing a check on the efficiency of quality control procedures.

(b) **Deliveries late: deliveries on schedule**. This ratio can be applied both to sales made to customers and to receipts from suppliers. When applied to customers it provides an indication of the efficiency of production and production scheduling.

(c) **Flexibility measures** indicate how well able a company is to respond to customers' requirements. Measures could be devised to measure how quickly and efficiently **new products** are launched, and how well procedures meet **customer needs**.

(d) **Number of people served and speed of service**, in a shop or a bank for example. If it takes too long to reach the point of sale, future sales are liable to be lost.

(e) **Customer satisfaction questionnaires,** for input to the organisation's management information system.

7 PERFORMANCE MEASURES FOR PROFIT CENTRES

7.1 Profit margin

Definition

The **profit margin** (profit to sales ratio) is calculated as (profit ÷ sales) × 100%.

The profit margin provides a simple measure of performance for profit centres. Investigation of unsatisfactory profit margins enables control action to be taken, either by reducing excessive costs or by raising selling prices.

Profit margin is usually calculated using operating profit.

NOTES

EXAMPLE: THE PROFIT TO SALES RATIO

A company compares its year 2 results with year 1 results as follows.

		Year 2	*Year 1*
		£	£
Sales		160,000	120,000
Cost of sales			
Direct materials		40,000	20,000
Direct labour		40,000	30,000
Production overhead		22,000	20,000
Marketing overhead		42,000	35,000
		144,000	105,000
Profit		16,000	15,000
Profit to sales ratio	$\left(\frac{16,000}{160,000}\right) \times 100\%$	10%	
	$\left(\frac{15,000}{120,000}\right) \times 100\%$		12½%

The above information shows that there is a decline in profitability in spite of the £1,000 increase in profit, because the profit margin is less in year 2 than year 1.

7.2 Gross profit margin

The profit to sales ratio above was based on a profit figure which included non-production overheads. The **pure trading activities of a business can be analysed** using the gross profit margin, which is calculated as (gross profit ÷ turnover) × 100%.

For the company in the above example the gross profit margin would be:

$$\text{Year 1: } \left(\frac{(16,000 + 42,000)}{160,000}\right) \times 100\% = 36.25\%$$

$$\text{Year 2: } \left(\frac{(15,000 + 35,000)}{120,000}\right) \times 100\% = 41.67\%$$

7.3 Cost/sales ratios

When target profits are not met, further ratios may be used to shed some light on the problem.

- Production cost of sales ÷ sales
- Distribution and marketing costs ÷ sales
- Administrative costs ÷ sales

Subsidiary ratios can be used to examine problem areas in greater depth. For example, for production costs the following ratios might be used.

- Material costs ÷ sales value of production
- Works labour costs ÷ sales value of production
- Production overheads ÷ sales value of production

EXAMPLE: COST/SALES RATIOS

Look back to the previous example. A more detailed analysis would show that higher direct materials are the probable cause of the decline in profitability.

		Year 2	*Year 1*
Material costs/sales	$\left(\frac{40,000}{160,000}\right) \times 100\%$	25%	
	$\left(\frac{20,000}{120,000}\right) \times 100\%$		16.7%

Other cost/sales ratios have remained the same or improved.

Activity 5 **(10 minutes)**

Use the following summary profit and loss account to answer the questions below.

	£
Sales	3,000
Cost of sales	1,800
	1,200
Manufacturing expenses	300
Administrative expenses	200
Operating profit	700

Calculate (a) the profit margin
(b) the gross profit margin

7.4 Resources

Traditional measures for materials compare actual costs with expected costs, looking at differences (or variances) in price and usage. Many traditional systems also analyse **wastage**. Measures used in **modern manufacturing environments** include the number of **rejects** in materials supplied, and the **timing and reliability of deliveries** of materials.

Labour costs are traditionally measured in terms of **standard performance** (ideal, attainable and so on) and rate and efficiency **variances**.

Qualitative measures of labour performance concentrate on matters such as **ability to communicate, interpersonal relationships** with colleagues, **customers' impressions** and **levels of skills** attained.

Managers can expect to be judged to some extent by the performance of their staff. High profitability or tight cost control are not the only indicators of managerial performance!

For variable overheads, differences between actual and budgeted costs (ie variances) are traditional measures. Various time based measures are also available, such as:

(a) **Machine down time: total machine hours.** This ratio provides a measure of machine usage and efficiency.

(b) **Value added time: production cycle time.** Value added time is the direct production time during which the product is being made. The production cycle time includes non-value-added times such as set-up time, downtime, idle time and so on. The 'perfect' ratio is 100%, but in practice this optimum will not be achieved. A high ratio means non-value-added activities are being kept to a minimum.

7.5 Measures of performance using the standard hour

Sam Ltd manufactures plates, mugs and eggcups. Production during the first two quarters of 20X5 was as follows.

	Quarter 1	*Quarter 2*
Plates	1,000	800
Mugs	1,200	1,500
Eggcups	800	900

The fact that 3,000 products were produced in quarter 1 and 3,200 in quarter 2 does not tell us anything about Sam Ltd's performance over the two periods because plates, mugs and eggcups are so different. The fact that the production mix has changed is not revealed by considering the total number of units produced. The problem of how to **measure output when a number of dissimilar products are manufactured** can be overcome, however, by the **use of the standard hour.**

The standard hour (or standard minute) is the **quantity of work achievable at standard performance, expressed in terms of a standard unit of work done in a standard period of time.**

The standard time allowed to produce one unit of each of Sam Ltd's products is as follows.

	Standard time
Plate	$^1/_2$ hour
Mug	$^1/_3$ hour
Eggcup	$^1/_2$ hour

By measuring the standard hours of output in each quarter, a more useful output measure is obtained.

		Quarter 1		*Quarter 2*	
	Standard hours		*Standard*		*Standard*
Product	*per unit*	*Production*	*hours*	*Production*	*hours*
Plate	$^1/_2$	1,000	500	800	400
Mug	$^1/_3$	1,200	400	1,500	500
Eggcup	$^1/_4$	800	200	900	225
			1,100		1,125

The output level in the two quarters was therefore very similar.

7.6 Efficiency, activity and capacity ratios

Standard hours are useful in computing levels of **efficiency, activity and capacity**. Any management accounting reports involving budgets and variance analysis should incorporate control ratios. The three main control ratios are the **efficiency, capacity** and **activity** ratios.

(a) The capacity ratio compares actual hours worked and budgeted hours, and measures the extent to which planned utilisation has been achieved.

(b) The activity or production volume ratio compares the number of standard hours equivalent to the actual work produced and budgeted hours.

(c) The efficiency ratio measures the efficiency of the labour force by comparing equivalent standard hours for work produced and actual hours worked.

WORKED EXAMPLE: RATIOS AND STANDARD HOURS

Given the following information about Sam Ltd for quarter 1 of 20X5, calculate a capacity ratio, an activity ratio and an efficiency ratio and explain their meaning.

Budgeted hours	1,100 standard hours
Standard hours produced	1,125 standard hours
Actual hours worked	1,200

ANSWER

$$\text{Capacity ratio} = \frac{\text{Actual hours worked}}{\text{Budgeted hours}} \times 100\% = \frac{1{,}200}{1{,}100} \times 100\% = 109\%$$

$$\text{Activity ratio} = \frac{\text{Standard hours produced}}{\text{Budgeted hours}} \times 100\% = \frac{1{,}125}{1{,}100} \times 100\% = 102\%$$

The overall activity or production volume for the quarter was 2% greater than forecast. This was achieved by a 9% increase in capacity.

$$\text{Efficiency ratio} = \frac{\text{Standard hours produced}}{\text{Actual hours worked}} \times 100\% = \frac{1{,}125}{1{,}200} \times 100\% = 94\%$$

The labour force worked 6% below standard levels of efficiency.

Activity 6 **(5 minutes)**

If X = Actual hours worked
Y = Budgeted hours
Z = Standard hours produced

What is $\frac{Z}{Y}$?

A Capacity ratio
B Activity ratio
C Efficiency ratio
D Standard hours produced ratio

8 PERFORMANCE MEASURES FOR INVESTMENT CENTRES

8.1 Return on investment (ROI)

Definition

> **Return on investment (ROI)** (also called **Return on capital employed (ROCE)**) is calculated as (profit/capital employed) × 100% and shows how much profit has been made in relation to the amount of resources invested.

ROI is generally used for measuring the performance of investment centres; profits alone do not show whether the return is sufficient when different values of assets are used. Thus if company A and company B have the following results, company B would have the better performance.

	A	*B*
	£	£
Profit	5,000	5,000
Sales	100,000	100,000
Capital employed	50,000	25,000
ROI	10%	20%

The profit of each company is the same but company B only invested £25,000 to achieve that profit whereas company A invested £50,000.

ROI may be calculated in a number of ways, but **profit before interest and tax** is usually used.

Similarly **all assets of a non-operational nature** (for example trade investments and intangible assets such as goodwill) **should be excluded** from capital employed.

Profits should be related to average capital employed. In practice many companies calculate the ratio **using year-end assets**. This can be misleading. If a new investment is undertaken near to the year end, the capital employed will rise but profits will only have a month or two of the new investment's contribution.

What does the ROI tell us? What should we be looking for? There are **two principal comparisons** that can be made.

- The change in ROI from one year to the next
- The ROI being earned by other entities

8.2 Residual income (RI)

An alternative way of measuring the performance of an investment centre, instead of using ROI, is residual income (RI). **Residual income** is a **measure of the centre's profits after deducting a notional or imputed interest cost**, and **depreciation** on capital equipment.

Definition

> **Residual income (RI)** is 'Pretax profits less a notional interest charge for invested capital'.

Activity 7 **(10 minutes)**

A division with capital employed of £400,000 currently earns a ROI of 22%. It can make an additional investment of £50,000 for a 5 year life with nil residual value. The average net profit from this investment would be £12,000 after depreciation of £2,000. A notional interest charge amounting to 14% of the amount invested is to be charged to the division each year.

Calculate the residual income of the division after the investment.

Chapter roundup

- Responsibility accounting is a system of accounting that segregates revenue and costs into areas of personal responsibility in order to monitor and assess the performance of each part of an organisation.
- A responsibility centre is a function or department of an organisation that is headed by a manager who has direct responsibility for its performance.
- A cost centre is any unit of an organisation to which costs can be separately attributed.
- A profit centre is any unit of an organisation to which both revenues and costs are assigned, so that the profitability of the unit may be measured.
- An investment centre is a profit centre whose performance is measured by its return on capital employed.
- Controllable costs are items of expenditure which can be directly influenced by a given manager within a given time span.
- Materiality, controllability and variance trend should be considered before a decision about whether or not to investigate a variance is taken.
- One way of deciding whether or not to investigate a variance is to only investigate those variances which exceed pre-set tolerance limits.
- Control limits may be illustrated on a control chart.
- A variance should only be investigated if the expected value of benefits from investigation and any control action exceed the costs of investigation.
- If the cause of a variance is controllable, action can be taken to bring the system back under control in future. If the variance is uncontrollable, but not simply due to chance, it will be necessary to review forecasts of expected results, and perhaps to revise the budget.
- Performance measurement aims to establish how well something or somebody is doing in relation to a planned activity.
- Ratios and percentages are useful performance measurement techniques.
- Cost per unit is total costs ÷ number of units produced.
- The profit margin (profit to sales ratio) is calculated as (profit ÷ sales) × 100%.

Chapter roundup (cont'd)

- The gross profit margin is calculated as gross profit ÷ sales × 100%.
- Return on investment (ROI) or return on capital employed (ROCE) shows how much profit has been made in relation to the amount of resources invested.
- Residual income (RI) is an alternative way of measuring the performance of an investment centre. It is a measure of the centre's profits after deducing a notional or imputed interest cost.
- Performance measures for materials and labour include differences between actual and expected (budgeted) performance. Performance can also be measured using the standard hour.

Quick quiz

1 Fill in the blank.

.... is a system of accounting that makes revenues and costs the responsibility of particular managers so that the performance of each part of the organisation can be monitored and assessed.

2 What is the difference between a cost centre and a profit centre?

3 What three types of variance would lie within tolerance limits?

4 What are the four basic reasons why variances occur?

5 What is meant by interdependence between variances?

6 What is the main aim of performance measurement?

7 Fill in the blanks.

To become useful, performance indicators should be compared against yard-sticks including .... , ... , ... or ....

8 How do quantitative and qualitative performance measures differ?

9 What types of measure are profit margin and ROCE?

	Profit margin	*ROCE*
A	Of efficiency	Of productivity
B	Of effectiveness	Of effectiveness
C	Of productivity	Of effectiveness
D	Of efficiency	Of efficiency

10 Profit margin = $\frac{C}{D} \times 100\%$

C =..........................

D = ...

11 $ROI = \frac{A}{B} \times 100\%$

A =...........................

B = ...

Answers to Quick quiz

1 Responsibility accounting

2 A profit centre collects information on both costs and revenue but a cost centre collects only cost information.

3 Normal variations around average performance, minor operational variances and variances due to minor planning errors in the standard cost will lie within tolerance limits.

4 Variances occur because of measurement errors, out of date standards, efficient or inefficient operations and random/chance fluctuations.

5 Interdependence between variances means that the cause of one variance can be wholly or partly explained by the cause of another variance.

6 To establish whether objectives or targets are being met.

7 standards, budgets or targets
trends over time
results of other parts of the organisation
results of other organisations

8 Quantitative measures are expressed in numbers whereas qualitative measures are not.

9 D

10 C = profit
D = sales

11 A = profit
B = capital employed

Answers to Activities

1 (a) Revenue centre (responsible for revenue from centrally made room bookings only).

(b) Investment centre (responsible for investment in some fixed assets, as well as hotel expenses and income).

(c) Profit centre (The restaurant manager will be responsible for the income and costs of the restaurant).

(d) Cost centre (There will only be costs in relation to cleaning and maintenance).

NOTES

2 This could indicate that prices are seasonal and perhaps stock could be built up in cheap seasons.

(a) Such variances usually indicate the workings of general inflation.

(b) These variances may indicate a sudden scarcity of a resource. It may soon be necessary to seek out cheaper substitutes.

(c) These may signal the existence of a learning curve, or the success of a productivity bonus scheme.

(d) These may indicate that equipment is deteriorating and will soon need repair or even replacement.

3 Minimum possible cost saving = 6 × £1,500 = £9,000

Expected value of the benefit of investigating the variance	= 70% × £9,000
	= £6,300
Cost of investigation	= £5,000

∴ Expected benefits exceed the costs
∴ The investigation is worthwhile.

4 *Total variance*

The total variance may only be 1.57% of total costs but this total disguises a number of significant adverse and favourable variances which need investigating.

Materials variances

The fact that there is a favourable price variance and an adverse usage variance could indicate interdependence. The purchasing department may have bought cheap materials but these cheaper materials may have been more difficult to work with so that more material was required per unit produced. The possibility of such an interdependence should be investigated. Whether or not there is an interdependence, both variances do require investigation since they represent 5.5% (usage) and 3.5% (price) of the actual material cost for the month.

Labour variances

Again there could be an interdependence between the adverse efficiency variance and the favourable rate variance, less skilled (and lower paid) employees perhaps having worked less efficiently than standard. Discussions with factory management should reveal whether this is so. Both variances do need investigation since they again represent a high percentage (compared with 1.57%) of the actual labour cost for the month (3.75% for the efficiency variance and 1.875% for the rate variance).

Overhead variances

An investigation into the fixed and variable components of the overhead would facilitate control information. The cause of the favourable expenditure variance, which represents 6% of the total overhead costs for the month, should be encouraged.

The adverse overhead variances in total represent 6.67% of actual overhead cost during the month and must therefore be investigated. The capacity variance signifies that actual hours of work were less than budgeted hours of work. The company is obviously working below its planned capacity level. Efforts should therefore be made to increase production so as to eradicate this variance.

CONCLUSION

It is not the total of the monthly variances which should be considered but the individual variances, as a number of them represent significant deviations from planned results. Investigations into their causes should be performed and control action taken to ensure that either performance is back under control in future if the cause of the variance can be controlled, or the forecasts of expected results are revised if the variance is uncontrollable.

5 (a) $\frac{700}{3,000} \times 100\% = 23\%$

The profit margin usually refers to operating profit/sales.

(b) $\frac{1,200}{3,000} \times 100\% = 40\%$

The gross profit margin takes the gross profit/sales.

6 B

7

	£
Divisional profit after investment (400,000 × 22% + 12,000)	100,000
Notional interest (450,000 × 0.14)	63,000
Residual income	37,000

Part B

Financial Reporting

Chapter : 11
THE REGULATORY FRAMEWORK

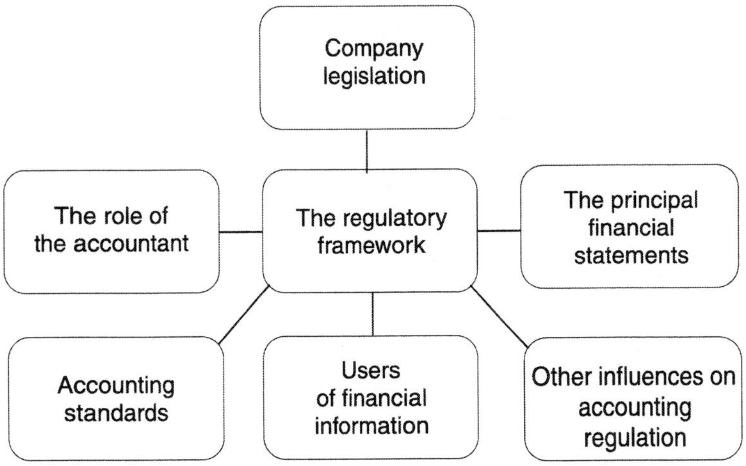

Introduction

The preparation of financial accounts of limited liability companies is closely regulated. The regulation comes from three main sources: company law, accounting standards, and Stock Exchange listing requirements. Further pervasive influence comes from the users of the accounts.

In many countries, the form and content of the financial statements is prescribed by national legislation. In the UK, the main statute governing the form and content of financial statements is the Companies Act 2006.

The form and content of company financial statements must also comply with accounting standards. These may be either International Accounting Standards (IFRSs) or national accounting standards. In many countries, including the UK, listed groups must prepare their consolidated financial statements in accordance with IFRSs.

Companies whose shares are listed on a stock exchange must also comply with the requirements of that stock exchange.

Your objectives

In this chapter you will learn about the following.

(a) Company legislation

(b) Accounting standards and other sources of regulation

(c) The different users of financial statements and their needs.

1 COMPANY LEGISLATION

Limited liability companies may be required by law to prepare and publish accounts annually. The form and content of the accounts may be regulated primarily by national legislation.

In the UK, limited liability companies must prepare their financial statements in accordance with the requirements of the Companies Act 2006. This requires companies to prepare accounts annually for distribution to their shareholders. A copy of these accounts must be lodged with the Registrar of Companies and is available for inspection by any member of the public. For this reason a company's statutory annual accounts are often referred to as its published accounts.

The Companies Act 2006 also prescribes the form and content of published accounts. and requires that accounts should show a 'true and fair view'. This is a slippery phrase which is nowhere defined in the Companies Acts. Also, there is no agreement in the accounting profession about the precise meaning of the phrase. It continues to be a cause of much argument and debate. What it certainly does *not* mean is that company accounts are to be exact to the penny in every respect. For one thing, as we shall see later, many of the figures appearing in a set of accounts are derived at least partly by the exercise of judgement. For another, the amount of time and effort that such a requirement would cost would be out of all proportion to the advantages arising from it.

We now look at another source of accounting regulation, namely accounting standards.

2 ACCOUNTING STANDARDS

2.1 Individual judgement and the need for accounting standards

Financial statements are prepared on the basis of a number of **fundamental accounting assumptions and conventions**. Many figures in financial statements are derived from the application of judgement in putting these assumptions into practice.

It is clear that different people exercising their judgement on the same facts can arrive at very different conclusions.

For example, an accountancy training firm has an excellent **reputation** amongst students and employers. How would you value this? The firm may have relatively little in the form of assets that you can touch, perhaps a building, desks and chairs. If you simply drew up a statement of financial position showing the cost of the assets owned, then the business would not seem to be worth much, yet its income earning potential might be high. This is true of many service organisations where the people are among the most valuable assets.

Other examples of areas where the judgement of different people may vary are as follows.

(a) Valuation of buildings in times of changing property prices.

(b) Research and development: is it right to treat this only as an expense? In a sense it is an investment to generate future revenue.

(c) Accounting for inflation.

(d) Brands such as 'Snickers' or 'Walkman'. Are they assets in the same way that a fork lift truck is an asset?

Working from the same data, different groups of people produce very different financial statements. If the exercise of judgement is completely unfettered, there will be no comparability between the accounts of different organisations. This will be all the more significant in cases where deliberate manipulation occurs, in order to present accounts in the most favourable light.

2.2 National standards and international standards

Accounting standards are statements that set out the way in which particular types of transaction and event should be reflected in the financial statements. They aim to narrow areas of difference and choice in financial reporting and to improve comparability between the financial statements of different organisations.

Accounting standards are developed at both a national level (in most countries) and an international level. Limited liability companies are generally required to follow the requirements of either national standards or international standards when preparing financial statements for publication.

International standards (IFRSs) are having a growing influence on national accounting requirements and practices.. In many countries, including the UK, some or all companies are required to follow IFRSs, rather than national standards.

In this text, we will normally assume that a business is using IFRSs.

2.3 Accounting standards and other businesses

Accounting standards apply to all kinds of entity, whether or not they have limited liability. If financial statements are intended to show a true and fair view or to give a fair presentation of an entity's performance and financial position they must be prepared in accordance with accounting standards.

Businesses that are not limited liability companies (for example, sole traders and partnerships) do not normally 'publish' their financial statements and therefore do not normally have to comply with accounting standards. However, accounting standards represent current best practice and many sole traders and partnerships choose to follow them.

Activity 1 **(10 minutes)**

You will be aware from your reading that attempts to regulate financial reporting have not yet been entirely successful. For fun, list a few of the more recent accounting scandals you can think of.

Having explained the need for accounting standards, we will now look at IFRSs and UK standards in turn.

3 INTERNATIONAL FINANCIAL REPORTING STANDARDS AND THE IASB

International Financial Reporting Standards (IFRSs) are produced by the **International Accounting Standards Board (IASB)**. The IASB develops IFRSs through an international process that involves the world-wide accountancy profession, the preparers and users of financial statements, and national standard setting bodies. Prior to 2003 standards were issued as International Accounting Standards (IASs). In 2003 IFRS 1 was issued and all new standards are now designated as IFRSs. Throughout this text, we will use the abbreviation IFRSs to include **both** IFRSs **and** IASs.

The objectives of the IASB are:

(a) To **develop**, in the public interest, a single set of high quality, understandable and enforceable **global accounting standards** that require high quality, transparent and comparable information in financial statements and other financial reporting to help participants in the world's capital markets and other users make economic decisions.

(b) To promote the use and **rigorous application** of those standards.

(c) To bring about **convergence of national accounting standards** and International Financial Reporting Standards to high quality solutions.

3.1 Standards Advisory Council (SAC)

The Standards Advisory Council assists the IASB in standard setting. It has about 50 members drawn from organisations all over the world, such as national standard–setting bodies, accountancy firms, the IMF and the World Bank.

The SAC meets the IASB at least three times a year and puts forward the views of its members on current standard–setting projects.

3.2 International Financial Reporting Interpretations Committee (IFRIC)

IFRIC was set up in December 2001 and issues Interpretations. Interpretations are guidance on applying IFRSs in cases where unsatisfactory or conflicting interpretations of standards have developed. In these situations, IFRIC works closely with similar national committees with a view to reaching consensus on the appropriate accounting treatment.

3.3 The International Accounting Standards Committee Foundation (IASCF)

The IASCF is an independent body that oversees the |ASB. It was formed as a not-for-profit corporation in the USA.

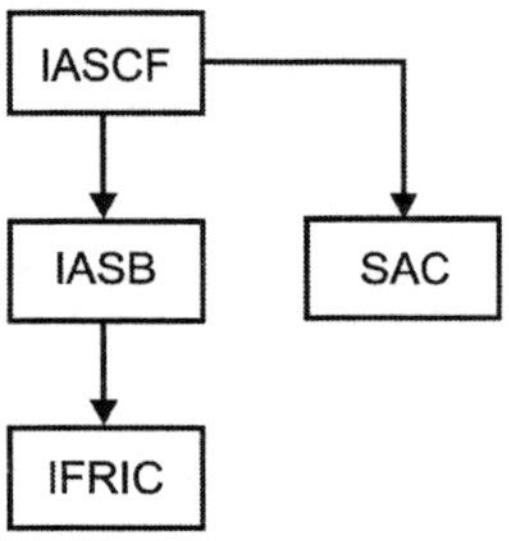

3.4 The use and application of IASs and IFRSs

IASs and IFRSs have helped to both improve and harmonise financial reporting around the world. The standards are used in the following ways.

(a) As **national requirements**, often after a national process
(b) As the **basis** for all or some **national requirements**
(c) As an **international benchmark** for those countries which develop their own requirements
(d) By **regulatory authorities** for domestic and foreign companies
(e) **By companies** themselves

3.5 Benchmark and allowed alternatives

IASs often allowed more than one accounting treatment (a benchmark (or preferred) treatment and an allowed alternative). Recent IFRSs and amendments to IASs have sought to disallow alternative treatments.

3.6 Application of IFRSs

Within each individual country **local regulations** govern, to a greater or lesser degree, the issue of financial statements. These local regulations include accounting standards issued by the national regulatory bodies and/or professional accountancy bodies in the country concerned.

The IASB **concentrates on essentials** when producing standards. This means that the IASB tries not to make standards too complex, because otherwise they would be impossible to apply on a worldwide basis.

3.7 Fair presentation

Financial statements prepared under IFRSs are required to present fairly the financial position, financial performance and cash flows of the entity. 'Fair presentation' is often held to be a similar concept to the 'true and fair view' required by the Companies Act.

The term fair presentation is not defined in IFRSs. However, IAS 1 *Presentation of financial statements* states that the application of IFRSs, with additional disclosure when necessary, is presumed to result in financial statements that achieve a fair presentation. The requirement to 'present fairly' also applies to transactions which are not covered by any specific accounting standard..

Despite this, a company's managers may depart from any of the provisions of accounting standards **in exceptional circumstances** if these are inconsistent with the requirement to give a fair presentation. This is commonly referred to as the ' fair presentation override'. In practice, use of the 'fair presentation override' is **very rare**.

4 UK ACCOUNTING STANDARDS

The current system consists of the following four bodies:

(a) the Financial Reporting Council (FRC)
(b) the Accounting Standards Board (ASB)
(c) the Financial Reporting Review Panel (FRRP)
(d) the Urgent Issues Task Force (UITF).

4.1 The Financial Reporting Council (FRC)

This acts as a kind of umbrella organisation to all the bodies involved in standard setting. It is responsible for funding and ensures the smooth running of the standard setting process. It is also responsible for the enforcement of standards, particularly in relation to the Review Panel. Its most important task is to set a general work programme for the ASB, along with a guide to broad policy issues. This role means that it is the FRC which determines what matters should come to the attention of the ASB..

The FRC has two operating arms: the ASB; and the Financial Reporting Review Panel (FRRP).

4.2 The Accounting Standards Board (ASB)

The ASB is responsible for the issue of accounting standards. Accounting standards issued by the ASB are called **Financial Reporting Standards** (FRSs). Prior to publication, the ASB circulates its proposals in the form of a **Financial Reporting Exposure Draft** (inevitably referred to as a FRED) and invites comments. The ASB has also adopted the Statements of Standard Accounting Practice (SSAPs) issued by its predecessor, the Accounting Standards Committee. The SSAPs have now largely been replaced by FRSs.

4.3 The Financial Reporting Review Panel (FRRP)

The FRRP examines accounts published by companies if it appears that Companies Act requirements have been breached – in particular, the requirement that accounts should show a true and fair view. The panel has legal backing: if a company departs from an accounting standard, the panel may go to the courts, which may in turn instruct the company to prepare revised accounts.

4.4 The Urgent Issues Task Force (UITF)

The UITF is an offshoot of the ASB. Its role is to assist the ASB in areas where an accounting standard or Companies Act provision already exists, but where unsatisfactory or conflicting interpretations have developed. As its name suggests, the UITF is designed to act quickly (more quickly than the full standard-setting process is capable of) when an authoritative ruling is urgently needed. The UITF pronouncements, which are called abstracts, are intended to come into effect quickly. They therefore tend to become effective within approximately one month of publication date. The UITF has so far issued over 30 abstracts, some of which have been incorporated into new accounting standards and some of which still stand alone.

FOR DISCUSSION

It has sometimes been suggested that to have too many rules encourages dishonesty as people obey the letter but not the spirit of those rules. Do you agree?

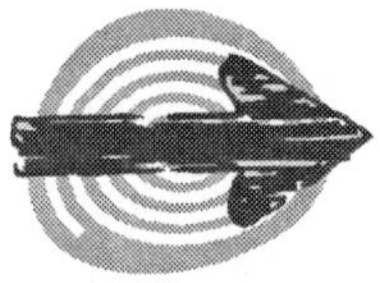

Different countries have different approaches to regulation. In some countries, all limited liability companies may have to publish financial statements for external users and comply with company law and accounting standards. In other countries, smaller companies may be exempt from some of the requirements. We now look briefly at the current situation in the UK.

5 THE REGULATORY FRAMEWORK IN THE UK

5.1 The current position

As we have seen, all UK limited companies must comply with the requirements of the Companies Act 2006 and accounting standards.

The Companies Act 2006 requires large companies to include a note to the accounts stating that the accounts have been prepared in accordance with applicable accounting standards or, alternatively, giving details of significant departures from those standards, with reasons. The Review Panel and the Secretary of State for Business, Enterprise and Regulatory Reform have the power to apply to the courts for revision of the accounts where non-compliance is not justified. These provisions mean that in the UK accounting standards have the force of law. It is now generally accepted that financial statements must comply with accounting standards in order to give a true and fair view.

Since 2005, listed companies have been required to prepare their group accounts in accordance with IFRSs. This requirement does not apply to the separate financial statements of the holding company or the separate financial statements of any subsidiaries, although it is permissible to use IFRSs for these as well.

All other companies have a choice: they can either prepare financial statements in accordance with UK standards or with IFRSs. However, when a company chooses to change from UK standards to IFRSs, it cannot subsequently change back to using UK standards.

Many companies have chosen to continue using UK standards. One reason for this is that under UK standards small companies can choose to follow a separate, much simpler, set of regulations known as the *Financial Reporting Standard for Small Entities* (the FRSSE). This is a single standard that contains all the accounting, disclosure and measurement requirements for smaller entities plus the requirements of the Companies Act 2006 relating to small companies. There is no equivalent option available to small companies under IFRSs.

5.2 Possible future developments

Over the last few years the influence of the International Accounting Standards on the UK standard setting process has gradually increased. For example, all UK FRSs state the level of compliance with the relevant IFRS. Some UK standards are based directly on IFRSs, or have been developed jointly with IFRSs, as happened with FRS 12 and IAS 37, *Provisions, contingent liabilities and contingent assets*

The ASB is committed to reducing the differences between UK standards and IFRSs, so that UK financial reporting practice will eventually converge with IASs and IFRSs.. However, although the main requirements of UK standards and IFRSs are now broadly very similar, there are still many differences in the detail..

The ASB accepts that there is no case for maintaining differences between UK accounting standards and IFRS. Consistency between UK standards and IFRS is not only important for the credibility and understandability of financial reporting; it is also important for those companies which, whilst choosing to continue to prepare their financial statements under UK standards, also wish to ensure that their financial statements are consistent with IFRS.

The ASB has been consulting with preparers and users of financial statements and at the time of writing, it looks as if the UK could eventually move to the following system:

(a) All UK publicly traded and other publicly accountable entities would be required to apply full IFRS, irrespective of size and whether they present group accounts or not.

(b) Small companies would apply the ASB's Financial Reporting Standard for Smaller Entities.

(b) All other companies would apply a new IFRS for Small and Medium-sized Entities. This is expected to be issued in 2009. It is intended to be a simplified version of the regulations in IFRSs and has been designed for use by entities that are not publicly accountable (such as privately owned companies). The new IFRS is expected to be more detailed and complex than the ASB's FRSSE and therefore not suitable for very small entities in the UK.

We now look at other major sources of influence on accounting regulation, including Generally Accepted Accounting Principles (GAAP).

6 OTHER INFLUENCES ON ACCOUNTING REGULATION

6.1 Stock Exchanges

Stock Exchanges are markets for stocks and shares, and a company whose securities are traded in on a Stock Exchange is known as a 'quoted' or 'listed' company.

Shares quoted on a Stock Exchange are said to be 'listed' or to have obtained a 'listing'. In order to receive a listing for its securities, a company must conform with the regulations of the exchange on which it is listed. The company commits itself to certain procedures and standards, including matters concerning the disclosure of accounting information, which are normally more extensive than the disclosure requirements of companies legislation.

6.2 European Directives

All member countries of the European Union (EU), including the UK, are required to implement the Union's legislation. They do this by enacting legislation to implement what are called Directives. A number of Directives have been issued but, from the point of view of financial reporting, the two most important ones were the Fourth and the Seventh Directives. The Fourth Directive dealt with the format and content for the published accounts, while the Seventh Directive addressed the issue of financial reporting for companies that come together to form a group..

UK financial reporting has been significantly affected by these developments. In particular, the Fourth Directive laid down for the first time, in law, the form and content of final accounts, greatly reducing the flexibility previously enjoyed by UK accountants.

6.3 Generally Accepted Accounting Practice (GAAP)

Generally accepted accounting practice (GAAP) is an important term which has become widely used in recent years. GAAP means all the rules, from whatever source, which govern accounting.

The rules may derive from:

- Local (national) company legislation
- National and international accounting standards
- Statutory requirements in other countries (particularly the US)
- Stock exchange requirements

GAAP varies from country to country. In the UK, GAAP does not have any statutory or regulatory authority or definition (unlike other countries, such as the US). The term is mentioned rarely in legislation, and only then in fairly limited terms.

GAAP is in fact a dynamic concept: it changes constantly as circumstances alter through new legislation, standards and practice. The IASB and national standard setters issue new standards and amend old ones in response to 'evolving business practices, new economic developments and deficiencies identified in current practice.'

The problem of what is 'generally accepted' is not easy to settle, because new practices will obviously not be generally adopted yet. The criteria for a practice being 'generally accepted' will depend on factors such as whether the practice is addressed by accounting standards or legislation, and whether other companies have adopted the practice. Most importantly perhaps, the question should be whether the practice is consistent with the needs of users and the objectives of financial reporting and whether it is consistent with the 'true and fair' concept or 'fair presentation'.

We will now look at the organisations and people who are interested in the financial information about a business. We will also look at the type of information each of them desires.

7 USERS OF FINANCIAL INFORMATION

7.1 The need for financial statements

Why do businesses need to produce financial statements? If a business is being run efficiently, why should it have to go through all the bother of accounting procedures in order to produce financial information?

The International Accounting Standards Board states in its document *Framework for the preparation and presentation of financial statements* (which we will examine in detail later in this text):

'The objective of financial statements is to provide information about the financial position, performance and changes in financial position of an entity that is useful to a wide range of users in making economic decisions.'

In other words, a business should produce information about its activities because there are various groups of people who want or need to know that information. This sounds rather vague: to make it clearer, we will study the classes of people who need information about a business. We need also to think about what information in particular is of interest to the members of each class.

Large businesses are of interest to a greater variety of people and so we will consider the case of a large public company, whose shares can be purchased and sold on a stock exchange.

7.2 Users of financial statements and their information needs

The following people are likely to be interested in financial information about a large company with listed shares.

(a) **Managers of the company**. These are people appointed by the company's owners to supervise the day-to-day activities of the company. They need information about the company's financial situation as it is currently and as it is expected to be in the future.. This enables them to manage the business efficiently and to take effective control and planning decisions.

(b) **Shareholders of the company**, ie the company's owners. They will want to assess how effectively management is performing its function. They will want to know how profitable the company's operations are and how much profit they can afford to withdraw from the business for their own use.

(c) **Trade contacts**, including suppliers who provide goods to the company on credit and customers who purchase goods or services provided by the company. Suppliers will want to know about the company's ability to pay its debts; customers need to know that the company is a secure source of supply and is in no danger of having to close down.

(d) **Providers of finance** to the company. These might include a bank which permits the company to operate an overdraft, or provides longer-term finance by granting a loan. The bank will want to ensure that the company is able to keep up with interest payments, and eventually to repay the amounts advanced.

(e) **The taxation authorities** who will want to know about the business profits in order to assess the tax payable by the company, including sales taxes.

(f) **Employees** of the company. They should have a right to information about the company's financial situation, because their future careers and the level of their wages and salaries depend on it.

(g) **Financial analysts and advisers** need information for their clients. Or their audience. For example, stockbrokers will need information to advise investors in stocks and shares; credit agencies will need information to advise potential suppliers of goods to the company; and journalists will need information for their reading public.

(h) **Government and their agencies** are interested in the allocation of resources and therefore in the activities of business entities. They also require information in order to provide a basis for national statistics.

(i) **The public** are affected by businesses in a variety of ways. For example, they may make a substantial contribution to a local economy by providing employment and using local suppliers. Another important factor is the effect of an entity on the environment, for example as regards pollution.

The purpose of financial statements is to provide useful information to these various groups of people. The regulatory framework does not only prevent preparers of financial statements from misleading users; it has also developed in order to ensure that the information in the financial statements actually does meet users' needs.

8 THE PRINCIPAL FINANCIAL STATEMENTS

The two principal financial statements drawn up by accountants are the **statement of financial position** (often called the **balance sheet)** and the income statement (often called the **profit and loss account**).

Definition

The **statement of financial position** is simply a list of all the assets owned by a business and all the liabilities owed by a business as at a particular date. It is a snapshot of the financial position of the business at a particular moment. **Assets** are the business's resources so, for example, a business may buy buildings to operate from, plant and machinery, goods to sell and cars for its employees. These are all resources which it uses in its operations. Additionally, it may have bank balances, cash and amounts of money owed to it. These provide the funds it needs to carry out its operations, and are also assets. On the other hand, it may owe money to the bank or to suppliers. These are **liabilities**.

The statement of financial position expresses the **accounting equation**: the rule that the assets of a business will at all times equal its liabilities.

Definition

In accounting, **capital** is an investment of money (funds) with the intention of earning a return. A business proprietor invests capital with the intention of earning profit. As long as that money is invested, accountants will treat the capital as money owed to the proprietor by the business.

Definition

The accounting equation is:

ASSETS = CAPITAL + LIABILITIES. Or

ASSETS – LIABILITIES = CAPITAL

Definition

> An **income statement** is a record of income generated and expenditure incurred over a given period. The period chosen will depend on the purpose for which the statement is produced. The income statement, which forms part of the published annual accounts of a limited company, will be made up for the period of a year, commencing from the date of the previous year's accounts. On the other hand, management might want to keep a closer eye on a company's profitability by making up quarterly or monthly income statements . The income statement shows whether the business has had more income than expenditure (a profit) or vice versa (a loss). Organisations which are not run for profit (charities etc) produce a similar statement called an income and expenditure account which shows the surplus of income over expenditure (or a deficit where expenditure exceeds income).

Both the statement of financial position and the income statement are summaries of accumulated data. For example, the income statement will show a figure for revenue earned from selling goods to customers. This will be a total amount derived by summing the revenue earned from numerous individual sales made during the period. One of the jobs of an accountant is to devise methods of recording such individual details and eventually to produce summarised financial statements from them.

The statement of financial position and the income statement represent the basis of the accounts of most businesses. For limited companies, other information by way of statements and notes must be shown according to company law and accounting standards, for example, a statement of cash flows. These will be considered in more detail later in this book.

> **Activity 2** **(5 minutes)**
>
> What is the purpose of an income statement? How does it differ from the purpose of a statement of financial position?

9 ROLE OF THE ACCOUNTANT

9.1 Major accounting disciplines

To a greater or lesser extent, accountants aim to satisfy the information needs of all the different groups mentioned earlier. Managers of a business need the most information so they can take their planning and control decisions; and they obviously have 'special' access to information about the business. When managers want a large amount of information about the cost and profitability of individual products, or different parts of their business, they can arrange to obtain it through a system of **cost and management accounting**. The preparation of accounting reports for external use is called **financial accounting**. Bookkeeping and costing are the bases of financial and management accounting respectively.

9.2 Management accounting

Management accounting refers to the internal reporting function of accounting. This 'branch' of accounting provides managers with information needed for day-to-day operations of the business as well as for short and long-term planning.

Management accounting systems produce detailed information often split between different departments within an organisation (sales, production, finance etc). Although much of the information necessarily deals with past events and decisions, management accountants are also responsible for preparing budgets, helping to set price levels and other decisions about the future activities of a business. Management (or cost) accounting is a management information system which analyses data to provide information as a basis for managerial action. The concern of a management accountant is to present accounting information in the form most helpful to management.

9.3 Financial accounting

Financial accounting is mainly a method of reporting the financial performance (profit or loss) and financial position of a business; it is not primarily concerned with providing information as a guide to the more efficient conduct of the business. Although financial accounts may be of interest to management, their principal function is to satisfy the information needs of persons not involved in the day-to-day running of the business.

Financial accounting is usually solely concerned with summarising historical data, often from the same basic records as management accounts, but in a different way. This difference arises partly because external users have different interests from management and have neither the time nor the need for very detailed information, but also because financial statements are prepared under constraints which do not apply to management accounts produced for internal use.

These constraints apply particularly to the accounts of limited companies. The owners of a limited company (the shareholders or members of the company) enjoy limited liability, which means that as individuals they are not personally liable to pay the company's debts. If the company's own assets are not sufficient to do so, the company may have to cease trading, but the shareholders are not obliged to make up any shortfall from their own private assets.

Clearly this system is open to abuse, and one of the safeguards is that limited companies are subject to a number of accounting regulations that do not apply to other forms of organisation. As we have seen, they must prepare financial statements in accordance with companies legislation and accounting standards.

In addition, the annual accounts of many limited companies must be audited (ie checked) by an independent person with defined qualifications. The auditor must make a report on the accounts, and will highlight any significant areas where they do not comply either with the legal regulations or with other regulations laid down by the accounting profession.

Chapter roundup

- The development of financial reporting has been influenced by:
  - company legislation
  - accounting standards
  - Stock Exchange Regulations
  - Generally Accepted Accounting Principles (GAAP)
  - the needs of users.
- Limited liability companies are required by law to prepare accounts annually for their shareholders.
- Financial statements are required to give 'a true and fair view' or to 'present fairly' the financial performance and position of the entity. These terms are not defined.
- International Accounting Standards (IASs) and International Financial Reporting Standards (IFRSs) are issued by the International Accounting Standards Board (IASB).
- UK accounting standards are issued by the Accounting Standards Board (ASB). It issues Financial Reporting Standards (FRSs).
- Listed UK groups must now prepare their consolidated financial statements in accordance with IAS/IFRS.
- Accounting information is required by a wide range of interested parties both within and outside the organisation.
- The principal financial statements of a business are the statement of financial position and the income statement.
- Management accounting is primarily concerned with providing information for the efficient running of the business, whereas financial accounting is concerned with reporting results and the financial position.

Quick quiz

1 What are the main factors which have influenced the development of financial reporting?

2 What is the main statute governing the content of limited company accounts in the UK?

3 What is an IFRS?

4 What is the IFRIC?

5 What are FRSs and FREDs?

6 What is a 'listed' company?

7 Identify seven user groups who need accounting information.

Answers to Quick quiz

1 Company law, accounting standards (National and international), Stock Exchange regulations.

2 Companies Act 2006.

3 International Financial Reporting Standard.

4 The IFRIC issues guidance (Interpretations) on applying IFRSs in cases where unsatisfactory or conflicting interpretations of standards have developed. In these situations.

5 Financial Reporting Standards and Financial Reporting Exposure Drafts, produced by the ASB. FRSs are developed from FREDs.

6 One quoted on the Stock Exchange.

7 Managers, shareholders, trade contacts, providers of finance, tax authorities, employees, financial analysts and advisers, government and their agencies, the public..

Answers to Activities

1 The list is almost endless but among the more recent ones you will have certainly thought of are Enron and WorldCom.

2 The purpose of an income statement is to show whether a business has made a profit or a loss over a certain period of time. The statement of financial position, on the other hand, shows the overall financial position of a business at a given point in time.

NOTES

Chapter : 12

THE STATEMENT OF FINANCIAL POSITION AND THE INCOME STATEMENT

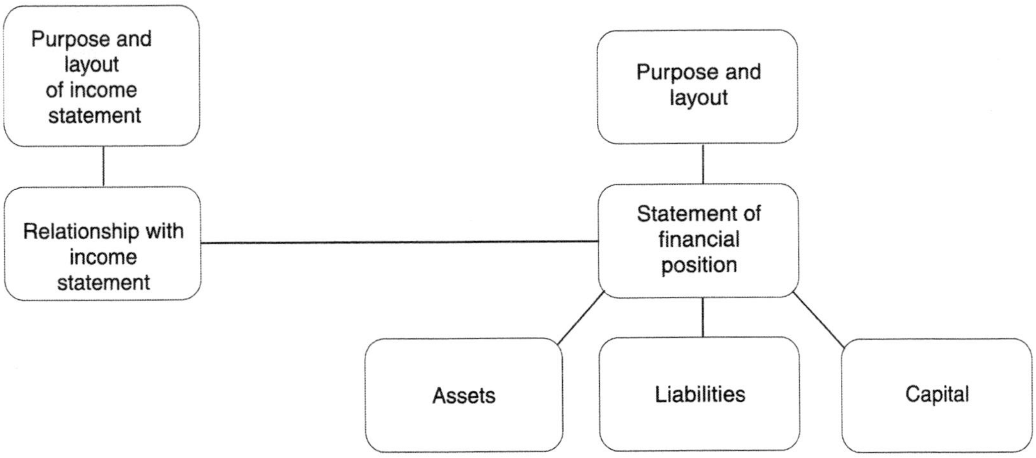

Introduction

The statement of financial position shows the assets, liabilities and capital of a business as at the end of the accounting period, to which the financial accounts relate. In other words, it is a statement of the assets, liabilities and capital of a business at a single moment in time – like a snapshot photograph.

One of the items which you will see in the capital section of the statement of financial position is the profit earned by the business. The income statement is the statement in which revenues and expenditures are compared to arrive at a figure of a profit or loss. It is a statement which shows in detail how the profit (or loss) for a period has been made. The basic reason for its preparation is that the details in the income statement enable business managers to exercise effective control over income and expenditure.

Your objectives

In this chapter you will learn about the following.

(a) What a statement of financial position is and how it is compiled

(b) The standard layout of a statement of financial position

(c) The categories of assets and liabilities found in a typical statement of financial position

(d) The income statement and how it is compiled

(e) How an income statement is usually presented

(f) The main items appearing in an income statement

(g) The difference between capital and revenue items

1 PURPOSE AND LAYOUT OF A STATEMENT OF FINANCIAL POSITION

1.1 Purpose

A statement of financial position is a list of the assets, liabilities and capital of a business at a given moment. Its purpose is to show the financial position of a business on a certain date.

The statement of financial position is sometimes called the balance sheet. It is a listing of balances 'on a particular day' (more accurately, 'at a particular moment'). It is sometimes compared to a snapshot of a business: it captures on paper a still image, frozen at a single moment of time, of something which is as a matter of course dynamic and continually changing. Typically, a statement of financial position is prepared to show the liabilities, capital and assets of a business at the end of the accounting period to which the accounts relate.

A statement of financial position is therefore very similar to the accounting equation: assets equal liabilities plus capital. In fact, the only differences between a statement of financial position and an accounting equation are:

(a) the manner or format in which the liabilities and assets are presented; and
(b) the extra detail which a statement of financial position usually goes into.

Activity 1 **(5 minutes)**

Answer the following questions to make sure you are familiar with the purpose of the statement of financial position.

(a) In one sentence describe the statement of financial position.

(b) Is the statement of financial position included in financial or management accounts?

1.2 Layout

A statement of financial position is divided into two halves. It may show assets (debit balances) in one half and capital and liabilities (credit balances) in the other.

NAME OF BUSINESS
STATEMENT OF FINANCIAL POSITION AS AT (DATE)

	£	£
Non-current assets		xxx
Current assets		xxx
		xxx
Capital		xxx
Non-current liabilities	xxx	
Current liabilities	xxx	
Total liabilities		xxx
		xxx

Another way of setting out a statement of financial position is to show capital in one half and net assets (ie assets less liabilities) in the other.

NAME OF BUSINESS
STATEMENT OF FINANCIAL POSITION AS AT (DATE)

	£	£
Non-current assets		xxx
Current assets	xxx	
Current liabilities	(xxx)	
Net current assets		xxx
		xxx
Non-current liabilities		(xxx)
Net assets		xxx
Capital		xxx

The total value of one half of the statement of financial position always equals the total value on the other half.

In this book, we will normally use the first method: assets in the top half and capital and liabilities in the bottom half. In practice, you may come across different formats. The second method of presenting the statement of financial position is widely used in the UK.

The format below, with specimen figures, should help you see how a typical statement of financial position is compiled.

HARVEY CARD
STATEMENT OF FINANCIAL POSITION AS AT 30 JUNE 20X1

Non-current assets	£	£
Land and buildings	30,000	
Plant and machinery	20,000	
Fixtures and fittings	17,000	
		67,000
Current assets		
Inventories	6,000	
Receivables	10,000	
Cash in hand	900	
		16,900
		83,900
Capital		
At 1 July 20X0		43,600
Profit for the year		8,000
At 30 June 20X1		51,600
Non-current liabilities		
Loan		25,000
Current liabilities		
Payables	7,000	
Bank overdraft	300	
		7,300
		83,900

Activity 2 **(5 minutes)**

Using the figures in the statement of financial position above, check that the accounting equation holds good in the form assets = capital + liabilities by putting figures in the appropriate parts of the equation.

At the beginning of the chapter, we said that a major difference between a statement of financial position and the accounting equation is the extra details in a statement of financial position. We now look at the first category of detail namely, assets.

2 ASSETS

Assets are divided into non-current and current assets.

2.1 Non-current assets

A non-current asset is an asset acquired for use within the business (rather than for selling to a customer), with a view to earning income or making profits from its use, either directly or indirectly.

For example:

(a) In a manufacturing industry, a production machine would be a non-current asset, because it makes goods which are then sold.

(b) In a service industry, equipment used by employees giving service to customers would be classed as non-current assets (eg the equipment used in a garage, and furniture in a hotel).

These are only examples. You may well have included other assets such as factory premises, office furniture, computer equipment, company cars, delivery vans or pallets in a warehouse.

To be classed as a non-current asset in the statement of financial position of a business, an item must satisfy two further conditions.

(a) Clearly, it must be used by the business. For example, the proprietor's own house would not normally appear on the business statement of financial position.

(b) The asset must have a 'life' in use of more than one year (strictly, more than one 'accounting period' which might be more or less than one year).

All of the above examples of non-current assets have one thing in common. They have a physical existence. However, not all assets have physical forms.

Definition

1 A **tangible asset** is a physical asset, ie one that can be touched. It has a real, 'solid' existence. All of the examples of non-current assets mentioned above are tangible.

2 An **intangible asset** is an asset which does not have a physical existence. It cannot be 'touched'. Patents or copyrights or expenses of developing a new product would be classified as intangible assets.

2.2 Depreciation

Non-current assets might be held and used by a business for a number of years, but they wear out or lose their usefulness over time. Nearly every tangible non-current asset has a limited life. The only exception is freehold land.

The accounts of a business try to recognise that the cost of a non-current asset is gradually consumed as the asset wears out. This is done by gradually writing off the asset's cost over several accounting periods. For example, in the case of a machine costing £1,000 and expected to wear out after ten years, it might be appropriate to reduce the amount at which it is shown in the statement of financial position by £100 each year. This process is known as depreciation.

If a statement of financial position were drawn up, say, four years after the asset was purchased, the amount of depreciation which would have accumulated would be 4 × £100 = £400. The machine would then appear in the statement of financial position as follows:

£

Machine at original cost	1,000
Less accumulated depreciation	400
Carrying amount*	600

* ie the value of the asset in the books of account, net of depreciation. After ten years the asset would be fully depreciated and would have a carrying amount of zero.

Activity 3 **(5 minutes)**

Here is a little test which brings in the concept of residual value. Suppose a business buys a car for £10,000.

It expects to keep the car for three years and then to trade it in at an estimated value of £3,400. How much depreciation should be accounted for in each year of the car's useful life?

In the statement of financial position layout in section 1, non-current assets are followed by current assets.

2.3 Current assets

Current assets are either:

(a) items owned by the business with the intention of turning them into cash within one year; or

(b) cash, including money in the bank, owned by the business.

These assets are 'current' in the sense that they are continually flowing through the business.

The definition in (a) above needs explaining further. Let us suppose that a trader, Chris Rhodes, runs a business selling motor cars, and purchases a showroom which he stocks with cars for sale. We will also suppose that he obtains the cars from a manufacturer, and pays for them in cash on delivery.

(a) If he sells a car in a cash sale, the goods are immediately converted into cash. The cash might then be used to buy more cars for re-sale.

(b) If he sells a car in a credit sale, the car will be given to the customer, who then owes money to the business. Eventually, the customer will pay what he owes, and Chris Rhodes will receive cash. Once again, the cash might then be used to buy more cars for sale.

In this example the cars, amounts receivable from customers and cash are all current assets. Why?

(a) The cars (goods) held in inventory (in stock) for re-sale are current assets, because Chris Rhodes intends to sell them within one year, in the normal course of trade.

(b) Any receivables are current assets, if customers are expected to pay what they owe within one year.

(c) Cash is a current asset.

The transactions described above could be shown as a cash cycle.

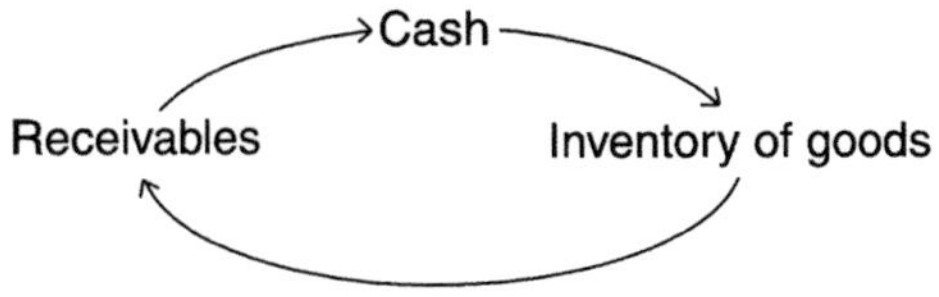

Cash is used to buy goods which are sold. Sales on credit create accounts receivable, but eventually cash is earned from the sales. Some, perhaps most, of the cash will then be used to replenish inventories.

The main items of current assets are therefore:

- inventories (sometimes called stocks);
- receivables (sometimes called debtors);
- cash.

Another item of current asset often found particularly in the statement of financial position of large companies is short term investments. These are stocks and shares of other businesses. For example, if a business has a lot of spare cash for a short time, its managers might decide to buy shares in, say, Marks and Spencer, ICI or British Airways. The shares will later be sold when the business needs the cash again. If share prices rise in the meantime, the business will make a profit from its short term investment.

2.4 The value of current assets in the statement of financial position

Current assets must never be valued at more than their net realisable value (sometimes called **fair value less costs to sell**).

Definition

> **Net realisable value** is the selling price of an item *less* reasonable selling costs; in other words, it is the amount of cash a business will earn when the asset is sold *minus* the further cost required to get it into a condition for sale and to sell it.

Current assets should never be reported in the statement of financial position at more than the money the business will make on selling off the asset and after reducing the sales price by the expense incurred in bringing the asset to a saleable condition. Thus, if the historic cost of the asset is more than the net realisable value, then the asset should be reported at the net realisable value.

Activity 4 **(5 minutes)**

This activity should help ensure you understand asset classification. Decide which of the following assets falls into the 'non-current' category and which should be treated as 'current'.

ASSET	BUSINESS	CURRENT OR NON-CURRENT
Van	Delivery firm	
Machine	Manufacturing Company	
Car	Car Trader	
Investment	Any	

Activity 5 **(5 minutes)**

How would you value (a) receivables and (b) inventories in the statement of financial position?

A statement of financial position not only lists all the assets of a business, it provides a list of the liabilities of the business as well.

3 LIABILITIES

Just like the assets, the various liabilities should be itemised separately, with a distinction being made between:

(a) current liabilities and

(b) non-current liabilities.

3.1 Current liabilities

Current liabilities are debts of the business that must be paid within a fairly short period of time (by convention, within one year). They include amounts payable to suppliers (sometimes called creditors) and bank overdrafts (because these are technically repayable at short notice).

3.2 Non-current liabilities

Non-current liabilities (sometimes called long term liabilities) are debts which are not payable within the 'short term. If a liability is non-current it is normally payable after more than one year.

Activity 6 **(5 minutes)**

Try to classify the following items as non-current assets, current assets or liabilities.

(a) A computer used in the accounts department of a retail store

(b) A computer on sale in an office equipment shop

(c) Wages due to be paid to staff at the end of the week

(d) A van for sale in a motor dealer's showroom

(e) A delivery van used in a grocer's business

(f) An amount owing to a bank for a loan for the acquisition of a van, to be repaid over 9 months

In a statement of financial position, liabilities are followed by capital.

4 CAPITAL

The 'capital' section of the statement of financial position may vary, depending on the nature of the entity. However, it will include:

- amounts invested by the owner(s) ie capital
  plus
- profit earned by the business
  less
- drawings (amounts withdrawn by the owner), if any.

Activity 7 **(15 minutes)**

Prepare a statement of financial position for the Sunken Arches Shoes and Boots Shop as at 31 December 20X0, given the information below.

	£
Capital as at 1 January 20X0	47,600
Profit for the year to 31 December 20X0	8,300
Freehold premises, carrying amount at 31 December 20X0	50,000
Motor vehicles, carrying amount at 31 December 20X0	9,000
Fixtures and fittings, carrying amount at 31 December 20X0	8,000
Long term loan (mortgage)	25,000
Bank overdraft *	2,000
Goods held in inventory for resale	16,000
Amounts receivable from customers	500
Cash in hand*	100
Amounts payable by suppliers	4,700
Drawings	4,000

* A shop might have cash in its cash registers, but still have an overdraft at the bank.

5 THE INCOME STATEMENT

5.1 Purpose

Any organisation will generate income (or revenue) from one or more sources. A business will sell its goods or services to customers in exchange for cash. A charity will raise money through donations, charitable events and perhaps trading activities. A police force will be granted funds from local or central government, and may also charge for providing its services (for example at sporting events).

The income generated will be used to finance the activities of the organisation: purchasing raw materials for use in manufacturing goods, purchasing ready-made goods for onward sale, purchasing equipment, paying expenses such as staff salaries, stationery, lighting and heating, rent and so on.

Periodically, the organisation will prepare an accounting statement showing the revenue generated and the amounts spent (the 'expenditure' of the organisation). Such a statement is called the income statement. The total revenue earned during a period is compared with the expenditure incurred in earning it. The difference is either a profit or a loss.

Thus, the income statement shows in detail how the profit (or loss) of a period has been made. The owners and managers of a business obviously want to know how much profit or loss has been made, but there is only a limited information value in the profit figure alone. In order to exercise financial control effectively, managers need to know how much income has been earned, what various items of costs have been and whether the performance of sales or the control of costs appears to be satisfactory. This is the basic reason for preparing the income statement.

The income statement is sometimes called the profit and loss account.

We next look at the layout of the income statement.

5.2 Layout

The main sections of the income statement, are as follows.

NAME OF BUSINESS
INCOME STATEMENT
FOR THE YEAR ENDED (DATE)

	£
Sales	xxx
Cost of sales	(xxx)
Gross profit	xxx
Expenses	(xxx)
Net profit	xxx

In the first part of the statement revenue from selling goods is compared with direct costs of acquiring or producing the goods sold to arrive at gross profit.; In the second part of the statement, indirect costs (expenses) are deducted to arrive at net profit. An example is shown below.

HARVEY CARD
INCOME STATEMENT
FOR THE YEAR ENDED 30 JUNE 20X1

	£	£
Sales		57,010
Cost of sales		30,690
Gross profit		26,320
Selling expenses	5,780	
Distribution expenses	5,150	
Administrative expenses	7,390	
		18,320
Net profit		8,000

The first 'section' of the income statement shows the gross profit for the accounting period. We now look at this section in more detail.

6 GROSS PROFIT

6.1 Gross profit

Gross profit is the difference between:

(a) the sales revenue for a given period and

(b) the purchase cost or production cost of the goods that have been actually sold in that period.

Thus, if 20 items were produced in, say, January at a cost of £6 each but only 15 of those items were sold at £10 each, then the gross profit would be as follows.

	£
Sales (£10 × 15) =	150
Cost of sales (£6 × 15) =	90
Gross profit	60

The unsold items (five in this example) would be shown in the statement of financial position as 'inventory' in the current assets section until such time as they are sold.

In a retail business, the cost of sales (or as it is often called the cost of goods sold) is their purchase cost from the suppliers. In a manufacturing business, the production cost of goods sold is the cost of raw materials in the finished goods, plus the cost of the labour required to make the goods, and certain other costs.

Activity 8 **(5 minutes)**

What does a gross loss signify about the way in which goods are being bought and sold?

The second part of the income statement shows the net profit of the business.

7 NET PROFIT

Net profit is calculated as follows.

Gross profit – Expenses = Net profit

The expenses in the income statement are the expenses that are incurred in running the business eg advertising, rent on the office etc, which have not been included in the cost of goods sold. (Remember: cost of sales or cost of goods sold are costs incurred in buying and/or producing goods for resale.)

Expenses are mainly classified into three categories: selling, distribution and administrative.

Selling expenses might include any or all of the following.

(a) Salaries of a sales director and sales management

(b) Salaries and commissions of salesmen

(c) Travelling and entertainment expenses of salesmen

(d) Marketing costs (eg advertising and sales promotion expenses)

(e) Discounts allowed to customers for early payment of their debts. For example, a business might sell goods to a customer for £100 and offer a discount of 5% for payment in cash. If the customer takes the discount, the accounts of the business would not record the sales value at £95; they would instead record sales at the full £100, with a cost for discounts allowed of £5

Distribution costs are the costs of getting goods to customers, for example the costs of running and maintaining delivery vans.

Administrative expenses are the expenses of providing management and administration for the business.

An example will show how an income statement is compiled.

EXAMPLE: INCOME STATEMENT

On 1 June 20X1, Jock Heiss commenced trading as an ice-cream salesman, selling ice-creams from a van which he drove around the streets of his town.

(a) He rented the van at a cost of £1,000 for three months. Running expenses for the van averaged £300 per month.

(b) He hired a part-time helper at a cost of £100 per month.

(c) He borrowed £2,000 from his bank, and the interest cost of the loan was £25 per month.

(d) His main business was to sell ice-cream to customers in the street, but he also did some special catering arrangements for business customers, supplying ice-creams for office parties. Sales to these customers were usually on credit.

(e) For the three months to 31 August 20X1, his total sales were:

(i) cash sales £8,900;

(ii) credit sales £1,100.

(f) He purchased his ice-cream from a local manufacturer, Floors Ltd. The cost of purchases in the three months to 31 August 20X1 was £6,200, and at 31 August he had sold every item of inventory. He still owed £700 to Floors Ltd for unpaid purchases on credit.

(g) He used his own home for his office work. Telephone and postage expenses for the three months to 31 August were £150.

(h) During the three month period he paid himself £300 per month.

The income statement for the three months 1 June – 31 August 20X1 will be as follows.

JOCK HEISS
INCOME STATEMENT
FOR THE THREE MONTHS ENDED 31 AUGUST 20X1

	£	£
Sales		10,000
Cost of sales		6,200
Gross profit		3,800
Expenses		
Wages	300	
Van rental	1,000	
Van expenses	900	
Telephone and postage	150	
Interest charges	75	
		2,425
Net profit (transferred to the statement of financial position)		1,375

Note the following points.

(a) The net profit is the profit for the period, and it is transferred to the statement of financial position of the business as part of the proprietor's capital.

(b) Drawings are appropriations of profit and not expenses. They must not be included in the income statement. In this example, the payments that Jock Heiss makes to himself (£900) are drawings.

(c) The cost of sales is £6,200, even though £700 of the costs have not yet been paid and this amount is shown as a payable in the statement of financial position.

The income statement deals with the activities of a business over time. The statement of financial position shows the state of a business at a particular point in time. The two statements are connected through the capital section of the statement of financial position.

8 RELATIONSHIP WITH THE STATEMENT OF FINANCIAL POSITION

The relationship between the income statement and the statement of financial position is through the capital section of the statement of financial position as shown below.

8.1 Income statement and statement of financial position

SAMINA SUPERMARKET
INCOME STATEMENT
FOR THE YEAR ENDED 31 MARCH 20X1

	£	£
Sales		100,000
Cost of goods sold		60,000
Less expenses		40,000
Selling	8,000	
Distribution	5,000	
Administration	7,000	
		20,000
Net profit		20,000

SAMINA SUPERMARKET
STATEMENT OF FINANCIAL POSITION
AS AT 31 MARCH 20X1

	£	£
Non-current assets		
Buildings		50,000
Van		15,000
Furniture		10,000
		75,000
Current assets		
Inventory	20,000	
Receivables	5,500	
Cash	7,200	
		32,700
		107,700
Capital		
Capital as at 1 April 20X0		62,600
Profit for the year		20,000
		82,600
Less: drawings		(3,500)
Capital as at 31 March 20X1		79,100
Non-current liabilities		
Loan		20,000
Current liabilities		
Payables		8,600
		107,700

The owner's investment, ie capital at the beginning of the financial year, stood at £62,600. It increased by the profit made by the business (£20,000). However, the resulting capital total of £82,600 was reduced by drawings of £3,500, resulting in a final balance of £79,100.

8.2 Capital and revenue expenditure

Now that you understand the relationship between the income statement and the statement of financial position, you need to be able to decide which items appear in a statement of financial position and which appear in an income statement. In order to do this we need to turn our attention to the distinctions between capital and revenue items.

Definition

> **Capital expenditure** is expenditure which results in the acquisition of non-current assets, or an improvement in their earning capacity.

(a) Capital expenditure results in the recognition of a non-current asset in the statement of financial position of the business.

(b) Capital expenditure is not charged as an expense in the income statement. Instead, the capital expenditure is gradually reduced in the statement of financial position and written-off over a period of time. The amount of the annual write-off is called the depreciation expense (introduced earlier in this chapter) and it is this annual expense (rather than the capital expenditure itself) that appears in the income statement.

Definition

> **Revenue expenditure** is expenditure which is incurred either:
>
> (a) for the purpose of running the business, including expenditure classified as selling and distribution expenses, administration expenses and finance charges eg interest expense; or
>
> (b) to maintain the non-current assets in their present condition (improving the non-current assets is capital expenditure).

Revenue expenditure is charged to the income statement of a period, provided that it relates to the trading activity and sales of that particular period. For example, if a business buys ten widgets for £200 (£20 each) and sells eight of them during an accounting period, it will have two widgets left in inventory at the end of the period. The full £200 is revenue expenditure but only £160 is a cost of goods sold during the period. The remaining £40 (cost of two units) will be included in the statement of financial position in the inventory of goods held ie as a current asset valued at £40.

Activity 9 **(5 minutes)**

Suppose that a business purchases a building for £30,000. It then adds an extension to the building at a cost of £10,000. The building needs to have a few broken windows mended, its floors polished and some missing roof tiles replaced. These cleaning and maintenance jobs cost £900. Should these three separate amounts be treated as capital or revenue expenditure?

8.3 Capital income and revenue income

Capital income is the proceeds from the sale of non-trading assets (ie proceeds from the sale of non-current assets, including non-current asset investments). The profits (or losses) from the sale of non-current assets are included in the income statement of a business, for the accounting period in which the sale takes place.

Revenue income is income derived from:

(a) the sale of inventory; or
(b) interest and dividends received from investments held by the business.

The categorisation of capital and revenue items given above does not mention raising additional capital from the owner(s) of the business, or raising and repaying loans. These are transactions which either:

(a) add to the cash assets of the business, thereby creating a corresponding liability (capital or loan); or

(b) when a loan is repaid, reduce the liabilities (loan) and the assets (cash) of the business.

None of these transactions would be reported through the income statement.

8.4 Why is the distinction between capital and revenue items important?

Since revenue items and capital items are accounted for in different ways, the correct and consistent calculation of profit for any accounting period depends on the correct and consistent classification of items as revenue or capital.

Activity 10 **(5 minutes)**

Complete the missing words to ensure you fully understand the difference between capital and revenue items.

Revenue expenditure results from the purchase of goods and services that will either:

(a) be ___________ fully in the accounting period in which they are _________, and so be a cost or expense in the income statement; or

(b) result in a ___________asset as at the end of the accounting period (because the goods or services have not yet been consumed or made use of).

Capital expenditure results in the purchase or improvement of _____________assets, which are assets that will provide benefits to the business in more than ____________ accounting period, and which are not acquired with a view to being resold in the normal course of trade. The cost of purchased non-current assets is not charged _________ to the income statement of the period in which the purchase occurs. Instead, the non-current asset is gradually ________________ over a number of accounting periods.

NOTES

Chapter roundup

- A statement of financial position is a statement of the financial position of a business at a given moment. It lists the assets, liabilities and capital of a business in a logical and informative manner.
- A standard layout for the statement of financial position is prescribed for limited companies; other entities may adopt other formats.
- The main groupings to remember are: non-current assets; current assets; current liabilities; non-current liabilities; capital.
- 'Current' means within one year. Current assets are expected to be converted into cash within one year. Current liabilities are debts which are payable within one year.
- Non-current assets are those acquired for long term use in the business. They are normally valued at cost less depreciation.
- An income statement shows the revenue generated during a period and the expenditure incurred in earning that revenue. The difference between them is the profit or loss for the period.
- The income statement is related to the statement of financial position through the capital section of the statement of financial position.
- The correct accounting treatment of an item depends partly on whether it is of a capital or a revenue nature.

Quick quiz

1 What is the purpose of a statement of financial position?

2 List two main categories of non-current assets.

3 What is meant by depreciation?

4 What are the main items of current assets in a statement of financial position?

5 Give three examples of current liabilities.

6 What will be included in the capital section of a statement of financial position?

7 What are the main categories of expenditure shown in the accounts of a limited company?

8 Where in the financial statements do the proprietor's drawings appear?

Answers to Quick quiz

1 It shows the financial position of the business on a certain date.

2 Intangible, tangible.

3 A measure of the wearing out of a non-current asset over its life.

4 Inventories, receivables, short term investments, cash, bank.

5 Trade payables, bank overdraft, taxation payable.

6 Amounts invested and withdrawn by the owner and profits earned by the business.

7 Check your answer with the examples given in the chapter.

8 As a deduction from net profit in the capital section of the statement of financial position.

Answers to Activities

1 Your answers should have covered the following points.

(a) A statement of financial position is a listing of asset and liability balances (including capital) on a certain date.

(b) Both. A statement of financial position will be included in financial accounts, showing the position at the year end. A forecast statement of financial position may also be used in management decision making.

2

Assets	=	*Capital*	+	*Liabilities*
£(67,000 + 16,900)	=	£51,600	+	£(7,300 + 25,000)
£83,900	=	£83,900		

3 The point in this case is that the car has a residual value of £3,400. It would be inappropriate to account for depreciation in such a way as to write off the asset completely over three years; the aim should be to account only for its loss of value (£10,000 – £3,400 = £6,600), which suggests depreciation of £2,200 per annum.

4

Asset	**Business**	**Current or Non-current**
Van	Delivery Firm	*Non-current*
Machine	Manufacturing Company	*Non-current*
Car	Car Trader	*Current*
Investment	Any	*Either**

*The classification of the investment will depend on the purpose for which it is held. If the intention is to make a long term investment it will be a non-current asset, but if it is a short term way of investing spare cash it will be a current asset.

5 (a) Receivables are valued at the cash value of the debt – ie at their realisable value.

(b) Inventories of goods are usually valued at historical cost. However, if the net realisable value (NRV) of inventories is less than their cost, the goods will be valued at NRV instead of cost. In other words, inventories of goods are valued at the lower of their cost and net realisable value. In normal circumstances, the lower of the two amounts is cost.

6 Non-current asset = N Current asset = C Liabilities = L

(a)	A computer used in the accounts department of a retail store	N
(b)	A computer on sale in an office equipment shop	C
(c)	Wages due to be paid to staff at the end of the week	L
(d)	A van for sale in a motor dealer's showroom	C
(e)	A delivery van used in a grocer's business	N
(f)	An amount owing to a bank for a loan for the acquisition of a van, to be repaid over 9 months	L

7

SUNKEN ARCHES STATEMENT OF FINANCIAL POSITION
AS AT 31 DECEMBER 20X0

	£	£
Non-current assets		
Freehold premises		50,000
Fixtures and fittings		8,000
Motor vehicles		9,000
		67,000
Current assets		
Inventories	16,000	
Receivables	500	
Cash	100	
		16,600
		83,600
Capital		
Capital as at 1 January 20X0		47,600
Profit for the year		8,300
		55,900
Less drawings		(4,000)
		51,900
Non-current liabilities		
Loan		25,000
Current liabilities		
Bank overdraft	2,000	
Payables	4,700	
		6,700
		83,600

8 A common reason for offering discount is to encourage a higher volume of sales. This is often seen in a retail context ('one ball point pen for 25p or five for £1'), and is common too on a larger scale (for example, a publisher will sell his books to customers, ie bookshops, at a discount level reflecting the purchasing 'clout' of the individual bookshop). By generating more activity the business aims to increase the total amount of profit from the amount it would have earned on a lower activity level.

9 The original purchase (£30,000) and the cost of the extension (£10,000) are capital expenditure because they are incurred to acquire and then improve a non-current asset. The other costs of £900 are revenue expenditure, because these merely maintain the building and thus the 'earning capacity' of the building.

10 The missing words are: used; purchased; current; non-current; one; in full; depreciated.

Chapter : 13
FINANCIAL RECORDS

Introduction

The income statement and the statement of financial position provide a summary of the activities and the resulting financial position of a business. Accounting needs evidence that these activities and events, called transactions, have taken place. This evidence is provided by a number of documents. These documents are the source of all the information recorded by a business and are therefore called source documents. Examples of source documents are many including sales and purchase invoices.

Records of source documents are kept in 'books of prime entry' which, as the name suggests, are the first stage at which a business transaction enters into the accounting system. The various books of prime entry are discussed in Section 2.

Your objectives

In this chapter you will learn about the following.

(a) The role of source documents

(b) The books of prime entry

(c) The purpose of sales and purchase day books and how they are prepared

(d) The sales and purchases returns day books and how they are prepared

(e) The cash book and how it is prepared

Source documents and books of prime entry were covered in Unit 2, Managing Financial Resources and Decisions. Some of the content of this chapter will therefore be familiar to you from that unit.

1 SOURCE DOCUMENTS

From the previous chapters you should have grasped some important points about the nature and purpose of accounting. You should have realised that most organisations exist to provide products and services in the ultimate hope of making profit for their owners, which they do by receiving payment in money for goods and services provided. Whenever such activities take place, they need to be recorded. They are recorded on what is called a document.

Whenever a business transaction takes place, involving sales or purchases, receiving or paying money, or owing or being owed money, it is usual for the transaction to be recorded on a document. These documents are the source of all the information recorded by a business. The documents used to record the business transactions of a business include:

(a) the sales order
(b) the purchase order
(c) the invoice
(d) the credit note
(e) the debit note
(f) the goods received note

We will now look at each of these documents in turn.

1.1 Sales order

A document showing the goods or services the customer wishes to buy.

1.2 Purchase order

A document sent by a business to a supplier ordering specified goods or services.

1.3 Invoice

An invoice relates to a sales order or a purchase order. When a business sells goods or services on credit to a customer, it sends out an invoice. The details on the invoice should match up with the details on the sales order. The invoice is a request for the customer to pay what he owes. Similarly, when a business buys goods or services on credit it receives an invoice from the supplier. The details on the invoice should match up with the details on the purchase order.

The invoice is primarily a demand for payment, but it is used for other purposes as well. Because it has several uses, an invoice is often produced on multi-part stationery, or photocopied, or carbon-copied. The top copy will go to the customer and other copies will be used by various people within the business.

1.4 What does an invoice show?

Most invoices are numbered, so that the business can keep track of all the invoices it sends out. Information usually shown on an invoice includes the following.

(a) Name and address of the seller and the purchaser

(b) Date of the sale

(c) Description of what is being sold

(d) Quantity and unit price of what has been sold (eg 20 pairs of shoes at £25 a pair)

(e) Details of trade discount, if any (eg 10% reduction in cost if buying over 100 pairs of shoes). We shall look at discounts in a later chapter

(f) Total amount of the invoice including (in the UK) any details of VAT

(g) Sometimes, the date by which payment is due, and other terms of sale

1.5 Credit note

A document issued by the seller to show a reduction in the amount owed by the buyer. The reduction could be due to a variety of reasons such as:

(a) goods were not according to specifications
(b) goods were damaged during packing or transit
(b) goods were faulty.

A credit note is sometimes printed in red to distinguish it from an invoice. Otherwise, it will be made out in much the same way as an invoice, but with less detail and 'Credit Note Number' instead of 'Invoice Number'.

1.6 Debit note

A document issued by the buyer to show a reduction in the amount owed to the seller/supplier. More commonly, a debit note is issued by the buyer to the seller as a means of formally requesting a credit note. It may also be issued by the seller to increase the amount already owed by the buyer.

1.7 Goods Received Note (GRN)

This is a document which is filled in to record a receipt of goods, most commonly in a warehouse. It may be used in addition to suppliers' advice notes. Often the accounts department will require to see the relevant GRN before paying a supplier's invoice. Even where GRNs are not routinely used, the details of a consignment from a supplier which arrives without an advice note must always be recorded.

Activity 1 **(5 minutes)**

Answer the following questions to make sure you are familiar with source documents.

(a) Explain how an invoice relates to a sales order.
(b) Why is a credit note issued?
(c) Who fills in the GRNs?

The source documents provide the evidence needed for recording business transactions in the accounting system. The transactions are first recorded in what are called books of prime entry.

2 BOOKS OF PRIME ENTRY

We have seen that in the operation of a business, source documents are created. The details on these source documents need to be summarised, as otherwise the business might forget to ask for some money, or forget to pay some, or even accidentally pay something twice. In other words, it needs to keep records of source documents – of transactions – so that it can keep tabs on what is going on. When a business is small, it can keep all these details in a single binder or book. However, as the firm grows, it becomes impossible to keep all records in just one binder/book. Maintaining separate binders/books for similar transactions, eg a separate book only for credit sales, another one only for credit purchases and so on makes the process of recording and retrieving information far more manageable and efficient (as more than one person can work on recording information at the same time).

Definition

> **Books of prime entry** or **day books** refer to a set of 'books' in which transactions are initially recorded in the accounting system; it is in these 'books' that information is recorded from the source documents at the start of the accounting process. Each of the books record only a particular type of transaction eg credit sales, credit purchases etc.

The main books of prime entry which we need to look at are:

(a) the sales day book
(b) the purchase day book
(c) the sales returns day book
(d) the purchases returns day book
(e) the journal (described in the next chapter)
(f) the cash book
(g) the petty cash book.

It is worth bearing in mind that, for convenience, this chapter describes books of prime entry as if they are actual books. Nowadays, books of prime entry are often not books at all, but rather files hidden in the memory of a computer. However, the principles remain the same whether they are manual or computerised.

2.1 The sales day book

The sales day book is used to keep a list of all invoices sent out to customers each day. An extract from a sales day book might look like this.

SALES DAY BOOK

Date	*Invoice*	*Customer*	*Sales ledger folio*	*Total amount invoiced*
20X1				£
Jan 10	247	Jones & Co	SL 14	105.00
	248	Smith Ltd	SL 8	86.40
	249	Alex & Co	SL 6	31.80
	250	Enor College	SL 9	1,264.60
				1,487.80

The column called 'sales ledger folio' is a reference to the sales ledger. We will explain ledger accounting in the next chapter.

Most businesses 'analyse' their sales. For example, suppose that the business sells boots and shoes, and that the sale to Smith was entirely boots, the sale to Alex was entirely shoes, and the other two sales were a mixture of both.

Then the sales day book might look like this.

SALES DAY BOOK

Date	*Invoice*	*Customer*	*Sales ledger folio*	*Total amount invoiced*	*Boot sales*	*Shoe sales*
20X1				£	£	£
Jan 10	247	Jones & Co	SL 14	105.00	60.00	45.00
	248	Smith Ltd	SL 8	86.40	86.40	
	249	Alex & Co	SL 6	31.80		31.80
	250	Enor College	SL 9	1,264.60	800.30	464.30
				1,487.80	946.70	541.10

This sort of analysis gives the managers of the business useful information which helps them to decide how best to run the business.

2.2 The purchase day book

A business also keeps a record in the purchase day book of all the invoices it receives. An extract from a purchase day book might look like this.

PURCHASE DAY BOOK

Date	*Supplier*	*Purchase ledger folio*	*Total amount invoiced*	*Purchases*	*Electricity etc*
20X1			£	£	£
Mar 15	Cook & Co	PL 31	315.00	315.00	
	W Butler	PL 46	29.40	29.40	
	EEB	PL 42	116.80		116.80
	Show Fair Ltd	PL 12	100.00	100.00	
			561.20	444.40	116.80

You should note the following points.

(a) The 'purchase ledger folio' is a reference to the purchase ledger just as the sales ledger folio was to the sales ledger. Again, we will see the purpose of this in the next chapter.

(b) There is no 'invoice number' column, because the purchase day book records other people's invoices, which have all sorts of different numbers.

(c) Like the sales day book, the purchase day book analyses the invoices which have been sent in. In this example, three of the invoices related to goods which the business intends to re-sell (called simply 'purchases') and the fourth invoice was an electricity bill.

2.3 The sales returns day book

When customers return goods for some reason, the returns are recorded in the sales returns day book or as it is sometimes called, the returns inwards journal. An extract from the sales returns day book might look like this.

SALES RETURNS DAY BOOK

Date	*Customer and goods*	*Sales ledger folio*	*Amount*
20X1			£
30 April	Owen Plenty		
	3 pairs 'Texas' boots	SL 82	135.00

Not all sales returns day books analyse what goods were returned, but it makes sense to keep as complete a record as possible.

The source document is the credit note.

2.4 The purchase returns day book

There are no prizes for guessing that the purchase returns day book is kept to record goods which the business sends back to its suppliers. The business might expect a cash refund from the supplier. In the meantime, however, it might issue a debit note to the supplier, indicating the amount by which the business expects its total debt to the supplier to be reduced. An extract from the purchase returns day book might look like this.

PURCHASE RETURNS DAY BOOK

Date	*Supplier and goods*	*Purchase ledger folio*	*Amount*
20X1			£
29 April	Boxes Ltd		
	300 cardboard boxes	PL 123	46.60

Activity 2 **(5 minutes)**

Why do you think businesses maintain separate returns day books rather than recording the returns in the respective sales and purchase day books?

2.5 Journal

Earlier in this chapter, we defined the books of prime entry as the first stage at which a business transaction enters into the accounting system. The journal is one such book of prime entry.

We shall consider the journal in greater detail in chapter 14, once we have introduced double entry bookkeeping.

2.6 The cash book

The cash book is also a day book, which is used to keep a cumulative record of money received and money paid out by the business. The cash book deals with money paid into and out of the business bank account. This could be money received on the business premises in notes, coins and cheques. There are also receipts and payments made by bank transfer, standing order, direct debit and, in the case of bank interest and charges, directly by the bank. Some cash, in notes and coins, is usually kept on the business premises in order to make occasional payments for odd items of expense. This cash is usually referred to as petty cash and is accounted for separately.

One part of the cash book is used to record receipts of cash, and another part is used to record payments. The best way to see how the cash book works is to follow through an example.

EXAMPLE

At the beginning of 1 July 20X1, Robin Plenty had £900 in the bank. On 1 July 20X1, Robin Plenty had the following receipts and payments:

(a) Cash sale – receipt of £80
(b) Payment from credit customer Jo £400 less discount allowed £20
(c) Payment from credit customer Been £720
(d) Payment from credit customer Seed £150 less discount allowed £10
(e) Cheque received for cash to provide a short-term loan from Len Dinger £1,800
(f) Second cash sale – receipts of £150
(g) Cash received for sale of machine £200
(h) Payment to supplier Kew £120
(i) Payment to supplier Hare £310
(j) Payment of telephone bill £400
(k) Payment of gas bill £280
(l) £100 in cash withdrawn from bank for petty cash
(m) Payment of £1,500 to Hess for new plant and machinery

If you look through these transactions, you will see that seven of them are receipts and six of them are payments.

The receipts part of the cash book for 1 July would look like this.

CASH BOOK (RECEIPTS)

Date	*Narrative*	*Folio*	*Total*
20X1			£
1 July	Balance b/d*		900
	Cash sale		80
	Receivable: Jo		380
	Receivable Been		720
	Receivable: Seed		140
	Loan: Len Dinger		1,800
	Cash sale		150
	Sale of machine		200
			4,370
2 July	Balance b/d*		1,660

* 'b/d' = brought down (ie brought forward from the previous period)

You should note the following points.

(a) There is space on the right hand side of the cash book so that the receipts can be analysed under various headings – for example, 'receipts from customers', 'cash sales' and 'other receipts'.

NOTES

(b) The cash received in the day amounted to £3,470. Added to the £900 at the start of the day, this comes to £4,370. But this is not, of course, the amount to be carried forward to the next day, because first we have to subtract all the payments made on 1 July.

The payments part of the cash book for 1 July would look like this.

CASH BOOK (PAYMENTS)

Date	*Narrative*	*Folio*	*Total*
20X1			£
1 July	Payable: Kew		120
	Payable: Hare		310
	Telephone		400
	Gas bill		280
	Petty cash		100
	Machinery purchase		1,500
	Balance c/d*		1,660
			4,370

*'c/d' = carried down

As you can see, this is very similar to the receipts part of the cash book. The only points to note are as follows.

(a) The analysis on the right would be under headings like 'payments to suppliers', 'payments into petty cash', 'wages' and 'other payments'.

(b) Payments during 1 July totalled £2,710. We know that the total of receipts was £4,370. That means that there is a balance of £4,370 – £2,710 = £1,660 to be 'carried down' to the start of the next day. As you can see this 'balance carried down' is noted at the end of the payments column, so that the receipts and payments totals show the same figure of £4,370 at the end of 1 July. And if you look to the receipts part of this example, you can see that £1,660 has been brought down ready for the next day.

With analysis columns completed, the cash book given in the examples above might look as follows.

CASH BOOK (RECEIPTS)

Date	*Narrative*	*Folio*	*Total*	*Receivables*	*Cash sales*	*Other*
20X1			£	£	£	£
1 July	Balance b/d		900			
	Cash sale		80		80	
	Receivable – Jo		380	380		
	Receivable – Been		720	720		
	Receivable – Seed		140	140		
	Loan – Len Dinger		1,800			1,800
	Cash sale		150		150	
	Sale of machine		200			200
			4,370	1,240	230	2,000

NOTES

CASH BOOK (PAYMENTS)

Date	*Narrative*	*Folio*	*Total* £	*Payables* £	*Petty cash* £	*Wages* £	*Other* £
20X1							
1 July	Payable – Kew		120	120			
	Payable – Hare		310	310			
	Telephone		400				400
	Gas bill		280				280
	Petty cash		100		100		
	Machinery purchase		1,500				1,500
	Balance c/d		1,660				
			4,370	430	100	-	2,180

2.7 Petty cash book

Most businesses keep a small amount of cash on the premises to make occasional small payments in cash – eg to pay the milkman, to buy a few postage stamps, to pay the office cleaner, to pay for some bus or taxi fares etc. This is often called the cash float or petty cash account. The cash float can also be the resting place for occasional small receipts, such as cash paid by a visitor to make a phone call, or take some photocopies etc. There are usually more payments than receipts, and petty cash must be 'topped up' from time to time with cash from the business bank account to keep petty cash at an agreed level, say, £100. Expense items are recorded on vouchers as they occur, so that at any time:

	£
Cash remaining in petty cash	X
Plus voucher payments	X
Must equal the agreed sum	X

The balance is made up regularly (to £100, or whatever the agreed sum is) by means of a cash payment from the bank account into petty cash. The amount of the 'top-up' into petty cash will be equal to the total of the voucher payments since the previous top-up.

The format of a petty cash book is much the same as for the cash book, with analysis columns (chiefly for expenditure items, such as travel, postage, cleaning etc).

2.8 Summary

The following table may help you remember the various day books and what is recorded in each book.

Day book		**Transactions recorded**
(a)	Sales day book	credit sales
(b)	Purchase day book	credit purchases
(c)	Sales returns day book (also: returns inwards journal)	returns from customers
(d)	Purchase returns day book (also: returns outwards journal)	returns to suppliers
(e)	Journal	not recorded in the other books (see next chapter)

Day book		Transactions recorded
(f)	Cash book	cash receipts and payments
(g)	Petty cash book	small (petty) cash receipts and payments

Activity 3 **(5 minutes)**

State which books of prime entry the following transactions would be entered into.

(a) Your business pays A Brown (a supplier) £450.

(b) You send D Smith (a customer) an invoice for £650.

(c) Your accounts manager asks you for £12 urgently in order to buy some envelopes.

(d) You receive an invoice from A Brown for £300.

(e) You pay D Smith £500.

(f) F Jones (a customer) returns goods to the value of £250.

(g) You return goods to J Green to the value of £504.

(h) F Jones pays you £500.

Chapter roundup

- Business transactions are recorded on source documents. These include:
  - sales orders
  - purchase orders
  - invoices
  - credit notes
  - debit notes
  - goods received notes (GRNs).
- These transactions are recorded in books of prime entry of which there are seven:
  - the sales day book
  - the sales returns day book
  - the purchase day book
  - the purchase returns day book
  - the cash book
  - the petty cash book
  - the journal.
- Most businesses keep petty cash on the premises which is topped up from the main bank account.
- You should be aware of which transactions go in a given book of prime entry.

Quick quiz

1 Name four pieces of information normally shown on an invoice.

2 What is the difference between a debit and a credit note?

3 Name the seven books of prime entry.

4 What information is summarised in the sales day book?

5 What is the purchase returns day book used for?

6 What is the difference between the cash book and the petty cash book?

Answers to Quick quiz

1 There are a number of possibilities which you may have chosen and you should refer back to section 1.3 of the chapter to check your answer.

2 A credit note shows a reduction in the amount owed by the buyer, whereas a debit note is a formal way of requesting a credit note.

3 Sales day book, purchase day book, sales returns day book, purchase returns day book, journal, cash book, petty cash book.

4 All invoices sent out to customers.

5 Details of goods sent back to suppliers.

6 The petty cash book details small amounts of cash relating to cash kept on the premises, usually in a petty cash box and the cash book records all cash received and paid by the business through its bank account.

Answers to Activities

1 (a) An invoice relates to both a sales order and a purchase order. When a business sells goods or services on credit to a customer, it sends out an invoice. It receives an invoice when it buys goods and services on credit.

(b) A credit note is issued by the seller of goods to the buyer in cases where the buyer is not satisfied with the goods. The credit note shows the allowance that has been given to the buyer for the faulty goods. As a result of the credit note, the amount owed by the buyer is reduced by the amount of the credit note.

(c) Goods received notes (GRNs) are filled in by the buyer (receiver) of goods to record the receipt of goods.

2 The maintenance of separate returns day books helps to ensure that goods returned to the business and by the business are separately identified and accounted for rather than being 'lost' (ie netted) in the sales and purchase day books. Returning goods or receiving returned goods involves time and money. By keeping a separate record of such activity, a business is able to keep a close tab on it and be in a position to take preventive measures, when needed.

3 (a) Cash book
(b) Sales day book
(c) Petty cash book
(d) Purchases day book
(e) Cash book
(f) Sales returns day book
(g) Purchase returns day book
(h) Cash book

Chapter : 14

LEDGER ACCOUNTING AND DOUBLE ENTRY

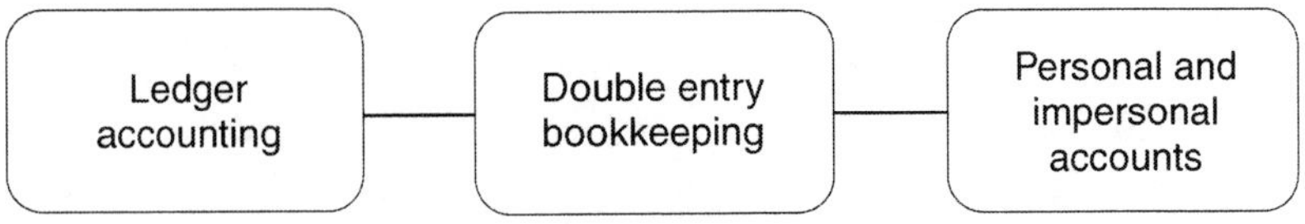

Introduction

Once accounting information has been recorded, it is summarised by means of a nominal or general ledger. The ledger accounts work on the principle of double entry bookkeeping which means that every transaction is recorded twice in the accounts. While some variations are found in practice in the way transactions are recorded using the double entry system, the rules of recording are firmly established.

While transactions can be entered directly into the ledger, they are first recorded in the books of prime entry. The journal is one such book and is used to record those transactions which cannot be recorded in the other books of prime entry discussed in that previous chapter.

Your objectives

In this chapter you will learn about the following.

(a) The need for a nominal ledger

(b) The rules of debit and credit

(c) How to record a variety of transactions in the ledger

(d) The purpose of the sales and purchase ledgers and how they are prepared

(e) The purpose of the journal and how it is prepared.

If you studied Unit 2 under the revised Edexcel guidelines, much of this chapter should be familiar.

1 LEDGER ACCOUNTING

1.1 What is ledger accounting?

In earlier chapters we looked at the income statement and the statement of financial position. We saw that by means of the accounting equation and the business equation, it would be possible to prepare a statement of the affairs of a business at any time we like, and that an income statement and a statement of financial position could be drawn up on any date, relating to any period of time. A business is continually making transactions, buying and selling etc, and we would not want to prepare an income statement and a statement of financial position on completion of every individual transaction. To do so would be a time-consuming and cumbersome administrative task.

However, it is common sense that a business should keep a record of the transactions that it makes, the assets it acquires and liabilities it incurs so that when the time comes to prepare an income statement and a statement of financial position, the relevant information can be taken from those records.

Ledger accounting is the process by which business keeps a record of its transactions:

(a) in chronological order, and dated so that transactions can be related to a particular period of time; and

(b) built up in cumulative totals. For example, a business may build up the total of its sales:

 (i) day by day (eg total sales on Monday, total sales on Tuesday)
 (ii) week by week
 (iii) month by month
 (iv) year by year.

Every business generates a large amount of financial information. The nominal ledger is a means of summarising such information.

1.2 The nominal ledger

Every business needs a means of summarising information required to meet the needs of internal and external users of accounting information.

Definition

> The **nominal** or **general ledger** is a file, binder, floppy disc or some other device which contains all the separate accounts of a business. In other words, a general ledger is an accounting record which summarises the financial affairs of a business.

The general or nominal ledger contains details of assets, liabilities and capital, income and expenditure and so profit or loss. It consists of a large number of different accounts, each account having its own purpose or 'name' and an identity or code. There may be various subdivisions, whether for convenience, ease of handling, confidentiality, security, or to meet the needs of computer software design.

Examples of accounts in the nominal or general ledger include:

(a) plant and machinery at cost (non-current asset)
(b) motor vehicles at cost (non-current asset)
(c) proprietor's capital (liability)
(d) inventory – raw materials (current asset)
(e) inventory – finished goods (current asset)
(f) total receivables (current asset)
(g) total payables (current liability)
(h) wages and salaries (expense item)
(i) rent and rates (expense item)
(j) advertising expenses (expense item)
(k) bank charges (expense item)
(l) motor expenses (expense item)
(m) telephone expenses (expense item)
(n) sales (income)
(o) total cash or bank overdraft (current asset or liability).

We next look at the layout of a ledger account.

1.3 The format of a ledger account

If a ledger account were to be kept in an actual book rather than as a computer record, its format might be as follows.

ADVERTISING EXPENSES

Date	*Narrative*	*Folio*	£	*Date*	*Narrative*	*Folio*	£
20X0							
15 April	JFK Agency for quarter to 31 March	PL 348	2,500				

Only one entry in the account is shown here, because the example is introduced simply to illustrate the general format of a ledger account.

There are two sides to the account, and an account heading on top. Thus, it is convenient to think in terms of 'T' accounts:

(a) on top of the account is its name eg capital, advertising expense etc;
(b) there is a left hand side, or *debit side*; and
(c) there is a right hand side, or *credit side*.

NAME OR TITLE OF ACCOUNT

Left hand side DEBIT SIDE	£	*Right hand side* CREDIT SIDE	£

The words debit and credit have no other meaning in accounting except the left and the right side of an account respectively. As will be explained later, neither debit nor credit implies good or bad news – they simply mean the left or the right side of an account. Similarly, debiting an account only means recording a transaction on the left side of an account (any account) and crediting an account only means entering a transaction on the right hand side of an account.

FOR DISCUSSION

Are the terms debit and credit either good or bad? Or are they simply factual?

We will now look at the way transactions are recorded, using the system of double-entry accounting, in ledger accounts.

2 DOUBLE ENTRY BOOKKEEPING

2.1 Dual effect

Double entry bookkeeping is the method used to transfer our weekly/monthly totals from our books of prime entry into the nominal ledger.

Central to this process is the idea that every transaction has two effects, the **dual effect**. This feature is not something peculiar to businesses. If you were to purchase a car for £1,000 cash for instance, you would be affected in two ways.

(a) You own a car worth £1,000.
(b) You have £1,000 less cash.

If instead you got a bank loan to make the purchase:

(a) You own a car worth £1,000.
(b) You owe the bank £1,000.

A month later if you pay a garage £50 to have the exhaust replaced:

(a) You have £50 less cash.
(b) You have incurred a repairs expense of £50.

Ledger accounts, with their debit and credit side, are kept in a way which allows the two-sided nature of business transactions to be recorded. This system of accounting is known as the '**double entry**' system of bookkeeping, so called because **every transaction is recorded twice** in the accounts.

2.2 The rules of double entry bookkeeping

The basic rule which must always be observed is that **every financial transaction gives rise to two accounting entries, one a debit and the other a credit**. The total value of debit entries in the nominal ledger is therefore always equal at any time to the total value of credit entries. Which account receives the credit entry and which receives the debit depends on the nature of the transaction.

Definitions

- An **increase** in an **expense** (eg a purchase of stationery) or an **increase in an asset** (eg a purchase of office furniture) is a **debit**.
- An **increase** in **income** (eg a sale) or an **increase in a liability** (eg buying goods on credit) is a **credit**.
- A **decrease** in an **asset** (eg making a cash payment) is a **credit**.
- A **decrease** in a **liability** (eg paying a supplier) is a **debit**.

Have a go at the activity below before you learn about this topic in detail.

Activity 1 **(5 minutes)**

Complete the following table relating to the transactions of a bookshop. (The first two are done for you.)

(a) Purchase of books on credit

(i) payables increase	CREDIT	payables (increase in liability)
(ii) purchases expense increases	DEBIT	purchases (item of expense)

(b) Purchase of cash register

(i) own a cash register	DEBIT	cash register (increase in asset)
(ii) cash at bank decreases	CREDIT	cash at bank (decrease in asset)

(c) Payment received from a customer

(i) receivables decrease
(ii) cash at bank increases

(d) Purchase of van

(i) own a van
(ii) cash at bank decreases

How did you get on? Learners coming to the subject for the first time often have difficulty in knowing where to begin. A good starting point is the cash account, ie the nominal ledger account in which receipts and payments of cash are recorded. The rule to remember about the cash account is as follows.

(a) A cash **payment** is a **credit** entry in the cash account. Here the **asset is decreasing**. Cash may be paid out, for example, to pay an expense (such as rates) or to purchase an asset (such as a machine). The matching debit entry is therefore made in the appropriate expense account or asset account.

(b) A cash **receipt** is a **debit** entry in the cash account. Here the **asset is increasing.** Cash might be received, for example, by a retailer who makes a cash sale. The credit entry would then be made in the sales account.

Definition

> **Double entry bookkeeping** is the method by which a business records financial transactions. An account is maintained for every supplier, customer, asset, liability, and income and expense. Every transaction is recorded twice so that for every *debit* there is an equal, corresponding *credit.*

EXAMPLE: DOUBLE ENTRY FOR CASH TRANSACTIONS

In the cash book of a business, the following transactions have been recorded.

(a) A cash sale (ie a receipt) of £2
(b) Payment of a rent bill totalling £150
(c) Buying some goods for cash at £100
(d) Buying some shelves for cash at £200

How would these four transactions be posted to the ledger accounts? For that matter, which ledger accounts should they be posted to? Don't forget that each transaction will be posted twice, in accordance with the rule of double entry.

ANSWER

(a) The two sides of the transaction are:

(i) Cash is received (debit entry in the cash account).
(ii) Sales increase by £2 (credit entry in the sales account).

CASH ACCOUNT

	£		£
Sales a/c	2		

SALES ACCOUNT

	£		£
		Cash a/c	2

(Note how the entry in the cash account is cross-referenced to the sales account and vice-versa. This enables a person looking at one of the accounts to trace where the other half of the double entry can be found.)

(b) The two sides of the transaction are:

(i) Cash is paid (credit entry in the cash account).
(ii) Rent expense increases by £150 (debit entry in the rent account).

CASH ACCOUNT

	£		£
		Rent a/c	150

RENT ACCOUNT

	£		£
Cash a/c	150		

(c) The two sides of the transaction are:

(i) Cash is paid (credit entry in the cash account).

(ii) Purchases increase by £100 (debit entry in the purchases account).

CASH ACCOUNT

	£		£
		Purchases a/c	100

PURCHASES ACCOUNT

	£		£
Cash a/c	100		

(d) The two sides of the transaction are:

(i) Cash is paid (credit entry in the cash account).

(ii) Assets - in this case, shelves - increase by £200 (debit entry in shelves account).

CASH ACCOUNT

	£		£
		Shelves a/c	200

SHELVES (ASSET) ACCOUNT

	£		£
Cash a/c	200		

If all four of these transactions related to the same business, the cash account of that business would end up looking as follows.

CASH ACCOUNT

	£		£
Sales a/c	2	Rent a/c	150
		Purchases a/c	100
		Shelves a/c	200

2.3 Credit transactions

Not all transactions are settled immediately in cash. A business might purchase goods or non-current assets from its suppliers on credit terms, so that the suppliers would be creditors (payables) of the business until settlement was made in cash. Equally, the business might grant credit terms to its customers who would then be debtors (receivables) of the business. Clearly no entries can be made in the cash book when a credit transaction occurs, because initially no cash has been received or paid. Where then can the details of the transactions be entered?

The solution to this problem is to use **receivables and payables accounts**. When a business acquires goods or services on credit, the credit entry is made in an account designated 'payables' instead of in the cash account. The debit entry is made in the appropriate expense or asset account, exactly as in the case of cash transactions. Similarly, when a sale is made to a credit customer the entries made are a debit to the total receivables account (instead of cash account) and a credit to sales account.

EXAMPLE: CREDIT TRANSACTIONS

Recorded in the sales day book and the purchase day book are the following transactions.

(a) The business sells goods on credit to a customer Mr A for £2,000.
(b) The business buys goods on credit from a supplier B Ltd for £100.

How and where are these transactions posted in the ledger accounts?

ANSWER

(a)

RECEIVABLES ACCOUNT

	£		£
Sales a/c	2,000		

SALES ACCOUNT

	£		£
		Receivables account	2,000

(b)

PAYABLES ACCOUNT

	£		£
		Purchases a/c	100

PURCHASES ACCOUNT

	£		£
Payables a/c	100		

2.4 When cash is paid to suppliers or by customers

What happens when a credit transaction is eventually settled in cash? Suppose that, in the example above, the business paid £100 to B Ltd one month after the goods were acquired. The two sides of this new transaction are:

(a) Cash is paid (credit entry in the cash account)

(b) The amount owing to suppliers is reduced (debit entry in the payables account).

CASH ACCOUNT

	£		£
		Payables a/c (B Ltd)	100

PAYABLES ACCOUNT

	£		£
Cash a/c	100		

If we now bring together the two parts of this example, the original purchase of goods on credit and the eventual settlement in cash, we find that the accounts appear as follows.

CASH ACCOUNT

	£		£
		Payables a/c	100

PURCHASES ACCOUNT

	£		£
Payables a/c	100		

PAYABLES ACCOUNT

	£		£
Cash a/c	100	Purchases a/c	100

The two entries in the payables account cancel each other out, indicating that no money is owing to suppliers any more. We are left with a credit entry of £100 in the cash account and a debit entry of £100 in the purchases account. These are exactly the entries which would have been made to record a *cash* purchase of £100 (compare example above). This is what we would expect: after the business has paid off its suppliers it is in exactly the position of a business which has made cash purchases of £100, and the accounting records reflect this similarity.

Similar reasoning applies when a customer settles his debt. In the example above when Mr A pays his debt of £2,000 the two sides of the transaction are:

(a) Cash is received (debit entry in the cash account)

(b) The amount owed by customers is reduced (credit entry in the receivables account).

CASH ACCOUNT

	£		£
Receivables a/c	2,000		

RECEIVABLES ACCOUNT

	£		£
		Cash a/c	2,000

The accounts recording this sale to, and payment by, Mr A now appear as follows.

CASH ACCOUNT

	£		£
Receivables a/c	2,000		

SALES ACCOUNT

	£		£
		Receivables a/c	2,000

RECEIVABLES ACCOUNT

	£		£
Sales a/c	2,000	Cash a/c	2,000

The two entries in the receivables account cancel each other out; while the entries in the cash account and sales account reflect the same position as if the sale had been made for cash (see above).

Now try the following activity.

Activity 2 **(15 minutes)**

See if you can identify the debit and credit entries in the following transactions.

(a) Bought a machine on credit from A, cost £8,000.
(b) Bought goods on credit from B, cost £500.
(c) Sold goods on credit to C, value £1,200.
(d) Paid D (a supplier) £300.
(e) Collected £180 from E, a debtor.
(f) Paid wages £4,000.
(g) Received rent bill of £700 from landlord G.
(h) Paid rent of £700 to landlord G.
(i) Paid insurance premium £90.

FOR DISCUSSION

Take a look at your bank statement, which is prepared from the bank's point of view. When your account is in credit, the bank owes you money and vice versa. How does this compare with a cash or bank account prepared by a business?

We next look at certain types of accounts which, although not part of the double-entry system, are crucial to the efficient running of a business.

3 PERSONAL AND IMPERSONAL ACCOUNTS

The accounts in the nominal ledger (ledger accounts) relate to types of revenue, expense, asset, liability – rent, rates, sales, receivables, payables etc – rather than to the person to whom the money is paid or from whom it is received. They are therefore called **impersonal** accounts. However, there is also a need for personal accounts, most commonly for receivables and payables and these are contained in the sales ledger and purchase ledger.

3.1 Personal accounts

Personal accounts include details of transactions which have already been summarised in ledger accounts (eg sales invoices are recorded in sales and total receivables, payments to suppliers in the cash and payables accounts). The personal accounts do not therefore form part of the double entry system, as otherwise transactions would be recorded twice over (ie two debits and two credits for each transaction). They are memorandum accounts only.

3.2 The sales ledger

The sales day book provides a chronological record of invoices sent out by a business to credit customers. For many businesses, this might involve very large numbers of invoices per day or per week. The same customer might appear in several different places in the sales day book, for purchases he has made on credit at different times. So at any point in time, a customer may owe money on several unpaid invoices. Therefore, in addition to keeping a chronological record of invoices, a business should also keep a record of how much money each individual credit customer owes, and what this total debt consists of. The need for a personal account for each customer is a practical one.

(a) A customer might telephone, and ask how much he currently owes. Staff must be able to tell him.

(b) It is a common practice to send out statements to credit customers at the end of each month, showing how much they still owe, and itemising new invoices sent out and payments received during the month.

(c) The managers of the business will want to keep a check on the credit position of an individual customer, and to ensure that no customer is exceeding his credit limit by purchasing more goods.

(d) Most important is the need to match payments received against debts owed. If a customer makes a payment, the business must be able to set off the payment against the customer's debt and establish how much he still owes on balance.

Sales ledger accounts are written up as follows.

(a) When entries are made in the sales day book (invoices sent out), they are subsequently also made in the debit side of the relevant customer account in the sales ledger.

(b) Similarly, when entries are made in the cash book (payments received), or in the sales returns day book, they are also made in the credit side of the relevant customer account.

Each customer account is given a reference or code number, and it is that reference which is the 'sales ledger folio' in the sales day book. We say that amounts are posted from the sales day book to the sales ledger. An example of how a sales ledger account is laid out is as follows.

ENOR COLLEGE			A/c no: SL 9
	£		£
Balance b/f	250.00		
10.1.X0 Sales – SDB 48			
(invoice no 250)	1,264.60	Balance c/d	1,514.60
	1,514.60		1,514.60
11.1.X0 Balance b/d	1,514.60		

The debit side of this personal account, then, shows amounts owed by Enor College. When Enor pays some of the money it owes it will be entered into the cash book (receipts) and subsequently 'posted' to the credit side of the personal account. For example, if the college paid £250 on 10.1.20X0, it would appear as follows.

ENOR COLLEGE			A/c no: SL 9
	£		£
Balance b/f	250.00	10.1.X0 Cash	250.00
10.1.X0 Sales – SDB 48			
(invoice no 250)	1,264.60	Balance c/d	1,264.60
	1,514.60		1,514.60
11.1.X0 Balance b/d	1,264.60		

The opening balance owed by Enor College on 11.1.X0 is now £1,264.60 instead of £1,514.60, because of the £250 receipt which came in on 10.1.X0.

3.3 The purchase ledger (bought ledger)

The purchase ledger, like the sales ledger, consists of a number of personal accounts. These are separate accounts for each individual supplier, and they enable a business to keep a continuous record of how much it owes each supplier at any time. After entries are made in the purchase day book, cash book, or purchase returns day book – ie after entries are made in the books of prime entry – they are also made in the relevant supplier account in the purchase ledger. Again we say that the entries in the purchase day book are posted to the suppliers' personal accounts in the purchase ledger.

Following is an example of how a purchase ledger account is laid out.

COOK & CO			A/c no: SL 31
	£		£
		Balance b/f	200.00
		15.3.X8 Invoice received	
Balance c/d	515.00	PDB 37	315.00
	515.00		515.00
		16.3.X8 Balance b/d	515.00

The credit side of this personal account, then, shows amounts owing to Cook & Co. If the business paid Cook & Co some money, it would be entered into the cash book (payments) and subsequently posted to the debit side of the personal account. For example, if the business paid Cook & Co £100 on 15 March 20X8, it would appear as follows:

COOK & CO			A/c no: SL 31
	£		£
15.3.X8 Cash	100.00	Balance b/f	200.00
		15.3.X8 Invoice received	
Balance c/d	415.00	PDB 37	315.00
	515.00		515.00
		16.3.X8 Balance b/d	415.00

The opening balance owed to Cook & Co on 16.3.X8 is now £415.00 instead of £515.00 because of the £100 payment made during 15.3.X8.

The roles of the sales day book and purchases day book are very similar, with one book dealing with invoices sent out and the other with invoices received. The sales ledger and purchases ledger also serve similar purposes, with one consisting of personal accounts for credit customers (receivables) and the other consisting of personal accounts for suppliers (payables).

Transactions can be recorded directly in the ledger accounts. However, with a large number of transactions, detecting errors or following individual transactions through the accounting system can be very difficult. It is the journal where unusual movement between accounts is first recorded.

3.4 The journal

In the previous chapter, we defined the books of prime entry as the first stage at which a business transaction enters into the accounting system. The journal is one such book of prime entry.

Definition

A **journal** is a book of prime entry in which are entered those transactions which cannot be recorded in chronological order. Such transactions are generally non-routine in nature such as sale or purchase of non-current assets, correction of errors etc.

Whatever type of transaction is being recorded, the format of a journal entry is:

Date	*Folio*	*Debit*	*Credit*
		£	£
Account to be debited		X	
Account to be credited			X
(Narrative to explain transaction)			

Remember: in due course, the ledger accounts will be written up to include the transactions listed in the journal.

A narrative explanation must accompany each journal entry. It is required for audit and control.

EXAMPLES: JOURNAL ENTRIES

The following is a summary of the transactions of Jo's hairdressing business of which Jo Ruth is the sole proprietor and which Jo started on 1 January.

1 January Put in cash of £2,000 as capital

Purchased brushes and combs for cash £50

Purchased hair driers from Z Ltd on credit £150

The journal entries for these transactions would be as follows.

JOURNAL

			£	£
1 January	DEBIT	Cash	2,000	
	CREDIT	Jo Ruth – capital account		2,000
	Initial capital introduced			
1 January	DEBIT	Brushes and combs account	50	
	CREDIT	Cash		50
	The purchase for cash of brushes and combs as non-current assets			
1 January	DEBIT	Hair dryer account	150	
	CREDIT	Sundry payables account*		150
	The purchase on credit of hair driers as non-current assets			

* Note: Suppliers who have supplied non-current assets are included amongst sundry payables, as distinct from suppliers who have supplied raw materials or goods for resale, who are trade payables. It is quite common to have separate 'total payabless' accounts, one for trade payables and another for sundry other payables.

Activity 3 **(5 minutes)**

Prepare journal entries for the following transactions for Hacker who commenced business as a retail butcher on 1 February 20X1.

1 Feb Put in cash of £4,000 as capital
10 Feb Bought a delivery van at a cost of £900 for cash

Chapter roundup

- A general or nominal ledger is a file, binder, computer disc or floppy containing all the accounts of a business.
- In its most basic form, an account has three elements: a title, the left hand or the debit side and the right hand or the credit side.
- The only meaning of the term debit is the left side of the account and similarly the only meaning of the term credit is the right side of the account.
- In a double entry system, every transaction must be entered in the ledger accounts twice: once as a debit and once as an equal and opposite credit.
- The rules of double entry bookkeeping are:

Account 'type'	*Debit*	*Credit*
Asset	Increase	Decrease
Expense	Increase	Decrease
Liability	Decrease	Increase
Capital	Decrease	Increase
Income/Revenue	Decrease	Increase

- The rules of double entry bookkeeping are best learnt by considering the cash book. In the cash book a credit entry indicates a payment made by the business; the matching debit entry is then made in an account denoting an expense paid, an asset purchased or a liability settled. A debit entry in the cash book indicates cash received by the business; the matching credit entry is then made in an account denoting revenue received, a liability created or a debt paid off.
- Some accounts in the nominal ledger represent the total of very many smaller balances. For example, the receivables account represents all the balances owed by individual customers of the business, while the payables account represents all amounts owed by the business to its suppliers.
- To keep track of individual customer and supplier balances, it is common to maintain subsidiary ledgers (called the sales ledger and the purchase ledger respectively). Each account in these ledgers represents the balance owed by or to an individual customer or supplier. These subsidiary ledgers are kept purely for reference and are therefore known as memorandum records. They do not normally form part of the double entry system.
- The journal is a book of prime entry where non-routine transactions which cannot be recorded in other books are recorded.

Quick quiz

1 What do the terms debit and credit mean?

2 List the rules of debit and credit bookkeeping.

3 What is the double entry to record a cash sale of £50?

4 What is the double entry to record a purchase of office chairs for £1,000 cash?

5 What is the double entry to record a credit sale?

6 What is the difference between the payables account in the nominal ledger and the purchase ledger?

Answers to Quick quiz

1 They relate to the two sides of ledger accounts.

2 Every debit must have a corresponding credit in the double entry system and the chapter gives further details depending on the type of transaction.

3 DEBIT: Cash £50
CREDIT: Sales £50.

4 DEBIT: Office furniture (or similar account) £1,000
CREDIT: Cash £1,000.

5 DEBIT: Receivables
CREDIT: Sales.

6 The payables account in the nominal ledger represents amounts owed by the business to suppliers and the purchase ledger provides memorandum entries for each individual supplier.

Answers to Activities

1 (c) Payment received from a customer

(i)	receivables decrease	CREDIT	receivables (decrease in asset)
(ii)	cash at bank increases	DEBIT	cash at bank (increase in asset)

(d) Purchase of van

(i)	own a van	DEBIT	van (increase in asset)
(ii)	cash at bank decreases	CREDIT	cash at bank (decrease in asset)

NOTES

2

			£	£
(a)	DEBIT	Machine account (fixed asset)	8,000	
	CREDIT	Payables (A)		8,000
(b)	DEBIT	Purchases account	500	
	CREDIT	Payables (B)		500
(c)	DEBIT	Receivables (C)	1,200	
	CREDIT	Sales		1,200
(d)	DEBIT	Payables (D)	300	
	CREDIT	Cash		300
(e)	DEBIT	Cash	180	
	CREDIT	Receivables (E)		180
(f)	DEBIT	Wages account	4,000	
	CREDIT	Cash		4,000
(g)	DEBIT	Rent account	700	
	CREDIT	Payables (G)		700
(h)	DEBIT	Payables (G)	700	
	CREDIT	Cash		700
(i)	DEBIT	Insurance costs	90	
	CREDIT	Cash		90

3

	JOURNAL		£	£
1 February	DEBIT	Cash	4,000	
	CREDIT	Hacker – Capital		4,000
	Initial capital introduced			
10 February	DEBIT	Delivery van	900	
	CREDIT	Cash		900
	The purchase of delivery van for cash			

Chapter : 15

PREPARATION OF ACCOUNTS FROM A TRIAL BALANCE

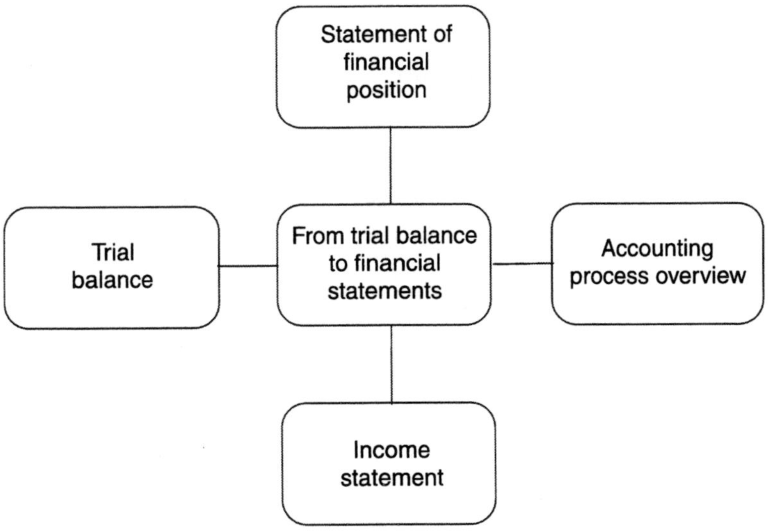

Introduction

You have learned the principles of double entry and how to post the ledger accounts. Once all the transactions have been posted, it is usual to test the accuracy of double entry bookkeeping records by preparing a trial balance. Its preparation also provides a convenient stepping stone to the preparation of the final accounts (and the related financial statements).

The trial balance is prepared by taking the balance of each and every account and aggregating separately the accounts with debit balances and those with credit balances. If the two totals equal, it will show that the basic principle of double entry has been correctly applied. Although such equality does not guarantee error-free accounting, it is possible to prepare final accounts directly from a trial balance without going through the time consuming process of referring to the ledger accounts. Once the final accounts have been prepared, preparation of financial statements is merely a matter of rearranging the information.

Your objectives

In this chapter you will learn about the following.

(a) The purpose of a trial balance and how it is prepared

(b) The circumstances when a trial balance might balance despite certain types of errors

(c) How to prepare an income statement from the trial balance

(d) How to balance accounts and prepare a statement of financial position

(e) All the accounting steps involved from entering transactions in the ledger accounts to preparing the financial statements

NOTES

1 TRIAL BALANCE

The earlier chapter on double entry would have shown you the following.

(a) Each transaction is entered at least twice in the ledger: once as a debit and once as a credit.

(b) The £ amounts of debit and credit entered for each transaction are equal.

Since equal £ amounts of debits and credits are recorded for each and every transaction, it follows that if all the debits in the ledger are added up, they must equal the total of all the credits in the ledger.

Total debit £ amount = Total credit £ amount

It is desirable that this equality is proven after all the transactions have been posted to the ledger but before the final accounts and the related financial statements are prepared. This proof of equality of debits and credits is obtained through the preparation of a trial balance.

The steps involved in preparing a trial balance are as follows.

(a) Find the balance on the ledger accounts

(b) Record the ledger account balances in the appropriate column of the trial balance

(c) Total each column

(d) Compare the totals of the two columns of the trial balance

Before you draw up a trial balance, you will have a collection of ledger accounts, such as below.

CASH

	£		£
Capital - Ron Knuckle	7,000	Rent	3,500
Bank loan	1,000	Shop fittings	2,000
Sales	10,000	Trade payables	5,000
Receivables	2,500	Bank loan interest	100
		Incidental expenses	1,900
		Drawings	1,500
			14,000
		Balancing figure	6,500
	20,500		20,500

CAPITAL (RON KNUCKLE)

	£		£
		Cash	7,000

BANK LOAN

	£		£
		Cash	1,000

PURCHASES

	£		£
Trade payables	5,000		

NOTES

TRADE PAYABLES

	£		£
Cash	5,000	Purchases	5,000

RENT

	£		£
Cash	3,500		

SHOP FITTINGS

	£		£
Cash	2,000		

SALES

	£		£
		Cash	10,000
		Receivables	2,500
			12,500

RECEIVABLES

	£		£
Sales	2,500	Cash	2,500

BANK LOAN INTEREST

	£		£
Cash	100		

OTHER EXPENSES

	£		£
Cash	1,900		

DRAWINGS ACCOUNT

	£		£
Cash	1,500		

Given a series of accounts in which transactions have been recorded, the process of preparing a trial balance is as follows.

1.1 *Step 1:* Finding the balance on the ledger accounts

At the end of an accounting period all ledger accounts are 'balanced'. This means finding the balance in each account by going through the following procedure.

(a) Total all the debits in the account, ie find the total of the left side of the account.

(b) Total all the credits on the account, ie total the right side of the account.

(c) Subtract the lower side total from the higher side total.

(d) If the higher side is the debit side, ie if total debits exceed total credits, the account has a debit balance.

NOTES

(e) If, on the other hand, the higher side is the credit side, ie if total credits exceed total debits, the account has a credit balance.

(f) If the debit and credit sides of an account are equal, the account has a zero balance.

In our example of Ron Knuckle, there is very little balancing to do.

(a) The trade payables account and the receivables account balance off to zero.
(b) The cash account has a debit balance of £6,500.
(c) The total on the sales account is £12,500, which is a credit balance.

The remaining accounts have only one entry each, so there is no totalling to do.

1.2 *Step 2:* Recording the balances

Once all the accounts have been 'balanced', a list of all the accounts along with their balances is prepared. The crucial thing is that the debit balances are entered in the debit column and the credit balances are recorded in the credit column of the trial balance. This is illustrated below for Ron Knuckle's accounts.

	Debit	*Credit*
	£	£
Cash	6,500	
Capital		7,000
Bank loan		1,000
Purchases	5,000	
Trade payables	-	-
Rent	3,500	
Shop fittings	2,000	
Sales		12,500
Receivables	-	-
Bank loan interest	100	
Other expenses	1,900	
Drawings	1,500	

1.3 *Step 3:* Totalling each column

After all the accounts and their balances have been entered in the proper columns (debit balances in the left-hand column and credit balances in the right-hand column), the two columns are then totalled.

	Debit	*Credit*
	£	£
Cash	6,500	
Capital		7,000
Bank loan		1,000
Purchases	5,000	
Trade payables	-	-
Rent	3,500	
Shop fittings	2,000	
Sales		12,500
Receivables	-	-
Bank loan interest	100	
Other expenses	1,900	
Drawings	1,500	
	20,500	20,500

1.4 *Step 4:* Comparing the totals

The final step in preparing the trial balance is to make sure that the totals of the debit and the credit columns are equal.

In our example, the two columns do total to £20,500. But what if the trial balance shows unequal debit and credit balances?

If the two columns of the trial balance are not equal, this means that there are error(s) in recording the transactions in the accounts or that mistake(s) have been made in entering the balances in the trial balance. These errors need to be corrected before going any further.

However, it is possible for the trial balance to balance, ie for debit and credit column totals to be equal, and still to have errors present. The errors that a trial balance will not disclose are the following.

(a) The complete omission of a transaction, because neither a debit nor a credit is made

(b) The posting of a debit or credit to the correct side of the ledger, but to a wrong account, eg debiting furniture account as opposed to cash

(c) Compensating errors, eg an error of £100 is exactly cancelled by another £100 error elsewhere

(d) Errors of principle, eg cash received from customers being debited to the receivables account and credited to cash instead of the other way round

---

EXAMPLE

As at 30.3.20X1, your business has the following balances on its ledger accounts.

Accounts	*Balance*
	£
Bank loan	12,000
Cash	11,700
Capital	13,000
Rates	1,880
Trade payables	11,200
Purchases	12,400
Sales	14,600
Sundry payables	1,620
Receivables	12,000
Bank loan interest	1,400
Other expenses	11,020
Vehicles	2,020

During the next day the business made the following transactions.

(a) Bought materials for £1,000, half for cash and half on credit.
(b) Made £1,040 sales, £800 of which was for credit.
(c) Paid wages to shop assistants of £260 in cash.

We will now draw up a trial balance showing the balances as at the end of 31.3.X1.

First it is necessary to put the original balances into a trial balance – ie decide which are debit and which are credit balances.

Account	*Debit*	*Credit*
	£	£
Bank loan		12,000
Cash	11,700	
Capital		13,000
Rates	1,880	
Trade payables		11,200
Purchases	12,400	
Sales		14,600
Sundry payables		1,620
Receivables	12,000	
Bank loan interest	1,400	
Other expenses	11,020	
Vehicles	2,020	
	52,420	52,420

1.5 The Rule of Thumb

With practice you will be able to distinguish between debit and credit balances at a glance. What may help you in the beginning is a simple rule of thumb: **accounts are likely to reflect the balance on the side on which increases are recorded in that account**. In other words, if the increases in an account are recorded on the debit side, the account is likely to have a debit balance and similarly if the increases are recorded on the credit side, the account will show a credit balance. In the above example, cash is shown as having a debit balance. Cash is an asset and hence increases are recorded on the debit side. Trade payables, on the other hand, is a liability account. Increases in liability accounts are recorded on the credit side and hence trade payables is showing a credit balance (as are sundry payables).

Now we must take account of the effects of the three transactions which took place on 31.3.X1:

			£	£
(a)	DEBIT	Purchases	1,000	
	CREDIT	Cash		500
		Trade payables		500
(b)	DEBIT	Cash	240	
		Receivables	800	
	CREDIT	Sales		1,040
(c)	DEBIT	Other expenses	260	
	CREDIT	Cash		260

When these figures are included in the trial balance, it becomes:

Account	*Debit*	*Credit*
	£	£
Bank loan		12,000
Cash (11,700 – 500 + 240 – 260)	11,180	
Capital		13,000
Rates	1,880	
Trade payables (11,200 + 500)		11,700
Purchases (12,400 + 1,000)	13,400	
Sales (14,600 + 1,040)		15,640
Sundry payables		1,620
Receivables (12,000 + 800)	12,800	
Bank loan interest	1,400	
Other expenses (11,020 + 260)	11,280	
Vehicles	2,020	
	53,960	53,960

Activity 1 **(15 minutes)**

S Trader carries on a small business. The following balances have been extracted from his books on 30 September 20X0.

	£
Capital	24,239
Office furniture	1,440
Drawings	4,888
Inventory	14,972
Purchases	167,760
Sales	184,269
Rent	1,350
Lighting and heating	475
Insurance	304
Salaries	6,352
Receivables	19,100
Payables	8,162
Petty cash in hand	29

Prepare a trial balance as at 30 September 20X0.

Now that you understand how a trial balance is prepared and what it is supposed to do, we will give you a concise definition of a trial balance, something we have avoided doing so far.

Definition

A **trial balance** is a schedule which lists all the accounts of the ledger along with their balances in the appropriate debit or credit column. It is used to ensure that the equality of debits and credits has been maintained in preparing the ledger accounts.

Once a trial balance has been balanced, the next step is to start preparing the financial statements. We start by looking at the income statement.

2 INCOME STATEMENT

The first step in the process of preparing the financial statements is to open up another ledger account, called the income and expense account. In it a business summarises its results for the period by gathering together all the ledger account balances relating to income and expenses. This account is still part of the double entry system, so the basic rule of double entry still applies: every debit must have an equal and opposite credit entry.

This income and expense account contains the same information as the financial statement we are aiming for, ie the income statement, and in fact there are very few differences between the two. However, the income statement lays the information out differently and it may be much less detailed.

So what do we do with this new ledger account? The first step is to look through the ledger accounts and identify which ones relate to income and expenses. In the case of Ron Knuckle, the income and expense accounts are the following.

(a) Purchases
(b) Sales
(c) Rent
(d) Bank loan interest
(e) Other expenses

The balances on these accounts are transferred to the new income and expense account. For example, the purchases account has a debit balance of £5,000. To transfer this balance we need to make a credit entry of £5,000 to the account. However, we cannot write £5,000 on the credit side of the purchases account without making a debit entry somewhere else in the ledger (it would be against the rules of double entry). The debit entry would go to the new income and expense account. Now the balance on the purchases account has been moved to the income and expense account.

If we do the same thing with all the separate accounts of Ron Knuckle dealing with income and expenses, the result is as follows.

PURCHASES

	£		£
Trade payables	5,000	Income and expense account	5,000

RENT

	£		£
Cash	3,500	Income and expense account	3,500

BANK LOAN INTEREST

	£		£
Cash	100	Income and expense account	100

OTHER EXPENSES

	£		£
Cash	1,900	Income and expense account	1,900

NOTES

SALES

	£		£
Income and expense account	12,500	Cash	10,000
		Receivables	2,500
	12,500		12,500

INCOME AND EXPENSE ACCOUNT

	£		£
Purchases	5,000	Sales	12,500
Rent	3,500		
Bank loan interest	100		
Other expenses	1,900		

(Note that the income and expense account has not yet been balanced off but we will return to that later.)

If you look at the items we have gathered together in the income and expense account, they should strike a chord in your memory. They are the same items that we need to draw up the income statement in the form of a financial statement. With a little rearrangement they could be presented as follows:

RON KNUCKLE: INCOME STATEMENT

	£	£
Sales		12,500
Cost of sales (= purchases in this case)		(5,000)
Gross profit		7,500
Expenses		
Rent	3,500	
Bank loan interest	100	
Other expenses	1,900	
		(5,500)
Net profit		2,000

The income statement is followed by the preparation of the statement of financial position.

3 THE STATEMENT OF FINANCIAL POSITION

Look back at the ledger accounts of Ron Knuckle. Now that we have dealt with those relating to income and expenses, which ones are left? The answer is that we still have to find out what to do with cash, capital, bank loan, trade payables, shop fittings, receivables and the drawings account.

Are these the only ledger accounts left? No: don't forget there is still the last one we opened up, called the income and expense account. The balance on this account represents the profit earned by the business, and if you go through the arithmetic, you will find that it has a credit balance – a profit – of £2,000. (Not surprisingly, this is the figure that is shown in income statement.) These remaining accounts must also be balanced and ruled off.

However, since these accounts represent assets and liabilities of the business (not income and expenses) their balances are not transferred to the income and expense account. Instead they are carried down in the books of the business. This means that they become opening balances for the next accounting period and indicate the value of the assets and liabilities at the end of one period and the beginning of the next. This should be contrasted with the income and expenses accounts which are closed off at the end of the accounting period and transferred to the income and expense account. This means that at the start of each accounting period, income and expenditure accounts always have a zero starting balance.

The conventional method of ruling off a ledger account at the end of an accounting period is illustrated by the bank loan account in Ron Knuckle's books.

BANK LOAN ACCOUNT

	£		£
Balance carried down (c/d)	1,000	Cash	1,000
		Balance brought down (b/d)	1,000

Ron Knuckle therefore begins the new accounting period with a credit balance of £1,000 on this account. A credit balance brought down denotes a liability. An asset would be represented by a debit balance brought down.

One further point is worth noting before we move on to complete this example. You will remember that a proprietor's capital comprises any cash introduced by him, plus any profits made by the business, less any drawings made by him. At the stage we have now reached these three elements are contained in different ledger accounts:

(a) Cash introduced of £7,000 appears in the capital account

(b) Drawings of £1,500 appear in the drawings account

(c) £2,000 profit made by the business is reflected by the credit balance in the income and expense account.

It is convenient to gather together all these amounts into one capital account, in the same way as we earlier gathered together income and expense accounts into one income and expense account. If we go ahead and gather the three amounts together, the results are as follows.

DRAWINGS

	£		£
Cash	1,500	Capital a/c	1,500

INCOME AND EXPENSE ACCOUNT

	£		£
Purchases	5,000	Sales	12,500
Rent	3,500		
Bank loan interest	100		
Other expenses	1,900		
Capital a/c	2,000		
	12,500		12,500

CAPITAL

	£		£
Drawings	1,500	Cash	7,000
Balance c/d	7,500	Income and expense account	2,000
	9,000		9,000
		Balance b/d	7,500

A re-arrangement of these balances will complete Ron Knuckle's simple statement of financial position.

RON KNUCKLE
STATEMENT OF FINANCIAL POSITION AT END OF FIRST TRADING PERIOD

	£
Assets	
Non-current assets	
Shop fittings	2,000
Current assets	
Cash	6,500
Total assets	8,500
Capital and liabilities	
Proprietor's capital	7,500
Non-current liabilities	
Bank loan	1,000
Total capital and liabilities	8,500

When a statement of financial position is drawn up for an accounting period which is not the first one, it ought to show the capital at the start of the accounting period and the capital at the end of the accounting period.

Activity 2 **(5 minutes)**

If you totalled up an income and expense account and found that it had a debit balance, what would that mean? Where would that balance go?

We next briefly review all the accounting steps involved from the moment transactions enter the accounting system until the preparation of financial statements.

4 ACCOUNTING PROCESS OVERVIEW

The accounting process described to this point may be summarised in the following eight steps.

Step 1: Enter the transactions in the books of prime or original entry.

Step 2: Post the transactions to the nominal ledger.

Step 3: Prepare a trial balance.

Step 4: Make any non-routine or special entries using the journal eg correcting the errors etc.

Step 5: Close all income and expenditure accounts by transferring their balance to income and expense account.

Step 6: Balance all asset, liabilities and capital accounts.

Step 7: Clear profit and drawings balances to the capital account.

Step 8: Prepare the financial statements.

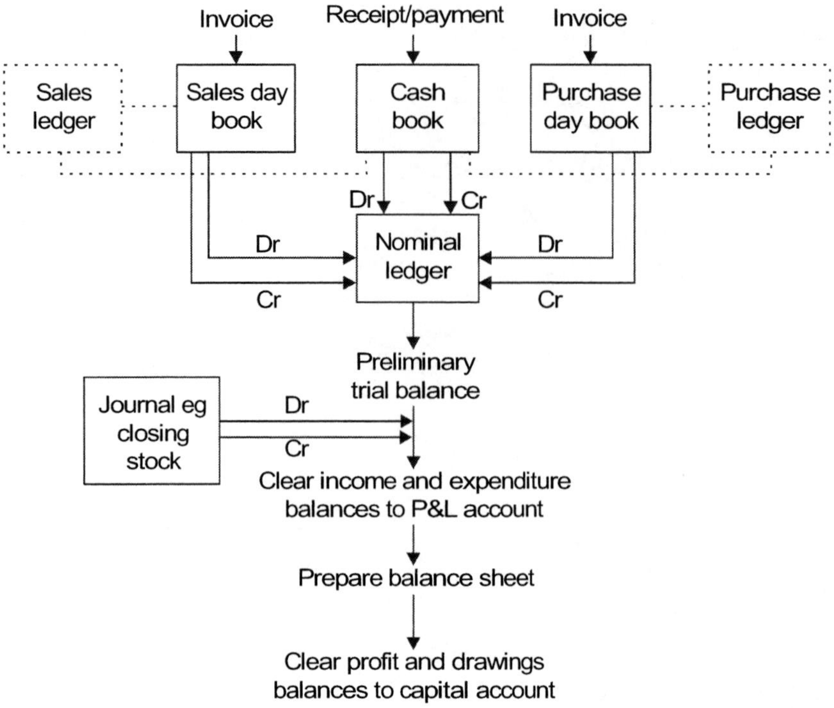

Figure 15.1 Accounting process overview

Chapter roundup

- At suitable intervals, the entries in each ledger account are totalled and a balance is struck. Balances are usually collected in a trial balance which is then used as a basis for preparing an income statement and a statement of financial position.
- A trial balance can be used to test the accuracy of the double entry accounting records. It works by listing the balances on ledger accounts, some of which will be debits and some credits, to see if they balance off to zero.
- The balancing off of the trial balance does not mean that the accounting process, so far, has been error free. There are a number of errors which are not revealed by a balanced-off trial balance.
- An income and expense ledger account is opened up to gather all items relating to income and expenses. When rearranged, the items make up the income statement.
- The balances on all remaining ledger accounts (including the income and expense account) can be listed and rearranged to form the statement of financial position.

Quick quiz

1. What is the purpose of a trial balance?
2. Give four circumstances in which a trial balance might balance although some of the balances are wrong.
3. What is the difference between the ledger account and the financial statement called the income and expense account?
4. What is the difference between balancing off an expense account and balancing off a liability account?

Answers to Quick quiz

1 To test the accuracy of the double entry system.

2 Complete omission of transaction; posting correct amount to incorrect account; compensating error; error of principle.

3 The income statement is the end of year financial statement comprising some of the ledger accounts, and is used to determine profit, whereas the ledger account shows the position in respect of specific expense, income, assets and liabilities.

4 An expense account is 'closed' at the end of the financial year by a transfer to the income and expense account and a liability account remains 'open' for the next accounting period and appears in the statement of financial position.

Answers to Activities

1 TRADER
TRIAL BALANCE
30 SEPTEMBER 20X0

	Dr	*Cr*
	£	£
Capital		24,239
Office furniture	1,440	
Drawings	4,888	
Inventory	14,972	
Purchases	167,760	
Sales		184,269
Rent	1,350	
Lighting and heating	475	
Insurance	304	
Salaries	6,352	
Receivables	19,100	
Payables		8,162
Petty cash	29	
	216,670	216,670

2 A debit balance in the income and expense account would show that the business has suffered a loss for that period.

The debit balance will be transferred to the capital account of the business by crediting the income and expense account and debiting the capital account.

Chapter : 16

PERIOD END ADJUSTMENTS

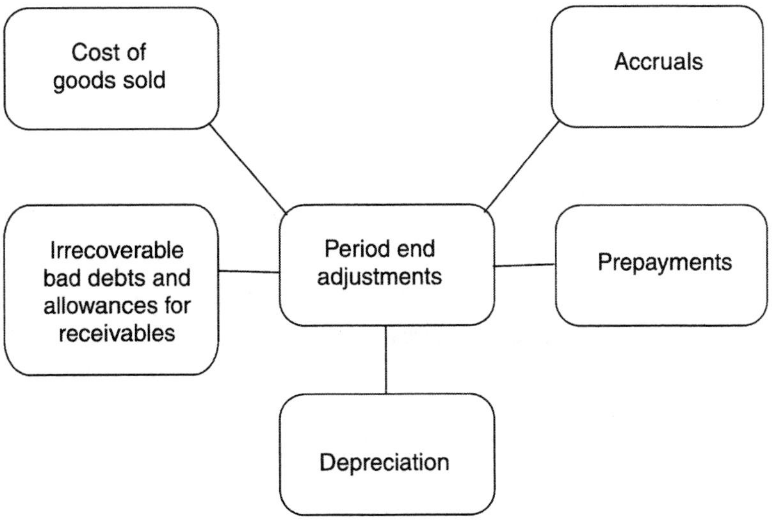

Introduction

The trial balance lists the balances on the ledger accounts at the period end date. It does not take into account various items which can only be calculated right at the end of the period once the final position is known. These adjustments include the cost of goods sold, accruals (expenditure incurred which has not yet been invoiced or paid) prepayments (payments made, some of which relate to the next accounting period) depreciation (the consumption of non-current assets) and irrecoverable debts and allowances for receivables (debts due to the business which may or may not be paid).

It is important that these items are treated correctly in the accounts, to avoid the profit or loss for the year from being over or under estimated.

Your objectives

In this chapter you will learn about the following.

(a) The accruals concept

(b) Accrued expenses and prepayments and their accounting treatment

(c) The main differences between irrecoverable debts and doubtful debts

(d) How to write off an irrecoverable debt and create an allowance for receivables

(e) How to adjust the allowance for receivables

(f) Accounting for depreciation at the period end

1 COST OF GOODS SOLD

1.1 Definition

When we looked at the income statement earlier in this book, we defined profit as:

Sales *less* **Cost of sales** *less* **Expenses**

This definition might seem simple enough; however, it is not always immediately clear how much are the cost of sales or expenses. A variety of difficulties can arise in measuring them: some of these problems can be dealt with fairly easily, whereas others are more difficult to solve. The purpose of this chapter is to describe some of these problems and their solutions.

1.2 Unsold goods

Cost of goods sold has been defined as the cost of the goods that have been sold by a business in a particular period. Thus, if Durham Enterprises bought 20 pairs of shoes in, say, October for £30 each and sold all of them in October, then the cost of goods sold for October would be £600 (£30 × 20). If, on the other hand, Durham Enterprises was only able to sell, say, 15 pairs in October then its cost of goods sold for October will be £450 (£30 × 15). The cost of the unsold pairs of shoes should not be included in the cost of goods sold for October since the pairs are still in inventory and have not been sold in October. Only those items which have been sold in a given period should be included in the cost of goods sold of that period.

EXAMPLE: CLOSING INVENTORY

Suppose that Perry P Louis, trading as the Umbrella Shop, ends his financial year on 30 September each year. On 1 October 20X0 he had no goods in inventory. During the year to 30 September 20X1, he purchased 30,000 umbrellas costing £60,000 from umbrella wholesalers and suppliers. He resold the umbrellas for £5 each, and sales for the year amounted to £100,000 (20,000 umbrellas). At 30 September there were 10,000 unsold umbrellas left in inventory, valued at £2 each.

Perry P Louis's cost of goods sold for the year can be calculated as follows.

Cost of each umbrella is £2 (£60,000 ÷ 30,000)

Umbrellas sold: 20,000	=	Purchases	–	Unsold
		30,000		10,000

Therefore, cost of goods sold = £40,000 (£2 × 20,000)

We can put this calculation in a more formal way as follows.

	£
Purchases	60,000
Closing inventory	20,000
Cost of goods sold	40,000

Purchases in accounting refers to goods bought for resale to customers; it reflects only those goods which have been acquired for resale. Assets acquired for use in the business such as buildings, office supplies etc are recorded by debiting the appropriate asset account, not the purchases account.

Goods or items unsold at the end of the year (or at the end of any period) is called *closing inventory*. Thus, the correct way of presenting the above information is as follows:

	£
Purchases	60,000
Closing inventory	20,000
Cost of goods sold	40,000

You already know that gross profit is calculated as follows:

Sales – Cost of goods sold

The gross profit for Umbrella shop for the year ending 30 September 20X1 can be calculated as follows.

	£	£
Sales (20,000 × £5)		100,000
Purchases	60,000	
Closing inventory	20,000	
Cost of goods sold		40,000
Gross profit		60,000

We shall continue the example of the Umbrella Shop into its next accounting year, 1 October 20X1 to 30 September 20X2. Suppose that during the course of this year, Perry P Louis purchased 40,000 umbrellas at a total cost of £95,000. During the year he sold 45,000 umbrellas for £230,000. At 30 September 20X2 he had 5,000 umbrellas left in inventory, which had cost £12,000. Let us now calculate his gross profit for the year.

In this accounting year, he purchased 40,000 umbrellas to add to the 10,000 he already had in inventory at the start of the year. He sold 45,000, leaving 5,000 umbrellas in inventory at the year end. Once again, gross profit should be calculated by matching the value of 45,000 units of sales with the cost of those 45,000 units.

The cost of sales is the value of the 10,000 umbrellas in inventory at the beginning of the year, plus the cost of the 40,000 umbrellas purchased, less the value of the 5,000 umbrellas in inventory at the year end.

	£	£
Sales (45,000 units)		230,000
Opening inventory (10,000 units)*	20,000	
Add purchases (40,000 units)	95,000	
	115,000	
Less closing inventory (5,000 units)	12,000	
Cost of sales (45,000 units)		103,000
Gross profit		127,000

*Taken from the closing inventory value of the previous accounting year.

The cost of goods sold

The cost of goods sold is found by applying the following formula.

	£
Opening inventory	X
Add cost of purchases	X
	X
Less closing inventory	(X)
Equals cost of goods sold	X

In other words, to match 'sales' and the 'cost of goods sold', it is necessary to adjust the cost of goods purchased to allow for increases or reduction in inventory levels during the period.

Activity 1 **(5 minutes)**

On 1 January 20X1, the Grand Union Food Stores had goods in inventory valued at £6,000. During 20X1 its proprietor, who ran the shop, purchased supplies costing £50,000. Sales revenue for the year to 31 December 20X1 amounted to £80,000. The cost of goods in inventory at 31 December 20X1 was £12,500.

Calculate the gross profit for the year.

Sometimes the buyer pays the delivery costs on his purchases. In such cases, the delivery charges become part of the cost of goods sold.

1.3 Carriage inwards and outwards

'Carriage' refers to the cost of transporting purchased goods from the supplier to the premises of the business which has bought them. Someone has to pay for these delivery costs: sometimes the supplier pays, and sometimes the purchaser pays.

Definitions

Carriage inwards is the cost to the purchaser of having goods transported to his business. It is paid by the purchaser.

Carriage outwards is the cost to the seller, paid by the seller, of having goods transported to the customer.

The cost of carriage inwards is usually added to the cost of purchases and is therefore part of the cost of goods sold.

The cost of carriage outwards is a selling and distribution expense in the income statement.

EXAMPLE: CARRIAGE COSTS

Gwyn Tring, trading as Clickety Clocks, imports and resells cuckoo clocks and grandfather clocks. He must pay for the costs of delivering the clocks from his supplier in Switzerland to his shop in Wales.

He resells the clocks to other traders throughout the country, paying the costs of carriage for the consignments from his business premises to his customers.

On 1 July 20X0, he had clocks in inventory valued at £17,000. During the year to 30 June 20X1, he purchased more clocks at a cost of £75,000. Carriage inwards amounted to £2,000. Sales for the year were £162,100. Other expenses of the business amounted to £56,000 excluding carriage outwards which cost £2,500. Gwyn Tring took drawings of £20,000 from the business during the course of the year. The value of the goods in inventory at the year end was £15,400.

The income statement of Clickety Clocks for the year ended 30 June 20X1 would be as follows.

CLICKETY CLOCKS
INCOME STATEMENT
FOR THE YEAR ENDED 30 JUNE 20X1

	£	£
Sales		162,100
Opening inventory	17,000	
Purchases	75,000	
Carriage inwards	2,000	
	94,000	
Less closing inventory	15,400	
Cost of goods sold		78,600
Gross profit		83,500
Carriage outwards	2,500	
Other expenses	56,000	
		58,500
Net profit (transferred to statement of financial position)		25,000

1.4 Goods written off or written down

A trader might be unable to sell all the goods that he purchases, because a number of things might happen to the goods before they can be sold. For example:

(a) goods might be lost or stolen;

(b) goods might be damaged, and so become worthless. Such damaged goods might be thrown away;

(c) goods might become obsolete or out of fashion. These might have to be thrown away, or possibly sold off at a very low price in a clearance sale.

When goods are lost, stolen or thrown away as worthless, the business will make a loss on those goods because their 'sale value' will be nil. Similarly, when goods lose value because they have become obsolete or out of fashion, the business will make a loss if their clearance sales value is less than their cost. For example, if goods which originally cost £500 are now obsolete and could only be sold for £150, the business would suffer a loss of £350.

If, at the end of an accounting period, a business still has goods in inventory which are either worthless or worth less than their original cost, the value of the inventory should be written down to:

(a) zero, if they are worthless; or
(b) their net realisable value, if this is less than their original cost.

This means that the loss will be reported as soon as it is foreseen, even if the goods have not yet been thrown away or sold off at a cheap price.

The costs of inventory written off or written down should not usually cause any problems in calculating the gross profit of a business, because the cost of goods sold will include the cost of inventories written off or written down, as the following example shows.

NOTES

EXAMPLE: INVENTORIES WRITTEN OFF AND WRITTEN DOWN

Lucas Wagg, trading as Fairlock Fashions, ends his financial year on 31 March. At 1 April 20X0 he had goods in inventory valued at £8,800. During the year to 31 March 20X1, he purchased goods costing £48,000. Fashion goods which cost £2,100 were still held in inventory at 31 March 20X1, and Lucas Wagg believes that these could only now be sold at a sale price of £400. The goods still held in inventory at 31 March 20X1 (including the fashion goods) had an original purchase cost of £7,600. Sales for the year were £81,400.

The calculation of gross profit of Fairlake Fashion would be a two-step process:

Step 1.

Initial calculation of closing inventory values:

INVENTORY COUNT

	At cost	*Realisable value*	*Amount written down*
	£	£	£
Fashion goods	2,100	400	1,700
Other goods (balancing figure)	5,500	5,500	-
	7,600	5,900	1,700

Step 2.

FAIRLOCK FASHIONS
INCOME STATEMENT FOR THE YEAR ENDED 31 MARCH 20X1

	£	£
Sales		81,400
Value of opening inventory	8,800	
Purchases	48,000	
	56,800	
Less closing inventory	5,900	
Cost of goods sold		50,900
Gross profit		30,500

Just as cost of goods sold for a period needs to be matched with the revenue for that period to calculate gross profit, similarly expenses need to be matched with revenue to calculate net profit. We now look at those situations where matching is not completely straightforward.

2 ACCRUALS AND PREPAYMENTS

We have already seen that the gross profit for a period should be calculated by matching sales and the cost of goods sold. In the same way, the net profit for a period should be calculated by charging the expenses which relate to that period only. For example, in preparing the income statement of a business for a period of, say, six months, it would be appropriate to charge only six months' expenses for rent and rates, insurance costs, telephone costs etc.

2.1 Introduction

Expenses might not be paid for during the period to which they relate. For example, a business rents a shop for £20,000 per annum and pays the full annual rent on 1 April each year. If we calculate the profit of the business for the first six months of the year 20X1, the correct charge for rent in the income statement is £10,000, even though the rent paid is £20,000 in that period. Similarly, the rent charge in the income statement for the second six months of the year is £10,000, even though no rent was actually paid in that period.

Definitions

(1) **Accruals** or accrued expenses are expenses which are charged against profit for a particular period, even though they have not yet been paid for.

(2) **Prepayments** are payments which have been made in one accounting period, but should not be charged against profit until a later period, because they relate to that later period.

2.2 Examples

Accruals and prepayments might seem difficult at first, but the following examples might help to clarify the principle involved, that expenses should be matched against the period to which they relate.

Adjustments for accruals and prepayments are the means by which we move charges into the correct accounting period. If we pay in this period for something which relates to the next accounting period, we use a prepayment to transfer that charge forward to the next period. If we have incurred an expense in this period which will not be paid for until next period, we use an accrual to bring the charge back into this period.

EXAMPLE: ACCRUALS

Horace Goodrunning, trading as Goodrunning Motor Spares, ends his financial year on 28 February each year. His telephone was installed on 1 April 20X0 and he receives his telephone account quarterly at the end of each quarter. He pays it promptly as soon as it is received. On the basis of the following data, we can calculate the telephone expense to be charged to the income statement for the year ended 28 February 20X1.

Goodrunning Motor Spares – telephone expense for the three months ended:

	£
30.6.20X0	23.50
30.9.20X0	27.20
31.12.20X0	33.40
31.3.20X1	36.00

The telephone expenses for the year ended 28 February 20X1 are:

	£
1 March-31 March 20X0 (no telephone)	0.00
1 April – 30 June 20X0	23.50
1 July-30 September 20X0	27.20
1 October-31 December 20X0	33.40
1 January-28 February 20X1 (two months)	24.00
	108.10

The charge for the period 1 January – 28 February 20X1 is two-thirds of the quarterly bill received on 31 March. As at 28 February 20X1, no telephone bill has been received for the quarter because it is not due for another month. However, it is inappropriate to ignore the telephone expenses for January and February, and so an accrued charge of £24 should be made, being two-thirds of the quarter's bill of £36.

This affects both the income statement and the statement of financial position:

(a) The telephone expense for the period is increased by £24 (in the income statement)

(b) An accrual of £24 is recognised as at current liability at 28 February 20X1 (in the statement of financial position).

EXAMPLE: PREPAYMENTS

The Square Wheels Garage pays fire insurance annually in advance on 1 June each year. The firm's financial year end is 28 February. From the following record of insurance payments, we will calculate the charge to the income statement for the financial year to 28 February 20X2.

Insurance paid	£
1.6.20X0	600
1.6.20X1	700

Insurance cost for year end 28 February 20X2:	£
(a) the 3 months, 1 March – 31 May 20X1 (3/12 × £600)	150
(b) the 9 months, 1 June 20X1 – 28 February 20X2 (9/12 × £700)	525
Insurance cost for the year, charged to the income statement	675

At 28 February 20X2 there is a prepayment for fire insurance, covering the period 1 March – 31 May 20X2. This insurance premium was paid on 1 June 20X2, but only nine months worth of the full annual cost is chargeable to the accounting period ended 28 February 20X2. The prepayment of (3/12 × £700) £175 as at 28 February 20X2 is recognised as a current asset in the statement of financial position of the Square Wheels Garage as at that date.

In the same way, there was a prepayment of (3/12 × £600) £150 in the statement of financial position one year earlier as at 28 February 20X1.

NOTES

Summary

	£
Prepaid insurance premiums as at 28 February 20X1	150
Add insurance premiums paid 1 June 20X1	700
	850
Less insurance costs charged to the income statement for the year ended 28 February 20X2	675
Equals prepaid insurance premiums as at 28 February 20X2	175

This diagram summarises the situation.

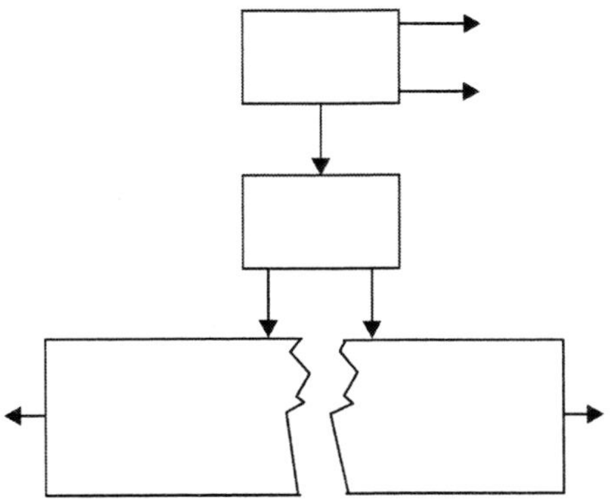

In the next period, charge the income statement with the amount of the prepayment brought forward.

Activity 2 **(5 minutes)**

Included in the statement of financial position of Kate's Coffee House at 30 June 20X0 were the following.

	£
Prepayment (insurance)	450
Accrual (electricity)	80

The following invoices were received and paid during the year to 30 June 20X1.

Date paid		£
5.9.20X0	Electricity (quarter to 31 August 20X0)	309
8.12.20X0	Electricity (quarter to 30 November 20X0)	320
2.1.20X1	Insurance (year to 31 December 20X1)	1,000
7.3.20X1	Electricity (quarter to 28 February 20X1)	340
6.6.20X1	Electricity (quarter to 31 May 20X1)	321

Calculate the electricity and insurance expenses for the year ended 30 June 20X1.

NOTES

FURTHER EXAMPLE: ACCRUALS

Willie Woggle opens a shop on 1 May 20X1 to sell hiking and camping equipment. The rent of the shop is £12,000 per annum, payable quarterly in arrears (with the first payment on 31 July 20X1). Willie decides that his accounting period should end on 31 December each year.

The rent account as at 31 December 20X1 records only two rental payments (on 31 July and 31 October) and there are two months' accrued rental expenses for November and December 20X1 (£2,000) since the next rental payment is not due until 31 January 20X2. The charge to the income statement for the period to 31 December 20X1 is for 8 months' rent (May-December inclusive). The total rental expense for the period is £8,000.

So far, the rent account appears as follows.

RENT ACCOUNT

		£			£
20X1			*20X1*		
31 Jul	Cash	3,000			
31 Oct	Cash	3,000	31 Dec	Income statement	8,000

To complete the picture, the accrual of £2,000 has to be put in, to bring the balance on the account up to the full charge for the year. This is a balance carried forward (a current liability) at 31 December 20X1. At the beginning of the next year the accrual is a balance brought down.

.

RENT ACCOUNT

		£			£
20X1			*20X1*		
31 Jul	Cash*	3,000			
31 Oct	Cash*	3,000	31 Dec	Income statement	8,000
31 Dec	Balance c/d (accruals)	2,000			8,000
		8,000			
			20X2		
			1 Jan	Balance b/d	2,000

* The corresponding credit entry would be cash if rent is paid without the need for an invoice – eg with payment by standing order or direct debit at the bank. If there is always an invoice where rent becomes payable, the double entry would be:

DEBIT	Rent account	£2,000	
CREDIT	Payables		£2,000

Then when the rent is paid, the ledger entries would be:

DEBIT	Payables	£2,000	
CREDIT	Cash		£2,000

The rent account for the *next* year to 31 December 20X2, assuming no increase in rent in that year, would be as follows.

RENT ACCOUNT

		£			£
20X2			*20X2*		
31 Jan	Cash	3,000	1 Jan	Balance b/d	2,000
30 Apr	Cash	3,000			
31 Jul	Cash	3,000			
31 Oct	Cash	3,000			
31 Dec	Balance c/d (accruals)	2,000	31 Dec	Income statement	12,000
		14,000			14,000
			20X3		
			1 Jan	Balance b/d	2,000

A full twelve months' rental charges are taken as an expense to the income statement.

Activity 3 **(5 minutes)**

At 1 January 20X1, the accounts of John Smith showed accrued rent payable of £500. During the year, he pays rent bills totalling £2,550, including one bill for £750 in respect of the quarter ending 31 January 20X2.

What is the expense for rent for the year ended 31 December 20X1 in the income statement?

FURTHER EXAMPLE: PREPAYMENTS

Terry Trunk commences business as a landscape gardener on 1 September 20X0. He immediately decides to join his local trade association, the Confederation of Luton Gardeners, for which the annual membership subscription is £180, payable annually in advance. He paid this amount on 1 September. Terry decides that his accounting period should end on 30 June each year.

In the first period to 30 June 20X1 (10 months), a full year's membership is paid, but only ten twelfths of the subscription should be charged to the period (ie $10/12 \times £180 = £150$). There is a prepayment of two months of membership subscription ie $2/12 \times £180 = £30$ and this is recognised in the ledger account for subscriptions. This is done in much the same way as accounting for accruals, by using the balance carried down/brought down technique.

DEBIT	Subscriptions account with the same balance b/d	£30
CREDIT	Subscription with prepayment as a balance c/d	£30

The remaining expenses in the subscriptions account should then be taken to the income statement. The balance on the account (ie the prepayment) will appear as a current asset (prepaid subscriptions) in the statement of financial position as at 30 June 20X1.

SUBSCRIPTIONS ACCOUNT

		£			£
20X0			*20X1*		
1 Sep	Cash	180	30 Jun	Income statement	150
			30 Jun	Balance c/d (prepayment)	30
		180			180
20X1					
1 Jul	Balance b/d	30			

The subscriptions account for the next year, assuming no increase in the annual charge and that Terry Trunk remains a member of the association, will be:

SUBSCRIPTIONS ACCOUNT

		£			£
20X1			*20X2*		
1 Jul	Balance b/d	30	30 Jun	Income statement	180
1 Sept	Cash	180	30 Jun	Balance c/d (prepayment)	30
		210			210
20X2					
1 Jul	Balance b/d	30			

Again, the charge to the income statement is for a full year's subscriptions.

2.3 Summary

- **Prepayments** are included in **receivables** in current assets in the statement of financial position. They are **assets** as they represent money that has been paid out in advance of the expense being incurred.
- **Accruals** are included in **payables** in **current liabilities** as they represent liabilities which have been incurred but for which no invoice has yet been received.

Double entry for accruals and prepayments

Transaction	DR	CR	Description
Accrual	Expense	Liability	Expense incurred in period, not recorded
Prepayment	Asset	(Reduction in) expense	Expense recorded in period, not incurred until next period

Effect on profit and net assets

You may find the following table a useful summary of the effects of accruals and prepayments.

	Effect on income/expenses	Effect on profit	Effect on assets/liabilities
Accruals	Increases expenses	Reduces profit	Increases liabilities
Prepayments	Reduces expenses	Increases profit	Increases assets

3 IRRECOVERABLE DEBTS AND ALLOWANCES FOR RECEIVABLES

3.1 Irrecoverable debts

Customers who buy goods on credit might fail to pay for them, perhaps out of dishonesty or perhaps because they have gone bankrupt and cannot pay. Customers in another country might be prevented from paying by the unexpected introduction of foreign exchange control restrictions by their country's government during the credit period. For one reason or another, a business might decide to give up expecting payment and to write the debt off as a 'lost cause'.

Irrecoverable debts are often called 'bad' debts. A debt that has 'gone bad' is a debt that is irrecoverable.

Definition

An **irrecoverable (bad) debt** is a debt which is not expected to be paid.

3.2 Accounting treatment

When a business decides that a particular debt is unlikely ever to be repaid, the amount of the debt should be 'written off' as an expense in the income statement.

For example, Alfred's Mini-Cab Service sends an invoice for £300 to a customer who subsequently does a 'moonlight flit' from his office premises, never to be seen or heard of again. The debt of £300 must be written off. It might seem sensible to record the business transaction as:

Sales £(300 – 300) = £0.

However, irrecoverable debts written off are accounted for as follows:

(a) Sales continue to be shown at their invoice value in the income statement. The fact that a debt has gone 'bad' has no effect whatsoever on sales.

(b) The irrecoverable debt written off is shown as an expense in the income statement.

(c) The trade receivables account in the statement of financial position is reduced by the amount of the debt written off, ie receivables in the statement of financial position are shown net of irrecoverable debts.

The double entry to write off an irrecoverable debt is:

DR IRRECOVERABLE DEBTS

CR TRADE RECEIVABLES

3.3 Irrecoverable debts written off and subsequently paid

An irrecoverable debt which has been written off might occasionally be unexpectedly paid. If it is paid in the same accounting period, the write-off journal can simply be reversed. The only accounting problem to consider is when a debt written off as irrecoverable in one accounting period is subsequently paid in a later accounting period.

NOTES

The amount paid should be recorded as additional income in the income statement of the period in which the payment is received.

DR	Trade receivables
CR	Irrecoverable debts recovered

For example, an income statement for the Blacksmith's Forge for the year to 31 December 20X1 could be prepared as shown below from the following information.

	£
Inventories of goods in hand, 1 January 20X1	6,000
Purchases of goods	122,000
Inventories of goods in hand, 31 December 20X1	8,000
Cash sales	100,000
Credit sales	70,000
Discounts allowed	1,200
Discounts received	5,000
Irrecoverable debts written off	9,000
Debts paid in 20X1 which were previously written off as irrecoverable in 20X0	2,000
Other expenses	31,800

BLACKSMITH'S FORGE
INCOME STATEMENT FOR THE YEAR ENDED 31.12.20X1

	£	£
Sales		170,000
Opening inventory	6,000	
Purchases	122,000	
	128,000	
Less closing inventory	8,000	
Cost of goods sold		120,000
Gross profit		50,000
Add: discounts received		5,000
Debts paid, previously written off as irrecoverable		2,000
		57,000
Expenses		
Discounts allowed	1,200	
Irrecoverable debts written off	9,000	
Other expenses	31,800	
		42,000
Net profit		15,000

Whether or not a business actually incurs an irrecoverable debt, it always faces the possibility that some of its customers may not pay. This possibility is reflected in the accounting records by means of an allowance for receivables.

3.4 Allowances for receivables

When irrecoverable debts are written off, specific debts owed to the business are identified as unlikely ever to be collected.

However, because of the risks involved in selling goods on credit, it might be accepted that a certain percentage of outstanding debts at any time are unlikely to be collected. But although it might be estimated that, say, 5% of debts will turn out to be irrecoverable, the business will not know until later which specific debts are irrecoverable.

NOTES

Definition

> The **allowance for receivables** shows the estimated portion of the debts which is unlikely to be collected.

An allowance for receivables is sometimes called a 'provision for doubtful debts'.

The following information is available for Niel's Hardware Store after the first year of operation to 30 June 20X1.

	£
Credit sales during the year	300,000
Add trade receivables at 1 July 20X0	0
Total debts owed to the business	300,000
Less cash received from credit customers	244,000
	56,000
Less irrecoverable debts written off	6,000
Receivables outstanding at 30 June 20X1	50,000

Now, some of these outstanding debts might turn out to be bad. The business does not know on 30 June 20X1 which specific debts in the total £50,000 owed will be bad, but it might guess (from experience perhaps) that 5% of debts will eventually be found to be irrecoverable.

When a business expects irrecoverable debts amongst its current receivables, but does not yet know which specific debts will be bad, it can make an allowance for doubtful receivables.

An allowance for receivables provides for future irrecoverable debts, as a prudent precaution by the business. The business will be more likely to avoid claiming profits which subsequently fail to materialise because some debts turn out to be irrecoverable.

(a) When an allowance is first made

Income statement	*Statement of financial position*
Initial allowance charged as expense	Initial allowance shown as a reduction from trade receivables in the current asset section
Example A 5% allowance in the above example would lead to an expense of £2,500 being shown in the income statement for the year ending 30 June 20X1	*Example* Trade receivables 50,000 less: allowance for doubtful debts 2,500 47,500

(b) When an existing allowance is increased

Income statement	*Statement of financial position*
The amount of the increase in the allowance is charged as expense to the income statement	The new higher total of the allowance is shown as a deduction from receivables
Example Assume no change in receivables balance of £50,000; allowance is increased from 5% to 7% for the year ending 30 June 20X2	
Charged as expense to income statement for the year ending 30 June 20X2: £1,000	Statement of financial position as at 30 June 20X2

Calculation			Trade receivables	50,000
	£		less: allowance for doubtful debts	3,500
New total allowance	3,500	(7% × 50,000)		46,500
Existing allowance	2,500			
Amount of increase	1,000			

(c) When an existing allowance is reduced

Income statement	*Statement of financial position*
The amount of decrease in the allowance is recorded as an item of 'income' in the income statement	The new reduced total is shown as a deduction from receivables

---

EXAMPLE: ALLOWANCE FOR RECEIVABLES

Corin Flakes owns and runs the Aerobic Health Foods Shop in Dundee. He commenced trading on 1 January 20X1, selling health foods to customers, most of whom make use of a credit facility that Corin offers. (Customers are allowed to purchase up to £200 of goods on credit but must repay a certain proportion of their outstanding debt every month.)

This credit system gives rise to a large number of irrecoverable debts, and Corin Flake's results for his first three years of operations are as follows.

Year to 31 December 20X1

Gross profit	£27,000
Irrecoverable debts written off	£8,000
Debts owed by customers as at 31 December 20X1	£40,000
Allowance for receivables	2½ % of outstanding receivables
Other expenses	£20,000

Year to 31 December 20X2

Gross profit	£45,000
Irrecoverable debts written off	£10,000
Debts owed by customers as at 31 December 20X2	£50,000
Allowance for receivables	2½ % of outstanding receivables
Other expenses	£28,750

Year to 31 December 20X3

Gross profit	£60,000
Irrecoverable debts written off	£11,000
Debts owed by customers as at 31 December 20X3	£30,000
Allowance for receivables	3% of outstanding receivables
Other expenses	£32,850

For each of these three years we would prepare the income statement of the business, and state the value of trade receivables appearing in the statement of financial position as at 31 December as follows.

AEROBIC HEALTH FOODS SHOP
INCOME STATEMENTS FOR THE YEARS ENDED 31 DECEMBER

	20X1		*20X2*		*20X3*	
	£	£	£	£	£	£
Gross profit		27,000		45,000		60,000
Sundry income:						
Reduction in						
allowance for receivables*						350
						60,350
Expenses:						
Irrecoverable debts written off	8,000		10,000		11,000	
Increase in allowance						
for receivables*	1,000		250		-	
Other expenses	20,000		28,750		32,850	
		29,000		39,000		43,850
Net (loss)/profit		(2,000)		6,000		16,500

* At 1 January 20X1 when Corin began trading the allowance for receivables was nil. At 31 December 20X1 the allowance required was 2.5% of £40,000 = £1,000. The increase in the allowance is therefore £1,000. At 31 December 20X2 the allowance required was 2.5% of £50,000 = £1,250. The allowance must therefore be increased by £250. At 31 December 20X3 the allowance required is 3% × £30,000 = £900. The 20X2 allowance is therefore reduced by £350.

VALUE OF TRADE RECEIVABLES IN THE STATEMENT OF FINANCIAL POSITION

	As at 31.12.20X1	*As at 31.12.20X2*	*As at 31.12.20X3*
	£	£	£
Total value of trade receivables	40,000	50,000	30,000
Less allowance for receivables	1,000	1,250	900
	39,000	48,750	29,100

Activity 4 **(5 minutes)**

At 31 December 20X0, the ledger of X included a £1,270 allowance for doubtful debts. During 20X1, irrecoverable debts of £680 were written off. Trade receivables balances at 31 December 20X1 totalled £60,500 and X wished to carry forward an allowance of 2%. Which of the following is the charge for irrecoverable and doubtful receivables in the income statement for 20X1?

(a) £620
(b) £740
(c) £1,800
(d) £1,890

3.5 Irrecoverable debts written off: ledger accounting entries

For irrecoverable debts written off, there is an irrecoverable debts account. The double-entry bookkeeping is fairly straightforward, but there are two separate transactions to record.

(a) *When it is decided that a particular debt will not be paid*

DEBIT Irrecoverable debts account (expense)
CREDIT Trade receivables account

(b) *At the end of the accounting period*

At the end of the year, the balance on the irrecoverable debts account is transferred to the income and expense ledger account (like all other expense accounts):

DEBIT I & E account
CREDIT Irrecoverable debts account

EXAMPLE: IRRECOVERABLE DEBTS WRITTEN OFF

At 1 October 20X0 a business had total outstanding debts of £8,600. During the year to 30 September 20X1:

(a) credit sales amounted to £44,000

(b) payments from various customers (accounts receivable) amounted to £49,000

(c) two debts, for £180 and £420, were declared irrecoverable and the customers are no longer purchasing goods from the company. These are to be written off.

The trade receivables account and the irrecoverable debts account for the year will be as follows.

TRADE RECEIVABLES

	£		£
Opening balance b/f	8,600	Cash	49,000
Sales	44,000	Irrecoverable debts	180
		Irrecoverable debts	420
		Closing balance c/d	3,000
	52,600		52,600
Opening balance b/d	3,000		

IRRECOVERABLE DEBTS

	£		£
Trade receivables	180	I&E a/c	600
Trade receivables	420		
	600		600

In the sales ledger, personal accounts of the customers whose debts are irrecoverable will be taken off the ledger. The business should then take steps to ensure that it does not sell goods on credit to those customers again.

NOTES

The accounting entries for doubtful debts are different from those for irrecoverable debts.

3.6 Allowance for receivables: ledger accounting entries

A business might know from past experience that, say, 2% of receivables balances are unlikely to be collected. It would then be considered prudent to make a general allowance of 2%. It may be that no particular customers are regarded as suspect and so it is not possible to write off any individual customer balances as irrecoverable debts. The procedure is then to leave the total receivables balances completely untouched, but to open up an allowance account by the following entries:

DEBIT Irrecoverable debts account (expense)
CREDIT Allowance for receivables

When preparing a statement of financial position, the credit balance on the allowance account is deducted from the total debit balances in the receivables ledger.

In subsequent years, adjustments may be needed to the amount of the allowance. The procedure to be followed then is:

(a) Calculate the new allowance required

(b) Compare it with the existing balance on the allowance account (ie the balance b/f from the previous accounting period)

(c) Calculate increase or decrease required.

(i) **If a higher allowance is required**:

DEBIT Irrecoverable debts expense
CREDIT Allowance for receivables

with the amount of the increase.

(ii) **If a lower allowance is needed now than before**:

DEBIT Allowance for receivables
CREDIT irrecoverable debts expense

with the amount of the decrease.

Activity 5 **(5 minutes)**

Select the appropriate option to complete the following sentence. A decrease in the allowance for receivables would result in:

(a) an increase in liabilities
(b) a decrease in net assets
(c) a decrease in net profits
(d) an increase in net profits

NOTES

EXAMPLE: ACCOUNTING ENTRIES FOR ALLOWANCE FOR RECEIVABLES

Alex Gullible has total trade receivables balances outstanding at 31 December 20X0 of £28,000. He believes that about 1% of these balances will not be collected and wishes to make an appropriate provision. Before now, he has not made any allowance for receivables at all.

On 31 December 20X1 his trade receivables balances amount to £40,000. His experience during the year has convinced him that an allowance of 5% should be made.

What accounting entries should Alex make on 31 December 20X0 and 31 December 20X1, and what figures for trade receivables will appear in his statements of financial position as at those dates?

At 31 December 20X0

Allowance required = 1% × £28,000 = £280

Alex will make the following entry.

DEBIT	Irrecoverable debts expense	£280	
CREDIT	Allowance for receivables		£280

In the statement of financial position trade receivables will appear as follows under current assets.

	£
Trade receivables	28,000
Less allowance for receivables	280
	27,720

At 31 December 20X1

Following the procedure described above, Alex will calculate the allowance as follows.

	£
Allowance required now (5% × £40,000)	2,000
Existing allowance	(280)
∴ Additional allowance required	1,720

He will now make the following entry:

DEBIT	Irrecoverable debts expense	£1,720	
CREDIT	Allowance for receivables		£1,720

The allowance account will by now appear as follows.

ALLOWANCE FOR RECEIVABLES

		£			£
20X0			*20X0*		
31 Dec	Balance c/d	280	31 Dec	I&E account	280
20X1			*20X1*		
31 Dec	Balance c/d	2,000	1 Jan	Balance b/d	280
			31 Dec	I&E account	1,720
		2,000			2,000
			20X2		
			1 Jan	Balance b/d	2,000

For the statement of financial position at 31 December 20X1, trade receivables will be valued as follows.

	£
Trade receivables	40,000
Less allowance for receivables	2,000
	38,000

In practice, it is unnecessary to show the total receivables balances and the allowance as separate items in the statement of financial position. Normally only the net figure is shown (£27,720 in 20X0, £38,000 in 20X1). .

4 DEPRECIATION

4.1 Definition

Where assets held by an entity have a limited useful life, it is necessary to apportion the value of an asset used in a period against the revenue it has helped to create. If an asset's life extends over more than one accounting period, it earns profits over more than one period. It is a non-current asset. Current assets, such as inventory and cash, are continually being used and replaced. Non-current assets such as plant and vehicles are intended for long-term use in the business.

With the exception of land, every non-current asset eventually wears out over time. Machines, cars and other vehicles, fixtures and fittings, and even buildings do not last for ever. When a business acquires a non-current asset, it will have some idea about how long its useful life will be, and it might decide either:

(a) to keep on using the asset until it becomes completely worn out, useless, and worthless; or

(b) to sell off the asset at the end of its useful life, either by selling it as a second-hand item or as scrap.

Since a non-current asset has a cost and a limited useful life, and its value eventually declines, it follows that a charge should be made in the income statement to reflect the use that is made of the asset by the business. This charge is called depreciation.

Definition

Depreciation (depreciation expense) is the allocation of the depreciable amount of an asset over its estimated useful life.

The **depreciable amount** of an asset is its cost less its estimated residual value.

One way of defining depreciation is to describe it as a means of **spreading the cost** of a non-current asset over its useful life, and so matching the cost against the full period during which it earns profits for the business. Depreciation charges are an example of the application of the accrual assumption to calculate profits.

Suppose that a business buys a machine for £40,000. Its expected life is four years, and at the end of that time it is expected to be worthless.

Since the machine is used to make profits for four years, it would be reasonable to charge the cost of the machine over those four years (perhaps by charging £10,000 per annum) so that at the end of the four years the total cost of £40,000 would have been charged against profits. The key points to remember about depreciation are as follows.

(a) Depreciation is a measure of the wearing out or depletion of a non-current asset through use, time or obsolescence.

(b) Depreciation charges should be spread fairly over an asset's useful life, and so allocated to the accounting periods which are expected to benefit (ie make profits) from the asset's use.

The total charge for depreciation: the depreciable amount

The total amount to be charged over the life of a non-current asset ('the depreciable amount') is usually:

Cost less residual value

Residual value is the value a business expects to receive at the end of the useful life of the asset by selling or trading-in the asset. It is also sometimes referred to as **salvage value** or **scrap value**.

EXAMPLES

(a) A non-current asset costing £20,000 which has an expected life of five years and an expected residual value of nil would have the depreciable amount of £20,000.

(b) A non-current asset costing £20,000 which has an expected life of five years and an expected residual value of £3,000 should be depreciated by £17,000 in total over the five year period.

4.2 Accounting for depreciation

When a non-current asset is depreciated, two things must be accounted for.

(a) The depreciation charge is an expense of the period and is charged to the income statement.

(b) At the same time, the non-current asset is wearing out and diminishing in value, and so the value of the non-current asset in the statement of financial position must be reduced by the amount of depreciation charged. The carrying amount of a non-current asset (the amount at which the asset is measured in the statement of financial position) is its cost less the depreciation charged to date. The cost of an asset less depreciation is often called the 'net book value'.

For each separate category of non-current assets (for example, plant and machinery, land and buildings, fixtures and fittings) there are two accounts:

The **cost account**. This records the cost of non-current assets.
The **accumulated depreciation account**.

The amount of depreciation deducted from the cost of a non-current asset to arrive at its carrying amount will build up (or 'accumulate') over time, as more depreciation is charged in each successive accounting period. The accumulated depreciation is sometimes called a 'provision for depreciation' because it provides for the fall in value of the non-current asset.

The double entry to record the depreciation charge is:

DEBIT: DEPRECIATION EXPENSE (in the income statement)

CREDIT ACCUMULATED DEPRECIATION (in the statement of financial position)

EXAMPLE: DEPRECIATION

Jo McGowan bought a used car on 1 January 20X0 for £1,200 cash. She planned to use it for four years. Jo does not expect the car to have any salvage value after four years.

The car has a depreciable amount of £1,200 (1,200 – 0) and a useful life of four years. The depreciation expense would be £300 (1,200 ÷ 4) per year.

The accounting entries would be as follows.

(a) To record the depreciation charge for the year:

The debit is to the depreciation expense account

DEPRECIATION EXPENSE

	£		
31 Dec 20X0	300		

The credit is to the 'accumulated depreciation' account..

ACCUMULATED DEPRECIATION

	£		£
		31 Dec 20X0	300

(b) Entries at year-end 20X0

The depreciation expense is transferred to the income statement (in the same way as for any other expense item).

The balance on the accumulated depreciation account is brought forward as the opening balance for next year.

DEPRECIATION EXPENSE

	£		£
31 Dec 20X0 Accumulated dep'n	300	31 Dec 20X0 Income statement	300

ACCUMULATED DEPRECIATION

	£		£
31 Dec 20X0 Bal c/d	300	31 Dec 20X0 Dep'n expense	300
		1 Jan 20X1 Bal b/d	300

(c) Entries at year-end 20X1

The depreciation expense for 20X1 is also £300.

DEPRECIATION EXPENSE

	£		£
31 Dec 20X1 Accumulated dep'n	300	31 Dec 20X1 Income statement	300

ACCUMULATED DEPRECIATION

	£		£
31 Dec 20X1 Bal c/d	600	1 Jan 20X1 Bal b/d	300
		31 Dec 20X1 Dep'n expense	300
	600		600
		1 Jan 20X2 Bal b/d	600

While the depreciation expense account shows only the depreciation charge for the year, the accumulated depreciation account shows the total depreciation charged on that asset since its acquisition by the business. Depreciation will continue to be credited to the accumulated depreciation account until the asset is completely written off or disposed of.

In this example, depreciation will be charged for another two years (20X2 and 20X3) at which time the total accumulated depreciation will be £1,200 and the carrying amount of the vehicle will be zero.

The motor vehicle cost account continues to show the asset at cost. It is unaffected by depreciation and will appear as follows.

MOTOR VEHICLE: COST

	£		£
1 Jan 20X0 Cash	1,200	31 Dec 20X0 Bal c/d	1,200
1 Jan 20X1 Bal b/d	1,200	31 Dec 20X1 Bal c/d	1,200
1 Jan 20X2 Bal b/d	1,200		

In the statement of financial position, non-current assets are shown at their **carrying amount (net book value)** which is :

Cost *less* accumulated depreciation

In Jo McGowan's example the car would appear in the statement of financial position as follows.

MOTOR VEHICLE

	Cost	*Accumulated depreciation*	*Carrying amount*
	£	£	£
At year end 20X0	1,200	300	900
At year end 20X1	1,200	600	600
At year end 20X2	1,200	900	300
At year end 20X3	1,200	1,200	0

The carrying amount of the non-current asset is reduced in every accounting period by the amount of depreciation. The key thing to remember is that the reduction takes place indirectly through the accumulated depreciation account.

If Jo continues to use the car in 20X4 and beyond, the statement of financial position in each of those years will continue to show the motor vehicle as a non-current asset with a carrying amount of zero. Only when the motor vehicle is disposed of will it stop being listed in the statement of financial position.

To summarise:

(a) There is an accumulated depreciation account for each separate category of non-current assets, for example, plant and machinery, land and buildings, fixtures and fittings.

(b) The depreciation charge for an accounting period is a charge against profit. It is accounted for as follows.

DEBIT	Depreciation expense (income statement)
CREDIT	Accumulated depreciation account (statement of financial position)

with the depreciation charge for the period.

(c) The balance on the statement of financial position accumulated depreciation account is the total accumulated depreciation. This is always a credit balance brought forward in the ledger account for depreciation.

(d) The non-current asset cost accounts are unaffected by depreciation. Non-current assets are recorded in these accounts at cost.

(e) In the statement of financial position of the business, the total balance on the accumulated depreciation account is set against the value of non-current asset accounts to derive the net book value of the non-current assets.

This is how the non-current asset accounts might appear in a trial balance:

	DR	CR
Freehold building – cost	2,000,000	
Freehold building – accumulated depreciation		500,000
Motor vehicles – cost	70,000	
Motor vehicles – accumulated depreciation		40,000
Office equipment – cost	25,000	
Office equipment – accumulated depreciation		15,000

And this is how they would be shown in the statement of financial position:

Non current assets	
Freehold building	1,500,000
Motor vehicles	30,000
Office equipment	10,000

While the accounting treatment of depreciation expense is always the same, there are several methods to calculate the expense itself.

4.3 Methods of depreciation

There are several different methods of depreciation. The three methods covered in this text are:

(a) the straight line method;
(b) the reducing balance method; and
(c) the machine hour method (sometimes called the units of output method).

4.4 The straight line method

This is the method of depreciation we have used so far. It is the most commonly used method of all. The total depreciable amount is charged in equal instalments to each accounting period over the expected useful life of the asset. The carrying amount of the non-current asset declines at a steady rate, or in a 'straight line' over time.

The formula for the annual depreciation charge is as follows:

$$\frac{\textbf{Cost of asset minus residual value}}{\textbf{Expected useful life of the asset}}$$

The depreciation charge on an asset is the same each year.

EXAMPLE: STRAIGHT LINE DEPRECIATION

(a) A non-current asset costing £20,000 with an estimated life of 10 years and no residual value would be depreciated at the rate of:

$$\frac{£20,000}{10 \text{ years}} = £2,000 \text{ per annum}$$

(b) A non-current asset costing £60,000 has an estimated life of 5 years and a residual value of £7,000. The annual depreciation charge using the straight line method would be:

$$\frac{£(60,000 - 7,000)}{5 \text{ years}} = £10,600 \text{ per annum}$$

The carrying amount of the non-current asset would be:

	After 1 year	*After 2 years*	*After 3 years*	*After 4 years*	*After 5 years*
	£	£	£	£	£
Cost of the asset	60,000	60,000	60,000	60,000	60,000
Accumulated depreciation	10,600	21,200	31,800	42,400	53,000
Carrying amount	49,400	38,800	28,200	17,600	7,000*

* ie its estimated residual value.

Since the depreciation charge per annum is the same amount every year with the straight line method, it is often convenient to state that depreciation is charged at the rate of x per cent per annum on the cost of the asset. In the example in '(a)' above, the depreciation charge per annum is 10% of cost (ie 10% of £20,000 = £2,000).

The straight line method of depreciation is a fair allocation of the total depreciable amount between the different accounting periods, provided that it is reasonable to assume that the business enjoys equal benefits from the use of the asset in every period throughout its life.

Activity 6 **(5 minutes)**

Can you name two assets which are likely to be depleted or worn out on a constant basis?

4.5 Assets acquired in the middle of an accounting period

A business can purchase new non-current assets at any time during the course of an accounting period. It might therefore seem fair to charge an amount for depreciation in the period when the purchase occurs. This will then reflect the limited amount of use the business has had from the asset in that period.

Suppose that a business which has an accounting year which runs from 1 January to 31 December purchases a new non-current asset on 1 April 20X0, at a cost of £24,000. The expected life of the asset is 4 years, and its residual value is nil. What should be the depreciation charge for 20X0?

The annual depreciation charge will be $\frac{\text{£24,000}}{\text{4 years}} = \text{£6,000 per annum}$

However, since the asset was acquired on 1 April 20X0, the business has only benefited from the use of the asset for 9 months instead of a full 12 months. It would therefore seem fair to charge depreciation in 20X0 of only:

$$\frac{9}{12} \times \text{£6,000} = \text{£4,500}$$

In practice, many businesses charge a full year's depreciation on non-current assets in the year of their purchase (regardless of the point in time during the year at which they were acquired) and no depreciation in the year of sale/disposal of the asset.

4.6 The reducing balance method

The reducing balance method of depreciation calculates the annual depreciation charge as a fixed percentage of the carrying amount of the asset, as at the end of the previous accounting period. (This should not be confused with the straight line method where annual depreciation charge is a fixed percentage of the cost of the asset.)

For example, a business purchases a non-current asset at a cost of £10,000. Its expected useful life is 3 years and its estimated residual value is £2,160. The business wishes to use the reducing balance method to depreciate the asset, and calculates that the rate of depreciation should be 40% of the reducing carrying amount (or net book value) of the asset. (The method of deciding that 40% is a suitable annual percentage is a problem of mathematics, not financial accounting, and is not described here.)

The total depreciable amount is £(10,000 – 2,160) = £7,840.

The depreciation charge per annum and the carrying amount of the asset as at the end of each year will be as follows:

		Accumulated depreciation
	£	**£**
Asset at cost	10,000	
Depreciation in year 1 (40%)	4,000	4,000
Carrying amount at end of year 1	6,000	
Depreciation in year 2		6,400
(40% of reducing balance ie £6,000)	2,400	(4,000+2,400)
Carrying amount at end of year 2	3,600	
Depreciation in year 3 (40%)	1,440	7,840
		(6,400+1,440)
Carrying amount at end of year 3	2,160	

You should note that with the reducing balance method, the annual charge for depreciation is higher in the earlier years of the asset's life, and lower in the later years. In the example above, the annual charges for years 1, 2 and 3 are £4,000, £2,400 and £1,440 respectively (as compared to a constant charge per annum under straight line).

The reducing balance method might therefore be used when it is considered fair to allocate a greater proportion of the total depreciable amount to the earlier years and a lower proportion to later years, on the assumption that the benefits obtained by the business from using the asset decline over time.

Activity 7 **(5 minutes)**

In the above example (cost £10,000; residual value £2,160), what will be the depreciation charge under the straight line method?

4.7 The machine hour method of depreciation

This method of depreciation may be suitable for plant and machinery, where it is assumed that the non-current asset wears out through use rather than over time. Instead of calculating a depreciation charge relating to a period of time, depreciation is calculated according to the number of hours of use made of the machine by the business during the course of the period.

The life of the asset is estimated in hours (or miles or other conventional units) and each unit is given a money value for depreciation purposes. The rate of depreciation in a particular year is calculated as:

$$\frac{\textbf{Cost of asset minus estimated residual value}}{\textbf{Expected useful life of the asset in hours}} \times \textbf{Hours used that year}$$

EXAMPLE: THE MACHINE HOUR METHOD

A business purchases a machine at a cost of £45,000. Its estimated useful life is 8,000 hours of running time, and its estimated residual value is £5,000.

The rate of depreciation by the machine hour method will be:

$$\frac{\pounds(45{,}000 - 5{,}000)}{8{,}000 \text{ hours}} = \pounds5 \text{ per machine hour}$$

Suppose that the actual use of the machine each year is:

	Hours
Year 1	3,000
Year 2	1,500
Year 3	2,500
Year 4	1,000
	8,000

We can calculate the annual depreciation charge and net book value of the machine as at the end of each year as follows.

Year	*Depreciation charge for the year*	*Accumulated depreciation as at end of the year*	*Non-current asset at cost*	*Carrying amount as at end of the year*
	£	£	£	£
Start of life			45,000	45,000
Year 1 (3,000 × £5)	15,000	15,000	45,000	30,000
Year 2 (1,500 × £5)	7,500	22,500	45,000	22,500
Year 3 (2,500 × £5)	12,500	35,000	45,000	10,000
Year 4 (1,000 × £5)	5,000	40,000	45,000	5,000
	40,000			

This method is sometimes modified so as to calculate each year's depreciation on the number of units produced by the machine in that year, rather than on the number of hours in which the machine is active. In this case the depreciation method is referred to as **the units of output method.**

4.8 Applying a depreciation method consistently

It is up to the business concerned to decide which method of depreciation to apply to its non-current assets. Once that decision has been made, however, it should not be changed – the chosen method of depreciation should be applied consistently from year to year.

Similarly, it is up to the business to decide what a sensible life span for a non-current asset should be. Again, once that life span has been chosen, it should not be changed unless something unexpected happens to the asset.

It is permissible for a business to depreciate different categories of non-current assets in different ways. For example, if a business owns three cars, then each car would normally be depreciated in the same way (eg by the straight line method) but another category of non-current asset, say, photocopiers, might be depreciated using a different method (eg by the machine hour method).

Regardless of the depreciation method chosen, changes in circumstances may require adjustments to the depreciation charge.

4.9 Changes to depreciation expense

(a) **Change in method of depreciation**

The depreciation method should be applied consistently and should not normally be changed. However, it should be reviewed for appropriateness. If there are any changes in the expected pattern of use of the asset, then the method used should be changed. In such cases, the remaining carrying amount is depreciated under the new method, ie only current and future periods are affected; the change is not retrospective.

NOTES

EXAMPLE: CHANGE IN METHOD OF DEPRECIATION

Jakob purchased an asset for £100,000 on 1 January 20X1. It had an estimated useful life of 5 years and it was depreciated using the reducing balance method at a rate of 40%. On 1 January 20X3 it was decided to change the method to straight line.

The depreciation charge for each year (to 31 December) of the asset's life is shown below:

Year		*Depreciation charge*	*Aggregate depreciation*
20X1	100,000 × 40%	40,000	40,000
20X2	60,000 × 40%	24,000	64,000
20X3	$\frac{£100{,}000 - £64{,}000}{3}$	12,000	76,000
20X4		12,000	88,000
20X5		12,000	100,000

(b) **A fall in the value of a non-current asset**

When the 'market' value of a non-current asset falls so that it is worth less than its carrying amount, the asset should be written down to its new low market value. The reduction in value should then be charged to the income statement . This loss of value is known as an impairment.

	£
Carrying amount at the beginning of the period	X
Less: new reduced value	(X)
Equals: the charge to the income statement for impairment in the asset's value	X

EXAMPLE: FALL IN ASSET VALUE

A business purchases a building on 1 January 20X0 at a cost of £100,000. The building has a 20 year life. After five years' use, on 1 January 20X5, the business decides that since property prices have fallen sharply, the building is now worth only £60,000, and that the value of the asset should be reduced in the accounts of the business.

The building was being depreciated at the rate of 5% per annum on cost.

Before the asset is reduced in value, the annual depreciation charge is:

$$\frac{£100{,}000}{20\ \text{years}} = £5{,}000 \text{ per annum } (= 5\% \text{ of } £100{,}000)$$

After five years, the accumulated depreciation would be £25,000 (£5,000 × 5), and the carrying amount of the building £75,000, which is £15,000 more than the new asset value. This £15,000 should be written off as:

(i) a charge for depreciation; or

(ii) fall in the asset's value in year 5, so that the total charge in year 5 is:

	£
Carrying amount of the building after 4 years £(100,000-20,000)	80,000
Revised asset value at end of year 5	60,000
Charge against profit in year 5	20,000

An alternative method of calculation is:

	£
'Normal' depreciation charge per annum	5,000
Impairment charge	15,000
Charge against profit in year 5	20,000

The building has a further life of 15 years, and its value is now £60,000. From year 6 to year 20, the annual charge for depreciation will be:

$$\frac{£60,000}{15 \text{ years}} = £4,000 \text{ per annum}$$

(c) **Change in expected life of an asset**

The depreciation charge on a non-current asset depends not only on the cost (or value) of the asset and its estimated residual value, but also on its estimated useful life.

For example, a business purchased a non-current asset costing £12,000 with an estimated life of four years and no residual value. If it used the straight line method of depreciation, the annual depreciation charge would be 25% of £12,000 = £3,000.

Now what would happen if the business decided after two years that the useful life of the asset has been underestimated, and it still had five more years in use to come (making its total life seven years)?

For the first two years, the asset would have been depreciated by £3,000 per annum, so that its carrying amount after two years would be £(12,000 – 6,000) = £6,000. If the remaining life of the asset is now revised to five more years, the remaining amount to be depreciated (here £6,000) should be spread over the remaining life. This would give an annual depreciation charge for the final five years of:

$$\frac{\textbf{Carrying amount at time of life readjustment, minus residual value}}{\textbf{New estimate of remaining useful life}}$$

$$= \frac{£60,000}{5 \text{ years}} = £1,200 \text{ per annum}$$

4.10 The disposal of non-current assets

Non-current assets are not purchased by a business with the intention of reselling them in the normal course of trade. However, they might be sold off at some stage during their life, either when their useful life is over or before then. A business might decide to sell off a non-current asset long before its useful life has ended.

Whenever a business sells something, it will make a profit or a loss. When non-current assets are disposed of, there will be a profit or loss on disposal. As it is a capital item being sold, the profit or loss will be a capital gain or a capital loss. These gains or losses are reported in the income and expenses part of the income statement of the business (not as sales revenue from the entity's normal trading operations). They are commonly referred to as '**profit on disposal of non-current assets**' or '**loss on disposal**'.

The profit or loss on the disposal of a non-current asset is the difference between (a) and (b) below.

(a) The carrying amount (net book value) of the asset at the time of its sale.
(b) Its net sale price, which is the price minus any costs of making the sale.

A profit is made when the sale price exceeds the carrying amount, and a loss is made when the sale price is less than the carrying amount.

EXAMPLE: DISPOSAL OF A NON-CURRENT ASSET

A business purchased a non-current asset on 1 January 20X1 for £25,000. It had an estimated life of six years and an estimated residual value of £7,000. The asset was eventually sold after three years on 1 January 20X4 to another trader who paid £17,500 for it.

What was the profit or loss on disposal, assuming that the business uses the straight line method for depreciation?

$$\text{Annual depreciation} = \frac{£(25{,}000 - 7{,}000)}{6 \text{ years}} = £3{,}000 \text{ per annum}$$

	£
Cost of asset	25,000
Less accumulated depreciation (three years)	9,000
Carrying amount at date of disposal	16,000
Sale price	17,500
Profit on disposal	1,500

This profit will be shown in the income statement of the business where it will be an item of other income added to gross profit.

4.11 The disposal of non-current assets: ledger accounting entries

We have already seen how the profit or loss on disposal of a non-current asset should be computed. A profit on disposal is an item of 'other income' in the income statement, and a loss on disposal is an item of expense in the income statement

It is customary in ledger accounting to record the disposal of non-current assets in a **disposal of non-current assets account.**

(a) The profit or loss on disposal is the difference between:

  (i) the sale price of the asset (if any); and
  (ii) the carrying amount of the asset at the time of sale.

(b) The following items must appear in the disposal of non-current assets account:

  (i) The value of the asset (at cost, or revalued amount*)
  (ii) The accumulated depreciation up to the date of sale
  (iii) The sale price of the asset

  *To simplify the explanation of the rules, we will assume now that the non-current assets disposed of are valued at cost.

(c) The ledger accounting entries are as follows.

  (i) DEBIT Disposal of non-current asset account
  CREDIT Non-current asset account

  with the cost of the asset disposed of.

NOTES

(ii) DEBIT Accumulated depreciation account
CREDIT Disposal of non-current asset account

with the accumulated depreciation on the asset as at the date of sale.

(iii) DEBIT Receivable account or cash book
CREDIT Disposal of non-current asset account

with the sale price of the asset. The sale is therefore not recorded in a sales account, but in the disposal of non-current asset account itself. You will notice that the effect of these entries is to remove the asset, and its accumulated depreciation, from the statement of financial position.

The balance on the disposal account is the profit or loss on disposal and the corresponding double entry is recorded in the income and expenditure account itself.

EXAMPLE: DISPOSAL OF ASSETS: LEDGER ACCOUNTING ENTRIES

A business has £110,000 worth of machinery at cost. Its policy is to charge depreciation at 20% per annum straight line. The total accumulated depreciation now stands at £70,000. The business sells for £19,000 a machine which it purchased exactly two years ago for £30,000.

PLANT AND MACHINERY ACCOUNT

	£		£
Balance b/d	110,000	Plant disposals account	30,000
		Balance c/d	80,000
	110,000		110,000
Balance b/d	80,000		

PLANT AND MACHINERY ACCUMULATED DEPRECIATION

	£		£
Plant disposals (20% of $30,000 for 2 years)	12,000	Balance b/d	70,000
Balance c/d	58,000		
	70,000		70,000
		Balance b/d	58,000

PLANT DISPOSALS

	£		£
Plant and machinery account	30,000	Accumulated depreciation	12,000
I & E a/c (profit on sale)	1,000	Cash	19,000
	31,000		31,000

Check

	£
Asset at cost	30,000
Accumulated depreciation at time of sale	12,000
Carrying amount at time of sale	18,000
Sale price	19,000
Profit on sale	1,000

Chapter roundup

- This chapter has illustrated how the amount of profit is calculated when:
  - there are opening or closing inventories of goods in hand
  - there is carriage inwards and/or carriage outwards
  - inventories are written off or written down in value
  - there are accrued charges
  - there are prepayments of expenses.
- The cost of goods sold is calculated by adding the value of opening inventory in hand to the cost of purchases and subtracting the value of closing inventory.
- Accrued expenses are expenses which relate to an accounting period but have not yet been paid for. They are a charge against the profit for the period and are shown in the statement of financial position as at the end of the period as a current liability.
- Prepayments are expenses which have already been paid but relate to a future accounting period. They are not charged against the profit of the current period and are shown in the statement of financial position as at the end of the period as a current asset.
- Accruals and prepayments are aspects of the accruals concept which is one of the underlying assumptions in accounting (see later chapter).
- Irrecoverable debts written off are an expense in the income statement.
- An increase in the allowance for doubtful receivables is an expense in the income statement whereas a decrease in the allowance for doubtful receivables is shown as 'income' in the income statement.
- Trade receivables are valued in the statement of financial position after deducting any allowance for doubtful receivables.
- Depreciation is the allocation of the cost of a non-current asset to the income statement over its estimated useful life.
- The depreciation charge is an expense in the income statement.
- The value of the non-current asset in the statement of financial position is reduced by the amount of depreciation charged.
- Commonly used methods of depreciation are: the straight line method; the reducing balance method; and the machine hour method.

Quick quiz

1 How is the cost of goods sold calculated?

2 Distinguish between carriage inwards and carriage outwards.

3 How is carriage inwards treated in the income statement?

4 Give three reasons why goods purchased might have to be written off.

5 If a business has paid rates of £1,000 for the year on 1 January 20X1, what is the prepayment in the accounts for the year to 31 March 20X1?

6 Define an accrual.

7 Where are the prepayments reported in the financial statements?

8 If allowance for doubtful receivables is increased, what is the effect on the income statement?

Answers to Quick quiz

1 Opening inventory plus purchases less closing inventory and any other appropriate adjustments associated with inventory.

2 Carriage inwards is the delivery cost of goods purchased, carriage outwards is the delivery cost of goods sold.

3 Added to the cost of purchases.

4 They may be lost or stolen, damaged or obsolete or out of fashion.

5 £750 (3/4 × £1,000).

6 An expense incurred by a business but which has not yet been paid for.

7 Under current assets.

8 The increase is included as an expense in the income statement.

Answers to Activities

1 **GRAND UNION FOOD STORES**
INCOME STATEMENT FOR THE YEAR ENDED 31 DECEMBER 20X0

	£	£
Sales		80,000
Opening inventory	6,000	
Add purchases	50,000	
	56,000	
Less closing inventory	12,500	
Cost of goods sold		43,500
Gross profit		36,500

2

	£
Electricity paid:	309
	320
	340
	321
Add closing accrual (321 × 1/3)	107
Less opening accrual	(80)
	1,317

3 £1,800.

John paid £2,550 of which £500 was applicable to the previous year. Therefore only £2,050 out of £2,550 was applicable to the year ended 31 December 20X1. However, £2,050 needs to be reduced by the amount applicable to the quarter ending 31 January 20X2, ie by one month's rent of £250 (1/3 × £750). The charge to the income statement is therefore £1,800 £(2,050 – 250).

4 (a):£620

	£
Irrecoverable debts written off	680
Less: decrease in the allowance for receivables £1,270 – (2% × 60,500)	(60)
	620

5 (d): an increase in net profits because lowering the allowance is a credit to the income statement.

6 Assets likely to be worn out on a constant basis and which hence might be suitable for straight line depreciation are:

(a) furniture
(b) buildings
(c) fixtures and fittings.

7 $\frac{10{,}000 - 2{,}160}{3}$ = £2,613.33 per annum

Chapter : 17

PREPARING ACCOUNTS FROM INCOMPLETE RECORDS

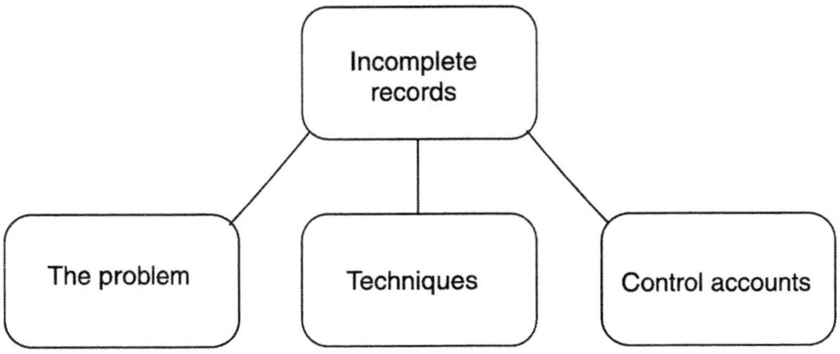

Introduction

Incomplete records problems occur when a business does not have a full set of accounting records. The problems can arise for two reasons.

(a) The proprietor of the business does not keep a full set of accounts, ie it has **limited accounting records.**

(b) Some of the business accounts are **accidentally lost or destroyed**.

However, as long as there is some basic information, it is often possible to reconstruct the accounting records and then from those draw up the accounts themselves.

There are several specific techniques which can be applied, depending on the availability of information.

Your objectives

In this chapter you will learn about the following.

(a) The use of control accounts

(b) The differences between limited and incomplete accounting records

(c) How to calculate the net asset position and the profit for a sole trader business which has incomplete accounting records

1 CONTROL ACCOUNTS

Control accounts are a useful tool if you have to write up accounts from incomplete records.

1.1 What are control accounts?

Definitions

A **control account** is an account in the nominal ledger in which a record is kept of the total value of a number of similar but individual items. Control accounts are used chiefly for trade receivables and trade payables.

- A **receivables control account** is an account in which records are kept of transactions involving all accounts receivable in total. The balance on the receivables control account at any time will be the total amount due to the business at that time from its customers.
- A **payables control account** is an account in which records are kept of transactions involving all accounts payable in total, and the balance on this account at any time will be the total amount owed by the business at that time to its suppliers.

Although control accounts are used mainly in accounting for trade receivables and trade payables, they can also be kept for other items, such as inventories of goods, wages and salaries. The first important idea to remember, however, is that a control account is an account which keeps a **total record for a collective item** (eg trade receivables) which in reality consists of many individual items (eg individual trade accounts receivable).

A control account is an **(impersonal) ledger account** which will appear in the nominal ledger. Before we look at the reasons for having control accounts, we will first look at how they are made up.

1.2 Control accounts and personal accounts

The personal accounts of individual customers are kept in the **sales ledger**; the amount owed by each customer will be a balance on his personal account. The amount owed by all the customers together will be a balance on the **trade receivables control account**.

At any time the balance on the receivables control account should be **equal** to the sum of the individual balances on the personal accounts in the sales ledger.

EXAMPLE

For example, if a business has three customers, H Duckworth who owes £200, T Carter who owes £450 and J Matthews who owes £320, the debit balances on the various accounts would be:

Sales ledger (personal accounts)	
	£
H Duckworth	200
T Carter	450
J Matthews	320
Nominal ledger - receivables control account	970

What has happened here is that the three entries of £200, £450 and £320 were first entered into the sales day book. They were also recorded in the three personal accounts of Duckworth, Carter and Matthews in the sales ledger - but remember that this is not part of the double entry system.

Later, the **total** of £970 is posted from the sales day book into the receivables (control) account. It is fairly obvious that if you add up all the debit figures on the personal accounts, they also should total £970.

---

2 THE OPERATION OF CONTROL ACCOUNTS

2.1 Accounting for receivables

It will be useful first of all to see how transactions involving receivables are accounted for by means of an illustrative example. Folio numbers are shown in the accounts to illustrate the cross-referencing that is needed, and in the following example folio numbers beginning:

(a) SDB, refer to a page in the sales day book
(b) SL, refer to a particular account in the sales ledger
(c) NL, refer to a particular account in the nominal ledger
(d) CB, refer to a page in the cash book.

EXAMPLE: ACCOUNTING FOR RECEIVABLES

At 1 September 20X0, the Earthminder Garden Business had no accounts receivable at all. During September, the following transactions affecting credit sales and customers occurred.

(a) Sept 3 Invoiced H Duckworth for the sale on credit of plants: £170

(b) Sept 11 Invoiced T Carter for the sale on credit of garden tools: £260

(c) Sept 15 Invoiced J Matthews for the sale on credit of plants: £330

(d) Sept 10 Received payment from H Duckworth of £150, in settlement of his debt in full, having taken a permitted discount of £20 for payment within seven days

(e) Sept 18 Received a payment of £108 from T Carter in part settlement of £120 of his debt. A discount of £12 was allowed for payment within seven days of invoice

(f) Sept 28 Received a payment of £200 from J Matthews, who was unable to claim any discount

Account numbers are as follows.

SL 028	Personal account: H Duckworth
SL 105	Personal account: T Carter
SL 017	Personal account: J Matthews
NL 200	Receivables control account
NL 207	Discounts allowed
NL 401	Sales: plants
NL 402	Sales: garden tools

NL 100 Cash control account

Required

Write up all the accounts listed above for the transactions which took place in September.

ANSWER

The accounting entries, suitably dated, would be as follows.

SALES DAY BOOK — SDB 090

Date	*Name*	*Folio*	*Total*	*Plants*	*Garden tools*
20X0			£	£	£
Sept 3	H Duckworth	SL 028 Dr	170.00	170.00	
11	T Carter	SL 105 Dr	260.00		260.00
15	J Matthews	SL 017 Dr	330.00	330.00	
			760.00	500.00	260.00
			NL 200 Dr	NL 401 Cr	NL 402 Cr

Note. The personal accounts in the sales ledger are debited on the day the invoices are sent out. The double entry in the ledger accounts might be made at the end of each day, week or month; here it is made at the end of the month, by posting from the sales day book as follows.

			£	£
DEBIT	NL 200	Receivables control account	760	
CREDIT	NL 401	Sales: plants		500
	NL 402	Sales: garden tools		260

CASH BOOK EXTRACT

RECEIPTS CASH BOOK: SEPTEMBER 20X0 — CB 079

Date	*Narrative*	*Folio*	*Total*	*Discount*	*Receivables*
20X0			£	£	£
Sept 10	H Duckworth	SL 028 Cr	150.00	20.00	170.00
18	T Carter	SL 105 Cr	108.00	12.00	120.00
28	J Matthews	SL 017 Cr	200.00	-	200.00
			458.00	32.00	490.00
			NL 100 Dr	NL 207 Dr	NL 200 Cr

The personal accounts in the sales ledger are memorandum accounts, because they are not a part of the double entry system.

Memorandum sales ledger

H DUCKWORTH — A/c no: SL 028

Date	*Narrative*	*Folio*	£	*Date*	*Narrative*	*Folio*	£
20X0				*20X0*			
Sept 3	Sales	SDB 090	170.00	Sept 10	Cash	CB 079	150.00
					Discount	CB 079	20.00
			170.00				170.00

T CARTER A/c no: SL 105

Date	Narrative	Folio	£	Date	Narrative	Folio	£
20X0				20X0			
Sept 11	Sales	SDB 090	260.00	Sept 18	Cash	CB 079	108.00
					Discount	CB 079	12.00
				Sept 30	Balance	c/d	140.00
			260.00				260.00
Oct 1	Balance	b/d	140.00				

J MATTHEWS A/c no: SL 017

Date	Narrative	Folio	£	Date	Narrative	Folio	£
20X0				20X0			
Sept 15	Sales	SDB 090	330.00	Sept 28	Cash	CB 079	200.00
				Sept 30	Balance	c/d	130.00
			330.00				330.00
Oct 1	Balance	b/d	130.00				

In the nominal ledger, the accounting entries can be made from the books of prime entry to the ledger accounts, in this example at the end of the month.

Nominal ledger (extract)

TOTAL RECEIVABLES (SALES LEDGER CONTROL ACCOUNT) A/c no: NL 200

Date	Narrative	Folio	£	Date	Narrative	Folio	£
20X0				20X0			
Sept 30	Sales	SDB 090	760.00	Sept 30	Cash and discount	CB 079	490.00
				Sept 30	Balance	c/d	270.00
			760.00				760.00
Oct 1	Balance	b/d	270.00				

Note. At 30 September the closing balance on the receivables control account (£270) is the same as the total of the individual balances on the personal accounts in the sales ledger (£0 + £140 + £130).

DISCOUNT ALLOWED A/c no: NL 207

Date	Narrative	Folio	£	Date	Narrative	Folio	£
20X0							
Sept 30	Receivables	CB 079	32.00				

CASH CONTROL ACCOUNT A/c no: NL 100

Date	Narrative	Folio	£	Date	Narrative	Folio	£
20X0							
Sept 30	Cash received	CB 079	458.00				

SALES: PLANTS A/c no: NL 401

Date	Narrative	Folio	£	Date	Narrative	Folio	£
				20X0			
				Sept 30	Receivables	SDB 090	500.00

SALES: GARDEN TOOLS A/c no: NL 402

Date	Narrative	Folio	£	Date	Narrative	Folio	£
				20X0			
				Sept 30	Receivables	SDB 090	260.00

If we took the balance on the accounts shown in the above example as at 30 September 20X0 the trial balance (insofar as it is appropriate to call these limited extracts by this name) would be as follows.

TRIAL BALANCE

	Debit	*Credit*
	£	£
Cash (all receipts)	458	
Receivables	270	
Discount allowed	32	
Sales: plants		500
Sales: garden tools		260
	760	760

The trial balance is shown here to emphasise the point that a trial balance **includes the balances on control accounts, but excludes the balances on the personal accounts** in the sales ledger and purchase ledger.

2.2 Accounting for payables

If you were able to follow the example above dealing with the receivables control account, you should have no difficulty in dealing with similar examples relating to purchases/payables. If necessary refer back to revise the entries made in the purchase day book and purchase ledger personal accounts.

2.3 Entries in control accounts

Typical entries in the control accounts are listed below. Folio reference Jnl indicates that the transaction is first lodged in the journal before posting to the control account and other accounts indicated. References SRDB and PRDB are to sales returns and purchase returns day books.

SALES LEDGER (RECEIVABLES) CONTROL

	Folio	£		*Folio*	£
Opening debit balances	b/d	7,000	Opening credit balances (if any)	b/d	200
Sales	SDB	52,390	Cash received	CB	52,250
Dishonoured bills or cheques	Jnl	1,000	Discounts allowed	CB	1,250
Cash paid to clear credit balances	CB	110	Returns inwards from receivables	SRDB	800
Closing credit balances	c/d	120	Irrecoverable debts	Jnl	300
			Closing debit balances	c/d	5,820
		60,620			60,620
Debit balances b/d		5,820	Credit balances b/d		120

Notes. Opening credit balances are unusual in the receivables control account. They represent customers to whom the business owes money, probably as a result of the over payment of debts or for advance payments of debts for which no invoices have yet been sent.

PURCHASES LEDGER (PAYABLES) CONTROL

	Folio	£		Folio	£
Opening debit balances			Opening credit balances	b/d	8,300
(if any)	b/d	70	Purchases and other		
Cash paid	CB	29,840	expenses	PDB	31,000
Discounts received	CB	30	Cash received clearing		
Returns outwards to	PRDB		debit balances	CB	20
suppliers		60	Closing debit balances		
Closing credit balances	c/d	9,400	(if any)	c/d	80
		39,400			39,400
Debit balances	b/d	80	Credit balances	b/d	9,400

Note. Opening debit balances in the payables control account would represent suppliers who owe the business money, perhaps because debts have been overpaid or because debts have been prepaid before the supplier has sent an invoice.

Posting from the journal to the memorandum sales or bought ledgers and to the nominal ledger may be effected as in the following example, where J Matthews has returned goods with a sales value of £100.

Journal entry	*Folio*	*Dr*	*Cr*
		£	£
Sales	NL 401	100	
To receivables control	NL 200		100
To J Matthews (memorandum)	SL 017	-	100

Return of electrical goods inwards

2.4 Contra entries

Sometimes the same business may be both a receivable and a payable. For example, C Cloning buys hardware from you and you buy stationery from C Cloning. In the receivables ledger, C Cloning owes you £130. However, you owe C Cloning £250. You may reach an agreement to offset the balances receivable and payable. This is known as a 'contra'. The double entry is as follows:

DEBIT	Payables control	£130	
CREDIT	Receivables control		£130

You will also need to make the appropriate entries in the memorandum receivables and payables ledger. After this, C Cloning will owe you nothing and you will owe C Cloning £120 (£250 – £130).

NOTES

Activity 1 **(10 minutes)**

A payables control account contains the following entries:

	£
Bank	83,000
Credit purchases	86,700
Discounts received	4,130
Contra with receivables control account	5,200
Balance c/f at 31 December 20X0	13,700

There are no other entries in the account. What was the opening balance brought forward at 1 January 20X0?

Activity 2 **(15 minutes)**

On examining the books of Archright Ltd, you ascertain that on 1 October 20X0 the receivables ledger balances were £20,347 debit and £228 credit, and the payables ledger balances on the same date £18,024 credit and £319 debit.

For the year ended 30 September 20X1 the following particulars are available.

	£
Sales	176,429
Purchases	108,726
Cash received from customers	148,481
Cash paid to suppliers	95,184
Discount received	2,798
Discount allowed	5,273
Returns inwards	3,180
Returns outwards	1,417
Irrecoverable debts written off	1,079
Cash received in respect of debit balances in payables ledger	319
Amount due from customer as shown by receivables ledger, offset against amount due to the same firm as shown by payables ledger (settlement by contra)	949
Allowances to customers on goods damaged in transit	553

On 30 September 20X1 there were no credit balances in the receivables ledger except those outstanding on 1 October 20X0, and no debit balances in the payables ledger.

You are required to write up the following accounts recording the above transactions bringing down the balances as on 30 September 20X1:

(a) receivables control account; and
(b) payables control account.

3 THE PURPOSE OF CONTROL ACCOUNTS

3.1 Accuracy check

Control accounts provide a **check on the accuracy of entries made in the personal accounts** in the sales ledger and purchase ledger. It is very easy to make a mistake in posting entries, because there might be hundreds of entries to make. Figures might get transposed. Some entries might be omitted altogether, so that an invoice or a payment transaction does not appear in a personal account as it should. By comparing:

(a) the total balance on the receivables control account with the total of individual balances on the personal accounts in the sales ledger; and

(b) the total balance on the payables control account with the total of individual balances on the personal accounts in the purchase ledger;

it is possible to identify the fact that errors have been made.

3.2 Discovering errors

The control accounts could also assist in the **location of errors**, where postings to the control accounts are made daily or weekly, or even monthly. If a clerk fails to record an invoice or a payment in a personal account, or makes a transposition error, it would be a formidable task to locate the error or errors at the end of a year, say, given the hundreds or thousands of transactions during the year. By using the control account, a comparison with the individual balances in the sales or purchase ledger can be made for every week or day of the month, and the error found much more quickly than if control accounts did not exist.

3.3 Internal check

Where there is a separation of clerical (bookkeeping) duties, the control account provides an **internal check**. The person posting entries to the control accounts will act as a check on a different person whose job it is to post entries to the sales and purchase ledger accounts.

3.4 Provides a total balance

To provide receivables and payables balances more quickly for producing a trial balance or statement of financial position. A single balance on a control account is obviously **extracted more simply and quickly** than many individual balances in the sales or purchase ledger. This means also that the number of accounts in the double entry bookkeeping system can be kept down to a manageable size, since the personal accounts are memorandum accounts only and the control accounts instead provide the accounts required for a double entry system.

However, particularly in **computerised systems**, it may be feasible to use sales and purchase ledgers without the need for operating separate control accounts. In such a system, the sales or purchase ledger printouts produced by the computer constitute the list of individual balances as well as providing a total balance which represents the control account balance.

3.5 Balancing and agreeing control accounts with sales and purchase ledgers

The control accounts should be **balanced regularly** (at least monthly), and the balance on the account agreed with the sum of the individual receivables or payables balances extracted from the sales or bought ledgers respectively. It is one of the sad facts of an accountant's life that more often than not the balance on the control account does not agree with the sum of balances extracted, for one or more of the following reasons.

(a) An **incorrect amount** may be **posted** to the control account because of a miscast of the total in the book of prime entry (ie adding up incorrectly the total value of invoices or payments). The nominal ledger debit and credit postings will then balance, but the control account balance will not agree with the sum of individual balances extracted from the (memorandum) sales ledger or purchase ledger. A journal entry must then be made in the nominal ledger to correct the control account and the corresponding sales or expense account.

(b) A **transposition** error may occur in posting an individual's balance from the book of prime entry to the memorandum ledger, eg the sale to J Matthews of £330 might be posted to his account as £303. This means that the sum of balances extracted from the memorandum ledger must be corrected. No accounting entry would be required to do this, except to alter the figure in J Matthews's account.

(c) A transaction may be recorded in the control account and not in the memorandum ledger, or vice versa. This requires an entry in the ledger that has been **missed out** which means a double posting if the control account has to be corrected, and a single posting if it is the individual's balance in the memorandum ledger that is at fault.

(d) The sum of balances extracted from the memorandum ledger may be **incorrectly extracted** or **miscast**. This would involve simply correcting the total of the balances.

Reconciling the control account balance with the sum of the balances extracted from the (memorandum) sales ledger or bought ledger should be done in two stages.

(a) Correct the total of the balances extracted from the memorandum ledger. (The errors must be located first of course.)

	£	£
Sales ledger total		
Original total extracted		15,320
Add difference arising from transposition error (£95 written as £59)		36
		15,356
Less		
Credit balance of £60 extracted as a debit balance (£60 × 2)	120	
Overcast of list of balances	90	
		210
		15,146

(b) Bring down the balance before adjustments on the control account, and adjust or post the account with correcting entries.

NOTES

RECEIVABLES CONTROL

	£		£
Balance before adjustments	15,091	Cash: posting omitted	10
		Returns inwards: individual posting omitted from control account	35
Undercast of total invoices issued in sales day book	100	Balance c/d (now in agreement with the corrected total of individual balances in (a))	15,146
	15,191		15,191
Balance b/d	15,146		

4 THE INCOMPLETE RECORDS PROBLEM

The problem is to **prepare a set of year-end accounts** for the business; an income statement and a statement of financial position. Since the business does not have a full set of accounts, preparing the final accounts is not a simple matter of closing off accounts and transferring balances to the income statement, or showing outstanding balances in the statement of financial position. Preparing the final accounts involves the following tasks.

(a) Establishing the cost of **purchases and other expenses**

(b) Establishing the total amount of **sales**

(c) Establishing the amount of **payables, accruals, receivables and prepayments** at the end of the year

Questions may take incomplete records problems a stage further, by introducing an 'incident' such as fire or burglary which leaves the owner of the business uncertain about how much **inventory has been destroyed or stolen.**

To understand what incomplete records are about, it will obviously be useful now to look at what exactly might be incomplete. We shall consider the following items in turn.

- The opening position
- Credit sales and trade receivables
- Purchases and trade payables
- Purchases, inventories and the cost of sales
- Stolen goods or goods destroyed
- The cash book
- Accruals and prepayments
- Drawings (for a sole trader)

5 THE OPENING POSITION

In practice there should not be any missing item in the opening statement of financial position of the business, because it should be available from the preparation of the previous year's final accounts. However, a problem might provide information about the assets and liabilities of the business at the beginning of the period under review, but then leave the balancing figure unspecified. This **balancing figure** represents the opening balance of the proprietor's business capital.

EXAMPLE: OPENING STATEMENT OF FINANCIAL POSITION

For example, a business has the following assets and liabilities as at 1 January 20X0.

	£
Fixtures and fittings at cost	7,000
Accumulated depreciation, fixtures and fittings	4,000
Motor vehicles at cost	12,000
Accumulated depreciation, motor vehicles	6,800
Inventory	4,500
Trade receivables	5,200
Cash at bank and in hand	1,230
Trade payables	3,700
Prepayment	450
Accrued rent	2,000

Required

Prepare a statement of financial position for the business inserting a balancing figure for proprietor's capital.

ANSWER

The statement of financial position of the business can be prepared and the balancing figure is the proprietor's capital at the year-end.

STATEMENT OF FINANCIAL POSITION AS AT 1 JANUARY 20X0

	£	£
Assets		
Non-current assets		
Fixtures and fittings at cost	7,000	
Less accumulated depreciation	4,000	
		3,000
Motor vehicles at cost	12,000	
Less accumulated depreciation	6,800	
		5,200
Current assets		
Inventory	4,500	
Trade accounts receivable	5,200	
Prepayment	450	
Cash	1,230	
		11,380
Total assets		19,580
Capital and liabilities		
Proprietor's capital as at 1 January 20X3 (balancing figure)		13,880
Current liabilities		
Trade accounts payable	3,700	
Accrual	2,000	
		5,700
Total capital and liabilities		19,580

The opening statement of financial position should now provide some of the information needed to prepare the final accounts for the current period.

6 CREDIT SALES AND TRADE RECEIVABLES

If a business does not keep a record of its **sales on credit**, the value of these sales can be derived from the opening balance of trade receivables, the closing balance of trade receivables, and the payments received from trade receivables during the period.

6.1 Credit sales

Credit sales are calculated as follows.

Definition

	£
Credit sales	
Payments received from trade receivables	X
Plus closing balance of trade receivables (since these represent sales in the current period for which cash payment has not yet been received)	X
Less opening balance of trade receivables(unless these become irrecoverable debts, they will pay what they owe in the current period for sales in a previous period)	(X)
Credit sales during the period	X

For example, suppose that a business had trade receivables of £1,750 on 1 April 20X0 and trade receivables of £3,140 on 31 March 20X1. If payments received from trade receivables during the year to 31 March 20X1 were £28,490, and if there are no irrecoverable debts, then credit sales for the period would be as follows.

	£
Cash from trade receivables	28,490
Plus closing trade receivables	3,140
Less opening trade receivables	(1,750)
Credit sales during the period	29,880

If there are **irrecoverable debts** during the period, the value of sales will be increased by the amount of irrecoverable debts written off, no matter whether they relate to opening trade receivables or credit sales during the current period.

The same calculation could be made in a ledger account, with credit sales being the balancing figure to complete the account.

TRADE RECEIVABLES

	£		£
Opening balance b/f	1,750	Cash received	28,490
Credit sales (balancing figure)	29,880	Closing balance c/f	3,140
	31,630		31,630

The same interrelationship between credit sales, cash from receivables, and opening and closing receivables balances can be used to derive a missing figure for cash from receivables, or opening or closing trade receivables, given the values for the three other items. For example, if we know that opening trade receivables are £6,700, closing trade receivables are £3,200 and credit sales for the period are £69,400, then cash received during the period would be as follows.

NOTES

TRADE RECEIVABLES

	£		£
Opening balance	6,700	Cash received (balancing figure)	72,900
Sales (on credit)	69,400	Closing balance c/f	3,200
	76,100		76,100

There is an alternative way of presenting the same calculation.

	£
Opening balance of trade receivables	6,700
Plus credit sales during the period	69,400
Total money owed to the business	76,100
Less closing balance of trade receivables	3,200
Equals cash received during the period	72,900

6.2 Control account

You may be asked to **reconcile control accounts** in an incomplete records question or assessment. You should also remember the complications which might arise in a sales ledger control account, which might include the following.

SALES LEDGER CONTROL ACCOUNT

	£		£
Opening debit balances	X	Opening credit balances (if any)	X
Sales	X	Cash received	X
Dishonoured bills or cheques	X	Discounts allowed	X
Cash paid to clear credit balances	X	Returns inwards	X
Irrecoverable debts recovered	X	Irrecoverable debts	X
Closing credit balances	X	Cash from irrecoverable debts recovered	X
		Contra with purchase ledger control a/c	X
		Allowances on goods damaged	X
		Closing debit balances	X
	X		X

If you have to find a balancing figure in the sales ledger control account, you may have to consider all the above items.

Activity 3 **(10 minutes)**

A trade receivables control account contains the following entries:

	£
Balance b/f 1 January	42,800
Bank	204,000
Discounts allowed	16,250
Credit sales	240,200

Assuming there are no other entries into the account, what is the closing balance at 31 December?

NOTES

7 PURCHASES AND TRADE PAYABLES

A similar relationship to that discussed above exists between **purchases of inventory** during a period, the opening and closing balances for trade payables, and amounts paid to trade payables during the period.

If we wish to calculate an unknown amount for purchases, the amount would be derived as follows.

Definition

	£
Payments to suppliers (trade payables) during the period	X
Plus closing balance of trade payables (since these represent purchases in the current period for which payment has not yet been made)	X
Less opening balance of trade payables (these debts, paid in the current period, relate to purchases in a previous period)	(X)
Purchases during the period	X

EXAMPLE

Suppose that a business had trade payables of £3,728 on 1 October 20X0 and trade payables of £2,645 on 30 September 20X1. If payments to suppliers during the year to 30 September 20X1 were £31,479, then purchases during the year can be derived as follows.

	£
Payments to suppliers (trade payables)	31,479
Plus closing balance of trade payables	2,645
Less opening balance of trade payables	(3,728)
Purchases	30,396

The same calculation could be made in a ledger account, with purchases being the balancing figure to complete the account.

TRADE PAYABLES

	£		£
Cash payments	31,479	Opening balance b/f	3,728
Closing balance c/f	2,645	Purchases (balancing figure)	30,396
	34,124		34,124

7.1 Control account

Once again, various complications can arise in the purchase ledger control account which you may have to consider.

PURCHASE LEDGER CONTROL ACCOUNT

	£		£
Opening debit balances (if any)	X	Opening credit balances	X
Cash paid	X	Purchases and other expenses	X
Discounts received	X	Cash received clearing debit balances	X
Returns outwards	X	Closing debit balances	X
Contras with sales ledger control a/c	X		
Allowances on goods damaged	X		
Closing credit balances	X		
	X		X

8 PURCHASES, INVENTORIES AND COST OF SALES

8.1 Purchases

When the **value of purchases is not known**, a different approach might be required to find out what they were, depending on the nature of the information given to you.

One approach would be to use information about the cost of sales, and opening and closing inventories rather than the trade payables account to find the cost of purchases.

Definition

		£
Since	opening inventory	X
	plus purchases	X
	less closing inventory	(X)
	equals the cost of goods sold	X
then	the cost of goods sold	X
	plus closing inventory	X
	less opening inventory	(X)
	equals purchases for the period	X

EXAMPLE

Suppose that the inventory of a business on 1 July 20X0 has a carrying amount of £8,400, and an inventory count at 30 June 20X1 showed inventory to be valued at £9,350. Sales for the year to 30 June 20X1 are £80,000, and the business makes a mark up of $33^1/_3$% on cost for all the items that it sells. What were the purchases during the year?

ANSWER

The cost of goods sold can be derived from the value of sales, as follows.

		£
Sales	($133^1/_3$%)	80,000
Gross profit	($33^1/_3$%)	20,000
Cost of goods sold	(100%)	60,000

The cost of goods sold is 75% (100% ÷ $133\frac{1}{3}\%$) of sales value.

	£
Cost of goods sold	60,000
Plus closing inventory	9,350
Less opening inventory	(8,400)
Purchases during the period	60,950

Activity 4 **(10 minutes)**

An extract from a company's income statement stood as follows for the year ended 31 March 20X0.

	£	£
Sales		150,000
Opening inventory	12,000	
Purchases	114,500	
	126,500	
Closing inventory	14,000	
		112,500

(a) Calculate the gross profit as a percentage of cost of sales.

(b) Calculate the gross profit as a percentage of sales.

8.2 Stolen goods or goods destroyed

A similar type of calculation might be required to derive the value of goods stolen or destroyed. An example will show how to determine the cost of an unknown quantity of goods lost.

EXAMPLE: INVENTORY LOST IN A FIRE

Fairmount Boutique is a shop which sells fashion clothes. On 1 January 20X0, it had inventory which cost £7,345. During the nine months to 30 September 20X0, the business purchased goods from suppliers costing £106,420. Sales during the same period were £154,000. The shop makes a mark-up of 40% on cost for everything it sells. On 30 September 20X0, there was a fire in the shop which destroyed most of the inventory in it. Only a small amount of inventory, known to have cost £350, was undamaged and still fit for sale.

How much inventory was lost in the fire?

ANSWER

		£
(a)	Sales (140%)	154,000
	Gross profit (40%)	44,000
	Cost of goods sold (100%)	110,000

(b)	Opening inventory, at cost	7,345
	Plus purchases	106,420
		113,765
	Less closing inventory, at cost	350
	Equals cost of goods sold and goods lost	113,415

		£
(c)	Cost of goods sold and lost	113,415
	Cost of goods sold	110,000
	Cost of goods lost	3,415

EXAMPLE: INVENTORY STOLEN

Ashley Guerrard runs a jewellery shop in the High Street. On 1 January 20X0, his inventory, at cost, amounted to £4,700 and his trade payables were £3,950.

During the six months to 30 June 20X0, sales were £42,000. Ashley Guerrard makes a gross profit of $33^{1/3}$% on the sales value of everything he sells.

On 30 June, there was a burglary at the shop, and all the inventory was stolen.

In trying to establish how much inventory had been taken, Ashley Guerrard was able to provide the following information.

(a) He knew from his bank statements that he had paid £28,400 to suppliers in the six month period to 30 June 20X0.

(b) He currently owed suppliers £5,550.

Required

(a) Calculate how much inventory was stolen.
(b) Calculate gross profit for the six months to 30 June 20X0.

ANSWER

Step 1. We must establish some 'unknowns' before we can calculate how much inventory was stolen. The first 'unknown' is the amount of purchases during the period. This is established by the method previously described in this chapter.

TRADE PAYABLES

	£		£
Payments to suppliers	28,400	Opening balance b/f	3,950
Closing balance c/f	5,550	Purchases (balancing figure)	30,000
	33,950		33,950

Step 2. The cost of goods sold is also unknown, but this can be established from the gross profit margin and the sales for the period.

		£
Sales	(100%)	42,000
Gross profit	($33^1/_3$%)	14,000
Cost of goods sold	($66^2/_3$%)	28,000

Step 3. The cost of the goods stolen is as follows.

	£
Opening inventory at cost	4,700
Purchases	30,000
	34,700
Less closing inventory (after burglary)	0
Cost of goods sold and goods stolen	34,700
Cost of goods sold (see (ii) above)	28,000
Cost of goods stolen	6,700

Step 4. The cost of the goods stolen will not be a charge against gross profit, and so the gross profit for the period is as follows.

ASHLEY GUERRARD
GROSS PROFIT FOR THE SIX MONTHS TO 30 JUNE 20X0

	£	£
Sales		42,000
Less cost of goods sold		
Opening inventory	4,700	
Purchases	30,000	
	34,700	
Less inventory stolen	6,700	
		28,000
Gross profit		14,000

8.3 Terminology

You may have noticed that we have used two terms for the relationship between gross profit and either cost or sales.

- **Mark-up** is where the gross profit is calculated as a percentage of cost, for example the company makes a mark up of 30% on cost.
- **Gross profit margin** is usually used to denote the relationship between profit and sales, for example the company makes a gross profit of 25% on sales.

	Mark-up	*Gross profit percentage*
	%	%
Sales	130	100
Cost of sales	100	75
Mark up/gross profit margin	30	25

8.4 Accounting for lost inventory

When inventory is stolen, destroyed or otherwise lost, the loss must be accounted for somehow. Since the loss is **not a trading loss,** the cost of the goods lost is not included in the cost of sales, as the previous example showed.

The accounting double entry is therefore

DEBIT	See below
CREDIT	Cost of sales

There are two possible accounts that could be **debited** with the other side of the accounting double entry, depending on whether or not the lost goods were insured.

(a) If the lost goods were **not insured** the business must bear the loss and the loss is shown in the income statement.

DEBIT	Income statement (I & E account)
CREDIT	Cost of sales

(b) If the lost goods were **insured** the business will not suffer a loss because the insurance will pay back the cost of the lost goods. This means that there is no charge at all in the income statement, and the appropriate double entry for the cost of the loss is as follows.

DEBIT	Insurance claim account (receivable account)
CREDIT	Cost of sales

The insurance claim will then be a current asset, and shown in the statement of financial position of the business as such. When the claim is paid, the account is then closed.

DEBIT	Cash
CREDIT	Insurance claim account

Activity 5 **(10 minutes)**

Janey Jennings's business had opening inventory of £71,300. Purchases and sales for 20X0 were £282,250 and £455,000 respectively. The gross profit margin is a constant 40% on sales. On 31 December 20X0 a fire destroyed all the inventory on Janey Jennings's premises, except for small sundry items with a cost of £1,200.

Required

Calculate the cost of the inventory destroyed.

9 THE CASH BOOK

The construction of a cash book (**largely from bank statements** showing receipts and payments of a business during a given period) is often an important feature of incomplete records problems. This is because the purpose of an incomplete records exercise is largely to test your understanding about how various items of receipts or payments relate to the preparation of a final set of accounts for a business.

We have already seen in this chapter that information about cash receipts or payments might be needed to establish the amount of credit sales or of purchases during a period.

Other receipts or payments figures might be needed to establish the following amounts.

- Cash sales
- Certain expenses in the income statement
- Drawings by the business proprietor

It might therefore be helpful, if a business does not keep a cash book on a daily basis, to **construct a cash book** at the end of an accounting period. A business which typically might not keep a daily cash book is a shop.

(a) Many sales, if not all sales, are cash sales and payment is received in the form of notes and coins, cheques, or credit cards at the time of sale.

(b) Some payments are made in notes and coins out of the till rather than by payment out of the business bank account by cheque.

Where there appears to be a sizeable volume of receipts and payments in cash then it is also helpful to construct a **two column cash book**. This is a cash book with one column for receipts and payments, and one column for money paid into and out of the business bank account.

EXAMPLE: PREPARING A CASH BOOK

Franklin George owns and runs a bookshop, making a gross profit of 25% on the cost of everything he sells. He does not keep a cash book.

ON 1 JANUARY 20X0 THE STATEMENT OF FINANCIAL POSITION OF HIS BUSINESS WAS AS FOLLOWS.

	£	£
Non-current assets (cost less accumulated depreciation)		20,000
Current assets		
Inventory	10,000	
Cash in the bank	3,000	
Cash in the till	200	
		13,200
		33,200
Proprietor's capital		32,000
Trade payables		1,200
		33,200

You are given the following information about the year to 31 December 20X0.

(a) There were no sales on credit.

(b) £41,750 in receipts were banked.

(c) The bank statements of the period show these payments.

(i)	To trade payables	£36,000
(ii)	Sundry expenses	£5,600
(iii)	In drawings	£4,400

(d) Payments were also made in cash out of the till.

(i)	To trade payables	£800
(ii)	Sundry expenses	£1,500
(iii)	In drawings	£3,700

At 31 December 20X0, the business had cash in the till of £450 and trade payables of £1,400. The cash balance in the bank was not known and the value of closing inventory has not yet been calculated. There were no accruals or prepayments. No further non-current assets were purchased during the year. The depreciation charge for the year is £900.

(a) Prepare a two-column cash book for the period.

(b) Prepare the income statement for the year to 31 December 20X0 and the statement of financial position as at 31 December 20X0.

ANSWER

A two-column cash book is completed as follows.

Step 1. Enter the opening cash balances.

Step 2. Enter the information given about cash payments (and any cash receipts, if there had been any such items given in the problem).

Step 3. The cash receipts banked are a 'contra' entry, being both a debit (bank column) and a credit (cash in hand column) in the same account.

Step 4. Enter the closing cash in hand (cash in the bank at the end of the period is not known).

CASH BOOK

	Cash in hand	*Bank*		*Cash in hand*	*Bank*
	£	£		£	£
Balance b/f	200	3,000	Trade payables	800	36,000
Cash receipts			Sundry expenses	1,500	5,600
banked (contra)		41,750	Drawings	3,700	4,400
Sales	*48,000		Cash receipts banked		
Balance c/f		*1,250	(contra)	41,750	
			Balance c/f	450	
	48,200	46,000		48,200	46,000
* Balancing figures					

Step 5. The closing balance of money in the bank is a balancing figure.

Step 6. Since all sales are for cash, a balancing figure that can be entered in the cash book is sales, in the cash in hand (debit) column.

It is important to notice that since not all receipts from cash sales are banked, the value of cash sales during the period is as follows.

	£
Receipts banked	41,750
Plus expenses and drawings paid out of the till in cash £(800 + 1,500 + 3,700)	6,000
Plus any cash stolen (here there is none)	0
Plus the closing balance of cash in hand	450
	48,200
Less the opening balance of cash in hand	(200)
Equals cash sales	48,000

The cash book constructed in this way has enabled us to establish both the closing balance for cash in the bank and also the volume of cash sales. The income statement and the statement of financial position can also be prepared, once a value for purchases has been calculated.

TRADE PAYABLES

	£		£
Cash book:		Balance b/f	1,200
payments from bank	36,000	Purchases (balancing figure)	37,000
Cash book:			
payments in cash	800		
Balance c/f	1,400		
	38,200		38,200

The mark-up of 25% on cost indicates that the cost of the goods sold is £38,400, as follows.

	£
Sales (125%)	48,000
Gross profit (25%)	9,600
Cost of goods sold (100%)	38,400

The closing inventory is now a balancing figure in the calculation of cost of sales.

FRANKLIN GEORGE INCOME STATEMENT
FOR THE YEAR ENDED 31 DECEMBER 20X0

	£	£
Sales		48,000
Less cost of goods sold		
Opening inventory	10,000	
Purchases	37,000	
	47,000	
Less closing inventory (balancing figure)	8,600	
		38,400
Gross profit (25/125 × £48,000)		9,600
Expenses		
Sundry £(1,500 + 5,600)	7,100	
Depreciation	900	
		8,000
Net profit		1,600

FRANKLIN GEORGE
STATEMENT OF FINANCIAL POSITION AS AT 31 DECEMBER 20X0

	£	£
Net non-current assets £(20,000 – 900)		19,100
Current assets		
Inventory	8,600	
Cash in the till	450	
		9,050
		28,150

Proprietor's capital		
Balance b/f		32,000
Net profit for the year		1,600
		33,600
Drawings £(3,700 + 4,400)		(8,100)
Balance c/f		25,500
Current liabilities		
Bank overdraft	1,250	
Trade payables	1,400	
		2,650
		28,150

9.1 Theft of cash from the till

When cash is stolen from the till, the amount stolen will be a credit entry in the cash book, and a debit in either the expenses section of the income statement or insurance claim account, depending on whether the business is **insured**. The missing figure for cash sales, if this has to be calculated, must take account of cash received but later stolen.

9.2 Using the receivables account to calculate both cash sales and credit sales

Another point which needs to be considered is how a missing value can be found for **cash sales and credit sales**, when a business has both, but takings banked by the business are not divided between takings from cash sales and takings from credit sales.

EXAMPLE: DETERMINING THE VALUE OF SALES DURING THE PERIOD

Suppose that a business had, on 1 January 20X0, trade receivables of £2,000, cash in the bank of £3,000, and cash in hand of £300.

During the year to 31 December 20X0 the business banked £95,000 in takings. It also paid out the following expenses in cash from the till.

Drawings	£1,200
Sundry expenses	£800

On 29 August 20X0 a thief broke into the shop and stole £400 from the till.

At 31 December 20X0 trade receivables amounted to £3,500, cash in the bank £2,500 and cash in the till £150.

What was the value of sales during the year?

ANSWER

If we tried to prepare a trade receivables account and a two column cash book, we would have insufficient information, in particular about whether the takings which were banked related to cash sales or credit sales.

TRADE RECEIVABLES

	£		£
Balance b/f	2,000	Payments from customers	
Credit sales	*Unknown*	(credit sales)	*Unknown*
		Balance c/f	3,500

CASH BOOK

	Cash	*Bank*		*Cash*	*Bank*
	£	£		£	£
Balance b/f	300	3,000	Drawings	1,200	
			Sundry expenses	800	
Trade receivables: cash received		*Unknown*	Cash stolen	400	
Cash sales		*Unknown*	Balance c/f	150	2,500

All we do know is that the combined sums from trade receivables and cash takings banked is £95,000.

The value of sales can be found instead by using the trade receivables account, which should be used to record cash takings banked as well as payments by customers. The balancing figure in the trade receivables account will then be a combination of credit sales and some cash sales. The cash book only needs to have single columns.

TRADE RECEIVABLES

	£		£
Balance b/f	2,000	Cash banked	95,000
Sales	96,500	Balance c/f	3,500
	98,500		98,500

CASH (EXTRACT)

	£		£
Balance in hand b/f	300	*Payments in cash*	
Balance in bank b/f	3,000	Drawings	1,200
Trade receivables a/c	95,000	Expenses	800
		Other payments	?
		Cash stolen	400
		Balance in hand c/f	150
		Balance in bank c/f	2,500

The remaining 'undiscovered' amount of cash sales is now found as follows.

	£
Payments in cash out of the till	
Drawings	1,200
Expenses	800
	2,000
Cash stolen	400
Closing balance of cash in hand	150
	2,550
Less opening balance of cash in hand	(300)
Further cash sales	2,250
Total sales for the year	£
From trade receivables account	96,500
From cash book	2,250
Total sales	98,750

NOTES

10 ACCRUALS AND PREPAYMENTS

Where there is an accrued expense or a prepayment, the charge to be made in the income statement for the item concerned should be found from the opening balance b/f, the closing balance c/f, and cash payments for the item during the period. The charge in the income statement is perhaps most easily found as the balancing figure in a ledger account.

EXAMPLE: ACCRUALS AND PREPAYMENTS

For example, suppose that on 1 April 20X0 a business had prepaid rent of £700 which relates to the next accounting period. During the year to 31 March 20X1 it pays £9,300 in rent, and at 31 March 20X1 the prepayment of rent is £1,000. The cost of rent in the income statement for the year to 31 March 20X1 would be the balancing figure in the following ledger account. (Remember that a prepayment is a current asset, and so is a debit balance brought forward.)

RENT

	£		£
Prepayment: balance b/f	700	I & E account (balancing figure)	9,000
Cash	9,300	Prepayment: balance c/f	1,000
	10,000		10,000
Balance b/f	1,000		

Similarly, if a business has accrued telephone expenses as at 1 July 20X0 of £850, pays £6,720 in telephone bills during the year to 30 June 20X1, and has accrued telephone expenses of £1,140 as at 30 June 20X1, then the telephone expense to be shown in the income statement for the year to 30 June 20X1 is the balancing figure in the following ledger account. (Remember that an accrual is a current liability, and so is a credit balance brought forward.)

TELEPHONE EXPENSES

	£		£
Cash	6,720	Balance b/f (accrual)	850
Balance c/f (accrual)	1,140	I & E a/c (balancing figure)	7,010
	7,860		7,860
		Balance b/f	1,140

11 DRAWINGS

In the case of a sole trader, drawings would normally represent no particular problem at all in preparing a set of final accounts from incomplete records, but it is not unusual for questions or assessments to involve the following situations.

(a) The business owner **pays income into his bank account** which has nothing to do with the business operations. For example, the owner might pay dividend income or other income from investments into the bank, from stocks and shares which he owns personally, separate from the business itself.

(b) The business owner **pays money out of the business bank account** for items which are not business expenses, such as life insurance premiums or a payment for his family's holidays.

(c) The owner takes inventory for his personal use.

11.1 Accounting treatment

These personal items of receipts or payments should be dealt with as follows.

(a) **Receipts should be set off against drawings**. For example, if a business owner receives £600 in dividend income from investments not owned by the business and pays it into the business bank account, then the accounting entry is as follows.

DEBIT Cash
CREDIT Drawings

(b) Payments of cash for personal items should be charged to drawings.

DEBIT Drawings
CREDIT Cash

(c) **Goods taken for personal use (drawings of inventory)**: the traditional way of dealing with this has been to charge the goods to drawings at cost. The required entries are:

DEBIT Drawings
CREDIT Purchases

However, the recommended treatment, according better with modern practice and the requirements of HM Revenue and Customs, is as follows.

DEBIT Drawings at selling price (including VAT)
CREDIT Sales
CREDIT VAT

12 COMPREHENSIVE APPROACH

A suggested approach to dealing with incomplete records problems brings together the various points described so far in this chapter. The nature of the 'incompleteness' in the records will vary from problem to problem, but the approach, suitably applied, should be successful in arriving at the final accounts whatever the particular characteristics of the problem might be.

12.1 The approach

The approach is as follows.

Step 1. If it is not already known, establish the opening statement of financial position and the brought forward proprietor's capital if possible.

Step 2. Open up four accounts.

- Income and expense account
- A cash book, with two columns if cash sales are significant and there are payments in cash out of the till
- A trade receivables account
- A trade payables account

Step 3. Enter the opening balances in these accounts.

Step 4. Work through the information you are given line by line. Each item should be entered into the appropriate account if it is relevant to one or more of these four accounts.

You should also try to recognise each item as an 'income and expense item' or a 'closing statement of financial position item'.

It may be necessary to calculate an amount for drawings and an amount for non-current asset depreciation.

Step 5. Look for the balancing figures in your accounts. In particular you might be looking for a value for credit sales, cash sales, purchases, the cost of goods sold, the cost of goods stolen or destroyed, or the closing bank balance. Calculate these missing figures and make any necessary double entry (for example to the income and expense account from the trade payables account for purchases, to the income and expense account from the cash book for cash sales, and to the income and expense account from the trade receivables account for credit sales).

Step 6. Now complete the income statement and statement of financial position. Working ledger accounts might be needed where there are accruals or prepayments.

Chapter roundup

- Preparation of accounts from incomplete records may be necessary where a business has limited accounting records or where accounting information has been accidentally lost or destroyed.
- Control accounts are usually used for trade receivables and trade payables and they record all relevant transactions on a totals basis.
- The opening statement of financial position can be reconstructed using the information available.
- Using gross profit percentages or mark up can help to provide missing figures.
- Reconstruction of a two column cash book is another technique.

Quick quiz

1 In the absence of a sales account or sales day book, how can a figure of sales for the year be computed?

2 In the absence of a purchase account or purchases day book, how can a figure of purchases for the year be computed?

3 What is the accounting double entry to record the loss of inventory by fire or burglary?

4 If a business proprietor pays his personal income into the business bank account, what is the accounting double entry to record the transaction?

Answers to Quick quiz

1 Sales can be found using the formula:

	£
Payments received from trade receivables	X
Plus closing balance of trade receivables	X
Less opening balance of trade receivables	(X)
Credit sales	X

2 Again, the following formula can be used.

	£
Payments to trade payables	X
Plus closing balance of trade payables	X
Less opening balance of trade payables	(X)
Credit purchases	X

3 (a) If the goods are not insured:

DEBIT I & E account
CREDIT Cost of sales

(b) If the loss is insured:

DEBIT Insurance claim a/c
CREDIT Cost of sales

4 For a receipt from a proprietor, the double entry is:

DEBIT Cash
CREDIT Drawings

Answers to Activities

1

	£	£
Amounts due to suppliers (trade payables) at 1 January (balancing figure)		19,330
Purchases in year		86,700
		106,030
Less: cash paid to suppliers in year	83,000	
discounts received	4,130	
contra with trade receivables control	5,200	
		92,330
Amounts still unpaid at 31 December		13,700

NOTES

2 (a)

TRADE RECEIVABLES CONTROL ACCOUNT

20X0		£	*20X0*		£
Oct 1	Balances b/f	20,347	Oct 1	Balances b/f	228
20X1			*20X1*		
Sept 30	Sales	176,429	Sept 30	Cash received from customers	148,481
	Balances c/f	228		Discount allowed	5,273
				Returns	3,180
				Irrecoverable debts written off	1,079
				Transfer trade payables control account	949
				Allowances on goods damaged	553
				Balances c/f	37,261
		197,004			197,004

(b)

TRADE PAYABLES CONTROL ACCOUNT

		£			£
20X0			*20X0*		
Oct 1	Balances b/f	319	Oct 1	Balances b/f	18,024
20X1			*20X1*		
Sept 30	Cash paid to suppliers	95,184	Sept 30	Purchases	108,726
	Discount received	2,798		Cash	319
	Returns outwards	1,417			
	Transfer trade receivables control account	949			
	Balances c/f	26,402			
		127,069			127,069

3 The ledger account will look like this.

TRADE RECEIVABLES CONTROL ACCOUNT

	£		£
1 January balance b/f	42,800	Bank	204,000
Sales	240,200	Discounts allowed	16,250
		31 December balance c/f	62,750
	283,000		283,000

4 The gross profit is £150,000 – £112,500 = £37,500.

(a) The gross profit as a percentage of cost of sales is:

$$\frac{£37,500}{£112,500} \times 100\% = 33^1/_3\%$$

(b) The gross profit as a percentage of sales is:

$$\frac{£37,500}{£150,000} \times 100\% = 25\%$$

5

	£	£
Sales		455,000
Less cost of sales		
Opening inventory	71,300	
Purchases	282,250	
	353,550	
Closing inventory (balance)	80,550	
		273,000
Gross profit (40% × £455,000)		182,000

Cost of inventory destroyed = £80,550 – £1,200 = £79,350.

Chapter 18
COMPANY ACCOUNTS

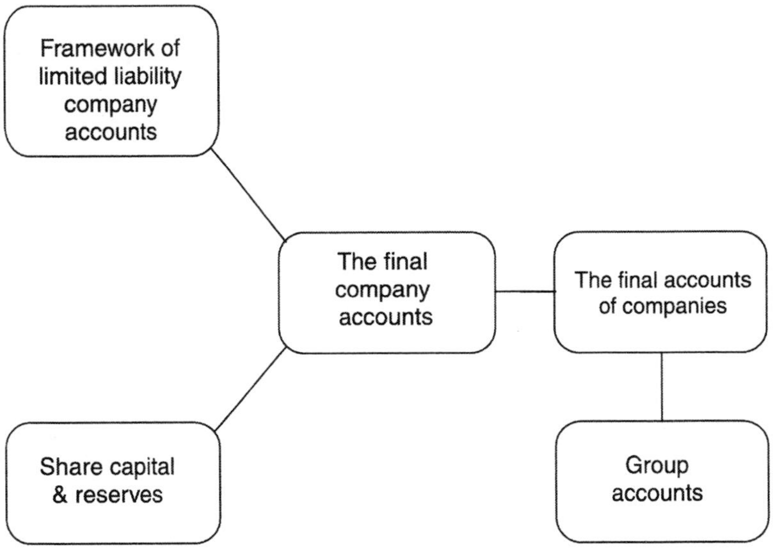

Introduction

So far we have dealt mainly with the accounts of businesses in general. In this chapter, we shall turn our attention to the accounts of limited liability companies (often simply called limited companies). Limited companies are businesses whose owners are called shareholders and who offer limited liability for their owners. It will come as no surprise to you that the accounting rules and conventions for recording the business transactions and preparing the final accounts of limited liability companies are much the same as for sole traders. There is, however, extensive regulation governing the activities of limited liability companies.

This chapter will highlight the main features of the accounts of limited liability companies and provide a detailed worked example. It will also explain how to prepare accounts for a simple group of companies.

Your objectives

In this chapter you will learn about the following.

(a) The nature of limited liability and the legal safeguards that surround it

(b) The capital structure of limited liability companies

(c) The main features of the accounts of limited liability companies

(d) Simple group accounts

1 FRAMEWORK OF LIMITED LIABILITY COMPANY ACCOUNTS

Sole traders and partnerships are, with some significant exceptions, generally fairly small concerns. The amount of capital involved may be modest, and the proprietors of the business usually participate in managing it.

As a business grows, it needs more capital to finance its operations, and significantly more than the people currently managing the business can provide themselves. One way of obtaining more capital is to invite investors from outside the business to invest in the ownership or 'equity' of the business. These new co-owners, called shareholders or equity holders, would not usually be expected to help with managing the business. To such investors, limited liability is very attractive. The shareholders know that if the company goes into liquidation the maximum amount they stand to lose is their share of capital in the business. Since investments are always risky undertakings, this is a very attractive prospect to investors.

Definition

Limited liability means that the maximum amount that an owner stands to lose in the event that the company becomes insolvent and cannot pay off its debts, is his or her share of the capital in the business.

Thus limited liability is a **major advantage** of turning a business into a limited liability company. However, in practice, banks will normally seek personal guarantees from shareholders before making loans or granting an overdraft facility and so the advantage of limited liability is lost to a small owner managed business.

There are two classes of limited liability company.

(a) **Public companies**. Public companies can invite members of the general public to invest in their equity (ownership), and the 'shares' of these companies are usually traded on a stock exchange, (that is to say, public companies are usually also listed companies, though this is not always the case). In the UK, public companies must have the words **public limited company**, usually shortened to PLC or plc, at the end of their name.

(b) **Private companies**. Private companies cannot invite members of the public to invest in their equity. In the UK, private companies must have the word limited (often shortened to Ltd) at the end of their name.

The accounting rules and conventions for recording the business transactions of limited liability companies, and then preparing their final accounts, are much the same as for sole traders. For example, companies will have basic accounting records similar to a sole trader. They also prepare in income statement annually, and a statement of financial position at the end of the accounting year.

There are, however, some differences in the accounts of limited liability companies. The **national legislation** governing the activities of limited liability companies tends to be very extensive. Amongst other things such legislation may define certain minimum accounting records which must be maintained by companies; they may specify that the annual accounts of a company must be filed with a government bureau and so available

NOTES

for public inspection; and they often contain detailed requirements on the minimum information which must be disclosed in a company's accounts. Businesses which are not limited liability companies (non-incorporated businesses) often enjoy comparative freedom from statutory regulation.

Activity 1 **(5 minutes)**

Mark the following statements as true or false.

(a) Where there are numerous owners of an entity it will always be incorporated.

(b) The capital of a company is shown differently from that of a sole trader.

(c) Sole traders usually manage their businesses on a day-to-day basis, unlike shareholders.

(d) Shareholders in a limited liability company may appropriate profits through drawings.

One of the main differences between the accounts of a sole trader and a limited company is in the area of capital accounts.

2 SHARE CAPITAL AND RESERVES

2.1 Share capital

The proprietors' capital in a limited company consists of share capital. When a company is set up for the first time, it issues shares, which are paid for by investors, who then become shareholders of the company. Shares are denominated in units of 25 pence, 50 pence, £1 or whatever seems appropriate. This 'face value' of the shares is called their *nominal value*.

Activity 2 **(5 minutes)**

Fill in the gaps in the following table.

Number of shares	Nominal value	Total value £
100,000		100,000
	50p	100,000
500,000	40p	
	10p	85,000

The nominal value is set by the company and is not the same as the market value, which is the price someone is prepared to pay for the share.

A distinction is made between authorised and issued share capital.

Definitions

1 The **authorised share capital** is the maximum amount of share capital that a company is empowered to issue. It is also sometimes known as nominal capital.

2 The **issued share capital** is the amount of authorised share capital that has already been issued to the shareholders.

The amount of authorised share capital varies from company to company, and can change by agreement.

The issued share capital obviously cannot exceed the authorised share capital. It can be equal to the authorised capital if all of the authorised share capital has been issued.

In the UK, from 1 October 2009, limited companies no longer need to have an authorised share capital.

Shareholders expect to earn a return on their investment. However, before any profit can be distributed to the shareholders, companies must pay taxes.

2.2 Taxes

Companies are taxed on the profits they earn. This tax is sometimes called **corporation tax**. The amount of tax is based on the amounts of profits made – the larger the profit, the higher the tax.

Unlike other types of business such as a sole trader or a partnership, a limited liability company is a separate legal entity. When sole trader or a partnership makes a profit it is the owners, rather than the business, that pays tax on those profits, but when a limited liability company makes a profit it is the company itself that is taxed. For this reason, tax is not recognised in the accounts of sole traders and partnerships, but limited liability companies must recognise the amount of tax that they owe to the taxation authorities.

(a) In the income statement, the amount of tax on profits for the year is shown as a deduction from profits.

	£
Profit before tax	X
Tax	(X)
Profit after tax	X

(b) In the statement of financial position, tax payable is shown as a current liability as it is normally due within twelve months of the year end.

A portion or all of the profit left after payment of taxes can be distributed to the shareholders. Profit paid out to shareholders is called dividends.

2.3 Dividends

Shareholders in a company are rewarded in the form of a dividend.

Definition

Dividends are that portion of the profit after tax that is distributed to the shareholders.

A company might pay dividends in two stages during the course of its accounting year.

(a) In mid year, after the half-year financial results are known, the company might pay an **interim dividend**.

(b) After the end of the year, the company might pay a further **final dividend**.

The total dividend for the year is:

Interim plus final

Not all companies pay an interim dividend. Interim dividends are, however, commonly paid out by listed companies.

At the end of an accounting year a company's directors will often propose a final dividend payment. If this is proposed after the year end then it is not a liability of the company at the year end and therefore does not appear in the financial statements. However the amount of the proposed dividend should be disclosed in a note to the financial statements.

The dividend paid during the accounting period (often last year's proposed final dividend plus the current year interim dividend) is not shown as a deduction from profit in the income statement but is instead deducted directly from the retained earnings (accumulated profits or profits made to date) of the company.

The terminology of dividend payments can be confusing, since they may be expressed either in the form:

(a) x pence per share eg 2p per share
(b) y per cent eg 5% per share

In the latter case, the meaning is always 'y per cent of the nominal value of the shares in issue'. For example, suppose a company's issued share capital consists of 100,000 50p ordinary shares. The company's statement of financial position would include the following.

Issued share capital: 100,000 50p ordinary shares £50,000

If the directors wish to pay a dividend of £5,000, they may propose either:

(a) A dividend of 5p per share (100,000 × 5p = £5,000); or
(b) a dividend of 10% (10% × £50,000 = £5,000).

Dividends are paid to shareholders who may own more than one type of share, each with its own rights and privileges.

2.4 Ordinary and preference shares

At this stage it is relevant to distinguish between the two types of shares most often encountered, preference shares and ordinary shares.

Preference shares carry the right to a final dividend which is expressed as a percentage of their nominal value: eg a 6% £1 preference share carries a right to an annual dividend of 6p. Preference dividends have priority over ordinary dividends. If the directors of a company wish to pay a dividend (which they are not obliged to do) they must pay any preference dividend first. Otherwise, no ordinary dividend may be paid.

The rights attaching to preference shares are set out in the company's constitution. They may vary from company to company and country to country, but typically:

(a) Preference shareholders have a **priority right** over ordinary shareholders to a return of their capital if the company goes into liquidation.

(b) Preference shares do not **carry a right to vote**.

Preference shares may be classified in one of two ways.

(a) Redeemable
(b) Irredeemable

Redeemable preference shares mean that the company will redeem (repay) the nominal value of those shares at a later date. For example, 'redeemable 5% £1 preference shares 20X9' means that the company will pay these shareholders £1 for every share they hold on a certain date in 20X9. The shares will then be cancelled and no further dividends paid. Redeemable preference shares are treated like loans and are included as non-current liabilities in the statement of financial position. Dividends paid on redeemable preference shares are treated like interest paid on loans and are included in financial costs in the income statement.

Irredeemable preference shares are treated just like other shares. They form part of equity and their dividends are treated as appropriations of profit.

Ordinary shares are by far the most common. They carry no right to a fixed dividend but are entitled to all profits left after payment of any preference dividend. Generally however, only a part of such remaining profits is distributed, the rest being kept in reserve (see below).

The amount of ordinary dividends fluctuates although there is a general expectation that it will increase from year to year. Should the company be wound up, any surplus is shared between the ordinary shareholders.

Ordinary shares normally carry voting rights, and ordinary shareholders are the effective owners of the company. They own the 'equity' of the business, and any reserves of the business (described later) belong to them. Ordinary shareholders are sometimes referred to as **equity shareholders**. In contrast, preference shareholders are in many ways more like loan creditors of the company (although legally they are members, not lenders).

It should be emphasised that the precise rights attached to preference and ordinary shares vary from company to company; the distinctions noted above are generalisations.

NOTES

Activity 3 **(5 minutes)**

The share capital of X Ltd is as follows.

	Authorised	*Issued*
	£	£
7% preference shares of £1 each	20,000	12,000
Ordinary shares of 20p each	100,000	80,000
	120,000	92,000

The directors declare an ordinary dividend for the year of 12%. How much in total will be paid out by the company in dividends?

One of the key differences between ordinary and preference shareholders not mentioned above, is the fact that ordinary shareholders own what are called reserves.

2.5 Reserves

The ordinary shareholders' total investment in a limited liability company is called the *equity* and consists of share capital plus reserves. Reserves are difficult to define since different reserves arise for different reasons, but one way of defining them is:

Reserves = net assets less share capital

The total amount of reserves in a company varies, according to changes in the net assets of the business. The important point to note is that all reserves are owned by the *ordinary* shareholders.

A distinction should be made between two types of reserves.

(a) **Non-distributable reserves** are reserves established in circumstances defined by companies legislation. They are not available for distribution as dividends. Companies legislation often restricts the amounts that companies are allowed to pay out to their shareholders in order to protect the claims of lenders and other creditors.

(b) **Distributable reserves** are reserves consisting of profits which are distributable as dividends, if the company so wishes.

Retained earnings

This is the most significant distributable reserve, and it is variously described as:

(a) revenue reserve;
(b) retained profits;
(c) accumulated profits;
(d) undistributed profits;
(e) profit and loss account;
(f) unappropriated profits.

These are profits earned by the company and not appropriated by dividends, taxation or transfer to another reserve account.

Assuming the company is making profits, this reserve generally increases from year to year, as most companies do not distribute all their profits as dividends.

Dividends can be paid from it: even if a loss is made in one particular year, a dividend can be paid from previous years' retained profits. For example, if a company makes a loss of £100,000 in one year, yet has unappropriated profits from previous years totalling £250,000, it can pay a dividend not exceeding £150,000 (ie £250,000 – £100,000).

One reason for retaining some profit each year is to enable the company to pay dividends even when profits are low (or non-existent). Another reason is usually shortage of cash. Very occasionally, you might come across a debit balance on retained earnings. This would indicate that the company has accumulated losses.

2.6 Other distributable reserves

The company directors may choose to set up other reserves. These may have a specific purpose (for example plant and machinery replacement reserve) or not (for example general reserve).
Profits are transferred to these reserves by making an appropriation out of profits, usually profits for the year.

The establishment of a 'plant and machinery replacement reserve' (or something similar) indicates an intention by a company to keep funds in the business to replace its plant and machinery. However, the reserve would still, legally, represent distributable profits, and the existence of such a reserve does not guarantee the company's ability to replace its plant and machinery in the future.

2.7 The share premium account

There are a number of non-distributable reserves, the most important of which is the **share premium account**.

Definition

Share premium: whenever shares are issued at a price in excess of their nominal value, the excess is called share premium and it is credited to a share premium account.

A share premium arises when a company sells shares for a price which is higher than their nominal value. By 'premium' is meant the difference between the issue price of the share and its nominal value.

For example, if X Ltd issues 1,000 £1 ordinary shares at £2.60 each the proceeds will be recorded as follows:

Accounts	*Debit*	*Credit*
	£	£
Cash	2,600	
Ordinary share capital		1,000
Share premium account		1,600

In the statement of financial position, they would be classified as follows.

	£
Share capital	1,000
Share premium	1,600

A share premium account only comes into being when a company, at the time of issue of shares, receives money in excess of their nominal value. The market price of the shares, once they have been issued, has no bearing at all on the company's accounts, and so if their market price goes up or down, the share premium account would not be affected.

Activity 4 **(5 minutes)**

Here are extracts from a company's statement of financial position at 30 June 20X0 and 30 June 20X1.

	20X1	*20X0*
	£	£
Equity		
Issued share capital: 50p ordinary shares	9,000	7,500
Share premium account	3,500	2,000

How many shares were issued during the year, and at what price?

2.8 Revaluation reserve

A revaluation reserve must be created when a company revalues one or more of its non-current assets. Freehold property is frequently revalued, as the market value of property rises or falls. The company's directors might wish to show the current value of an asset in the statement of financial position. .This may provide more useful information to shareholders and other users of the financial statements than historic cost.

When an asset is revalued, the revaluation reserve is credited with the difference between the revalued amount of the asset, and its carrying amount (net book value) before the revaluation took place.

EXAMPLE: REVALUATION

X Ltd bought a freehold property for £20,000 ten years ago; its carrying amount (after depreciation of the building) is now £19,300. At 31 December 20X1, the market value of the property was £390,000 and the directors wish to reflect this in the accounts for the year ended 31 December 20X1.

(a) The revaluation surplus is £390,000 – £19,300 = £370,700.

(b) In the statement of financial position:
– freehold property is restated to reflect the revaluation;
– a revaluation reserve of £370,700 is recognised as part of equity.

(c) The revaluation has no immediate effect on the income statement.

(d) In future periods, depreciation is charged on the revalued amount, not the historic cost. If the property has a remaining useful life of 50 years at 1 January 20X2, depreciation for the year ended 31 December 20X2 is £7,800 (390,000 ÷ 50). At 31 December 20X2 the carrying amount of the property is £382,200 (390,000 – 7,800).

It is important to understand that not all gains and losses are recognised as part of profit or loss. A company can make substantial gains and losses through changes in the value of its assets. Where property, plant or equipment is revalued, accounting standards state that the resulting gain or loss cannot be recognised in profit or loss. Revaluation gains are not included in retained earnings, but in a separate revaluation reserve (as in the example above).

Activity 5 **(5 minutes)**

Can you think of another type of gains and losses which might be recognised during a period but which are not included in profit or loss (recognised in the income statement)?

Having looked at some of the unique features of the accounts of limited liability companies, we now look at the final accounts of limited liability companies.

3 THE FINAL ACCOUNTS OF COMPANIES

3.1 Format of the final accounts

We saw in an earlier chapter that limited liability companies must prepare their financial statements either in accordance with international accounting standards (IFRSs) or in accordance with UK accounting standards and the detailed regulations in the Companies Act 2006.

We will concentrate on the requirements of IFRSs, but will also look briefly at the form of company final accounts prepared in the UK under the Companies Act 2006.

IAS *1 Presentation of financial statements* lists the required contents of a company's income statement and statement of financial position. It also give guidance on how items should be presented in the financial statements.

IAS 1 requires a company to prepare:

(a) a statement of financial position at the end of the period;

(b) a statement of comprehensive income for the period;

(c) a statement of changes in equity for the period;

(d) a statement of cash flows for the period

(e) notes, comprising a summary of significant accounting policies and other information.

The statement of cash flows is covered in a later chapter.

It is normal for entities to present financial statements **annually** and IAS 1 states that they should be prepared at least as often as this.

IAS 1 requires a **statement of comprehensive income**. An entity's comprehensive income consists of:

(a) its profit or loss; and
(b) other comprehensive income.

Definitions

Profit or loss is income less expenses.

Other comprehensive income is items of income and expense that are not recognised in profit or loss. For example, when a non-current asset is revalued, the difference between its original cost less depreciation and its fair or market value is not included in profit or loss for the period. Instead, it is recognised as part of other comprehensive income.

IAS 1 allows a company to choose the presentation: one statement (statement of comprehensive income) or two statements (income statement and statement of other comprehensive income).

If an item is recognised 'in profit or loss', this means that it is included in the income statement section of the statement of comprehensive income or in the separate income statement (if two statements are prepared).

The format of the statement of comprehensive income and the statement of financial position are shown below.

ABC CO
STATEMENT OF FINANCIAL POSITION AS AT 31 DECEMBER 20X2

	20X2		*20X1*	
	£'000	£'000	£'000	£'000
Assets				
Non-current assets				
Property, plant and equipment	X		X	
Goodwill	X		X	
Other intangible assets	X		X	
		X		X
Current assets				
Inventories	X		X	
Trade receivables	X		X	
Other current assets	X		X	
Cash and cash equivalents	X		X	
		X		X
Total assets		X		X

NOTES

	20X2		20X1	
	£'000	£'000	£'000	£'000
Equity and liabilities				
Equity				
Share capital	X		X	
Retained earnings	X		X	
Other components of equity	X		X	
		X		X
Non-current liabilities				
Long-term borrowings	X		X	
Long-term provisions	X		X	
		X		X
Current liabilities				
Trade and other payables	X		X	
Short-term borrowings	X		X	
Current portion of long-term borrowings	X		X	
Current tax payable	X		X	
Short-term provisions	X		X	
		X		X
Total equity and liabilities		X		X

ABC CO

STATEMENT OF COMPREHENSIVE INCOME FOR THE YEAR ENDED 31 DECEMBER 20X2

	20X2	20X1
	£'000	£'000
Revenue	X	X
Cost of sales	(X)	(X)
Gross profit	X	X
Other income	X	X
Distribution costs	(X)	(X)
Administrative expenses	(X)	(X)
Other expenses	(X)	(X)
Finance cost	(X)	(X)
Profit before tax	X	X
Income tax expense	(X)	(X)
Profit for the year	X	X
Other comprehensive income:		
Gains on property revaluation	X	X
Total comprehensive income for the year	X	X

Now that we have dealt with the format of company accounts, we explain some of the items that appear in the statement of financial position and statement of comprehensive income.

Intangible assets

These are assets that do not have a physical existence. If a company purchases some patent rights, or a concession from another business, or the right to use a trademark, the cost of the purchase can be accounted for as the purchase of an intangible non-current asset. These assets must then be amortised (depreciated) over their useful life.

Goodwill is an intangible asset and we will be looking at it later in this chapter, in the section on group accounts.

Other components of equity

Other components of equity are reserves, such as share premium and the revaluation reserve.

Long-term borrowings

Long-term borrowings may include loan stock (sometimes called debenture stock or bonds). These are long-term liabilities and in some countries they are described as *loan capital* because they are a means of raising finance, in the same way as issuing share capital raises finance. They are different from share capital in the following ways.

(a) **Shareholders** are **members** of a company, while **providers of loan capital** are **creditors**.

(b) **Shareholders** receive **dividends** (appropriations of profit) whereas the **holders of loan capital** are entitled to a **fixed rate of interest** (an expense charged against revenue).

(c) Loan capital holders can take legal action against a company if their interest is not paid when due, whereas **shareholders cannot enforce the payment of dividends**.

(d) Loan stock is **often secured on company assets**, whereas shares are not.

The holder of loan capital is generally in a less risky position than the shareholder. He has greater security, although his income is fixed and cannot grow, unlike ordinary dividends. As remarked earlier, preference shares are in practice very similar to loan capital, not least because the preference dividend is normally fixed.

Interest is calculated on the par or legal value of loan capital, regardless of its market value. If a company has £700,000 (par value) 12% loan stock in issue, interest of £84,000 will be charged in the income statement per year. Interest is usually paid half-yearly; so it is often necessary to make an accrual for interest due at the year-end.

For example, if a company has £700,000 of 12% loan stock in issue, pays interest on 30 June and 31 December each year, and ends its accounting year on 30 September, there would be an accrual of three months' unpaid interest (3/12 × £84,000) = £21,000 at the end of each accounting year that the loan stock is still in issue.

Provisions

Provisions are liabilities that are uncertain in timing and amount. For example, a company may guarantee that it will replace or repair faulty goods sold to customers. At some point the company will have to incur expenditure, but it cannot know exactly when or how much. Therefore it recognises a provision for its best estimate of the eventual liability.

Accumulated depreciation and allowances for receivables are sometimes called provisions. However, these are not strictly provisions at all, because they are accounting estimates, rather than actual liabilities.

Finance cost

This is interest payable during the period.

We now pull together several of the items described in this chapter into a comprehensive example.

EXAMPLE OF LIMITED COMPANY ACCOUNTS

The accountant of Tehreem Ltd has prepared the following list of balances as at 31 December 20X0.

	£'000
50p ordinary shares	450
10% loan stock	200
Retained earnings 1 January 20X0	92
General reserve 1 January 20X0	71
Freehold land and buildings 1 January 20X0	430
Plant and machinery 1 January 20X0 (cost)	830
Accumulated depreciation:	
freehold buildings 1 January 20X0	20
plant and machinery 1 January 20X0	222
Sales	2,695
Cost of sales	2,156
Ordinary dividend (interim) paid	15
Loan stock interest paid	10
Wages and salaries	274
Light and heat	14
Sundry expenses	107
Suspense account	420
Receivables	179
Payables	195
Cash	126

Notes

(a) The suspense account is in respect of the following items.

	£'000
Proceeds from the issue of 100,000 ordinary shares	120
Proceeds from the sale of plant	300
	420

(b) The freehold property was acquired some years ago. The buildings element of the cost was estimated at £100,000 and the estimated useful life of the assets was fifty years at the time of purchase. As at 31 December 20X0 the property is to be revalued at £800,000.

(c) The plant which was sold had cost £350,000 and had a carrying amount of £274,000 as on 1 January 20X0. £36,000 depreciation is to be charged on plant and machinery for 20X0.

(d) The loan stock has been in issue for some years.

(e) The directors wish to provide for:

(i) loan stock interest due
(ii) a transfer to general reserve of £16,000
(iii) audit fees of £4,000.

(f) Inventory as at 31 December 20X0 was valued at £224,000 (cost). The cost of sales has been adjusted for this inventory. There was no inventory at 1 January 20X0.

(g) Taxation is to be ignored.

Now, let us prepare the final accounts of Tehreem Ltd.

Approach

(a) The loan stock interest accrued is calculated as follows.

	£'000
Charge needed in income statement (10% × £200,000)	20
Amount paid so far, as shown in trial balance	10
Accrual – presumably six months' interest now payable	10

(b) Depreciation on the freehold building is calculated as = £2,000.

The carrying amount of the freehold property is then £430,000 – £20,000 – £2,000 = £408,000 at the end of the year. When the property is revalued a revaluation reserve of £800,000 – £408,000 = £392,000 is then created.

(c) The profit on disposal of plant is calculated as proceeds £300,000 (per suspense account) less net book value £274,000, ie £26,000. The cost of the remaining plant is calculated at £830,000 – £350,000 = £480,000. The accumulated depreciation at the year end is made up of the following.

	£'000
Balance 1 January 20X0	222
Charge for 20X0	36
Less depreciation on disposal (350-274)	(76)
	182

(d) The other item in the suspense account is dealt with as follows.

	£'000
Proceeds of issue of 100,000 ordinary shares	120
Less nominal value 100,000 × 50p	50
Excess of consideration over nominal value (= share premium)	70

(e) The transfer to general reserve increases that reserve to £71,000 + £16,000 = £87,000.

We can now prepare the financial statements.

TEHREEM LIMITED

STATEMENT OF COMPREHENSIVE INCOME FOR THE YEAR ENDED 31 DECEMBER 20X0

	£'000	£'000
Revenue		2,695
Less cost of sales		2,156
Gross profit		539
Profit on disposal of plant		26
		565
Less expenses		
Wages and salaries	274	
Sundry expenses	107	
Light and heat	14	
Depreciation: freehold building	2	
plant	36	
Audit fees	4	
Loan stock interest	20	
		457
Profit for the year		108

NOTES

TEHREEM LIMITED

STATEMENT OF FINANCIAL POSITION AT 31 DECEMBER 20X0

	£'000	£'000
ASSETS		
Non-current assets		
Property, plant land and equipment		
Property at valuation		800
Plant: cost	480	
depreciation	182	
		298
		1,098
Current assets		
Inventory	224	
Trade receivables	179	
Cash	126	
		529
Total assets		1,627
EQUITY AND LIABILITIES		
Equity		
50c ordinary shares	500	
Share premium	70	
Revaluation reserve	392	
General reserve	87	
Retained earnings (92 + 108 – 15 – 16)	169	
		1,218
Non-current liabilities		
10% loan stock (secured)		200
Current liabilities		
Trade payables	195	
Accrued expenses	14	
		209
Total equity and liabilities		1,627

To finish this section, we show below an example of financial statements prepared in accordance with the Companies Act 2006. Many companies in the UK still prepare their financial statements in this format.

NOTES

TYPICAL COMPANY LIMITED BALANCE SHEET AS AT ...			
Fixed assets	£	£	£
Intangible assets			
Concessions, patents, licences, trademarks		15,000	
Goodwill		4,000	
			19,000
Tangible assets			
Land and buildings		75,000	
Plant and machinery		24,000	
Fixtures, fittings, tools and equipment		8,000	
Motor vehicles		13,000	
			120,000
Investments			2,500
			141,500
Current assets			
Stocks		6,000	
Debtors and prepayments		8,500	
Investments		1,500	
Cash at bank and in hand		300	
		16,300	
Creditors: amounts falling due within one year			
(ie current liabilities)			
Debenture loans (nearing their repayment date)	4,000		
Bank loans and overdrafts	1,300		
Trade creditors	7,200		
Taxation	2,800		
Accruals	800		
		16,100	
Net current assets			200
Total assets less current liabilities			141,700
Creditors: amounts falling due after more than one year			
Debenture loans			(8,000)
			133,700
Capital and reserves			
Ordinary shares		20,000	
Preference shares		5,000	
			25,000
Reserves			
Share premium account		11,000	
Revaluation reserve		15,000	
Other reserves		6,000	
Profit and loss account (retained profits)		76,700	
			108,700
			133,700

TYPICAL COMPANY LIMITED
PROFIT AND LOSS ACCOUNT FOR THE YEAR ENDED…

	£	£
Turnover		91,700
Cost of sales		(32,000)
Gross profit		59,700
Distribution costs	17,000	
Administrative expenses	24,000	
		(41,000)
		18,700
Other operating income	1,000	
Income from fixed asset investments	200	
Other interest receivable and similar income	500	
		1,700
		20,400
Interest payable		(3,200)
Profit before taxation		17,200
Tax		(3,500)
Net profit for the year		13,700

In addition, companies following UK standards prepare a **statement of total recognised gains and losses**. This shows items such as gains and losses on revaluation that are not included in profit or loss. The profit and loss account is equivalent to the income statement. As its name suggests, it shows profit or loss for the period. The statement of total recognised gains and losses shows total comprehensive income for the period.

Now that we have looked at the statement of total comprehensive income and statement of financial position, we move on to consider the notes to these financial statements..

3.2 Notes to the accounts

The published accounts of companies are required to include a large number of supporting notes. These analyse the total figures in more detail or provide additional information or explanations. The accounts of other types of organisations such as sole traders may also include notes.

Notes to the financial statements provide information about the accounting policies adopted by management.

Definition

> **Accounting policies** are the specific principles, bases, conventions, rules and practices applied by an entity in preparing and presenting financial statements.

As we have seen, some companies revalue assets such as freehold land and buildings, while other companies do not. There are several generally accepted ways of measuring other types of asset, such as inventories and investments, all of which can produce different results and affect the financial statements in different ways.

Users of the financial statements need to be aware of the accounting policies that management has adopted in order to properly understand the entity's financial performance and position. Information about accounting policies also helps users to compare the financial statements of different entities.

The notes to the financial statements also explain significant accounting estimates, such as the rates and methods of depreciation adopted for different types of non-current asset.

One of the commonest notes to company financial statements is shown below

NOTES TO THE ACCOUNTS

Property, plant and equipment

	Land and Buildings	*Plant and machinery*	*Fixtures and fittings*	*Motor vehicles*	*Total*
	£	£	£	£	£
Cost (or valuation)					
At the beginning of the year	66,000	31,000	10,000	24,000	131,000
Additions	-	9,000	1,000	4,000	14,000
Revaluations	10,000	-	-	-	10,000
Disposals	-	(3,000)	-	-	(3,000)
At the end of the year	76,000	37,000	11,000	28,000	152,000
Depreciation					
At the beginning of the year	5,000	10,000	2,500	9,000	26,500
Charge for the year	1,000	5,000	500	6,000	12,500
Revaluation	(5,000)	-	-	-	(5,000)
Disposals	-	(2,000)	-	-	(2,000)
At the end of the year	1,000	13,000	3,000	15,000	32,000
Carrying amount					
At the end of the year	75,000	24,000	8,000	13,000	120,000
At the beginning of the year	61,000	21,000	7,500	15,000	104,500

We now look briefly at some other aspects of limited company financial statements.

3.3 Statement of changes in equity

Definition

> The **statement of changes in equity** shows the movements on equity capital and on each reserve during the period.

An example is shown over the page.

STATEMENT OF CHANGES IN EQUITY FOR THE YEAR ENDED 31 DECEMBER 20X6

	Share capital	*Share premium*	*Revaluation reserve*	*Retained earnings*	*Total*
Balance at 1.1.X6	X	X	X	X	X
Changes in equity for 20X6					
Dividends	-	-	-	(X)	(X)
Total comprehensive income for the year	-	-	X	X	X
Issue of share capital	X	X	-	-	X
Balance at 31.12.X6	X	X	X	X	X

Note that the statement of changes in equity simply takes the equity section of the statement of financial position and shows the movements during the year. The bottom line shows the amounts for the current statement of financial position. Total comprehensive income for the year is taken from the statement of comprehensive income.

Dividends paid during the year are not shown on the income statement; they are shown in the statement of changes in equity.

The statement of changes in equity provides a 'bridge' between the statement of comprehensive income and the statement of financial position. It is similar to the 'capital' section of the statement of financial position of a sole trader because it shows all the transactions of the company with its owners:

Company	**Sole trader**
Opening equity	Opening capital
Issue of share capital	Capital introduced
Total comprehensive income for the period	Profit for the period
Dividends paid	Drawings
Closing equity	Closing capital

3.4 The annual report

The annual report is the name sometimes given to the published financial statements of a limited company.

All companies are required to prepare a statement of comprehensive income, statement of financial position, statement of changes in equity, statement of cash flows and supporting notes. The published financial statements of most companies also include a directors' report and an auditors' report (there are exemptions available for small companies).

For most private companies, the financial statements are only 'published' in the sense that they are distributed to the shareholders and filed with the Registrar of Companies. However, most public companies treat the annual report as an important way of advertising the company to potential investors, the financial press, and the general public. The report is normally attractively designed and printed and contains much more information than the minimum required by law, for example:

- a Chairman's Statement;
- highlights and summary indicators (key figures showing trends over a number of years);
- environmental and social reports (these are sometimes issued as separate documents).

Often an Operating and Financial Review (sometimes called a Business Review or Management Commentary) is also included, which is a discussion of the main factors underlying a company's performance and financial position. It is intended to help users of the financial statements to assess the future performance of the company. It includes non-financial information, such as the objectives of the business, the risks that it faces, the influences on its performance and factors likely to affect it in future. Environmental and social reports contain information about the way in which the company has interacted with the natural environment and the wider community.

This additional information can be very useful and often provides a more balanced picture of a company's performance and activities than the financial statements by themselves. However, it is important to remember that, unlike the financial statements, it is not audited. Companies can publish whatever information they wish and inevitably the directors will wish to present the company in the best possible light.

So far, we have only considered the financial statements of single companies. We will now explain how to prepare the financial statements of a group of companies.

4 GROUPS OF COMPANIES

4.1 Parent and subsidiary

You will probably know that many large businesses actually consist of several companies controlled by one central or administrative company. Together these companies are called a **group**. The controlling company, called the parent or **holding company**, will own some or all of the shares in the other companies, called subsidiary and associated companies.

There are many reasons for businesses to operate as groups; for the goodwill associated with the names of the subsidiaries, for tax or legal purposes and so forth. Accounting standards require that the results of a group should be presented as a whole. In some countries, including the UK, this is often also a requirement of companies legislation.

In traditional accounting terminology, a **group of companies** consists of a **holding company** (or parent company) and one or more **subsidiary companies** which are controlled by the holding company.

The legal definitions of parent companies (sometimes called parent undertakings) and subsidiaries (sometimes called subsidiary undertakings) are very detailed, but the basic idea behind them is simple. A company is a parent if it has one or more subsidiaries. A company is a subsidiary if it is controlled by the parent. Control is the power to direct the financial and operating policies of another entity so as to obtain benefits from its activities.

There are several ways in which one company can gain control of another, but the most common ways are:

(a) by holding a majority of voting rights; or

(b) by holding shares in the company and having the right to appoint or remove directors holding a majority of the voting rights at meetings of the board.

In practice, if a company holds more than 50% of the equity (ordinary) shares in another company it is normally able to control that company.

4.2 The consolidated statement of financial position

The preparation of a consolidated statement of financial position, in a very simple form, consists of two procedures.

(a) Take the individual accounts of the parent and each subsidiary and **cancel out items** which appear as an asset in one company and a liability in another.

(b) **Add together all the uncancelled assets and liabilities** throughout the group.

Items requiring cancellation may include the following.

(a) The asset '**investment in subsidiary**' which appears in the parent company's accounts will be matched with the liability 'share capital' in the subsidiaries' accounts.

(b) There may be **inter-company trading** within the group. For example, S Ltd may sell goods to P Ltd. P Ltd would then be a receivable in the accounts of S Ltd, while S Ltd would be a payable in the accounts of P Ltd.

EXAMPLE: H GROUP

P Ltd regularly sells goods to its one subsidiary company, S Ltd. The statements of financial position of the two companies on 31 December 20X6 are given below.

STATEMENT OF FINANCIAL POSITION AS AT 31 DECEMBER 20X6

	P Ltd	*S Ltd*
	£	£
Assets		
Non-current assets		
Property, plant and equipment	35,000	45,000
Investment in 40,000 £1 shares in S Ltd at cost	40,000	
	75,000	
Current assets		
Inventories	16,000	12,000
Receivables: S Ltd	2,000	
Other	6,000	9,000
Cash at bank	1,000	
Total assets	100,000	66,000
Equity and liabilities		

NOTES

Equity		
40,000 £1 ordinary shares		40,000
70,000 £1 ordinary shares	70,000	
Retained earnings	16,000	19,000
	86,000	59,000
Current liabilities		
Bank overdraft		3,000
Payables: P Ltd		2,000
Payables: Other	14,000	2,000
Total equity and liabilities	100,000	66,000

Prepare the consolidated statement of financial position of P Ltd at 31 December 20X6.

ANSWER

The cancelling items are:

(a) P Ltd's asset 'investment in shares of S Ltd's (£40,000) cancels with S Ltd's liability 'share capital' (£40,000);

(b) P Ltd's asset 'receivables: S Co' (£2,000) cancels with S Ltd's liability 'payables: P Ltd's (£2,000).

The remaining assets and liabilities are added together to produce the following consolidated statement of financial position.

P Ltd
CONSOLIDATED STATEMENT OF FINANCIAL POSITION AS AT 31 DECEMBER 20X6

Assets	£	£
Non-current assets		
Property, plant and equipment		80,000
Current assets		
Inventories	28,000	
Receivables	15,000	
Cash at bank	1,000	
		44,000
Total assets		124,000
Equity and liabilities		
Equity		
70,000 £1 ordinary shares	70,000	
Retained earnings	35,000	
	105,000	
Current liabilities		
Bank overdraft	3,000	
Payables	16,000	
		19,000
Total equity and liabilities		124,000

Note the following.

(a) P Ltd's bank balance is **not netted off** with S Ltd's bank overdraft. To offset one against the other would be less informative and would conflict with the principle that assets and liabilities should not be netted off.

(b) The share capital in the consolidated statement of financial position is the **share capital of the parent company alone**. This must *always* be the case, no matter how complex the consolidation, because the share capital of subsidiary companies must *always* be a wholly cancelling item.

4.3 Non-controlling interests

It was mentioned earlier that the total assets and liabilities of subsidiary companies are included in the consolidated statement of financial position, even in the case of subsidiaries which are only partly owned. A proportion of the net assets of such subsidiaries in fact belongs to investors from outside the group (non-controlling interests or minority interests).

In the consolidated statement of financial position it is necessary to distinguish this proportion from those assets attributable to the group and financed by shareholders' funds (equity).

There are two alternative ways of calculating non-controlling interest in the group statement of financial position. Non-controlling interest can be valued at:

(a) Its proportionate share of the fair value of the subsidiary's net assets; or

(b) Full (or fair) value (usually based on the market value of the shares held by the non-controlling interest).

Most groups value non-controlling interest using method (a) and this is the method that we will use throughout.

EXAMPLE: NON-CONTROLLING INTERESTS

P Ltd has owned 75% of the share capital of S Ltd since the date of S Ltd's incorporation. Their latest statements of financial position are given below.

P LTD
STATEMENT OF FINANCIAL POSITION

	£	£
Assets		
Non-current assets		
Property, plant and equipment	50,000	
30,000 £1 ordinary shares in S Ltd at cost	30,000	
		80,000
Current assets		45,000
Total assets		125,000
Equity and liabilities		
Equity		
80,000 £1 ordinary shares	80,000	
Retained earnings	25,000	

		105,000
Current liabilities		20,000
Total equity and liabilities		125,000

S LTD
STATEMENT OF FINANCIAL POSITION

	£	£
Assets		
Property, plant and equipment		35,000
Current assets		35,000
Total assets		70,000
Equity and liabilities		
Equity		
40,000 £1 ordinary shares	40,000	
Retained earnings	10,000	
		50,000
Current liabilities		20,000
Total equity and liabilities		70,000

Prepare the consolidated statement of financial position.

ANSWER

All of S Ltd's net assets are consolidated despite the fact that the company is only 75% owned. The amount of net assets attributable to non-controlling interests is calculated as follows.

	£
Non-controlling share of share capital (25% × £40,000)	10,000
Non-controlling share of reserves (25% × £10,000)	2,500
	12,500

Of S Ltd's share capital of £40,000, £10,000 is included in the figure for non-controlling interest, while £30,000 is cancelled with P Ltd's asset 'investment in S Limited'.

The consolidated statement of financial position can now be prepared.

P GROUP
CONSOLIDATED STATEMENT OF FINANCIAL POSITION

	£	£
Assets		
Property, plant and equipment		85,000
Current assets		80,000
Total assets		165,000
Equity and liabilities		
Equity attributable to owners of the parent		
Share capital	80,000	
Retained earnings £(25,000 + (75% × £10,000))	32,500	
		112,500
Non-controlling interest		12,500
		125,000
Current liabilities		40,000
Total equity and liabilities		165,000

Procedure

(a) Aggregate the assets and liabilities in the statement of financial position ie 100% P + 100% S irrespective of how much P actually owns.

This shows the amount of net assets **controlled** by the group.

(b) Share capital is that of the parent only.

(c) Calculate the non-controlling interest share of the subsidiary's net assets (share capital plus reserves).

(d) Balance of subsidiary's reserves are consolidated (after cancelling any intra-group items).

4.4 Goodwill arising on consolidation

In the examples we have looked at so far the cost of shares acquired by the parent company has always been equal to the nominal value of those shares. This is seldom the case in practice. To begin with, **we will examine the entries made by the parent company in its own statement of financial position when it acquires shares.**

When a company P Ltd wishes to **purchase shares** in a company S Ltd it must pay the previous owners of those shares. Suppose P Ltd purchases all 40,000 £1 shares in S Ltd and pays £60,000 cash to the previous shareholders in consideration. The entries in P Ltd's books would be:

DEBIT	Investment in S Ltd at cost	£60,000	
CREDIT	Bank		£60,000

The amount which P Ltd records in its books as the cost of its investment in S Ltd may be more or less than the carrying amount (book value) of the assets it acquires. Suppose that S Ltd in the previous example has nil reserves, so that its share capital of £40,000 is balanced by net assets with a carrying amount of £40,000. For simplicity, assume that the carrying amount of S Ltd's assets is the same as their market or fair value.

Now when the directors of P Ltd agree to pay £60,000 for a 100% investment in S Ltd they must believe that, in addition to its tangible assets of £40,000, S Ltd must also have intangible assets worth £20,000. This amount of £20,000 paid over and above the value of the tangible assets acquired is called **goodwill arising on consolidation** (sometimes **premium on acquisition**).

Following the normal cancellation procedure the £40,000 share capital in S Ltd's statement of financial position could be cancelled against £40,000 of the 'investment in S Limited' in the statement of financial position of P Ltd. This would leave a £20,000 debit uncancelled in the parent company's accounts and this £20,000 would appear in the consolidated statement of financial position under the caption 'Intangible non-current assets. Goodwill arising on consolidation.'

4.5 Goodwill and pre-acquisition profits

Up to now we have assumed that S Ltd had nil reserves when its shares were purchased by P Ltd. Assuming instead that S Ltd had earned profits of £8,000 in the period before acquisition, its statement of financial position just before the purchase would look as follows.

	£
Total assets	48,000
Share capital	40,000
Reserves	8,000
	48,000

If P Ltd now purchases all the shares in S Ltd it will acquire net tangible assets worth £48,000 at a cost of £60,000. Clearly in this case S Ltd's intangible assets (goodwill) are being valued at £12,000. It should be apparent that any **reserves** earned by the subsidiary **prior to its acquisition** by the parent company must be **incorporated in the cancellation** process so as to arrive at a figure for goodwill arising on consolidation. In other words, not only S Ltd's share capital, but also its **pre-acquisition retained earnings,** must be cancelled against the asset 'investment in S Ltd' in the accounts of the parent company. The uncancelled balance of £12,000 appears in the consolidated statement of financial position.

The consequence of this is that **any pre-acquisition retained earnings of a subsidiary company are not aggregated with the parent company's retained earnings** in the consolidated statement of financial position. The figure of consolidated retained earnings comprises the retained earnings of the parent company plus the post-acquisition retained earnings only of subsidiary companies. The post-acquisition retained earnings are simply retained earnings now less retained earnings at acquisition.

EXAMPLE: GOODWILL AND PRE-ACQUISITION PROFITS

Sing Ltd acquired the ordinary shares of Wing Ltd on 31 March when the draft statements of financial position of each company were as follows.

SING LTD
STATEMENT OF FINANCIAL POSITION AS AT 31 MARCH

	£
Assets	
Non-current assets	
Investment in 50,000 shares of Wing Ltd at cost	80,000
Current assets	40,000
Total assets	120,000
Equity and liabilities	
Equity	
Ordinary shares	75,000
Retained earnings	45,000
Total equity and liabilities	120,000

WING LTD
STATEMENT OF FINANCIAL POSITION AS AT 31 MARCH

	£
Current assets	60,000
Equity	
50,000 ordinary shares of £1 each	50,000
Retained earnings	10,000
	60,000

Prepare the consolidated statement of financial position as at 31 March.

ANSWER

The technique to adopt here is to produce a new working: 'Goodwill'.

	£	£
Cost of investment		80,000
Share of net assets acquired as represented by:		
Ordinary share capital	50,000	
Retained earnings on acquisition	10,000	
	60,000	
Group share 100%		60,000
Goodwill		20,000

SING LTD
CONSOLIDATED STATEMENT OF FINANCIAL POSITION AS AT 31 MARCH

	£
Assets	
Non-current assets	
Goodwill arising on consolidation	20,000
Current assets	100,000
	120,000
Equity	
Ordinary shares	75,000
Retained earnings	45,000
	120,000

FOR DISCUSSION

Companies with subsidiaries are required to publish group accounts. Why do you think this is? Do group accounts have any limitations?

4.6 Consolidated income statement

The principles are exactly the same as for the consolidated statement of financial position.

EXAMPLE

P Ltd acquired 75% of the ordinary shares of S Ltd on that company's incorporation. The summarised income statements of the two companies for the year ending 31 December 20X0 are set out below.

	P Ltd	*S Ltd*
	£	£
Revenue	75,000	38,000
Cost of sales	30,000	20,000
Gross profit	45,000	18,000
Administrative expenses	14,000	8,000
Profit before tax	31,000	10,000
Income tax expense	10,000	2,000
Profit for the year	21,000	8,000

Note: Movement on retained earnings

Retained earnings brought forward	87,000	17,000
Profit for the year	21,000	8,000
Retained earnings carried forward	108,000	25,000

Required

Prepare the consolidated income statement and extract from the statement of changes in equity showing retained earnings and non-controlling interest.

ANSWER

P LTD
CONSOLIDATED INCOME STATEMENT
FOR THE YEAR ENDED 31 DECEMBER 20X6

	£
Revenue (75 + 38)	113,000
Cost of sales (30 + 20)	50,000
Gross profit	63,000
Administrative expenses (14 + 8)	22,000
Profit before tax	41,000
Income tax expense	12,000
Profit for the year	29,000
Profit attributable to:	
Owners of the parent	27,000
Non-controlling interest (£8,000 × 25%)	2,000
	29,000

STATEMENT OF CHANGES IN EQUITY (EXTRACT)

	Retained Earnings	*Non-controlling Interest*	*Total Equity*
	£	£	£
Balance b/f	99,750	4,250	104,000
Profit for the year	27,000	2,000	29,000
	126,750	6,250	133,000

Notice how the non-controlling interest is dealt with.

(a) Down to the line '**profit for the year** the **whole** of S Ltd's results are included without reference to group share or minority share. A **one-line**

adjustment is then inserted to deduct the non-controlling share of S Ltd's profit.

(b) The non-controlling share (£4,250) of S Ltd's retained earnings brought forward is excluded from group retained earnings. This means that the carried forward figure of £126,750 is the figure which would appear in the statement of financial position for group retained earnings (see below).

This last point may be clearer if we construct the working for group retained earnings.

Group retained earnings

	£
P Ltd (87,000 + 21,000)	108,000
Share of S Ltd's pre-acquisition retained earnings (75% × £25,000 (17,000 + 8,000))	18,750
	126,750

The non-controlling share of S Ltd's retained earnings comprises the non-controlling interest in the £17,000 profits brought forward plus the non-controlling interest (£2,000) in £8,000 retained earnings for the year.

Notice that a consolidated income statement **links up** with a consolidated statement of financial position exactly as in the case of an individual company's accounts: the figure of retained earnings carried forward at the bottom of the income statement appears as the figure for retained earnings in the statement of financial position.

Chapter roundup

- The financial statements of a limited liability company are strictly regulated by accounting standards and (often) by national legislation.
- Ordinary shareholders are in effect the owners of the company.
- Profits paid out to shareholders are called dividends; profits not paid out in the form of dividends and taxation are kept in the retained earnings reserve.
- The total amount of reserves in a company varies according to changes in the net assets of the business.
- Share premium is the cash received by a company in excess of the nominal value of shares at the time of issue of the shares.
- The difference between the carrying amount of an asset before revaluation and the revalued amount of the asset is credited to the revaluation reserve.
- The form and content of company financial statements is prescribed by accounting standards and national legislation.
- Where one company controls another, that company has a subsidiary. Group accounts present the results, assets and liabilities of a parent and its subsidiaries as if they were a single company.

Quick quiz

1 Who owns a limited liability company? Who manages its day-to-day activities?

2 What are the two classes of limited company?

3 A public limited company is the same as a listed company. True or false?

4 Who receives dividends?

5 Distinguish between a preference share and an ordinary share.

6 Name two kinds of non-distributable reserve.

7 What are the four main financial statements that a company is required to prepare?

8 What is 'goodwill arising on consolidation'?

Answers to Quick quiz

1 Shareholders own a limited company and directors manage the day-to-day activities.

2 Public and private.

3 False, as not all public companies need to be listed.

4 Shareholders.

5 Preference shares have a right to a fixed level of dividend prior to dividends for ordinary shareholders.

6 Share premium account and revaluation reserve.

7 Statement of comprehensive income; statement of financial position; statement of changes in equity; statement of cash flows.

8 The amount paid over and above the fair value of the net assets acquired.

Answers to Activities

1 True.

(b) Yes, and similarly the appropriation account of a company is different.

(c) True. With companies, the owners (shareholders) appoint directors to be responsible for management. However, even if shareholders and directors are the same people there is a legal distinction between the two roles. Where a director receives a salary he is an employee and his salary is an expense; as a shareholder he receives a dividend which is an appropriation.

False.

(a) Generally where there are numerous owners an entity will be incorporated, the obvious exception being partnerships.

(d) Shareholders receive dividends rather than take drawings from the business. Both dividends and drawings are appropriations.

2

Number of shares	Nominal value	Total value £
100,000	**£1**	100,000
200,000	50p	100,000
500,000	40p	**200,000**
850,000	10p	85,000

3 To begin with, ignore the figures for authorised capital: dividends are paid only on shares actually in issue.

If an ordinary dividend is proposed, the preference dividends will also have to be paid. The total to be paid is therefore as follows:

	£
Preference dividend (7% × £12,000)	840
Ordinary dividend (12% × £80,000)	9,600
	10,440

4 Issued share capital has increased from £7,500 to £9,000; this means that 3,000 shares (nominal value 50p each) have been issued. The amount received for the shares was £1,500 nominal value, plus £1,500 share premium (£3,500 – £2,000), ie £3,000 in total. The issue price was therefore £1 per share.

5 Gains or losses arising on the translation of foreign currency, for example with overseas investments.

Chapter : 19

ACCOUNTING CONCEPTS AND CONVENTIONS

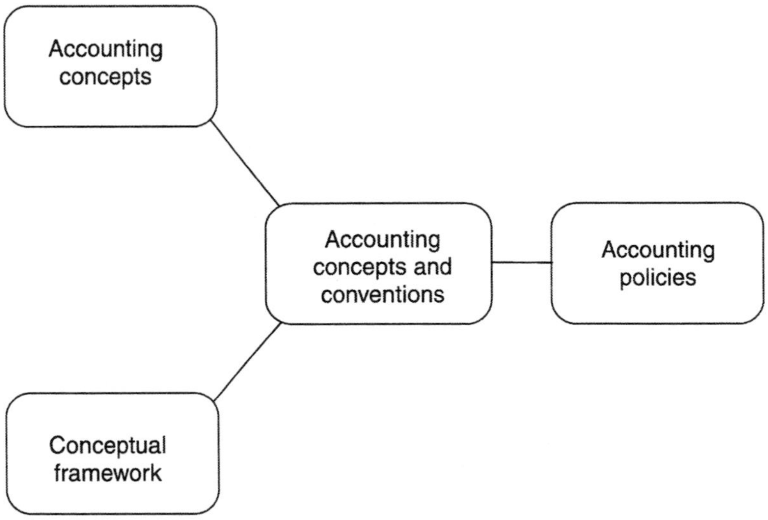

Introduction

Accounting standards are one of the major sources of accounting regulation. Two fundamental assumptions should be taken into account when preparing financial statements: going concern and accruals. In addition to these two assumptions, a number of additional concepts and ideas have been highlighted by various people as being important to accounting.

Whereas the concepts and conventions are designed to help in the preparation of accounts, the accounting information itself is expected to have certain qualities. Four such qualities have been identified: relevance; reliability; comparability; and understandability.

Your objectives

In this chapter you will learn about the following.

(a) The more widely accepted concepts underlying the preparation of accounts

(b) Some of the main conventions applied in the preparation of accounts

(c) The conceptual framework

1 ACCOUNTING CONCEPTS

Accounting practice has developed gradually over a matter of centuries. Many of its procedures are operated automatically by people who have never questioned whether alternative methods exist which have equal validity. However, the procedures in common use imply the acceptance of certain concepts which are by no means self-evident; nor are they the only possible concepts which could be used to build up an accounting framework.

Our first step is to look at some of the more important concepts which are taken for granted in preparing accounts. Accountants have traditionally regarded four concepts as fundamental accounting concepts: they are going concern, prudence, accruals and consistency. Nowadays, going concern and accruals are regarded as the most important assumptions underpinning the preparation of financial statements. But there is no universally agreed list of fundamental concepts, and others besides these have been described as fundamental by various authors.

We will begin by discussing the two most important underlying assumptions: going concern and accruals.

1.1 Going concern

Definition

> The **going concern** concept implies that the business will continue to operate for the foreseeable future, and that there is no intention to close the company down or to make drastic cutbacks to the scale of operations.

This concept assumes that, when preparing a normal set of accounts, the business will **continue to operate** in approximately the same manner for the foreseeable future (at least the next 12 months). In particular, the entity will not go into liquidation or scale down its operations in a material way.

The main significance of the going concern concept is that the assets of the business should not be valued at their 'break-up' value, which is the amount that they would sell for if they were sold off piecemeal and the business were thus broken up.

EXAMPLE

Suppose, for example, that Emma acquires a T shirt printing machine at a cost of £60,000 which is expected to last six years. Since the asset has an estimated useful life of six years, it is normal to gradually write off the cost of the asset over this time. This practice of gradually writing off the cost of an asset over its useful life helps to ensure that as the asset physically or operationally deteriorates, its cost in the accounting records is also reduced to reflect the physical/operational deterioration. The yearly reduction in the cost of the asset is called depreciation. In this example the depreciation will be £10,000 per year (£60,000 ÷ 6 years).

Using the going concern concept, it would be presumed that the business will continue its operations and so the asset will live out its full six years in use. A depreciation charge of £10,000 will be made each year, and the value of the asset will be reduced each year by the amount of yearly depreciation. After one year, the value of the asset would therefore appear in the accounting records as £(60,000 – 10,000) = £50,000, after two years it would be £40,000, after three years £30,000 and so on, until it has been written down to a value of 0 after 6 years.

Now suppose that this asset has no other operational use outside the business, and in a forced sale, it would only sell for scrap. After one year of operation, its scrap value might be, say, £8,000. What would the value be after one year?

The value of the asset in the accounting records, applying the going concern concept, would be £50,000 after one year, but its immediate sell-off value is only £8,000. It might be argued that the asset is over-valued at £50,000 and that it should be written down to its break-up value. However, provided that the going concern concept is valid, it will be assumed that the asset will continue to be used; hence, it will not be written down to its sell off value but will gradually be reduced in value over time.

Activity 1 **(5 minutes)**

Your friend John has just started a business on 1 January. He bought inventory of 20 second-hand washing machines, each costing £100. During the year he sold 17 machines at £150 each.

John is not completely happy with this venture and is considering closing down the business. However, before he can make up his mind, John has asked for your help in determining the value of the remaining machines on 31 December.

John has asked you to calculate the value of the remaining machines if

(a) he is forced to close down his business at the end of the year and the remaining machines will realise only £60 each in a forced sale; or

(b) he intends to continue his business into the next year.

How will you respond to John's request for help?

1.2 Accruals

Definition

The **accruals basis of accounting** (sometimes called the **accruals concept** or the **matching concept**) states that, in computing profit, revenue earned must be matched against the expenditure incurred in earning it.

Entities should prepare their financial statements on the basis that transactions are recorded in them, not as the cash is paid or received, but as the revenues or expenses are **earned or incurred** in the accounting period to which they relate.

EXAMPLE

Emma prints 20 T-shirts in her first month of trading (May) at a cost of £5 each. She then sells all of them for £10 each. Emma has therefore made a profit of £100, by matching the revenue (£200) earned against the cost (£100) of acquiring them.

If, however, Emma only sells 18 T-shirts, it is incorrect to charge her income statement with the cost of 20 T-shirts, as she still has two T-shirts in inventory. If she sells them in June, she is likely to make a profit on the sale. Therefore, only the purchase cost of 18 T-shirts (£90) should be matched with her sales revenue (£180), leaving her with a profit of £90.

Her statement of financial position will look like this.

	£
Assets	
Inventory (at cost, ie 2 × £5)	10
Accounts receivable (18 × £10)	180
	190
Capital and liabilities	
Proprietor's capital (profit for the period)	90
Accounts payable (20 × £5)	100
	190

However, if Emma had decided to give up selling T-shirts, then the going concern assumption no longer applies and the value of the two T-shirts in the statement of financial position is break-up valuation not cost. Similarly, if the two unsold T-shirts are unlikely to be sold at more than their cost of £5 each (say, because of damage or a fall in demand) then they should be recorded on the statement of financial position at their *net realisable value* (ie the likely eventual sales price less any expenses incurred to make them saleable) rather than cost. This shows the application of the **prudence concept**, which we will look at shortly.

In this example, the concepts of going concern and accrual are linked. Since the business is assumed to be a going concern, it is possible to carry forward the cost of the unsold T-shirts as a charge against profits of the next period.

Next, we will look at the other important accounting concepts, starting with two more that have traditionally been regarded as important: prudence; and consistency.

1.3 Prudence

Definition

> **Prudence** is the inclusion of a degree of caution in the exercise of the judgements needed in making the estimates required under conditions of uncertainty, such that assets or income are not overstated and liabilities or expenses are not understated.

Prudence must be exercised when preparing financial statements because of the **uncertainty** surrounding many transactions.

Thus, for example, in the case of John's washing machines (Activity 1), the washing machines will be recorded in the accounting records at £100 each (their original cost) rather than £150 each (the selling price). To record the machines at £150 before they have been sold would be to anticipate a profit before the profit has actually been made.

On the other hand, in the case where a loss can be foreseen, it should be anticipated and taken into account immediately. If a business purchases inventory for £1,200 but because of a sudden slump in the market only £900 is likely to be realised when the goods are sold, prudence dictates that the inventory should be valued at £900. It is not enough to wait until the goods are sold, and then recognise the £300 loss; it must be recognised as soon as it is foreseen.

Another example might help to explain the application of prudence.

EXAMPLE

A company begins trading on 1 January 20X5 and sells goods worth £100,000 during the year to 31 December. At 31 December there are accounts receivable outstanding of £15,000. Of these, the company is now doubtful whether £6,000 will ever be paid.

The company should make an allowance for receivables of £6,000. Sales for 20X5 are shown in the income statement at their full value of £100,000, but the allowance for receivables is a charge of £6,000. Since there is some uncertainty that the sales will be realised in the form of cash, prudence dictates that the £6,000 should not be included in the profit for the year.

1.4 Revenue recognition

At this point we can consider the issue of when revenue should be recognised (ie recorded) in the accounting records. Let us suppose that John sold his washing machines (Activity 1) on credit. Should John be allowed to show a revenue of £2,550 (£150 × 17)? Would allowing John to show the revenue be prudent, given that the customers have purchased on credit and have not yet paid cash to John?

Accruals accounting is based on the **matching of costs with the revenue they generate**. It is crucially important under this convention that we establish the point at which revenue is recognised, so that the correct treatment can be applied to the related costs. For example, the costs of producing an item of finished goods should be carried as an asset in the statement of financial position until such time as it is sold; they should then be written off as a charge to the income statement. Which of these two treatments should be applied cannot be decided until it is clear at what moment the sale of the item takes place.

The decision has a **direct impact on profit** since, under the prudence concept, it is unacceptable to recognise the profit on sale until a sale has taken place.

Revenue is generally recognised as **earned at the point of sale**, because at that point four criteria will generally have been met.

(a) The product or service has been **provided to the buyer**.

(b) The buyer has **recognised his liability** to pay for the goods or services provided. The converse of this is that the seller has recognised that ownership of goods has passed from himself to the buyer.

(c) The buyer has indicated his **willingness to hand over cash** or other assets in settlement of his liability.

(d) The **monetary value** of the goods or services has been established.

However, sometimes revenue is **recognised at other times than at the completion of a sale**. For example, where an entity has a contract to construct an asset (such as a motorway, a housing estate or an aircraft) over more than one accounting period, contract revenue and contract costs are recognised by reference to the stage of completion of the contract activity at the reporting date.

Generally, revenue recognition occurs when it is probable that **future economic benefits** (normally in the form of cash) will flow to the entity and when these benefits can be **measured reliably**.

1.5 Consistency

Accounting is not an exact science. There are many areas in which judgement must be exercised in attributing money values to items appearing in accounts. Over the years certain procedures and principles have come to be recognised as good accounting practice, but within these limits there are often various acceptable methods of accounting for similar items.

The consistency concept states that in preparing accounts consistency should be observed in two respects.

(a) Similar items within a single set of accounts should be given similar accounting treatment.

(b) The same treatment should be applied from one period to another in accounting for similar items. This enables valid comparisons to be made from one period to the next.

Activity 2 **(5 minutes)**

Peter Axon has a trading year which runs from 1 January to 31 December. In the year to 31 December 20X0, he sold goods, produced in his industrial unit, for £30,000 and expects to earn a similar revenue for 20X1.

Peter pays rent for a year in advance on 1 July annually. On 1 July 20X0 he paid £2,400 rent and on 1 July 20X1 £3,000.

(a) How much rent should Peter include in his accounts for the year ended 31 December 20X1?

(b) If Peter's landlord agreed, could he alter his payment date for rent to 1 January or would this conflict with the consistency concept?

We next look at certain other accounting concepts considered equally fundamental by various authors.

1.7 The separate valuation principle

The separate valuation principle states that, in determining the amount of an asset or liability in the statement of financial position, each component item of the asset or liability must be valued separately. These separate valuations must then be aggregated to arrive at the total figure. For example, if a company's inventory comprises 50 separate items, a valuation must (in theory) be arrived at for each item separately; the 50 figures must then be aggregated and the total is the inventory figure which should appear in the accounting records.

1.8 Materiality

Definition

> Information is **material** if its omission or misstatement could influence the economic decisions of users taken on the basis of the financial statements.

An error which is too trivial to affect anyone's understanding of the accounts is referred to as immaterial (ie insignificant). In preparing accounts it is important to assess what is material (ie significant) and what is not, so that time and money are not wasted in the pursuit of excessive detail.

Determining whether or not an item is material is a very subjective exercise. There is no absolute measure of materiality. It is common to apply a convenient rule of thumb (for example, to define material items as those with a value greater than 5% of the profit disclosed by the accounts). But some items disclosed in accounts are regarded as particularly sensitive and even a very small misstatement of such an item would be regarded as a material error. An example might be the amount of remuneration paid to directors of the company.

The assessment of an item as material or immaterial may **affect its treatment in the accounts**. For example, the income statement of a business shows the expenses incurred grouped under suitable captions (heating and lighting, rent and local taxes, etc); but in the case of very small expenses it may be appropriate to lump them together as 'sundry expenses', because a more detailed breakdown is inappropriate for such immaterial amounts.

In assessing whether or not an item is material, it is not only the amount of the item which needs to be considered. The context is also important.

(a) If a company shows assets of £2 million and inventories of £30,000, an error of £20,000 in the asset valuation might not be regarded as material, whereas an error of £20,000 in the inventory valuation would be. In other words, the total of which the erroneous item forms part must be considered.

(b) If a business has a bank loan of £50,000 and a £55,000 balance on bank deposit account, it might well be regarded as a material misstatement if these two amounts were netted and the total shown as 'cash at bank £5,000'.

(These two items should be shown separately, even though the net effect of showing separately or netting would be identical.) In other words, incorrect presentation may amount to material misstatement even if there is no monetary error.

Activity 3 **(5 minutes)**

You have recently paid £4.95 for a waste paper bin which should have a useful life of about five years. Should you treat it as a non-current asset and capitalise it in the statement of financial position?

1.9 Offsetting

Assets and liabilities should not be offset (netted off against each other) unless such a treatment is required or permitted by an accounting standard.

Income and expenses can be offset only when one of the following applies.

(a) An accounting standard requires/permits it.

(b) Gains, losses and related expenses arising from the same/similar transactions are not material.

1.10 Substance over form

Definition

Substance over form. is the principle that transactions and other events are accounted for and presented in accordance with their substance and economic reality and not merely their legal form.

EXAMPLE

A Ltd leases a machine from a leasing company for five years. Under the terms of the lease, A Ltd pays annual lease rentals of £10,000 and is responsible for insuring and repairing the machine. It would have cost A Ltd £48,000 to buy the machine outright and it has a useful life of five years. The machine remains the property of the leasing company throughout the five year lease term.

The legal form of the lease agreement is that the leasing company owns the machine and A Ltd is renting it.

The substance of the lease agreement is that A Ltd has bought the right to use the machine for the whole of its useful life. The leasing company has made a loan to A Ltd, which is secured on the machine. When A Ltd pays the lease rentals, it is repaying the loan by instalments. The difference between the cost of the machine (£48,000) and the total lease rentals (£50,000) is interest.

To recognise the substance of the lease in the financial statements, A Ltd recognises the machine as an asset in the statement of financial position and depreciates it over five years. A Ltd also recognises a liability for the outstanding lease rentals.

Substance over form usually applies to transactions which are fairly complicated. It is very important because it acts as a 'catch-all' to stop entities distorting their results by following the **letter of the law,** instead of showing what the entity has really been doing.

1.11 The money measurement concept

This concept states that accounts will only deal with those items to which a monetary value can be attributed. For example, monetary values can be attributed to such assets as machinery (eg the original cost of the machinery; or the amount it would cost to replace the machinery) and inventories of goods (eg the original cost of the goods, or, theoretically, the price at which the goods are likely to be sold).

However, a business may have assets such as the flair of a good manager or the loyalty of its workforce which although important are difficult to quantify. These may be important enough to give it a clear superiority over an otherwise identical business, but because they cannot be evaluated in monetary terms they do not appear anywhere in the accounts.

The fact that some assets cannot be expressed in monetary terms and therefore are not recorded in the accounting records does not mean that they are less important than the assets which can be expressed in monetary terms. In fact, recognising the importance of non-quantifiable assets, accountants in recent years have tried to come up with ways of attributing values to them. These methods are beyond the scope of this text, but you should at least be aware of the problems such attempts try to address.

1.12 The entity concept

Briefly, the concept is that accountants regard a business as a separate entity, distinct from its owners or managers. The concept applies whether the business is a limited company (and so recognised in law as a separate entity) or a sole proprietorship or partnership (in which case the business is not separately recognised by the law).

Acceptance of this concept has important practical consequences, particularly in the case of a small business run by a single individual where the owner's personal affairs and business affairs may appear to be inextricably linked.

EXAMPLE

Suppose, for example, John runs a DIY shop but at times keeps some of the inventory at home. In preparing the business accounts, it is essential to distinguish his private activities and keep them separate from the business activities.

Suppose that John withdraws some paint boxes from his inventory to give to friends. How would this be reflected in the accounts?

ANSWER

The correct accounting treatment is to regard John as having purchased the goods from the business, which is a completely separate entity; the subsequent gift to his friends is then a private transaction and is not recorded anywhere in the books of the business. John should pay for the paint by taking money from his own purse and putting it into the till, or he should regard the taking of the paint boxes as a partial withdrawal of the investment he has made in the business. Otherwise, the accounts will give a misleading picture.

Activity 4 **(5 minutes)**

This activity will help to ensure that you have understood the concepts and conventions covered so far in this chapter.

Are the following statements true or false?

(a) The entity concept is that accountants regard a business as a separate legal entity, distinct from its owners or managers.

(b) Accounts deal only with items to which a monetary value can be attributed.

2 ACCOUNTING POLICIES

Accounting policies are the specific principles, bases, conventions, rules and practices that a business applies in order to specify the way in which particular items are reflected in the accounts. For example, if a business decides to revalue its non-current assets, rather than measuring them at historic cost, this is its accounting policy.

Accounting policies should be chosen in order **to comply with accounting standards.** Where there is **no specific requirement** in an accounting standard, policies should be developed so that information provided by the financial statements is:

(a) **Relevant** to the decision-making needs of users.

(b) **Reliable** in that they:

  (i) Represent faithfully the **results and financial position** of the entity.

  (ii) Reflect the **economic substance** of events and transactions and not merely the legal form.

  (iii) Are **neutral**, that is free from bias.

  (iv) Are **prudent**.

  (v) Are complete in all material respects.

(c) Comparable

(d) Understandable

We will look at these four characteristics in more detail in Section 3 of this chapter

There should be a specific section for accounting policies in the notes to the financial statements and the following should be disclosed there.

(a) **Measurement bases** used in preparing the financial statements.

(b) Each **specific accounting policy** necessary for a proper understanding of the financial statements)

To be clear and understandable it is essential that financial statements disclose the accounting policies used in their preparation. This is because **policies may vary,** not only from entity to entity, but also from country to country. As an aid to users, all the major accounting policies used should be disclosed in the same note.

An accounting policy can only be changed if:

(a) the change is required by an accounting standard; or

(b) the change results in the financial statements providing reliable and more relevant information to users.

We next look at the IASB's Framework for the preparation and presentation of financial statements. This is the conceptual framework upon which all IFRSs are based and hence which determines how financial statements are prepared and the information they contain.

3 THE CONCEPTUAL FRAMEWORK

A conceptual framework is a system of concepts and principles that underpin the preparation of financial statements. Both the IASB and the UK Accounting Standards Board (ASB) have developed documents that set out their conceptual frameworks. The IASB's conceptual framework is *The Framework for the preparation and presentation of financial statements.* The ASB's conceptual framework is the *Statement of Principles for Financial Reporting*. We will discuss the IASB's *Framework*, but the *Statement of Principles* is very similar.

The *Framework* deals with the following issues:

(a) The objective of financial statements.
(b) Underlying assumptions
(c) Qualitative characteristics of financial statements
(d) The elements of financial statements
(e) Recognition of the elements of financial statements
(f) Measurement of the elements of financial statements

The *Framework* is not an IFRS and so does not overrule any individual IFRS. In the (rare) cases of conflict between an IAS or IFRS and the *Framework*, the IAS or IFRS will prevail.

3.1 Users and their information needs

We have already looked at the users of accounting information in Chapter 1. They consist of investors, employees, lenders, suppliers and other creditors, customers, government and their agencies and the public.

Financial statements cannot meet all these users' needs, but financial statements which meet the **needs of investors** (providers of risk capital) will meet most of the needs of other users.

3.2 The objective of financial statements

The *Framework* states that:

> 'The objective of financial statements is to provide information about the financial position, performance and changes in financial position of an entity that is useful to a wide range of users in making economic decisions.'

The statements also show the results of the **management's stewardship**.

3.3 Underlying assumptions

We have met two of the assumptions discussed earlier in this chapter. They are:

(a) **Accruals basis**

Financial statements prepared under the accruals basis show users past transactions involving cash and also obligations to pay cash in the future and resources which represent cash to be received in the future.

(b) **Going concern**

It is assumed that the entity has no intention to liquidate or curtail major operations. If it did, then the financial statements would be prepared on a different (disclosed) basis.

3.4 Qualitative characteristics of financial statements

The *Framework* states that qualitative characteristics are the attributes that make the information provided in financial statements useful to users. The four principal qualitative characteristics are **understandability, relevance, reliability and comparability**.

Understandability

Users must be able to understand financial statements. They are assumed to have some business, economic and accounting knowledge and to be able to apply themselves to study the information properly. Complex matters should not be left out of financial statements simply due to its difficulty if it is relevant information.

Relevance

Only relevant information can be useful. Information is relevant when it helps users evaluate past, present or future events, or it confirms or corrects previous evaluations. The predictive and confirmatory roles of information are interrelated.

Information on financial position and performance is often used to predict future position and performance and other things of interest to the user, eg likely dividend, wage rises. The **manner of showing information** will enhance the ability to make predictions, eg by highlighting unusual items.

The relevance of information is affected by its nature and **materiality**. Information may be judged relevant simply because of its nature (eg remuneration of management). In other cases, both the nature and materiality of the information are important. Materiality is not a primary qualitative characteristic itself (like reliability or relevance), because it is merely a threshold or cut-off point.

Reliability

Information must also be **reliable** to be useful, ie **free from material error and bias**. The user must be able to depend on it being a faithful representation.

Even if information is relevant, if it is very unreliable it may be misleading to recognise it, eg a disputed claim for damages in a legal action.

The *Framework* discusses several aspects of reliability. These are:

(a) **Faithful representation**

Information must represent faithfully the transactions it purports to represent in order to be reliable. There is a risk that this may not be the case, not due to bias, but due to inherent difficulties in identifying the transactions or finding an appropriate method of measurement or presentation.

Where measurement of the financial effects of an item is so uncertain, an entity should not recognise such an item. For example, an entity may have developed valuable brands, but because it is difficult to measure their value reliably, they are not recognised on the statement of financial position.

(b) **Substance over form**

Transactions should be accounted for according to their substance and economic reality, not according to their legal form.

(c) **Neutrality**

Information must be free from bias to be reliable. Neutrality is lost if the financial statements are prepared so as to influence the user to make a judgement or decision in order to achieve a predetermined outcome.

(d) **Prudence**

Uncertainties exist in the preparation of financial information, eg the collectability of doubtful receivables. These uncertainties are recognised through disclosure and through the application of prudence.

Prudence does not, however, allow the creation of hidden reserves or excessive provisions, understatement of assets or income or overstatement of liabilities or expenses.

(e) **Completeness**

Financial information must be complete, within the restrictions of materiality and cost, to be reliable. Omissions may cause information to be misleading.

(f) **Comparability**

Users must be able to compare an entity's financial statements:

(i) through time to identify trends; and

(ii) with other entity's statements, to evaluate their relative financial position, performance and changes in financial position.

FOR DISCUSSION

Some of these qualities may not be compatible, for example relevance and reliablity. For example, if an entity revalues its non-current assets, it provides users of its financial statements with information that is relevant, but not necessarily reliable. The historic cost of an sset is an objective fact. Its market value is someone's subjective opinion. Another potential conflict exists between prudence and neutrality. How do you think any incompatability between qualities should be resolved?

3.5 The elements of financial statements

The *Framework* lays out these elements as follows.

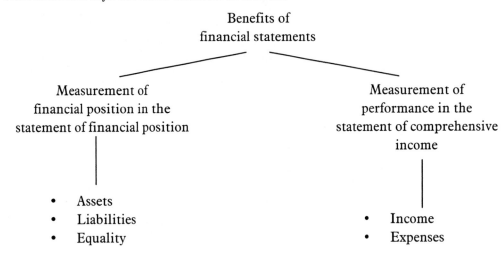

Benefits of financial statements

Measurement of financial position in the statement of financial position

- Assets
- Liabilities
- Equality

Measurement of performance in the statement of comprehensive income

- Income
- Expenses

Definition

An **asset** is a resource controlled by the entity as a result of past events and from which future economic benefits are expected to flow to the entity.

There are two important things to note.

An entity often owns its assets, but this need not be the case as long as it controls them. For example, a business may lease a motor vehicle under an agreement which gives it the right to use the vehicle throughout its useful life, even though it will never legally own it. The motor vehicle is an asset of the business because the business controls the motor vehicle.

An asset is something that provides future economic benefit. This means that it should eventually result in an inflow of cash. For example, a factory is used to produce goods that will be sold for cash.

NOTES

Definition

> A **liability** is a present obligation of the entity arising from past events, the settlement of which is expected to result in a outflow from the entity of resource embodying economic benefits.

Here there are three important things to note.

There must be an obligation, in other words, an entity only has a liability if it cannot avoid an outflow of economic benefit.

An outflow of economic benefits normally means incurring expenditure or paying cash to somebody, but this is not always the case. An entity might have a liability to provide goods or services in return for cash or another benefit.

If an entity recognises a liability in its statement of financial position, the transaction or event giving rise to the liability must have happened before the year-end.

Definition

> **Equity** is the residual interest in the assets of the entity after deducting all its liabilities.

In other words, equity is what the entity 'owes' to its owners.

3.6 Recognition of the elements of financial statements

Recognition. is the process of incorporating in the statement of financial position or statement of comprehensive income an item that meets the definition of an element.

For an item to be recognised it must meet the following conditions:

(a) it is probable that any future economic benefit associated with the item will flow to or from the entity; and

(b) the item has a cost or value that can be measured with reliability.

3.7 Measurement of the elements of financial statements

There are a number of different ways of measuring items in financial statements. We will discuss each of these in turn.

Historical cost

A basic principle of accounting (some writers include it in the list of fundamental accounting assumptions) is that items are normally stated in accounts at historical cost, ie at the amount which the business paid to acquire them. An important advantage of this procedure is that the objectivity of accounts is maximised: there is usually documentary evidence to prove the amount paid to purchase an asset or pay an expense.

In general, accountants prefer to deal with costs, rather than with 'values'. This is because valuations tend to be subjective and to vary according to what the valuation is for.

Replacement cost

Definition

Replacement cost means the amount needed to replace an items with an identical item.

For example, XY Ltd bought a machine five years ago for £15,000. It is now worn out and needs replacing. An identical machine can be purchased for £20,000.

Historical cost is £15,000 and replacement cost is £20,000

Net realisable value

Definition

Net realisable value is the expected price less any costs still to be incurred in getting the item ready for sale and then selling it.

For example, XY Ltd's machine from the example above can be restored to working order at a cost of £5,000. It can then be sold for £10,000. What is its net realisable value?

Net realisable value = £10,000 – £5,000 = £5,000

Economic value

Definition

Economic value is the value derived from an asset's ability to generate income.

A machine's economic value is the amount of profits it is expected to generate for the remains of its useful life.

Suppose XY Ltd buys the new machine for £20,000. It is estimated that the new machine will generate profits of £4,000 per year for its useful life of 8 years. What is its economic value?

Economic value = £4,000 × 8 = £32,000

There is a further important measurement base that is **not** mentioned in the *Framework*. This is **fair value.**

NOTES

Fair value

Definition

> **Fair value** is the amount for which an asset could be exchanged between knowledgeable, willing parties in an arm's length transaction

In practice, fair value is normally open market value.

The IASB wants to encourage greater use of fair values. Accounting standards allow many types of non-current asset to be measured at fair value and actually **require** certain types of investment (financial instruments) to be measured at fair value.

FOR DISCUSSION

The main advantage of measuring assets at fair value is that this normally provides more useful information to users than measuring assets at cost. But there are many possible disadvantages of using fair values too. What might they be? Can you think of any further advantages?

Chapter roundup

- In preparing financial statements, certain fundamental concepts are adopted as a framework.
- There are two important assumptions underlying the preparation of financial statements.
  - Going concern. Unless there is evidence to the contrary, it is assumed that a business will continue to trade normally for the foreseeable future.
  - Accruals (or matching). Revenue earned must be matched against expenditure incurred in earning it.
- A number of other concepts may be regarded as fundamental. These include:
  - The prudence concept. Where alternative accounting procedures are acceptable in conditions of uncertainty, choose the one which gives the less optimistic view of profitability and asset values.
  - The consistency concept. Similar items should be accorded similar accounting treatments.
  - The entity concept. A business is an entity distinct from its owner(s).
  - Substance over form. Financial statements should reflect the economic substance of transactions, not their legal form, where these are different.
  - The money measurement concept. Accounts only deal with items to which monetary values can be attributed.
  - The separate valuation principle. Each component of an asset or liability must be valued separately.
  - The materiality concept. Items are material where their misstatement or omission would influence a user of the financial statements.
- The objective of financial statements is to provide information about the financial position, performance and changes in financial position of an entity that is useful to a wide range of users in making economic decisions.
- Accounting information is expected to possess a number of qualities.
- They are, among others, relevance, reliability, comparability and understandability.
- The elements of financial statements are: assets; liabilities; equity; income and expenses.

Quick quiz

1 What are the two assumptions underlying the preparation of financial statements?

2 Briefly re-cap what is meant by: the entity concept; the money measurement concept; the going concern concept; the prudence concept; the accruals concept; the consistency concept; the separate valuation principle; and the materiality concept.

3 At what stage is it normal to recognise the revenue arising from a credit sale?

4 What are the qualities of useful accounting information?

Answers to Quick quiz

1 Accruals, going concern, prudence.

2 Check your answers in respect of these concepts in the chapter.

3 Refer to the various aspects detailed in Paragraph 1.4.

4 Check the various qualities in the chapter, Paragraph 3.4.

Answers to Activities

1 (a) If the business is to be closed down, the remaining three machines must be valued at the amount they will realise in a forced sale, ie 3 × £60 = £180.

(b) If the business is regarded as a going concern, the inventory unsold at 31 December will be carried forward into the following year, when the cost of the three machines will be matched against the eventual sale proceeds in computing that year's profits. The three machines will therefore appear in the statement of financial position at 31 December at cost, 3 × £100 = £300.

2 (a) The matching concept is applied so that £1,200 rent applies to the first half of the year and £1,500 to the second half of the year – a total of £2,700.

(b) Consistency is concerned with the application of accounting concepts and policies and so long as matching and accruals are applied, it does not matter when the actual payment of rent takes place.

3 No, because of the materiality concept. The cost of the bin is very small. Rather than cluttering up the statement of financial position for five years, treat the £4.95 as an expense in this year's income statement.

4 (a) False. Although it is certainly true that the entity concept is that accountants regard a business as a separate entity, it is not always a legal difference. For example, legally a sole trader is not separate from his business.

(b) True, although attempts have been made to account for a number of non-monetary items.

Chapter : 20
STATEMENTS OF CASH FLOWS

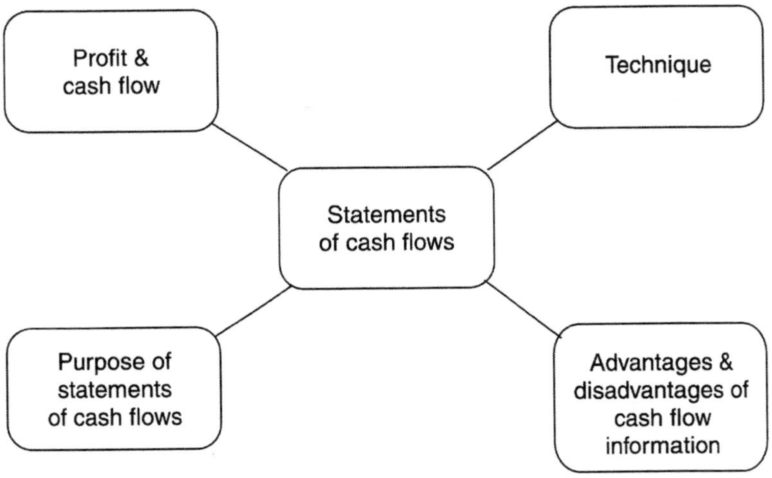

Introduction

If a firm is unable to pay its bills when they are due it can be forced into liquidation, regardless of how profitable the firm may happen to be. In the long run, profit will result in an increase in the company's cash balance but, as Keynes observed, 'in the long run we are all dead'. In the short run, the making of a profit will not necessarily result in an increased cash balance.

This observation leads us to two questions. The first relates to the importance of the distinction between cash and profit. The second is concerned with the usefulness of the information provided by the statement of financial position and income statement in the problem of deciding whether the company has, or will be able to generate, sufficient cash to finance its operations.

The importance of the distinction between cash and profit and the fact that this is not reflected in the income statement has resulted in the development of statements of cash flows (sometimes called cash flow statements). Section 1 of this chapter discusses the distinction between profit and cash while the preparation of statements of cash flows is covered in Sections 2 and 3.

Your objectives

In this chapter you will learn about the following.

(a) The differences between profits and cash surpluses

(b) The purpose of statements of cash flows and their preparation

(c) The strengths and weaknesses of cash flow accounting

1 PROFITS AND CASH FLOW

To be successful in business, an entity must make a profit. Profits are needed to pay dividends to shareholders and to reward partners or proprietors. Some profits are retained within the business as reserves to finance the development and growth of the business. We can therefore say that although a firm may be able to bear occasional losses, it must be profitable in the long term.

In addition to being *profitable*, in order to survive and grow, it is also necessary for a firm to 'pay its way': to *pay cash* for the goods and services and capital equipment it buys, the workforce it employs and the other expenses (such as rent, rates and taxation) that it incurs. If a firm does not pay its bills when they are due, it will first of all lose the goodwill of its suppliers or workforce and may then be driven into liquidation. *It is therefore necessary to be not just profitable, but also capable of obtaining cash to meet demand for payments.*

Activity 1 **(5 minutes)**

Profits and cash surpluses are not the same thing for a number of reasons. For example, cash may be obtained from a transaction which has nothing to do with profit or loss, such as a share issue. Fill in the missing entries in the following table to ensure you understand the impact on cash flow and profit of the items listed.

Item	*Effect on cash flow*	*Effect on profit*
Motor vehicle purchased 2 years ago		
New issue of shares for cash		
Increase in bank loan		
New machine purchased for cash		
Computer equipment sold during year		

The income statement reports the total sales in a year. If goods are sold on credit, the cash receipts will differ from sales. The relationship between sales and receipts is as follows, with illustrative figures.

	£
Customers owing money at the start of the year (opening trade receivables)	20,000
Sales during the year	300,000
Total money due from customers	320,000
Less customers owing money at the end of the year (closing trade receivables)	30,000
Cash receipts from customers during the year	290,000

Similarly, the income statement reports the cost of goods sold during the year. However, if materials are bought on credit, the cash payments to suppliers will be different from the value of materials purchased.

NOTES

	£
Payments owed to suppliers at the start of the year (opening trade payables)	6,000
Add purchases during the year	70,000
	76,000
Less payments still owing to suppliers at the end of the year (closing trade payables)	4,000
Equals cash payments to creditors during the year	72,000

Information about cash receipts and payments can add to our understanding of a firm's operations and financial stability. Whereas an income statement reports on profitability, statements of cash flows report on the ability of the firm to pay its bills.

It can be argued that 'profit' does not always give a useful or meaningful picture of a company's operations. Readers of a company's financial statements might even be misled by a reported profit figure. Shareholders, employees and lenders might interpret a company's making profit in different ways.

(a) **Shareholders** might believe that if a company makes a profit after tax, of say, £100,000 then this is the amount which it could afford to pay as a dividend. Unless the company has sufficient cash available to stay in business and also to pay a dividend, the shareholders' expectation would be wrong.

(b) **Employees** might believe that if a company makes profits, it can afford to pay higher wages next year. This opinion may not be correct: the ability to pay wages depends on the availability of cash.

(c) **Lenders** might consider that a profitable company is a going concern. But this may not be so. For example, if a company builds up large amounts of inventory, their cost would not be chargeable against profits. However, cash would have been used up in making them, thus weakening the company's liquid resources.

Moreover, the income statement and statement of cash flows are subject to manipulation by the use of different accounting policies, eg different inventory valuation methods, depreciation methods, etc.

The survival of a business entity therefore depends not so much on profits as on its ability to pay its debts when they fall due. Such payments might include 'profit and loss' items such as material purchases, wages, interest and taxation etc, but also capital payments for new non-current assets and the repayment of a loan when it falls due.

From these examples, it is apparent that a company's performance and prospects depend not so much on the 'profits' earned in a period, but more realistically on cash flows.

Since cash flows are so vital to the survival and growth of a business, regulatory bodies require that information about cash flows be made available to external users as well.

2 PURPOSE OF STATEMENTS OF CASH FLOWS

2.1 Aims

Both IFRSs and UK standards require entities to prepare and present a statement of cash flows as part of their published financial statements.

The main purpose of the statement is to provide information about a company's cash receipts and cash payments during an accounting year. Some of the information provided by the statement of cash flows can be obtained by analysing the income statement and the statement of financial position. However, it is the statement of cash flows that brings together all those transactions which affect a company's cash position.

The statement of cash flows provides information to users of financial statements about an entity's **ability to generate cash and cash equivalents,** as well as indicating the cash needs of the entity. The statement of cash flows provides *historical* information about cash and cash equivalents, classifying cash flows between operating, investing and financing activities.

2.2 Cash and cash equivalents

Definitions

Cash comprises cash on hand and demand deposits.

Cash equivalents are short-term, highly liquid investments that are readily convertible to known amounts of cash and which are subject to an insignificant risk of changes in value.

Many entities invest surplus cash in short term investments or deposits, so as to earn interest on cash that they are unlikely to need immediately. This is part of cash management, rather than part of operating, investing or financing activities. Therefore cash equivalents are treated as part of an entity's cash, rather than as investments or sources of finance. Movements between different types of cash and cash equivalent are not included in cash flows.

Cash equivalents are not held for investment or other long-term purposes, but rather to meet short-term cash commitments. To fulfil the above definition, an investment's **maturity date should normally be three months from its acquisition date**. It would usually be the case then that equity investments (ie shares in other companies) are *not* cash equivalents. An exception would be where redeemable preference shares were acquired with a very close redemption date.

Loans and other borrowings are **not** normally included in cash and cash equivalents. However, in some countries, including the UK, **bank overdrafts** are repayable on demand and are treated as part of an entity's total cash management system. In these circumstances an overdrawn balance will be included in cash and cash equivalents. Such banking arrangements are characterised by a balance which fluctuates between overdrawn and credit.

2.3 Classifying cash flows

IAS 7 requires statements of cash flows to report cash flows during the period classified by **operating, investing and financing activities.**

The manner of presentation of cash flows from operating, investing and financing activities **depends on the nature of the entity**. By classifying cash flows between different activities in this way users can see the impact on cash and cash equivalents of each one, and their relationships with each other. We can look at each in more detail.

2.4 Operating activities

This is perhaps the key part of the statement of cash flows because it shows whether, and to what extent, companies can **generate cash from their operations**. It is these operating cash flows which must, in the end pay for all cash outflows relating to other activities, ie paying loan interest, dividends and so on.

Most of the components of cash flows from operating activities will be those items which **determine the net profit or loss of the entity**, ie they relate to the main revenue-producing activities of the entity. The standard gives the following as examples of cash flows from operating activities.

(a) Cash receipts from the sale of goods and the rendering of services
(b) Cash receipts from royalties, fees, commissions and other revenue
(c) Cash payments to suppliers for goods and services
(d) Cash payments to and on behalf of employees

Certain items may be included in the net profit or loss for the period which do *not* relate to operational cash flows, for example the profit or loss on the sale of a piece of plant will be included in net profit or loss, but the cash flows will be classed as **investing**.

2.5 Investing activities

The cash flows classified under this heading show the extent of new investment in **assets which will generate future profit and cash flows**. The standard gives the following examples of cash flows arising from investing activities.

(a) Cash payments to acquire property, plant and equipment, intangibles and other non-current assets, including those relating to capitalised development costs and self-constructed property, plant and equipment

(b) Cash receipts from sales of property, plant and equipment, intangibles and other non-current assets

(c) Cash payments to acquire shares or debentures of other entities

(d) Cash receipts from sales of shares or debentures of other entities

(e) Cash advances and loans made to other parties

(f) Cash receipts from the repayment of advances and loans made to other parties

2.6 Financing activities

This section of the statement of cash flows shows the share of cash which the entity's capital providers have claimed during the period. This is an indicator of **likely future interest and dividend payments**. The standard gives the following examples of cash flows which might arise under these headings.

(a) Cash proceeds from issuing shares

(b) Cash payments to owners to acquire or redeem the entity's shares

(c) Cash proceeds from issuing debentures, loans, notes, bonds, mortgages and other short or long-term borrowings

(d) Cash repayments of amounts borrowed

Activity 2 **(10 minutes)**

The statement of cash flows should classify cash receipts and payments under one of three headings. Try classifying the following receipts and payments.

(a) Purchase of an asset for cash
(b) Cash repayment of a loan
(c) Issue of shares for cash
(d) Borrowing money
(e) Receipts from customers

Before we start looking at how to construct a statement of cash flows, an example will help our understanding of the issues discussed so far.

2.7 Example of a statement of cash flows

Flail Ltd commenced trading on 1 January 20X0 with a medium-term loan of £21,000 and a share issue which raised £35,000. The company purchased non-current assets for £21,000 cash, and during the year to 31 December 20X0 entered into the following transactions.

(a) Purchases from suppliers were £19,500, of which £2,550 was unpaid at the year end.

(b) Wages and salaries amounted to £10,500, of which £750 was unpaid at the year end.

(c) Interest on the loan of £2,100 was fully paid in the year and a repayment of £5,250 was made.

(d) Sales revenue was £29,400, including £900 receivable at the year end.

(e) Interest on cash deposits at the bank amounted to £75.

(f) A dividend of £4,000 was proposed as at 31 December 20X0.

The statement of cash flows for the year ended 31 December 20X0 will be as follows.

NOTES

FLAIL LTD
STATEMENT OF CASH FLOWS FOR
THE YEAR ENDED 31 DECEMBER 20X1

	£	£
Cash flows from operating activities		
Cash received from customers (£29,400 – £900)	28,500	
Cash paid to suppliers (£19,500 – £2,550)	(16,950)	
Cash paid to and on behalf of employees (£10,500 – £750)	(9,750)	
Interest paid	(2,100)	
Net cash used in operating activities		(300)
Cash flows from investing activities		
Purchase of non-current assets	(21,000)	
Interest received	75	
Net cash used in investing activities		(20,925)
Cash flows from financing activities		
Issue of shares	35,000	
Proceeds from medium-term loan	21,000	
Repayment of medium-term loan	(5,250)	
Net cash from financing activities		50,750
Net increase in cash and cash equivalents		29,525
Cash and cash equivalents at 1 January 20X1		–
Cash and cash equivalents at 31 December 20X1		29,525

Note that the dividend is only proposed and so there is no related cash flow in 20X1.

Preparing a statement of cash flows is straightforward. We next look at the various steps involved in preparing the statement.

3 TECHNIQUE

3.1 Cash flows from operating activities

There are two possible methods of presenting this part of the statement of cash flows.

(a) **Direct method:** disclose major classes of gross cash receipts and gross cash payments

(b) **Indirect method**: net profit or loss is adjusted for the effects of transactions of a non-cash nature, any deferrals or accruals of past or future operating cash receipts or payments, and items of income or expense associated with investing or financing cash flows

The example above used the **direct method**. This method discloses information not available elsewhere in the financial statements which could be of use in estimating future cash flows. However, the **indirect method** is simpler and more widely used.

Both IFRSs and UK accounting standards encourage the use of the direct method, but do not require it.

NOTES

3.2 Using the direct method

There are different ways in which the **information about gross cash receipts and payments** can be obtained. The most obvious way is simply to extract the information from the accounting records.

In examinations and assessments you are normally asked to prepare a statement of cash flows from the statement of financial position at the beginning and end of the year and the income statement for the year. The easiest way to produce the information is to draw up ledger accounts or T accounts, as shown below:

TRADE RECEIVABLES

	£		£
Opening balance (statement of financial position)	X	**Cash received from customers (balancing figure)**	**X**
Sales revenue (income statement)	X	Closing balance (statement of financial position)	X
	X		X

TRADE PAYABLES

	£		£
Cash paid to suppliers (balancing figure)	**X**	Opening balance (statement of financial position)	X
Closing balance (statement of financial position)	X	Purchases (see below)	X
	X		X

If the purchases figure is not provided it can be found by breaking down the figure for cost of sales:

	£
Cost of sales (income statement)	X
Add closing inventory (statement of financial position)	X
Less opening inventory (statement of financial position)	(X)
Purchases for the period	**X**

Activity 3 **(10 minutes)**

The following information relates to the cash flows of Flail Ltd for the year ended 31 December 20X2.

(a) Sales revenue was £36,000 (£900 receivables at the start of the year; £450 receivables at the year end).

(b) Further expenses were:

(i) purchases from suppliers – £18,750 (£2,550 owed at the start of the year; £4,125 owed at the year end);

(ii) wages and salaries – £11,250 (£750 owed at the start of the year; £600 owed at the year end);

(iii) loan interest – £1,575.

(c) Income taxes of £2,300 was paid in respect of 20X1.

Calculate net cash from operating activities for the year ended 31 December 20X2, using the direct method.

NOTES

3.3 Using the indirect method

This method is undoubtedly **easier** from the point of view of the preparer of the statement of cash flows. The net profit or loss for the period is adjusted for the following.

(a) Changes during the period in inventories, operating receivables and payables

(b) Non-cash items, eg depreciation, provisions, profits/losses on the sales of assets

(c) Other items, the cash flows from which should be classified under investing or financing activities.

A **proforma** of such a calculation is as follows.

	£
Profit before interest and tax (income statement)*	X
Add depreciation	X
Loss (profit) on sale of non-current assets	X
(Increase)/decrease in inventories	(X)/X
(Increase)/decrease in receivables	(X)/X
Increase/(decrease) in payables	X/(X)
Cash generated from operations	X
Interest (paid)/received	(X)
Income taxes paid	(X)
Net cash flows from operating activities	X

* Take profit before tax and add back any interest expense

It is important to understand why **certain items are added and others subtracted**. Note the following points.

(a) **Depreciation**. To arrive at a figure for profit we deduct an amount to reflect depreciation of the non-current assets. But although this is correctly shown as a reduction in profit, it is not a cash outflow. To arrive at cash generated from operations, we must add back amounts deducted in respect of depreciation.

(b) **Profits and losses on disposal of non-current assets**. The above logic also applies to any gain or loss on disposal of non-current assets. A loss is added back and a profit is deducted.

(c) **Increase/decrease in inventories**. Inventory in the statement of financial position at the year end represents an asset for which money has been paid, but which has not been charged against profits for the period. If closing inventory exceeds opening inventory the income statement understates the amount of cash paid out to suppliers. To compensate for this, the increase in inventory over the year is deducted from profit. A decrease in inventory levels over the year is added back to profit.

		Profit + decrease in inventories
To arrive at cash flow from operations	=	**or**
		Profit – increase in inventories

(d) **Increase/decrease in receivables**. An increase in the receivables balance over an accounting period means that cash receipts have been less than the sales for the period (no change in receivables over a period means that cash receipts from sales were exactly equal to sales).

NOTES

Since the profit for the year includes all sales (whether for cash or credit), it is important that the profit figure is adjusted for changes in receivables to arrive at cash flow from operations.

		Profit + decrease in receivables
To arrive at cash flow from operations	=	**or**
		Profit – increase in receivables

A decrease in receivables means that cash receipts from sales were greater than the sales for the period. As profit only includes the sales for the period, we need to add the excess cash collections (excess of cash receipts over sales shown by the decrease in receivables) to the profit in order to include all the cash receipts for the period in our calculations.

The opposite applies, of course, if receivables have increased over the year.

(e) **Increase/decrease in payables**. The situation here is the reverse of that described under receivables. Thus, the rule is:

		Profit – decrease in payables
To arrive at cash flow from operations	=	**or**
		Profit + increase in payables

The reason for an increase in payables being added to the profit is that not all purchases are being bought for cash. In fact, cash is being retained and not used to pay off suppliers.

Activity 4 **(10 minutes)**

The summarised statements of financial position of Cashflow Ltd at 30 June 20X0 and 20X1 are given below. Calculate the net cash flow from operating activities for the year ended 30 June 20X1, assuming no tax or interest was paid.

	30 June 20X0	*30 June 20X1*
	£	£
Non-current assets: cost	12,000	13,600
Depreciation	6,500	7,800
	5,500	5,800
Inventory	4,000	5,200
Receivables	6,000	4,700
Cash	1,800	850
	17,300	16,550
Equity	13,000	14,700
Payables	4,300	1,850
	17,300	16,550

3.4 Interest and dividends

Cash flows from interest and dividends received and paid should each be **disclosed separately**. Each should be classified in a consistent manner from period to period as either operating, investing or financing activities.

Dividends paid by the entity can be classified in **one of two ways**.

(a) As a **financing cash flow**, showing the cost of obtaining financial resources.

(b) As a component of **cash flows from operating activities** so that users can assess the enterprise's ability to pay dividends out of operating cash flows.

3.5 Taxes on income

Cash flows arising from taxes on income should be **separately disclosed** and should be classified as cash flows from operating activities *unless* they can be specifically identified with financing and investing activities.

Taxation cash flows are often **difficult to match** to the originating underlying transaction, so most of the time all tax cash flows are classified as arising from operating activities.

3.6 Example of a statement of cash flows

EXAMPLE: DIRECT METHOD

STATEMENT OF CASH FLOWS YEAR ENDED 20X7

	£m	£m
Cash flows from operating activities		
Cash receipts from customers	30,330	
Cash paid to suppliers and employees	(27,600)	
Cash generated from operations	2,730	
Interest paid	(270)	
Income taxes paid	(900)	
Net cash from operating activities		1,560
Cash flows from investing activities		
Purchase of property, plant and equipment	(900)	
Proceeds from sale of equipment	20	
Interest received	200	
Dividends received	200	
Net cash used in investing activities		(480)
Cash flows from financing activities		
Proceeds from issuance of share capital	250	
Proceeds from long-term borrowings	250	
Dividends paid*	(1,290)	
Net cash used in financing activities		(790)
Net increase in cash and cash equivalents		290
Cash and cash equivalents at beginning of period (Note)		120
Cash and cash equivalents at end of period (Note)		410

* This could also be shown as an operating cash flow

EXAMPLE: INDIRECT METHOD

STATEMENT OF CASH FLOWS YEAR ENDED 20X7

	£m	£m
Cash flows from operating activities		
Net profit before taxation	3,570	
Adjustments for:		
Depreciation	450	
Investment income	(500)	
Interest expense	400	
Operating profit before working capital changes	3,920	
Increase in trade and other receivables	(500)	
Decrease in inventories	1,050	
Decrease in trade payables	(1,740)	
Cash generated from operations	2,730	
Interest paid	(270)	
Income taxes paid	(900)	
Net cash from operating activities		1,560
Cash flows from investing activities		
Purchase of property, plant and equipment	(900)	
Proceeds from sale of equipment	20	
Interest received	200	
Dividends received	200	
Net cash used in investing activities		(480)
Cash flows from financing activities		
Proceeds from issuance of share capital	250	
Proceeds from long-term borrowings	250	
Dividends paid*	(1,290)	
Net cash used in financing activities		(790)
Net increase in cash and cash equivalents		290
Cash and cash equivalents at beginning of period (Note)		120
Cash and cash equivalents at end of period (Note)		410

* This could also be shown as an operating cash flow

The statement of cash flows above is in the format required by IFRSs (IAS 7 *Statement of cash flows*). You may see statements presented in a slightly different format. For example, in the UK, the cash flow statement classifies cash flows under different headings. It also shows movements in cash only; cash equivalents are shown under a separate heading (management of liquid resources).

NOTES

EXAMPLE

OUTFLOW LIMITED
CASH FLOW STATEMENT FOR THE YEAR ENDED 30 JUNE 20X1

Reconciliation of operating profit to net cash outflow from operating activities

	£
Operating profit (£23,350-£22,150)	1,200
Depreciation (£2,800-(£1,900-£1,650))	2,550
Profit on sale of tangible fixed assets	(250)
Increase in stocks	(4,200)
Increase in debtors	(1,700)
Increase in creditors	250
	(2,150)

	£	£
Net cash outflow from operating activities		(2,150)
Capital expenditure		
Payments to acquire tangible fixed assets	(4,500)	
Receipts from sale of tangible fixed assets	800	
Net cash outflow from capital expenditure		(3,700)
Net cash flow before financing		(5,850)
Financing		
Issue of share capital	2,500	
Repayment of loan	(1,000)	
Net cash outflow from financing		1,500
Decrease in cash (3,500 + 850)		(4,350)

Now we will work through a more detailed example. As usual, we will assume that financial statements are being prepared according to the requirements of IFRSs.

3.7 Example: Preparation of a statement of cash flows

Colby Ltd's income statement for the year ended 31 December 20X2 and statements of financial position at 31 December 20X1 and 31 December 20X2 were as follows.

COLBY LTD
INCOME STATEMENT FOR THE YEAR ENDED 31 DECEMBER 20X2

	£'000	£'000
Sales		720
Raw materials consumed	70	
Staff costs	94	
Depreciation	118	
Loss on disposal of non-current asset	18	
		(300)
		420
Interest payable		(28)
Profit before tax		392
Taxation		(124)
Profit for the period		268

NOTES

COLBY LTD
STATEMENT OF FINANCIAL POSITION AS AT 31 DECEMBER

	20X2		*20X1*	
	£'000	£'000	£'000	£'000
Assets				
Property, plant and equipment				
Cost	1,596		1,560	
Depreciation	318		224	
		1,278		1,336
Current assets				
Inventory	24		20	
Trade receivables	76		58	
Bank	48		56	
		148		134
Total assets		1,426		1,470
Equity and liabilities				
Capital and reserves				
Share capital	360		340	
Share premium	36		24	
Retained earnings	716		514	
		1,112		878
Non-current liabilities				
Non-current loans		200		500
Current liabilities				
Trade payables	12		6	
Taxation	102		86	
		114		92
		1,426		1,470

During the year, the company paid $90,000 for a new piece of machinery.

Dividends paid during 20X2 totalled $66,000.

Required

Prepare a statement of cash flows for Colby Ltd for the year ended 31 December 20X2, using the indirect method.

Step 1 **Set out the proforma statement of cash flows** with the headings required by IAS 7. You should leave plenty of space. Ideally, use three or more sheets of paper, one for the main statement, one for the notes and one for your workings. It is obviously essential to know the formats very well.

Step 2 **Begin with the reconciliation of profit before tax to net cash from operating activities** as far as possible. When preparing the statement from statements of financial position, you will usually have to calculate such items as depreciation, loss on sale of non-current assets, profit for the year and tax paid (see Step 4). Note that you may not be given the tax charge in the income statement. You will then have to assume that the tax paid in the year is last year's year-end liability and calculate the charge as the balancing figure.

NOTES

Step 3 Calculate the cash flow figures for **dividends paid, purchase or sale of non-current assets, issue of shares and repayment of loans** if these are not already given to you (as they may be).

Step 4 If you are not given the profit figure, open up a **working**. Using the opening and closing balances, the taxation charge and dividends paid, you will be able to calculate profit for the year as the balancing figure to put in the net profit to net cash flow from operating activities section.

Step 5 You will now be able to **complete the statement** by slotting in the figures given or calculated.

COLBY LTD
STATEMENT OF CASH FLOWS FOR THE YEAR ENDED 31 DECEMBER 20X2

	£'000	£'000
Net cash flow from operating activities		
Profit before tax	392	
Depreciation charges	118	
Loss on sale of property, plant and equipment	18	
Interest expense	28	
Increase in inventories	(4)	
Increase in receivables	(18)	
Increase in payables	6	
Cash generated from operations	540	
Interest paid	(28)	
Dividends paid	(66)	
Tax paid (86 + 124 – 102)	(108)	
Net cash flow from operating activities		338
Cash flows from investing activities		
Payments to acquire property, plant and equipment	(90)	
Receipts from sales property, plant and equipment	12	
Net cash outflow from investing activities		(78)
Cash flows from financing activities		
Issues of share capital (360 + 36 – 340 – 24)	32	
Long-term loans repaid (500 – 200)	(300)	
Net cash flows from financing		(268)
Decrease in cash and cash equivalents		(8)
Cash and cash equivalents at 1.1.X2		56
Cash and cash equivalents at 31.12.X2		48

Working: property, plant and equipment

COST

	£'000		£'000
At 1.1.X2	1,560	At 31.12.X2	1,596
Purchases	90	Disposals (balance)	54
	1,650		1,650

BPP LEARNING MEDIA

ACCUMULATED DEPRECIATION

	£'000		£'000
At 31.1.X2	318	At 1.1.X2	224
Depreciation on disposals		Charge for year	118
(balance)	24		
	342		342

NBV of disposals	30
Net loss reported	(18)
Proceeds of disposals	12

Preparing a statement of cash flows takes time. In business, time is money. Why does a business then spend time preparing such a statement?

4 ADVANTAGES AND DISADVANTAGES OF CASH FLOW INFORMATION

The advantages of cash flow accounting are as follows.

(a) Survival in business depends on the ability to generate cash. Cash flow information directs attention towards this critical issue.

(b) Cash flow is more objective than 'profit', which is less 'dependent' on somewhat arbitrary accounting conventions and concepts.

(c) Lenders (loan creditors) and suppliers are more interested in an entity's ability to repay them than in its profitability. Whereas 'profits' might indicate that cash is likely to be available, cash flow accounting is more direct with its message.

(d) Cash flow reporting provides a better means of comparing the results of different companies than traditional profit reporting, since profit can be easily manipulated by choosing the more favourable accounting policies.

(e) Cash flow reporting satisfies the needs of all users better:

  (i) for management, it provides the sort of information on which decisions should be taken; traditional profit accounting does not help with decision making;

  (ii) for shareholders and auditors, cash flow accounting can provide a satisfactory basis for judging the performance of management;

  (iii) as described previously, the information needs of loan creditors and employees will be better served by cash flow accounting.

(f) Cash flow forecasts are easier to prepare, as well as more useful, than profit forecasts.

(g) Cash is an easy, familiar concept for users to understand.

FOR DISCUSSION

You should give some thought to the possible disadvantages of cashflow accounting which are essentially the advantages of accruals accounting. There is also the practical problem that few businesses keep historical cash flow information in the form needed to prepare a historical statement of cash flows and so extra record keeping is likely to be necessary.

Chapter roundup

- Cash is vital to the survival of a business.
- Profits are not the same as cash flows. A company can have healthy profits, but poor cash flow or vice versa.
- Whereas income statements report on profitability, statements of cash flows report on a firm's ability to pay its bills.
- A statement of cash flows shows changes in cash over a period.
- The statement classifies cash flows under three headings: operating activities; investing activities; and financing activities.
- The possible disadvantages of cash flow accounting are essentially the advantages of accrual accounting.

Quick quiz

1 List four examples of transactions which affect profit differently from their effect on cashflow.

2 Explain the limitations of a profit figure for:

(a) shareholders
(b) employees
(c) lenders (loan creditors)
(d) management.

3 What are the aims of a statement of cash flows?

4 Why is an increase in inventory treated as negative in a statement of cash flows?

Answers to Quick quiz

1 Check your answer against the details given in Section 1 of the chapter.

2 Compare your answer with the chapter.

3 To provide information to users of financial statements about an entity's ability to generate cash and cash equivalents, as well as indicating the cash needs of the entity. To provide historical information about cash and cash equivalents.

4 To compensate for impact of inventory in the profit calculation.

Answers to Activities

1

	Effect on cash flow	*Effect on profit*
Motor vehicle purchased 2 years ago	None	Depreciation charge
New issue of shares for cash	Cash inflow	None
Increase in bank loan	Cash inflow	Increase in interest charges
New machine purchased for cash	Cash outflow	Depreciation charge
Computer equipment sold during year	Cash inflow	Profit or loss on sale

2 You should have included (a) as investing activities, (b), (c) and (d) as financing activities and (e) as operating activities.

3

	£
Cash received from customers (36,000 + 900 – 450)	36,450
Cash paid to suppliers (18,750 + 2,550 – 4,125)	(17,175)
Cash paid to and on behalf of employees (11,250 + 750 – 600)	(11,400)
Interest paid	(1,575)
Taxation	(2,300)
	4,000

4

	£
Profit for the year (14,700 – 13,000)	1,700
Depreciation (7,800 – 6,500)	1,300
Increase in inventory	(1,200)
Decrease in receivables	1,300
Decrease in payables	(2,450)
	650

Chapter : 21

PARTNERSHIPS

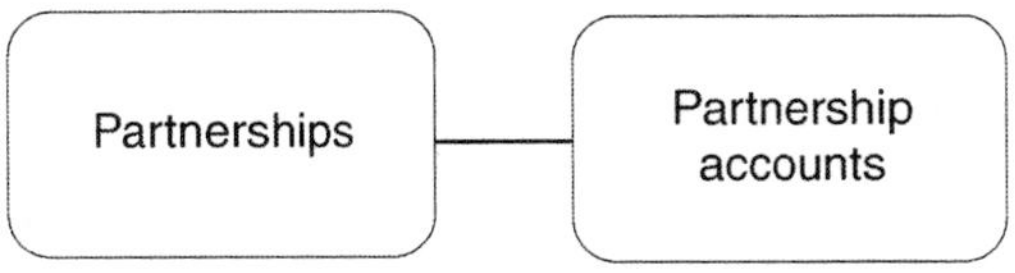

Introduction

The Edexel Guidelines make it clear that you are expected to be able to prepare and present financial statements for sole traders, limited companies and partnerships. So far we have concentrated on the first two of those three, so this chapter introduces partnership accounting.

Your objectives

In this chapter, you will learn about the following.

(a) The nature of a partnership

(b) Partnership accounts

1 PARTNERSHIP ACCOUNTS

1.1 What is a partnership?

Definition

> A **partnership** is the relationship which subsists between persons carrying on a business in common with a view of profit.

In other words, a partnership is an arrangement between two or more individuals in which they undertake to share the risks and rewards of a joint business operation.

In a partnership:

(a) The **personal liability** of each partner for the firm's debts is **unlimited**, and so an individual's personal assets may be used to meet any partnership liabilities in the event of partnership bankruptcy.

(b) All partners usually **participate in the running of the business**, rather than merely providing the capital.

(c) Profits or losses of the business are **shared** between the partners.

> **Activity 1** **(5 minutes)**
>
> Try to think of reasons why a business should be conducted as a partnership rather than:
>
> (a) as a sole trader
> (b) as a company

1.2 The partnership agreement

It is usual for a partnership to be established formally by means of a *partnership agreement.* The partnership agreement is a written agreement in which the terms of the partnership are set out, and in particular the financial arrangements as between partners.

However, if individuals act as though they are in partnership even if no written agreement exists, then it will be presumed that a partnership does exist and that its terms of agreement are reflected in the way the partners conduct the business, ie the way profits have been divided in the past, etc.

The partnership agreement should cover include the following.

(a) **Capital.** Each partner puts in a share of the business capital. If there is to be an agreement on how much each partner should put in and keep in the business, as a minimum fixed amount, this should be stated.

(b) **Profit-sharing ratio**. Partners can agree to share profits in any way they choose. For example, if there are three partners in a business, they might agree to share profits equally but on the other hand, if one partner does a greater share of the work, or has more experience and ability, or puts in more capital, the ratio of profit sharing might be different.

(c) **Interest on capital**. Partners might agree to pay themselves interest on the capital they put into the business. If they do so, the agreement will state what rate of interest is to be applied.

(d) **Partners' salaries**. Partners might also agree to pay themselves salaries. These are not salaries in the same way that an employee of the business will be paid a wage or salary, because partners' salaries are an appropriation of profit, and not an expense in the income statement of the business. The purpose of paying salaries is to give each partner a satisfactory basic income before the residual profits are shared out.

(e) **Drawings.** Partners may draw out their share of profits from the business. However, they might agree to put a limit on how much they should draw out in any period. If so, this limit should be specified in the partnership agreement. To encourage partners to delay making withdrawals from the business until the financial year has ended, the agreement might also be that partners should be charged interest on their drawings during the year.

In the absence of an agreement, express or implied, between the partners, or where an agreement is silent on particular points, legislation may apply. In the UK, the Partnership Act 1890 states that, where there is no agreement:

(a) Partners share equally in the profits and losses of the partnership

(b) Partners are not entitled to receive salaries

(c) Partners are not entitled to interest on their capital

(d) Partners may receive interest at 5% per annum on any advances over and above their agreed capital

(e) A new partner may not be introduced without the consent of all the existing partners

(f) A retiring partner is entitled to receive interest at 5% per annum on his share of the partnership assets (his capital) retained within the partnership after his retirement

(g) On the dissolution of a partnership the assets of the firm must be used (in the following order)

(i) to repay outside creditors (loans and other payables)
(ii) to repay partners' advances
(iii) to repay partners' capital
(iv) to distribute any residue to the partners in profit sharing ratio

1.3 Preparing partnership accounts

Partnership accounts are identical in many respects to the accounts of sole traders.

(a) The assets of a partnership are like the assets of any other business, and are accounted for in the same way. The assets side of a partnership statement of financial position is the same as for a sole trader.

(b) The net profit of a partnership is calculated in the same way as the net profit of a sole trader. The only minor difference is that if a partner makes a loan to the business (as distinct from capital contribution) then interest on the loan will be an expense in the income statement, in the same way as interest on any other loan from a person or organisation who is not a partner. We will return to partner loans later in the chapter.

There are two respects in which partnership accounts are different, however.

(a) The funds (capital) put into the business by each partner are shown differently.

(b) The net profit must be **appropriated** by the partners, ie shared out according to the partnership agreement. This appropriation of profits must be shown in the partnership accounts.

1.4 Partnership capital

Just as capital contributed by a sole trader to his business is recorded in his capital account, the capital contributed to a partnership is recorded in a series of **capital accounts, one for each partner**. The amount of each partner's contribution usually depends upon the partnership agreement, and since each partner is ultimately entitled to repayment of his capital it is vital to keep a continuous record of his interest in the firm.

1.5 Current accounts

A **current account** for each partner is maintained to record a wide range of items on a continuous basis, for example, to charge drawings and other personal benefits and to credit salaries, interest on capital, share of profits etc.

The main differences between the capital and current account in accounting for partnerships are as follows.

(a) (i) The balance on the capital account remains static from year to year (with one or two exceptions).

(ii) The current account is continually fluctuating up and down, as the partnership makes profits which are shared out between the partners, and as each partner makes drawings.

(b) A further difference is that when the partnership agreement provides for interest on capital, partners receive interest on the balance in their capital account, but *not on the balance in their current account*.

The drawings accounts serve exactly the same purpose as the drawings account for a sole trader. Each partner's drawings are recorded in a separate account. At the end of an accounting period, each partner's drawings are cleared to his current account.

DEBIT	Current account of partner
CREDIT	Drawings account of partner

(If the amount of the drawings exceeds the balance on a partner's current account, the current account will show a debit balance. However, in normal circumstances, we should expect to find a credit balance on the current accounts.)

The partnership statement of financial position will therefore consist of:

(a) the capital accounts of each partner; and
(b) the current accounts of each partner, net of drawings.

1.6 Loans to the partnership

Where an existing or previous partner makes a **loan to the partnership** he becomes a **creditor** of the partnership.

(a) If the partnership is short of cash (which often happens) and the existing partners do not wish to contribute further capital which would be tied up in the business for many years, one or more of them may be prepared to enter into a formal loan agreement for a specified period and at a realistic interest rate.

(b) When a partner retires, if there is insufficient cash to pay the balance owed to him (the total of his capital and current account balances), the amount which he cannot yet be paid is usually transferred to a loan account.

In the partnership statement of financial position a loan is shown separately as a non-current liability (unless it is repayable within twelve months), whether or not the loan creditor is also an existing partner.

However, **interest on such loans will be credited to the partner's current account.** This is administratively more convenient, especially when the partner does not particularly want to be paid the loan interest in cash immediately it becomes due. You should bear in mind the following.

(a) Interest on loans from a partner is accounted for as an expense in the income statement, and not as an appropriation of profit, even though the interest is added to the current account of the partners.

(b) If there is no interest rate specified, national legislation *may* provide for interest to be paid at a specified percentage on loans by partners. In the UK, loans to the partnership attract interest at 5% per annum (Partnership Act 1890) unless there is agreement to the contrary.

1.7 Presentation of capital accounts

In the statement of financial position, the **funds employed** (partnership capital) is shown in the following way.

	£	£
Capital accounts		
Jill	10,000	
Susan	6,000	
		16,000
Current accounts		
Jill	2,500	
Susan	(1,000)	
		1,500
		17,500

Note that, unlike in a sole trader's statement of financial position, the profit and drawings figures are not shown separately. They have been absorbed into the current accounts and only the balances appear on the final accounts.

1.8 Appropriation of net profits

When a sole trader's net profit has been ascertained it is appropriated by him, ie credited to his capital account. He may or may not remove it from the business in the form of drawings. The net profit of a partnership is appropriated by the partners, according to whatever formula they choose, and the sharing out of profit between them is detailed in an **appropriation account**. The appropriation account is normally shown below the income statement.

The following factors have to be taken into consideration.

(a) **Interest**. Partners can agree to credit themselves with interest on capital account balances and, more rarely, interest may be allowed (or charged) on current accounts. This is a means of compensating partners for funds tied up in the business that could be earning interest if invested elsewhere. However, the rate of interest agreed upon often bears little relation to current market rates.

(b) **Salaries**. Partners can agree to credit one or more partners with fixed salaries. This can be a means of compensating a partner for particularly valuable services rendered, especially if his share of profits is otherwise small.

(c) **Share of residual profits (or losses).** After allowing any interest and salaries, partners share remaining profits (or losses) according to their profit sharing ratio. Unless fixed by the partnership agreement they are divided equally.

All these appropriations of profit (or loss) are credited (or debited) to the partners' current accounts.

Remember that interest on a loan account represents an expense charged against profit, whereas **interest on a capital account** is an appropriation of profit. Loan interest must therefore be deducted before arriving at the figure of net profit available for appropriation.

1.9 Format of partnership accounts

In the statement of financial position, partners' capital and current ledger accounts are normally shown side by side, in **columnar form**.

EXAMPLE: PARTNERSHIP ACCOUNTS

Crossly, Steels and Nabs are partners in a music business, sharing profits in the ratio 5:3:2 respectively. Their capital and current account balances on 1 January 20X1 were as follows.

	Capital accounts	*Current accounts*
	£	£
Crossly	24,000	2,000
Steels	18,000	(1,000) Dr
Nabs	13,000	1,500

Interest at 10% per annum is given on the fixed capitals, and salaries of £8,000 per annum are credited to Steels and Nabs.

Crossly made a personal loan of £20,000 to the partnership on 1 July 20X1. The loan was to be repaid in full on 30 June 20X4 and loan interest at the rate of 15% per annum was to be credited to Crossly's account every half year.

The partnership profit (before charging loan interest) for the year ended 31 December 20X1 was £63,000 and the partners had made drawings of: Crossly £16,000; Steels £16,500; Nabs £19,000, during the year.

Prepare the appropriation account, the partners' capital and current accounts and the partnership statement of financial position in respect of the year ended 31 December 20X1.

ANSWER

APPROPRIATION ACCOUNT
FOR THE YEAR ENDED 31 DECEMBER 20X1

	£	£
Net profit*		61,500
Interest on capital accounts		
Crossly	2,400	
Steels	1,800	
Nabs	1,300	
	5,500	
Salaries		
Steels	8,000	
Nabs	8,000	
	16,000	
		21,500
		40,000
Partners' shares of balance		
Crossly (5/10)		20,000
Steels (3/10)		12,000
Nabs (2/10)		8,000
		40,000

	£
*Profit per question	63,000
Less loan interest to Crossly: 15% × £20,000 × 1/2	1,500
Net profit available for appropriation	61,500

PARTNERS' CAPITAL ACCOUNTS

	Crossly	Steels	Nabs		Crossly	Steels	Nabs
	£	£	£		£	£	£
				Balances b/f	24,000	18,000	13,000

PARTNERS' CURRENT ACCOUNTS

	Crossly	Steels	Nabs		Crossly	Steels	Nabs
	£	£	£		£	£	£
Balances b/f	-	1,000	-	Balances b/f	2,000	-	1,500
Drawings				Loan interest	1,500	-	-
Balances c/d	9,900	4,300	-	Appropriation a/c			
				Interest	2,400	1,800	1,300
				Balance	20,000	12,000	8,000
				Balance c/d			200
	25,900	21,800	19,000		25,900	21,800	19,000

STATEMENT OF FINANCIAL POSITION AS AT 31 DECEMBER 20X1

		£
Total assets less current liabilities (balancing figure)		89,000
Partners' capital accounts		
Crossly	24,000	
Steels	18,000	
Nabs	13,000	
		55,000
Partners' current accounts		
Crossly	9,900	
Steels	4,300	
Nabs	(200)	
		14,000
		69,000
Non-current liabilities		
Crossly: loan		20,000
		89,000

It is possible that salaries and interest on capital may **exceed the partnership profit**, or indeed, increase a partnership loss. The usual treatment is to credit the partners with their salaries, interest on capital etc and divide the total loss between them in the usual profit sharing ratio.

Activity 2 **(10 minutes)**

Suppose Bill and Ben are partners sharing profit in the ratio 2:1 and that they agree to pay themselves a salary of £10,000 each. If profits before deducting salaries are £26,000, how much income would each partner receive?

Chapter roundup

- This chapter has introduced the basic principles of accounting for partnerships. In general, in income statement may be prepared for a partnership in exactly the same way as for a sole trader. In the appropriation account the net profit is then apportioned between the partners according to the partnership agreement.
- In the partnership statement of financial position, net assets are financed by partners' capital and current accounts. Current accounts must be credited with the profits appropriated to each partner for the year, and debited with partners' drawings. It is essential to remember that drawings, salaries and interest on capital are *not* expenses. Drawings only affect the statement of financial position. Salaries and interest on capital are appropriations of profit.

Quick quiz

1 A partner's salary is an expense of the partnership. Is this statement:

(a) True

(b) False

2 In the statement of financial position of a partnership, how is a loan from a partner disclosed?

3 Interest on a loan made by a partner is shown as an appropriation of profit, not as an expense. True or false?

Answers to Quick quiz

1 (b) False. It is an appropriation of profit.

2 A loan from a partner is shown separately as a long-term liability.

3 False. Interest on a loan is an expense charged against profit.

Answers to Activities

1 (a) The main problem with trading as a sole trader is the limitation on resources it implies. As the business grows, there will be a need for:

(i) additional capital. Although some capital may be provided by a bank, it would not be desirable to have the business entirely dependent on borrowing;

(ii) additional expertise. A sole trader technically competent in his own field may not have, for example, the financial skills that would be needed in a larger business;

(iii) additional management time. Once a business grows to a certain point, it becomes impossible for one person to look after all aspects of it without help.

(b) The main disadvantage of incorporating is the regulatory burden faced by limited companies. In addition, there are certain 'businesses' which are not allowed to enjoy limited liability; you may have read about the Lloyd's 'names' who face personal bankruptcy because the option of limited liability was not available to them.

There are also tax factors to consider, but these are beyond the scope of this book.

2 First, the two salaries are deducted from profit, leaving £6,000 (£26,000 – £20,000).

This £6,000 has to be distributed between Bill and Ben in the ratio 2:1. In other words, Bill will receive twice as much as Ben. You can probably work this out in your head and see that Bill will get £4,000 and Ben £2,000, but we had better see how this is calculated properly.

Add the 'parts' of the ratio together. For our example, 2 + 1 = 3. Divide this total into whatever it is that has to be shared out. In our example, £6,000 ÷ 3 = £2,000. Each 'part' is worth £2,000, so Bill receives 2 × £2,000 = £4,000 and Ben will receive 1 × £2,000 = £2,000.

So the final answer to the question is that Bill receives his salary plus £4,000 and Ben his salary plus £2,000. This could be laid out as follows:

	Bill	*Ben*	*Total*
	£	£	£
Salary	10,000	10,000	20,000
Share of residual profits (ratio 2:1)	4,000	2,000	6,000
	14,000	12,000	26,000

Chapter : 22

INTERPRETING FINANCIAL STATEMENTS

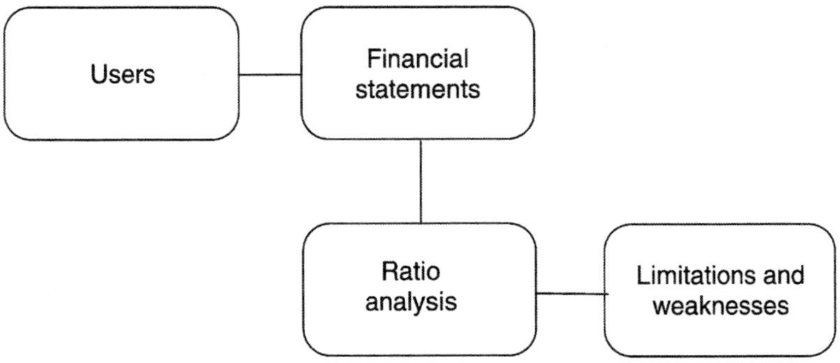

Introduction

Financial statements are prepared for a reason: to provide information. Users need information in order to make decisions about a business. For example, shareholders of a limited company often need to decide whether to sell their shares or continue to hold them.

Users and their advisers must interpret the figures in the financial statements. How do they decide whether a company is performing well or badly? Or whether it is a safe investment or a risky investment? What do they look at in the figures in the income statement and the statement of financial position to help them to make their judgement?

Ratio analysis is the main technique used to interpret a set of financial statements. It involves comparing one figure with another to calculate a ratio and then assessing whether the ratio indicates a weakness or a strength.

In this chapter we concentrate on ratio analysis: the main ratios and what they measure; how to interpret them; how to report your conclusions; and the limitations of this type of analysis.

Your objectives

In this chapter, you will learn about the following.

(a) User needs and how they relate to ratio analysis

(b) Calculating ratios that reflect profitability, liquidity, efficiency and gearing

(c) Comparing these ratios with other ratios and interpreting the results

(d) The limitations of ratio analysis

1 USERS OF THE FINANCIAL STATEMENTS AND THEIR INFORMATION NEEDS

1.1 Purpose of financial statements

Both the ASB and the IASB have developed and published statements that explain the purpose of financial statements and the general principles that should be followed in preparing and presenting financial statements. Accounting standards reflect these principles.

The ASB **Statement of Principles for Financial Reporting** and the IASB **Framework for the Preparation and Presentation of Financial Statements** are very similar. Both of them state that the objective of financial statements is to provide information about a company's financial performance and financial position that is useful to a **wide range of users** for **assessing the stewardship** of the entity's management and for **making economic decisions**.

Financial information about a company is of interest to a wide range of users. Some of these users are able to obtain special-purpose reports about a company specific to their information needs. Management can obtain internal management accounting reports, and on occasion, someone else, such as a lending bank or the tax authorities, can obtain specially-prepared reports. Many users of accounts, however, do not have access to special-purpose reports, and must rely for their information on general purpose financial statements, normally the company's published financial statements.

1.2 Users of financial statements

Both the ASB and the IASB identify a number of different groups of users of financial statements

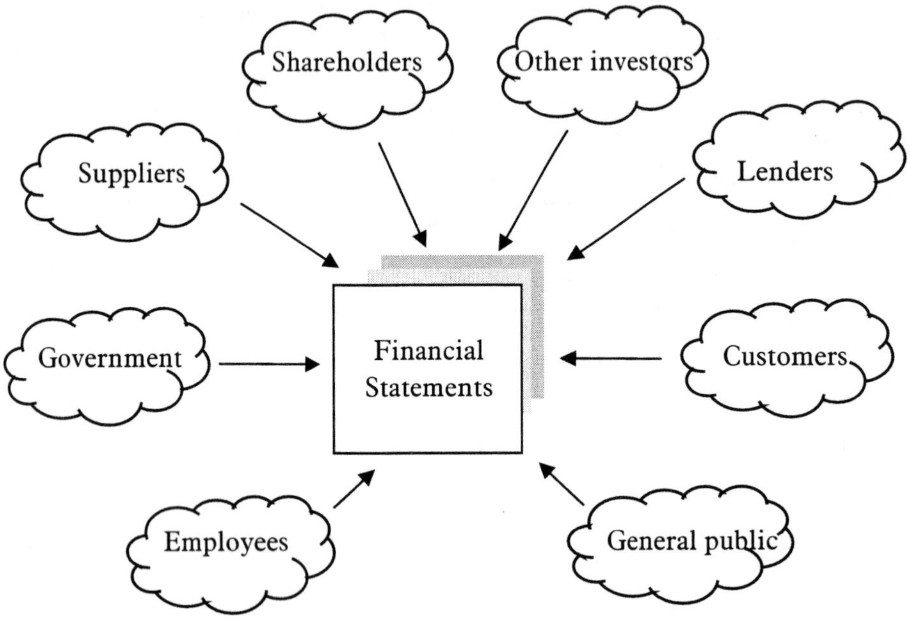

The ASB and the IASB suggest that although there are many different users of general purpose financial statements, the needs of all these users will be met if the information provided in the statements meets the requirements of present and future investors in the company.

1.3 Financial statements for assessing stewardship

Management is accountable to investors for the stewardship of the company. To understand this, you might find it useful to think of the stewardship of an estate, which involves looking after the assets and condition of the estate, and managing it in the interest of the owner. In much the same way, managers are responsible for the safeguarding of the assets and other resources of the company, and for putting these resources to an efficient and profitable use. Investors will be interested in any **information that helps them to judge how well management has carried out their stewardship responsibility**.

1.4 Using financial statements to make economic decisions

Various groups make use of a company's financial statements to make economic decisions.

(a) Present and potential **investors** in the company will consider their investment decision. Should they buy shares in the company? Should they sell their shares? To make an investment decision, the investor needs information about profitability and the ability to generate cash to pay dividends, and also about the risks in the investment. Financial statements should help an investor to assess both the cash-generating capabilities of a company, and also its ability to respond to risks and change (its financial adaptability).

(b) **Lenders** to a company will be interested in any information that helps them to assess whether the company will have the ability to meet its obligations: to pay interest and repay the loan principal on time. Potential lenders need similar information to decide whether to lend to the company, and if so, how much and on what terms.

(c) **Suppliers** to the company need to know how reliable the company will be in paying its debts, and how much credit can safely be given.

(d) **Employees** want information about the financial stability and profitability of their employer, particularly in the part of the company's business where they work. Their decision to remain with the company will depend to a large extent on the ability of the company to continue to offer them secure and well-paid employment. They will also be interested in how much the company is earning in order to reach a view on what remuneration levels should be.

(e) **Customers** are interested in the financial performance and position of a company in order to decide whether to continue buying from it. Where a customer relies on a long-term warranty, or expects to purchase replacement parts from the company over a long period, it will want reassurance that the company is financially stable, with good long-term future prospects.

(f) The **government** (and its agencies) can often obtain the information it needs from a company from special-purpose reports. Even so, general purpose financial statements can provide additional useful information. For example, the tax authorities are provided with specially-prepared information about the company's trading and profits to determine how much tax is payable. A comparison with general purpose financial statements can then help the tax authorities to assess whether the amounts payable in tax seem consistent with the published information. They would certainly be interested if a company declares profits of several million pounds but pays no corporation tax.

(g) A company's activities have an influence on the **community at large**. A major employer in a local community, for example, will help to boost the local economy and stimulate business and employment. Members of the general public might therefore use the financial statements of a company to assess trends and recent developments in its business, and the implications these might have in the future.

1.5 Types of financial information available to users

The information needs of different users are not the same. Financial statements do not provide all the information that individuals need, or would like, to make their decisions, and the **limitations** of a company's report and accounts should be understood. Financial statements are **backward-looking,** reporting what has happened in the past, when users are more often concerned with the **future**. They also report on the company in purely **financial** terms, and do not properly address **non-financial** matters.

Managers responsible for the running of a business are likely to find **detailed management accounts** showing actual performance against budget, usually on a monthly basis, to be more useful than statutory financial statements. Moreover, these are likely to be used alongside **business plans** projected into the future usually over a period of three to five years.

1.6 Investor focus

In reaching their decisions about what financial statements should disclose, the ASB and IASB take the view that **investors are the 'defining class of user'**. Investors need information about the ability of a company to generate profits and cash flows from its operations and on the company's financial adaptability (ie its ability to respond to unexpected events and new opportunities). Essentially, other user groups are interested in the same information. 'Therefore, in preparing financial statements, it is assumed that financial statements that **focus on the interest** that **investors** have in the company's financial performance and financial position will, in effect, also be focusing on the common interest that all users have in the company's financial performance and financial position.'

1.7 The information required by investors

Investors need information about a company's financial performance and financial position.

(a) **Financial performance** relates to the **return** that the company has made on the **resources** at its disposal. Information about performance provides an account of the **stewardship** by management, and can also be used to assess the ability of the company to **generate** cash from its **existing resources**. Information about historical performance can help investors to make judgements about future prospects.

(b) The **financial position** of a company relates to the assets that it owns (including its cash position), the liabilities it owes and the amount of capital invested. This information helps investors to assess the **stewardship of management**. It also helps them to understand how the **future cash flows** generated by the business will be distributed among those with an interest in or a claim on the company (eg lenders, suppliers, employees and shareholders). Information about the cash position and liquidity helps investors to assess the **ability** of the company to **meet** its **financial obligations** as they fall due. Information about the **risk profile** of a company will help them to judge the **financial adaptability** of the company, and its ability to deal with **unexpected future setbacks and opportunities**.

(c) The extent to which a company needs to be **financially adaptable** depends on the **risks** that it faces, and the appetite of its shareholders for risk in their investment. Financial adaptability can be provided in several ways, but many relate to the **ability** of the company to **raise new cash** should the need arise. For example, a company is financially adaptable if it is able to raise new capital at **short notice**, for example by borrowing or issuing new debt securities. Alternatively, financial adaptability exists if the company could **sell off assets quickly** without disrupting its **continuing business operations**, or if it can achieve a **rapid improvement** in its ability to generate cash flows from its **ongoing business operations**.

(d) The financial statements consist of the **statement of financial position**, a **statement of comprehensive income** for the period under review and a **statement of cash flows** for the same period. In broad terms, profits and cash flow information can be used to assess the **ability of the company to generate cash**. A statement of financial position provides information about the **financial position**. Taken together, they provide information on **performance** and the **stewardship of management**.

Activity 1 **(10 minutes)**

It is easy to see how 'internal' people get hold of accounting information. A senior manager, for example, can just go along to the accounts department and ask the staff there to prepare whatever accounting statements he needs. But external users of accounts cannot do this. How, in practice, can (a) a business contact, (b) a financial analyst, (c) a bank or (d) an employee of the company obtain financial statements about the company?

2 THE BROAD CATEGORIES OF RATIOS

Broadly speaking, basic ratios can be grouped into five categories.

(a) Profitability and return
(b) Long-term solvency and stability
(c) Short-term solvency and liquidity
(d) Efficiency (turnover ratios)
(e) Shareholders' investment ratios

Within each heading we will identify a number of standard measures or ratios that are normally calculated and generally accepted as meaningful indicators. One must stress however that each individual business must be considered separately, and a ratio that is meaningful for a manufacturing company may be completely meaningless for a financial institution. Try not to be too mechanical when working out ratios and constantly think about what you are trying to achieve.

The key to obtaining meaningful information from ratio analysis is **comparison**. This may involve comparing ratios over time within the same business to establish whether things are improving or declining, and comparing ratios between similar businesses to see whether the company you are analysing is better or worse than average within its specific business sector.

It must be stressed that ratio analysis **on its own is not sufficient for interpreting** company accounts, and that there are other items of information which should be looked at, for example:

(a) Comments in the Chairman's report and directors' report

(b) The age and nature of the company's assets

(c) Current and future developments in the company's markets, at home and overseas

(d) Any other noticeable features of the report and accounts, such as notes describing events after the reporting period, a qualified auditors' report, the company's taxation position, and so on

---

EXAMPLE: CALCULATING RATIOS

To illustrate the calculation of ratios, the following statement of financial position and income statement figures will be used.

FURLONG PLC INCOME STATEMENT
FOR THE YEAR ENDED 31 DECEMBER 20X8

	Notes	*20X8*	*20X7*
		£	£
Revenue	1	3,095,576	1,909,051
Profit from operations	1	359,501	244,229
Finance costs	2	17,371	19,127
Profit before taxation		342,130	225,102
Income tax expense		74,200	31,272
Profit for the year		267,930	193,830
Earnings per share		12.8p	9.2p

NOTES

FURLONG PLC STATEMENT OF FINANCIAL POSITION AS AT 31 DECEMBER 20X8

	Notes	20X8	20X7
		£	£
Assets			
Non-current assets			
Property, plant and equipment		802,180	656,071
Current assets			
Inventory		64,422	86,550
Receivables	3	1,002,701	853,441
Cash at bank and in hand		1,327	68,363
		1,068,450	1,008,354
Total assets		1,870,630	1,664,425
Equity and liabilities			
Equity			
Ordinary shares 10p each		210,000	210,000
Share premium account		48,178	48,178
Retained earnings		651,721	410,591
		909,899	668,769
Non-current liabilities			
10% loan stock 20X4/20Y0		100,000	100,000
Current liabilities	4	860,731	895,656
Total equity and liabilities		1,870,630	1,664,425

NOTES TO THE ACCOUNTS

		20X8	20X7
		£	£
1	*Sales revenue and profit*		
	Sales revenue	3,095,576	1,909,051
	Cost of sales	2,402,609	1,441,950
	Gross profit	692,967	467,101
	Administrative expenses	333,466	222,872
	Profit from operations	359,501	244,229
	Depreciation charged	151,107	120,147
2	*Interest*		
	Payable on bank overdrafts and other loans	8,115	11,909
	Payable on loan stock	10,000	10,000
		18,115	21,909
	Receivable on short-term deposits	744	2,782
	Net payable	17,371	19,127
3	*Receivables*		
	Amounts falling due within one year		
	Trade receivables	905,679	807,712
	Prepayments and accrued income	97,022	45,729
		1,002,701	853,441
4	*Current liabilities*		
	Trade payables	627,018	545,340
	Accruals and deferred income	81,279	280,464
	Corporate taxes	108,000	37,200
	Other taxes	44,434	32,652
		860,731	895,656
5	Dividends paid	20,000	–

3 PROFITABILITY AND RETURN ON CAPITAL

3.1 PBIT

In our example, the company made a profit in both 20X8 and 20X7, and there was an increase in profit on ordinary activities between one year and the next:

- Of 52% before taxation
- Of 38% after taxation

Profit ***before*** **taxation** is generally thought to be a **better** figure to use **than profit after taxation,** because there might be unusual variations in the tax charge from year to year which would not affect the underlying profitability of the company's operations.

Another profit figure that should be calculated is **PBIT, profit before interest** and tax. This is the amount of profit which the company earned before having to pay interest to the providers of loan capital. By providers of loan capital, we usually mean longer-term loan capital, such as loan stock and medium-term bank loans, which will be shown in the statement of financial position as non-current liabilities.

Profit before interest and tax is therefore:

- Profit before taxation; PLUS
- Interest charges on long-term loan capital

Published accounts do not always give sufficient detail on interest payable to determine how much is interest on long-term finance. We will assume in our example that the whole of the interest payable (£18,115, note 2) relates to long-term finance.

PBIT in our example is therefore:

	20X8	*20X7*
	£	£
Profit before tax	342,130	225,102
Interest payable	18,115	21,909
PBIT	360,245	247,011

This shows a 46% growth between 20X7 and 20X8.

3.2 Return on capital employed (ROCE)

It is impossible to assess profits or profit growth properly without relating them to the amount of funds (capital) that were employed in making the profits. The most important profitability ratio is therefore return on capital employed (ROCE), which states the profit as a percentage of the amount of capital employed.

Definitions

$$\textbf{ROCE} = \frac{\text{Profit before interest and taxation}}{\text{Capital employed}}$$

Capital employed = Shareholders' equity plus non-current liabilities (*or* total assets less current liabilities).

NOTES

The underlying principle is that we must compare like with like, and so if capital means share capital and reserves plus non-current liabilities and debt capital, profit must mean the profit earned by all this capital together. This is PBIT, since interest is the return for loan capital.

EXAMPLE: ROCE

In our example, capital employed = 20X8 1,870,670 – 860,731 = £1,009,899
20X7 1,664,425 – 895,656 = £768,769

These total figures are the total assets less current liabilities figures for 20X8 and 20X7 in the statement of financial position.

		20X8	*20X7*
ROCE	=	$\frac{360,245}{1,009,899} = 35.7\%$	$\frac{247,011}{768,769} = 32.1\%$

What does a company's ROCE tell us? What should we be looking for? There are three comparisons that can be made.

(a) The change in ROCE from one year to the next can be examined. In this example, there has been an increase in ROCE by about 4 percentage points from its 20X7 level.

(b) The ROCE being earned by other companies, if this information is available, can be compared with the ROCE of this company. Here the information is not available.

(c) A **comparison** of the ROCE with **current market borrowing** rates may be made.

    (i) What would be the cost of extra borrowing to the company if it needed more loans, and is it earning a ROCE that suggests it could make profits to make such borrowing worthwhile?

    (ii) Is the company making a ROCE which suggests that it is getting value for money from its current borrowing?

    (iii) Companies are in a risk business and commercial borrowing rates are a good independent yardstick against which company performance can be judged.

In this example, if we suppose that current market interest rates, say, for medium-term borrowing from banks, are around 10%, then the company's actual ROCE of 36% in 20X8 would not seem low. On the contrary, it might seem high.

However, it is **easier to spot a low ROCE than a high one**, because there is always a chance that the company's **non-current assets**, especially property, **are undervalued** in its statement of financial position, and so the capital employed figure might be unrealistically low. If the company had earned a ROCE, not of 36%, but of, say only 6%, then its return would have been below current borrowing rates and so disappointingly low.

3.3 Return on equity (ROE)

Another measure of profitability and return is the return on shareholders' equity (ROE), sometimes called return on owners' equity (ROOE):

Definition

$$\text{ROE} = \frac{\text{Profit after tax}}{\text{Equity shareholders' funds}}$$

It is intended to focus on the return being made by the company for the benefit of its shareholders, and in our example, the figures are:

20X8	*20X7*
$\frac{267,930}{909,899} = 29.4\%$	$\frac{193,830}{668,769} = 29\%$

These figures show an improvement between 20X7 and 20X8, and a return which is clearly in excess of current borrowing rates.

ROE is not a widely-used ratio, however, because there are more useful ratios that give an indication of the return to shareholders, such as earnings per share and dividend per share, which are described later.

3.4 Analysing profitability and return in more detail: the secondary ratios

We often sub-analyse ROCE, to find out more about why the ROCE is high or low, or better or worse than last year. There are two factors that contribute towards a return on capital employed, both related to sales turnover.

(a) **Profit margin**. A company might make a high or low profit margin on its sales. For example, a company that makes a profit of 25p per £1 of sales is making a bigger return on its turnover than another company making a profit of only 10p per £1 of sales.

(b) **Asset turnover**. Asset turnover is a measure of how well the assets of a business are being used to generate sales. For example, if two companies each have capital employed of £100,000 and Company A makes sales of £400,000 per annum whereas Company B makes sales of only £200,000 per annum, Company A is making a higher turnover from the same amount of assets (twice as much asset turnover as Company B) and this will help A to make a higher return on capital employed than B. Asset turnover is expressed as 'x times' so that assets generate x times their value in annual turnover. Here, Company A's asset turnover is 4 times and B's is 2 times.

Profit margin and asset turnover together explain the ROCE and if the ROCE is the primary profitability ratio, these other two are the secondary ratios. The relationship between the three ratios can be shown mathematically.

NOTES

Definition

Profit margin × Asset turnover = ROCE

$$\therefore \frac{\text{PBIT}}{\text{Sales}} \times \frac{\text{Sales}}{\text{Capital employed}} = \frac{\text{PBIT}}{\text{Capital employed}}$$

In our example:

	Profit margin		*Asset turnover*		*ROCE*
(a) 20X8	$\frac{360,245}{3,095,576}$	×	$\frac{3,095,576}{1,009,899}$	=	$\frac{360,245}{1,009,899}$
	11.64%	×	3.06 times	=	35.6%
(b) 20X7	$\frac{247,011}{1,909,051}$	×	$\frac{1,909,051}{768,769}$	=	$\frac{247,011}{768,769}$
	12.94%	×	2.48 times	=	32.1%

In this example, the company's improvement in ROCE between 20X7 and 20X8 is attributable to a higher asset turnover. Indeed the profit margin has fallen a little, but the higher asset turnover has more than compensated for this.

It is also worth commenting on the change in sales revenue from one year to the next. You may already have noticed that Furlong plc achieved sales growth of over 60% from £1.9 million to £3.1 million between 20X7 and 20X8. This is very strong growth, and this is certainly one of the most significant items in the income statement and statement of financial position.

3.5 A warning about comments on profit margin and asset turnover

It might be tempting to think that a high profit margin is good, and a low asset turnover means sluggish trading. In broad terms, this is so. But there is a **trade-off between profit margin and asset turnover**, and you cannot look at one without allowing for the other.

(a) A high profit margin means a high profit per £1 of sales, but if this also means that sales prices are high, there is a strong possibility that sales revenue will be depressed, and so asset turnover lower.

(b) A high asset turnover means that the company is generating a lot of sales, but to do this it might have to keep its prices down and so accept a low profit margin per £1 of sales.

Consider the following.

Company A		*Company B*	
Sales	£1,000,000	Sales	£4,000,000
Capital employed	£1,000,000	Capital employed	£1,000,000
PBIT	£200,000	PBIT	£200,000

These figures would give the following ratios.

ROCE	$= \frac{200,000}{1,000,000}$	= 20%	ROCE	$= \frac{200,000}{1,000,000}$	= 20%
Profit margin	$= \frac{200,000}{1,000,000}$	= 20%	Profit margin	$= \frac{200,000}{4,000,000}$	= 5%
Asset turnover	$= \frac{1,000,000}{1,000,000}$	= 1	Asset turnover	$= \frac{4,000,000}{1,000,000}$	= 4

The companies have the same ROCE, but it is arrived at in a very different fashion. Company A operates with a low asset turnover and a comparatively high profit margin whereas company B carries out much more business, but on a lower profit margin. Company A could be operating at the luxury end of the market, whilst company B is operating at the popular end of the market.

Activity 2 **(5 minutes)**

Which one of the following formulae correctly expresses the relationship between return on capital employed (ROCE), profit margin (PM) and asset turnover (AT)?

A PM $= \frac{AT}{ROCE}$

B ROCE $= \frac{PM}{AT}$

C AT = PM × ROCE

D PM $= \frac{ROCE}{AT}$

3.6 Gross profit margin, net profit margin and profit analysis

Depending on the format of the income statement, you may be able to calculate the gross profit margin as well as the net profit margin. Looking at the two together can be quite informative.

For example, suppose that a company has the following summarised income statement for two consecutive years.

	Year 1	*Year 2*
	£	£
Revenue	70,000	100,000
Cost of sales	42,000	55,000
Gross profit	28,000	45,000
Expenses	21,000	35,000
Net profit	7,000	10,000

Although the net profit margin is the same for both years at 10%, the gross profit margin is not.

In year 1 it is: $\frac{28,000}{70,000} = 40\%$

and in year 2 it is: $\frac{45,000}{100,000}$ = 45%

The improved gross profit margin has not led to an improvement in the net profit margin. This is because expenses as a percentage of sales have risen from 30% in year 1 to 35% in year 2.

4 LIQUIDITY, GEARING AND WORKING CAPITAL

4.1 Long-term solvency: debt and gearing ratios

Debt ratios are concerned with **how much the company owes in relation to its size**, whether it is getting into heavier debt or improving its situation, and whether its debt burden seems heavy or light.

(a) When a company is heavily in debt banks and other potential lenders may be unwilling to advance further funds.

(b) When a company is earning only a modest profit before interest and tax, and has a heavy debt burden, there will be very little profit left over for shareholders after the interest charges have been paid. And so if interest rates were to go up (on bank overdrafts and so on) or the company were to borrow even more, it might soon be incurring interest charges in excess of PBIT. This might eventually lead to the liquidation of the company.

These are two big reasons why companies should keep their debt burden under control. There are four ratios that are particularly worth looking at, the **debt** ratio, **gearing** ratio, **interest cover** and **cash flow** ratio.

4.2 Debt ratio

The **debt ratio** is the ratio of a **company's total debts to its total assets.**

Assets consist of non-current assets at their carrying amount, plus current assets. Debts consist of all liabilities, whether they are current liabilities or non-current liabilities (due after more than one year).

There is no absolute guide to the maximum safe debt ratio, but as a **very general guide**, you might regard **50% as a safe limit** to debt. In practice, many companies operate successfully with a higher debt ratio than this, but 50% is nonetheless a helpful benchmark. In addition, if the debt ratio is over 50% and getting worse, the company's debt position will be worth looking at more carefully.

In the case of Furlong plc the debt ratio is as follows.

	20X8	*20X7*
Total debts	(860,731 + 100,000)	(895,656 + 100,000)
Total assets	1,870,630	1,664,425
	= 51%	= 60%

In this case, the debt ratio is quite high, mainly because of the large amount of current liabilities. However, the debt ratio has fallen from 60% to 51% between 20X7 and 20X8, and so the company appears to be improving its debt position.

4.3 Gearing ratio

Capital gearing is concerned with a company's **long-term capital structure**. We can think of a company as consisting of non-current assets and net current assets (ie working capital, which is current assets minus current liabilities). These assets must be financed by **long-term capital** of the company, which is **one of two** things.

(a) Issued share capital which can be divided into:

  (i) Ordinary shares plus other equity (eg reserves)
  (ii) Non-redeemable preference shares (these are unusual)

(b) Long-term debt including redeemable preference shares.

Preference share capital is normally classified as a non-current liability, and preference dividends (paid or accrued) are included in finance costs in the income statement.

The **capital gearing ratio** is a measure of the proportion of a company's capital that is prior charge capital. It is measured as follows:

Definition

$$\textbf{Capital gearing ratio} = \frac{\text{long term debt}}{\text{shareholders' equity + long term debt}}$$

As with the debt ratio, there is no absolute limit to what a gearing ratio ought to be. A company with a gearing ratio of **more than 50%** is said to be **high-geared** (whereas low gearing means a gearing ratio of less than 50%). Many companies are high geared, but if a high geared company is becoming increasingly high geared, it is likely to have difficulty in the future when it wants to borrow even more, unless it can also boost its shareholders' capital, either with retained profits or by a new share issue.

A similar ratio to the gearing ratio is the **debt/equity ratio**, which is calculated as follows.

Definition

$$\textbf{Debt/equity ratio} = \frac{\text{long term debt}}{\text{shareholders' equity (share capital and reserves)}}$$

This gives us the same sort of information as the gearing ratio, and a ratio of 100% or more would indicate high gearing.

In the example of Furlong plc, we find that the company, although having a high debt ratio because of its current liabilities, has a low gearing ratio. It has no preference share capital and its only long-term debt is the 10% loan stock.

	20X8	*20X7*
Gearing ratio	$\frac{100{,}000}{1{,}009{,}899} = 10\%$	$\frac{100{,}000}{768{,}769} = 13\%$
Debt/equity ratio	$\frac{100{,}000}{909{,}899} = 11\%$	$\frac{100{,}000}{668{,}769} = 15\%$

4.4 The implications of high or low gearing

We mentioned earlier that gearing is, amongst other things, an attempt to quantify the **degree of risk** involved in holding equity shares in a company, risk both in terms of the company's ability to remain in business and in terms of expected ordinary dividends from the company. The problem with a high geared company is that by definition there is a lot of debt. Debt generally carries a fixed rate of interest (or fixed rate of dividend if in the form of preference shares), hence there is a given (and large) amount to be paid out from profits to holders of debt before arriving at a residue available for distribution to the holders of equity. The riskiness will perhaps become clearer with the aid of an example.

	Company A	*Company B*	*Company C*
	£'000	£'000	£'000
Ordinary share capital	600	400	300
Retained earnings	200	200	200
Revaluation reserve	100	100	100
	900	700	600
6% preference shares (redeemable)	-	-	100
10% loan stock	100	300	300
Capital employed	1,000	1,000	1,000
Gearing ratio	10%	30%	40%

Now suppose that each company makes a profit before interest and tax of £50,000, and the rate of corporation tax is 30%. Amounts available for distribution to equity shareholders will be as follows:

	Company A	*Company B*	*Company C*
	£'000	£'000	£'000
Profit before interest and tax	50	50	50
Interest/preference dividend	10	30	36
Profit before tax	40	20	14
Taxation at 30%	12	6	6
Available for ordinary shareholders	28	14	8

If in the subsequent year profit before interest and tax falls to £40,000, the amounts available to ordinary shareholders will become:

	Company A	*Company B*	*Company C*
	£'000	£'000	£'000
Profit before interest and tax	40	40	40
Interest/preference dividends	10	30	36
Profit before tax	30	10	4
Taxation at 30%	9	3	3
Available for ordinary shareholders	21	7	1

Note the following.

Gearing ratio	10%	30%	40%
Change in PBIT	– 20%	– 20%	– 20%
Change in profit available for ordinary shareholders	– 25%	– 50%	– 87.5%

The more highly geared the company, the greater the risk that little (if anything) will be available to distribute by way of dividend to the ordinary shareholders.

(a) The example clearly displays this fact in so far as the more highly geared the company, the greater the percentage change in profit available for ordinary shareholders for any given percentage change in profit before interest and tax.

(b) The relationship similarly holds when profits increase, and if PBIT had risen by 20% rather than fallen, you would find that once again the largest percentage change in profit available for ordinary shareholders (this means an increase) will be for the highly geared company.

(c) This means that there will be greater volatility of amounts available for ordinary shareholders, and presumably therefore greater volatility in dividends paid to those shareholders, where a company is highly geared. That is the risk: you may do extremely well or extremely badly without a particularly large movement in the PBIT of the company.

The risk of a company's ability to remain in business was referred to earlier. Gearing is relevant to this. A high geared company has a large amount of interest to pay annually (assuming that the debt is external borrowing rather than preference shares). If those borrowings are 'secured' in any way (and loan stock in particular is secured), then the holders of the debt are perfectly entitled to force the company to realise assets to pay their interest if funds are not available from other sources. Clearly the more highly geared a company the more likely this is to occur when and if profits fall.

4.5 Interest cover

The interest cover ratio shows whether a company is earning enough profits before interest and tax to pay its interest costs comfortably, or whether its interest costs are high in relation to the size of its profits, so that a fall in PBIT would then have a significant effect on profits available for ordinary shareholders.

Definition

$$\textbf{Interest cover} = \frac{\text{profit before interest and tax}}{\text{interest charges}}$$

An interest cover of 2 times or less would be low, and should really exceed 3 times before the company's interest costs are to be considered within acceptable limits.

Returning first to the example of Companies A, B and C, the interest cover was as follows.

	Company A	*Company B*	*Company C*
(a) When PBIT was £50,000 =	$\frac{50,000}{10,000}$	$\frac{50,000}{30,000}$	$\frac{50,000}{30,000}$
	5 times	1.67 times	1.67 times

(b) When PBIT was £40,000 =	$\frac{40,000}{10,000}$	$\frac{40,000}{30,000}$	$\frac{40,000}{30,000}$
	4 times	1.33 times	1.33 times

Note. Although preference share capital is included as prior charge capital for the gearing ratio, it is usual to exclude preference dividends from 'interest' charges. We also look at all interest payments, even interest charges on short-term debt, and so interest cover and gearing do not quite look at the same thing.

Both B and C have a low interest cover, which is a warning to ordinary shareholders that their profits are highly vulnerable, in percentage terms, to even small changes in PBIT.

> **Activity 3** **(5 minutes)**
>
> Returning to the example of Furlong plc above, what is the company's interest cover?

4.6 Cash flow ratio

The **cash flow ratio** is the ratio of a company's net cash inflow to its total debts.

(a) Net cash inflow is the amount of cash which the company has coming into the business from its operations. A suitable figure for net cash inflow can be obtained from the statement of cash flows.

(b) Total debts are short-term and long-term payables, together with provisions. A distinction can be made between debts payable within one year and other debts and provisions.

Obviously, a company needs to be earning enough cash from operations to be able to meet its foreseeable debts and future commitments, and the cash flow ratio, and changes in the cash flow ratio from one year to the next, provide a useful indicator of a company's cash position.

4.7 Short-term solvency and liquidity

Profitability is of course an important aspect of a company's performance and debt or gearing is another. Neither, however, addresses directly the key issue of **liquidity**.

Liquidity is the amount of cash a company can put its hands on quickly to settle its debts (and possibly to meet other unforeseen demands for cash payments too).

Liquid funds consist of:

(a) Cash

(b) Short-term investments for which there is a ready market

(c) Fixed-term deposits with a bank or building society, for example, a six month high-interest deposit with a bank

(d) Trade receivables (because they will pay what they owe within a reasonably short period of time)

In summary, **liquid assets** are current asset items that will or could soon be **converted into cash, and cash itself**. Two common definitions of liquid assets are:

(a) All current assets without exception
(b) All current assets with the exception of inventories

A company can obtain liquid assets from sources other than sales, such as the issue of shares for cash, a new loan or the sale of non-current assets. But a company cannot rely on these at all times, and in general, obtaining liquid funds depends on making sales and profits. Even so, profits do not always lead to increases in liquidity. This is mainly because funds generated from trading may be immediately invested in non-current assets or paid out as dividends. You should refer back to the chapter on the statement of cash flows to examine this issue.

The reason why a company needs liquid assets is so that it can meet its debts when they fall due. Payments are continually made for operating expenses and other costs, and so there is a cash cycle from trading activities of cash coming in from sales and cash going out for expenses. This is illustrated by the diagram below.

4.8 The cash cycle

To help you to understand liquidity ratios, it is useful to begin with a brief explanation of the cash cycle. The cash cycle describes the flow of cash out of a business and back into it again as a result of normal trading operations.

Cash goes out to pay for supplies, wages and salaries and other expenses, although payments can be delayed by taking some credit. A business might hold inventory for a while and then sell it. Cash will come back into the business from the sales, although customers might delay payment by themselves taking some credit.

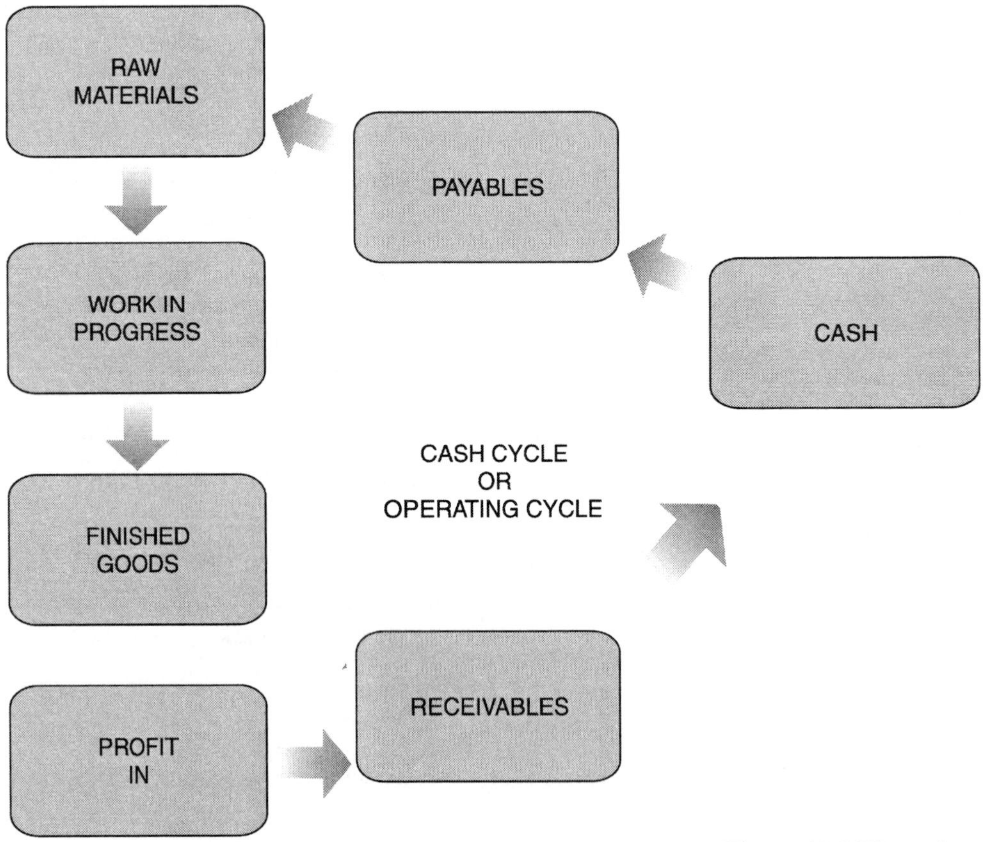

Figure 22.1 The cash cycle

The main points about the cash cycle are as follows.

(a) The **timing of cash flows in and out of a business does not coincide with the time when sales and costs of sales occur**. Cash flows out can be postponed by taking credit. Cash flows in can be delayed by having receivables.

(b) **The time between making a purchase and making a sale also affects cash flows**. If inventories are held for a long time, the delay between the cash payment for inventories and cash receipts from selling them will also be a long one.

(c) Holding inventories and having receivables can therefore be seen as two reasons why cash receipts are delayed. Another way of saying this is that **if a company invests in working capital, its cash position will show a corresponding decrease**.

(d) Similarly, **taking credit from suppliers can be seen as a reason why cash payments are delayed**. The company's liquidity position will worsen when it has to pay the suppliers, unless it can get more cash in from sales and receivables in the meantime.

The liquidity ratios and working capital turnover ratios are used to test a company's liquidity, length of cash cycle, and investment in working capital.

4.9 Liquidity ratios: current ratio and quick ratio

The 'standard' test of liquidity is the **current ratio**. It can be obtained from the statement of financial position, and is calculated as follows.

Definition

$$\textbf{Current ratio} = \frac{\text{current assets}}{\text{current liabilities}}$$

The idea behind this is that a company should have enough current assets that give a promise of 'cash to come' to meet its future commitments to pay off its current liabilities. Obviously, a **ratio in excess of 1** should be expected. Otherwise, there would be the prospect that the company might be unable to pay its debts on time. In practice, a ratio comfortably in excess of 1 should be expected, but what is 'comfortable' varies between different types of businesses.

Companies are not able to convert all their current assets into cash very quickly. In particular, some manufacturing companies might hold large quantities of raw material inventories, which must be used in production to create finished goods inventories. Finished goods inventories might be warehoused for a long time, or sold on lengthy credit. In such businesses, where inventory turnover is slow, most inventories are not very 'liquid' assets, because the cash cycle is so long. For these reasons, we calculate an additional liquidity ratio, known as the **quick ratio** or **acid test** ratio.

Definition

The **quick ratio**, or **acid test ratio** is: $\frac{\text{current assets less inventories}}{\text{current liabilities}}$

This ratio should ideally be at least 1 for companies with a slow inventory turnover. For companies with a fast inventory turnover, a quick ratio can be comfortably less than 1 without suggesting that the company should be in cash flow trouble.

Both the current ratio and the quick ratio offer an indication of the company's liquidity position, but the absolute figures should not be interpreted too literally. It is often theorised that an acceptable current ratio is 1.5 and an acceptable quick ratio is 0.8, but these should only be used as a guide.

EXAMPLE

Different businesses operate in very different ways. For example, a supermarket has a current ratio of 0.52 and a quick ratio of 0.17. The business has low receivables (people do not buy groceries on credit), low cash (good cash management), medium inventories (high inventories but quick turnover, particularly in view of perishability) and very high payables (the business buys its supplies of groceries on credit).

Compare these ratios with another company which is a manufacturer and retailer. This company has a current ratio of 1.44 and a quick ratio of 1.03. and operates with liquidity ratios closer to the standard. At the same date, another company's figures give a current ratio of 1.18 and a quick ratio of 0.80. This company is a refiner and seller of sugar.

What is important is the **trend** of these ratios. From this, one can easily ascertain whether liquidity is improving or deteriorating. If the supermarket has traded for the last 10 years (very successfully) with current ratios of 0.52 and quick ratios of 0.17 then it should be supposed that the company can continue in business with those levels of liquidity. If in the following year the current ratio were to fall to 0.38 and the quick ratio to 0.09, then further investigation into the liquidity situation would be appropriate. It is the relative position that is far more important than the absolute figures.

Don't forget the other side of the coin either. **A current ratio and a quick ratio can get bigger than they need to be**. A company that has large volumes of inventories and receivables might be over-investing in working capital, and so tying up more funds in the business than it needs to. This would suggest poor management of receivables (credit) or inventories by the company.

4.10 Efficiency ratios: control of receivables and inventory

A rough measure of the average length of time it takes for a company's customers to pay what they owe is the 'receivable days' ratio, or **average receivables payment period**.

Definition

Receivables payment period = $\frac{\text{trade receivables}}{\text{sales}} \times 365$ days

The estimated average **receivables payment period** is calculated as follows.

The figure for sales should be taken as the revenue figure in the income statement. Note that any **cash sales should be excluded** – this ratio only uses credit sales.

The trade receivables are not the total figure for receivables in the statement of financial position, which includes prepayments and non-trade receivables. The trade receivables figure will be itemised in an analysis of the receivables total, in a note to the accounts.

The estimate of receivables days is only approximate.

(a) The carrying amount of receivables might be abnormally high or low compared with the 'normal' level the company usually has.

(b) Sales revenue in the income statement is exclusive of sales taxes (eg, VAT), but receivables in the statement of financial position are inclusive of sales taxes. **We are not strictly comparing like with like.**

Sales are usually made on 'normal credit terms' of payment within 30 days. Receivables days significantly in excess of this might be representative of poor management of funds of a business. However, **some companies must allow generous credit terms to win customers**. Exporting companies in particular may have to carry large amounts of receivables, and so their average collection period might be well in excess of 30 days.

The **trend** of the collection period (receivables days) **over time is probably the best guide**. If receivables days are increasing year on year, this is indicative of a poorly managed credit control function (and potentially therefore a poorly managed company).

EXAMPLE: RECEIVABLES DAYS

Using the same examples as before, the receivables days of those companies were as follows.

Company	*Trade receivables/sales*	*Receivables days (× 365)*	*Previous year*	*Receivables days (× 365)*
Supermarket	$\frac{£5{,}016k}{£284{,}986k} =$	6.4 days	$\frac{3{,}977k}{£290{,}668k} =$	5.0 days
Manufacturer	$\frac{£458.3m}{£2{,}059.5m} =$	81.2 days	$\frac{£272.4m}{£1{,}274.2m} =$	78.0 days
Sugar refiner and seller	$\frac{£304.4m}{£3{,}817.3m} =$	29.3 days	$\frac{£287.0m}{£3{,}366.3m} =$	31.1 days

The differences in receivables days reflect the differences between the types of business. The supermarket has hardly any trade receivables at all, whereas the manufacturing companies have far more. The receivables days are fairly constant from the previous year for all three companies.

4.11 Inventory turnover period

Another ratio worth calculating is the **inventory turnover period**, or **inventory days**. This is another estimated figure, obtainable from published accounts, which indicates the average number of days that items of inventory are held for. As with the average debt collection period, however, it is only an approximate estimated figure, but one which should be reliable enough for comparing changes year on year.

Definition

The number of **inventory days** is calculated as:

$$\frac{\text{Inventory}}{\text{Cost of sales}} \times 365$$

The reciprocal of the above fraction, ie:

$$\frac{\text{cost of sales}}{\text{inventory}}$$

is termed the inventory turnover, and is another measure of how vigorously a business is trading. A lengthening inventory turnover period from one year to the next indicates one of two things:

(a) A slowdown in trading

(b) A build-up in inventory levels, perhaps suggesting that the investment in inventories is becoming excessive

Presumably if we add together the inventories days and the receivables days, this should give us an indication of how soon inventory is convertible into cash. Both receivables days and inventory days therefore give us a further indication of the company's liquidity.

EXAMPLE

The estimated inventory turnover periods for a supermarket were as follows.

Company	*Inventory /cost of sales*	*Inventory turnover period (days × 365)*	*Previous year*
Supermarket	$\frac{£15{,}554K}{£254{,}751K}$	22.3 days	$\frac{£14{,}094K}{£261{,}368K} \times 365 =$ 19.7 days

---

Activity 4 **(5 minutes)**

Butthead Ltd buys raw materials on six weeks credit, holds them in store for three weeks and then issues them to the production department. The production process takes two weeks on average, and finished goods are held in store for an average of four weeks before being sold. Customers take five weeks credit on average.

Calculate the length of the cash cycle.

Activity 5 **(5 minutes)**

During a year a business sold goods which had cost £60,000. The inventory held at the beginning of the year was £6,000 and at the end of the year £10,000.

What was the annual rate of inventory turnover?

4.12 Payables turnover

This is a measure of the average length of time that a company takes to pay its suppliers.

Definition

Payables turnover (sometimes called payables days) is ideally calculated by the formula

$$\frac{\text{Trade payables}}{\text{Purchases}} \times 365 \text{ days}$$

It is rare to find purchases disclosed in published accounts and so cost of sales serves as an approximation. The payment period often helps to assess a company's liquidity; an increase in payables days is often a sign of lack of long-term finance or poor management of current assets, resulting in the use of extended credit from suppliers, increased bank overdraft and so on.

NOTES

Activity 6 **(10 minutes)**

Calculate liquidity and working capital ratios from the accounts of Services plc, a business which provides service support (cleaning etc) to customers worldwide.

	20X7	*20X6*
	£'000	£'000
Sales revenue	2,176.2	2,344.8
Cost of sales	1,659.0	1,731.5
Gross profit	517.2	613.3
Current assets		
Inventories	42.7	78.0
Receivables (note 1)	378.9	431.4
Short-term deposits and cash	205.2	145.0
	626.8	654.4
Current liabilities		
Loans and overdrafts	32.4	81.1
Tax liabilities	67.8	76.7
Accruals	11.7	17.2
Other payables (note 2)	487.2	467.2
	599.1	642.2

Notes

1 Trade receivables	295.2	335.5
2 Trade payables	190.8	188.1

5 INVESTMENT RATIOS

5.1 Information provided by investment ratios

These are the ratios that help shareholders and other investors to assess the value and quality of an investment in the ordinary shares of a company. The value of an investment in ordinary shares in a company listed on a stock exchange is its market value, and so investment ratios must have regard not only to information in the company's published accounts, but also to the current price. The market price of the company's shares is used to calculate some of these ratios.

5.2 Earnings per share

Earnings per share (EPS) is often regarded as the most important single measure of a company's performance. It is used to compare the results of a company over a period of time and to compare the performance of one company's shares against the performance of another company's shares (and also against the returns obtainable from loan stock and other forms of investment). It shows the amount of residual profit available to the holder of one ordinary share.

Definition

$$\textbf{EPS} = \frac{\text{Profit for the year available for equity (ordinary) shareholders}}{\text{Number of ordinary shares in issue during the period}}$$

The profit which 'belongs' to ordinary shareholders is the profit that is left after all other appropriations have been made: interest on debt; taxation; and preference dividends (if any). It can be paid out directly in the form of ordinary dividends or retained in the company (where, hopefully, it will help to generate increased profits in future periods).

Returning to our example of Furlong plc, earnings per share is as follows:

20X8	*20X7*
$\frac{£267{,}930}{2{,}100{,}000} = 12.8\text{p}$	$\frac{£193{,}830}{2{,}100{,}000} = 9.2\text{p}$

5.3 Dividend cover

Dividend cover measures the number of times the current dividend could have been paid from available earnings.

Definition

$$\textbf{Dividend cover} = \frac{\text{Earnings per share}}{\text{Dividend per ordinary share}}$$

Dividend cover shows the **proportion of profit for the year that is available for distribution to shareholders that has been paid (or proposed) and what proportion will be retained in the business to finance future growth.** A dividend cover of 2 times would indicate that the company had paid 50% of its distributable profits as dividends, and retained 50% in the business to help to finance future operations. Retained profits are an important source of funds for most companies, and so the dividend cover can in some cases be quite high.

A **significant change** in the dividend cover from one year to the next would be worth looking at closely. For example, if a company's dividend cover were to fall sharply between one year and the next, it could be that its profits had fallen, but the directors wished to pay at least the same amount of dividends as in the previous year, so as to keep shareholder expectations satisfied.

In practice, the simplest way to calculate this is by dividing the profit available to ordinary shareholders by the ordinary dividend paid for the year.

For Furlong plc, dividend cover for 20X8 is as follows:

$$\frac{267{,}930}{20{,}000} = 13.4 \text{ times}$$

5.4 Price earnings ratio (P/E ratio)

Definition

The **price earnings ratio (P/E ratio)** = $\frac{\text{Share price}}{\text{Earnings per share}}$

A high P/E ratio indicates strong shareholder confidence in the company and its future (for example, profits are likely to increase) and a lower P/E ratio indicates lower confidence. The P/E ratio of one company can be compared with other companies in the same business sector and with other companies generally. It is generally used by investment analysts and other experts.

Suppose that the market price of a share in Furlong plc is 45p per share. The P/E ratio for 20X8 is:

$$\frac{45}{12.8} = 3.5$$

6 PRESENTATION OF A RATIO ANALYSIS REPORT

6.1 Basic approach

You should begin your report with a heading showing who it is from, the name of the addressee, the subject of the report and a suitable date.

A good approach is often to head up a **schedule of ratios** which will form an **appendix to the main report**. Calculate the ratios in a logical sequence, dealing in turn with operating and profitability ratios, use of assets (eg turnover periods for inventories and receivables), liquidity and gearing.

As you calculate the ratios you are likely to be struck by **significant fluctuations and trends**. These will form the basis of your comments in the body of the report. The report should begin with some introductory **comments**, setting out the scope of your analysis and mentioning that detailed figures have been included in an appendix. You should then go on to present your analysis under any categories called for by the question (eg separate sections for management, shareholders and lenders, or separate sections for profitability and liquidity).

Finally, look out for opportunities to **suggest remedial action** where trends appear to be unfavourable.

6.2 Focusing on user needs

Users of financial information are likely to fall into a few key categories:

- shareholders and potential investors
- loan creditors
- bankers and other providers of finance.

Most users are interested in a range of performance indicators. However, they are likely to interpret them from their own perspective, based on their own particular needs and interests. For example, shareholders will focus on profitability and return on investment, whereas a bank manager may be more concerned with a company's cash flow and its ability to pay debts as they fall due.

When preparing a report, ask yourself the following questions:

- Who are the users of the report and what are their interests?
- What is the purpose of the report?
- What is wanted, definite recommendations or less specific advice?

Ratio analysis is not foolproof. There are many problems in trying to identify trends and make comparisons.

7 LIMITATIONS OF RATIO ANALYSIS

7.1 General limitations

(a) Financial statements are based on historic information, not forecast information. They may be several months out of date by the time that they are published.

(b) Financial statements normally ignore the effects of inflation (although some non-current assets may be measured at current value). This means that trends can be distorted.

(c) Information in published accounts is generally summarised information, so that analysis based on published information alone is likely to be superficial. (However, proper analysis of ratios should identify areas about which more information is needed.)

7.2 Comparing different businesses

It can be useful to compare the ratios of a business with industry averages, or with ratios for another business in the same industry sector. However, such a comparison may be misleading.

(a) Ratios may not always be calculated in the same way. For example, there are several different ways of calculating the return on capital. It can be calculated based on total capital employed or on ordinary shareholders' capital. It can be based on average capital employed, rather than on the closing figure.

(b) The businesses may adopt different accounting policies. For example, if a business that revalues non-current assets is compared with one that measures them at historic cost, ratios such as ROCE, profit margin and gearing will not be strictly comparable.

(c) A small business may not be directly comparable with a large company, because it is probably managed in a completely different way. For example, a large company is likely to be able to take advantage of extended credit terms and trade discounts for bulk buying which may not be available to a smaller business.

(d) Businesses within the same industry sector can operate in completely different markets. For example, one clothes store may sell a very large number of cheap items at low margins, while another may sell a relatively small number of expensive items.

Activity 7 **(1 hour)**

Bimbridge Hospitals Trust has just lost its supplier of bandages. The company that has been supplying it for the last five years has gone into liquidation. The Trust is concerned to select a new supplier which it can rely on to supply it with its needs for the foreseeable future. You have been asked by the Trust managers to analyse the financial statements of a potential supplier of bandages. You have obtained the latest financial statements of the company, in summary form, which are set out below.

PATCH LIMITED
SUMMARY INCOME STATEMENT
FOR THE YEAR ENDED 30 SEPTEMBER 20X8

	20X8	*20X7*
	£'000	£'000
Revenue	2,300	2,100
Cost of sales	1,035	945
Gross profit	1,265	1,155
Expenses	713	693
Net profit before interest and tax	552	462

PATCH LIMITED
SUMMARY STATEMENT OF FINANCIAL POSITION
AS AT 30 SEPTEMBER 20X8

	20X8		*20X7*	
	£'000	£'000	£'000	£'000
Non-current assets				
Property, plant and equipment		4,764		5,418
Current assets				
Inventories	522		419	
Receivables	406		356	
Cash	117		62	
		1,045		837
		5,809		6,255
Share capital		1,100		1,000
Share premium		282		227
Retained earnings		2,298		2,073
		3,680		3,300
Non-current liabilities				
Loan		1,654		2,490
Current liabilities				
Trade payables	305		254	
Taxation	170		211	
		475		465
		5,809		6,255

You have also obtained the relevant industry average ratios which are as follows:

	20X8	*20X7*
Return on capital employed	9.6%	9.4%
Net profit percentage	21.4%	21.3%
Quick ratio/acid test	1.0:1	0.9:1
Gearing (debt/capital employed)	36%	37%

Tasks

Prepare a report for the managers of Bimbridge Hospitals Trust recommending whether or not to use Patch Ltd as a supplier of bandages. Use the information contained in the financial statements of Patch Ltd and the industry averages supplied.

Your answer should:

(a) Comment on the company's profitability, liquidity and financial position
(b) Consider how the company has changed over the two years
(c) Include a comparison with the industry as a whole

The report should include calculation of the following ratios for the two years.

(a) Return on capital employed
(b) Net profit percentage
(c) Quick ratio/acid test
(d) Gearing

Chapter roundup

- The ASB and the IASB have identified several different groups of users of financial statements; each with particular information needs. Investors are assumed to be the most important group of users.
- Profitability is measured by:
  - return on capital employed
  - net profit as a percentage of sales
  - asset turnover ratio
  - gross profit as a percentage of sales
- Debt and gearing are measured by:
  - debt ratio
  - gearing ratio
  - interest cover
  - cash flow ratio
- Liquidity and efficiency are measured by:
  - current ratio
  - quick ratio (acid test ratio)
  - receivables days (average debt collection period)
  - average inventory turnover period
- Investment ratios include earnings per share, dividend cover and the price earnings (P/E) ratio
- Ratios provide information through comparison:
  - **trends** in a company's ratios from one year to the next, indicating an improving or worsening position;
  - in some cases, against a **'norm'** or 'standard';
  - in some cases, against the **ratios of other companies**, although differences between one company and another should often be expected.
- Ratio analysis is not foolproof. There are several **problems** inherent in making comparisons over time and between organisations.

Quick quiz

1. List three groups of people who might be interested in a company's financial statements.
2. Why might a bank be interested in the financial statements of a company?
3. Apart from ratio analysis, what other information might be helpful in interpreting a company's accounts?
4. What is the usual formula for ROCE?
5. ROCE can be calculated as the product of two other ratios. What are they?
6. Define the 'debt ratio'.

NOTES

7 Give two formulae for calculating gearing.

8 What are the formulae for:

(a) The current ratio?
(b) The quick ratio?
(c) The receivables collection period?
(d) The inventory turnover period?

Answers to Quick quiz

1 Managers of the company, shareholders, trade contacts, providers of finance, tax authorities, employees, financial analysts and advisers, government agencies, the public.

2 In order to satisfy itself as to the company's financial position before giving it a loan.

3 (a) Comments in the Chairman's report and directors' report.
(b) The age and nature of the company's assets.
(c) Current and future developments in the company's markets.
(d) Events after the reporting period, contingencies, qualified audit report and so on.

4 $\frac{\text{Profit before interest and tax}}{\text{Capital employed}}$

5 Asset turnover and profit margin.

6 The ratio of a company's total debts to its total assets.

7 (a) Capital gearing ratio $= \frac{\text{long term debt}}{\text{shareholders' equity + long term debt}}$

(b) Debt/equity ratio $= \frac{\text{long term debt}}{\text{shareholders' equity (share capital and reserves)}}$

(4.3)

8 (a) $\frac{\text{Current assets}}{\text{Current liabilities}}$

(b) $\frac{\text{Current assets less inventory}}{\text{Current liabilities}}$

(c) $\frac{\text{Trade receivables}}{\text{Sales}} \times 365$

(d) $\frac{\text{Inventory}}{\text{Cost of sales}} \times 365$

Answers to Activities

1 In some countries, including the UK, it may be possible for any of these user groups to obtain the latest filed statutory accounts for the company. Listed companies whose shares are traded on a stock exchange are required to provide copies of their most recent published accounts to anyone who asks for them. Listed companies often publish their financial statements on the Internet and in some countries they are required to do so.

There is a greater problem in obtaining financial information from private companies. A trade contact, such as a supplier, can demand to see financial statements as a condition of doing business with the company. Similarly, a bank can demand to see financial information as a condition of granting a loan or overdraft facility.

Employees, as members of the public, are entitled to see the statutory accounts of their company employer. Some companies choose to provide financial statements prepared specifically for the benefit of their employees, but this is not a legal requirement.

2 $$\text{ROCE} = \frac{\text{Profit}}{\text{Capital employed}}$$

$$\text{PM} = \frac{\text{Profit}}{\text{Sales}}$$

$$\text{AT} = \frac{\text{Sales}}{\text{Capital employed}}$$

It follows that ROCE = PM × AT, which can be re-arranged to the form given in option D.

3 Interest payments should be taken gross, from the note to the accounts, and not net of interest receipts as shown in the income statement.

	20X8	*20X7*
$\frac{\text{PBIT}}{\text{Interest payable}}$	$\frac{360{,}245}{18{,}115}$	$\frac{247{,}011}{21{,}909}$
	= 20 times	= 11 times

Furlong plc has more than sufficient interest cover. In view of the company's low gearing, this is not too surprising and so we finally obtain a picture of Furlong plc as a company that does not seem to have a debt problem, in spite of its high (although declining) debt ratio.

4 The cash cycle is the length of time between paying for raw materials and receiving cash from the sale of finished goods. In this case Butthead Ltd stores raw materials for three weeks, spends two weeks producing finished goods, four weeks storing the goods before sale and five weeks collecting the money from customers (receivables): a total of 14 weeks. However, six weeks of this period is effectively financed by the company's suppliers (payables) so that the length of the cash cycle is eight weeks.

5 $$\text{Inventory turnover} = \frac{\text{Cost of goods sold}}{\text{Average inventory}} = \frac{£60{,}000}{£8{,}000}$$

$$= 7.5 \text{ times}$$

NOTES

6

	20X7		20X6	
Current ratio	$\frac{626.8}{599.1}$	= 1.05	$\frac{654.4}{642.2}$	= 1.02
Quick ratio	$\frac{584.1}{599.1}$	= 0.97	$\frac{576.4}{642.2}$	= 0.90
Receivables payment period	$\frac{295.2}{2,176.2} \times 365$	= 49.5 days	$\frac{335.5}{2,344.8} \times 365$	= 52.2 days
Inventory turnover period	$\frac{42.7}{1,659.0} \times 365$	= 9.4 days	$\frac{78.0}{1,731.5} \times 365$	= 16.4 days
Payables turnover period	$\frac{190.8}{1,659.0} \times 365$	= 42.0 days	$\frac{188.1}{1,731.5} \times 365$	= 40.0 days

The company's current ratio is a little lower than average but its quick ratio is better than average and very little less than the current ratio. This suggests that inventory levels are strictly controlled, which is reinforced by the low inventory turnover period. It would seem that working capital is tightly managed, to avoid the poor liquidity which could be caused by a high receivables collection period and comparatively high payables.

Services plc is a service company and hence it would be expected to have very low inventories and a very short inventory turnover period. The similarity of receivables collection period and payables payment periods means that the company is passing on most of the delay in receiving payment to its suppliers.

7 **Note**. Do not be put off by the fact that you are writing to the managers of a hospitals trust – this is ratio analysis in its normal form. Don't forget – you need to *comment* on the ratios as well as calculating them correctly.

REPORT

To: The Managers, Bimbridge Hospitals Trust
From: Business Adviser
Date: 20 November 20X8

Performance and position of Patch Ltd

As requested, I have analysed the performance and position of Patch Ltd with special reference to selected accounting ratios. The calculation of the ratios is shown in the Appendix attached to this report. The purpose of the analysis is to determine whether we should use Patch Ltd as a supplier of bandages.

General comments

Both sales revenue and profits have increased over the two years. The company is clearly expanding, although not at an exceptionally fast rate. The growth seems to have been achieved without investing heavily in property, plant and equipment, the fall in this figure presumably being due to depreciation. Shares were issued in 20X8 at a premium, while a sizeable portion of the long-term loan has been paid off. Expansion appears to be financed by share capital and profits.

Return on capital employed

This has increased from 8% in 20X7 to 10.3% in 20X8. It had also gone from being below the industry average in 20X7 to above it in 20X8. These are encouraging signs. As indicated above, the company has not invested significantly in non-current assets to finance its expansion – the assets/capital employed is simply working harder.

Net profit percentage

This has also increased from 22% in 20X7 to 24% in 20X8. In both years it was higher than the industry average. This is obviously good news. Sometimes when a company grows, it is at the expense of lower margins, but this is clearly not the case for Patch Ltd.

Quick ratio or acid test

The quick ratio shows how many assets, excluding inventory, are available to meet the current liabilities. Inventory is excluded because it is not always readily convertible into cash. The quick ratio or acid test is therefore a better indicator of a company's true liquidity than the current ratio which does not exclude inventory. Patch Ltd's quick ratio is healthy (around 1) in both years, and has in fact improved from) 0.9:1 to 1.1:1. While Patch's quick ratio was the same as the industry average in 20X7, it was better than average in 20X8.

These are encouraging signs. Sometimes growth can lead to overtrading to the detriment of liquidity, but Patch Ltd has not fallen into this trap.

Gearing

The gearing ratio is also favourable. This can be calculated in two ways: debt/capital employed and debt/equity. Debt/capital employed shows a fall from 43% in 20X7 to 31% in 20X8. In 20X7 it was higher than the industry average, but in 20X8 it is lower. Calculated as debt/equity, the ratio shows an even more significant decline.

This is reassuring. A high geared company is more risky than a low geared one in that, if profits are falling, it is more difficult for a high geared company to meet interest payments. A high geared company is therefore more likely to go into liquidation, as our last supplier of bandages did.

Conclusion

On the basis of the above analysis, I see every reason to use Patch Ltd as our supplier. The company's profitability and liquidity are improving and the gearing is at a lower level than last year. In addition the company compares favourably with other companies operating in the same sector.

NOTES

APPENDIX – CALCULATION OF RATIOS

	20X8	*Industry average 20X8*	*20X7*	*Industry average 20X7*
Return on capital employed	$\frac{552}{5,334} = 10.3\%$	9.6%	$\frac{462}{5,790} = 8.0\%$	9.4%
Net profit percentage	$\frac{552}{2,300} = 24\%$	21.4%	$\frac{462}{2,100} = 22\%$	21.3%
Quick ratio/acid test	$\frac{1,045 - 522}{475} = 1.1:1$	1.0:1	$\frac{837 - 419}{465} = 0.9:1$	0.9:1
Gearing:				
Debt/capital employed	$\frac{1,654}{5,334} = 31\%$	36%	$\frac{2,490}{5,790} = 43\%$	37%
Debt/equity	$\frac{1,654}{3,680} = 45\%$		$\frac{2,490}{3,300} = 75\%$	

BPP LEARNING MEDIA

Appendix: Edexcel Guidelines

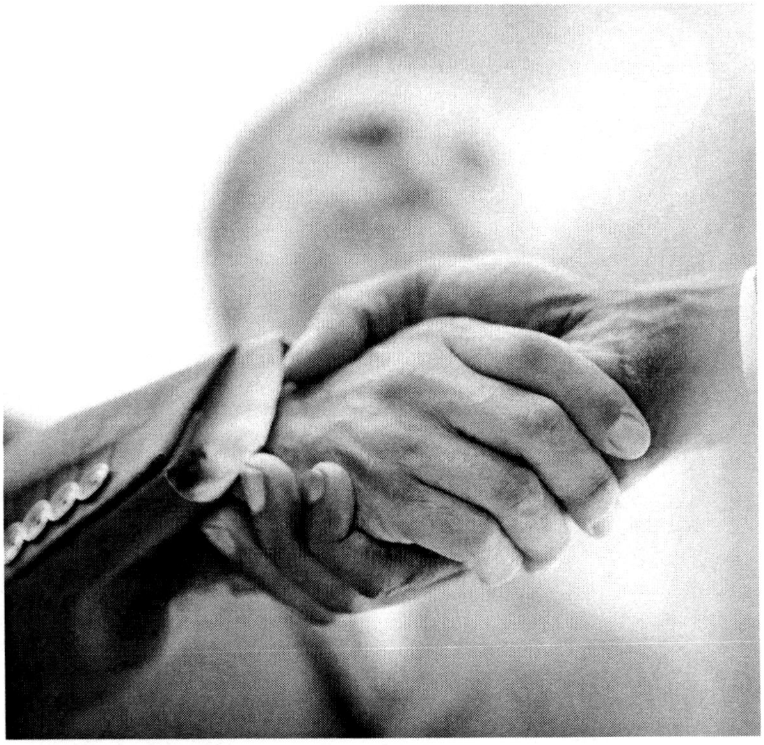

Edexcel Guidelines for the BTEC Higher Nationals in Business

This book is designed to be of value to anyone who is studying finance, whether as a subject in its own right or as a module forming part of any business-related degree or diploma.

However, it provides complete coverage of the topics listed in the Edexcel Guidelines for Units 9 (Management Accounting: Costing and Budgeting) and 10 (Financial Accounting and Reporting), of the BTEC Higher Nationals in Business (revised 2010). We include the Edexcel Guidelines here for your reference, mapped to the topics covered in this book.

Edexcel Guidelines
Unit 9 Management Accounting: Costing and Budgeting

Description of the Unit

The aim of this unit is to provide learners with the understanding and ability to use cost information for budgeting and forecasting purposes in the management of business.

This unit looks at the cost information, both current and future, of businesses. It looks at how cost data is collected, compiled and analysed, and processed into information that is useful for business managers. Learners will have the opportunity to apply these principles to practice.

The unit then deals with budgetary planning and control. It looks at how to prepare forecasts and budgets and to compare these to actual business results. Learners will again have practical experience of this.

Finally, the unit considers different costing and budgetary systems and the causes of resulting variances, together with the possible implications and the corrective action the business will need to take.

The unit links with the following units within the specification: *Unit 2: Managing Financial Resources and Decisions*, *Unit 6: Business Decision Making*, *Unit 10: Financial Accounting and Reporting*, *Unit 11: Financial Systems and Auditing* and *Unit 12: Taxation*.

Additionally it covers some of the underpinning knowledge and understanding for NVQ in Accounting as mapped in *Annexe B*.

The unit covers topics essential to learners aiming for a career in management accounting and who would like to become members of professional accounting bodies.

On successful completion of this unit a learner will:

1. Be able to analyse cost information within a business
2. Be able to propose methods to reduce costs and enhance value within a business
3. Be able to prepare forecasts and budgets for a business
4. Be able to monitor performance against budgets within a business.

Content

		Chapter coverage
1	**Be able to analyse cost information within a business**	
	Types of costs and classification: materials; labour; overheads; direct and indirect; fixed; variable and semi-variable	1
	Costing methods: job costing; batch costing; process costing; contract costing; service costing	6, 7
	Cost measurement: absorption and marginal costing; traditional overhead absorption and activity-based costing; stock valuation methods (FIFO, LIFO, AVCO, standard costing)	2, 3, 4
	Costing as basis for pricing and stock valuation: cost plus pricing; market pricing; target costing	5
	Data collection and analysis: sampling methods and purpose; presentation of data eg tabular, diagrammatical, graphical; index numbers	
2	**Be able to analyse cost information within a business**	
	Cost reports: preparation; comparison with other data; explanation and implication of variances	5, 10
	Performance indicators: monitor and assess to identify potential improvements	
	Quality and value: definitions and interaction; added value; total quality management	
3	**Be able to prepare forecasts and budgets for a business**	
	The budgeting process: purpose; benefits; links with organisational objectives/strategy; the budget manual; budgets as planning, coordinating, motivation and control devices	8
	Budget preparation: limiting or key factors; master, subsidiary and functional budgets; cash budgets; the preparation of sales budget, debtors' budgets, creditors' budgets, production costs, raw materials and finished goods budgets	
	Budgeting methods: incremental; zero-based; fixed and flexible	
	Behavioural consequences of budgets: padding the budget; spending to budget; creative budgets	
4	**Be able to monitor performance against budgets within a business**	
	Variances: types; analysis; calculation; possible causes; corrective action	9, 10
	Reporting: operating statement; reconciliation of budgeted and actual results	
	Responsibility centres: relevance to budgeting; identification of responsibility for variances	

Outcomes and assessment criteria

The learning outcomes and the criteria used to assess them are shown in the table below.

Outcomes	Assessment criteria To achieve each outcome a learner must demonstrate the ability to:
LO1 Be able to analyse cost information within a business	1.1 classify different types of cost 1.2 use different costing methods 1.3 calculate costs using appropriate techniques 1.4 analyse cost data using appropriate techniques
LO2 Be able to propose methods to reduce costs and enhance value within a business	2.1 prepare and analyse routine cost reports 2.2 use performance indicators to identify potential improvements 2.3 suggest improvements to reduce costs, enhance value and quality
LO3 Be able to prepare forecasts and budgets for a business	3.1 explain the purpose and nature of the budgeting process 3.2 select appropriate budgeting methods for the organisation and its needs 3.3 prepare budgets according to the chosen budgeting method 3.4 prepare a cash budget
LO4 Be able to monitor performance against budgets within a business	4.1 calculate variances, identify possible causes and recommend corrective action 4.2 prepare an operating statement reconciling budgeted and actual results 4.3 report findings to management in accordance with identified responsibility centres.

Edexcel Guidelines
Unit 10 Financial Accounting and Reporting

Description of the Unit

In this unit learners will prepare financial statements for different types of business, complying with relevant legal and regulatory provisions and the basic principles of group accounts. Learners will also develop tools for the interpretation of financial statements.

It is essential for the success of any business that it has good financial control and record keeping. Lack of effective control, planning and recording can ultimately lead to poor financial results. Owners and managers need to be able to recognise the indications of potential difficulties and take remedial action when required.

The unit considers the current regulations governing financial reporting, the formats of financial statements and the purpose of these statements for different users.

Learners will use records to complete financial statements. They will consider various categories of business income and expenditure and use cash flow forecasts, monitoring and adjusting for the effective management of cash flow. They will measure financial performance using a profit and loss account and balance sheet and analyse the profitability, liquidity and efficiency of a business through the application of ratio analysis.

The unit links with the following units within the specification: *Unit 2: Managing Financial Resources and Decisions*, *Unit 6: Business Decision Making*, *Unit 9: Management Accounting: Costing and Budgeting*, *Unit 11: Financial Systems and Auditing* and *Unit 12: Taxation*.

Additionally, the unit covers some of the underpinning knowledge and understanding for the NVQ in Accounting as mapped in *Annexe B*.

The unit covers topics essential for learners aiming to make a career in this field and who would like to become members of professional accounting bodies.

Summary of learning outcomes

To achieve this unit a learner must:

1 Understand the regulatory framework for financial reporting

2 Be able to prepare financial statements from complete or incomplete records

3 Be able to present financial information in accepted formats for publication

4 Be able to interpret financial statements.

		Chapter coverage
1	**Understand the regulatory framework for financial reporting**	
	User groups: owners; managers; employees; suppliers; customers; lenders; government; potential investors; different needs from financial statements	11
	User needs: profitability; liquidity; gearing; cash flow; job security; Accounting Standards Board (ASBs) statement of principles; International Accounting Standards Board (IASBs) framework for the presentation of financial statements	
	Legislation: current legislation including Companies Acts 1985, 1989 and 2006; Partnership Act 1890; European directives	
	Other regulations: International Accounting Standards (IASs); International Financial Reporting Standards and the main differences from UK Statements of Standard Accounting Practice (SSAPs) and Financial Reporting Standards (FRSs); The Accounting Standards Board (ASB)	
2	**Be able to prepare financial statements from complete or incomplete records**	
	Statements: trial balance; assets, liabilities, income, expenses, capital; profit and loss accounts; balance sheet; cash flow statement; notes to the accounts; statement of recognised gains and losses; international equivalents under the International Accounting Standards (IAS)	12, 15, 16, 18, 20, 21
	Types of business: sole trader; partnership; limited company (public and private); manufacturing/service/retail, group of companies	
	Preparation: from trial balance with adjustments eg stock, prepayments, accruals, bad debts, depreciation; from incomplete records; basic consolidation of accounts; changes to reporting requirements under the International Accounting Standards (IAS) eg statement of comprehensive income, statement of financial position	
3	**Be able to present financial information in accepted formats for publication**	
	Types of business: different formats for the businesses described in learning outcome 2 above; annual report	18, 21
	Formats: requirements of law and generally accepted accounting practice; changes to reporting requirements under the International Accounting Standards (IAS)	
4	**Be able to interpret financial statements**	
	Ratios: calculate ratios to reflect profitability, liquidity, efficiency, gearing, investment; comparison of these ratios both externally (other companies, industry standards) and internally (previous periods); interpretation of results	22
	Reporting: present findings in a format appropriate to users; weaknesses and limitations of analysis	

Outcomes and assessment criteria

The learning outcomes and the criteria used to assess them are shown in the table below.

Outcomes	Assessment criteria To achieve each outcome a learner must demonstrate the ability to:
LO1 Understand the regulatory framework for financial reporting	1.1 describe the different users of financial statements and their needs 1.2 explain the legal and regulatory influences on financial statements 1.3 assess the implications for users 1.4 explain how different laws/regulations are dealt with by accounting and reporting standards
LO2 Be able to prepare financial statements from complete or incomplete records	2.1 prepare financial statements for a variety of businesses from a trial balance, making appropriate adjustments 2.1 prepare financial statements from incomplete records 2.3 prepare a consolidated balance sheet and profit and loss account for a simple group of companies
LO3 Be able to present financial information in accepted formats for publication	3.1 explain how the information needs of different user groups vary 3.2 prepare financial statements in a form suitable for publication by a sole trader, partnership and limited company
LO4 Be able to interpret financial statements	4.1 calculate accounting ratios to assess the performance and position of a business 4.2 prepare a report incorporating and interpreting accounting ratios, including suitable comparisons.